BRITISH SOCIALIST FICTION, 1884-1914

CONTENTS OF THE EDITION

VOLUME 1
General Introduction
1884–1891

VOLUME 2
1892–1900

VOLUME 3
1901–1906

VOLUME 4
1907–1910

VOLUME 5
1911–1914

BRITISH SOCIALIST FICTION, 1884–1914

Volume 3
1901–1906

Edited by
Deborah Mutch

PICKERING & CHATTO
2013

Published by Pickering & Chatto (Publishers) Limited
21 Bloomsbury Way, London WC1A 2TH

2252 Ridge Road, Brookfield, Vermont 05036-9704, USA

www.pickeringchatto.com

All rights reserved.
No part of this publication may be reproduced,
stored in a retrieval system, or transmitted in any form or by any means,
electronic, mechanical, photocopying, recording, or otherwise
without prior permission of the publisher.

Copyright © Pickering & Chatto (Publishers) Limited 2013
Copyright © Editorial material Deborah Mutch 2013

To the best of the Publisher's knowledge every effort has been made to contact
relevant copyright holders and to clear any relevant copyright issues.
Any omissions that come to their attention will be remedied in future editions.

BRITISH LIBRARY CATALOGUING IN PUBLICATION DATA

British socialist fiction, 1884–1914.
1. Political fiction, English – 19th century. 2. Political fiction, English – 20th century. 3. Socialism – Fiction.
I. Mutch, Deborah, 1965– editor of compilation.
823.8'0803581-dc23

ISBN-13: 9781848933576

This publication is printed on acid-free paper that conforms to the American
National Standard for the Permanence of Paper for Printed Library Materials.

Typeset by Pickering & Chatto (Publishers) Limited
Printed and bound in the United Kingdom by Berforts Information Press

CONTENTS

Introduction	vii
Clarion	1
Alex M. Thompson, 'The Labyrinth. A Caution to Husbands: a Warning to Wives' (1902)	5
R. B. Suthers, 'The Adventures of a Drop of Water' (1903)	15
'By the Author of "Arthur's"' [A. Neil Lyons], 'Little Pictures of the Night' (1903–4)	21
Harry Beswick, 'Brother Eli on Tramps' (1904)	133
Robert Blatchford, 'Dismal Dan's Story. "The Only Chance He Ever Gave."' (1905)	137
A. Neil Lyons, 'A Distressed Gentlewoman. A True History' (1906)	141
Justice	145
Joseph Grose, 'The Golden Egg' (1901)	147
R. B. Cunninghame Graham, 'A Fisherman' (1902)	149
J. W. B., 'Men and Things' (1904)	155
Anon., 'The "Smart Set"' (1905)	159
Labour Leader	163
Hugo, 'The Blackleg, an Agitator's Yarn' (1901)	165
Anon., 'The Marchioness' (1902)	169
Frank Starr, 'The Doll Shop' (1903)	173
I. O. Ford, 'Aunt Caroline's Christmas Eve' (1904)	175
Fred Plant, 'Our Story. "The Far Land." (A Fragment of Fact.)' (1905)	179
J. Bruce Glasier, 'Andrew Carnegie's Ghost. A Red-Letter Day at Skibo Castle. A Christmas Story' (1906)	183
Social Democrat	189
Maxime Görki, 'On the Steppes. Told by a Tramp', trans. Emily Jakowleff and Dora B. Montefiore (1901)	191
Anatole France, 'Crainquebille', trans. Jacques Bonhomme (1902)	203
M. Winchevsky, 'He, She, and It' (1906)	215

Teddy Ashton's Northern Weekly	219
Charles Allen Clarke, 'The Cotton Panic' (1900–1)	221
Teddy Ashton, 'Bill Spriggs an Bet: Their Matrimony an their Marlocks. Bet Turns Bill Eaut' (1901)	385
Frank Starr, 'An Unpremeditated Crime' (1902)	391
E. Whittaker, 'When Death Crossed the Threshold' (1903)	397
Alfred H. Pearce, 'An Angel of Humanity' (1904)	403
Teddy Ashton, 'Th' Female Fister' (1905)	409
Harford Willson, 'The Scarlet Shoes. (The Story of a Serio-comic Walking Tour and its Tragic End.)' (1906)	413
Editorial Notes	419
Silent Corrections	465

INTRODUCTION

The range and variety of fiction published through the many socialist periodicals in the preceding volume continues to be a feature in the period covered by this volume. A multitude of genres again creates a richly textured literary landscape within both the individual periodical and the socialist movement as a whole. Similarly, the multitude of authors creates a multitude of perspectives from which the iniquities of capitalism are critiqued. This volume includes fiction by authors from a range of backgrounds – upper class (R. B. Cunninghame Graham (1852–1936)); middle class (Alex M. Thompson (1861–1948), Isabella O. Ford (1855–1924), John Bruce Glasier (1859–1920)); and working class (Robert Blatchford (1851–1943), Charles Allen Clarke (1863–1935), Harry Beswick (n.d.)) – and from a range of nationalities, as the predominantly British authors are joined by the Russian Maxime Görki (1868–1936) and the French Anatole France (1844–1924).

The apparently comradely world of socialist fiction was not carried through to the British socialist movement generally, and there was a growing schism between parliamentary and anti-parliamentary socialism. The foundation of the Independent Labour Party (ILP) in 1893 brought parliamentary socialism to the fore, and an agreement between the ILP and the Trades Union Congress in 1899 had resulted in the formation of the Labour Representation Committee (LRC) in 1900. Representatives of all socialist groups attended the founding conference, but the LRC's conscious movement towards the Liberal Party alienated many. There was a friendly relationship between the LRC executive board and the Fabian Society because the Fabians already had connections with the Liberal Party, but a working relationship with the Liberals was aided by the withdrawal of the Social Democratic Federation (SDF) from the LRC in 1902.[1] The rapprochement between the LRC and the Liberals arose out of an overlap of a number of their policies, including the opposition of both Liberal Radicals and the ILP to the Second Boer War, and the shared outcry against indentured Chinese labour in South Africa.[2] The secret 1903 Gladstone–MacDonald pact between James Ramsay MacDonald (1866–1937), secretary of the LRC, and Herbert Gladstone (1854–1930), Liberal Chief Whip and son of William

Gladstone (1809–98), ensured both Liberal and Labour candidates stood unopposed by the other in certain key constituencies.[3] To achieve this agreement, the LRC had to scale back their promotion of socialism: 'While MacDonald could hardly control local socialist societies, he could emasculate their efforts by denying them the official LRC nomination – effective because it warned local trade unions that a rebel candidate was a socialist'.[4] This was a pragmatic decision by the LRC executive board, based on the weak position of LRC candidates in a three-cornered contest against both Liberal and Tory opposition, but it was one that caused rifts in the socialist movement as a whole.

There was little attempt to use fiction to persuade the reader of the necessity of LRC pragmatism, as James Keir Hardie's (1856–1915) *Labour Leader* serialized only one sustained piece of fiction in the periodical, Margaret McMillan's (1860–1931) 'Handel Stumm' (1900–1). There was an abridged serialization of George Eliot's (1819–80) *Adam Bede* published over the winter of 1901–2, which ended with Arthur Donisthorne's last-minute reprieve for Hetty Sorrell, and that was all. The short fiction had as much variety of sub-genres as this periodical, and the others in this collection, had carried up to this point. The most realistic of the short stories selected are Isabella O. Ford's 'Aunt Caroline's Christmas Eve' (1904) and Hugo's (n.d.) 'The Blackleg, an Agitator's Yarn' (1901). Ford tells the story of the narrator's encounter with Aunt Caroline on two railway journeys as she visits her nephew, who was injured by an accident at work, while Hugo's tale concerns the revelation to a union leader of the consequences of his intransigent approach to union affiliation and, by extension, the difficulties of change by means of industrial action alone. Each story maintains the tradition of multiple sub-genres in the explication of working-class experience: the realism of Ford's story is tinged with tragedy for both the injured man and his worried family; Hugo's realism is mitigated by the actions of the trade unionist as *deus ex machina* for the blackleg and his family. The other stories selected to represent the *Labour Leader* for this period display a range of non-realist sub-genres, including the sentimentalism of 'The Marchioness' (1902), as a French aristocrat is given the opportunity during the revolution to marry the peasant she loves and symbolically draw together 'high' and 'low'; the fable of 'The Doll Shop' (1903), where the usefulness of different classes of occupation are presented through the attractiveness and durability of a child's toy; and the ghost story of 'Andrew Carnegie's Ghost' (1906), in which Carnegie is confronted by his own ghost and forced to accept his own greed and hypocrisy.

The same variation of sub-genres is found in the rest of the volume, ranging from Grose's (n.d.) fable of good intentions stifled by cynicism in 'The Golden Egg' (*Justice*, 1901), through Blatchford's army tale 'Dismal Dan's Story' (*Clarion*, 1905), to Clarke's Bill Spriggs dialect comedies (*Teddy Ashton's Northern Weekly*, 1901, 1905). Realism ranges through Maxime Görki's 'On the Steppes'

(*Social Democrat*, 1901), which deals with the desperation of starving men, Harry Beswick's 'Brother Eli on Tramps' (*Clarion*, 1904), which criticizes the inhumane complaints of the *Telegraph* columnist on the unsightliness of the homeless, and R. B. Cunninghame Graham's 'A Fisherman' (*Justice*, 1902), on the life of a poor Scottish worker. The two long serializations featured in this volume similarly combine realism with other genres, creating two very different fictions to make very similar points.

The first is A. Neil Lyons's (1880–1940) 'Little Pictures of the Night', which was published in the *Clarion* between October 1903 and April 1904. Lyons is unnamed, and the authorship is attributed to 'the Author of "Arthur's"'. Subsequent criticisms of Lyons and *Arthur's* cite the 1909 bound publication, but it is evident that he had already gained a reputation through the publication of earlier chapters of his work (see the *Clarion* headnote in this volume for further details). Lyons was a popular and respected author of working-class life: D. H. Lawrence placed Lyons's work alongside H. G. Wells's depictions of working-class life in *Tono Bungay*, *Love and Mr Lewisham* and *The History of Mr Polly*,[5] while Alex Thompson recollected in his autobiography that 'he [Lyons] saw life as it was really lived between Brixton and the Obelisk and his reports of what he saw were tinged with a wide humanity, a mellow humour, and a vein of biting satire that no short-story writer of his time has equalled'.[6] Similarly, C. F. G. Masterman quotes at length from *Arthur's* when discussing London nightlife in *The Condition of England*.[7]

Thompson's praise acknowledges the difficulty in placing Lyons's writing: was he a journalist writing 'reports of what he saw', or was he an author of short stories? The question is not resolved by reading Lyons's work as his narrator is invariably placed within the fiction, representing the position of the journalist: within the frame of action, but as an observer rather than a participant. The identity of the narrative voice is suggested to be Lyons himself, as the narrator occasionally refers to his employment; in 'Little Pictures' he mentions 'the acting-editor of the great newspaper by means of which I live' (p. 78). Thus the difficulty arises of separating Lyons's work into categories of 'fiction' and 'journalism'.

In all of Lyons's work the default 'norm' is the inherent democratic attitude of the working class, practised without the framework socialist ideology. Such a non-political approach chimes closely with that of Blatchford, who stated in the inaugural issue of the *Clarion* that 'The policy of THE *CLARION* is a policy of humanity; a policy not of party, sect, or creed; but of justice, of reason and mercy'.[8] This apolitical approach to socialism caused fractures between the ILP and the editor of the periodical read by most of its members, as Blatchford's consistent calls for political independence went unheeded by the pragmatic LRC executive board. Lyons perpetuates Blatchford's rejection of party politics, as he focuses on the communal nature of working-class life, the spirit of community support and the celebration of a culture that others wish to re-mould in their own image. In 'Little Pictures' the natural empathy of the working class is demonstrated through the actions of the regulars at Arthur's coffee stall. Lyons consistently reinforces the collective self-help of the workers – Arthur employs the tramp Beaky; Mr Honeybunn employs Miss Hopper, Beaky's female companion on tramp; Trooper Alfred greets arrivals at his father's coffee stall with the offer to ''Ave a corfee' (p. 61) – and the critical perspectives of the middle class are shown as ignorant, supercilious and intrusive.

One of the most forthright expositions of this defence of working-class culture against the imposition of middle-class values is given in the chapter entitled 'Concerning a Benevolent Idiot'. The eponymous idiot is the sociologist Mr Fothergill, MA, who approaches the *Clarion* in order to get a closer view of the London underworld of coffee stalls. In his portrayal of Fothergill, Lyons recognizes the general compassion of some philanthropists in their dealings with workers, but also the stupidity of attempting to understand, critique and remodel one social group in the image of another. An exchange between Fothergill and the narrator reinforces the dominance of the narrator's perspective on the coffee stall crowd specifically and the working class generally, and the perversion of the scene by its refraction through middle-class values. During his visit to Arthur's coffee stall, what Fothergill sees is not the gathering of like-minded souls in a place of comfort, inclusion and harmony, but rather drunkenness in the merry sailors, prostitution in the drab, theft by the drayman's boy of his employer's coffee and industrial subversion in the debaters discussing trade unionism. Thus without expressly referring to either socialist ideology or that of philanthropic capitalism, Lyons juxtaposes the two opposing ends of the political spectrum. Through the eyes of the narrator, he asks the reader to judge the pressures of 'normalizing' or standardizing in the manner of the middle classes applied by those whose whim of philanthropy is one of the few safety nets for the working class. Rather, the default position of the narrator normalizes the attitudes, actions and emotions of the working class and prioritizes that perspective on working-class culture in opposition to the judgmental Fothergill. By placing the narrative voice in the position of the journalist, Lyons emphasizes the 'reality' of his narrative, and the reader is encouraged to come to their own conclusions of the well-intentioned but patronizing efforts of Fothergill and his ilk.

Lyons removes his working-class characters from the usual class indicators of employment through which many other socialist (and non-socialist) authors have defined their characters. In H. J. Bramsbury's 'A Working Class Tragedy' (*Justice*, Volume 1), Frank Wilson is defined through his employment in the Cranston ironworks, his subsequent unemployment and his reinvention as a land steward and collective farm manager. His whole character is built around the work he does and his attempts to reinstate himself into the working world when employment is removed. Similarly, 'The Blackleg' by 'Citizen' (James Sexton; *Workman's Times*, Volume 2) defines John Goodman through his employment on the docks, and his political work is also filtered through his employment as he forms and helps manage the dockworkers' trade union. The indication of class position through employment is not restricted to the male worker in socialist fiction, as 'Connie' by 'John Law' (Margaret Harkness; *Labour Elector*, Volume 2) is similarly defined by her employment as a dancer until she is rescued from unemployment through her relationship with her upper-class lover, Humphry Munro. Connie is later rescued from homelessness by two women, Flora and Bess, who are similarly defined by their work as prostitutes.

The second serialization included in this volume, Charles Allen Clarke's 'The Cotton Panic' (*Teddy Ashton's Northern Weekly*, 1900–1), similarly defines its working-class characters through the class indicators of work (or in this case, unemployment) by setting the fiction during the Lancashire cotton famine caused by the blockade of cotton during the American Civil War. In this fiction, Clarke creates his working-class characters through what Joanna Bourke defines as the main sites through which working-class individuals are constructed: 'the body, the home, the marketplace, the locality, and the imagined "nation".[9] The inhabitants of Preston, divested of their 'normal' indicators of class by their unemployment, are defined by the struggle to feed the body and maintain the home (via the maintenance of life through food, the maintenance of the house which is the family home, and the unity of the family within that house by resisting – as far as possible – the fragmentation of the home through entry to the workhouse), the support networks which had been formed in the locality before the famine, and the construction of 'nation' through the British involvement in the American Civil War.

In 'Little Pictures of the Night', however, Lyons lifts his characters free of even these looser class indicators, although he does not remove them altogether. The most common indicator of class, work, is only depicted through Arthur and Beaky at work in the coffee stall, and there is very little description of the work involved in the business. The regular visitors to the coffee stall have various forms of employment – Kitty and Miss Hopper are employed as seamstresses, Mr Honeybunn is a printer, Arthur's son Alfred is a soldier, and there is a stream of visits from sailors (drunk and sober), draymen and an omnibus driver – but while all are employed, their location at the coffee stall removes them from that work so that they are defined by other means. The location of the coffee stall similarly disturbs even Bourke's broader ways of defining the working class. The story is set in London but the location of Arthur's stall is deliberately vague, although occasional descriptions of the narrator's travels indicate its position in a working-class area south of the river Thames. While this does suggest a particular class position, the characters' homes are not made visible to the reader and therefore are not available as a signifier of class; the coffee stall itself draws customers from all social levels, including drunk 'toffs', the middle-class narrator and the criminal underclass as well as the recognizably working-class regulars. What Lyons creates in this fiction (and in others) is a community network that stretches beyond the coffee shop and which is flexible and inclusive. The regulars show support for each other (Alfred and the narrator track down Miss Hopper's elusive boyfriend; Arthur gives Beaky employment and arranges, through Kitty, for the employment of Miss Hopper) and for the transient visitor (Kitty and Miss Hopper, at different times, give food and drink to a starving tramp and a hungry prostitute; Arthur and Beaky attempt to soothe a customer's crying baby). Removed from the usual indicators of social rank, often used by the likes of Fothergill to demonize the poor, Lyons's characters show a wide empathy and sense of humanity to the troubles and suffering of others. They suggest a broad sense of community in conflict with the cult of individualism and self-help, a kind of unconscious generosity and sympathy that bound the working class beneath the disconnecting structures of hierarchy of employment, trade unions, location and political affiliation.

The inclusiveness of community is also evident in Clarke's 'The Cotton Panic' but projected through lenses of different perspectives. Clarke's fiction as a whole creates a recognizable community of working-class people, as readers became familiar with the 'Tum Fowt' (Tonge Fold) community through the 'Bill Spriggs' short stories. Although the stories were primarily focused on the character of Bill, they gave almost as much attention to Bill's wife, Bet, and Bill's friends in the 'Menociation', Ben Roke, Joe Lung, Sammy Snokes and the fictional embodiment of Clarke's pseudonym, Teddy Ashton. Following a long dialect tradition, Clarke's characters were presented as superficially stupid, but they would invariably get the better of the 'toffs' and those in authority.[10] However, Clarke's specific positioning of his stories in recognizable areas of Lancashire gives a greater importance to location in the development of working-class communities than there is in Lyons's fiction.

Clarke's longer fiction similarly creates communities of Lancashire working-class characters, evident in 'The Cotton Panic' as the reader becomes immersed in the lives of the Preston operatives through the characters of Sid Clifton and Ada Milner. These characters are not presented as being extraordinarily involved in the lives of others; they are simply representative of the interaction of working-class people in Lancashire urban life. Many of Clarke's novels also create a working-class community arising out of a shared sense of experience, as the characters suffer in similar ways. These communal experiences would often rely on the workplace as the basis of cohesion between characters. For instance, the unemployed weaver Sid Clifton is employed on the Confederate warship the *Alabama* alongside Sandy Aspinall, who had courted Ada Milner's sister, and '[h]e found that he knew several of the crew, including the brawny lads from the Fylde, and nimble Bob Hagan ... from Chorley' (p. 311); Sid and Ada also witness the seduction of Lucy Clayton, who worked with Ada in the weaving shed. In 'The Cotton Panic', the suffering caused by the North's blockade of the Confederate states' cotton exports during the American Civil War creates mass unemployment in Lancashire and amplifies the sense of shared experience through its effect on the broader sites of class identity.

Like Lyons, Clarke's sense of inclusion in his fiction is not restricted to those who live in the locality, as illustrated by the visit of dialect poet Edwin Waugh to the Virgin's Inn, the Preston public house. Waugh initially appears to be an outsider, using Standard English rather than the dialect of the characters. There is a suggestion by one of the group in the inn that he should be the victim of a practical joke; but by taking the suggestion in good part, evincing general friendliness and changing his register to dialect, Waugh is welcomed by the members of this community. Although Waugh is now a journalist (a form of employment associated with middle-class status) rather than a manual worker, his background, his place of birth and his language establish common ground and a shared body of experiences.

The development of community had a material basis as well as psychological ties, as the network would provide a safety net for those struggling during periods of trouble. As Wally Seccombe recognizes, working-class communities would pull together in times of distress: 'Such gestures of solidarity were based on an implicit assumption of community reciprocity. This was not so much a bilateral calculus of indebtedness ... it was more the conviction that "what goes round, comes round"'.[11] Just as they are in Lyons's, empathy and care for others are threaded through Clarke's fiction, demonstrating his belief in 'the solidarity and warmth between ordinary working class people'.[12] Ada Milner's actions express this aspect of working-class empathy when she tries to prevent the fallen Lucy Clayton from knowing she and Sid have seen her, and she practises material solidarity when she invites the Chartist Grimshaw to live with her and her mother after his family are taken to the workhouse. The community does what it can to alleviate the worst of its members' sufferings, mitigating the worst excesses of capitalism and indicating what might be done on a national scale through the community created under socialism.

Clarke's fictional presentation of working-class community and mutual aid has been criticized for undermining his realism. In *Class Fictions*, Pamela Fox repeats Mary Ashraf's criticism of Clarke, whose 'text as a whole is arguably "marred" by other forms of "sentimentality" and "idealism"'.[13] Fox recognizes that Clarke is taking 'a "realistic," expansive look at a particular working-class community',[14] but she appears to consider the sense of community as unrealistic and ideal. Both Lyons and Clarke build their fictional communities on their own experiences with the working class, as both had witnessed the support the poor provide one another, and their fiction connects that provision with the arguments for 'self-help' in Parliament – an argument more important than they realized, as the LRC executive board worked secretly to tie the Labour Party to the Liberals.

Notes

1. M. Pugh, *Speak for Britain! A New History of the Labour Party* (London: Vintage, 2011), p. 61.
2. H. Pelling and A. J. Reid, *A Short History of the Labour Party* (Basingstoke: Macmillan, 1996), p. 12.
3. D. Howell, *British Workers and the Independent Labour Party, 1888–1906* (Manchester: Manchester University Press, 1983), p. 4.
4. Pugh, *Speak for Britain!*, pp. 64–5.
5. D. H. Lawrence to August de Wit, 1916, *The Letters of D. H. Lawrence*, ed. J. T. Boulton, 8 vols (Cambridge: Cambridge University Press, 2000), vol. 8, p. 18.
6. A. M. Thompson, *Here I Lie* (London: Routledge, 1937), p. 134.
7. C. F. G. Masterman, *The Condition of England*, ed. J. T. Boulton (1909; London: Faber and Faber, 2012); see the last pages of Chapter V.
8. Editorial, *Clarion*, 12 December 1891, p. 1.
9. J. Bourke, *Working Class Cultures in Britain, 1890–1960: Gender, Class and Ethnicity* (London: Routledge, 1994), p. 1.
10. P. Salveson, *Lancashire's Romantic Radical: The Life and Writings of Allen Clarke/Teddy Ashton* (Huddersfield: Little Northern Books, 2009), p. 74.
11. W. Seccombe, *Weathering the Storm: Working-Class Families from the Industrial Revolution to the Fertility Decline* (London: Verso, 1995), p. 140.
12. Salveson, *Lancashire's Romantic Radical*, p. 64.
13. P. Fox, *Class Fictions: Shame and Resistance in the British Working-Class Novel, 1890–1945* (Durham, NC: Duke University Press, 1994), p. 123.
14. Ibid.

CLARION

Alex M. Thompson, 'The Labyrinth. A Caution to Husbands: a Warning to Wives', *Clarion*, 26 December 1902, p. 5.

R. B. Suthers, 'The Adventures of a Drop of Water', *Clarion*, 11 December 1903, p. 3.

'By the Author of "Arthur's"' [A. Neil Lyons], 'Little Pictures of the Night', *Clarion*, Chapter I, 16 October 1903, p. 1; Chapter II, 23 October 1903, p. 1; Chapter III, 30 October 1903, p. 8; Chapter IV, 6 November 1903, p. 1; Chapter V, 13 November 1903, p. 8; Chapter VI, 20 November 1903, p. 8; Chapter VII, 27 November 1903, p. 8; Chapter VIII, 4 December 1903, p. 1; Chapter IX, 18 December 1903, p. 1; Chapter X, 25 December 1903, p. 1; Chapter XI, 1 January 1904, p. 1; Chapter XII, 8 January 1904, p. 8; Chapter XIII, 15 January 1904, p. 8; Chapter XIV, 22 January 1904, p. 1; Chapter XV, 29 January 1904, p. 8; Chapter XVI, 5 February 1904, p. 3; Chapter XVII, 12 February 1904, p. 1; Chapter XVIII, 19 February 1904, p. 1; Chapter XIX, 26 February 1904, p. 1; Chapter XX, 4 March 1904, p. 1; Chapter XXI, 11 March 1904, p. 1; Chapter XXII, 18 March 1904, p. 3; Chapter XXIII, 26 March 1904, p. 1; Chapter XXIV, 1 April 1904, p. 1; Chapter XXV, 8 April 1904, p. 1; Chapter XXVI, 15 April 1904, p. 1; Chapter XXVII, 22 April 1904, p. 1.

Harry Beswick, 'Brother Eli on Tramps', *Clarion*, 6 May 1904, p. 5.

Robert Blatchford, 'Dismal Dan's Story. "The Only Chance He Ever Gave."', *Clarion*, 21 July 1905, p. 5.

A. Neil Lyons, 'The Distressed Gentlewoman. A True History', *Clarion*, 7 September 1906, p. 3.

The *Clarion* (1891–1935) continued to maintain high sales during the period covered by this volume, despite editor Robert Blatchford's increasingly controversial opinions. His support for British military action in South Africa during the Second Boer War (1899–1902) lost him friends in the socialist movement and also lost the *Clarion* some readers. Then in 1903 a debate on religion in the *Clarion* was started in Blatchford's review of a cheap edition of Haeckel's *The Riddle of the Universe*, when Blatchford made the controversial claim that 'this book of Professor Haeckel's demolishes the entire structure upon which the religions of the world are built. There is no escape from that conclusion. The case for science is complete'.[1] The ensuing response, which Blatchford published in the *Clarion*, came from socialists, non-socialists and members of the clergy. Blatchford later published his arguments in *God and my Neighbour* (1903) and followed it with *Not Guilty: A Defence of the Bottom Dog* (1905), an argument for the force of heredity and environment, which he had begun in the *Clarion*. Nevertheless, the circulation of the *Clarion* rose to 74,000 after the general election of 1906. For Blatchford's full biographical details, see the headnote to the *Clarion* in Volume 2, pp. 1–3.

As well as controversial ideas, Blatchford continued to publish fiction, both his own and that of his *Clarion* colleagues. Alexander Mattock Thompson (1861–1948),[2] co-founder of the *Clarion* and close friend of Robert Blatchford, was born in Carlsruhe, Germany, to wealthy English parents. His father had wanted him to train as a barrister, but Thompson drifted into journalism and met Blatchford while both were working for Edward Hulton (1869–1925) on the *Sunday Chronicle*. When Blatchford left Hulton's employ to begin the *Clarion*, Thompson became one of the periodical's founding members, along with Edward Fay and Montagu Blatchford. He also wrote under the pseudonym 'Dangle', a name taken from Richard Brinsley Sheridan's (1751–1816) satirical play *The Critic* (1779), as he was the *Clarion* theatre critic. He continued to work on the *Clarion* after Blatchford left in 1913, and he also began writing and adapting for the theatre, collaborating with Robert Courtneidge (1859–1939) in the production of pantomimes, musical comedies and plays. Thompson's short story included in this selection is the only piece of fiction he published in the *Clarion*.

Robert Bentley Suthers (1870–1950), the son of a Chorlton draper, met Blatchford while working as a clerk at the *Sunday Chronicle*. He left the *Chronicle* to work on the *Clarion* in 1891 and was employed as the *Clarion* accountant, among other jobs. Although he did not begin contributing to the *Clarion* until 1901, he became renowned as a skilled propagandist for municipal socialism; his first novel, *A Man, a Woman and a Dog*, was published in 1901. He left the *Clarion* in 1910 to edit Hulton's Manchester journal *Ideas*, around the time Blatchford first withdrew from the *Clarion*. When Blatchford returned in 1913, he asked Suthers to rejoin him. Suthers did so and remained with the paper until 1925, after which he continued as a freelance contributor, while also contributing to other labour papers such as the 1930s *Labour Magazine*.

'The Author of "Arthur's"' refers to A. (Albert Michael) Neil Lyons (1880–1940), who also published fiction in the *Clarion* under the pseudonym 'Edwin Smallweed'. Lyons was born in Kimberley, South Africa, but moved to Britain as a youth; he came to the attention of Blatchford and the *Clarion* through his fictional vignettes, collected under the title *Arthur's*, that appear to have been first published in 1901. The first eleven vignettes introduce Arthur and his coffee stall patrons, and the opening of the longer *Clarion* serial rests on the reader's prior knowledge of the coffee stall, as we plunge into the stories *in media res*. In the 1914 book edition of *Arthur's*, the stories are divided into two sections, 'Book 1 A.D. 1901' and 'Book 2 A.D. 1904'. The only difference between the *Clarion* serial and the book version is that one of the original 1901 vignettes, 'Hush-a-by Baby', is repeated in the serial as Chapter XVI, published on 5 February 1904. Lyons was a prolific author of fiction for the *Clarion*, and his output included a great many short stories and longer fiction such as *Sixpenny Pieces* (1907–8) and *Simple Simon: The History of a Fool* (1911). He also published bound fiction, such as *Moby Lane* (1915), wrote a biography of Robert Blatchford entitled *Robert Blatchford: The Sketch of a Personality* (1910), and has writing credits for the 1929 film *The Return of the Rat*, starring Ivor Novello.

Harry Beswick (n.d.) was a regular contributor to the *Clarion* under both his own name and the pseudonym 'Bezique'. Alex M. Thompson termed him a 'merry sprite' and recorded Beswick giving up well-paid employment in insurance to join the *Clarion* group.[3] Beswick's 'Brother Eli' dialect short stories were regular contributions.

Notes
1. R. Blatchford, 'In the Library', *Clarion*, 23 January 1903, p. 3.
2. Efforts to trace Thompson's living descendants have so far been fruitless, but any copyright acknowledgements will be included in later editions if owners of the copyright are later identified.
3. Thompson, *Here I Lie*, pp. 134–5.

Alex M. Thompson, 'The Labyrinth. A Caution to Husbands: a Warning to Wives' (1902)

Wives should never be cross with their husbands. Husbands should always be true to their wives. If you don't believe me, ask Andreas Springmühl.

A few weeks ago, Andy was sitting in the kitchen at the back of his shop in Hull, when his wife brought him a letter. On opening it, he found this:

"The Labyrinth"
    Cottingham, near Hull.

Dear Mr. Andy. – I have changed my mind since yesterday. I will now consent. Meet me to-night at the colonel's summer-house at nine. I am afraid I am acting foolishly, But I do it for your sake. – Yours affectionately
                              ANNIE LASCELETT.

Andy rubbed his eyes, and stared. It was plain enough. Colonel Francis's buxom housekeeper had fallen in love with him. Yesterday when she called at the shop, he had asked, in jest, whether she wouldn't show him over the grounds of "The Labyrinth" one of these fine moonlight nights; and this was her answer. She had taken the proposal quite seriously. The poor woman's passion, thought Andy, was natural; for he was a fine man of his inches (five foot three), with eyes soft and tender (his wife said they were of a squashed gooseberry hue), and an extensive smile.

Now what was to be done? Should he go? No, thought Andy. He would stand by his wife and his domestic hearth. He would –

"Move off," said Kathleen, sharply, "an' don't be intrudin' on the fire," says she.

Absorbed in his meditations, he did not notice the interruption. She came over to the fire with a spoon in her hand, and spilled boiling soup over his shins. Andy roared enough to frighten off all the nightingales in Hull.

"Hould your tongue," says she. "Ye'll rouse the town." And she tapped his head with the back of the spoon.

Her temper was not good at the best. To-day it was unbearable.

"Lieber. Himmel!"[1] said Andy. "Dis cannot any longer be ge-stood. I vill go out."

"You ungovernable brute," says she, throwing his walking-stick after him.

That settled it. His numerous excellences were not appreciated at home. He would go and see Mrs. Lascelett.

Chapter II.

That commodious and desirable messuage known as "The Labyrinth," the residence of Colonel Stewart Francis, situated near Cottingham, on the highway between Hull and Beverley, is known throughout the district for its maze, whose complexity is heightened by the precise similarity and cunningly-designed juxtaposition of two summer-houses, known respectively as "The Colonel's" and "The Young Master's" pavilions.

Andy had been to "The Labyrinth" once or twice, but did not know that there were two summer-houses in the grounds; therefore, when he reached the "Young Master's Pavilion" he felt confident of having found the place of appointment, and sat down to wait for her whom he had already began to call "his own bonnie Annie Lassled." The moon tipped the edge of the distant wolds with silvery light intensifying the blackness of the shadows over Cottingham Plain. Time flew with drowsy, slow, and flagging wings. Andy perspired and shivered in turns. Every breath of wind alarmed him.

"Vas I but now safe to house," he said to himself, "vould I my vife kiss as I her nefer before ge-kissed hev."

His feverish mood filled the air with visionary terrors. Catching sight of his light dust coast, with the conspicuous black buttons, he felt that it must be visible ten miles away; and hurriedly pulling it off, bestowed it in a dark corner, with his grey chimney-pot.[2] At this moment, hearing a light step crushing the gravel, he rushed out of the pavilion. There was somebody moving. He heard his name in faint whispers. It was she! How to get at her? She was only a few yards away; but a few yards such as the melting soul might not pierce without many a winding bout of linked terror long drawn out. For there were now several persons' steps to be heard in the garden – one a stealthy step, that followed him behind, driving the unhappy Teuton into a very frenzy of fear. Who was his pursuer? Could it be his poor, injured little wife? – with the poker? – without?

At the turn of the path, he found himself face to face with a woman.

"Is that Mr. Andy?" she asked.

Ah, what a relief! It was Mrs. Lascelett.

"Yes, ma'am," gasped the heavy-breathing German, "I am ge-come."

"Why," exclaimed Mrs. Lascelett, "it is Mr. Springmühl!"

"Vell, who should I be if I vas not meself?" asked Andy, struggling to smile lovingly.

Mrs. Lascelett had no time to reply. The figure of a man appeared at the bend of the path, and the buxom housekeeper hurriedly told the portly German that if he wanted her he had better go to the house and wait for her.

Mr. Springmühl had never been so much surprised.

"I am to oblige a lady ge-come," said he, "and so am I ge-treated. I vill not remain here to be made a Dummkopf. I vill go home to my loafing vife, and never mitout her vill I any more out-go."

He tried to retract his stops to the pavilion where he had left his hat and coat; but hadn't gone far when he hear a sound of scuffling, and then, startlingly sudden, the crack of a pistol.

Looking round in fear and trembling, he saw a man running. A ray of moonlight shone across the path, and Andy observed that the man carried a light overcoat.

"Woa!" said Andy. "Let me look at that coat," and made a grab at the garment.

He had just time to ascertain that the buttons on it were black, when the stranger struck him on the head with a stick, and Andy tumbled into the hedge. He was only half-conscious when, a few moments later, he heard two men talking.

"He went this way," said one man.

"What a blessing he didn't hurt anybody," said the other.

("Auch!" thought Andy, "didn't he, though?")

"And a comfort that the colonel didn't shoot him," said the first speaker.

"Especially if it was really Master Andy, as Mrs. Lascelett thinks," said the second speaker.

("Ei? Vat ist das?" thought Andy.)

The men walked on, and Andy cautiously arose.

"So! Dat wollüstige[3] voman has dis bloottirsty colonel to shoot me incited!" thought Andy, trembling more than ever. And, wishing himself a thousand times home again with his "loafing frau," he crept as quietly and as quickly as he could out of these "verflüchte gardens of the Teufel."[4] Yet, as he passed the pavilion, he could not resist the temptation to look whether the stranger had taken his hat, as well as his coat. No, the hat was gone. But – hallo! what's this? A coat! A light dust coat with black buttons!

"Hoora!" said Andy; "he must have brought it back!" And, putting it on, he pursued his way to Hull.

After a long and anxious walk he safely reached the town, and, finding a hat shop open in Waterworks Street, secured a cover for his head. He was accounting for his hatless condition by telling the shopkeeper that the wind had blown his hat into the docks, when Detective Brown, with whom he was acquainted, rushed in to buy a cap. The detective was full of business.

"Hallo! Springmühl!" he said. "Just off to investigate a mysterious affair at Cottingham: you know the place. Colonel Francis's house. Attempted burglary, I expect. The thieves got the colonel's coat, containing his pocket-book. Easy job for me, though. One of 'em has left his hat, and the housekeeper knows him. Just going up to get particulars. Hi! Cabby! Good-night Springmühl."

And the detective, stepping into the cab, was driven off.

Andreas stood like one petrified. He might be locked up. How should he clear himself? What was he to do? He saw the hatter keenly watching him. "Ach. Gott in Himmel!"[5] thought Andy. "I am suspected."

He paid for the hat, and went out. Wither should he go? If he went home, he would be dragged out of bed by Detective Brown, and his shame would be proclaimed from the house-tops. No, he could not go home. He must go away. But where? To London. London was a big place. Nobody would know him in London. But it was too late to catch a train to London to-night. He must go to a hotel, and catch the 6.35 in the morning.

In his dazed condition, it was an immense relief to have decided even that. He walked on, looking right and left, to see whether he was watched. At last he reached the hotel. Could he have a bedroom and be called in time for the 6.35 train?

A chambermaid showed him to his room, and, having locked the door, he sat down on the bed to consider the situation. What money had he? He fumbled in his trousers' pockets. Six shillings and ninepence! He felt in his overcoat. Hallo! A pocket-book! Bank-notes! Gracious heaven! Whose were they? An envelope dropped out. In a frenzy Andreas read the address:

> Colonel Stewart Francis
>   The Labyrinth
>   Cottingham
>   Near Hull.

With excitement, he now examined the coat. It wasn't his at all. He *was* the thief who had stolen the colonel's coat.

* * *

Poor Andy had a sleepless, anxious night. In the morning, distracted by conflicting fears, he took one ten-pound note from the pocket-book, put the rest back in the coat, and left his room. As he walked down the passage, he saw a bedroom door standing open. Happy thought! He would throw the coat in there. That might divert the police on a false track. He went downstairs, and paid his bill. The man took the note, and brought back the change. No suspicion so far. Springmühl glanced nervously up the platform. No sign of Detective Brown. He hung back till the train was nearly starting, then jumped in, and was whirled away.

Thank heaven! he was safe. He had brought an "Eastern Morning news" on the platform, and now proceeded to read it. Ha!

MYSTERIOUS AFFAIR AT COTTINGHAM

There it was. What said the report?

A very mysterious affair occurred at an advanced hour last evening at Cottingham at the residence of that well-known and justly popular officer and magistrate, Colonel Stewart Francis. The particulars of the affair are steeped in mystery; but, as far as we have been able to ascertain, the gallant officer was smoking his cigar in the grounds, according to this post-prandial custom, when he saw a person of sinister aspect lurking in the hedge behind him. Colonel Francis, with characteristic courage, turned to seize the intruder, when the latter struck him on the head with some heavy instrument, and rapidly escaped. The gallant colonel, notwithstanding the blow he had received, retained sufficient presence of mind to pull out the revolver which he invariably carries, and to shoot at the retreating malefactor's legs; but, owing probably to the injury which he suffered, the aim miscarried and the miscreant escaped. Nothing has been missed from the premises except the colonel's light-grey dust coat, in which was a pocket-book containing a rather considerable amount of bank-notes (numbers known), and which he had somewhat carelessly deposited on a seat of one of the summer-houses in the grounds. No trace of the criminal has yet been discovered; but a grey tall hat, which has been identified as the property of a well-known local tradesman, has been found, and certain remarks dropped in our reporter's presence by the colonel's housekeeper, Mrs. Lasellett, tend to connect this individual in some manner with this remarkable affair. Detective-sergeant Brown is conducting an investigation into the circumstances of the case, and may be trusted to bring the guilty person or persons to justice within a very short time; but the police at present preserve great reticence in the communications to the Press.

What did it all mean? Why had that wicked Jezebel lured him from his happy home and his "loafing frau," to embroil him in her dark, unfathomed iniquities? Why – why, in short, was everything? His muddled brain could make nothing of it – except that Mrs. Lascelett had denounced him as a burglar, that his famous white hat had been found on the spot to convict him, that the detective in charge of the case had actually seen him buying another hat, that he had carried away the only thing stolen from "The Labyrinth" that night, that he had negotiated one of the bank-notes ("numbers known") in paying his hotel bill, and that *he had run away.*

Poor Andreas felt his sinews slacken with his fears. His imagination framed fantastic shapes of hideous punishments. "If I am discovered," thought he, "I am lost. No; if I am discovered, I am found." This, somehow, seemed to sooth him. He kept on repeating it to himself, and after an while observed that the train had taken it up, and had translated its ponderous rattle into "If I'm discovered, I am found; if I'm discovered I am lost; if I'm discovered, I am found." This association of ideas between the train and himself comforted Andy as, with a sense of pleasant companionship, and still muttering "If I'm discovered," he fell at last into a deep and balmy sleep.

Chapter III.

Sleep is the best thing in the cosmic scheme. By enabling a man to forget that he lives, it makes life, while sleep lasts, worth living. That man does well who sleeps well. While he remains insensible to the wisdom of the world, he continues sensible. It is when men wake, and begin to spin round on their heels, and skip and jump on each other's corns, and twist, and rush, and run, and rotate each on his own axis, as if their fussing, and fretting, and foaming at the mouth were of some consequence – it is then that men cease to be respectable. What is the difference between the man whom business men call a "wide-awake man" and the swift-crawling, nimble-wriggling, limb-waggling centipede? Depend on it, fleas, mosquitoés, centipedes, and wide-awake men, they are all of one species – sleep-killers every one of them, enemies of repose, and sworn foes to true wisdom. There is no wretch so miserable as the man who can't sleep, no assassin so loathsome as he who murders sleep. Some poet, who must have been a wise, and good, and accomplished sleeper, calls sleep "a momentary respite from despair,"[6] and the man who snatches the longest moments of respite is, therefore, the wisest of men, even as they who provoke such respites are the noblest and most deserving of men. That is why the profession of letter is respected.

When Andreas woke, his massive Teutonic intellect had recovered from the previous day's unaccustomed excitements, and he was able to face the situation with comparative calmness. He saw now that he had done foolishly to leave Hull. He saw equally that it was useless coming all the way to London for a sleep in a railway carriage. He could not mend matters by going back in the next train to surrender himself to justice. Therefore, let justice have a bit of excitement, too; he had had his share.

No patent in existence rectifies disordered judgments so effectually as sleep. After his long arrears of rest, Andy was as wise as Sancho Panza.[7] For two days he did his best to enjoy himself; but on the morning of the third day he chanced to find a copy of the "Eastern Morning News" in a Strand restaurant, and therein he read the following:

THE COTTINGHAM MYSTERY

At the Police Court yesterday, Andrew Francis, the son of Colonel Francis, was once again charged on remand under circumstances fully reported in our former issues.

Detective-sergeant Brown having given evidence of his discovery in the accused's bedroom at the Paragon Hotel of the colonel's coat and pocket-book, as described by us yesterday, informed the court that the missing bank-note had been traced to the banking account of the hotel. A clue to Springmühl's whereabouts had been discovered, and if the court would adjourn the case for a week, he hoped then to be able to place the court in full possession of all the facts of the case.

At the request of the magistrates, Thomas Vokes, cashier at the Paragon Hotel, was called and deposed that he was not able to state with certainty whether the bank-note to which reference had been made had been paid by the prisoner or by another visitor to the hotel, whose movements, he understood, were being traced by Detective Brown.

Detective-sergeant Brown signified that such was the case.

A very painful scene occurred in court when the magistrates desired Colonel Francis to give evidence. The gallant officer, in a voice broken with emotion, repeated that he had nothing to say, that he and his son had quarreled some months ago, and that he had not seen him from that day till he saw him here in the dock. The unhappy position of the gallant gentleman provoked general commiseration, and a murmur of respectful sympathy went round the court when he descended from the witness-box.

Annie Lascelett, housekeeper at "The Labyrinth," was next called, and she testified, as stated by us yesterday, that she had been in correspondence with Mr. Francis, jun., during his stay at the Paragon Hotel, with a view to bringing about a reconciliation between him and his father; that she had, in compliance with his request, agreed to bring about an interview between him and his father on the night of the robbery. But she swore positively that she had not seen Mr. Andrew Francis that night. She could not account for his failing to come when he himself had entreated her to make the appointment. She had met Mr. Springmühl in the ground while looking for Mr. Andrew, but was too much agitated at the time to speak to him, and she had not seen him since.

Kathleen Springmühl, who wept repeatedly, and whose evidence could scarcely be heard –

Andy could read no more. The tears gathered in his eyes, and it was in a voice tremulous with subdued passion that he ordered his next pint of lager. O, what a villain he had been! A tear actually trickled down his nose as he thought of his diabolical treatment of that angelic woman, his wife; and then, ashamed of his sensibility, he stretched out his hand for the paper to resume his study of Kathleen's evidence.

"I beg your pardon," said a man, "this is my paper."

"Oh, I did not know," answered Springmühl. "I – hallo!" he suddenly exclaimed, "ver hev I you before ge-seen?"

The stranger sullenly answered that he was sure he didn't know and was rising to depart, when Andy jumped up, to, shouting at the top of his voice:

"I hev you ge-caught! It is you. *Jawohl! Also*, then, come mit me."

Instead of which, the stranger hit Andy in the midst of his capacious nose, and attempted to escape; but Andy, bellowing "Police!" "Murder!" with a voice like the deep-mouthed roar of thunder, clung tight to the stranger till five constables and two sergeants had arrived. And he would have continued to shout "Police!" and "Murder!" after that, had not the constabulary treated his excessive enthusiasm with coercive measures.

Andrew Springmühl was in earnest.

* * *

The intelligent reader has already guessed the rest of the story – how the letter which Springmühl had received from Mrs. Lascelett had been written for her master's son, Mr. Andrew Francis; how, in her agitation, Mrs. Lascelett had directed the order for the week's groceries to Mr. Francis, and the letter of appointment with Mr. Andy Francis to Mr. Andy Springmühl. Now that they knew all about it, the police understood the case perfectly, the more especially when it proved that the man captured in London by Springmühl was one of a gang of burglars who had been 'touring' somewhat extensively of late in the North of England. They had intended to "crack" The Labyrinth," but the unusual stir in the grounds had upset their designs, and Andy's evidence had completed their conviction. Colonel Francis was so relived by the lifting of the charge against his son, that he was glad to forgive and forget the youthful errors which had estranged him from his boy. And all this had been accomplished by the astuteness and determination of Andrew Springmühl! No wonder that he thought himself a hero! No wonder that Kathleen was proud of him! But, if you don't mind, we will borrow a little light upon this point from a conversation which Andy had with Kathleen on the day of his return. It shows how truly Solomon spoke when he declared that all men are, as one may say, poets; it shows how much women can believe when they want to; and it also shows several things.

"But what were you doin' at 'The Labyrinth' that blessed night?" asked Kathleen.

"Vat *I* vas doing? I was to catch de burglars ge-gone."

"But how did you know about them at all, darlin'?" says she.

"Ach! Mein Gott![8] I got a glue, and ven I a glue ge-gotten hev, I stick to it. But vimmen can not dese dings understand."

"Sure enough, that's thrue," says she; "divil a bit do I understand. But how did you get the colonel's coat from the colonel's pavilion, darling?" says she.

"De colonel's coat? Ach, I saw de burglar in de pavilion put it down, so I tought dere's money in dat coat, and ven de burglar vas not looking, I put my coat down in de place of de colonel's coat, and so de burglar got my coat, and I took de colonel's"

"By jabbers!" says she. "I should never ha' thought o' that. An' you followed the man all the way to London? But how was it," says she, "that you left your hat in the young master's pavilion?"

"In de – young master's pavilion? O, joost to put de police off the scent, so dat I could catch dem all by mineself."

"Och! By the hokey," says she, "yer're a cliver man, Andy, an' I'll never cross ye any more in the wide world, at all," says she.

"No, Kathleen, don't you neffer do it no more, und I vill try to forgif you," said Andy.

That is nearly a month ago, and Kathleen has since been as gentle as a zephyr's breath. As for Andy, he turns his head away when any woman – except his wife – looks at him.

R. B. Suthers, 'The Adventures of a Drop of Water' (1903)

Master Percy Bunting, being in a hot and breathless condition after half-an-hour spent in vigorous exercise on the long slides outside the school-gates, made haste to quench his thirst with a cup of icy-cold water from the scullery tap. Dashing the last quarter of its contents into the sink, he hung up the cup and went, gasping and panting, to a chair before the kitchen fire.

"Shouldn't think there's much fun in being a drop of water," he said, as he noticed a splash on his hand.

"O! wouldn't you?" replied a voice, as he was about to wipe his hand on the leg of his trousers.

Master Percy Bunting looked quickly up to the door. "Was that you, mother?"

Silence reigned. "I'm sure someone spoke!" said Percy, rising and lifting the tablecloth, and looking into all the corners suspiciously. "It didn't sound like Jim!" he said.

"Of course, it didn't! It was me," said the voice again.

Percy glanced with startled eye in every direction at once.

"You needn't be afraid; I'm only a drop of water," the voice continued. "Here I am, right under your nose."

Percy lifted his hand suddenly to his organ of smell.

"Well, I am under it now," said the voice, "if I wasn't then. I'm on your hand."

Percy looked at his hand, and saw that it was still wet. He couldn't really believe that the voice had come from *that*.

"O! you needn't look so unbelieving," said the voice, in a somewhat injured tone. "'My finger's wet, my finger's dry'[1] – you know that, don't you?"

"Of course, I do!" said Percy. "But I didn't know water could *talk*."

"Why, were do you keep your ears? Do you mean to say you've never heard us babbling in the brooks and wrangling over the stones, and singing in the April showers, and complaining on the panes, and rollicking and roaring on the sands? Good gracious! are you a deaf boy?"

"No – no. Only I didn't know water could talk like us!"

"Ah! There's a lot of things you don't know yet. Don't think a drop of water can have much fun, don't you? Why, I could tell you things –"

"I know," said Percy, "that would freeze my –"

"Ugh! Don't talk about freeing if *you* please; and, I say, just sit a little further away from that fire, will you? Thanks. I shall have to evaporate soon, anyhow, but I don't want to go in a hurry, by way of the chimney. Dear me! It *is* a long time since I was allowed to talk to a human. I think the last occasion was when I had a conversation with Napoleon in the Alps."

"Napoleon!" said Percy, "Why he's been dead years!"

"Dead? O! yes, of course; lost all his moisture long since, and how he's being blown about the Sahara Desert, and he'll be getting into that new-fangled Emperor's eyes – what's his name? – Lebaudy.[2] How things do get unmixed to be sure! But, bless you! I'd been half over the universe before I met Nappy. I remember he asked me a lot about the Milky Way – Milky Way, indeed! as if our family wasn't clustered there thicker than any other. Why, if the County Council ever got their hands on that, our business up there would be ruined.

"Heard about Noah's Ark, I suppose? Well, I was there, too. My word! that was a day out for us. We simply snowed everything under. No fun in being a drop of water? If you'd seen the way we hustled that poor boat up and down the watery waste, you'd have given your back teeth to have had a hand in it! Football? Well, you are innocent. It was football, and battledore and shuttlecock, and pitch and toss, and shinny, and golf and ping-pong,[3] all rolled up in one. And no umpire and no touch-lines! We *did* have a game. You should have seen a few millions of us standing on each other like the acrobats you saw at the Hippodrome (O! I was *there*), and making awful yawning hollows, and tumbling Noah and his menagerie down at a thousand miles an hour. Then we'd stand mountains high, and pretend not to see the Ark wanted to pass, and hang over it like forty million Niagras.[4] You should have heard the language of the man at the wheel, and the row the animals under hatches made! That was another time when I was allowed to talk to a human. I had to comfort poor old Noah. He was awfully sick – they all were – so I asked him a riddle: 'Where was Moses when the light went out?'[5] He got that mad because he couldn't find the answer he broke the window and I fell into the crowd. Hurt? No, we have the pull of you there. *You* couldn't be thrown out of a window onto a mob of boys without breaking something.

"No, we don't get permission often. This time I'm talking because of a poor journalist chap who has been scratching his head for a story. O! he'll hear me right enough. You see, we've got means of telegraphing that you people don't know much about yet. He's asleep now, and I'm in communication with another drop of water in his head – see? Water in his head? Should think he has! *All* journalists have. He'll wake up, and think he's invented this brilliant conversation of mine. Ah! We never get credit for half the good turns we do.

"Talking about turns reminds me of the time I once went to school. *My*! Never again. What I went through that day.

"Through the tap? O! yes. Funny boy. Yes, I went through the tap, and you'd open your eyes if I told how I came to be *in* that tap. Well, I tumbled into a sort of bottle, and found we were in a room on a big table, with a crowd of bottles, and pipes, and tubes and a gas-jet. There were a lot of boys sitting at seats, like you do at a theatre. One of the boys said they were learning 'stinks,' and the smell was certainly chronic, and I've been in some niffy corners in my time.

"Presently, a man in goggles came in, and all the boys stopped talking, and the man said: 'I will now proceed to show the composition of water by an analytical demonstration. You will see I have here a retort containing the water. This I shall boil, by lighting the spirit lamp placed underneath. The steam produced is conducted along this tube into the gun-barrel, which you see is carried above the little furnace, which keeps it at a red heat. At this end of the gun-barrel is another tube, and in a moment – now, you –'

"Then I fainted. All that time I have been simply boiling, because he had poured me into the retort when I wanted to see the show. Then I swelled with indignation, and disguised myself as Steam, and ran along the gun-barrel, hoping to escape in that way. I had not gone many steps when I felt the most awful sundering sensation, just as you might feel if the butcher were to chop you right down the middle. I fainted dead away. I don't know how long I was unconscious; but when I came to, my master, Heat, seemed to be giving me a most awful whacking, and I could just hear the voice of the goggle-eyed man saying: 'The steam which escaped into the gun-barrel was decomposed by the heated metal, the oxygen of the water was retained by the metal, and the hydrogen passed on to the end of the tube where I lit it as it came out. I will now partly cover the flame with this cold vessel, and you will see the water which results from the burning of the hydrogen, or by the union of the hydrogen with the oxygen present in the air, drop into this other vessel placed underneath.'

"And, somehow, I seemed to come strong and vigorous as ever all in a second, and yet there was something different – felt as if I'd got a new inside, like. I was in a glass at the other end of the torture-machine, and I was in an awful funk for fear he should put me in the retort again, and re-torture me. But I was left in peace till the end of the show, and then all the boys and the master trooped out.

"One boy came to the table on his way, and, pouring some more of us on top of me, tipped us into his tummy. I didn't mind that, because – well, I could tell you some things about people's interiors, if I'd time, that would knock that Arabian Nights chap[6] into a dust storm. I've been inside millions. I wasn't in him long, though.

"As soon as he got outside, he stood on his head against a wall, and I slipped down his lachrymal duct,[7] and about five minutes after another boy gave him a punch in the eye and I came out to see who was at the door, and while I was looking round I rolled down his cheek, and dropped into a puddle in the playground. I felt a bit wild at that because it was a damp sort of day, and there didn't seem to be much chance of me being lifted out of it for some time.

"However, I was in luck again. A boy came along, and stooped down, and stuck a sort of tube into us, and all at once a lot of us were sucked up into it. Well, I nearly dried up with fright. It was very like being in the gun-barrel. But in a minute we were all squirted out again as fast as if we'd been coming down in a thunderstorm, and I found myself having a ride on the moustache of the goggle-eyed master that taught you – I mean tortured me. My! how he did carry on. It seems the boy had meant to squirt us on to another boy, and he's done it from behind a wall without making sure of his target. I think they put him on report[8] for it.

"Of course, the master wiped a lot of us on to his handkerchief, but he missed me, and when he got home a little later, and kissed his wife, I got transferred to her lips, and nice red lips they were. I'd have given worlds to be allowed to talk to her. It made me fret and fume so, when she went and bent over the fire, that I fell off, and was carried up the chimney, and out into the air; and I knew I was ordered abroad as soon as I felt the wind. I put on my travelling dress of Vapour, and in about a week I was hanging over the Himalayas, getting ready for our bargain sale. We are simply given away at those times.

"My word! The things I've seen in India. If I could only talk oftener! Know what the Victoria Cross is, don't you? Valour? Yes, O! yes, valour. But not always. Listen. One day I found myself inside one of your Tommies.[9] He was one of an expedition which had been sent to put down an Afridi[10] rising. This chap had never been in action before, and he was in such a shaky condition he couldn't hold a lot of us. He kept chucking us out in a cold perspiration, but I hung on, and tried to get back into his blood, and rush the red corpuscles round; but it was no use. Then we tumbled on the enemy one day about dusk. All was noise and confusion, and swearing and shooting. The Afridis ran, and your Tommies ran after them, and the chap I was inside dropped behind a big stone, and lay there, shivering and quaking, with hundreds of us chaps half-frozen with his fear dropping off his white face on to the dust he was clenching with his fists.

"After a time, your men came back with a rush, and the Afridis behind them. My! How they ran. My bold soldier nearly died with fright, and hardly had strength enough to drag himself round the stone so as to hide from the Afridis when they returned. The Tommies turned them right about once more, but didn't follow them up, and after a while the firing ceased entirely.

"Then, when he thought all was safe, my man was for getting on to camp; but he was in an awful funk of a court-martial now. So he chucked a lot of cartridges away, and fired off his rifle, and waited to see if the Afridis replied. All was quiet, so he got up gingerly, and made a run for it. He hadn't gone two hundred yards when he heard a crack, and felt a whiff of air near his cheek, and he jumped about seventeen yards sideways. Then another bullet shaved his right boot and put two miles an hour on to his speed. Then more bullets came, the place seemed to be alive with Afridis, and there was no cover about. He shrieked with fear. All at once his foot caught in something, and he fell headlong and rolled over. He thought it was a dead man; but he wasn't. His hand touched a soft body. He felt it, and peered at it. It was a man, one of your men. He laid down alongside him, and crouched up against him away from the bullets.

"Then he had a inspiration. He took hold of the body, got on his feet, lifted it onto his back, and started running again. If they shoot, he thought, they will hit *him*. Soon the bullets whistled again, and he couldn't run so fast. But he stuck to the body, and stumbled frantically forward. Blindly, almost unconsciously, he went on, with an awful buzzing in his head. Then he seemed to hear a shout from a crowd of people and he thought he was in Fleet Street, reading an election result on a newspaper office window. He tried to cheer, and – fainted. He was in camp, and wounded in the ankle, though he didn't know it.

"I was out on his forehead by this time. His comrades crowded round, and cheered, and carried on like lunatics, because the man on his back was their captain, and they thought the Afridis had him. My man was a hero. Then I dropped off, and was ordered abroad. I was in Germany for three weeks, and then I was waltzing round the British Islands for a month or two in a cumulus cloud, and having a royal time. I was next sent to London, and one day we gathered in force, and gave it such a drenching as it hadn't had for months. I remember coming down on the umbrella of a poor woman who had been delivering some washing at a big house. She was standing at a street corner, reading a dirty bit of paper to a friend she had met, and as I hung on the rib I could see it was torn from your official 'Gazette'.[11]

"'God bless him!' she said. "I allus knew he was a brave lad. There you are, Maria. It's in print. 'Ow he saved the capting's life at the imminit peril of his own, and carried him on his back over a thousand yards, an' the bloomin' niggers firin' guns into his back all the time. An' the Queen, God bless her! is goin' to pin the Victoria Cross on to him with her own beautiful 'ands.'

"Then I fell into the gutter and – Ever been to Barking? Ugh! It isn't at *all* fun. But wouldn't you like to be a drop of water, and travel all over the world, and up to the sky, and down to the centre of the earth, and get locked up in an iceberg, and turn into a snowflake, and dance in the moonlight and act in the Rainbow Minstrel Troupe[12] – I'm a corner man, wear purple tights – and get inside boilers, and push trains and boats along, and drive machinery, and play touch with the lightning, and – By Jove! I must be off. I see all my pals have gone. Wonder where I'm booked for this journey? Guess that chap's got his two columns, anyhow. Good-bye! I'll come again if –"

* * *

"Percy! Percy! The idea of falling asleep at tea-time."

It was a real voice this time. Percy rubbed his eyes, and looked at his hand. It was quite dry.

"I've had such a funny dream, mother," he said, "about a drop of water."

"Ah! That's sitting in front of that roaring fire. Dreams always go by contraries."

'By the Author of "Arthur's"' [A. Neil Lyons], 'Little Pictures of the Night' (1903–4)

[16 October 1903]

I. "Beaky".

There are some people to whom Nature stands god-parent. She has marked them in plain figures. They are her show goods; put into the window, as it were, for a careful world to marvel at. Names, along with other gew-gaws of parental choice, may be thrust upon them at birth. Cakes may be cut to the glory of these names, and flagons broached. Great discourse, likewise, shall be framed and uttered. But if Nature hath taken the whim to act this part of god-parent, such vanities shall avail them nothing. Montressor Albert,[1] dreaming great vistas of warm milk in vats, bewrays[2] these titles by his very leer. One peep, how scant soever, beneath the curtain on Montressor Albert's crib shall inform you that Providence has anticipated the parson. Montressor Albert is destined to discard those names. He is set down upon the playbill of life, definitely, and in big print, as – "Ginger"! Thus he was born; thus for all his little ever, he must live: thus he shall die. Montressor Albert's lot in life may be to drive oxen, or to cure souls, or to direct a bank, or to beat a drum. He'll be "Ginger," just the same – always "Ginger." I don't think Montressor Albert need be pitied. People will not be curious about him. We know the names of all the common flowers, and they dwell in peace. With roses and rare pot-herbs it is otherwise.

Now Nature, by a like device, had marked her interest in my man of tatters. He surged out of the darkness so quickly that I did not have time to think about him. We were standing at the top of Waterloo Bridge,[3] and the blaze from the great arc light there fetched him out sharp and clear against the night, like a picture in white chalk upon a blackboard. He stood still only long enough to bellow a curse at the rain. Then he passed out of the light circle, and came on towards me, a noisy blur. But I had seen enough in that second of illumination to put a name to my man, "It was Beaky."

I couldn't tell you *why* his name was "Beaky," nor why I knew his name was "Beaky." One merely felt it. When he came nearer, and we fell to talking,

I observed in him a strange, distorted likeness to Benjamin Disraeli,[4] who was Earl of Beaconsfield. That, of course, helped to confirm the wisdom of Providence. But in that first glimpse I saw only a tall old man, with jerky features and a tramp's bend, and a body covering that had been dragged from twenty dustbins, and was lashed about his person with tags and ends of rope. He wore a kind of hat, and a kind of hair – blue-green, with a relish that was not all of time – hung down below it, half covering his eyes. All these things I knew, and saw, and felt; and I knew, also, that his name was "Beaky."

When he had come so close to me that we might almost have touched, he swung off suddenly into the bridge embrasure that was by my right hand. He shook his fist towards the river, and leant over the parapet, and spat – contemplatively. Then he contracted his body – so it seemed – and was seen to be sitting, rather than sat, upon a seat. After which he proceeded to reason with the elements. As thus:

"Call yerself a blighted summer, do ye? Not much. Got 'arf the blighted ormenack[5] laid out for ye. 'Arf the blighted ormenack, so 'elp me, and red print fur Sundays. There's a summer for ye! Don't even know its own blighted ormenack. Comes crawlin' 'ome in November, – crawlin' 'ome wiv the milk. Lorlumme, there *ain't* no blighted summer these days! Poor ole perisher's 'fraid to come in, 'e is. 'Arf a ormenack dead wasted! There's the blighter all ready, an' – an' whatffor? *Whaffor*, I say? F'r a blighted ole summer that never comes 'ome. I never see sich days – neether before nor since. O – ughh! –"

It ended with a shiver. Not a tickly back shiver. A real "six-o'clock-of-a-frosty-morning-sing-for-you-breakfast" sort of shiver. So I got out my tobacco pouch, and spoke him fair.

"Have a pipe, Beaky?" said I.

He started up and blinked at me through the rain. "Pipe?" he echoed. "Yus: an' a match, an' a loan o' one of them papers, an' a copper, too, guv'nor. For a night's lodgin', guv'nor. You'll 'elp a pore fellar to a night's lodgin', guv'nor?"

"Depends," said I. "Have the pipe first."

He took an old clay[6] from a hole in his coat, and filled it from my pouch. This, like any gentleman, he afterwards folded up, and returned to me with a "Thank you."

"Walked far?" I asked him.

He was not able to say. He didn't *count* the blessed miles. Walking them was bad enough. If pressed to name a figure he would say a trillion million billion blighted miles. His mate was on the road. Would be along here soon. Had this meeting-place been fixed upon between them? "Oh, no," said he, "we simply follow on."

"Your name, by the way," I suggested, "is Beaky." He assented.

"What else could it be? Blokes with a face like mine always *are* Beaky. It's Nature."

"Any news about the 'Ouse, guv'nor?" he enquired, presently glancing at the roll of papers beneath my arm. "Come along 'er through Surrey," he explained. "The amount o' brown paper goin' about in Surrey would break your 'eart. If they can't wrop up their bits of waste in noospaper, what's the use o' worppin' it up at all? Brown paper ain't no good to us. Anythink further about the 'Ouse, guv'nor?"[7]

"Which House?" I asked. It did not seem reasonable to suppose that this man should be interested in stocks.[8] To credit him with a thirst for knowledge concerning the seat of his country's laws seemed still less reasonable.

In answer to my question, Beaky waved an arm in the direction of Welling Street. "That's the 'Ouse I mean," he said. "*The* 'Ouse. Played there many a time I 'ave – *with* Irving an' without 'im. Notice they don't ask *my* vote abaht pullin' of it down.[9] Ho, no! No at all! I'm a back number, I am."

"What," I enquired, "was your particular line? Extra gentleman?"

"Extra *pancakes*," responded "Beaky," with a gesture of revolt. "If I wos ten year younger, it'd take more'n a yob in a squash 'at to call *me* a blighted sooper[10] to me face."

I offered a complete and unconditional apology. "I'm *sure*," said "Beaky – which I perceived to be sarcasm.

"My line," he made answer, "was *any* blighted line. Animals was considered my masterpiece. Bein' patronised be royalty was a common thing with me in them days – as the sayin' goes. Why, 'Er Late Lamented[11] come to see me one day at Astley's.[12] I was playin' one o' the rats in 'Dick Whittington,' ... Played every animal I the bill, I 'ave – bar kangaroo. There don't seem to be no call fur kangaroo, some'ow. An' at the time I'm speakin' of they was on'y jest invented – as the sayin' goes. I made me mark at Tragedy, too. I nigh killed a man in 'Dick Turpin' once. It was '*is* fault, mind you. 'E was a circus-bred man, really – never been on the legitimate at all before. Consequence was, yer back an' side fall was all one to 'im. If yo was to bend over that parapet, I could show you 'ow it 'appened. You won't? Oh! please yeself! Only I could 'a' showed you just 'ow Ted Purkis come to be crippled f'r life. 'Es's alive now – but very weak. Fractured 'is neck, they said. Very bad fracture, I believe.

"It was later on in life I took to Comedy. Made me reputation at that, really. I was in a circus, see, an' – Can ye spare me another fill o' baccy, guv'nor?"

I handed him my pouch. This time he did not fill his pipe. "There's more nourishment in a chaw,"[13] said he.

"... I was in a circus – see? An' you may not credit it, but they 'ad me name in the paper once. 'A painstaking humorist,' was what they said. Yus, that was what they said: 'A painstaking humorist named Fred Dillnutt.' That was the name I went by in them days. I disremember the name of the gentleman what printed that about me. 'E was a nice gentleman. 'Mine's gin' we useder call 'im.

"Well, well! I fetched 'em proper in them days. It was the verses what done it – that an' fallin' down. When I come on I useder trip over meself. Then I useder look at 'em ard, an' say:

> 'Ere I am: I just come in.
> There's a woman there a-drinkin' gin!

That fetched 'em. An' before goin' off I useder fall over meself again an' say:

> Before you go to sweet repose
> Don't forget to wipe yer nose.

That useder fair knock 'em. It was that that made the gentleman put me in print. Any more tobaccy to spare, guv'nor?"

He shivered again. Chawing tobacco, he explained, was a famous corrective to the shivers. "My mate says tobaccer'l be the Death o' *me*. But my mate's younger nor me – an' not so wore out like, with the rain an' trampin' an no teeth an' things. My mate's in better repair, like. You oughter *know* my mate."

"Do you still perform?" I asked him, then.

"I am still," said he, "open to accept engagements."

"Animals?" I enquired.

"No, mate – Comedy: strict Comedy. I'll give you a show now."

I should not like to witness many entertainments like that contributed by Beaky on the bridge. Can't you imagine the scene? That tired old body, tied up with rotten ropes, was no figure of Mirth at all. It was not good to watch its tottering simulation of a strut. It was not good to look upon its leers and gestures. Halfway through the second verse, however, Beaky gave up. "It's swallerin' that there 'bacca," he gasped out. "You ought never to do it on an empty stomach."

"*Did* you swallow it?" I asked.

"Did I 'arf?" he answered. "I ain't 'ad nothing but a bite of bread an' bacon fat since yesterday. An' that," he added, "were yesterday night. You'll spare a copper to 'elp a fellow to a night's lodging, won't you, guv'nor?"

This last in a loud and plaintive voice. Then aside in a cautious undertone: "Below! There's my mate comin' up." And a girl with bulrushes in her hand, stepped out of the darkness.

"Well, you ole fool," said the girl, "what's the latest? More trouble than fifty *'usbands*, you are. What mischief you bin up to eh?"

"I bin swallering tobacco – twice," Beaky made the announcement with an air of proud and conscious infamy.

"You done *what*?" asked the girl, slowly unbuttoning her sleeves. She was a freckled young person, tired and needy-looking as the man himself, but indescribably cleaner.

"I swallered two goes o' tobacco," repeated Beaky, triumphant in sin.

The girl flung down her bulrushes. "Put 'em up!" she cried. "I'll show you whose boss 'ere. I'll learn ye!"

[23 October 1903]

II. Beaky's Mate.

Those Honoured Patrons who were kind enough to glance at last week's picture will remember that it represented the author as being situated in a position of delicacy. He – which is I – stood on Waterloo Bridge holding discourse with two vagrom and dissentient hedge-roosters. And of these twain one was a wench, and scornful.

This fact she exhibited both in speech and gesture. "I will show you, ole soft-'ead," she remarked to her companion, "'oo is boss *'ere*" – and therewith proceeded (after the laying bare of a clean and dimpled fore-arm) to anoint him with blows. And when she had *quite* done, the companion, whose name was Beaky, turned to me with a quiet smile, saying:

"This is my mate: I'd like to introduce you." Quoth the maiden, "You are a saucy clown," and smote him once more upon the head. After repeating this act unto the thricely and fourthly, she addressed herself to me.

"As for you be'ind the pipe there," she exclaimed, "I wonder you got the face to stop here. Standin' there with your toes turned in like two-penn'orth of Gaudelpus!¹⁴ If you was a little bigger for your age I'd set about *you*, too. What do you mean be eggin' on this pore ole luniac 'ere to go swollerin' tobaccer? Gasp 'isself violet, 'e will. You oughter know better – *you*, with your education an' white spats¹⁵ an' what all."

It is possible that – given time – I could have framed a coherent answer to this charge. But the smiling Beaky stepped in to offer a repetition of his previous remark.

"*This* – when it's finished scatterin' itself – is my mate. I would liketer introdooce you."

"Would you, indeed? Is that so?" enquired the lady, with evident satire. "*My* likes don' count, I s'pose? In case they do, you may's well note that I am not a starter. Bit partickler what *I* git iterodooced to."

"That on'y shows your igerance," retorted Beaky. "Looks are very deceiving things. There's many a noble 'eart beneath a squash 'at an' always will be. What saith the Bard:

> It isn't long whiskers an' check pattern coats,
>   That makes a gentle*man*,
> Nor cheatin' your baker, nor sowin' wild hoats,
>   Nor sportin' the light rat*tan*.
> No! gimme the fellar that's trew to 'is word,
>   An' dresses in cord-u-o-roy;

> That to scoff at 'is neighbours 'as never been 'eard,
>   An would scorn 'is fond wife to annoy.
>
> Young Peter, the ploughman, is free with 'is gold,
>   An' sheds it wherever 'e can,
> On the sick an' the needy; the young and the old –
>   R! that is a trew gentle*man!*
> The rich city merchant, 'oo –[16]

To my extreme sorrow, Professor Beaky's first reading from the British poets was at this point forcibly suspended. No self-respecting elocutionist likes to be cut off at the main. There was a note almost of anger in the voice with which Beaky, after gently removing a hand from before his mouth, requested an explanation of its presence there.

"What did I stop you for?" responded the owner of this hand, "what do you *think* I stopped you for? Got quite enough 'ump as it is, without listenin' to *your* spasms. You'd 'a' gone on till you choked if I *'adn't* stopped you."

This assertion was warmly repudiated by my friend. "There is only seven more verses," said he, "and well you know it."

The girl, who had picked up the bundle of bull-rushes which she threw down in the last picture, offered no contradiction to this statement. She unrolled the sleeve which she had recently tucked up, and thumped and pinched her arm to restore its circulation. The plashing of the rain upon this limb, together with its hue, which had changed from pink to Liberty green,[17] produced an effect distinctly Morgue-like. When the girl had thumped for a little while, she left off to shiver, and then she thumped again. But the thumping did no good, and it seemed, somehow, to bring on the shivers; so she put the bull-rushes over her shoulder, and pushed the wet fringe away from her eyes, and stamped her feet upon the pavement, and swore, definitely and fearfully, at things in general. Then she spoke to Beaky, saying:

"Are you comin' on, Mister Irving, or *ain't* you? I ain't goin' to stop 'ere to be washed out an' warped. I'm goin' to look f'r a railway arch. A dry railway arch an' a wink o' sleep 'll do you more good than all the po'try as was ever wrote. Come on!"

"I'll come on," responded Beaky, "when I've interodooced you to this gentleman 'ere. This gentleman – *is* a gentleman. He's give me 'arf-a-dollar. Saith the Bard:

Oh –

"Bard be boiled!" cried Beaky's mate, which I did not consider to be a ladylike utterance. "If this gentleman give you 'arf-a-dollar," she continued, "I'll take back what I said. Shake 'ands, boy!"

We shook.

"She is my mate," explained Beaky, "an' I would like to interodooce you."

"You see," said the girl, "this ole blind-worm 'ere can't ever be relied upon to do anythink what's sensible. 'Stead o' givin' me the orfice soon's ever I come up, 'e stands gaspin' alongside, without so much as utterin' a word, whiles I give you the spikiest character I could lay me tongue to. I wasn't to *guess* you've be'aved so 'andosme, was I? People can only be looks, an' I put you down as a tract merchant.[18] No offence, of course."

"There is no vice in my mate, really," remarked Beaky, in a confidential manner. "If ye can bring ye'self to let bygones be bygones, I would –"

He stopped short. The girl had begun to tuck up her sleeve again. "You an' your interference is enough to drive a person stark staring," she exclaimed with wrath. If you don't keep that rat-trap shut, I'll – I'll –" she paused, being suddenly inspired. "Jest take an' count these bull-rushes. Go over 'em three times. An' don't talk to me again till you've got out two totals alike ... That," she explained in a confidential aside to myself, "won't be this sider Christmas."

"Goin' back to what I was sayin'. I daresay what I said was a bit crisp – about that tobaccer an' all. But you see, there's a lot of people takes liberties with Beaky. Bein' old an' a bit silly-like, an' past 'ittin' much, they likes to take a rise out of 'im. Nature, I sp'ose. On'y that sorter little game 'as gotter be watched. Beaky's a reg'lar she nanny-goat fur playin' the ox.[19] The things that man 'll eat if 'e's tempted! 'E wouldn't stop at potater-shavin's! But 'is worst fault is the tobaccer. It nigh kills 'im, it does; but a soon's ever 'e goes a bit 'ungry – Gawd! Look at 'im now!"

Beaky was gasping again. He provided a striking illustration of the evils of tobacco – when eaten on an empty stomach. We thumped him, and shook him, and tickled his ears, so that presently he "came round," and said several hard things concerning manufacturers who flood the market with indigestible tobacco. Then we walked southward in search of a quiet coffee-stall. A refreshment place of that kind is situated on the north end of the bridge, within a stone's throw of where we stood. But this we did not patronise, knowing it to be horribly police-ridden. We shuffled off to the south side, and made use of a little stall that stands almost on the bridge itself. Having fortified the inwards of us with a many beakers, we pushed forward again. For I had an object in view. And, on the journey, I learned the name of Beaky's mate.

"Is my name *what*?" she exclaimed, in reference to a question of mine. "Why, that's 'is name, stoopid. Fred Dillnutt, comedian: an' the best name for a fat-'ead ever I come across. 'E ain't no relative o' mine, y' know. My name's Primrose – leastways, that's what they tole me, 'long a' the cokernuts. Only the name I generally go by is 'Oppa – after me walk, y' know."

"There's lots of people takes me an' Beaky for relations. Us bein' always together is what does it. What we really are is on'y jest mates. You see, Beaky come with me when I done a bunk from the cokernuts.[20] 'E travelled along o' the same caravan, Beaky did. 'E does 'igh-class comedy turns between the rounds in the boxing booth. Well, when I begun to grow up, see there was a lotter fellows after me for no good. Gypsies, some on 'em, an' a great red-'aired bloke from the boxing, an' Professor Dinwaddy, of the Electric Shocks.

Beaky saw to the boxing bloke with a cooper's mallet. An' 'im an' Dinwaddy 'ad a dust-up in public. But it done no good, an' some on 'em was settin' by to get Beaky under a van wheel, or in a tent when the pole come down. An' then there was the young gentlemen in round 'ats an' leggin's[21] what come to see the fair. Made theirselves that at 'ome, they did, when I was in charge of the sticks, you'd 'a' took me fur part o' the game. So, one way 'n' another, there was nothing for it but a bunk. So Beaky got a pair of scissors, an' cut all the little bits of brown wire off the Professor's shock machine, a' the pair on us took the road. It was 'ard, after standin' by the cokernuts for all those years. But what's a girl to do?"

Then I raised a question which had agitated my mind during the whole course of the conversation. "But hadn't you a sweetheart?" I asked.

"Why, of *course*!" answered the girl.

"Then what was he doing all this time? Why did Professor Dinwaddy remain alive?"

"Why, don't you see," explained Miss Hopper, "my boy was out at sea. 'E's a sailor, 'e is. They'll be an end to all this trampin', an' the wet, an' dead flesh an' things, when 'e comes 'ome. Do you know Bewnezerry?"

I had read of a place called Bueos Ayres, and said so.

"Ah!" remarked the girl. "That's where he was last. 'E's comin' 'ome now. 'Ow soon might I expect 'im, would you fancy, now, guv'nor? They bin three years on the way already."

"Three years?" I echoed. "Three years since when?"

"Since leaving Bewnezerry. I know they've left all right, cos I see it in the paper. My boy showed me where to look, an' what for. 'S.S. "City of Lisbon." Cardiff to the Argentine. Ballast an' cattle.' An' I looked in the place 'e said in the paper 'e said every day for weeks an' weeks. An' sometimes 'is boat was there, an' sometimes it wasn't. An' one day – about a week before I left the sticks – I see: 'Bewnezerry' – that's the way they call it, y' know, 'cos my boy told me. 'E can't write, but 'e knows a heap more than lots as can. 'Bewnezerry: Left, s.s., "City of Lisbon." Homeward.' It'll be three years come Wednesday since they left. Ought to be 'ere soon, don't you think?"

I did think so.

"Whenever we passes a free library in I goes – tatters an' all – fur a look at the papers.[22] But the bit my boy tole me to look for don't seem to be there no more. Wonder what 'e'll say about it when 'e comes ome?"

At this we came to the object, and while I was wondering about it, too, we came to the end or our walk.

"While," remarked Beaky, "we are waitin' to 'ear about this objec' what you 'ave in view, I'd better see about interodoocin' you two. You *oughter* know each other."

[30 October 1903]

III. Coffee.

Owing to the gratuitous collaboration of Lord Noson (the gentleman who is always responsible for misprints), there seems to have been a little confusion at the end of last week's picture. What I tried to tell everybody was this: that my conversation with Beaky, the tramp, and his Lady Friend, was brought to a termination by reason of our arrival at Arthur's coffee-stall.[23]

Now, Arthur's coffee-stall is a rare, especial, and excellent good coffee stall – the property of an intimate friend of mine. At Arthur's stall – which esquires and dames of the honourable order of London nighthood prefer to call just "Arfur's" for short – you get the hottest coffee which Nature and energy can provide. You get, also, buns, butter, eggs, tea, and other things, all of the freshest. And you get Arthur himself, who is a sage and prophet of price.

"Strike a light, lad! You do find 'em," this person remarked upon our arrival at his counter. I suppose that Beaky's garments *were* remarkable – even for London night-wear. But Beaky ate seven hard-boiled eggs and half a cottage loaf. And he entertained us to Beaky's reliques of ancient poetry. And he performed a conjuring trick with Arthur's hat, and permanently disfigured that venerable property. Finally, he produced his precious half-dollar, and was for "treating" everybody at the stall to hot coffee and sardines. We forcibly restrained him from performing this rash deed.

"'Ave it yer own way," he snorted, at last. "'Ave it yer own way. It seems I'm took fur a pauper. Always like that wiv us Bo'eemians. A man can't ever dress a bit eccentric in these days. Reminds you of 'Oh! Spare Me the Lash.' Finest ballad goin'. Saith the Bard:

> O spare me the lash of a pityin' look!
>   Sigh not thus in superior fashion.
> Far, far would I rather my friends me forsook,
>   Than accept of their 'aughty compassion.
> What though my ole beaver is worn at the brim?
>   What though I and cetera an' so on?
> I something or other an' tiddlerly push
>   An' merrily chirp as I go on![24]

"An' so say I," continued Beaky, by way of annotation. "I don't mind civility, but I have pride. Spendin' money is no novelty wiv me, an' don't you think it. Stood drinks to a alderman in *my* time!"

"Don't you give 'im any more food, guv'nor. 'E'll go same's if 'e was drunk if you do. It's not bein' used to it." The girl said this.

"Don't you listen to 'er, gents," cried Beaky. "She on'y wants to show off 'er authority. *She* ain't no stomach specialist! She's my mate, really. I would like to interodooce 'er to everybody."

"Everybody," consisted of Arthur, Arthur's cat, two cabmen, and myself. It was three o'clock, which from the coffee-stall point of view is neither one thing nor the other, being too late for supper and somewhat in advance of breakfast. "'Arvest in England, I gen'lly call it," Arthur had once remarked. "Lot's o' rain, an' nothink to reap."

"Give over chatterin', now" said Miss Hopper to Beaky, "an' come along. Say 'Thank you' to the gentlemen."

Beaky turned a reproachful eye upon the girl. "You are fergittin' ye'sel'," said he; "you are showing your vulgarity. I must apologise fur my mate, gentlemen," he continued, addressing the company at large. "Let my mate pop off if she wants to, I will stand by. 'Manners before comfort' is *my* motter."

In accordance with this principle, Mr. Dillnutt proceeded, without further preface, to lift up our hearts with anecdotes of the circus tent. Miss Hopper at first stood coldly aloof, buttoning and unbuttoning her sleeve in an ominous manner, and tapping the ground with an impatient foot. But by the time Beaky reached his third episode, which was a masterpiece of romantic fiction, she, too yielded to the fascination of his genius; and a constable stepped up and stayed to listen, and the rain "left off", and the day drew closer, so that the charmed circle of his audience grew and grew.

This is how episode three terminated: "Believe me or not, gentlemen, it is trew what I am tellin' you. Little Alf the Clown put gin into the milk of the Boxing Kangaroo. So Vulcan the Strong Man was soon no more. An' Little Alf the Clown bein' the on'y thing 'andy, an' our Lady Lion Tamer bein' of a marryin' natur', she took an' married '*im*. So Little Alf the Clown got two things what 'e wanted – with one stone, as the sayin' were, got a bit of is 'is own back from Vulcan the Strong Man, an' married the lady what 'e loved. Very strange it was, I grant you. You might almost put it in a book."

"No doubt of that!" assented Arthur. "What become of the Boxing Kangaroo. We should all of us like to 'ear some more about the Boxing Kangaroo. 'Ave a sip o' corfee. It may strengthen you up a bit. We should like you to think of somethink *extra* about the Boxin' Kangaroo!!"

"Now you come to mention it," responded Beaky, with a reminiscent glance into his coffee cup, "now you come to mention it, there *is* a tale to tell about the

Kangaroo. Very sad it was. That drop o' gin what little Elfred put into 'is milk gave the pore ole animal a taste fur drink. It died o' drunkard's liver."

It was some time before Arthur could find words in which to express his admiration. Then, in a voice tremulous with emotion, he murmured a few unprintable superlatives, and re-filled Beaky's cup. These and other compliments were accepted by Beaky in a spirit of well-considered modesty. "That," he explained, "is far from bein' one o' my specials. If you want a really *strange* story, now, there is that little item about the piebald 'orse. You see –"

"I am sorry to interrup' you," interpolated Arthur, "but perhaps that 'air-restorer will keep. 'Oo knows but what it won't *improve* even be bein' pondered over for a bit? I like listenin' to these 'ere 'appy thoughts o' yourn very much indeed, but business is business. Customers must be attended, y' know – jest off an' on, like."

"It is your loss – not mine," responded Beaky, and wrapped himself in moody silence.

In the mean time, customers were arriving thick and fast. A voice which had cried, "G.H.!" in reference to one of Beaky's proudest feats of memory betrayed itself to my practised ear as being that of somebody connected with the printing trade. And, squinting into the blackness, I beheld in retirement, and partially obscured by a coffee cup, the countenance of my old friend and colleague, Mr. William Honeybunn.

"Go' bless my soul! Ain't you cut the line yet?" he remarked, on seeing me. This is Printer's Talk, and very charming. I proposed having discourse with Mr. Honeybunn; but Mr. Honeybunn was in no mood for discourse. "Go an' talk 'make-up' to your aunt," he suggested. "*I* don't want to talk to you. God knows I see enough of the editors all day long without takin' them to me supper. I'm in the mood for *killin'* editors, I am."

From this I concluded that the paper – *our* paper – had been late in getting to press. On these occasions Mr. Honeybunn is a gentleman to be avoided. I think I may go so far as to say that, under normal conditions, I am a friend of Mr. Honeybunn's. When Parliament rises early, and things are well with the "finals," we take snuff together (*all* Printers carry snuff), and exchange confidences. These confidences relate chiefly to the subject of wife management, concerning which question I am in the habit of collecting expert evidence. Mr. Honeybunn's method is simple, consisting – but it will keep. This night, at any rate, Mr. Honeybunn was *not* for confidence. I left him, and looked for friends among the early morning crowd which was fast collecting about the counter of Arthur's stall.

It was a curious crowd. Much of it consisted of draymen, but the market porters bulked largely too. Wholesale newspaper men were there to the number of three; but their presence and conversation, which related the subject of "returns", was offensive to me.[25] A couple of early labourers were present; but they drank their coffee quickly, and in silence, having roads to take up before breakfast. The usual sailor arrived with the usual lady, and quarreled about his change, and broke a teacup, and was dealt with by the draymen. And a real "toff," really drunk, came up, and tendered sixpence for a packet of Wild Dream cigarettes, and went on his way rejoicing. I seemed to see a "come-down" of the clerk variety lurking somewhere in the outskirts of the crowd. His skin was yellow, and his body shrunk, and there was hunger, and cold, and FEAR writ large upon him. But he wore a high white collar.[26] And there was a policeman, of course; and the women (God save the mark!)[27] were everywhere.

"I gotter thank you for bein' a pal," said a voice at my elbow. I looked, and beheld Miss Hopper, of the "cokernuts." "I'd give you my bull-rush," she continued, "on'y it would be kinder not to. Of all the stinkin' rubbish, give me bull-rushes. On'y people *do* buy 'em – sometimes." She wrung my hand in a fervid manner, and turned her back upon me. Then she pushed her way through his admiring audience, and made for Beaky, who, having stood on one leg in an imitation of a stork, and asked a number of remarkable riddles, had got definitely under weigh with the narrative of the pie-bald horse.

The owner of this animal, it seemed, was in the circus business. His name was Tooney, but his aliases were many. The piebald horse made ten appearances nightly, and was so called by reason of the marking which distinguished him when performing in association with Mademoiselle Loisette, Champion Lady Rider of the Universe.

"For 'Shaw the Life-Guardsman,'" explained Beaky, "ole Pie-Balls 'ad to be black. An' for the dashin 'Igh-School Act you wanted a friendly brown. When it come to little Tiny the Child Equestrienne, we give 'em a 'an'some cream direct from the royal stables; an' Mr. X (ole Tooney, reely) done 'is reckless jockey act on a dapple grey.

"As I said before, the ole bloomin' stud on'y totalled one 'orse. An' that was ole Pie-Balls. Mr. Tooney was that clever with the paint pot, it would 'a' took cleverer blokes than any o' *you* mugs to spot the fraud, an' don't you doubt it."

"Well – what of it?" demanded somebody.

"What of it"? echoed Beaky. "R, that is just what we are comin' to. That 'orse 'e up an' died, an' there was a post-mortem – wiv turpentine. We was all of us anxious to find out ole Pie-Balls' nat'ral colour. It took three strong men a matter of eight hours to work down to the last coat. An' when we got through that, what do you think we found?"

In reply to this enquiry, Beaky was favoured with a variety of suggestions embracing every colour ever associated with horseflesh. One competitor, indeed, suggested pink. Beaky smiling the smile of conscious triumph, shook his head.

"You are all wrong," said he, at last. "We found a blinkin' zebra!"

Sensible of the sensation produced by this anecdote, Beaky favoured us with a comprehensive bow, and prepared to depart.

"Look 'ere, ole Calamity," said Arthur, suddenly. "Could you clean plates an' keep sober?"

"I doubt it," stated Beaky.

"You bloomin' well say 'No' – that's all my beauty." It was Beaky's mate who spoke, turning up her sleeves as she did to.

"My mistake," conceded Beaky, with an affable smile. "My mistake: as you were. I *could* wipe dishes I *could* keep sober."

"Very well," said Arthur. "Come round to my copper-'ouse, 19, Little Turnbull Street, 2 a.m. termorrer."

Beaky was profuse in his thanks. Arthur advised him to keep them until called for.

"Say good-night to the gentlemen, an' come along at once," ordered the girl.

"Good-night, ole speed-gear," shouted Arthur, "Good-night, Miss What's-yer-name."

"I like that gal's face: she washes it," he added, half to himself.

We watched the curious couple until the blur of their two figures had merged into the early morning haze. And when we had almost looked long enough, the voice of Beaky came faintly out of the mist: "My mate ... Never interdooced her after all! Next time."

[6 November 1903]

IV. A Conspiracy of Kindness.

My friend Arthur has at least one characteristic beloved of Providence. He is a cheerful giver. "Live reg'lar an' save re'lar; but when you *do* spend, make a job of it." Such is his creed.

In view of this fact, I was not surprised to find that Beaky's visit to Arthur's copper-house resulted most happily for the former gentleman. As each of Arthur's "regulars" arrived that evening at the stall, he found himself confronted by a stately, suave, benign, clean-shaven personage, arrayed in mouse-coloured clothing of agreeable freshness. There was oil in the stranger's hair, a scarf of many colours about his throat, and (most arrestive feature of all) a "Superba" cigar,[28] very little used, within the riband of his head-dress. As customer after customer drew close to the "counter," our host, who stood beside it, performed a ceremony of introduction, in these terms:

"Bill (or Sid, or 'Erry, as the case might be), "this is Fred Dillnutt – my curate-in-charge."[29]

Beaky's object in removing his moustache and beard was, I think, not wholly clear to that gentleman himself. "I feel me responsibilities," was the nearest approach to an explanation which he vouchsafed to *us*. My own curiosity, however, was less tickled by the night change in Beaky (although *that* metamorphosis was sufficiently striking) than by an extraordinary departure in the conduct of Arthur himself.

During all the years of our acquaintanceship, and they embraced a period big with unexpected incident, Arthur had never been known to go "off duty." When you come to think about it, there is nothing really remarkable in this fact. The coffee-stall business provides a man with free evenings and free days. By a judicious variation of his hours of slumber, he may be out and about in the world at all the times when things happen. His hours of business clash with nothing, and, therefore, the temptation to shirk them is not great. For many reasons, therefore, it surprised me, even more than Beaky's brand-new smartness surprised me, to find Arthur leaning airily against the outer fabric of his own stall, and paying for coffees over the counter.

"You are noticin'," said Arthur, in reference to my scrutiny of his person, "you are noticin' the clobber".[30] He altered his position, so that the light in his stall shone full upon a new and noble suit of Sunday "blacks." After a minute search for any speck or fluff which might be clinging to the surface of this raiment he sighed in a manner suggestive of spiritual happiness, and spoke again:

"There is a lot of satisfaction in noo clobber. My one extravagance. Look at this yer 'at. 'As worn by the King,'[31] it says inside."

"His Majesty has a happy taste in linings," said I, in returning the article to Arthur, after due inspection.

"The linin' *is* a bit sudden, I grant you," responded Arthur; "but even a king can't wear 'is Trilby[32] inside out. Wore on the 'ead a little to one side, like this" (Arthur obliged us with a practical illustration) "toes at an angle o' forty-five degrees, right knee slightly bent, chest throwed out, arms 'angin' straight but not stiff at the sides – all that an' a ripe fourpenny[33] between yer lips – why, I'd guarantee to 'ave the guard out at Buckin'ham Palace any time I liked to blow me nose."

"You see," he continued, in a confidential "aside" to myself, "I couldn't be out-classed be me own bally Curate. So when we got to Mosenstein's[34] I made a 'olesale order of it. Thought you'd *look*!"

"The clothes," I answered, "are very interesting and effective – both the Curate's and yours. But I wasn't looking so much at them as at *you*. It is unusual to catch you playing customer at your own stall."

"Ah! It *is* a bit unusual!" assented Arthur. "I wanted to watch the Rev. Beaky conductin' service. And I wanted to judge them Swiss rolls from an outside point of view. Changed me baker, y' see. An' I wanted to get somewhere where the noo clobber could be seen; an'" (his voice dropped) "I wanted a little private confabulation with yere 'umble self."

"But," I pointed out, "you don't usually come outside the stall for that. We've discussed treason over that counter before now."

"It ain't no treason what I'm layin' for this time. You've on'y gotter look at me clothes to know that. A man can't vote Progressive[35] in a noo soot, let alone talk treason.

"What I wanter speak to you about (when you can tear yeself away from that corfee) is not for the Curate's ears. It's about that mate of 'is. What with that clobber, an' a reg'lar stipend, an' the things 'e'll steal from my copper-'ouse, Beaky oughter be all right. The question is – 'Ow're we goin' on fur 'is mate?"

I shook my head: I shrugged my shoulders.

"It's no good pertendin' you don't care," exclaimed Arthur. "You've bloomin' well *gotter* care. We're both of us in this. *You* dug the beauties up."

"But," I made answer, "it is your fault that I didn't put them back again. Why didn't you let them to their ways? Because I choose to buy coffee for a couple of loafers at your stall, I do not make myself responsible for their existence. *I* never asked you to invite Beaky home to tea; *I* never asked you to dress him up like a Labour Member,[36] and give him the run of your jam – *and* your till. He's a charming conversationalist, we know, but – well, for myself, I should have drawn the line at open tills. That's your business, however, I resent your attempting to make it *mine*."

"You do, do you?" responded Arthur. "Then p'raps you'll tell me 'oo it was as *tempted* me? When you brought that couple round to my stall you *knoo* that Beaky would find a job there. You *knoo* that a wonderful liar like 'e is would touch me on my softest spot."

I met this accusation with a guilty blush.

"That bein' so," pursued Arthur, "you are as much to blame as me. Also, you ain't the skulking rat you lay on to be. You wouldn't like to stand by an' see a gal like that go the same way as the rest on 'em. You've come down 'ere to 'ave another look at the pair on 'em – Beaky an' 'er – an' well you know it. So we will leave off bluffin', an come to business."

"Agreed!" quoth I.

"Well," continued Arthur, "it's said in one word – 'Oneybunn. We must work it, lad."

Arthur's reference was to my friend, the printer. Mr. Honeybunn supervises the appointment of young women to the jobbing department of his "house." In this connection Mr. Honeybunn possesses a wide power of choice, hampered, however, by one condition. "They must be deservin' cases," says Mr. Honeybunn. "It is the guv'nor's orders." Some few years ago we had occasion to approach Mr. Honeybunn in connection with the case of one, Kitty the Rake,[37] who was a friend of ours.

"If you give 'er a job," Arthur had explained, "she 'as promised to go off the streets an' eat three proper meals a day."

"Is she a deservin' case?" Mr. Honeybunn had enquired. "Has she consumption or a club foot?"

Kitty the Rake was called up, and made sorrowful confession of sound lungs and straight ankles.

Mr. Honeybunn, after shaking his head in an ominous manner, had enquired hopefully after a number of other diseases and ailment, none of which, however, poor Kitty had in stock.

"I am very sorry," Mr. Honeybunn had observed, "but your application cannot be considered. You cannot honestly describe yourself as a deservin' case. We *must* have deservin' cases – be the guv'nor's orders."

Then an inspiration came to Kitty. She had not got tuberculosis or a weak spine, but she *had* got a baby, and said so.

"A baby!" Mr. Honeybunn had exclaimed. "Good! Excellent!! The very thing! It'll please the guv'nor more'n if you was blind."

This episode had the effect of impressing the minds of Arthur and myself with the peculiarity of Mr. Honeybunn's requirements. It was these which constituted our difficulty in making arrangements for Miss Hopper. We knew that she was hungry and cold, and altogether unhappy; but a horrible doubt possessed us as to whether these things alone would make up a "deserving case" in the Honeybunn sense.

"If on'y *she's* had a baby, now!" said Arthur, half to himself, and in a tone which implied that Miss Hopper had made poor use of her time. "She is such an ennercent little thing," he continued, "that's where it comes in. If on'y we could prove a forger against her! We know what 'Oneybunn will say at once: 'What misfortunes 'as she 'ad?'"

"She's pretty miserable, anyhow," I pointed out.

"Misery ain't on 'Oneybunn's list," responded Arhtur. "Now I come to think of it," he added, more hopefully, "trudgin' in the rain an' damp ditches an' that does sometimes damage your lungs. P'aps we can work up a case of consumption, after all!"

"Honeybunn will be round here pretty soon if he's coming at all," I reminded him.

"That's so," he answered. "The gal's due now. We gotter make our arrangements afore he comes. Mrs. Walpole's comin', too. She's got the gal in charge, jest fur the time bein'."

"Mrs. *Who*?" I asked, and Arthur looked at me, and grinned. The question was certainly ridiculous. It was two years, then, since Kitty the Rake had settled down and married comfortably into the municipal service. Arthur and I had schemed and plotted to bring about that marriage as we had schemed and plotted, also, to put Miss Kitty in the way of clean living and a trousseau. But I had been out of London for a year, describing pig shows and prize pumpkins in an unappreciated vein of humour for the benefit of rustic readers. And, somehow, I found it a task requiring effort to associate our whimsical, calamitous Kitty of yesterday with unmitigated wifehood. Not that I doubted for a moment but what Kitty had proved herself as sweet and "managing" a helpmeet as was ever wed. It was merely the sound of the thing which seemed to challenge the congruities. The idea of Kitty – *our* Kitty – possessing a legal prefix and a vote for the School Board![38]

Just then these reflections were disturbed by the arrival of Kitty herself, with Miss Hopper duly and safely under convoy.

"'Oo's that calling me Mrs. Walpole?" demanded Kitty, in reference to my greeting. "Why, it's the Lad! Thank 'eavens, I see you in the dark! That thing on your lip would 'ave given me convulsions if I'd seen it in the daytime. And 'e's taken to a pipe, too, and – why – yes – no – yes! a spat on *each* foot! What's it the lady says in the play? 'My God! 'ow time *'as* changed you!'"

"And what of matrimony?" quoth I.

Kitty turned her eyes to heaven, and sighed tragically. "'E turns up 'is nose at cold mutton," she replied, "but we still speak."

"When the two of you 'ave done," exclaimed Arthur at this point, "there is business afore the meeting, to be discussed immediate. Touchin' this matter of deservin' cases –"

Kitty interrupted him. "You can set your little minds at rest," said she; "all that 'as bin attended to. This lady 'as done time."

We turned to Miss Hopper for confirmation of the charge. "It's true," said she.

"Even 'Oneybunn oughter be satisfied with *that*," asserted Arthur.

[13 November 1903]

V. "Which the Serpent Tempted."

Kitty's dramatic announcement and Miss Hopper's personal confirmation thereof, created a hopeful flutter in the breast of every coffee-stall conspirator amongst us. For, as Arthur so justly remarked, even Mr. Honeybunn ought to feel satisfied with a proved conviction. The most "deserving" case ever recorded on that gentleman's tablets had reference to a lady who, yielding to sudden temptation, had sought to stimulate the value of an insurance policy by the means of kerosene. This unfortunate creature was now a forewoman in Mr. Honeybunn's stitching department. Thus, as in the case of Kitty and all Mr. Honeybunn's other young ladies, her misfortune had proved a stepping-stone to higher things.

There were limits to this principle, of course. Arthur recognised this fact. He therefore said to Miss Hopper:

"It would be as well, young woman to 'ear the circs.[39] There's sich a thing 'as bein' *too* deservin' in a case of this sort."

"I was on'y in fur a day," explained Miss Hopper. "Through hittin' a lady of title on the mouth."

"That's what I call actin' clumsy," said Arthur.

"Daresay it was," assented the girl, "on'y she insulted me. It was rainin', see? an Beaky 'ad bin swallerin' tobaccer, an' we was 'ungry, an' 'e 'ad got delusions on 'is mind, so I put him in the pound.[40] We was on tramp, of course. I went round to this lady's 'ouse to cadge. You can generally get stale tea leaves an' that, if you play the game. Soon's ever I showed me 'ead inside the gate the lady come bouncin' out of a verander.

"'You bad, wicked girl,' says she, 'I know you,' she says. 'It was you what stole my collie dog.'

"'Lor' love you, lady,' says I, 'do I *look* as if I wanted to steal a 'ungry dog?'

"She was a gay-lookin' lady – diamonds, an' a muslin chest, an' what all. An' I daresay you've noticed that there ain't never no kindness in a woman like that. With men it's different. The sorter bloke that wears a black westcoat an' a smile ain't *never* no good fur anything – except a tract. It's the worldly kind that give you bobs an' blessings. Women are contrairy. A dowdy jacket an' a ready-made skirt *is* a sign of goodness with them. Well, the one I'm talkin' of was the other sort. An' she fetched up her gardener, an' called me a slut. So I darnsed on 'er strawberry bed (it bein' April), an slapped 'er mouth.

"An' they took me to Claverin' Gaol.[41] An' they kep' me there fur a day an' a 'arf. Then they fetched me up afore a deaf ole gentleman in a fur oat. An' a interferin' bloke that sat in a pitch lower down said it would be five bob.[42] So the ole genelman 'e *give* me the five bob, an' I give it back to '*im*, an' 'e said somethink about discredit bein' brought on to the county be manufacturers' wives, an I went away. That's all."

"Your deaf friend was a rash ole idiot. 'E will find himself chalked[43] for dis."

By this cryptic utterance we were made conscious of the presence of Mr. Honeybunn himself.

"I do not talk slang," responded Miss Hopper. "Come forward, 'oo ever you are, an' let's pipe your dial.[44] I dunno what it was you said in that sausage-talk of yours. But if it was an insult to my dear ole Deafie, I may's well say at once that you are a onion-faced liar."

We clutched at our throats, we breathed hard, we nudged Miss Hopper, and we whistled strenuously. All this with a view to disguising the horror which consumed us. Here was this maiden, the possessor of a record so "deserving" that you might consider her engagement as good as fixed, wantonly jeopardizing her future career by applying such epithets as onion-faced to a foreman printer!

Kitty caught the girl in a wild embrace, and poured disheveled whisperings into her ear.

"*I* don't care," cried Miss Hopper; "the sauce of the man! Runnin' down my dear old Deafie to me very face!"

Mr. Honeybunn cleared his throat. This was an ominous sign, and we feared the worst. "What I was about to add," said Mr. Honeybun, "when so rudely interrupted to my right, was this –"

Miss Hopper grabbed a dish-cloth from the stall. "You say it!" she exclaimed, "that's all – on'y jest you *say* it! Say *one* word against my Deafie, an' I'll wipe this 'ere acrost your mouth, so sure's my name is Primrose."

Mr. Honeybunn waved a condescending arm towards the multitude. "Explain to Miss Primrose '*oo* I am," said he.

"It don't need no explainin', thank ye kindly," retorted Miss Primrose. "I can tell you are a bit of a boss be the oil in ye're 'air. This'll lose me a job, I *dessay*: as well's the pleasure of 'avin' you always 'andy.⁴⁵ But rats to your job, an' you, too. I kin go on tramp ag'in, same's before, an' yearn me livin' with me feet. Mrs. Walpole 'as give me a pair of 'er 'usban's boots, so I don't care fur nobody. I *will not* 'ear ole Deafie scoffed at."

"What I was about to add," said Mr. Honeybunn, resuming the thread of his interrupted discourse, "what I was about to add will not be looked upon as a scoff by any person impartial judgment. I have nothing to say against the kind 'eart an' generosity of your benefactor. I pass no slur upon 'is *looks*. It's his bloomin' folly that erritates me. What does 'e want to go an' risk a good job for be castin' reflections on the productive classes? Once we admit the principle that the Bench, in its public capacity, shall permit itself to be influenced by caste distinctions, incalculable evil may be wrought. A court of justice is the last institution which should lend itself to the exploitation of social prejudice. This is a democratic age."

"God save us all!" remarked Arthur, at the conclusion of this address. I permitted myself the luxury of a chuckle.

"You may well larf!" exclaimed Mr. Honeybunn. "I ain't bin 'oldin over your two sticks o' tripe an' onions for nothing. Glad you reckernise your own sentiments."

"Leadin' article? Our friend 'ere's?" enquired Arthur, with warm and wondering interest.

"More or less," responded Mr. Honeybunn. "You don't take 'arf a column to say it is not a judge's job to be influenced be social influence in the fudge space, I give you *my* word. Nor you don't refer to the democracy of the age. That tag is a 'must' in all our leaderettes. The Party⁴⁶ expects it.

"Quite right, too," asserted Arthur. "You can't remind 'em of it too often."

"That is what *I* say," rejoined Mr. Honeybunn. "'Elps to keep the Stone 'Ands[47] in their place.

"But comin' back," he continued, "to sweet Kate O'Connor[48] 'ere. She kin put up the dish-cloth, an' smooth back 'er 'air. What I said was said in all kindness. No offence intended, an' if any was given, I express my sorrow."

"The King couldn't say no fairer than *that*," declared Arthur; a semintment which found its echo in all our hearts.

"Go on, silly, say somethink. An' fur Gawd's sake curtsey – 'e expects it." This in a loud undertone from Kitty, who knew her Honeybunn like a bankbook.

"Take me fur a parlour-maid, or what?" demanded Miss Hopper, in response to this suggestion. "Curtsey, indeed! I look like it, don't I, in your man's Number Forties?[49] Might as well arst me to stand on me 'ead."

Arthur coughed uneasily. "We was thinkin', Mr. 'Oneybun – that is, we was 'opin – me an' The Boy 'ere – but what per'aps you could see your way to –"

"The fact of the matter is," I began, in a loyal effort to support my fellow agent, "the fact of the matter is that – er – that –"

"R! That is the point." Not to be out done in fealty, Arthur now came to *my* assistance. "The fact of the matter is that we – me an' The Boy 'ere – was thinkin' – or, rather, we was 'opin – but what per'aps – er –"

"When," interpolated Mr. Honeybunn, "you 'ave *quite* done makin' yourselves clear, you will per'aps permit *me* to tell *you* what it really is you was 'opin'. You was 'opin' to git round me – to *defraud* me, as it were – into pushin' Miss Perky there into our firm. I ain't 'avin' any."

"Now, look 'ere, Mr. 'Oneybunn," began Arthur; but Kitty edged him into obscurity and silence. "You're fairly duffin' it between you," she exclaimed, in one of her very loudest whispers. "This is a case fur *me*!"

"Mr. Honeybunn, you ain't forgot me, I 'ope? My name's Kitty."

Mr. Honeybunn softened visibly. We – the ancient and admitted Freemen of Arthur's stall – knew that there was a frail and mortal side to Mr. Honeybunn's character. And when Kitty smiles ... Ye gods! If the firm and excellent wife of Mr. Honeybunn's bosom were but here to see that smile!

"Remember you?" responded Mr. Honeybunn. "Not 'arf! Why, my dear Miss Kitty – Mrs. Walpole, I suppose I *oughter* say –."

"Kitty to *you*, Mr. 'Oneybunn. Think what I owe to your kindness."

"Since you put it like that," replied the Printer, blushing painfully, "I may's well say that the shop 'as seemed a different place ever since you left it!"

Kitty smiled again. "There are some things, Mr. 'Oneybunn, which a married woman 'ad better leave unsaid. But we can't 'elp rememberin' past kindnesses, can we, Mr. 'Oneybunn? An' – – ah! well. Do you remember that dear old book you give me, Mr. 'Oneybunn? By the greatest writer as ever lived, you said it was. 'The Last days of Something or Other,' by Lord Somebody."[50]

"I remember it," said Mr. Honeybunn.

"I 'ave it still, ole friend. I read it *every* day. Do you remember the bunch of everlastin' vi'lets you give me that evenin in Fetter Lane?"[51]

The look of gratification vanished from Mr. Honeybunn's face. "That is an incident which I try to forget, Mrs. Walpole," said he. "You may have forgotten that you threw them in the gutter, and reminded me of my age."

Kitty's talent for improvisation did not desert her at this rather critical juncture. "Where was your eyes, Mr. Honeybunn?" she enquired. "Many's the time I arst meself that question – 'No Eyes' I useder call you. Perhaps if you had come back to Fetter Lane a quarter-of-an-hour later you *might* have seen – but there are some things a married woman 'ad better leave unsaid."

"You was a rare pal to me, at any rate. The little kindnesses you useder do me! The good advice you useder give me! And always such a gentleman with it all."

"I hope so!" exclaimed Mr. Honeybunn. "We are all of us liable to be 'asty at times; but if a man 'as got any taste for manners at all, they – well, there they are! Always! Overtime included!"

"No doubt of it," asserted Kitty. "Well, now, Mr. 'Oneybunn, I won't try to git over you be flattery, because I know you to be above it. But a gentleman is a gentleman always, as you say, an' I speak as I find. This gal 'ere is my lodger. She ain't bulging over with sense, or manners, neether, as you can see fur yeself; but she's a good girl sometimes. An' your influence would do a lot for 'er. Mind you, I aint' tryin to make excuses for 'er. What she said about your face was ugly – very ugly; and I admit it."

"It wasn't too stinkin' polite," assented Mr. Honeybunn.

"At the same time," pursued Kitty, "you oughter make allowances. Look at the life she's led, an' the state of 'er clothes. She ain't never wore stays since she was born. What can you expect from a girl like that? Never 'ad a chance to improve 'erself, even if she wanted to. A little trainin' (strict, mind you!) would make another woman of her. Look what *I* was till you took me in hand!"

"That's true," mused Mr. Honeybunn.

"An' she's a very deservin' case," added Kitty. "You 'eard 'er story – bin in prison an' all."

"*Unjustly*, mind you!" broke in Arthur.

"R! Unjustly! An' you gotter remember," Kitty reminded us, "that proper trainin' would 'a' prevented even *that*!"

"Well, well," said Mr. Honeybunn, in the midst of an expectant silence, "we will consider the matter."

"Coffees all round on that!" cried Arthur. "'Urry up, young Beaky, there: coffees all round – my call." And Arthur broke out into a series of spasmodic movements, which were understood to represent a dance of joy. And Beaky, with supplicating gesture, demanded to know what all this palaver was about. "You'll 'ear ter-morrer," said Arthur; whilst Kitty exultantly squeezed the waist of Beaky's mate, and offered to lay her stockings on something or other being a blooming cert. "Though, mind you," she added, "they're no beauties to work under, I give you my word. The pay is reg'lar, any'ow, an' they start you at fourteen.[52] Now, pull yeself together an' beg 'is pardon, an' then we'll go."

Miss Hopper went boldly to this task. "Please, mister, beg your pardon. I on'y said what I did because of ole Deafie bein' kind to me. I believe in standin' by them as stands by you. It'd be the same now with anybody as got sayin' things against you."

"Oh! yes. No doubt! I'm *sure*!" responded Mr. Honeybunn, with delicate irony.

Miss Hopper submitted her forefinger to an agitated sucking. "See this wet –" she began; but Mr. Honeybunn interrupted her.

"We'll take that for granted, my good girl," quoth he. "You can consider yourself took on – or you can consider yourself to 'ave *my* influence with the guv'nor which is the same thing."

"*There* now," exclaimed the ingeniuous Kitty. "Didn't I say so? *Nothink* could 'old Mr. 'Oneybunn back from a kind deed, an' so I said."

"Well, I don't lay on to be a saint," responded Mr. Honeybunn; "but what is good enough fur a magistrate is good enough for me. I'll see '*is* 'and at charity, any day."

Kitty and Miss Hopper had already said: "So long everybody; don't be late in the mornin'," which, among three-fifths of the population, at any rate, is now the London equivalent to "Good-night." But at mention of the word "charity" Miss Hopper turned back.

"I give 'im back 'is five shillin's – or as good," she informed us, with evident pain that a contrary impression should prevail. "I sent a pinkie valentine – the best that money could buy. You could almost smell the scent through the letter box."

"More fool you," declared Arthur. "What was you doin' with so much money, anyways?"

"That? Oh! *that*?" responded Miss Hopper. "Well, you see, we got a matter of ten bob fur the collie."

"Collie? *Which* collie?" asked everybody.

"Why, the yaller lady's collie, of course," replied Miss Hopper.

Arthur had to be supported by Mr. Honeybunn, and Mr. Honeybunn propped himself against the stall.

"Then you *did* pinch the dog?" they shouted, in chorus.

"Not before they lagged me,"[53] explained Miss Hopper. "It'd on'y follered the milkman, an' 'e fetched 'im back. But we 'ad 'im soon's I come out. What do you think!"

* * *

"An' the serpent tempted 'er!"[54] quoted Mr. Honeybunn. After a concerted pause for thought: "Think of it, lads! Think of a wrigglin' little worm settin' out to deceive a sex like that!"

[20 November 1903]

VI. "The Broomfield Squire."

It was on the occasion of our being entertained to coffee by one "Jerry the Twister," that Miss Primrose Hopper first definitely exhibited herself in the light of a sentimentalist. Jerry the Twister had been fortunate enough to make the acquaintance of a "college gentleman," cast drunk and derelict upon the highseas of the night.

"So, it's corfee for everybody," Jerry the Twister had explained upon his arrival at Arthur's stall. "Give me a quid, 'e did, as a start-off, an' then blighted well *fought* me fur it, the blighter. 'Where am I?' says 'e. 'Kennington Road,' says I. 'Lead me to the Strand,' says 'e. It was a 'lead,' I give you *my* word. 'E *was* a 'ot-un. Climbed down nigh every airey[55] we passed; stole the milk-cans, an' tied 'em up to knockers. Pinched a rozzer[56] in the leg, give 'im a visitin' card, an' stole his whistle. Put 'is dooks[57] up to a fireman, tossed 'im fur 'is chopper, an' kissed 'is wife. Run fur his very life into Covint Garden Market (me after 'im), bought a cabbidge, took it to a resterong[58] where all the nobs was dinin', sends fur the boss, an' ses, 'Cully,[59] cook this fur my dinner.' Boss says, 'You be damned.' Collidge genelman takes off 'is 'at. 'I call upon you in the name of King Edward,' says 'e 'to cook this cabbidge. It is the law.' 'I'll be shot if I do,' says the boss. 'You'll be endorsed if you don't,' says the toff. 'Give it 'ere,' says the boss, 'I'll cook it.' Cabbidge comes upon on a silver dish: charge, two thick 'uns.[60] Genelman pays the money, an' breaks a glass: charge, ten shillings. 'Grand lark,' says the toff. 'I seen cheaper,' says I. 'Put 'em up,' says the toff. "Where's ye're money?' says I. "Ere's a quid,' 'e says: an' afore I can start on 'im up comes a swaddy[61] in a red cap. 'Give you a bob for that 'at,' shouts the toff. "Old 'ard,' I tells 'im. 'That's a policeman – military policeman. Don't you 'ave no larks wiv 'im. 'Rats to you,' 'e says. 'I'll 'ave that to make a wescoat of,' says 'e. An' 'e up an' snatches it.

"*Then* the trouble began. 'Im an' the swaddy an' two constables an' a cab-tout they was mixed up proper for nigh on ten minutes. Put 'em up grand, 'e did – the toff, I mean. An' they squashed 'is 'at, an' tore 'is westcoat, an' the cab-tout bit 'is 'and. And 'e broke a window, an' lost 'is watch, an' they frog's-marched 'im off to Vine Street.⁶² "Ere's a lark!' says 'e, when they started."

"There's no understanin' these toffs," stated Arthur. "More like wild animals than 'uman beings."

"They ain't so bad when you know 'em," asserted the raconteur. "Got their failin's, same's us; but there's a lot of exaggeration goes on about their 'abits. This one chucked me another thick 'un – 'fur services rendered' – when we got to Vine Street. That made three in all. I followed up to give evidence about the soldier beginnin' the quarrel."

The heart of Arthur remained untouched even by this evidence of generosity in a despised race. "You can 'ave your toffs for me," he proclaimed. "I don't like to know 'em an' I don't like to 'ear about 'em. They ain't 'class.'"

["Your books *may* be very clever, and they *may* be true," says my excellent Aunt Elizabeth. "But I prefer not to read about such persons. Couldn't you choose *nice* people for your characters?"]

Jerry the Twister patted Arthur encouragingly upon the arm. "What you want is a touch o' sympathy, m' lad. We're all 'uman bein's alike, ain't we? What if ye're torf *does* go a bit free when the drink is in 'im? Go' bless my soul, 'tain't 's if *we* set 'em sich a perishin' good example."

"All I can say," responded Arthur, in tones of finality, "is that we didn't 'old with such notions in *my* young days." Wherein I seemed to catch a further echo of my excellent Aunt Elizabeth.

It was at this point that Miss Hopper edged into the controversy. She and Mrs. Walpole, *née* Kitty, were come for the purpose of bringing early breakfast to Mr. Walpole, whose employment is municipal. Miss Hopper had been duly taken into the service controlled by Mr. Honeybunn's guv'nor. She bore every appearance of thriving on it. Her apron and her kerchief were white; her cheek was faintly crimson. She looked altogether less hungry. If it were not for the expression in her eyes, which appeared to be looking, looking and yearning, as if for some half-shape in the darkness, you might have called her happy. Very old people have that look, and some very young ones.

"What Jerry says is *right*," she informed us. "There's a lot too much despisery goin' about in this world. 'Keep to your class,' is a very good rule; but you can go too fur with it. I've known one or two rare good-'earted toffs in my time – not women, mind you: parcel o' over-fed 'ussies, I call *them*. But there's a lotter the reg'lar right sort among the blokes. I speak from experience."

"Sorry to 'ear it," remarked Arthur, with intent to mortify.

"You got no call to be *sorry*," answered Miss Hopper, quietly. "These blokes didn't get their ideas from a coffee-stall. They took a girl's honesty fur granted."

"'Ave a cup o' corfee," cried Arthur hastily. "Go on – 'ave it with me; there's a good girl. I always was a bit 'asty-tongued. Don't you mind *me*."

"I ain't minding you, ole Arthur," Miss Hopper replied. "Think I don't know the difference between temper an' spite? I can talk a bit crisp meself, sometimes."

Arthur shyly patted her hand. "Pals again?" he enquired.

"Pals again, now," answered the girl. "Kiss you Christmas."

"Beaky – chalk that up!" Arthur shouted. "And now," he added "we will 'ear about these good, kind torfs o' yourn. Leave out the parsons."

"There ain't no parsons on *my* list," responded Miss Hopper, "not enough salt in parsons, unless – oh! well, if you count '*im* a parson! There *was* a young 'oly man in a clay pipe I got quite chummy with near Dorking. Rare lad 'e was. Lit 'is pipe with a tract, 'e did, an' gimme 'Scraps'[63] to read an' 'Robinson Crusoe.' 'Do you know your colics?'[64] 'e asks me.

"'Do I ''arf?' says I. 'The surest lay goin' I says, 'fur getting' cold beef outer the rectories.'

"'Blessed are the pure in 'eart,' 'e says. 'You come through Ambleworth?'[65] says 'e. 'What did they give you at the rectory there?'

"'They give me,' says I, 'they give me a sort of picture book,' I says, 'with Daniel in it, an' the lamb, an' the seventh little 'orn.'[66]

"''The Good Shepherd watcheth over 'Is flock'' wrote outside it?' 'e asks.

"'The same,' says I.

"'That's right,' 'e says. 'What would you do with tuppence?'

"'Pennorth o' tea, 'a'porth o' sugar, 'a'porth o' lard,' I says.

"'That'll do,' says 'e ''And over the book. I'm buyin' 'em all in,' 'e says ('to the glory o' God') 'an' sellin' 'em back (at a 'andsome profit to my blanket fund.)'[67]

"That's the sort o' bloke 'e was. Full o' spirits, full o' sense, an' bung up with ginger. You can't count '*im* a parson.

"But what I reely set out to tell you about was somebody different. My Broomfield Squire[68] I allus call 'im, after the bloke in the song. On'y a lad 'e was – not more'n seventeen. Fine eyes, an' a gal's laugh, an' a 'get-out-an-walk' sorter way with 'im. If it 'ad't 'a' bin fur his guarjian an' my Boy, we might be keepin' company be now. 'Ow'd I go, changin' 'ats with a Cabinet Minister? That's what 'e is, 'cos that's what 'e said 'e was gointer be. My Boy'd on'y bin gone two year at that time. An' I was more merry-like than I am now. Wasn't fur that bow-legged guarjian I might … Tole you about my Boy, didn't I? Started from Bewnezerry three year ago come Michaelmas. When 'is ship reaches England I'm to meet 'im at the Obelix,[69] an' there'll be a weddin'. Reckon it's getting' close up now. Three years is a good long time fur a ship to take – even from Bewnezerry.

"But goin' back to the lad. 'E was a rare toff, an' I met 'im first with the caravan. 'Im an' a lot of 'is schoolmates come to the fair, see, an' they didn't 'arf shake things up. Bought up the 'ole cokernut outfit as a start, an' give free shies to every gal as'd kiss 'em. Country gals, mind you! Cold mutton must 'a' bin excitin' to it. I '*ate* country gals.

"They did a rare trade, those lads. Wasn't them fat 'ussies 'arf on it, that's all. You ain't gotter orfer cokernuts to git kisses outer dairy-maids an' that, I give you *my* word. They got enough to say about us Cockneys. J'alousy, of course. I *'ate* j'alousy. 'Talk about London bred, under-fed,' I says to 'em. '*We* ain't got no call to guzzle ourselves purple. We got a bit o' shape be nature. *Our* plumpness is in the right place.'

"But I set out to tell you about my Broomfield Squire. Well, we – 'im an' me – we made friends at the fair because I talked over the Fat Woman's 'usband. In a rare state 'e was: wanted the lad to give 'im two sovereigns fur insultin' 'is wife. This Fat Woman (she was a bloomin' skeleton by the side o' some o' them dairy-maids), she put a kinder spell over my young toff. 'E paid to look at 'er three time; an' at last 'e couldn't 'old in 'is curiosity no longer so 'e took a scarf-pin out of 'is tie, an' shoved it in her leg, jest to satisfy 'is curiosity. 'E was soon satisfied all right. She up an' 'ollered that painful you could ear it over be the cokernuts; an' me young dook come runnin' out with the scarf-pin in is 'and, and the Fat Woman's 'usband come after with a linch-pin[70] in *'is* 'and. There looked like bein' trouble, I can tell you, until I went up and smoothed it over. I smoothed it over be 'oldin' on to the Fat Woman's 'usban's leg until the toff boy 'ad got away. 'You're a brick,' 'e 'ollers back.

"That was the last I saw of 'im *then*, an' I never expected to see 'im again. 'E didn't come back to the fair any more, an' two days afterwards the caravan shifted. An' about a month after *that* Beaky an' me we did our bunk.

"When we'd been trampin' it about two months, Mr. Beaky gets ill. Cramp in both 'is legs an' a tired feeling all over 'im. Obstinacy, *I* called it, 'e said rheumatic fever. The doctors believed 'im, an' so I left 'im in Bedford Infirmary, an' pushed along on me own – made a kinder circle of it, so's to be back in Bedford about the time 'e was due out.

"About a week arter I started the summer left off freezin' fur a bit, an' we got a spell o' sun. An' I found a job at ironing in a farm-'ouse. I got a night's lodgin' in the 'ayloft, an' come away next mornin' with two bob in me stockin' an' as much cold toke[71] as I could bloomin' well lift. So there was yere 'umble settin' under a May bush eatin' cold carrot an' dumplin', an' weavin' a wild-grass apron as contented as the Queen.

"Suddenly I sees a likely young bloke come swingin' up the road. An', barrin' the pipe an' the spotty weskit, an' 'im 'avin' no whiskers an' scarlet bedgown an' that, you might 'ave took – you might 'ave took 'im fur a pilgrim out of a church window when the sun's on it. 'E 'ad 'is stick over 'is shoulder, an' a parcel at the end of it. An 'e was singin' of a rare ole-fashioned song, with a tune to it that lifted you up like 'ome-brewed ale:

> Tho' I am but a country wench
>   A frolic mind I bear-a,
> I think myself as good as they
>   Which gay apparel wear-a:
> My smock is but of linsey grey
>   Yet is my skin as soft-a
> As they who with the chiefest wines
>   Do bathe their bodies oft-a.[72]

"He'd got as far as the 'soft-a' when he sees me. 'E raises 'is 'at, quite correct, an' as grave as a judge.

"Madame,' said 'e, 'I give you good-*den*.'[73]

"'Mornin', cully,' says I; an' I see it was the toff boy from the fair.

"'I seem to remember your ladyship's smile,' 'e says, 'but I can't set a name to it. You don't 'appen to be a popular actress, I suppose?'

"'Not to-day,' says I.

"'Um!' says 'e. 'I wonder – does your *roof* leak?'

"I looks up at the sky, like a blue silk tent stretched good an' tight. 'Not much,' I says.

"'Um!' says 'e. 'Is your floor silting?'

"I looks up the road, shinin' an' curlin' there like a noo white windin'-sheet. 'Floor's all right,' I tells 'im.

"'Um!' says 'e. 'What about your walls?'

"I sniffs at the May-blossom. 'Walls are a treat,' I says.

"'Roof all right, floor's all right, walls all right,' says 'e to 'imself. Then – 'Rent low enough?'

"I takes a sniff at everything, an' nods me 'ead.

"'That settles it,' says 'e. 'No tenant o' *mine*.'

"'E stood there whistlin', an' kickin' the road, an' smokin'. 'Pretty weeds you got there,' says 'e, after a bit. 'What do you call 'em?'

"'Fool's Parsley,' I says. 'Ave a bunch?'

"'E grins. 'Do I deserve to wear it?' says 'e.

"'As the fat woman o' Rugby Fair,' I tells 'im.

"*Then* 'e tumbled. "E –"

In the face of an exceedingly menacing reception, Kitty obtruded herself. "You can tell us what 'appened next to-morrow night," said she. "Time for a spinster girl to be in bed."

She seized Miss Hopper by the middle, and whisked her off, and left us darkling.[74]

[27 November 1903]
VII. The Broomfield Squire (*continued*).

Those of my readers who were of the party at Arthur's coffee-stall last week will remember that we were much disgruntled by the sudden and unexpected interruption of a story in process of narration by Miss Hopper. Quite a little regiment of Miss Hopper's admirers collected on the next evening; and the efforts of these gentlemen to stifle their curiosity by means of Swiss roll proved highly profitable to Arthur. When Miss Hopper, with whom was Mrs. Walpole and Mrs. Walpole's husband's dinner, did presently arrive, she found herself the object of homage.

"Here is corfee," stated Arthur, "an' here is sardine sandwiches, and here is butter cakes. There is a 'Wild Dream' cigarette to foller. When you have partaken, we are all ready to 'ear the rest of this precious little love affair o' yourn."

Miss Hopper blushed. "Go on with you," said she. "Love affair, indeed! 'Ooever 'eard of a love affair at breakfast-time? An' in the open road! Good job my boy don't 'ear you! 'E's on 'is way 'ome from Bewnezerry, an' don't you forgit it! Three year next Boxing Day since 'e sailed, so you can expect a lump in the mouth from 'im almost any night now. Don't say I never warned you."

"I'll go armed," replied Arthur. "Now you get along with that toke, an' fetch a start on the story. Nigh bu'stin' our braces with curiosity, we are!"

"'Ad enough, thank you," responded Miss Hopper, as she pushed plate and cup away from her. "You must 'a' got your notions of a lady's appetite from the Jew girls on a Saturday night.[75] Nobody can call me *dainty* – cold cabbage outer the dustbins is a great thing fur makin' you broad-minded about food – but three slabs o' Swiss roll, six butter cakes, *and* a cup o' your coffee would puzzle a policemen, let alone a young gal like me."

"Get on with the story, then," reiterated Arthur, who has long since left of wincing at reflections on his larder.

"I don't know," said Miss Hopper, "as there's reely so very much to get on with. 'Im an' me – the Toff Boy, I mean – 'im an' me, we 'ad a talk together, an' 'e nigh killed one of 'is own gamekeepers. An' we 'ad dinner in the coffee-room of the 'Ampton Arms,' an' the landlady fainted with shock, an' 'e cut open 'er corsets wiv a carving-knife, an' *she* said 'Oh mercy! oh mercy! 'Oo would 'a' thought of it Mr. Frank? An' 'im not yet turned twenty!' So they sent for 'is garjian, an' 'is garjian come round on a 'orse what was not big enough to kerry, let alone ride, an' the Broomfield Squire threw a loaf of bread, an' 'it 'is garjian in the stomick, an' –"

"'Old 'ard," interpolated Arthur. "Seems to me there's more to tell than you laid on to think. Start fair: begin from the beginning. Tell us what the young bloke said when you reminded 'im of the fat woman, an' 'e remembered 'oo you was. You got as fur as 'im jumpin, an' then you left off. What did 'e say?"

"'E says, 'Well, I'll be damned!' 'e says.

"'Nice language for a gentleman,' says I. 'Do you always talk to young women like that?'"

"'E rises 'is 'at very 'andsome. 'Slip o' the tongue,' says 'e; 'my feelin's overcome me. Will you give me some o' your breakfast?'

"'If cold carrots an' plain duff won't spoil your complexion,' says I, 'you can share, an' welcome. Will you 'ave it in bits, or do you prefer to gnaw?'

"'Why,' says "e, 'I'll 'ave it the way *you* 'ave it. May I come into the bood*wyer*?'

"'If it's the *ditch* you mean,' I answered 'im, 'it's public property.' So 'e come in alongside o' me. 'There is no need for you to sit so close,' says I, very severe; 'there's plenty o' room between me an' Bedford.

"'E jumps away as 'umble as you like. 'I reely beg your pardon,' says 'e, risin 'is 'at ag'in. 'It's the fault o' this May bush[76] you see. You *got* to sit close under a little May bush like this.'

"'That's true,' says I; an' 'e come close ag'in. I couldn't be selfish about the May bush, could I? There wasn't another fur fifty yards.

"'E slipped the little parcel off'n the end o' 'is stick, an' opened it. There was a bottle inside, an' some sandwiches. It was a pretty bottle with a gold paper nob to it. 'Now,' says 'e 'we'er gointer to do a deal. You 'and over some o' that round shot there, an' I'll give you my sandwiches.' Then 'e opened the bottle, an' it went off pop into my eye. 'Pretty eyes,' says 'e, when 'e put 'is 'andkerchief back into 'is pocket.

"Them sandwiches was not 'arf so dusty. There was all kinds. Some 'ad got pink stuff inside 'em – like tin salmon without the juice, an' not so pungent. An' some 'ad got red stuff that smelt like bloater paste an' tasted different. An' there was eggs in some others – chopped fine, with bits o' parsley like you get in stood eels.[77] An' the bread was that thin it felt like eatin' a echo.

"The Toff Boy poured some yaller stuff outer the bottle into a little cup that 'e carried squashed up in 'is pocket. 'E give me a cupful, an' I thought it middlin' – ginger beer with a dash more ginger, an' not quite so fillin'. Then the Toff Boy went back to 'is duff, while I eat the last o' the sandwiches. 'E worried away, pertendin' to like it for well on five minutes. Then 'e give in. 'I ain't 'ad the practice,' says 'e. 'If you carried a coal 'ammer, or a gimlet,[78] even, we might separate it. As it is, I ham powerless.'

"'It's a matter o' teeth,' says I. 'What you want is teeth like mine.'

"'Let me look at your teeth,' says 'e. 'Anything else?' says I, an' tried to look cross; but 'e sat so comic there, with a lump o' duff in one 'and an' a carrot in the other, an' 'is 'air all rumpled, that I started laughin'. So 'e bent forward, an' patted me cheek with the carrot, an' 'ad a look at the teeth, after all.

"'Pretty teeth,' says 'e. Of course, I fetched 'im a clout o' the 'ead. Then 'e jumps up laughin', an' 'olds out 'is 'and for to 'elp me up, as polite an' solemn as if I was a don't-touch-me-or-I'll-fall-to-pieces lady out of a picture book.

"When I was on me feet 'e stretched out an' took 'old o' my bundle o' cold vittles, what was done up in a old red 'an'kercher, with Beaky's braces round it.

"'We take the road together, fair lady,' says 'e. And 'e went up to the 'edge, an' started 'ackin' of it about with 'is knife.

"'You'll look silly, me lad,' says I, 'if anybody cops you at *that* game.'

"'What game?' says 'e. 'I'm cuttin' out a blackthorn staff to walk with *all*,' 'e says, in 'is funny-talk. 'I'm lendin' *you* my stick.'

"'Much better cut your 'ook,' I tells 'im; 'the owner of that 'edge 'll give you staffs to walk with if 'e 'appened to spot you.'

"'The owner of this 'edge,' says 'e, with a grin, 'is meself.'

"'Ho!' says I, not believin' 'im. 'Per'aps the field belongs to you, too?"

"'Yes,' says 'e.

"'I like your sauce,' says I. 'I like yours,' says 'e; an' we walked on, arm in arm, like Tommy Brooks an' Bessy Snooks in the rhyme.[79]

"''Ow long's all these woods an' fields an' skyes an' flowers an' things belonged to you?' I arsts him.

"'Since I was about two,' says he.

"'Got 'em for a birthday present?" I says.

"'You can call it that – a birthday present from a Zulu. 'E stuck my father in the neck.'

"*I* didn't know whether to believe 'im or not, so I says, 'Tip us your moniker.'[80]

"'With pleasure,' says 'e, 'if you'll tell me what my moniker 'appens to be.'

"'Your *name*, stoopid,' says I. 'Where *was* you brought up?'

"'My name,' says 'e, sorter puttin' a 'ead on 'isself, 'is John Richard Wilberforce Travers Taylor Travers-Taylor, Travers 'All, Under Petterling, Beds.'

"'Put a penny stamp on it,' says I, 'An' God will p'r'aps forgive you for it.'

"So we walked along as chuff as two pals on bend. It *was* a rare fine mornin', an' no mistake. Jest enough wind too lift your feet, an' the sun playin' 'ide-an'-seek with everything. The pinky May was pinker nor ever I seen it, an' the white May whiter. An' you couldn't see the 'edge-bank for lady-smocks, an' dog vi'lets, an enemies, an that.[81] Fair made you dance along, it did – what with the singin', an' all. We sang the 'Song o' the Jolly Beggars'.[82] Nice voice my Toff Boy 'ad, an' a comic way with 'is staff.

> Of all the occupations
>   A beggar's life's the best,
> For whene'er he's weary
>   'E lays 'im down to rest,
> All in a 'ollow tree
> 'E lives an' pays no rent.
> Providence provides for 'im

An' 'e is well content.
So a-begging we will, go, will go, will go, will go, will go,
An' so a-begging we will go,
A-begging we *will* go.

"That's what we sung – the top of our voices, an not so much as the shadow of a copper to come an' interrupt. Even the birds didn't seem to mind. Chipped in, some of 'em did. An' a cheeky young weasel come bounce into the shiny part o' the road an' made a long nose at us with 'is paw.

"'You must be very rich,' says I, to my Toff Boy. 'You must be very rich, with all this grass, an' wheat, an' road, an' stuff.'

"'Fifteen thousand a year my income is,' says 'e.

"'You're the lad I bin wantin' to walk out with for years,' I tells 'im. 'What do you do with most of it?'

"'Entertain the free-born Saxon,' says 'e – that was 'is word – 'Free-born Saxon. There's not much over when the free-born Saxon's finished, I can promise you.' 'E stopped, an' pulled me up to a bit o' the 'edge where there wasn't any. 'Look through there,' says 'e.

"I looked an' there was a nobby ole 'ouse, with a red roof, an' pointy ends, an' little comic drarf-board windows, like you see in the country. Smilin' an' twinklin' all over, it was, an' the windows seemed to be winkin' at us.

"'That's my 'ouse,' says the Toff Boy. 'It's got a oak 'all five 'undred year old inside it, an' the free-born Saxon walks round every Saturday an' Monday, an' cuts 'is name in the oak with a jack-knife. An' 'e leaves ginger-beer bottles in all the lower-beds, an' gets sick in the picture-gallery. Twelve thousand a year that 'ouse costs me, an' I couldn't sell it if I wanted to. Starve first, any'ow. But you can see what I do with "most of it."'

"'Why do you let 'em do it?' says I, '– the jack-knives, I mean, an' bein' sick, an that?'

"'Because I'm a landlord,' says 'e, 'livin' on the sweat o' the brow o' the free-born Saxon, an' this is the on'y way 'e knows o' gettin' 'is own back.'

> Read the Clarion,
> Price 1d., Weekly

"Then we started on again, an' 'e told me stories. Grand stories they was, about knights, an' dragons, an' 'ussies, an' that. There was a bloke called Sir Tristram, an' a lady named Isalt.[83] Rare spoony couple they was, an' not 'arf up to the moves, neether. An' there was another knight, be the name of Lancelot, an' a down-'earted young thing called *E*lane.

"'Takin' it all round,' says I, 'there seems to have been some catch in bein' a wench in them days.'

"'Depends,' says 'e. 'Some wenches in them days could tell you different. Girls – poor girls – was likely to be carried off from their cottage doors be any gentleman in a tin westkit[84] that 'appened to like their figure. 'Ow would *you* like a great big 'orse soldier, all ironmongery an' whiskers, to come gallopin' up, an' snatch you from the 'igh road, an' take you 'ome on 'is saddlebow without so much as a "thank you"?'

"'Depends on the man,' says I.

"'If I was a knight in armour eight 'underd years ago,' says 'e, 'maybe I should treat you so.'

"'Wouldn't 'a' suited you to try it on,' says I.

"'*Suited me*!' says 'e. 'Why, girl, all things suited us – eight 'undred years ago. We didn't take stock in a lady's pout. We come up on a 'orse, an' we laughed at 'er tears, an' we tugged 'er up to the saddle seat, an' we galloped away. An' if we put an arm around 'er waist, it was an arm o' steel, an' it pressed tight, an' be damned to your wriggles. We were *suited*, my girl.'

"'Eight 'undred year ago!' says 'e; an' 'e come close, and grew taller. An' 's face looked like the face o' God. 'E put 'is 'and on my shoulder, an' it bore down 'eavy as an 'and o' steel. '*I* should 'a' bin suited all right,' says 'e, ' – eight 'undred years ago.'

"Somehow or other, I couldn't see very clear. But I seemed to feel a shinin' an' glitterin' all over 'im. 'E threw 'is arm round my waist: it was like the arm of a giant, an' gripped me cruel an' sweet. 'E pulled me to 'im, an' I thought me clothes would burn for shame.

"'Eight 'undred years ago,' says 'e.

"I wanted to scream, but I couldn't see. An' 'e 'eld me close, an' I made out a big cloud with 'is eyes in it. So I lay quiet.

"'Eight 'undred years ago,' say 'e, again. An' I 'eard the beatin of 'is 'eart. It sounded strong an' brave.

"'Eight 'undred years ago!' I whispered to 'im. 'Eight 'undred years ago!' I said it over an' over again, an' I cried.[85]

"Then 'e let go of me very gently. An' I sat on a bank, an' covered my face. An after a while 'e took my 'and, an' patted it, an' I stood up. An' we walked on without lookin' at each other. I still couldn't see quite plain, an' I kept thinking of steel arms an' the face of God, and I felt burnin', an' afraid.

"But, presently, I looked up, an' saw jest a foolish young Toff Boy with wet eyes."

[4 December 1903]

VIII. The Broomfield Squire (*concluded*).

After refreshing herself from Beaky's coffee-cup – the effect whereof caused her to inform Arthur that the flavour of his tea seemed to have improved – Miss Hopper continued her narrative of the sentimental Toff Boy.

"Well," said she, "we went on like that – sayin' nothin', and feelin' silly – for a mile or more. The white road went windin' on. An' the sun kept a-shinin', an' the smell o' flowers an' 'oney-bees grew thicker an' thicker. On'y it seemed all mixed up like an imitation – like a good thing you dreamt about the week before last. 'Oo'd 'a' believed what 'ad jest 'appened, let alone the rest? Felt like being in a transformation scene – bar wearing clothes, of course. The more I thought of it, the more strange an imitation it all seemed. *I* couldn't think of anything to say, nor didn't want to. I'd got to remember that the Toff Boy had forgot 'isself. When a gentleman does that, it is the lady's place to keep silent until 'e 'as explained 'isself."

This statement was received with approval by all the gentlemen present at the stall. A certain cabdriver who was of our company requested Miss Hopper to put the aphorism into writing. "My missus," said he, "won't believe me else. I bin tellin' 'er the same thing for years. I'd give a day's money any day to let 'er 'ear it from the mouth of a woman."

Miss Hopper sniffed in a scornful manner. "I wasn't talkin' about *merried* people, my good fellar. If a married woman was to keep silent every time 'er man forgot 'isself, she would be *always* silent. Nice sort o' wife *that*'d be, wouldn't it?

"No," continued Miss Hopper, "the rule I'm talkin' about is for the single wenches; bein' married is a different game altogether. I'll tell you about that when I've tried it ... About the Toff Boy, now. 'E spoke at last.

"'Look 'ere,' says 'e, 'you're a jolly good sort, you know, an' I'm a rotter, you know. Awf-ly sorry for forgettin' meself,' says 'e; 'deserve a hiding, you know. But ... I wish to God you'd look another way. Thanks. I never *could* resist a 'azel eye.

"'I owe you a lot of thanks,' 'e went on, 'fur not encouraging me. I get fearfully desperate when encouraged. Kissed our vicar's wife once, through being encouraged. They betted me I wouldn't, you know. Gave the money to the "Distressed Clergy Relief Fund." I say though, you will forgive me, won't you?'

"'I ain't one for bearin' malice,' says I, 'an' you are on'y a yob, any'ow.'

"'Thanks, awf'ly,' says he. 'What *is* a yob, by the way?'

"I 'ad to explain to 'im, an' the road got very steep jest then, an' 'e said I looked tired, an' the explanation took more explainin' than you'd think, and so, somehow, without thinkin' like, we found ourselves goin' arm-in-arm again, as chuff an' friendly as before.

"'I bin readin' a very fine novel be a lady,' says 'e, after a bit. 'Never 'eard of it, I suppose?' 'E fetched a book out of 'is pocket – yaller coloured. 'Sir Godfrey's Bride'[86] it was called, an' a young gentleman in pink trahsers was 'oldin' a servint gal be the middle an' sayin 'Scoundrel – you lie' to an *old* gentleman in green trahsers. 'They say that women can't write good books,' says my Toff Boy, 'but that's all rot. They can't write *funny books*, perhaps; but give me women for sentiment, any day. There's a great deal of power in this book, an' a great deal of sense. An' bits of it are extremely beautiful. Let me read you some.

"So we sat down on the roadside, an' my young gentleman pockets 'is pipe, an' takes off 'is 'at, an' starts to chuck out slabs of 'Sir Godfrey.' I'll admit it was a fine book; but I ain't one for readin' much, an' I'd 'eard the story afore. It was 'Noble Sir Arthur an' Pretty Mollee'[87] told over again. You know 'ow 'Noble Sir Arthur' goes, of course? *Don't remember the song about 'Noble Sir Arthur'*? Well, you *are* a rare ole-fashioned lot at this stall an' no mistake! Why, a baby in the country would know that song! 'Arf the novelettes they bring out are took from it. An' *all* the dramas. Now let me see – the beginning goes like this:

> As nobel Sir Arthur one mornin' did ride,
> With 'is 'ounds at 'is feet an' 'is sord be 'is side,
> 'E saw a fair maid sittin' under a tree,
> So 'e arster 'er name an' she said 'twas Mollee.

"That's the first verse. Well, Sir Arthur 'e gets smit with this 'ere Molly, you see. So 'e starts in to play the flash game on 'er. This is one of the things 'e says in the song:

> I'll give you fine ribbons, I'll give you fine rings,
> I'll give you fine jewels an' many fine things;
> I'll give you a petticoat flounced to the knee,
> If you will but love me, my charming Mollee.

"But Molly knows a bit. *She* ain't 'avin' none o' your broom-stick business.[88] She up an' says so. Like this:

> I'll 'ave none o' yere ribbons an' none o' yere rings,
> None of yere jewels an' other fine things;
> And I've got a petticoat suits me degree,
> And I'll ne'er love a married man till 'is wife dee.

"After that, Sir Arthur Lies low a bit, an' plays the straight ticket game. So Mollee she makes 'im a promise:

> O, nobel Sir Arthur, it must not be so,
> Go 'ome to your wife an' let nobody know;
> For seven long years I will wait upon thee,
> But I'll ne'er love a married man till 'is wife dee!

So they make a bargain of it, an' shake 'ands. And in seven years to the very minute Sir Arthur's ole woman passes peacefully away. Then young Molly gets rewarded:

Now seven long years are gone and are past,
The ole woman went to 'er long 'ome at last,
The ole woman died, an' Sir Arthur was free,
An' he soon came a-courting to charming Mollee.

The last verse gives you the moral:

Now charmin' Mollee in 'er carriage does ride,
With 'er 'ounds at 'er feet and 'er man be 'er side;
Now all ye fair maids, take a warnin' by me,
An ne'er love a married man till 'is wife dee.

"There! Mean to say you ain't 'eard the story now?"

"I've 'eard *that* story, all right," responded Arthur. "Not the song, mind you, but the story. 'Eard it at every theayter in London, an' read it in every Christmas annual I looked at. Fine story."

"Don't read Christmas annuals, meself," Miss Hopper replied. "Never was one for readin', as I said before. Goin' back to the Toff Boy, now. 'E read that book out for an hour or more. 'E acted it in bits. 'E was that taken up, 'e would 'a' gone on till dark if I 'adn't interrupted 'im.

"'I must be gettin' on now,' says I.

"'Where to?' says 'e.

"'On me way,' says I. 'This may be a picnic to you, but I am out for business. *I* tramp fur me livin'.'

"'We'll go on, be all means,' says 'e; 'but you won't be givin' me the go-by yet awhile, and don't you think it. Before we discuss anything of that sort, we're goin' to have lunch. No cold dumpling, mind you. Hot lunch we're goin' to have, with wine and coffee. We're 'avin it at the "Taylor's Arms."'

"I tole 'im to give over, an' talk sense. ''Ow'd *I* go in a bar-parlour with clobber like this, an' odd boots, an me 'air all any'ow? You're mad,' says I.

"'There never was a woman yet,' says 'e, 'that didn't make the same excuse about everything. You're booked to lunch with me, an' the matter's settled. If Mrs. Druikshank objects to your dress, I'll raise her rent. *Now* we'll see.'

"It was all the same to me, of course. *I* like a beano, same's anybody else, an' I rather fancied meself drinkin' sherry out of a glass in the best bar-parlour, with wenches an' that fallin' over each other to do the 'umble.

"'What would you do with ten bob?' says the Toff Boy, all of a sudden. We 'adn't bin speakin' for some time when 'e said that – 'oldin' 'ands, but not speakin'. 'What would you do with ten bob?'

"'Depends,' says I. 'Five bob 'd go in toke, for a start. Pound o' tea, pound o' sugar, pound o' lard, pound o –'

"'Judgin' be the clay-pipe parson, I thought that 'ud please 'im. But 'e interrupted, quite impatient. 'I didn't mean that,' 'e said. 'We'll take that for granted.

Suppose you 'ad enough to eat already, an' enough to drink, an' a warm 'ouse, with plenty of furniture, an' firewood, an' that. If I give you ten bob *then*, what would you do with it?'

"I thought a minute. Then I says: 'Buy a pair o' corsets.'

"'E seemed disappointed. 'I thought per'aps you'd like to spend it all on books and improvin' your mind, like the girl in the story,' says 'e.

"'I never was one for readin',' I tells 'im. '"The more you read, the more you may read," is what I say. As for me *mind*, why, that's past improvin'. Cut an' dried this five years past. You might just as well ask a pair o' kid gloves to get up an' butt.'

"'That is silly talk,' says he. 'I am a Socialist meself. I believe in education, and free speech, an' vegetarianism, an' the same chances for everybody. What do you say to going to school in France? And then going to school in Germany? And learnin' to play the piano, and show your chest without blushin'? It'd be an awf'ly good idea, you know. When you had finished your education, we could get married, and brave the world. We could live down all the spite of the neighbourhood, and be kind to the poor. And you would be the most beautiful woman in the county, and I would write novels – like Lord Lytton.[89] And our children –'

"'Arf a mo cocky,' says I. 'We ain't even married yet. An' what would my young fellar say?'

"'Young fellar?' says 'e. 'What young fellar?'

"'*My* young fellar,' I gives back, 'sailor, on 'is way 'ome from Bewnezerry now. Where does 'e come in?'

"That seemed to puzzle 'im. Looked quite down-'earted, 'e did. All of a sudden, 'e brightened up. 'I know,' says 'e. 'We'll buy 'im a ship, an' send 'im to trade in the Pacific.' Full of ideas, that yob.

"Then we come to the 'Taylor Arms.' There was a bit of a barney to start with. A bloke in leggin's was sittin' outside. Dreckly 'e sees me, up 'e starts. 'That's the gal,' 'e 'ollers out to 'is pal, 'that's the gal! Stole two o' my settin pheasants yesterday mornin'. I know 'er be 'er 'air.' 'E comes up, an' collars 'old of me arm. 'You'll come along o' me, me gal,' says 'e. 'This is a tow-pickin' job.'[90]

"The Toff Boy grabs 'im be the collar. 'Leave go that lady's arm,' 'e shouts. ''Ow dare you insult my friends.'

"'I'll insult *you* in a minute,' says the man. Then 'e stops, an' 'as a look at the Toff Boy's face. 'Mr. Travers-Taylor, sir, I beg your pardon, sir,' says 'e. 'Didn't reckernise you sir.'

"'What do you mean by makin' unfounded charges against this young woman?' says the boy. 'Good mind to report you to Sir Robert.'

"'Beg your pardon, sir, but this young party 'as bin interferin' with your birds, sir. Sor 'er meself, sir, yest-day mornin', sir.'

"So the Toff Boy set on 'im, an' 'it 'is nose. An' banged 'is 'ead. 'I'll see Sir Robert about *you*, my man,' says 'e, when 'e'd done. Then we went in to lunch, an' I felt very glad I'd sold the birds, although the fat woman at the forge *did* on'y give me a tanner for 'em.

"Can't say I enjoyed the lunch. There was a pale young 'ussy, in a tinned-salmon-coloured blouse, turnin' up 'er nose at me all the time. An' there was whisperin' an' sniffin' goin' on all the time in the passage. An' I saw a fat woman, through the window, givin' orders to the bloke in gaiters what my Toff Boy 'ad bashed an' the bloke went runnin' off with a 'appy smile. An' the Toff Boy got sulky an' angry, an' kept on drinkin' more yellow stuff out of a bottle with a golden knob like 'e'd 'ad with 'im in the morning', an' 'e began to sing silly songs, an' 'e broke a plate, an' tried to kiss me, an' I felt afraid. Presently the fat woman come in, an' the Toff Boy tried to kiss *'er*. She was very crisp, an' reminded the Toff Boy of 'is mother, an' said she would never have believed it, an pulled her skirts away from *me*, an' acted the woman, proper. The Toff Boy called 'er 'Barbara Allen,'[91] an' silly names like that, an' chucked 'er under the chin. An' so she goes hystrikes, like I tole you, an' the Toff Boy got a carvin'-knife, an' cut open 'er stays. 'First aid,' 'e called it. She 'ollered somethink fearful. An' all 'er daughters – there were about five – come in, an' 'ung round 'is neck, an' pulled 'is 'air, an' screwed 'is collar, an' ordered me out of the 'ouse.

"Then a fat ole gentleman come ridin' up on a tiny 'orse. An' the Toff Boy opened the window, an threw bread at 'im, an' 'arf a loaf 'it 'im in the stomach, so 'e went 'Oof,' as if the place 'ad chilblains on it.

"But the ole gentleman didn't lose 'is temper. 'E got off 'is 'orse, an' come inside, quite smilin' an' cheerful.

"'My nephew a bit drunk?' says 'e. 'Dear! dear! Have to get a governess for the lad, I fear.'

"'This stupid ole fool is my gargian,' says the Toff Boy. 'He's fearfully unintelligent, an' nobody ever listens to a word 'e says.'

"'The Travers-Taylors were always witty in their cups,' says the gargian, still smilin'. 'But they usually drew the line at abduction. Who is this poor child?' He turned an' looked at me – very kind an' sympathetic like.

"'Hang your impudence,' says the Toff boy. 'This lady is my future wife. She –'

"'I quite understan',' says the gargian. 'Rude manner, but a priceless heart. She has an interesting method of eating pickles.'

"I felt meself burnin', an wanted to slap 'is mouth. But I sat quiet, an' looked at the Toff Boy. 'E was very red, an' opened 'is mouth to speak. But nothing came of it. 'E looked at me, an' then at the pickles, an' then at my fingers, what was covered with the juice (an' a bit grubby, any'ow), an' then back at 'is gargian again.

"'Yes,' the ole bloke went on, 'it *would* look well at Travers 'All, as you say. Underneath the picture of your mother. An' in full view of your grandmother.

She was the wittiest woman in London once, an' people read 'er memories to-day. She *would* enjoy this – ah – lady – at meal times.'

"I waited for the Toff boy to speak the. But 'e on'y got redder, an' 'ung 'is 'ead, an' looked silly. That settled it.

"'Time fur me to go,' says I. An I took me 'at an' went. The Toff Boy sorter looked at me – 's much to say, 'I'm sorry,' 'Is uncle on'y grinned.

"There was no sun on the road any more when I got outside."

[18 December 1903]
IX. Christmas Eve at "Arthur's".

At this generous season of the year English people are disposed to look kindly even upon the familiarity of strangers. For this once, therefore, I propose to make free with my readers. They – I should say he[92] – must be a lonely man, all things considered; and I will accordingly ask him to accept to-night a little hospitality from me.

But, my dear friend, I must ask you to quit your domestic hearth, and to deny yourself the comforts of wassail, and minstrelsy. Yea, even the wife of your bosom must be deserted. I fancy that her time will be quite adequately employed during your absence in disposing of those drums, and battledores, and that magic lantern, and the red flannel Gollywog. What *will* she do with the drum? Why, even the stocking of dear mamma, from which so much had been hoped, is not capable of comprehending *that* vast diameter.

Now, kiss the dear girl, and having permitted yourself the luxury of one last furtive tap with the poker-knob upon the drum, come forth with me. Our way leads us past terraces and tabernacles into certain dark lanes, where mist and mire and misery foregather. Thence we shall presently emerge into that comfortable space where Arthur's oil-lamp peeps through the slush.

And our reward?

A cup of coffee, hot and sweet, for the inwards. For the soul, a pinch of many spices, mostly fragrant.

What shall we see? That depends on our eyes. Some of us, I think, will see a sort of God.

Upon our first arrival at the stall there is some little uproar and disorder. The public-houses have barely closed their portals, and several bottle-bearers, in the first flush of intoxication, have come to revel in hard-boiled eggs and harmony. Weird and curious ditties, of music-hall origin, are these which they sing. Dirge-like in form, their chief business is tragedy, flavoured with a sort of bastard sentiment. "Break ver noos ter muvver," "Vere'll come a ti-i-me some di," and "Shike 'ands an' let us be frien's fur ole Ti-i-me's sike" are some of the cadences which most thoroughly shall rend you.

They are most solemn, these people. Of a certain coarse ribaldry there is much; but it is mirthless, joyless, merely loud. It reminds one strongly of those festivities which always welcome home the "squire" in melodrama. Occasionally there will arise the sound of breaking china, and sometimes the thud which betokens a lover's quarrel. In such cases, you may depend that the Victor will herself make haste to assist the vanquished in regaining a posture more befitting the traditions of his sex. And all this while you hear no word or hint of Christmas greeting.

Plaints there are in plenty, and admonition, as thus:

"Forty shillin', yus! Forty shillin' or seven days. That was *my* Christmus-box. An' a corshian. 'All right, me lord,' I says; ''ave it yere own way. The boy must go to school, an' I will starve'."[93]

Or, again:

"'Old hup there! – Once more, boys, chorus! – 'Oo're ye shuvin'? – Don't forget termorrer. – 'It 'er chest! – An' bring a corkscrew, mind!"

Some there be, amongst the married women, chiefly, who seem to wear, faintly, an aspect of reprobation. There was a time, perhaps, when "Christmas" brought to them something of the message which even unbelievers amongst those who wash all over go out to meet. But to the majority of the revellers there comes no message, no sentiment: only two days' holiday, and licence to make themselves insensible by means of foul beer. That, and a not very pristine gander, for which, week in, week out, they have pinched a little dole during the long night of days successive to the previous Yuletide of frenzied satiety.[94]

It is, perhaps, well that these carefully encouraged savages of ours should be granted this horrid, purple patch of limelight relief upon the daub which is their life. It is well, I say – since nothing better offers. But to-night good friend, you and I shall ask each other the unanswerable "Why?" We are no "thinkers." To eat, sleep, sometimes to do a little wickedness, and to view life in that light wherein its lines show deepest, is, perhaps, the sum of our joint philosophy. And yet must we wonder that, with all the glorious instruments of which our nation can boast – Party Politics, the Constitution, a Gambling Act, the Press, Bedlam, and Mr. Bernard Shaw[95] – such things should be. To me it seems just possible that the freedom of speech which our ancestors extorted is bad for the heart. Many a strong man hath died whilst his friends debated the choice of an apothecary ... Well, well!

Presently, in groups of three and four, these early visitors retire. But not, mind you, with that pantomime fairy's "trip"[96] which one, somehow associates with Yule-tide. In ragged echelon, they lurch from gutter to gutter along the wide road, their voices always uplifted in mirthless melody. Such of the women (and these are many) as carry babies wear them slung face downwards across the arm, easily, artlessly, in the manner of a mackintosh. This process must feel more comfortable than it looks – or else it is singularly effective in stifling comment, for the weanlings do not cry at all. It is seldom that one of them gives way even to a whimper, and, then only to be see-sawed back to silence by its mother, who, you will observe, flings the infant from arm to arm in a motion called "petting"!

Thus the furious legion passes away. Hogarth at his frankest has given us nothing more horrible than this Christmas-tide reality.

After this, it is a relief to press as close as may be to Arthur's stall, and to admire our old friend's Yule-tide gallantries. These consist, for the most part, of evergreens, dressed in a gay suiting of those little sweetmeats which are called "hundreds and thousands." How the vendors of these trappings came to think of so curious a method of improving upon Nature is, I suppose, one of those mysteries which will never be solved. Besides these striking articles of embellishment, there is a small piece of holly, some blatant mistletoe, and a large and gawdy specimen of what Houndsditch conceives to be the flag of our country.

Soon we have filed our way through the clamour, and are able to rest elbows, grown weary, upon the very ledge of Arthur's stall. Here we are welcomed with most generous greeting. For when the last of the absolute strangers has strolled off, Arthur delves stealthily amid the treasures of his little store-cupboard, and produces a goodly portion of black pudding. Also some determined-looking mince pies.

"Present from me sister in Berkshire," says Arthur. "Married to a major in the Salvation Army.[97] Station-master, too – when 'e's got time for it."

We accept a portion of these delicacies with fitting expressions of gratitude. Our chief concern for some little while thereafter is to convince Arthur that we do not consider ourselves stinted. By dint of lying, we avoid a second portion; and then Mr. and Mrs. Robert Walpole arrive, accompanied, of course, by Miss Hopper, and the privilege of engaging Arthur is transferred to them.

We get in conversation with Beaky, and learn strange facts about Christmas traditions in the dramatic profession. One of us is presented with a remarkable match-box, composed of vulcanite, and which contains a secret spring. Upon touching the same, you find yourself confronted with a realistic representation in colours of the bath of Psyche.

Our attention is subsequently drawn to an ominous bulge in Mr. Walpole's chest. We are somewhat nonplussed until Mr. Walpole, turning his back upon Kitty, winks humorously, and caresses this inscrutable growth, as who should say, "What ho!" Thus we are informed that his bosom bears a graceful burden, destined to awaken joy in the heart of that bosom's lady. Love, they say, is blind. To me, at any rate, it seemed that the expression of profound ignorance in the eyes of Mrs. Walpole savoured strongly of love, but not at all of blindness. And Mrs. Walpole has also *her* secrets. These she furtively displays in the full flare of the lamp behind Robert. A pipe, a pouch, and – oh! horror of horrors! – a tartan necktie! But such a tartan! Red and green and gold, with a touch of purple, the whole set off upon a background of pale magenta.

I look at the thing again, and, as I look, hold discourse with myself, and say: "Pshaw! This gift is kindly given. From hands so gentle, I would accept a worse. Aye! and flaunt it at the opera!" But, as I speak, Miss Hopper comes towards me, and draws from some secret nest about her person just another such iniquity. Then do I stagger and blench, and know myself for a coward.

For all that, I do not mean to part with Miss Hopper's gift, nor with the memory of her pretty words in giving it. And under Arthur's mistletoe, in the full light of – What! shocked, my friend? I think you ought to have stayed at home with the drums and stockings, after all.

But it is growing late, and we survivors of the great company must help Arthur prepare for an early bed. So we harness up the little pony, which has come – unattended, as usual – from their home to meet its master. And we secure the shutters of our quaint little inn, and bid each other good-night, and go our several ways. Then the dissolution of the picture is complete.

[25 December 1903]

X.

"What is all this?" said Mr. Honeybunn, the Master Printer.

The remark was occasioned by the unseemly conduct of a soldier. This warrior – a shambling young giant, all bone and gristle and grin, with a weather-proof eye[98] and scars, and a backward lip-growth – had lurched out from the stall and seized Mr. Honeybunn's hand in an unmistakably cordial manner. He committed the further indiscretion of saying "'Ow are we?"

That is why Mr. Honeybunn assumed his editorial room glare, and his editorial room tone, and said: "What is all this?"

"You know," explained the soldier, enlarging the grin and winking not quite confidently – "you know – young Alf?"

"I *don't* know young Alf," Mr. Honeybunn responded. "I don't know *any* swaddies."

Arthur behind the stall, rattled a teacup to attract attention, and exhorted Mr. Honeybunn to wake up and use his eyes. "You know *'im* all right," said Arthur. "That's young Alf what useder see you 'ome from my place after Lodge nights. That's *my* young Alf: my son Alf – jest 'ome from the front.[99]

"Ho!" retorted Mr. Honeybunn, obviously nettled by our host's masonic reminiscences – "Ho! This is *your* son Ellfred, is it? Then perhaps you would oblige me be kindly askin' him to kindly take his foot away. I am not a barrack-square for every clumsy young militia-man in London to come and stand on."

The grin on the face of the soldier grew broader still. "All right, Mr. 'Oney-bunn," said he, stepping back two paces in a very correct and military manner. "'Ave a corfee?"

"I will when I can use me foot to walk up to the stall with," responded Mr. Honeybunn; and so peace was restored.

"Allow me t'interjuce," said Arthur, turning to me. "My son Alf – jest 'ome from the front. One o' my customers, Alf."

The soldier favoured me with an edition de luxe of the grin. "'Ow are we?" he said; "'Ave a corfee."

Whilst having the coffee I was made conscious of the presence of another warrior. He was an older man than young Alf – much older – and of a build more meager. He had an enquiring manner and a dispassionate eye. His face, somehow, reminded one strongly of a note of interrogation. His manner towards young Alf was warmly sympathetic. He supported all that youth's remarks – which seldom diverged from the obvious – with a warmth of conviction and expletive that marked him out as one who knew the value of flattery in its relation to the human thirst.

This interesting rascal permitted himself presently – with a great show of bashfulness – to be dragged forth into publicity. He was introduced to us as Private Ducker, late of the Shrumphire Light Infantry, now a member of the Royal Garrison Regiment. Upon being introduced, he gratified us exceedingly by coming to the salute in a strictly correct and military manner. He also tapped his boot with his swagger cane[100] and remarked that he had known some stinking chill evenings but never a stinkinger. For summer, mind!

"What about that night outside Voetsvlei?"[101] remarked young Alf. "No corfees there, m'lad."

"R!" admitted Mr. Ducker: "I was forgettin' Voetsvlei. They served out rum at Voetsvlei."

Mr. Ducker then very deliberately unbuttoned his tunic and produced from beneath a green belt of webbed material upon the surface of which a large number of metal badges coruscated and glittered. From amongst these, he selected the badge of his old regiment – the Shrumpshire Light Infantry – and proceeded to supply us with a picturesque resumé of the regiment's history. He also called our attention to the fact that seventeen engagements were honourably inscribed upon the colours of his regiment. These battles he described to us with an abundance of surprising detail. A person to whom he referred as "Ole Stand By" occupied the foreground of every picture. "Ole Stand By" was blessed with a valuable collection of physical infirmities. Whenever the fortunes of England trembled in the balance, Old Stand By came to the rescue. He would remove one of his limbs – they were all detachable – and armed therewith would head devastating charges into the disheveled ranks of bloodthirsty but credulous foe. Mr. Ducker concluded his narrative by referring to the interesting coincidence that to-morrow was than anniversary of one of Old Stand By's most characteristic feats. This, he added, in an impartial manner, would be the first occasion in the whole course of his military career upon which he should fail to celebrate this anniversary in malted liquor. Feeling the cause to be national in its character some of us provided Mr. Ducker with a legitimate excuse for maintaining his record.

Then Mr. Walpole strolled up, and Arthur repeated the ceremony of introducing his son. "Fine lad!" said Robert, after a benevolent inspection. And the fine lad said:

"'Ow are we? 'Ave a corfee?"

Robert and Arthur and young Alf and Mr. Ducker were, of course, soon entered upon a professional discussion. Arthur had some severe things to say concerning the modern system of drilling companies without markers; and Robert Walpole had a poor opinion of the short sword bayonet. Young Alfred's share in the argument consisted of saying, at intervals:

"Well! P'raps you're right, but I don't 'old with you meself;" whilst Mr. Ducker said "'Ear, 'ear," to this observation, and poured infinite scorn upon any expression of opinion by the other two.

Mr. Ducker, I need hardly state, was the First Man to Enter Pretoria. He was also the man who fired the first shot at Belmont, and the man who fired the last shot at Graapan, and the man who brought the news of all the surrenders to the Commander-in-Chief.[102] Whenever challenged at to the accuracy of any of his statements, Mr. Ducker used the same invariable form of evidence:

"All I can say is," he would assert, "that I wish ole Soap-Suds 'Erry was 'ere to bear me out. 'E'd tell you all about it, an a bit in. 'E was with me when it 'appened. Counted the corpses for me afterwards."

On being questioned as to the whereabouts of Soap-Suds 'Erry, Mr. Ducker took on an air of grievous resignation, whilst describing the death and burial of that important witness. "After Magersfontein,"[103] he added, briefly.

"Thought you told me yesterday it was Paardeburg,"[104] remarked young Alf.

"Paardeburg it was. You are right. I know it was Paardeburg, because it was there we stole the whisky."

"Were you at Ladysmith?"[105] enquired Robert.

Mr. Ducker thought carefully for some moments. "No," he replied, at length, in grudging accents, "I was not at Ladysmith. I was every blighted where *bar* Ladysmith."

"Sanna's Post?"[106]

"Not 'arf. There was bottle beer served out after Sanna's Post – to them as come back."

Kitty and Miss Hopper joined the company at this point. Upon being presented, young Alf so far varied the first half of his accustomed address, as to say, "Delighted, I'm sure." He finished, as usual, with, "Ave a corfee?"

Miss Hopper appeared to interest him. He divided a Swiss roll into finger-slices, and proffered the same in silent token of esteem. He remarked upon the chilliness of the night, touched lightly upon the subject of music-halls, and suggested, in a general sort of way, that, really, what puzzled your soldier freed from war's alarms more than anything else was the difficulty of getting rid of his accumulated pay.

In a final burst of oratory, he extolled the virtues of Mr. Ducker. "Rare talker, my pal: rare frien's me an' 'im: travelled 'ome on the same troopship. Ducker be name; let me interjuce you; seen a lotter service."

"'As 'e ever been to Bewneserry?" enquired Miss Hopper.

"'Ave I been to blazes!" responded with Mr. Ducker, with great readiness. "Remember Bewnes-what-you-call-'em well. Most sanguarry little engagement."

"Never 'eard of it meself," said young Alf, who was, perhaps, a little envious of the extraordinary powers of recollection displayed by his friend.

"Never 'eard of Bewnes-what's-its-name?" cried Mr. Ducker, with an incredulous gesture. "You *must* 'a' 'eard of Bewnesjiggity! Come to think of it, you was there yourself. They served out 'ot porridge mornin' o' the scrap, an' you shared your lot with a little brown-eyed wench from a farm-'ouse what –"

"I'll thank you," exclaimed young Alf, with heat, "to keep my name outer your dam fairy tales. Brown-eyed wench! It is a lie; well you know it's a lie! On'y spoke to one gall all the time I was out there, an' *she* was a Bible-reader with a weak spine. Dam fairy tales," he remarked once more, in an earnest aside to Miss Hopper. "Gets beyond a joke sometimes, my pal does. Clever talker, mind you. But I'll break 'is neck."

"I arst about Bewnesarry," Miss Hopper explained, "because my boy was there. On 'is way 'ome now."

Young Alf inspected his boots, and whistled a polka in Psalm time.

"What is his regiment, miss?" enquired Mr. Ducker.

"Regiment!" echoed Miss Hopper. "'E ain't got no regiment. My boy is a sailor."

Mr. Ducker shrugged his shoulders, and spat. He had rather misunderstood Miss Hopper's drift, and begged her pardon for it. He did not know her lad was a sailor-man. He pitied her. The morals of sailor-men were despicably loose.

"I'll slap your face, or whatever it is, in about one minute," exclaimed Miss Hopper, beginning to unfasten her sleeve, as of yore. "What 'ave *you* gotter say about sailor-men?" she continued, turning to young Alf.

"Oh!" responded young Alf, "sailor-men are all right, in their way – same's coppers."

"You *are* a gentleman, at any rate," replied the girl.

"That's all right," said Alfred. "'Ave a corfee?"

"Don't mind if I do – with you," responded Miss Hopper.

And that was how the hobbing and nobbing of the twain first began.

[1 January 1904]
XI. The Devout Lover.

You may well suppose that the return from active service of Arthur's son created quite a stir among the faithful ranks of Arthur's reg'lars. For some evenings following Alfred's reappearance, that embarrassed youth found himself the object of a nightly ovation at the stall. Reformed night-birds of all ages and characters – chiefly the victims of matrimony – came forth from their little reformatories at Catford, or Tooting, or Walthamstow, or Ilford,[107] to clink the cup of friendship with Trooper Alfred. All brought homage, and some brought gifts. Most of these were of an edible character; but others took the form of pipes, and knives, and match-boxes, and wild things dubbed cigars.

Young Alfred wore these honours with a difference. At first, he made extensive use of that wonderful grin of his; but after the third night he lost heart, and the grin refused to come. On the fifth night he manifested unmistakable signs of impatience, and on the sixth night he absented himself from the stall.

When next I saw Alfred – a week or so later – it pained me to observe that, far from his having recovered his normal buoyancy of spirits, the air of impatience had given place to a settled expression of gloom.

We fell to coffee-drinking, of course, and I remarked with interest that Trooper Alfred disposed of three cups in a feverish and reckless manner. I also observed, from the expression of his eye, which was at once eager and tragic, that he was engaged in a hand-to-hand contest with his better judgment. At the end of exactly three minutes, the better judgment went under, and Alfred delivered himself of an ominous sigh. If you can imagine the probable conduct of a virile young hurricane let out on bail, you can form a tolerably close conception of Alfred's sigh.

"Indigestion, Alfred?" I enquired, with an air of sympathetic interest.

He looked at me reproachfully. Then: "You can call it that," he said, in a tone of melancholy resignation.

"Well, cheer up, anyhow," I exhorted him. He laughed the laugh of one whom experience has soured. He expressed, by look and gesture, an irrevocable sense of the hollowness of things. He also scowled.

So I emptied the contents of my emergency spirit flask into his cup.

"'Ere's to you: you are a pal," he remarked, and drained the vessel. The result fulfilled my hopes. Alfred began to display a power of conversation which, in a person of his normal restraint, amounted to positive garrulity. He said that this was a rummy world; that in the matter of tribulation, you might safely say that it never rained but it snowed; that London was a good place to be out of; that there were worse things than a soldier's grave; that he wondered people "had the nerve" to bring children into a world of such proved depravity; that nothing was what it seemed; that the more you looked at things, the more they mocked you; and that the art of being entirely happy consisted in being entirely bad. I dissented mildly from some of these doctrines; but Alfred shook his head, after the manner of one suffering fools kindly. He drank another cup of coffee, and lit a cigarette, and let it go out, and lit it again, and the next moment threw it away. Then he began to discuss cricket averages and half-way through the argument forgot that he was discussing cricket averages, and lapsed into silence, and bathed his soul in melancholy, and wallowed, and was glad.

Suddenly he beckoned me closer, and squared his chest, and opened his great mouth so wide, that I said to myself, "Oh! It's coming now!" But it wasn't. He subsided at the moment of climax, and confined himself to saying, with the abstract air of a philosopher:

"Rum blokes – fathers!"

I acquiesced. For the sake of agreement, chiefly; but also because I have reason to hold the memory of one father (whom, thank goodness, I never knew) a good deal cheaper than dirt.

After a short silence, Alfred began to manifest further symptoms of a kind precisely similar to those which I have just described. Again, I had hopes of the long-delayed outburst, and again I was disappointed. Once more the afflicted warrior contented himself with a harmless generalization:

"Rum creatures – gals!" he remarked this time.

Again I acquiesced.

"Some, mind you," he continued, after submitting the thought to a long process of gestation, "some, mind you, are a jolly sight rummer than others! Eh? What's that?"

"What's what?" I asked.

"That remark o' yourn. Something between a pig's grunt an' a bad cough."

"I made no remark," said I. "I merely chuckled!"

That did the business. Without stopping to consider the question either of effect or of discretion, Trooper Alfred gave full expression to his feelings.

"There you are," he said, "just like the rest of 'em: chuckle, chuckle, chuckle! That's what my father does – chuckle! 'Ere, dad,' I says, 'turn on the advice tap,' I says. 'I need it.'

"'Woman, o' course,' says 'e.

"'Bulls-eye,' says I.

"'Love,' says 'e, 'or – or – the other sorter thing?'

"'Love,' I says, an' looks at the 'earth-rug.

"Then I 'ears that fat-headed noise like you was makin' just now; and I looks up, an' there's the ole man suckin' at 'is ole black cutty,[108] an' chucklin' fit to bust 'isself.

"'You're a God-beloved nice off-spring-of-a-lady of a father, *you* are!' I says.

"''E went on chucklin'.

"'Take that stinkin' cutty out o' yere mouth, an' sit up, an' look sober,' I says. 'Took looney, or what is it? Nice thing my mother was after to go an' get spliced to a laughin' jackass, what's lost the switch o' the bray-box, an' can't turn the current off.'

"'E give over a minute at that, an' looked at me straight an' solemn. But soon's 'e started to talk, back comes the grin again, an' I was that savage I could 'a' banged 'is 'ead with the knife-board.

"After chucklin' to 'is old self like a tom-cat for nigh on twenty minutes, 'e pulls a straight face, an' keeps it straight, an' looks me all over, an; spits in the fender, an' speaks:

"'It's a very 'orrible sensation, this love-sickness – what, lad? Pricks, don't it? All day long – like skewers in ye're heart? Presses a bit, too – what? Like plummets on the brain? Ain't 'arf stifling, neether – what? Wet dish-cloth round your throat 'd be a necklace to it. You can't eat, an' you can't drink, an thinkin' 'urts you. There's nothing that don't 'urt, so there's nothin' to be done. An doin' nothin' 'urts more than everythink else put together. Oh! it's a 'orrible sensation this love-sickness. Eh? What?'

"I gives 'im a nod.

"'Very well, my boy,' 'e says. 'It's a very 'orrible sensation, an' I'll give you a word of advice about it. You lay on to that there 'orrible sensation with both 'ands, an you 'ug it, an' you nurse it. Come to my age, you'll know why. Come to my age, you'll find that Life ain't no telescope, for one thing, an' that you ain't so darned inquisitive, for another. Come to my age, an' start thinkin' with yere head instead o' yere stomick, you'll find the mildewed ole inaccurate route-map o' the past locked away in yere mind. An' when you go to study it, you'll find that most of the ink 'as faded, an' the rest of it 'as run. But 'ere an' there you'll strike a small patch marked out strong. An' when you come to look at them patches, an laugh at 'em, an' – an' frown at 'em, you'll find that every single blighted one on 'em belongs to a 'orrible sensation like this what's causin' you to wear odd boots in uniform to-day.'

"Well, 'e dried up then, an' *I* took *my* turn at the chucklin' fur a bit. 'You stick to the stall, ole man,' I says. 'Leave love to the young 'uns – more up-to-date in it than you. Now 'and up that advice.'

"'There ain't no advice,' says dad. 'I stick to the stall. But I'll tell you something what's been known for fifty billion years, an' yet it's quite up-to-date enough for you. There's no sich thing as "once in love" with *any* man. It's 'arf-a-dozen times, or *never*. An' if you said the same thing about women you wouldn't be tellin' no lie.'

"Then," continued Alfred, "'e stands up, looks me up an' down all over, 'as some more chuckles, an' shins off. So there I'm left, not a blinkin' soul to 'elp me – though when a father starts, what can you expect of the world!"

"Well! well!" said I, "I promise not to chuckle any more. Who is the lady?"

Trooper Alfred blushed. "You see, it –" He stopped, suddenly, glaring into the darkness, which seemed to be slowly retreating before a couple of figures which came nearer and nearer to the stall. Young Alfred, after gazing earnestly for some seconds, turned to me with an immense expression of defiance.

"'Who is the lady?' you want to know," he said. "Well, if you must know the truth, there's *two* on 'em!"

"*Two*!" I echoed.

"*Two*!" he repeated. "An, what is more, they are coming up this minute."

I turned and beheld the couple from the darkness now quite near. And, lo! the both of them were women, and both were raimented to kill.

[8 January 1904]

XII. One of England's Heroes.

"I suppose," said young Alfred, with an air of tentative enquiry – "I suppose you couldn't see your way to do a bit of love-makin' to oblige a pal?"

This question was addressed to me in a hoarse undertone, the elocutionary effect of which was not assisted by Alfred's hand held slantwise across his mouth. It was necessary for Alfred to stoop in order to reach within reasonable breathing distance of my collar. Alfred stood immediately beneath the great lamp of his father's stall – (You may think I have been studying Ollendorf,[109] but the fact is I am writing in bed) – and his crouching bulk enveloped in a romantic overcoat of military pattern, stood out boldly against the darkness which surrounded it. The whole proceeding had a pleasant flavor of the Drama.

"It depends on the lady – somewhat," I made answer, after due consideration.

"Oh, the lady," said Alfred, with an air of assurance, "is all right: all right so far as looks an' conversation an' style, y' know. Squidgin' of '*er* waist is no 'ardship, I promise you. The filly on the off-side there. 'Er with the yaller whatyoucallem an' peacock 'at."

Alfred pointed with his left thumb in the direction of the two damsels whom last week we caught a glimpse of as they approached the stall. Fixing my eye upon the middle of an imaginary line extending from Alfred's thumb to the coffee-urn, I beheld a wholly sufficient virgin. She wore pale brown boots. You may wonder that I should think it necessary to mention the matter at all: but the fact is that these boots formed so striking a feature of their wearer's amenities that to picture her without them would be to fail in justice to her charms. So might one paint the wild-rose without its blush. This beautiful creature grew – or should one say "soared"? – out of her boots like Venus rising from the waves. I shall not be so uncivil as to suggest that she was aware of this fact. The circumstance that she held her skirt in such a manner as to afford a welcome view of the boots, may, doubtless, be attributed to the refreshing ingenuousness of youth.

At any rate, the boots were there – bold and bee-eautiful. Likewise the yellow blouse and the peacock hat. You remember Thackeray's view of George IV?[110] How he conceived him to consist throughout of fancy waistcoats? You took off one waistcoat and found another: you undid that to discover another, and so the proceeding went on until the end when you found that his very elegant Majesty had no existence at all outside his clothes. Well, do you know that, as I looked upon this lady of the boots, a similar thought occurred to me. Supposing – if you can bring yourself to contemplate a proceeding so indelicate – that we were to strip this fair creature of pale-brown boots and her peacock hat and her yellow blouse and all the rest of it. Do you think that one would find the body and soul of a woman beneath it all? There would be more boots, of course, and more blouses, and yards and yards of ribbon. But what about the woman? What about her *heart*? Get a pitchfork and prod amongst the heap of clothing and perhaps you'll find it. Stop – what is that? It is a think little voice speaking. What does is say? "Go away," it says "and leave my nice new clothes alone. You have found my heart already ... Did I not show you my pale brown boots?"

These are the thoughts I thought. I repeat them here because they may help you to see the lady of the boots with my eyes. When I add that she was perfumed like a valentine and wore real Alaska jewellery[111] wherever feasible, and said "Granted" when you begged her pardon, I think the description may be considered adequate.

As to this attractive maiden's companion, I would describe her, too, but for the fact that description does not appear to be necessary. You happen to have met her before. I did not recognise her in the beginning myself, by reason of a very beautiful costume in purple velvet; also by reason of a profusely feathered "creation" in Sunday hats, both articles being worn without prejudice to a rose-coloured silk neckerchief and yellow canvas shoes. When I had finished marveling at this bold but effective study in colour contrasts, I examined the face of the wearer. And I was less astonished than gratified to recognise the features of Miss Primrose Hopper.

I turned to Trooper Alfred. He was eyeing me anxiously, with eager supplication in his gaze. "Make 'Yus' of it mate,' he urged, pathetically. 'All I arst of you is to go in an' fashinate[112] 'er. You *are* a kind of a gent, ain't you – in a manner of speakin', y' know? Very well, then. The job is done as soon as looked at. Give 'er eyes to be took up be a gent, she would. I call you a gent, because you *are* one, in a manner of speakin'."

It was my turn to look earnestly at Alfred now. "If there is any taking-up in this business, my seductive young friend, I do not deal."

"You've got a false impression altogether," Alfred assured me. "Don't you think I am asking you to take up with 'er permanent – far from it. Though, mind you, so far as looks an' kerridge is concerned, I've travelled to Inja an' back, an' found worse. Far worse. But don't you get no false impressions. All I arst of you is to fashinate 'er – you bein' next thing to a gent – an keep 'er interested an' busy for a few days – or a week, say, or two weeks. I'll do the same for you another time – so 'elp me, I will!"

Remark the verbosity of the youth! Such is the power of that stimulating emotion which we call love. If the charms of merely *two* young ladies could make an orator of Alfred, what wonders could not be worked by a trio? Then, again, suppose him to take service, say as instructor, with the Khedival Government.[113] What more natural in such circumstances than that he should set up a modest but comfortable harem in a suburban district of Cairo? I am myself in no position to speak authoritatively on the subject of harems; but I take it that at least a half-dozen of damsels must be required to form a quorum. Very well, then. Our Alfred, being subjected to the immediate influence of six soul-inspiring beauties, immediately achieves greatness. He becomes Commander-in-Chief (*Anglice*, Sirdar) of the Egyptian Army, Honorary Colonel of the Cork Militia, Knight Commander of the Bath, V.C., M.V.O. and G.P.O., besides receiving the Freedom of the City of London and the chest strap and button (third-class) of the Spread Eagle of Prussia.[114] Such, I repeat, is the power of LOVE.

Alfred, being no thought-reader, did not appreciate the highly prophetic and flattering character of my thoughts. "Seems to take some people a long time to make their minds up over trifles," was the only remark he made.

"Look here," I said to him, at length, "it seems to me that I am not at all the person to perform the duties which you so generously offer me. I give you my word of honour as the next thing to a gent that I cannot fashinate worth tuppence. On the other hand, you have a friend – Ducker, I believe, by name – who – well, fashinating is altogether too mild a word to apply to *his* remarkable gift for pleasing."

Trooper Alfred replied with a bitter laugh. "There you go," he said. "Anythink for an excuse! I mighta knowed it. Comin' to me with yere Duckers, indeed. Suppose I *wanted* 'im to 'elp, which I don't – beautiful sight too free with 'is fairy tales – but supposin' I did want 'im to, why – why, 'e bally well *couldn't*, an' well you know it."

I did not know it, and said so.

"Then you ain't 'eard about 'is bit o' luck? Went courtin' a gal at Tufnell Park last Sunday – plumber's daughter with 'ouse property – walks into a greengrocers to arst the time, an' falls back thunderstruck. 'Oo should 'e see standin' be'ind the counter with 'er 'and on the till, an' a good deal aged, but *'is first wife*! 'adn't met for thirteen years. Thought each other was dead!"

"What a remarkable situation!" I interpolated. "How dramatic and – romantic. Who spoke first?"

"Bill Ducker spoke first. 'We'll 'ave a pint on this,' 'e says.

"Soon's the greengrocer come 'ome," continued Alfred, "they – 'im an' Bill Ducker, I mean – 'ad a interview. Bill put the greengrocer into the coal-cellar, an' locked the door. Then 'e went outside, on to the pavement, an' spoke to 'im down the shute. 'I'm fetchin' a policeman to you, my fine fellar!' says Bill. 'Whaffor?' says the greengrocer. 'Bigamy,' says Bill. 'I am William Ducker, the lawful wedded 'usband of Maria Tute, what you feloniously entrapped into matrimony on March twenty-three, eighteen-'undred-an'-ninety-six. It is seven years for bigamy at best,' says Bill. 'They'd give a greengrocer ten.' 'But I didn't know nothin' about it; I thought she was a single woman,' says the greengrocer. 'Ignorance of the law is no excuse,' says Bill. 'You can 'ave the woman, an' welcome!' says the greengrocer. 'That will I,' says Bill, 'an' a bit in. 'Andin back the ole woman don't make us quits. They's a bit o' rental to come. 'And over the business along with 'er, an' we'll call it quits.' 'Is that all you want?' shouts the greengrocer. 'That's it,' says Bill Ducker. 'Let me out; it's a bargain,' says the greengrocer.

"Bill let 'im out, an' 'e goes upstairs, an' gets 'is bits o' traps together, an' shakes Bill be the 'and, an' cadges a pipe of baccy off 'im, an' goes away. Bill says 'e never see a fellar take a knock-down blow so cheerful afore. So Bill sent word to 'is third wife – the second one's out in Canada – to say that 'e was dead. An' we sent off a certificate this morning. An' next Sunday I'm booked to spend the day with Bill an' 'is missus in their little greengrocery. You can see as Bill is outer the question for this job, can't you?"

I didn't see it. The events just narrated by Alfred seemed, in my judgment, to mark out Mr. Ducker as a man predestined to succeed where I should fall. Alfred, however, refused to accept this view.

"You are my last straw," said he, "and 'elp me you must."

The discussion began anew, and at the end of it – "Well! well!" I said, "... for this occasion only."

I have reported the whole of this conversation as though it consisted of an uninterrupted sequence of debate. But you must know that in fact our discourse was interjectory. Trooper Alfred kept breaking off in the midst of his sentences and of mine to shout greetings and compliments to his lady friends in front. By the time we had reached a basis of agreement, each of the ladies in question was exhibiting distinct signs of a badly ruffled temper. No sooner had Alfred extracted from me my half-promise of complaisance, than he hurried me into their company. I had, therefore, no further opportunity for asking questions; and my only clue as to the exact nature of the situation was provided by the curious word, "Breacherprom,"[115] whispered hoarsely into my ear as we hurried.

Miss Cobworthy – Cissie Cobworthy – was the name of the booted one. Miss Cobworthy did not take kindly to me from the first. Were it not for a manly reluctance to speak in any such terms of a lady, I should say that her expression at the interesting moment of our introduction to each other strongly resembled a snarl. My strenuous attempts at fashination met with strange rebuffs. All Miss Cobworthy's serious attention was devoted to the complicated tasks of seeing an oblique view of Alfred and Miss Hopper whilst appearing to contemplate the urn, and of listening to their conversation whilst pretending to be listening to mine.

"Ha! ha!" I said to myself; likewise "Ho! ho!" And spilt hot coffee over my hand. Then I braced my sinews all, and started out to fashinate.

And here comes a chopper to chop off my head,[116] because I have reached two columns. The fashination, so please you, will be continued in our next.

[15 January 1904]

XIII.

I promised, last week, to tell you this week how I carried out the earnest entreaty of Trooper Alfred to "fashinate," for his salvation, a preposterous lady in pale brown boots. Very well, then.

I opened the procedings with a light and chivalrous reference to Miss Cobworthy's beauty. "You are a bit of all right," I said, basing my language upon the best coffee-stall models.

Miss Cobworthy's repoy was not encouraging. "If you want a cut lip, say so," she responded.

"There's a bad-tempered little puss, now," I remarked, in my turn; again making use of what I believed to be a recognised formula amongst fashinators.

This time Miss Cobworthy's response was of the vaguely ironic character: "I 'ope," she remarked, "that me standin' 'ere don't interfere with you actin' the corpuscular swain?"[117]

I therefore dropped the professional manner and the professional discourse, and switched on to the merely amateur subject of the weather.

Miss Cobworthy offered no reply.

So I nudged her arm, and said: "I was saying that it is a cold night, Miss Cobworthy."

"I know," she replied. "Don't trouble to say it again. You don't make things like that no better by 'arpin' on them."

"It is like this, cully," she said. "I do not want no coffee; I do not want no Swiss rolls; I do not want no sardines. I do not want nothing; but what I particulerry and espeshulerry and uncommonly do not want is you an' your gaff. You got an ugly 'at, an' a splay foot, an' no sense. You look like a pug dog, an' you talk like an owl. You are a silly fool, an' I don't like you."

Miss Cobworthy's extreme frankness quite disarmed me. In view of her implied unwillingness, it would be cruel, I argued, to continue the process of fashination. I, accordingly, had recourse to Beaky, who after exchanging a few commonplaces, beckoned me furtively to an unfrequented spot opposite the Bath buns. As soon as I had occupied this place, Beaky bent forward, and, comprehending Miss Hopper and Alfred and the lady to the boots in an anxious glance, said:

"What is the little game?"

I told him the truth, which was that I did not know. It was an interesting little game, and a curious little game, but its purpose and rules and "reason-to-be" seemed somewhat confused. I would gladly give money for an explanation.

"Money!" echoed Beaky. "I would give me 'ead, 'at throwed in. It ain't the gal in the peacock 'at I'm thinkin' of, nor yet Alfred. Good lad, but big an' ugly enough to look arter 'isself, as the sayin' were. It is my mate I'm thinkin' of. Rare goin's on there 'as bin; but what it all means I *don't* know. Can't make 'ead nor tail of it, nor yet sense. Seems to be a kinder game o' ''Ere we go round the mulberry bush,'[118] with a sorter walkin' match throwed in."

All the time Beaky was talking, Miss Cobworthy, out of earshot, so far as we were concerned, was edging closer and closer to Alfred and Miss Hopper, who stood at the farther end of the stall. She still made a pretence of being interested in the crockeryware and other fittings of the stall; but one could see that her faculties were, in reality, being directed to overhearing the conversation of the other two. Her manner suggested that she was eager, yet hesitant to interrupt.

"Yes," continued Beaky, "it seems to be a walkin' game. My mate ain't said nothink to me. We on'y meet at the stall these days, an' the stall ain't always convenient for private conversations, as the sayin' were. But I can see there's a game on. First, there's 'er noo clobber – not 'arf classy, ain't it?"

I gazed upon Miss Hopper's costume of purple velvet, and upon her yellow shoes and feather hat and magenta neckcloth, and I endorsed the criticism of Beaky.

"Well," continued that gentleman, "she 'as wore that clobber every night this week. She 'as bin round to the stall every night this week. She 'as come all hours – from as early as 'arf-past eleven, when we open, up to as late as three. Comes a different time each night; but whether it's early or whether it's late, that there gal in the yaller boots comes with 'er. Pickers 'er up an' follers 'er, an' stays 'ere till she goes away again."

"They are not pals, then?" I asked.

"*Pals*," cried Beaky. "Looks like a pal, don't she – with them teeth showin', an' that wicked chin, an' 'er eyes squintin' all ways at once, like a cat on the prowl? She ain't no *pal*. She is a common or garden mink, that's what she is – fit to bust with jallousy, an' waitin' 'er chance to give my mate a seidlitz powder".[119]

"She looks a little dangerous," I admitted.

"R! Dangerous is right," exclaimed Beaky. "Wouldn't like to owe 'er fur me washin'. Not that she'd come no seidlitz powders on me. One o' my very first wives, she was in the laundry, and what with rheumatism and bad temper, an' bein' muscular an' that, she was a reg'lar education, as the sayin' were. What saith the poet? –

> This is the grave of my wife, Matilda.
> Too much water is what killed 'er.
> Proud was 'er port: stiff-necked 'er gait.
> She was gettin' on for forty-eight.
> She died of dropsy, free from pain;
> We shall not look upon 'er like again.[120]

"So what your 'umble servant don't know about dealin' with them is a trifle. But it is different, like, fur my mate. She *ain't* the scrappin' sort – not with women. She ain't one fur arguin' much with women at all. 'Old 'er own against a man *any* time; but 'er way with a woman is 'Be pals or don't speak.' 'Oity-toity, like as the sayin' were. As for the spit-an-scratch game – why, that's outside 'er radius altogether. Never punched another woman in 'er life, I'll lay. If she did, she'd only slap – you know; 'Tut! tut! Naughty! naughty!' Like this." Beaky gave a pantomime illustration of a timid lady engaged in striking the air with the tips of her fingers.

"As for 'at-pins," concluded Beaky, "an' broken medicine bottles, an' the chest stroke – why, she don't know no more about them than – than – Mary Queen o' Scots! It'd go 'ard if Yaller Boots there was to set about 'er, I give you *my* word. Yaller Boots ain't no blue-eyed novice be a long chalk."

"Why don't you get rid of her?" I asked. "Send her away – refuse to serve her."

"Because I ain't a blighted juggins," answered Beaky. "That *would* be clever, wouldn't it, now? Go an' bloomin' well insult the woman, eh, an' get 'er dander up proper! Besides, she's with Trooper Alfred, in a manner o' speakin'. They're all in the same lot, like, an' you as well. Supposed to be Yaller Boots' partner, ain't you? Very well, then, if I sent 'er away, I should send you, too. Arthur'd look 'appy when 'e come back, wouldn't 'e? Four customers give the push for nothink, an' 'is own son among 'em.

"What is the matter with the own son, then?" I exclaimed. "What does he fetch the woman round for? Why does he let her stay? I suppose that – that –"

"You suppose that 'e is the pretty pet what all the trouble's over. You suppose right, young fellar. But when you arst me what '*is* game is, I – I pause fur a reply. That is jest the 'ole crux o' the mystery, as the sayin' were. That's why I arst you. Thought *you'd* know, any'ow; talkin' to 'im long enough, you was. What'd 'e tell you?"

"Told me nothing – oh! yes, he did whisper some word, but I couldn't make head or tail of it. We spent all that long time talking together because he was trying to persuade me to go and – er – fashinate Miss Cobworthy."

"Miss what? – oo – R! I see!" exclaimed Beaky. And we both looked at the lady. She had long since interpolated herself into the *tête-à-tête* of the other two; and, from the expressions on their faces, one might judge that she did not bring sweetness with her.

"Well," said Beaky, "whatever Alfred's game is, it is a mug's game. What *is* 'e playin' at? I keeps arstin meself; an' Echo answers."

"Come to that," said I (one soon acquires the coffee-stall vernacular), "what is Miss Hopper playing at? What is she here for, anyhow? She must see that the other girl means mischief. And what is the attraction, anyhow? It can't be Alfred."

"Oh!" answered Beaky. "Why can't it be Alfred?"

"His looks, for one thing," I replied. (Though why Miss Hopper should have created even a momentary fit of jealousy in my bosom, I cannot for the life of me now say.) "Also," I continued, "Miss Hopper is already in love, poor girl. The Buenos Ayres sailor-man, you know. Surely she isn't giving up that ghost for – for *Alfred*! I'd be glad to think it, mind you. Waiting and watching, and hoping and planning for the return of the dead is –"

"Sh!" cried Beaky, with trepidation. "She might 'ear. She's funny about that sailor-man. Wouldn't do at all for to let 'er know what we think about. But, so far as what you say about 'er an' Trooper Alfred, well –" Beaky paused.

"It is like this, you see, young fellar. There's a great difference between young people an' old people. I don't mean looks an' that. It's more in a way o' *thinkin'*, what I mean. Everythink's a matter o' make-believe with the young. They don't know nothink, an' they ain't tried nothink, but ain't they 'arf sure about it! Now, my mate there, she's very sure as she's in love with a sailor-man what's bin sailin' 'ome from Bewnezerry this three years past. Won't look at nobody, 'ardly; mopes be 'erself; cries over 'is pictur' each night, an' kids 'erself on that this long voyage of 'is is all as nat'ral as daylight, an' any mornin' may see 'im stepin' up to the Obelix with a weddin' ring in one 'and an' a licence in the other.

"That's what she reckons, young gentleman boy. An' you would very likely call it 'love.' But it ain't an' don't you think so. There she is, twenty-two, an' a good motherin build. Lives in a garrick a-top of the Walpoles, an' fancies 'erself in love with a ruddy corpse. An' 'fancy' it is, me lad. What! – do you think she ain't never lonely an' nervous? Think she don't often get tired o' squattin up there, an' shakin' 'ands with 'erself? Why don't she go out an' enjoy a bit o' life an' fun, then? Because she fancies 'erself in love with the sailor, an' she's made vows to 'erself, an' because she's young, an' reckons that you've only gotter think a thing to make it true.

"So she don't go out of the way to make no friends, and keeps 'erself to 'erself, an' 'as the chronic pip, an' *thinks* he's 'apppy. Then, without 'er thinkin', like, a young bloke comes along, what she 'as got to be nice to because 'e is the son of a good pal – which if you bet yourself that it was Mr. Arthur as I 'ad in me mind, you would not be fur wrong. So she gets talkin' to this young bloke, like, an' 'e gets talkin' to 'er, like; an' they goes to a theaytre, like, an' walks 'ome in company, like; an' the result is – well, the result is I give that Bewneserry sailor-man another two months. She'll *think* she's in love with 'im, mind you, up to the last; but – well! well! it's a great thing to be young."

I nodded sagely.

"You can make allowances for a person when they're young – ain't that so, guv'nor?"

I nodded again.

"You can make allowances for my mate, like – 'er bein' so young an' that, as the sayin' were. Three years is a long time to be in love with a skeleton. You can make allowanced for my mate – ain't that so, guv'nor."

My answer was drowned by a noise from the group to our left. Miss Hopper was heard to address heated remonstrances to Yaller Boots. Down the skirt of her purple dress a great mop of scalding tea trickles, and spread itself hungrily.

"You done it a-purpose," exclaimed Miss Hopper.

"No, I never," replied Yaller Boots. "It slipped from me 'and as I 'eld it. Think I'd go for to spoil a nice noo dress like that, when I could see you bought it so special? Be like robbin' you of a meal, wouldn't it – you bein' a factory girl? Gawd! – don't it spread, that tea? And ain't it 'arf walkin' off with the colour! You must 'a' spent a lot o' dinner money on that stuff – cost nigh eleven-pence a yard, I *dare* say."

"I don't want none o' your sarcasm," retorted Miss Hopper. "I don't want none o' your company, neether. Why don't you go away an' leave me? I ain't never done you no 'arm. Bin a reg'lar plague to me, you 'ave, this ten days past."

"Keep your temper, dear," urged Miss Cobworthy, with an ineffable air of patronage and possession, commencing to fluff Miss Hopper's fringe and to dab and pull and curl and tweak it, for all the world as though Miss Hopper were a barber's block or a paid model.

Of course, Miss Hopper resented it, and, of course, she showed her resentment by giving the other a slight push. That was the opportunity for which Yellow Boots had been waiting the whole night through. She raised her hand, and gave Miss Hopper a slap that sent her reeling against the side of the stall. Then she seized Alfred's half-filled cup of coffee, and flung it at the bodice part of Miss Hopper's dress. "May's well make a match of it," she said, with marked coolness.

Miss Hopper straightened herself up, and pulled back her hat, and pushed the fringe out of her eyes, and looked at the other woman strangely. She opened her mouth as though to speak, and lifted her hand as though to strike; and then – she sank back weakly, and burst into tears.

I looked at Alfred. He stood by, smiling a smile of anxious insanity, and twiddling his thumbs.

"I – I – never done – 'er – no – 'a – 'arm," sobbed Miss Hopper, pitifully. "W – what's she want to k – kerry on like this – fur? Let me g – go – home. I never done 'er no 'a – 'arm."

Yaller Boots, with a cruel laugh, went close, and pinched the poor girl's cheek.

"Go in, you great lout, and wring that hussy's neck! Why do you stand by and watch her behave like this? Kick her out!" I shouted all this to Alfred, in a frenzy of disgust. For the time being, I was a convinced wife-beater.

"That's enough, Cissie. 'Old 'ard, Cissie. Give over now, Cissie."

Thus Alfred, in a tone of mild and benevolent cajolery.

The girl laughed. Her answer to Alfred was to seize Miss Hopper by the shoulders, and push her right off the pavement onto the kerbstone.

"I blame you for this, you shirker," exclaimed Alfred to myself, in an undertone. "Precious lotter fashinatin' you done, didn't you? She was loose on us in less than two minutes."

"I never done you no 'arm," said the voice of Miss Hopper from the gutter. "Let me alone, or I'll set the men on you."

"Men? Pah! I'd watch the man as'd set on *me*. Lie down there, dearie!" And Miss Cobworthy pushed her victim down into the soft, oozy slimy mud of the gutter.

"Here's a man that will set on you, my good woman," and I made to step forward. But two strong arms – the arms of Alfred – held me back.

"Leave 'er alone, for Gawd's sake!" shrieked that youth. "Don't make 'er angry. Fashinate 'er, if you like, but do not irritate 'er."

I was helpless in Alfred's embrace; but I took what little satisfaction I might in kicking his shin-bones with my heels.

Miss Cobworthy, laughing derisively, stood regarding us. The other girl had gone; some faint, pitiable sobs, which sounded afar off, told us that she was creeping home.

"She'll look smart for the pantomime to-morrer, won't she, Alf?" And Miss Cobworthy turned and vanished, also.

[22 January 1904]

XIV. Concerning a Benevolent Idiot.

"It is all lies about me bruising her. I banged a part you *couldn't* bruise. She is a liar. I dident ought to be here. I will be dismist from the Army why ain't you doing nothing none of you."

This is an extract from a letter. I quote it from an epistle which Trooper Alfred wrote to his father on the evening of his sentence to three week's imprisonment. The charge, you will remember, was that of assaulting Miss Cobworthy with a knife-board. "Struck her about the head," said the police; but the police lied – or else their sense of delicacy caused them to make an exaggerated use of the language of euphemy.

"If 'e never banged 'er 'ead, an' if 'e never bruised 'er," said Arthur to us, "somethink oughter be done. A bruise or two is no more than what she deserves for 'er wickedness; but women is women, an' my Alf was always a gentleman, please Gawd, though 'asty when roused. Fair is fair. This must be looked to."

Looked to it was. There were investigations and re-investigations. A company officer came up from Aldershot to speak fair things concerning Alfred's general conduct. And Miss Cobworthy broke down under cross-examination, and the police revised their notes. So Alfred was discharged, ruffled, but stainless. And the newspapers which had printed paragraphs concerning licentious soldiery omitted to chronicle the fact of his discharge, and high festival was held at Arthur's.

There was quite a representative gathering at the stall when I arrived there that night in the company of Mr. Fothergill, M.A.

That gentleman had been an acquaintance of mine for something under six hours; but I had learnt in that short period to despise him as thoroughly as though he were my oldest fried. Mr. Fothergill was palmed off upon me, as one might express it, by the acting-editor of the great newspaper by means of which I live. He – Mr. Fothergill – had arrived with the post at 9 a.m. He expressed a desire to see the editor, and saw him.

"What is your business?" asked the editor.

Mr. Fothergill explained his business. "My name," said he, "is probably familiar to you as the author of several small works on sociologic subjects. I –"

The editor rang his bell. "I must refer you, sir, to our assistant editor. Boy, show this gentleman to Mr. Yapper's room. Good-day, Mr. Fothergill."

"Mr. Yapper don't come till eleven, sir," said the boy.

"I will call back at eleven," said Mr. Fothergill. He called back at eleven; also at twelve, at one, and at two. By half-past-two Mr. Yapper had lunched, and Fothergill, M.A., was allowed in under protest.

"My name," Mr. Fothergill explained, "is Fothergill. It is probably familiar to you by reason of its association with several small works of a sociologic character. I –"

"Full up," said Mr. Yapper. "Will bear your name in mind."

"You misunderstand me, sir," Mr. Fothergill replied. "I do not desire to contribute to your paper. That, perhaps, may come later. 'All in good time' is a useful motto, Mr. Yapper; also 'Festina lente'.[121] I am at present engaged upon a small treatise, or synthesis, to be entitled 'The Masses of London, Their Life and Environment: Does it make for good?' It occurred to my mind that many members of the staff of a great journal such as this must possess exceptional opportunity for forming an intimate first-hand acquaintance with –"

"Boy!" shouted Mr. Yapper, "show this gentleman to Mr. Dukes."

When Fothergill, M.A., had explained himself to Mr. Dukes, that gentleman said: "Quite so, quite so. Yes. The man you ought to see is our Mr. Brewer. Boy, show this gentleman in to Mr. Brewer." And Brewer, who was pouring some of yesterday's tea into a paste-pot which required moisture, said: "The chap to introduce you to the vices of London is our sporting man. Wash your face, boy, and take this gentleman to The Colonel."

"But I do not wish to be introduced to the vices of London," protested Mr. Fothergill. "I am in favour of the suppression of all forms of vice by Act of Parliament. My forthcoming book is to deal exclusively with the vital facts of life, Mr. Brewer. It will go deep; it will go deep."

Mr. Brewer, standing in an almost clerical attitude, as though in the act of bestowing a blessing with his past-brush, whistled intelligently. "Ah! My dear fellow," he exclaimed. "I begin to twig. You are on the 'How London Lives' lay?"

Mr. Fothergill bowed a dignified acquiescence.

"Then the fellow you want is young Stick-in-the-mud: young What's-His-Name – the new man. Boy, take Mr. Fothergill to the new man."

And thus this tedious person was bequeathed to me. He hung about the office all day and half the night, and waylaid me with question and greeting at intervals. When evasion and incivility had done their worst and failed, I capitulated, and took him out to a fish supper – wishing it might choke him – and so to Arthur's.

"Dear! dear!" said Mr. Fothergill, as we approached the stall, "this really is very interesting. I apprehended you to state that the institutions plied an exclusively nocturnal commerce?"

"You understood me to say that these stall-keepers only traded at night-time."

"One might, I take it, infer with accuracy, from the figures with which you have so kindly supplied me, that the proprietors of these enterprises supply a pressing need?"

"'Long-felt want' is a useful form," I suggested.

"A trifle hackneyed, don't you think?' queried Mr. Fothergill, with an indulgent smile. "Savours of that valuable, but hardly exquisite medium, 'The Reporter's Note Book.' I must certainly devote a chapter of my forthcoming volume to a survey of the history, scope, and ethical utility of this species of refectory. 'St. Boniface of the Benighted'[122] would, I think, form a descriptive and alluring title for that feature of the work. Does the suggestion command itself to your trained judgment?"

"'Midnight coffee-stalls' would do as well," I replied, for Mr. Fothergill was rasping me.

"I will consider the question," said he, a little coldly. "And this, I presume, is the object of our investigation?"

"That," I replied, "is Arthur's coffee-stall." And Mr. Fothergill, who was pointing an ebony stick before him, after the manner of an illustrated-journal explorer discovering waterfalls, carefully lowered that accessory, adjusted his waistcoat, pulled down his hat, pocketed his watch-chain, and assumed, generally an air of sympathetic, but cautious, enquiry.

We secured a place at the counter, and Arthur, with a cheerful nod of greeting, banged down two cups of coffee.

"One assumes to drink it, naturally?" enquired Mr. Fothergill, in a hoarse undertone.

"One drinks it," said I.

"This system of enquiry has certainly the merit of realism," said Mr. Fothergill, with a limp smile. He sipped at the coffee shyly, as though gall were in it, instead of honest, plain water and plain sugar and good chicory and the best bark.[123]

Mr. Fothergill then looked about him.

The company, beside ourselves, numbered some dozen. There was a sailor, with vine leaves in his hair,[124] singing love songs to another sailor, who had removed a boot, which he was labouriously polishing by means of natural moisture and a coat-sleeve. And a gentleman in a mauve squash hat was undertaking to explain to another gentleman in a fawn squash hat, exactly why the harness-buckle industry had left Birmingham for Belgium. "Mind you, I git this direct from me own brother at Ribstone's," said Mauve Hat, after each octave; whilst his companion exclaimed at intervals, "Well, all I can say is – the men must combine." Another group consisted of Trooper Alfred and Miss Hopper, and Kitty and her spouse, and a poor, verminous, hungry old tramp, who was there because his rags and filth covered a kind of a body, and because Kitty and Miss Hopper were women, and themselves had suffered hunger and desolation and the scorn of men. Over by the flare lamp there was the usual vain, half-witted, resentful little drab, of course. Publicity is at once the paradise and the hell of these women, and they seek and absorb it as a drunkard sups his gin – with a grand, exultant loathing. This poor little scrap of human merchandise was especially, and particularly, and wonderfully brazen of deportment. She thrust her pitiful clown's face, and her faded, yellow poll,[125] deeper and deeper into the lamp-glare; and she cast great hungry, ugly eyes of commerce upon the men, and glared aggressively at the women. And she straightened a tattered, gaudy skeleton of a hat upon her head, and flirted a grimy old handkerchief, and sipped exquisitely at her coffee, and giggled, and ogled, and reeled from hunger, and was altogether terrible. Anon she pulled her sodden skirt about her with an air ostentatiously exclusive, and gazed fixedly and provokingly, and scornfully at the other women, as who should say: "Think yourselves mighty superior in your cotton-print virtue, don't you? Perhaps it might interest you to know that I have been to Brighton with a stock-broker, in *my* time."

Then a drayman began to exchange witticisms with her, an occasion which the drayman's boy made of use to exchange coffee cups, to his own advantage, with the drayman.

And there you have a picture of the whole assembly: two cheerful sailors; two futile, but contented, debaters; an exceedingly flattered and happy old tramp; a chivalrous and conversational drayman; a resourceful drayman's boy; Trooper Alfred and party; and a drab being comforted with coffee and lies. Over all, a pervasive odour of hot coffee and fresh buns, the glitter of the urn, and the smiling face of Arthur.

Wherefore, Fothergill, M.A., did stroke his stomach, and wag his head, and roll his eyes in oily moisture, and cough in an emotional manner, and speak, saying:

"It is very, very sad!"

"What is sad?" I queried, a trifle nonplussed.

"This – all this!" responded Mr. Fothergill. "The extreme disharmony of it all. The misery! The want!! The sorrow!!! The pain!!!! The sordidness!!!!! It is a surprising, pathetic, and painful spectacle. It is a spectacle such as few could witness without distress, and none without emotion. This is England at her saddest. Such a sight is calculated to make humanitarians and reformers of the worst of us. Ah! me!"

From all of which I gathered that Mr. Fothergill, like some better men, and many prettier, cultivated his sympathies on behalf of his prefaces, and believed the opposite. He continued to hold forth in the strain indicated above for quite a while. The company began to look at him, and not wholly with approval.

After eventually terminating the outburst of feeling, Mr. Fothergill permitted himself to relapse into a state of merely contortional frenzy, and continued to stand as before, with his arms folded, and is eyes rolling, and his head wagging. Every now and then he sighed. He also made a note or two. Judge, then, of my delight then the drayman mentioned heretofore turned suddenly, and addressed the sociologist as "Toeface." Judge, also, of that gentleman's dismay.

"I beg your pardon?" he enquired, with dignity.

And the carman replied: "Don't beg my pardon; move yere 'ulkin' carcase. What I said was, if you jogged my arm again, I would knock yere 'ead. Come 'ere 'avin spasms an' contortions over a man when 'e is tryin' to eat 'is supper."

"I beg your pardon!" quothe Mr. Fotherill, again.

"Then it ain't blushin' well granted!" answered this excellent drayman. "Stinkin' sight too many o' your good-fur-nothin' sort 'angin' about o' nights. Why don't you go 'ome to bed? Get 'ome quick, an' you'll cop the pleeceman,[126] I'll be bound."

At this mystic reference there was a shout of laughter from the company. Mr. Fothergill was obviously not the kind of person to stand by and be laughed at, and he accordingly addressed himself to Arthur.

"My good man," said he, "I must insist upon your putting a stop to these proceedings."

Arthur is not accustomed to being "my good manned" by anybody. Mr. Fothergill's appeal, therefore, left him cold.

"It's your own fault," he replied curtly. "You should ha' left the man alone."

At one man, the company (by now considerably augmented in numbers) took up the cry. "R!" it shouted, in chorus, "why couldn't you let the man alone? 'E never done you no 'arm!"

"That's what I say!" asserted the drayman, pathetically. "Why couldn't 'e let me alone? I never done 'im no 'arm!"

Then somebody pushed Mr. Fothergill, and Mr. Fothergill fell forward into the drayman's arms, and the drayman moved Mr. Fothergill out of the way, as one might express it, and Mr. Fothergill fell on to Trooper Alfred. So Trooper Alfred pushed Mr. Fothergill on to one of the drunken sailors, and this person very deliberately began to feel in a hip pocket. He was, in reality, seeking for the flask that cements friendship; but long ere he could produce it, Fothergill, M.A., had flown.

So now you know why a whole chapter in Mr. Fothergill's lately published work is devoted to a denunciation of coffee-stalls. "The resort of thieves, and harpies, and prostitutes, and pimps, and bullies," says he, "these institutions may be regarded as veritable plague-spots upon the fair face of our Metropolis."

But we of Arthur's know better. We know that there is warmth at coffee stalls, and good cheer, and honest mirth. We know that the sweetest of all gospels – the gospel of tolerance – is practiced there as nowhere else. For twopence the poor man may obtain at Arthur's a rich man meal; and the rich man – well, gentlemen, Arthur's is open. Try your fortunes.

[29 January 1904]
XV. A Pinch of Salt.

The great point about this week's picture is its truth. I beg you will bear that fact in mind. Your evidence may be necessary to me on the Day of Judgment.

You may remember that when transcribing Miss Hopper's narrative of her adventures with the Broomfield Squire, I set down certain extracts from a ballad of the Shires – the which I did definitely declare to have been uttered, or sung, or intoned by Miss Hopper, in the course of the narrative aforesaid. It has since been laid to my charge that Miss Hopper and her song were not in keeping. I am told by certain sceptics (Nunquam[127] amongst them) that it is not from the lips of little ragamuffins like Miss Hopper that one shall learn such songs as those.

Now, as a matter of fact, there are far stranger things to be met with at my coffee-stall than a tramp who can tip you a stave from a Shire song. But, by way of putting the matter upon a friendly basis, so to speak, I may tell Nunquam that in these days it is only tramps and ostlers and the like who have any pride at all in the sweet old ballad literature of our country. I say this to Nunquam's face – him bein' a man o' letters, an' all.

A ballad of sorts is shortly to follow. And, taking one consideration with another, I am a little doubtful as to what everybody (Nunquam and the sceptics included) will think about it. Hence my insistence upon the absolute truth of that which shall follow.

It was a sailorman that sang the song – a sailorman with mumps. The bandages and scarves and plasters which bound and swathed his countenance led one at first to form the opinion that this sailorman had suffered some grand, heroic mischance of his calling. One thought of shipwreck, fire, and battle. When the thing eventually reduced itself to a mere question of mumps, we felt, vaguely, that the sailorman had defrauded us. He was a harmless fellow, though, and drunk enough to be lovable. And this (so near as I can reduce its metre to a typographical form) is the haunting sea-dirge with which he introduced himself to us. Repeat in a hoarse, guttural voice, with a moaning intonation, and strike a table with some hard instrument at appropriate intervals. That was the sailorman's method, anyhow. Follows:

> So theer 'e sot
> a spettin' op
> the purple blood
> like wine. So
> theer 'e sot a
> spettin' op the
> purple blood
> like wine, cos
> Joe,
> Joe Golightly
> stabbed 'im in
> the spine. When
> Joe Golightly
> very rightly
> knifed 'im in
> the spine, 'e
> sadly sot a
> spettin' op the
> purple blood like wine.

> Oah Wine,
>   Wine,
>   Wine,
> Ther pur-ah-pul blood like wine!
> O, Joe Golightly's
> 'and it was as jabbed
> 'im in the spine.
> So theer 'e sot
> a spettin' op
> the pur-ah-pul
> blood like wine.
> Oah, Joe,
>   Joe,
>   Wine,
>   Spine,
> The pur-ah-pul Joe[128]
> like – Gimme a
> blessed corfee and
> I will start again.

"I will give you a corfee, an' welcome," responded Arthur; "but as fur startin' again – well, I will put *that* to the vote. Gentlemen, do we want any more of this 'ere psalm?"

"We do not," replied the company, in chorus.

"Meeting is unanimous," said Arthur. "We like your company, but the concert can be dispensed with."

"Norra word!" responded the sailor, grasping Arthur's hand with cordiality. "Norra nura word. All friends 'ere, I make no doubt. Friends objeckn my singin', why – why – very well, then. Thas whar *I* say. Very well, then. If friends objec' – (hic) – if friends objec' – (hic) – they – they objec'. Ain't tharright? 'Course thas right. Gimme nurra corfee."

"Wharri say," pursued the sailorman, "is *right*. We are friends 'ere, and friends, Gawdammun, objecks my singin'. Very well, then."

"It ain't you *singin'* we objects to," Arthur explained. "It's you *song*."

The sailor banged his coffee cup against the urn, shattering the smaller vessel into fragments. "Ain't that warri said?" he demanded with heat. "Suppose I '*ave* gorra mumps? That don't make me a fool. Far from it. Very well, then. We are all friensere, an' I will sing you another song.

> My li-i-ttle love,
> My milkwhite dove,
> Is now, alsa! no moah;
> A cruel shark 'as eat my love,
> An' I am stricken soah.
> Ther shark 'e opened wide 'is jaws,

> An' choked 'er shrieks with brine.
> Ther purple blood it did run out
> Like wine, like wine, like wine.
> 'Er satin limbs 'e tore apart
> Like –"

The sailorman paused. "You finish it, guv'nor," he politely suggested to Arthur. "Gorra mumps, I 'ave. Bad things forra memory is mumps. Gimme nurra corfee."

"Great gift of 'armony you got," observed Arthur, as he handed a fresh cup to the sailorman.

"I believe you, ole mate," replied the sailorman. "'Armony it is.

> Ther smile upon 'er bonnie cheek
>   Was sweeter than the bee,
> Her voice eckshelled the cuckoo's song,
>   But R! 'Ow false was she.
> I bound 'er body to a mast,
>   I seized 'er tresses fine,
> I pierced 'er false 'eart through an' through,
>   An' 'er warm blood ran like wine."

"Seem to get prettier each time, your songs do," commented Arthur. "Muster took a precious lot o' learnin'."

"Noso precious," responded the sailor, modestly. "It all comes narral to me. A gift."

"A very useful gift, too," said Arthur, with approval. "So 'andy, like, fur soothin' the baby to sleep with."

At mention of the word "baby," the sailorman's countenance became suddenly overcast with gloom. "Tharreminds me," he exclaimed, in a peremptory voice. "Tharreminds me warri come 'ere for. I come 'ere for to find a man what stole my woollen monkey. Thas warri come 'ere for. Did *you* steal my woollen monkey?" The sailorman pointed an accusing finger at Arthur.

"You can search *me*," responded that individual. "Never stole a woollen monkey in me life – nor yet a live one. So I 'ope you will be good enough to leave *my* purple blood where it is for the present."

"No offence, guv'nor – no offence," exclaimed the sailorman. "All friends 'ere, I make no doubt. I gorra grudge aginner swine what stole my woollen monkey. Tha's on'y fair. I put it to you, guv'nor, ain't that on'y fair? Any swine what can be swine enough to steal the little woollen monkey what I brought from Monte Video for my baby daughter is a – is a – a swine. Thas what *'e* is – a swine. I can't speak no fairer nor that. Lord Kitchener couldn't speak no fairer nor that. Ain't that right, guv'nor?"

Arthur acquiesced. "So you got a baby daughter, 'ave you?" he continued. "An' a nice, kind, musical ole father you must make to 'er."

"Musical is right," assented the sailor. "Two year come Monday it'll be since last I seed 'er.

> For it's 'ome, dearie, 'ome,
>   An' it's 'ome I'd like to be,
> With me raw, gapin' wounds
>   Bein' bandaged up be thee.

"'Ow did you lose the monkey?" enquired Arthur, with sympathetic interest.

"Monkey? *What* monkey?" enquired the sailorman.

"That there woollen monkey what you jest bin makin' all this song about?'

"Song?" echoed the sailor. "R, yus:

> I sor my loved one's 'ands were red,
>   It looked to me like blood;
> 'Twas only monkey's gore, 'e said,
>   An' fainted where 'e stood!

Gimme another corfee," said the sailor.

"You ain't answered my question yet," Arthur reminded him. "What about that woollen monkey – the one you was bringin' 'ome to baby?'

Again the word "baby" supplied our sailorman with recollections. Again his face darkened, and he raised his coffee cup as if to throw it at Arthur. "You gimme back my woollen monkey," he shouted. "Go on – 'and it back. 'And it back or put 'em up. I give you option, fair an' square. 'And back the monkey, or put up yere dooks. There's the straight griffin."

"That's all right, cully," responded Arthur, with guile. "That's all right. We'll soon find your monkey for you; never fear. Now, let me see – what was we talkin' about? R, yus – Cardiff: that was it – Cardiff. Fine place, Cardiff."

The sailorman vehemently dissented from this view. Since Arthur had effected his object in creating a diversion, he did not permit the sailor's language on the subject of Cardiff to discomfort him. Cardiff, said the sailorman, was a disgrace to Wales; and Wales, he added was a disgrace to God. No, he repeated, Cardiff was out of the question. Give him London. Barring London, one might tolerate Plymouth. But the best of them, London included, were poor by the side of Rio. *That* was your sailorman's true paradise. You could get drunk for less than tuppence in Rio.

"I suppose," enquired Arthur, "that you bin nigh everywhere in your time?"

"If," replied the sailor, "you could name the name of any point what I aint't touched at, I would give you five shillin', an' welcome."

"What about Yarmouth?" asked Arthur, with a grin.

"Born at Yarmouth," said the sailor.

"What about Moscow?" asked another enquirer.

"Touched at Moscow a dozen times," said the sailor.
"And Port o' Spain?" suggested Trooper Alfred.
"Traded there for five year reg'lar."
"And Bristol?" asked somebody else.
"Born at Bristol," replied the sailorman. (You must remember that he was suffering from the mumps.)
"You know Bloemfontein,[129] I make no doubt?" This enquiry came from Trooper Alfred.

The sailorman knew Bloemfontein well. He last touched that port about four years since, and had a lively and detailed recollection of the visit, which was distinguished in his mumps by the fact that he had been drunk for five consecutive days of his sojourn there. Other ports included in the sailorman's itinerary were Michigan, Surbiton, Arizona and Bath.

Then came the inevitable enquiry form Miss Hopper. "Bin to Bewnezerry?"
"Not much!" replied the sailorman. "My very last week," he asserted, "was on a ship from Bewnezerry."

Miss Hopper flushed, and then turned pale. "What might be the name o' your ship?" she asked, excitedly.
"I disremember the name," asserted the sailorman, after a pause.
"Captain's name?" demanded Miss Hopper.
"Smith!" responded the sailor, promptly.

Miss Hopper's face fell; one more question occurred to her, and she asked it.
"I wonder if there was a shipmate sailin' with you be name of Joe Tuttle?"
"Joe Tuttle!" echoed the sailor. "Know 'im well. 'E owes me five bob!"

Then a night tram came whizzing out of the darkness, and pulled up with a grunt within sight of the stall. The sailorman lurched towards it.
"Oh! come back, sailor!" cried Miss Hopper. "Do come back, like a good fellar. Come back an' 'ave a coffee."

The sailor went stumbling on.
"Where does'e live?" shrieked Miss Hopper.

The sailorman began to sing, and climbed the tram. As that vehicle glided forward, we heard his voice uplifted in song.

> "So theer 'e sot
> a-spettin' op
> the purple blood
> like wine, and
> Joe Golightly
> very politely
> 'eaved 'im in ther brine
>   brine,
>   brine
> 'E-a-ved 'im in ther brine!

Then a faint ahout reached our ears concerning woollen monkeys and a baby girl and the sailorman's ole woman and home, sweet home.

Arthur then undertook to explain to Miss Hopper that sailormen were sometimes liars. I did not envy Arthur this task.

[5 February 1904]

XVI. Hush-a-by Baby.

"Yes," said the man with the baby, as he wearily changed arms, and pointed a hand with a penny in it towards the coffee-urn, "Yes, the startin' out is all right. It's the comin 'ome o' night what takes the flavor out o' these Sunday visits."

"Bin far?" quereied Arthur.

"Depends what you call 'far'." replied the man with the baby. "We ain't bin no distance, not to say *distance* really. We bin to Southgate Chase."

"I ain't no ruddy athlete meself," observed Arthur. "Southgate Chase an' back, with the weights all up, would satisfy my appetite fur distances a treat."

"As I say," affirmed the visitor, "it is the comin' back what pips you. Goin' out of a Sunday mornin' is all gay enough. What with trams an' trains an' tubes an' that, you got your choice to pick from. But the comin' back is a problem: that's what it is – a problem. Missed the last train to-night, I did, an' one way an' another – walkin' a bit 'ere, an' trammin' a bit there, an' doin a sprint for it now an' then by way of a change – I daresay I bin a matter of two hours on the road. Must be getting on for one o'clock – what, guv'nor?"

"Twenty past," replied Arthur, duly consulting a battered alarm clock which was buried somewhere amongst the manifold ornaments of his tobacco shelf.

"Twenty past, is it!" exclaimed the man with the baby. "Later than I thought for. There'll be a night-tram along sooner or later, I make no doubt. What do you say to me setting this little 'un on your counter for a spell, while I ease me arms a trifle?"

"Very welcome," responded Arthur. "We'll move the butter, if you don't mind, an' my man 'ere will jest run a cloth over the zincwork. Don't do to let 'em lie in the wet too much. They catch cold an' that sometimes."

"I believe you," replied the man, and whilst Beaky, in pursuance of Arthur's order, proceeded to mop the surface of the counter, our visitor offered us some views on the subject of babies.

"They don't grow no lighter as they grow up," said he, "nor they don't eat no less. At the same time, mind you, I don't begrudge 'em nothin', neether trouble nor food. I'm a believer in 'em myself – always 'ave bin. Rare comfortable things to 'ave about the 'ouse – in the daytime. Rare companions, too, took in the proper sperrit. There's the expense, of course; but what *does* that amount to, after all? That's what I always say to my missus o' Friday nights. *Somebody's* got to eat the leavin's, I says, an' it might swell be a nipper as anybody else."

"Very true, " observed Arthur, as he held out his arms towards the infant, saying: "Sling 'im over, mate. We can do 'im up in my old 'orse blanket. May's well lie warm as cold, an' my old nag ain't one to be pertickler."

But our friend the baby was not for having any horse blankets. He had a proper sense of the dignity and privileges of his age, besides (I daresay) possessing a precocious sensitiveness to the savour of things. Also, the blanket was of abnormal hairiness, and it tickled his nose. So he woke up, and sneezed, and swore – inaudibly, but with evident feeling. And when Arthur, after duly ascertaining which part of the bundle contained the head, was about to employ the blanket, our young visitor summoned forth his strength, and gave a vocal and muscular demonstration of his displeasure.

"Now you started 'im," remarked the father, with an air of pessimism.

"That's all right, ole pal," Arthur made answer. "I ain't no amatoor at this business, an' don't you think it. Soothin' down babies is one of my specialities. 'Old on to 'is middle, so's 'e don't fall an' 'urt 'isself, an jest you watch."

Arthur then proceeded to assume an expression of inanity fearful to look upon. He also banged his counter with the bread-board, and shouted "Oy! Oy! Oy!" with deafening effect. The suddenness of this outburst naturally caused the baby to leave off crying in order to get its eyes open. This was evidently the effect which Arthur had intended to produce. He immediately proceeded to turn it to account. "Ho! baby, ho!" he shouted, exultantly; "baby, watch! What price this for a puff-puff?"

Arthur then emitted a shrill shriek in alleged imitation of the whistle of a locomotive. He stamped his feet; he clapped his hands; he snorted. The veins stood out upon his forehead; his eyeballs revolved and, as it were, curvetted; his breath poured forth like steam. The whole performance was very unusual and distressing, and after one first glance of terror-struck bewilderment, the baby renewed his cries – this time with a note of poignant anguish.

But Arthur did not despair "I'll try the dawg on 'im," said he, and forthwith proceeded to bay like a bloodhound. Strange to relate, this entertainment failed also in its purpose of lulling the infant. Arthur's next sedative took the form of an imitation parrot squawk. He subsequently pretended to bray like a donkey, to crow like a cock, and to squooch like a motor-car. The whole concluded with a grand display of fireworks, in which a judicious selection of gurgles and whizzes and splutters and hisses were succeeded by a wonderfully realistic representation of the blowing-up of a powder factory.

And still the baby cried.

"You've struck a tough 'un this time, my man," said Trooper Alfred, who by this time had joined the party. It was a small party. The night was cold and damp and foggy, and the morrow was a working day. The man with the baby and Trooper Alfred and myself were the only visitors present – unless you care to count a furtive, hopeless old drab of a woman, who crouched in the gloom vainly thinking herself unseen, and content to be merely within sight of the warmth and goodness of the stall.

"Tough 'un is right," quoth Arthur, in response to the gibes of his son. "But I ain't beat yet, an' don't you think so. I got a little medicine 'eer will charm the lad a treat."

This medicine consisted of a bright tin can. By means of a table-spoon and extreme muscular effort, Arthur produced a reverberating clamour. "It is a quick-step," he explained, "an you work it faster as you go on." The effect was certainly startling. Even the chinaware rattled with emotion.

But still the baby cried.

"Well, well!" cried Arthur, after submitting this soothing treatment to a really exhaustive test. "I give it up. I own meself beat. This job is one too many for me."

"It is only what I expected," remarked the father not without emotion. "'Is voice is *always* at its best at this time o' night. If tin cans would calm it, I think I could 'a' trusted meself to find out the invention before now."

Here Beaky spoke:

"You will pardon me, genelmen," said he, "but if I might go so fur as to offer advice, there is a lot to be said for the ole-fashioned treatment. I know a dodge about babies, I do!"

"What is that?" we cried, in chorus.

"First of all," explained the specialist, "You turn 'im over on 'is chest. Then you say: 'Hups a daisy! *There's* a little man!' an' thump 'im on 'is back. Then you give 'im a fork or sich-like to play with. Then you say" 'Did 'e 'ave a dirty black-guard of a father, then?' (no offence to *you*, sir, on'y it's custom), and then you jerk 'im up an' down, an' 'old your breath till 'e falls asleep."

"There's nothink like tryin', anyhow," remarked Arthur, after due consideration. "S'pose you try the plan yourself." He handed the baby over to Beaky, and the treatment was duly applied. But the infant was pertinacious, and wept unmercifully.

"Your tram is due in about five minutes: that's *one* comfort," observed Arthur, during a pause. "P'raps, if you thought, you could remember 'ow your missus deals with 'im."

"My missus ain't good at that sort of thing," explained the man, reddening a little. "Rare good sort, my missus, mind you; but clever! Sings, y' know, an' plays the sither,[130] an reads novels. Great reader, she is. Fonder theaytres, too. I took 'er to 'The Ice-Cream Girl' t'other night, an' afore we was 'arf-way 'ome she's whistled over every bloomin' toon in the piece. She's practisin' the on 'er sither to-day. That's why she ain't with me now – that an' a sore throat. We live at Balham, see?

an' there was a fire at three o'clock on Wednesday mornin' and she was up an' out to see it in no time! Rare active one, she is. Bin laid up ever since.

"But my sister, now," continued the man, "my sister what I bin seein' to-day, she's a rare one for putting a stop to their cryin'. They bin unfortunate theirselves – two dead an' one stillborn. That makes 'er sorter extra mother-like with my kid, if you understand. Get on a treat, them two do. She's a good ole sort, my sister. Raspy an that in 'er temper, I admit; in fact, my wife can't stand 'er. For ever squabbling they are. My wife's very sensitive, you see, and Bella *is* 'asty with 'er tongue. I admit that meself. But she's a good ole sort is Bella, an' a good sister to me. Sewed 'arf-a-dozen buttons on me westkit this very day."

Arthur looked queerly at the urn. "Good old Cupid!" he said, derisively.

The man with the baby, who was an honest fellow of Teutonic build and conservative principles, did not hear this observation, so nothing came of it.

In the meantime, the baby had not ceased its lamentations. Trooper Alfred, being minded to restore his waning circulation, had indulged himself in a sort of cake-walk[131] up the tram-line. On his return journey he fell in with a certain furtive old drab, who sat on a kerbstone blinking at the glitter and goodness of his father's stall. This woman was immediately seized upon by Alfred. He dragged her back to the stall, and expanded her with quartern[132] cups of coffee. When sheer exhaustion caused her to desist from further imbibition, he put sardines and bread into her wallet, and bade her hence. "But before you go," said he, "jest take an' 'old that child, an' stop 'is 'ollerin'. If you can do the trick, I'll give you tuppence."

The old lady snorted scornfully. She seized the infant. She placed it face downward across her arm, she thumped its back, she gave it a tablespoon to play with, and bade it take no notice of the "dhirty blaygard min, thin." And, lo! this infant's lamentations immediately did cease, and its countenance took on a broad and beautiful smile. Then it noticed the medals which decorated the bosom of Trooper Alfred. It allowed itself to be reinstated upon the counter, and lay there beaming, its eye directed upon Trooper Alfred with an appreciative twinkle, as though one should say: "This is the *very* thing that I have been looking for all day!"

And the furtive old lady favoured us with a comprehensive curtsey, and retired. But before doing so, she delivered a speech of prophecy.

"The cheeild," quoth she, "which I have hild in me arrums will grow to be a foin tall man. He will lead armies and govern min. He will marry a purty gyurl, begad! an' live long, begad! an doi rich. God kape him!"

"Which his name," explained the father with a smile, "is Martha Victoria Constance Anne!"

XVII. The Red-Faced Man. [12 February 1904]

A red-faced man, wearing a horseshoe tie-pin and double-seamed kid gloves, came the other evening to Arthur's stall. He was a stranger to us regulars: but having spat all about him with amiable impartiality, and having also volunteered a fervid commentary on the day's racing intelligence, he gained an immediate welcome. The Brotherhood divined, as it were, that these were manifestations of a kindred spirit. The red-faced man exhibited by his manner that he was a person of Bohemian tendencies; his opinions signified that he had travelled; and his language afforded the most pleasing evidences of a mis-spent youth. We accordingly waived the question of references, and accepted the red-faced stranger as a man and a brother,[133] and one of the right sort to boot.

"Racing gent?" enquired Arthur, with friendly interest, as he handed the stranger his third cup of coffee.

"A bit that way," responded the other. "In the 'bus trade at present. Regarded as a trade," he added, confidentially, "the 'bus trade is a ruddy farce."

"So I hear: tube competition, I s'pose, an' the trams an' motor cars an' that?" Arthur made this enquiry with an air of respectful deference.

"It ain't the competition I'm a thinkin' of," replied the stranger. "The trade don't give a toad for competition. Dividends gone up again this year – so I 'ear; though I notice they ain't in no lurid 'urry to shove our wages up accordin'. When I say that the 'bus trade is a farce, it is us poor beggars what I am a thinkin' of. Where do *we* come in?"

"R! Where?" echoed Arthur, perhaps a little vaguely.

"My last trade 'ad its drawbacks, I will admit; but my last trade was a fiery paradise compared with *this* giddy trade."

"What might your last trade 'a' bin?" enquired Arthur.

"Druv a fever-van",[134] responded the stranger.

"Very ketchin' an' risky occupation, I should 'a' supposed?" suggested Arthur.

"Never done *me* no 'arm," the stranger answered. "Our cases was allus wropped up very thorough an' no expense spared for carbolix[135] an' that. Druv Fred Archer[136] in my van, once."

A silence, as of respectful awe, fell upon the company. "We cured 'im, too, by God!" the stranger added, by way of a culminating triumph.

"But goin' back to the 'bus trade, now," said Arthur. "What is your partickler complaint? What makes you so 'arsh about it all? Wages are good, I'm told."

"Depends what you call 'good,'" responded the stranger. "But it ain't the wages I object to. What I complains of is the indignity of it all. Give me a trade with a bit of dignity to it. A 'bus-driver in these days is no better than a lamp-post – at the beck an' call of everybody, an' never left in peace for 'arf a minute at a time."

"All the lamp-posts *I* ever see," said Arthur, "was left I peace all right. Only a lunatic would beck an' call a lamp-post."

"That is what *you* think, my cock-eyed coffee merchant," replied the red-faced man, with quiet contempt. "I daresay there's a thing or two you don't know, even about lamp-posts. If you want to make me out a liar, say so: that's all. Come out from be'ind that frowsy ole zareeba[137] an' say so. Take more'n a aged costermonger to get the better of *me*, man to man, an' don't you forget it. 'Arf a word more, my man, an' I will *put you through it!*"

A friendly customer intervened: "Be reasonable," he urged; "keep cool." Then, by way of appeal to the stranger's better nature – "let me orfer you a drop o' rum in the corfee."

"Well, well," remarked the stranger, "why not? Let bygones be bygones! 'Ere's *to* you, gentlemen all. May the best 'orse win, may your best pal never welsh[138] you, an' may a 'asty tongue never spoil friendship. 'Ere's to you, guv'nor. What was I a-sayin'?"

"You was sayin'," Arthur reminded him, "that what you asked for was a profession with a touch of dignity to it."

"R," quoth the red-faced man: "I remember. Well, what I say about it is as it's a bit of a come-down. Fancy me what's drove a fever van for two and twenty year – drove it, mind you, for one of the biggest 'orspitals in town an' drove it, *more*-over for some of the most interesting cases – fancy me, I say, bein' redooced to settin' up be'ind a giddy pill advertisement, with clurks an' females tuggin' at me elbow all day long to arsk ridiclous questions, an' a regiment of rozzers jerkin' their silly arms at me an' 'ollerin' their precious orders at me all up the blushin' street. *Fancy* it, I say."

"It is 'orrible," said Arthur.

"An' that, mind you," continued the red-faced man, is on'y the least of it! There's inspectors in the 'bus trade an over-seers an' a ridiclous bloomin' swain they calls a time-keeper. Fair set to I 'ad with our man, t'other mornin'.

"'I am reportin' you. No. 8,' 'e says to me, the other mornin'. 'This is the third journey runnin' you've fetched it early. There's three minutes to spare this time.'

"'Old me 'orses, Joe!' I says to the conductor. Then I 'ops down off my blanky seat an' I walk up to 'is blanky perch an' I makes 'im a blanky speech. Then I pay's 'im out."

"What did you do to 'im?" enquired Arthur.

"What did I *do* to 'im?" repeated the stranger; "I bloomin' well *put 'im through it*'.

"Then there's our over-seer. ''*E* bloomin' well starts on me next. Sends for me to 'is orfice. 'There are complaints about you, 'Uskings,' 'e says. 'Ho! *are* there!' says I. 'Yus!' says 'e. 'Ho!' says I. 'Yus!' says 'e. 'Well – spit 'em out,' says I.

"When 'e'd done – a bloomin' psalm it was about fetchin' up too early at the mark – when 'e'd done, I ups an; speaks a candid word or two. 'It's like this,' says I. 'There's such a thing as proper pride in this world,' I says. 'Now I comes,' I says, 'from a dignified profession', I says. 'When I was a drivin' of the fever van,' I tells 'im, 'there was no talk about sackings and fines. I done my work an' took a pride in it – thirteen cases of 'scarlet' between Lambeth an' 'Olloway in *one monrnin*' was *my* record – I done my work,' I says, 'an' I took a pride in it. I was found in clobber an' got a Christmas box.[139] In *your* ruddy service,' I says, 'it is like workin' fur the Govinment. I'd almost 's soon be a convict,' I says, ''as be in this 'ere 'bus trade.'

"'All right,' says 'e, 'you can take a month'.[140]

"'I can, can I?' says I. 'Then I'll tell you what.' An' I up's an' I *puts 'im through it*!'

"Wonder you don't go back to the fever business," Arthur remarked with an air of sympathy.

"Well you *may* wonder!" responded the stranger. "If it wasn't for some one 'avin' a spite agin me at the 'orspital, I would go back. But what can you expect from an institution when it's got a Jew for its secretary?[141] I never was one for toleratin' Sheenies,[142] an' when this noo young man come on, me an' 'im was at difference in no time. It ended be me leavin': but you can bet your 'at as 'e thumpin' well went through it afore I *did* go.

"All that's left for me now, I s'pose," continued the red-faced man, "is a blighted cab. From what I 'ear there ain't much joy to be got outer the cab business. Masters screwin' you all ends up – fifteen bob a day to be earned afore you can keep a single blanky stiver[143] for yourself – and the police banded together to make your life a misery and motor cars comin' in an' the Taxameter[144] comin' out. But *I* don't worry: Tom 'Uskings is a match for any on 'em yet. There ain't a swain in London from the Lord Mayor downwards as'll keep me from goin' about me business in me own way an' earnin' a honest livin'. Anybody as thinks different 'as got to *go through it*! That's all.

"At the same time, mind you, I ain't one fur choppin' an' changin' really: not in the ordinary way o' Natur'. Left alone an' treated reasonable I am easy to work in with as any man in the 'ole drivin' profession. But interference I will *not* stand an' it's that what's drivin' me outer the 'bus trade – that an' this war. I wouldn't take me Bible oath but what the disagreeables alone might a' bin smoothed over: but this war business settles it. *I leave the 'bus trade!*"

"What war is this?" asked Arthur with professional interest. "I wonder my boy ain't wrote about it. 'E's in the cavalry, my boy: went back to Aldershot last week. What is this war?"

"Lorlumme," exclaimed the red-faced man, "you can't lay on to us as you ain't 'erd of it. It's kep' the racin' down to a psalm for weeks past. Papers ain't printed nothink else – to speak of."

"Oh – I – you – it is this yer Jap business[145] what you allude to?"

"R! That is it. THE WAR; that's what I'm referring to – THE WAR. That's what druv me outer the 'bus trade."

"What 'as the war got to do with the 'bus trade?" This inquiry came from twenty sources at once.

"The war," responded our friend, "as got this much to do with the 'bus trade – it'll take away my 'osses. There ain't no stinkin' sentiment about me, mind you. I ain't one for weepin' tears about our dumb friends, an' the rest of it. But I believe in knowin' your beast an' makin' 'im know you. An' now – arter six weeks' steady trainin' – when I got my team well in 'and – back my thirteen, I would, to toe the line with any live stock in London – up comes a rotten war, an' I got the ole stinkin' job to do over again. I ain't 'avin' any. I'm leavin' the 'bus trade. That's what the war has done for me, an' that's the make o' man I am. I will not be put upon by nobody nor nothink. Anybody as takes liberties with me, must go *through* it."

"Pardon the liberty," interpolated Arthur at this point, "but it don't seem clear to me what this Japanese war 'as go to do with your 'orses."

"Artillery," barked the stranger by way of explanation.

"*What* artillery?" enquired Arthur.

"*The* artillery," responded the stranger.

Arthur then essayed to explain to the stranger that his fears of the immediate loss of his team were baseless. He tried to suggest the distinction between the effect on British commerce and the British people of a war conducted by Britain and one waged entirely between alien nations. "Your 'orses are all right," he concluded, reassuringly. "The Japanese won't touch your 'orses, nor yet the Russians. They're foreigners both."

"Foreigners be blowed!" exclaimed the stranger. "The Bowers[146] is blanky furriners, ain't they? They 'ad 'arf the 'bus 'orses in London not three years ago, an' don't you forget it."

"The Bowers," asserted Arthur, with heat, "never 'ad *no* 'bus 'orses. It was *our* Govinment what 'ad the 'bus 'orses."

"Very well," cried the stranger, "then it's our Govinment as'll 'ave 'em this time."

"But our Gov'nment ain't got no voice in the matter!" shrieked Arthur; "our Gov'm'nt –"

"Tut!" roared the stranger: "'Ere comes my tram. You are a bally ole fool. War is war, an' any child can tell you as the first thing that 'apens in war time is for all the 'bus 'orses to be called up. It's no use 'buttin'. You don't know enough to suck ye're thumb when you bang it. You are a erretatin' ole fool. An' if it was not for my tram comin' up, I'd – I'd –"

"Well, *what* would you do?" demanded Arthur, with menaces.

The red-faced man glowered ominously. "I would have you out into the open," said he, "an' I would blighted well *put you through it.*"

P.S. – What *is* the definition of this fearful threat?

[19 February 1904]

XVIII. Bertie's Partner.

"You seen my Partner, mate? I'm lookin' fur my partner."

'Twas a great, gentle, square-rigged mariner[147] that put this question to Arthur: a shambling, shy young fellow, with fair hair and tarry fingers, and a general air – an "altogether" – that was breezy and salt of the sea.

"I 'ave *not* seen your partner," Arthur said to him. "I got other things to do here than lookin' arter people's partners. Where d'you lose 'im?"

"I lorst 'im over be the Obelix," the mariner answered. "'E is sober, you see, an' when 'e is sober, it is 'is 'obby to spread The Word.[148] When last seed, 'e was spreadin' it over some cabmen. They was blasphemin' 'orrible."

"'Ow did ye come to lose 'im?" Arthur enquired.

"I left 'im," replied the sailor, "so soon's ever 'e started on the cabmen. I don't like cabmen, meself, an' it's my private opinion as they do not fight fair. They fights in packs, cabmen does. Also, they uses stable implements and language. Gimme a God-fearin' scrapper fur *my* money.'

"There is a lot," Arthur asserted, with a judicial manner, "to be said on both sides."

"Seein'," continued the mariner, "as 'e was about to start on the cabdrivers, I says to 'im, 'So long, 'Arry,' I says. 'So long, Bert,' says 'e. 'What about our evenin' out?' says I. 'This is a nice way to treat a pal.' I says.

"But my partner 'e 'ad got 'isself fairly planted on the step of the Obelix. 'My friends,' says 'e, 'I 'ave a few words to say unto you. What I want to say unto you is this:

> When the wicked man turneth away from his wickedness, which he hath committed, and doeth that which is lawful and right, he shall save his soul alive.[149]

"Soon's ever I 'ear that, I know as it was time to be goin'. My pal was sober, you see, an' when my pal *is* sober, you cannot trust 'im. 'Gather round my friends, an' rejoice,' says 'e. An' the cabmen, they *gathered* round, rejoicin' in seven different languages. 'If you are a blushin' missionary,' they says, 'where are the coal tickets?'[150]

"'Breverin,' says 'Arry, 'I 'ave no coal tickets. I come 'ere,' says 'e, 'not to minister unto your selfish wants,' says 'e 'but to spread The Word. R! my breverin,' says 'e, 'I do not offer you coal tickets. I offer you that which is also 'ope, an' faith, an' charity, an' beer, an' beef-steaks, an' pleasure, an' comfort, an' delight, an' all things lovely. Listen unto me,' says 'Arry, 'an' I can promise you as you will be drunk with a joy surpassin' the joy of drunkenness.'

"'The man's a liar,' says one of the cabmen.

"''E's a fool,' says another.

"''E's a pore blighted sailorman,' says another. 'Spit in 'is eye an' leave 'im.'

"So," continued our mariner, "I walked up the step, an' took ole 'Arry be the arm. 'Partner,' I says, 'you are sober,' I says. 'Come away outer this. You'll get yeself into trouble.'

"'Leggo my arm,' says 'Arry. 'Go away. Leave me. I am spreadin' of The Word.'

"'I will *not* leave you,' says I. 'You are sober; you *know* you are. Come along to the stall be the tramlines an' drink corfee. I got a gill o' rum in the back o' me trousers," I says.

"But ole 'Arry, 'e gives me a silly, sober look, an' says: 'Satan, get thee 'ence!'

"I fetched the rum-flask out of me trousers. ''Ave a pull, ole partner,' I says, 'an' punch these cabmen in the stummick, an' come along of me. We will buy some more rum,' I says, 'an' we will drink it; an' when we 'ave drunk it, we will shift over to the coffee-stall by the tram-lines, an' you can recite some ballads an' 'it a copper.'

"But my partner, 'e was sober. There was no arguin' with 'im. 'Get thee be'ind me,' 'e says. 'I am 'ere,' 'e says, to do a mericle fur the Lord,' 'e says. 'I am 'ere to turn these cabmen into cherubims,' 'e says, 'an' to 'old 'igh festival in the 'ouse of my dad,' 'e says, 'an' to blow the 'oly trumpet. For,' says 'e, 'if the trumpet give an uncertain voice, who shall prepare 'isself for war?"

"So," pursued the story-teller, "I says to 'im, 'Very well, then,' I says. 'I wash my 'ands of you. If you *will* go an' get sober,' I says, 'an' fall among cabmen while in that condition,' I says, 'you must bear the consequences. But,' I goes on, 'there is one thing I will say, an' that is this: you are a miserable paste-board imitation of a man,' I says, 'an' no seaman.'

"With that, I drors meself up to me full 'eight, steadies meself be 'oldin' the 'ead of a neighbourin' noos-boy, an' walks away. When I 'ad walked a few yards, I stops, an' turns round, an' gives 'im another chance. 'Look 'ere, my man,' I says 'it is no good arguin' with you now. But if you can manage to get a 'ead on you before to-morrow, come to the corfee-stall beside the tramlines. I'll be there from twelve onwards.' An' 'Ary 'e 'ollers back an' says, 'Friend, I thank thee. The Lord willing, I, thy brother, shalt be there.'

"The last I see on 'im, 'e was wavin' a psalm-book in the cabmen's faces, an' dodgin' the orange-skins, an' 'e was sayin', 'Take 'eed that no man deceive you.

Many false prophets shall rise up an' deceive many.' An' just as 'e said it, 'e give a sort o' gurgle, an rose down – owin' to the orange peel.

"You may well, laugh," continued the sailor; "but I'll ast you not to forget as the man was sober. Some of you, I daresay, would look funny if let loose at the Obelix in the same state. An' with ole 'Arry, mind you, it is worse than with other men; the soberness takes 'im *cruel*. Why, bless my soul, when sober, I 'ave seen that man kerry on more like a (blue-eyed) curate than a – a person.

"An' mind you onst more, there is this I will say for my partner: when 'e is quite 'isself – when not fuddled with soberness – there ain't a 'eartier, smarter, more gentlemanly cove from 'ere to Limus Reach.[151] Even the firemen[152] respect 'im – when 'isself.

"An' the sperits of the man! You should 'ear 'im sing! When at 'is best, I don't know nothink as I would rather 'ear – barrin', per'aps, a good Welsh choir. There's a little song of 'is about Joe Golightly an' the captain's spine[153] as would do honour to Our King 'isself.

"A good sailor, too – though dull on a voyage. What with skippers an' quartermasters an' sich, there's a lot of excuse fur a bloke gettin' sober aboard ship. My partner is a terror for soberness, sometimes, an' it is not good for 'is 'ealth. But 'e is one o' God's seamen: a seaman 'e is. Sailed everywhere an' round it an' back again. An' always a gentleman – even when sober. That's more'n some can say. Eh? What?"

Arthur nodded assent. "You must be dry – what with thinkin' of ye're friend an' that."

The mariner took this hint, and handed Arthur his empty coffee cup and a penny. Miss Hopper took the opportunity to ask the sailor whether he had ever visited, or touched at, or heard of, or had otherwise been associated with a port called Bewnezerry.

"Bin to Bewnezerry?" said the mariner. "That I 'ave. Was in gaol there."

"How was that?" we asked.

"Through gettin' sober," replied the mariner, and refused, amiably, but with firmness, to speak further on the subject.

"Ever knowed a sailorman named Joe Tuttle?" Miss Hopper enquired.

"Joe Buckle?" responded the mariner. "Know 'im well!"

"Not Buckle," said Miss Hopper, "Tuttle."

"R! Buckle!" said the sailor again. "I know 'im well. Rare man for getting married."

"Spell it for 'im, somebody," Miss Hopper requested of the audience in general. We debated the orthography of Mr. Tuttle's name for some minutes, and not without heat. When we had, finally arrived at a working compromise agreeable to everybody, the mariner informed us that, having been deserted by his parents in early youth, a knowledge of the alphabet had not been included in his education. But if, the mariner continued, the object of enquiry was a person named *Tuttle* (why hadn't we said the word afore?), the only gentleman of that name amongst his acquaintances was a gentleman of that name at present residing at his – the mariner's – boarding-house. Upon being requested to divulge the name of this hostel, the mariner spat cheerfully, and said, "Go to 'Ell the lot of you fur a set o' blear-eyed crimps." We bribed the mariner with flattery, and in the end Miss Hopper, sobbing exultantly, departed homewards with a scrap of dirty newspaper margin, in which, in Arthur's hand, was written: Shadwell:[154] Mrs. Pusby's.

And at that moment the sailorman was seized with a species of St. Vitus' Waltz.[155] He waved his arms, and pirouetted, and shouted with emotion at a shadowy figure that grew out of the darkness. "'Ere 'e comes, the dirty thief. Go' blessim. What o! 'Arry boy! Come 'ere ole pal, an' be kicked fur a stinkin' swine, Lor love you!"

And Harry Boy drew close, and turned up his eyes, and groaned and sighed, after the manner of the evangelically just. We examined him closely, from his somber habiliments to a loosely folded umbrella. And, presently, our eyes did light upon his face, and lo and behold! and likewise strike us, if that face was not the face of our lately encountered sailorman – he of the mumps and the blood and the monkey of wool.

"Perish me *pink*!" ejaculated Arthur, obviously amazed. "This is ole Purples for a soverink!"[156] Purples, ole friend, 'ow are you? Give us a song, ole Purples."

"He that asketh," responded Purples, as he produced from his coat-tail pocket a small accordion, "he that asketh shall be blessed." He contorted the accordion, and sang to us as follows:

> I 'ave a lit-t-t-tle sister
>   What's only two year old'
> To us as loves 'er dearly
>   She is worth 'er weight in gold.
> We must be ve-ry gentil,
>   Nor ever angry be,
> But we must love my sister,
>   What God 'as give to me.[157]

"Pithy!" said Arthur, with approval. "Pithy and improvin'. Now give us the little yarn about Joe What-you-call-'em and 'is purple blood. Put the music-box away. Music would spoil that song."

The sailorman removed his silk hat, and bowed his head in silent prayer. Then he looked at Arthur – looked at him wildly, with the hopeless resentment of a frog regarding a tadpole: "We are related, but *what* a gulf!" When he had looked at Arthur long enough, the sailor brushed up his silk hat the wrong way (a deliberate manifestation of meekness), and turned on his heel and departed.

"'Ere!" shouted Arthur, "you – Purples – ole friend, m' lad, come back! Come back! What 'as come over the man?"

The younger man jerked at Arthur's arm. "Shut up!" he commanded, in a loud whisper. "Leave the chap alone! Don't erritate 'im! Can't you see he's *sober*!"

[26 February 1904]

XIX. Miss Hopper's "Boy".

"Shadwell: Mrs. Pusby's" is not what you might term a full and particular direction. The man at the canary shop thought meanly of it.

"You are like all the no-river lubbers," he remarked. "Seem to take us for a set o' blue-eyed villagers. Now, what can I arst you for a real 'Artz Mountain[158] songster – warranted masculine an' free from parasites?"

"Y' see," responded Trooper Alfred – he was enjoying a day's "leave" from Aldershot, and he and I were devoting the same to a private and especial enterprise of our own – "y' see, it is like this 'ere. A certain party give us this yere paper, or, as you might say, the *gist* of it, when in liquor. It is a case, as it were, of this certain party bein' friends with another certain party what is a friend of ours. Me an' my friend 'ere, as a matter of friendship, like, we would wish, as it might be to run acrost this other certain party. The question is where to find 'im. That is the question. Shadwell is no village, but, on the contrary, it is a full-blown blooming wilderness, and does you proud, and I looks towards you. All we want is Mrs. Pusby. That, in a manner o' speakin, is the Problem."

"What you want, ole friend, is a ready reference book. *My* business is song birds. What is the opinion of your mate in the spats regardin' my orfer of a prize bullfinch fur two-pun-ten? Your choice of cage throwed in."

"My mate, explained Trooper Alfred, with a winning smile, "is no judge o' birds. 'Is 'obby is blood-'ounds."

"If it is a question," said the tradesman, "of sellin dawgs, I will go an change me jacket. I got a dawg-dealin jacket an' a dawg-dealin' at. I likes to feel a noo man afore I sells dawgs."

"Very intelligent, too," exclaimed Trooper Alfred, with approval. "But about this what you was sayin' in regard to reference books. I *quite* agree with you. Me an' a young lady friend of mine we 'ave spent two howers this very mornin' lookin through all the reference books as was ever made. The same young lady friend of mine 'as also spent all 'er evenin's for a week or more in searchin' the neighbourhood – this neighbourhood. You wouldn't think as so many tradesmen what 'ave never 'eard the name Pusby could be gathered together in one place!"

"'Vast heaving!"[159] commanded the man of the canary shop – not without sighs of impatience – "'vast heaving! an' come to bisness. What shall I say fur a throstle[160] in full song? Cage *and* bath included, and every feather complete!"

"We'll 'ave a lot to say about that in a minute or two,' rejoined my diplomatic young friend. "But, meanwhiles, I would like to arst a favour of you in regard to Mrs. Pusby. I would like –"

"Shiver my timbers!" exclaimed the canary man. Those were his words: "Shiver my timbers!" My recollection of the phrase is distinct. I would put this statement into affidavit form with all the pleasure of life. "Belay there!" was a subsequent observation of the canary man, as also "Port 'elm you lubber!" He characterized Trooper Alfred as the Creator-condemned son of a dead sea-cook, besides applying to that astonished youth a number of adjectives quite brilliantly unprintable. Nothing more nautical, I am sure, ever brightened the pages of Captain Marryat.[161]

"When you interrupted me," remonstrated Trooper Alfred – who, under all the circumstances, displayed a wonderful restraint – "when you interrupted me, I was about to say as I would like to buy that throstle."

"William – William, ahoy!' exclaimed the canary man in a voice that was all breeze and briskness, "'vast whistlin', an' leave that parrit's 'ead alone, an' fetch the steps. I am askin'," he continued, addressing himself to Trooper Alfred, "a matter of five shillin' fur this little bird. The little bird is cheap at the money."

With an air of the utmost cordiality, Trooper Alfred delved into a very tight little pocket situation in the most inaccessible portion of his overalls, and produced two florins. "I am not one to 'aggil," he exclaimed briefly. "Lend me a shillin' fur the time being," he whispered thickly down my spine.

The bargain being concluded, the canary dealer began to exhibit signs of the most surprising amiability. "Afore we was interrupted by this little matter o' trade," he said, "you was sayin' somethink or other in regards to this Mrs. Whatsername. It would give me satisfaction to 'elp you find this Mrs. Whatsername. Per'aps we could compose a plan."

"I thank you kindly," rejoined the soldier. "Perhaps I could arst you to be so obligin' as to oblige me be keepin' a friendly ear open, as one might say. What with sailors an' that comin' in an' out o' your shop so frequent, like, it – it –"

"Aye, aye, m'lad!" ejaculated the canary man, with pleasing alacrity. "I will make it so."

We were interested to learn at a later stage of the interview, that the canary man's connection with the sea was one purely of commerce.

"They brings me money, d' y' see, and I pervides 'em with live stock. A sailor-man comin' 'ome f'm a vige, d' y' see, fust thing 'e looks for is a pritty bird in a pritty cage. Part of 'is shore-goin' clobber, as you might say. 'Allmark of 'is trade, as you might say. There's many people won't believe a sailor *is* a sailor unless 'e's got a bird in a cage to prove, or a thumb missin', or that. An' very nat'ral, too. An' very proper. I'm a great believer, meself, in keepin up ole customs. What's to become of me an' other gentlemen in my perfession, I would like to know, if this ole rule about sailormen kerryin' dicky-birds[162] in cages was to die out?

"Yus," contined the canary dealer, "I am Shadwell born an' Shadwell bred. I 'ave lived in Shadwell, man an' boy, for forty year. It's 'ere I 'ope to die. Not at present, mind you – when the time comes. I don't arst much in this world, but I *would* like to feel, afore the end comes, as I'd sold jest *one* of them two-pun-ten prize bullfinches."

Asked subsequently whether he had ever enjoyed any actual experience of life at sea, the canary man demanded to know whether we took 'im for a rose-coloured unicorn. Why "unicorn" I cannot say. "On'y time I ever *see* the sea," he explained, "was at Yarmouth. And what I say is – *never no more*! Strewth! you oughter taste the blanky stuff they call *fish* there! No more flavour to it than a noo-laid egg! Give me *flavour* – 'specially in fish. That's a thing you *can* depend on gettin' in Shadwell.

"Two days o' Yarmouth was enough for *me*. I 'opped back 'ome to Shadwell, an' I've stayed there ever since. Sea soots some people, an' bein' a naturalist soots others. *I* am a naturalist. Belay there wi' that whistlin', m' lad. Stand by, an' attend to business. In less than two shakes of the mainbrace, I shall fetch a rope's end to *you*."

This last observation was addressed to the boy William, who did not appear to be greatly terrified by the threat which it conveyed. The strongly marine flavor of the canary man's speech caused me, at the time, to wonder. It was not until later that I came to realise its immense significance. Then I learnt that in Shadwell, at any rate, it is the utter absence of nautical illusion in his discourse which marks your true and proper sailorman. If, when in course of traversing this fragrant suburb, you should chance upon a citizen who does not under any circumstances chew tobacco or hitch his breeks, and who, above all things, does not introduce peak-halyards and marlinspikes[163] into his conversation, you may rejoice in that you have found a mariner.

It was not until we were on the point of leaving him that the canary man really endeared himself to us. Trooper Alfred, having subjected his newly purchased throstle to a long and distrustful scrutiny, at last prevailed upon himself to take hold of the cage. Holding it gingerly, and beyond reach of bodily contact, after the fashion of one suffering agonies from an attack of caste reserve, he advanced to the canary man's counter, and held out a hand.

"Well," said Trooper Alfred, "Time we was makin' a move. Glad to 'ave met you. See you soon."

"So long, ole messmate," responded the canary dealer. "Pleased to see you any time, y' know. Always 'ave a throstle or two on 'and."

"Good!" replied the soldier, a trifle dubiously. "An' I'll be glad if you can bear in mind that little promise of yours. Pusby's the name, remember, per'aps you'd like to make a note of it."

"No need for notes," rejoined the canary man, cheerfully; "I carried longer words than that in *my* head, an' remembered them in liquor!"

"While you are at it," remarked Alfred, "you might ask for Joe Tuttle at the same time. That'd be better still, though I doubt you'll 'ear of 'im. That's the name, any'ow – Joe Tuttle."

"Joe *Tuttle*, did you say?" demanded the canary man, with a sudden quickening of interest.

"That's what I said," answered Alfred.

The canary man took possession of the boy William's pocket handkerchief, and made use of it with reverberating effect.

"Do I understand you," he said, with a suggestion of ascerbity, to want a woman named Something or other, or the man Tuttle? Now, which is it? Speak up!"

"What I want," responded Alfred, "is a party be name of Tuttle: I would be glad to meet his body – dead or alive. I on'y arst for Mrs. Pusby because I 'eard a rumour of 'im lodgin' at 'er boardin' 'ouse. An' when I find it, like as not we shall discover it all a plant – or 'im gone back to sea, or still at the bottom of it, or else in gaol. You never know with sailors."

"You think all that, do you?" enquired the canary man, with a suggestion of sarcasm in his voice.

"I do," retorted Alfred.

"Then," said the naturalist, "you can consider ye'self a fool. If I'd knowed it was Joe Tuttle you was after, I could 'a' put you on to 'im a hower or more ago. Boy, William – mind the shop. Gentlemen, 'ave the goodness to foller me." And with these words our friend the canary dealer preceded us into the ancient thoroughfare of Ratcliffe Highway.[164]

The canary dealer followed a devious and intricate course. Trooper Alfred, carrying the bird-cage with an air of fine indifference, walked at his right. I walked in rear.

"Where am I takin' you to?" repeated the canary man, in reference to a question of Alfred's. "I am takin' you to 'The Friendly Grip' – that is where I'm takin' you to. A public? Of course it's a blinkin' public. Think it was a 'orspital? Why am I takin' you there? I am takin' you to find Joe Tuttle, m' lad. If Joe Tuttle ain't lyin' drunk in the four-ale[165] bar of 'The Friendly Grip,' my name is not Tom Pusey."

"Lyin drunk, you say?" repeated Trooper Alfred, with interest.

"So fur as that goes," responded the canary dealer, "I will not be dogmatic. Per'aps 'e'll be entertaining of the company. Quite a character round 'ere, Joe Tuttle is. Fine cake-walker,[166] an' fine singer, an' 'andy with the banjo. When able to stand up, 'e can keep you laughin' by the hower. Maybe 'e's 'ad another weddin' – said to be a 'abit with 'im is weddin's – an' if so we shall find 'im full o' knife-wounds, most likely. Lady's 'usband, you know: they don't see the joke in Joe's weddin's, the men don't. Some do, mind you – the old 'ands. But a lot o' the young fellars, they make as much fuss about lendin' you their wives as if it was a watch!"

"I'd *like* to set eyes on Joe Tuttle," said Alfred, wistfully.

"You won't 'ave long to wait, m' lad," answered the canary man. "That is 'The Friendly Grip' over yonder, acrost the road. A splendid 'ouse, too."

"It ain't *certain* 'e'll be drunk, then?" said Trooper Alfred, half to himself.

"Not be any manner o' means!" replied the naturalist. "'E might be givin' 'em a coon dance[167] this very minute."

Trooper Alfred turned briskly to me. "I'll get you to 'old this bird-cage," he said.

[4 March 1904]
XX. Miss Hopper's "Boy" (continued).

Trooper Alfred, Mr. Tom Pusey, and I, your servant, duly entered the four-ale bar of "The Friendly Grip."

To say merely that we found Mr. Joseph Tuttle inside this place would be to under-estimate facts. It is really more accurate to state that we found this place outside Mr. Tuttle. That gentleman quite dominated his surroundings. He was so distinctive, so original, so boldly designed. Until one looked closely, there didn't seem to be a four-ale bar at all – merely a brilliant view of Mr. Tuttle judiciously supported by a back and fore ground of barmaids, bad characters and beer-engines.[168]

Mr. Tuttle's personal appearance is best summed up in a phrase of Trooper Alfred's. He was a bandy-legged freckle in odd boots. Speaking broadly, I should be prepared to maintain that Mr. Tuttle's countenance was more affluent in the matter of freckles than anything that has been seen since the Hebrew patriarch devoted himself with such success to the scientific production of spotted cows.[169] Also Mr. Tuttle was sandy-haired, bull-throated, and muscular, with features of the *retroussé* type. Also, his mouth was something short of the orthodox number of teeth, and he suffered the disadvantage of a strabismus.[170] When first we came upon him, he was wearing a lady's "picture hat",[171] and though not manifestly drunk, it would be vain to describe him as rabidly sober. Assisted by the ministrations of two cup-bearers that looked as though they once were women, Mr. Tuttle thumbed a banjo, and sang as follows:

> Ow, Dinah, Dinah, Dinah, Doo!
> Be my 'Oney an' I'll swear to marry yew,
> For the yaller folk are rompin' neath the pale blue moon,
> And Hi am your dust-coat coloured coon.
> I may be yaller;
> But I'm yer faller;
> Not very rich;
> But trew as pitch:

No Broadway mash
With heaps of cash;
But just your Joe
Firm as the snow
My skin is dark;
But Hi'm yere spark,
As full of glee
As any bee;
So come right out
And dance with me.
   Chorus, with nasal obligato,
How Dinah,
Dinah, Dinah, Doo.
I'm a-waitin' in the pumpkin' patch,
A-waitin 'ere for yew.
And I know you can't be sleepin',
'Cos the possums are a peepin',
I'll meet you soon
Beneath the moon,
And you'll dance a rag-time polka
With your dust-coat coloured coon!
'Cos —[172]

But I don't suppose you want any more of it. I am sure I didn't. The audience – Mr. Tuttle's audience – could not, on the other hand, be appeased of its hunger for yaller girls and coons and moons and all the rest of the nauseating drivel which goes to the making of a twentieth-cenutry love lyric in England. The chorus of Mr. Tuttle's song ended with a sort of wail – consisting of "Loo-oo-oo's" and "Doo-oo-oo's," prolonged indefinitely. And when Mr. Tuttle arrives at this portion of his most lamentable ballad, he performed miracles of contortion with his spine, and his stomach had convulsions, and his eyes rolled and he shuffled his feet, and deflected his hips, and gurgled in his throat. So that, in any but an Anglo-Saxon country, you might suppose yourself to be viewing an Experimental Chemist in the act of conducting his last experiment. Being, however, situated in the heart of London, we knew ourselves to be participating in harmony. I am, personally, of opinion that they do these things better in Nigeria.

But, bless you, this opinion was not shared by the barmaids and the cup-bearers and the rest of them. When Mr. Tuttle was forced by fatigue to terminate the vocal and organic activity to which I have referred, the audience rose as one drunkard, and hiccupped with approval. The very beer engines foamed and spurted with joy. And one of the barmaids addressed herself to the company, saying:

"I 'ave 'eard Pug MacQueesy sing that song, and I 'ave 'eard our Joe. I know which I prefer."

Mr. Tuttle, who evidently possessed a gift of intuition, laughed indulgently. "Better not let some o' the boys 'ear you," he said. "They think a lot o' Pug Mac-Queesy."

"No bad judges, neether," said the voice of a sober, but undiplomatic critic in a remote corner of the taproom.

The company gazed upon this person with undisguised contempt.

"Did you 'ear what 'e said, Joe?" asked one of the cup-bearers, removing her arm from its resting-place about Joe's neck to point it accusingly at the critic.

"I *'eard*," responded Joe.

"'E said, 'No bad judges, neether.' Like 'is bloomin sauce! I'd 'no bad judge' 'im if *I* was a man."

Thus spoke the First Barmaid. Second Barmaid lent her moral support by gazing fixedly at the critic, and saying, in the tone of one putting forward a general enquiry: "Well – you can't expect manners from a Rangitang,[173] can you?"

"'E's only a gas-meter man, any'ow," said Barmaid No. 1. "An' if a person saw fit to say all that was in their minds, it might not be so difficult to make a guess at where the pennies come from what some people spends so free o' month-ends."

"I believe you," said Barmaid No. 2. "For me own part, its enough to see a so-called man for everlastin' drinking ginger-pop an that. Always somethink fishy with that sort, you may depend."

"No doubt of it, my dear," assented the First Barmaid. "You want a clear 'ead an' so forth fur ringin' the changes. Robert – where *is* that boy – Robert, go an' move them pewters away from the corner bench. Look *underneath* while you're about it."

In the meantime, cup-bearer No. 2 was offering counsel and comfort to the outraged Tuttle. "Go on, Joe," she was saying; "I'll 'old yere 'at; go an' break 'is ugly jawbone. My Gawd! you ain't 'arf a man to stand by an' be put on like this."

"I'll 'it 'im if you *want* me to, of course," responded Mr. Tuttle, not with cordiality. "This is a free country, they say, an' I s'pose a bloke is welcome to 'is opinion, even if 'e is a gas-fitter."

"Free country!" echoed all the ladies at once, with scorn. "Fine sort o' freedom," their tone implied, "which encourages gas-meter men to maintain their jawbones in an undislocated condition." And the second cup-bearer put her arms about the neck of Joseph, and kissed him fondly, and made it otherwise evident that by hitting the gas-meter man Mr. Tuttle would confer a favour upon herself.

"Aw right," responded Joseph; "as you wish. 'Ullo, you there – you with the face an' pigeon whiskers! Come out o' that corner an' stand up. There's a lady 'ere wishes me to knock yere 'ead off."

"What d'ye mean?" demanded the gentleman addressed, speaking in a voice tremulous with reproach. "What d'ye mean? I ain't done you no 'arm. You lemme alone."

"I give you," retorted Mr. Tuttle, "one vermillion minute to leave that carmine corner. If I 'ave to come an' fetch you, you'll be sorry for givin' me the trouble. You'll make me impatient; that's what you'll do an' if I start on that dial o' yourn when impatient, there'll come such a change over it, you won't know it from one o' your own meter faces."

The audience, which had grown considerably more sober at the mention of hostilities, grew visibly brighter during the delivery of this speech.

Most of the men in the tap-room managed to stand upright, and by holding on to things remained in that attitude for the desired length of time. Trooper Alfred – who, with Mr. Pusey and myself, had been watching events on behalf of another power concerned – drew closer to Joseph, and was, indeed, with difficulty prevented from assaulting that mariner without notice. We had been trying, since our entry, to impress upon Trooper Alfred the necessity of taking bearings before action. Trooper Alfred's face left no doubt as to the nature of his ambitions; and Mr. Pusey knew as well as I that his ultimate intention was to wage warfare with Joseph.

"Well," said that gentleman to the gas-fitter, "are you comin' on, or ain't you? On'y fifteen more seconds left."

At this point the elder barmaid became suddenly recollectful of her duty. She performed it by saying in a kind voice to Mr. Tuttle:

"You know, the Guv'nor don't like fightin' in the bar. A pity the Guv'nor is away for the day."

"Are you –?" began Joseph, again; when the gas-fitter, taking advantage of a convenient drunkard, rose suddenly from his seat, precipitated the inebriate in question into the arms of Mr. Tuttle, and made a hurried, but successful, exit.

"Well," said Joseph, when he had recovered from his surprise, "I ain't so sure arter all, as I'm sorry 'e's gone. It'd 'a' bin very much like 'ittin' of a pawnbroker. The gas-fittin' men is userly fragile."

Presently, Mr. Tuttle's face became absorbed into an expansive smile. "Tut! tut!" he remarked, warmly returning the congratulatory endearments of his lady friends. "Tut! tut! There ain't many on 'em seems anxious to stand up agin yere ole pal Joe – eh? What? Any swain in 'ere like to try 'is luck? Not Bill Walling, I'll lay money. Why, I'd back myself to *spit* 'arder'n ole Bill could 'it. Anybody else care to take me on?"

Mr. Tuttle's women were smiling their approval upon his bravery. And while they were doing so, Trooper Alfred stepped forward, and gurgled, and did a lot of things with his arms. And Mr. Tuttle lay on the floor in a sorry plight: and when we had torn Trooper Alfred away from his body by force, and had reminded that excited young man of certain rules of chivalry, Mr. Tuttle sat up and gulped.

"Good Gawd!" he exclaimed, "this takes it! Never bin so thunderstruck since I was a cabin 'and."

"Do ye want any more, ye swine?" gasped Trooper Alfred, straining in the grip of Mr. Pusey, and myself.

"Not to-day, cocky," responded Joseph. "I'll give you best to-day. Must be gettin' old. Time I went back to sea."

"Not much sea for you, me beauty," roared Trooper Alfred. "There's a lotter be settled between you an' me before you goes off to sea again. There's a little Primrose 'Opper to be settled, for a start."

"Why, what's all this?" demanded Mr. Tuttle, with obviously genuine surprise. "I never done the gel no 'arm. I never done *no* gel no 'arm."

Tooper Alfred explained things to Mr. Tuttle. Mr. Tuttle expressed his admiration of Trooper Alfred's dictum in suitable terms.

We jammed Mr. Tuttle into a cab. He assured us several times during the journey that his sentiments were honourable. "I dowanter do the gel no 'arm," he said. "I dowanter do *no* gel no 'arm."

[11 March 1904]

XXI.

So we hauled Mr. Tuttle to the dwelling-house of Trooper Alfred's father. Trooper Alfred's father – it being then an hour after sunset in early spring – was discovered in an outbuilding contiguous to his residence. He wore no upper garment save a vest and was conspiring with Beaky to produce miasma and coffee.

When we entered his laboratory, Arthur was closely inspecting a bucketful of very sugary sugar. But upon catching sight of Trooper Alfred, he withdrew his head from the bucket in order to address a paternal greeting to that youth.

"Get to 'ell out o' this, Young Alf," he said. "'Ow many more times am I to tell you that I will *not* 'ave you an' your mates 'angin' round my copper 'ouse. Bein' next fur stripes[174] don't seem to a' altered you much, I notice."

Trooper Alfred ignored this reproof. "Where's Beaky?" he enquired: "I got a friend of Beaky's 'ere. Beaky – come out an' 'elp identify a stinkin' rogue. Beaky, where are you?"

And Beaky emerged, as it were, from the depths of a copper cauldron. Certain tubular devices which I had heretofore supposed to be an appurtenance of "the copper" were, it seems, the property of Beaky: being, in fact, his legs. The rest of Beaky had been swallowed up by the cauldron, wherein he had been conducting mysterious rites with a large wooden ladle. This implement he now flourished menacingly, as he peered through the murk and addressed remonstrations to Alfred.

"If you want to see a 'ole copperful o' good cocoa turned the taste of oak-bark, go on interruptin' me – that's all!"

Trooper Alfred, with a reprehensible disregard for his father's feelings, suggested that nobody would know the difference.

"Leave that sort of joke to the customers," said Arthur. "I did not," he added with feeling, "bring you into the world to criticise my cocoa."

Then Arthur, coming closer, recognised the features of your servant. "It's you, is it, lad?" he therefore said. "I could a named a more convenient time fur callin', but come in an' welcome. Always pleased to see you. Though at the same time I *'ave* known moments when I'd be pleaseder. Jest my very busy hour, this is – liquid to boil, and stores to take, an' what not. Very pleased to see you though. And I daresay you won't be so *very* much in the way, though the hour is awkward. Come right in an' bring your friend."

I hastened to disown the honour of friendship with Mr. Tuttle. "Friend of your son's," I said.

"If you want a cut lip," ejaculated Trooper Alfred with heat, "say so. That red-'aired scavenger squattin' on the charcoal bin is no friend o' mine. If he's a friend of any blighted body's 'e is a friend o' Beaky. Hi, Beaky. Come outer the coffee bath you ole luniac an' listen to me. D' y'ear me? I want you to stand up an' identify a dirty blackguard."

This epithet called forth no protest from the person whom it most concerned. Mr. Tuttle, comfortably "enscoshioned" on the charcoal bin, continued to maintain an attitude of silence.

"I s'pose there's no peace fur the wicked," sighed Beaky, slowly relinquishing his ladle and assuming a posture of dignified resignation, which, in that hazy atmosphere, looked rather well: "I s'pose there's no peace fur the wicked. Saith the Bard:

> This life is but a 'oller sham,
>   All paint and patch and thread;
> The baker sighs in vain for jam,
>   The grocer pines for bread.
> If you and me was kings o' men
>   We'd alter things a lot;
> If we was kings, R, then R, then;
>   R, then, you see, we're not!"[175]

For all that, guv'nor, I see no excuse for ever takin' this boy o' yourn away from school."

"I often wonder what I was thinking of meself," responded Arthur. "It was 'is 'ight deceived me. You'd think, to look at 'im, as 'e was growed up. But bless yere 'eart, 'is mind 'as never left off playin' peg tops[176] to this minute."

"That'll do for to-day," said Alfred with the air of one who would say more if he could think of it. "Come into the light, Beaky, and identify this cut-throat 'ere. Stand up, you on the coal-box, an' prepare to meet your God. If 'e identifies you, through it you go!"

Mr. Tuttle offered no reply to this statement; neither did he stand up.

"Do you 'ear what I say," demanded Trooper Alfred, and drew near to the charcoal bin. The rest of us gathered round. It was then made evident to us that Mr. Tuttle slept. Trooper Alfred's taunts, therefore, had been lost upon him; a fact which caused Trooper Alfred to throb and glow with righteous indignation.

We had observed a certain languor – a dizziness – in Mr. Tuttle's comportment during the progress of our cab journey from Shadwell. He had displayed throughout that journey a marked inclination to nestle on Trooper Alfred's bosom. Trooper Alfred had not hesitated to remonstrate with Joseph in this respect. "Leave off 'uggin' me: Take your dirty 'ead away from me," he had more than once remarked. And to each of these rebukes Mr. Tuttle had replied as follows:

"Aw-right, ole Luvey – it's only Joe. You love yere ole Joe boy, don't ya?"

At last, being wrought into a condition of frenzy by the mariner's endearments, Trooper Alfred had thumped Mr. Tuttle upon the nose.

That gentleman, sitting up with a start, had raised his languid eye-lids and gazed about him in bewilderment. Then realizing the situation, he grasped Trooper Alfred warmly by the hand.

"Go' bless you, ole pal," he had said. "Go' bless you: you give me a fright. I was dozin', like, an' that push o' yourn made me dream I was married again. It's awright now. Go' bless you, ole pal."

Before we had proceeded another fifty yards Mr. Tuttle relapsed again, and was restored with further thumps. He continued thus to relapse and the rally under stimulant at frequent intervals during the rest of the journey. The process of lighting off from the cab, however, caused him no difficulty, and he entered Arthur's copper house as forthright and vivacious as any of us. This fact, perhaps, accounts for Trooper Alfred's obvious surprise at the discovery that his flowers of contumely had been wasted upon a desert ear.

"Now then – wake up, you tripe-'ound. D' year me? Get off my father's charcoal bin. Like your impudence to sit on it." And Trooper Alfred seized Mr. Tuttle by the shoulder and toppled him into the grime.

"Awright, old Lovey," said Mr. Tuttle. Then, sitting up, he collected his faculties and Trooper Alfred's legs, by the help of which he assumed a perpendicular attitude.

Then he banged Trooper Alfred's eye, saying:

"It's you again, is it? Seem to be a kind of pink rat,[177] you do. Wherever I look I see you. Sometimes you are my first wife: sometimes you are my Annie: sometimes you are ye're ugly self. But whatever you are, it's always there – in pubs, in cabs, in ruddy wash'ouses. Blow me if I don't shake the innards outer you."

There then ensued a prolonged and devastating conflict. Viewing it for some moments with stupefaction, we bystanders then began to rejoice and deprecate with one voice. And after a judicious interval, Beaky and Arthur (seconded in a mild and bashful manner by myself) rushed forward and forcibly unraveled the combatants.

"And now," said Arthur, holding Mr. Tuttle against the wall whilst Beaky and your servant sat on Alfred's chest – "Now, you will, per'aps, be so kind as to tell me what all this little dust up is about?"

"Arst Beaky," panted Alfred. "Beaky can identify the swine."

"You're a liar," interpolated Beaky. "Don't know the man from Adam."

Trooper Alfred's humour being of the sourest, and conflict being in the air, it looked, for a moment, as though Beaky would now be impelled to make use of physical force. But the situation was saved by Mr. Tuttle – of all persons.

"What do you mean – don't know me from Adam," he demanded in an aggrieved accent from Beaky. "You know me well enough. I am young Joe Tuttle what kept company along of Primrose 'Opper, an' you are ole Beaky as travelled along of the gaff."

"So help me angels," Beaky ejaculated, "the beggar speaks the truth."

Arthur spoke then. "So you," he remarked, "are the low and measly 'ound what sailed to Bewnezerry an' give Miss 'Opper the go by. If it wasn't for contaminatin' the brew, I would duck the ugly thing you call yer 'ead in the coffee-copper."

"Gents, all," responded Mr. Tuttle, in accents rife with restraint and dignity, "you do me a injustice. I never meant the gel no 'arm. I never *done* the gel no 'arm. I am a simple sailor man."

"We'll 'simple' ye, me pretty pickpocket!" and Arthur patted his biceps and spat on the floor in a manner most ominous to behold.

"We will not kill you for the present," he continued, still addressing himself to Mr. Tuttle. "We will lock you in here fur four hours and then we will take you in a sober state of mind to the coffee stall, and you shall meet Miss 'Opper face to face an' then – an' then – we shall see."

"But what about my revenge," demanded Trooper Alfred.

"We'll see about revenge so soon as your ole man lets go of my throat," rejoined the mariner with feeling. "I'm puzzled to know what call you got to interfere wi' me at all."

"What call?" echoed Trooper Alfred. "Why this, you freckled fish porter. You played fast an' loose an' acted the dirty tyke by a good little pal o' mine, be name o' Primrose 'Opper. That's *'what call'*!"

"I ain't played fast an' loose wi' no little pals," asserted Mr. Tuttle. "If so be the young party what you got in name is a young party be name of 'Opper – I love 'er square an' meant 'er fair an' don't want to do 'er, nor any other gel, no 'arm. Come to that I would give a pint to know what the fiery furnace *you* got to do with Miss 'Opper – my Miss 'Opper? 'Cos come to that, I love the young lady with flamin' passion, an' anybody interferin' will go through it! Come to that, I mean to merry the lady. What now?"

"I – I think I'll take some fresh air if you will let me up, ole frien's," said Trooper Alfred: and that was all the reply he offered.

And Mr. Tuttle was cribbed and cabined and confined within the four walls of the copper house until the very witching hour of night, when we un-ungaoled him and carried him off to Arthur's.

Miss Hopper awaited us there in a state of trepidation, having been previously warned of the joy the portended.

Mr. Tuttle, with a right ocean roll, lurched up to the stall. "Lass ahoy. Hurrah there! Pipe hands to grog. Sing hey!" These were the sentiments which I expected Mr. Tuttle to express. Instead of that he looked sheepish and said:

"'Ullo gel!"

And Miss Hopper? She blushed and shrank and looked happy but a little grave, and said:

"What-cher, boy!"

[18 March 1904]

XXII. Arthur's Holiday.

One actor-manager had said of another actor-manager that the latter's advocacy of a State-aided theatre smacked somewhat, he ventured to suspect, of cynicism. If this remark had emanated from the lips of anybody but an actor-manager, or if it had borne reference to the State aid of anything but theatres, I might have finished reading "Melincourt"[178] in office hours and comfort. But there is a superstition amongst editors that the people of England are interested in DRAMA, as apart from the trousers and millinery of its exponents. And so they packed me off to Brighton, where the other actor-manager, together with two private secretaries, a "publicity agent," and a motor-car, was enjoying the pleasures of repose.

On arriving at Brighton, I sought and found my actor-manager. He had nothing to say, but filled a column with it easily. So we drank sherry, and shook hands. It was then six o'clock of a Saturday evening. The actor-manager's views were duly forwarded, per railway guard, to London. The weather conditions seemed favourable, and to-morrow would be Sunday. I therefore said to my conscience:

"Mr. Conscience, sir, would you have any objection to my working another sovereign into this expenses slip, and staying here till to-morrow night?"

And my conscience said: "You have been a very well-conducted lad of late. Please yourself."

Behold me, therefore on Sunday morning partaking of air in the King's Road. Behold me also arrested in my meditation by a pair of checked trousers.

There was nothing really remarkable about the trousers. Broad checks are as common as bankrupts at Brighton.[179] It was the air of something familiar with the curves of the leg associated with these trousers that actually drew my attention. Some inward prompting, as Mrs. Sherwood[180] would remark, informed me that I had seen that leg before. I examined it closely. The sense of familiarity grew upon me. I allowed my eyes to travel upward until they lit upon a new mouse-coloured, soft felt hat with a white ribbon. One glance at the head inside the hat decided me. That head, rendered immediately distinguishable by the bump of caution[181] which its owner had produced by minutely investigating a lift-shaft, could belong to no one else but Arthur.

"Arthur at Brighton!" I said to myself. "What does this mean?" And I situated myself upon a spot favourable to viewing the front elevation of Arthur's figure.

Immediately I fell a-wondering. For, viewed from the situation which I had selected, Arthur's figure disclosed undreamt-of beauties. There was, to begin with, the famous cairngorm scarf-pin, which I had seen but once before, and then at a wedding – the wedding of Kitty. The most fabulous stories are connected with this article of Arthur's wardrobe. My eye also lit upon a tie, composed, appropriately enough, of some tartan texture, strong as to the high lights, and far from poorly furnished in the matter of scarlet foreground. Below the tie and scarf-pin, appeared a Baden-Powell waistcoat,[182] quite of the newest cut, and "very natty." The waistcoat supported a golden Albert chain[183] – an ornament which, like the scarf-pin, is associated with traditions – and the golden Albert chain supported a metal emblem of wonderful design, believed to be connected with the benefit society of which Arthur is a Worshipful Something.

The trousers I have already referred to. Likewise the HAT. But I should be failing in justice to the sartorial genius of my friend if I failed to mention one other feature of his costume. I refer, of course to his shoes, which combined in their aspect an equal suggestion of the democratic and gay dawg temperaments. They were of canvas – sand-paper colour – with porridge-coloured straps. Rose and diamond and ivy-leaf shaped sections had been punched out of the straps, thus imparting a distinct flavor of finish to those articles. I have often wondered what becomes of the ivy leaves and roses which get punched out of the straps that adorn the dressiest brands of seaside shoe. My own opinion is that these remnants are sold to the licenced trade, and that they subsequently masquerade as confetti in Fleet Street soup.[184]

Arthur's face was sombred o'er with frowns; his arms were folded sternly, and his shoulders hunched. He gazed upon the sunlit sea with an air of reprobation.

So I stepped up and slapped him heartily upon the back.

"Go' bless your soul!" and some reference to the letter "L" were (I think) the first observations made by Arthur. Then he recognised me, and his enthusiasm knew no bounds.

"Why, lad," he said, "if it was two hours later in the day, I should suppose meself to ha' bin drinkin'. I can 'ardly believe me eyes. It is like a dream!" All this time he was wringing my hand with a solid pump-handle movement that was highly affecting. His voice was hysterical.

"What finds you here, Arthur?" I asked of him.

"That is a question you may *well* arst," my friend responded. "I have bin arstin' it to meself fur hours. If it wasn't for an overworked young squirt in ridin' breeches what calls 'isself a doctor, I should be safe an' comfortable at 'ome – washin' the crockery most likely, an' 'earin' gossip, an' whistlin' to meself, an' damnin' Beaky's eyes like a gentleman. Instead o' that, 'ere I am alone at eleven o'clock in the mornin' leanin' up ag'in a lamp-post, an' gazin' at a puddle, an' tryin' to kid meself I am seein' life."

"What has the young man in riding breeches got to do with it?" I enquired, a little puzzled.

"My medical adviser," responded Arthur, with dignity. "What wi' one thing an another, I bin feelin' what you might call a trifle low o' late. So I sent my yard-boy round for sixpenn'orth o' physic, an' I took it all standin' – one gulp, you know: what we useder call the colonel's cure. Didn't seem to do me no good, some'ow, so I sent the lad round for another sixpenn'orth of physic – something nastier this time, I tells 'im. I took that lot all standin', too; but it never done me no good. Be next mornin' I 'ad come over real poorly. So I 'ad a drop of whisky and a word or two with Beaky to brace meself, and I took me 'at an' walked round to interview me medical in person. 'E punched me about a bit, like they all do, an' arst a lot o' cock-eyed questions. Was I vaccinated? A tee-totaller?[185] If so, 'ow often? Did I take much exercise? If I did, I shouldn't and if I didn't I should. So on, fur about three-quarters of a giddy hour. Then 'e says: 'What is the matter with you is want o' rest. You want a 'oliday an' change of air. If you could get a week's leave from your firm, an' go away to the seaside fur a complete rest, it would make another man of you. Fee fur consultation eighteenpence; certificate, shillin' extra. Thank you. Good-day.'

"So 'ere," continued Arthur, "I am. An' 'ere I wish to gracious blazes I wasn't! London-be-the-Sea,[186] they call it, don't they? Rotten insult to London, I say. *Pimlico*,[187] if you like; but not London. Take away all them stones and ventriloquists and the water,[188] and fasten your eye on the ladies, and you have the mornin' view o' Pimlico to the life.

"But then, again, I ain't so sure as what sayin' that ain't going too far. This 'ere Brighton is a slow little place at best, an' that ain't like Pimlico. You can say what you llke about Pimlico – dirt and character an' bad 'bus service granted – but you cannot call it slow. The last thing you can say about Pimlico is that it's slow."

"Slowness is not supposed by experts to be the most striking feature of Brighton," I said.

"Never mind the bespattered experts," answered Arthur. "Can you point out one single thing in the 'ole neighbour'ood what *ain't* slow?"

When you come to think about it, this was a difficult question. It was a comprehensive question, and, therefore, one which could not be answered quite satisfactorily either in detail or bulk. "There are the donkeys and – and – the band," I said, hesitantly.

"Why not bung in the Bath chairs,[189] an' make a trio of it?" Arthur enquired, with sarcasm.

There was the sea, I pointed out, and the – the architecture, and the people. "If," was Arthur's answer, "you find anything to entertain you in the people, you are a fool; if the archi-what-you-call-'em pleases you, you are welcome; and if you see anything to get delighted over in that water there, you are a ruddy lunatic. Give me good ole London."

So I took Arthur by the arm, and led him thence to some place where a joy existed that I felt *sure* would please him. "What do you think of *that*?" I said, when we got there.

"*You* may call it whisky," Arthur repled. "*I* call it Brighton methylated".[190]

"But it is your own favourite brand," I protested, "the brand which you have favourably commended to my notice every Saturday for years."

Arthur sniffed contemptuously. "Even the best whisky," he asserted, "would go off in a stinkin' atmosphere like this."

I did my best to cheer him up. There was a sacred concert in progress on the pier, and I offered to escort him there. His reply was unprintable. Very well, then, I answered, there was the sunlight? Was not that good enough for him? That and the dancing of a thousand elfin waves, and the dimples on a thousand pretty cheeks, and the laughter, and the colour, and the crisp, salt savour of things?

"Pah!" grunted Arthur. What was all this compared to the Walworth Road[191] on a Saturday night?

We wandered disconsolately down and sat about the sea-wall. Arthur's conversation was desultory, disagreeable, and depressing. The doctor's presecription looked like making a confirmed pessimist of him.

At last, my eye happening to catch a clock, I was minded of an appointment to eat cold mutton with my Aunt Elizabeth. "I must be going now," I said to Arthur, with an alacrity, I fear, that was but ill-concealed.

Arthur clutched my arm, and held on to it, and gazed upon me imploringly. "Don't say you mean to leave me, lad!" he urged. "What am I to do 'ere all be meself? I daresay I bin a bit rotten – what with grumblin' an' that. But I will buck up – strewth, I will! Come along an' 'ave some more o' that whisky. Not such bad stuff, after all."

But my Aunt Elizabeth is a lady whom it is not profitable to slight. That mutton of her's had to be devoured at all costs, and I told Arthur so. "Well, take me with you," he said; and again he looked upon me with imploring mien.

For a moment, I hesitated. Then I thought of Arthur's waistcoat and the tie, *and* my aunt's tame curate. Then I hesitated no longer. The thing could not be done; my courage would not run to it, and I told Arthur so. "My aunt," I explained to him, "is a Dame – Grand – Falconer of the Primrose League."[192]

"Well," answered Arthur, "If I can't come with you, I can wait outside for you. 'Ow long will you be?"

"Three hours," I said, giving it a stretch.

"I'll wait," said Arthur.

He did wait, pacing up and down before my Aunt Elizabeth's doorstep like a lion waiting for his share of Daniel.[193] Now and then he paused in his walk to hold discourse with an objectionable-looking crossing-sweeper. To him he frequently offered largesse.

When at last I tore myself away from Aunt Elizabeth – she did not seem loath to leave me; my manner has been *distrait* – I found Arthur patiently seated on the corner kerb-stone, waiting for me.

"Glad you've come," he said. "I was beginning to get lonesome."

"That crossing-sweeper," he continued, "is a fine fellar. 'E useder live in Kennington nine year ago. Says there is a matter o' three corfee-stalls in Brighton. We must look out for one to-night."

There was no "we" about it. Duty called me back to London by the five-something train, and so I told him.

He looked at me gratefully, the light of new-found happiness in his eye. "Will you wait till I goes round to me lodgings?" he asked, "jest to fetch me bag an' settle up? I ain't unpacked yet."

"Do you mean to say that you are coming, too?" I asked.

"I do," he said; and *did*.

And when we lit off at Victoria Station, Arthur sniffed the atmosphere of that popular resort with unfeigned pleasure. He strode out into the open and looked at the lights, and winked at a shoeblack, and exchanged some small-talk with a porter. Then (myself following) he boarded the roof of a 'bus, and spat over the side, and smiled at the lamps of an adjacent music-hall, and patted his chest, and beamed. "Doctor was right," he exclaimed, at last. "That 'oliday *did* do me good!"

[26 March 1904]
XXIII.

Now it is a strange thing to relate, but the homecoming of Joseph Tuttle did not cause any rose to bloom more vividly than usual in the cheek of Miss Hopper.

This fact was partly due to the circumstance that Miss Hopper's roses were blowing their hardest quite irrespective of Mr. Tuttle. So that it is difficult to see how his advent, even if thoroughly successful, could have added to their lustre. But in point of fact, one very soon began to fear that the return of Joseph was not attended with that perfect happiness to Miss Hopper which we all expected of it. Joseph in the flesh, you see – with red hair and a thirst – was not quite the same thing as a romantic, pathetic, enchanted Joseph of dreams. Also, the material Joseph was more expensive. This knowledge was borne in upon me one night when Miss Hopper paid for Joseph's supper (a handsome one) from her own little purse (a lean one). After which proceeding Joseph, in a condescending manner, said: "What about tobaccer?" and was provided with tobacco on the same terms. Even then his demands upon Miss Hopper's generosity did not cease, for I heard some whispering, and the reluctant, greasy jingle of coppers, and then I heard a sniff from Joseph, and then more whispers, and finally, more jingling. Whereupon our Joseph, who had hitherto been silent, became bright and talkative, and chid Miss Hopper for her reserve. "I'm firsty," said Miss Hopper. "Buy yesef a corfee, then, stoopid," quoth Joseph. "I left the *rest* o' me money at 'ome," explained the lady; in response to which revelation, Mr. Tuttle, after eyeing the clock in silence for some moments, exclaimed: "Wait till three o'clock, o' gel, an' I'll stand you one." Coffee is reduced to the price of a halfpenny a cup after 3 a.m. at the London stalls.

Miss Hopper evinced much genuine delight at this mark of Joseph's concern for her comfort; but she declined his offer, saying:

"You are a silly little yob. What do you want stayin' up till three – nor me eether? And what do you take me for – orfering to buy corfee? I don't want you to buy me corfee – you outer work an' all. Besides, I ain't thirsty for corfee. It's water *I* want. A drink o' water 'll suit me fine."

So Joseph smiled indulgently, and begged Miss Hopper to "have it her own way." He also said he thought he must be going (he had been hailed by a congenial spirit, one 'Erry the Nark, a chronic sufferer from black-eye), and presently took leave whistling cheerfully.

The departure of Mr Tuttle left Miss Hopper at liberty to take stock of her surroundings before adopting a like course. When she turned and observed myself, in company with Mr. Walpole, her landlord, she blushed a little, because we stood so near to her that part or all of the foregoing passage with Joseph must have been heard by us.

After greeting us, Miss Hopper remarked, in the tone of one casting about for a suitable topic of conversation, that it was wonderful what scarcity in work prevailed at present.

Mr. Walpole expressed the opinion that the truth of this statement depended on "circs."[194] He would ask the following questions: (1) When a party says "work", what do they mean by "work"? There is work and work. (2) When a party says "worker," what do they mean by "worker"? There are workers and workers. There are also shirkers.

"You see," explained Mr. Walpole, "you can't find work if you don't look fur it, and it's no good findin' of it if you won't do it."

"My boy's lookin' fur work," said Miss Hopper. "But 'e can't get none, my boy can't. Seems terrible times fur finding work."

"What is your boy's trade?" enquired Mr. Walpole.

"My boy's trade!" responded Miss Hopper. "Oh! any trade, bless you. Wonderful 'andy, my boy is. That's where the 'ardship comes in – 'e says to 'isself, very often. ''Tain't as if I on'y knoo one blighted trade,' 'e says, 'or was pertickler about soilin' me fingers,' 'e says. 'I know twenty trades, an' I can do anythink,' 'e says, 'from paintin' kerridge panels or makin' a marine flag to designin' evergreen crosses an' singin' songs.'"

"Reg'ler Jack-of-all-trades, your boy!" observed Mr. Walpole.

"Yes," said Primrose.

"Unless you told me," continued Mr. Walpole, "I should 'a' thought different. I got the idea 'e might be a 'ot-cross-bun maker."[195]

"No," said Miss Hopper, who did not discern the sarcasm which underlay this speech. "No, he is not a 'ot-cross-bun maker – leastways, I never 'ear 'im mention 'ot-cross-bun making along of 'is other trades."

"Per'aps," suggested Mr. Walpole, "'e does a bit at printin' leap-year awmanacs?"

"No," said Miss Hopper, again.

"You surprise me," responded Mr. Walpole. "I 'eerd say as your boy was lookin' fur work, an' I says to meself, says I, ''E will no doubt be a long time lookin' fur it, because,' I says, 'there is no doubt but what 'is trade is stampin' 'ot-cross-buns, or printin' leap-year awmanacs, or making brown glass for viewin' eclipses,' I says."

"You seem," said Miss Hopper, still perfectly unconscious of the serious reflections upon Joseph contained in Mr. Walpole's elaborate description of his thoughts, "you seem to 'a' thought of some funny trades while you was about it."

"Joseph," explained Mr. Walpole, "is a funny fellar."

"I believe you there," rejoined Miss Hopper, apparently glad of the opportunity for confiding her views in regard to the character of Joseph. "Sometimes, you know, I can 'ardly bring meself to believe as it *is* Joseph. It's on'y 'is face, an' 'is legs, an' 'is speech, an' 'is language, an' is appetite what makes me reckernise 'im at all. I'd 'a' knowed 'im in a thousand so fur as *they* goes. An' mind you, 'e is MY BOY, an' anybody as runs 'im down 'll learn about it. *I* can put 'em up all right, as is well known.

"An', mind you, I ain't runnin' 'im down, meself. I'm on'y sayin' as 'e seems diff'rent – diff'rent, I mean, from the Joseph as was three year comin' 'ome from Bewnezerry."

"The man," said Mr. Walpole, betrayed by his feelings into a tone of marked contempt, "the man ain't never been to Bewnez Thingamabob."

"Oo are you callin' names?" deamanded Miss Hopper, warmly. "Furgettin' yeself, I think. You an' ye're 'mans,' indeed!"

"Beg pardon!" pleaded Mr. Walpole. "'Young fellar' was what I *meant* to say."

"It is a good thing," asserted Miss Hopper, "to get into the way of sayin' what you *do* mean. There's a lotter people seems to 'a' got into the way o' bein' careless when they are talkin' of My Boy."

"You was sayin'?" remarked Mr. Walpole suavely.

"Never mind what I was sayin'," replied Miss Hopper. "I ougher knowed better than to get talkin' about my boy to a parcel o' men – an' you a *landlord*, too! Gawd 'elp you! I am thirsty, an' you can treat me to a corfee."

Robert hastened to perfom the gallantry suggested of him. In the temporary absence of Arthur (who was treating himself for an attack of what he called "too much 'alliterative' Brighton"), Beaky officiated; and, whilst handing her the loving-cup, he took occasion to remark upon an entirely supposititious lack of cordiality in Miss Hopper's recent manner towards himself.

"Too proud to go talkin' to 'mates' an' sich-like rubbish, ain't we, now that red-'air an' 'armony 'as grown so common."

"You are a liar," was Miss Hopper's reply. One felt entitled to expect more of her; but she was always kind and forbearing with Beaky.

"I am no liar," Beaky maintained. "If you was a barmaid, you couldn't 'a' bin more freezin' than what you acted since red-'aired turnips 'as begun to sprout everywhere."

"Don't be a silly ole fat-'eaded fool." said Miss Hopper, indulgently.

"You can deny, my gel, till Christmas, but it is there."

"What is there, chatterbox?" demanded Miss Hopper.

"Why, pride," said Beaky, "an' conceit, an' wicked tempers, an' turnin' up your nose at pals, an' crispness, an' sayin' 'Oh! indeed.'"

"No good arguin' with you," Miss Hopper affirmed. "I *called* you a liar, and I called you a fool. May's well say 'Lunatic,' an be done with it."

"What I said," declared Beaky, "I 'olds to. You can make what excuse you like, but *it is there*! Other people 'as noticed ti. What about pore ole Alfred? Week's leave, an' forced to stand clear of 'is father's stall, all along of you."

This intelligence produced the unlooked-for result of quenching Miss Hopper's thirst. She slammed down her coffee cup, and blushed eagerly, and glowed all over, and again called Beaky a liar – but with a distinct air of wishing otherwise.

"What you mean?" she enquired. "Trooper Alfred stayin' away along of me? Talk rational."

"What I say is true," protested Beaky, "so help me anythink. Your airs an' your fellow together is enough to make any gentleman stand clear."

"What's my fellow gotter do with Alfred, any'ow, you everlastin' ole box o' tricks, you?"

"There's a question for a growed-up gel to arst a bloke! Your fellar does not fancy 'im, that is all. Alfred knows it; an', fur all 'is cavalry legs, Alfred is a gentleman."

"My fellar does not fancy 'im!" echoed Miss Hopper, as she gulped her coffee, and made to depart. "My fellar don't fancyings are a 'andy sight too free. My fellar must be spoke to."

Which, when you come to think of it, was a strange remark for a growed-up gel to make to blokes.

[1 April 1904]

XXIV. Braces and a Mystery.

"It is like this Beaky," said Miss Hopper, in reference to certain observations of that gentleman. "It is like this: I don't mind you showin' your silly pleasure because of what 'as 'appened – no person can't 'elp their nature, and if yourn is a petty one, that is Gawd's fault. But you (or any other old monkey for that matter) *can* 'elp what they bloomin' well says. So take an' grin and wink an' giggle to yeself 's'much 'sever you please. But don't *talk*. It is only you *talkin'* what can make me angry. Your *face* I 'ave got used to."

"Put in a nutshell," said Arthur, smiling kindly.

Beaky also smiled. "What I said," he affirmed, "was the truth. And what I said I stick to, and will say again. *You are well shut of a dirty loafer.*"

"That settles it," exclaimed Miss Hopper, distinctly nettled. "Gimme back them braces!"

"Which braces?" enquired Beaky, paling visibly.

"*My* braces, you ungrateful ole liar," Miss Hopper responded. "You know well enough what braces I mean. The braces I made for you at Christmas. For two months," she affirmed, comprehending the entire body of Arthur's customers in a gesture of appeal, "for two months I c'lected cigarette pictures, an' gummed 'em on canvas – green canvas, mind you, and actress pictures – all for to make a pair of braces that my gentleman might wear with pride. There was a red silk frame to every picture, an' gold braid trimmin', and a owdy clone sachy[196] atop of all. Two months that job lasted, not to mention the expense an' a fair eightpenn'orth o' lamp oil. And all for this Barnum's-what-is-it as stands there wiping coffee cups with the lamp-cloth as if gettin' the sack an' wearin' braces was never 'eerd of. *That* is what they call gratitood."

Beaky was so far moved by this speech as to discard the lamp-cloth with a hot blush (the colour scheme of Beaky's blushes is unique), and to shake his head solemnly at Miss Hopper. "You are wrong about the braces," he said with evident sincerity. "I bear them well in mind, and always shall do. The acresses was a bit stiff, and their edges 'as frayed a trifle; but better braces for everythink but stroppin' your razor I never wish to see. Don't make any mistake about it. I bear the braces well in mind and so will continue. Amen."

"Then," retorted Miss Hopper, "why make a fuss about it all? Keep silent, and do as you are asked. 'And over the braces."

"I cannot 'and over the braces," responded Beaky.

Miss Hopper displayed signs of impatience. "That's enough monkey-talk," she said. "'And over the braces."

"I *will* not 'and them over," stated Beaky, with firmness.

"First you cannot, then you will not. Better not make me angry. I 'ave been quite civil so far. You are a impudent old ape, and you 'ave insulted my boy – you 'ave insulted Joe Tuttle. So now we are strangers. 'Ere is your sea-shell pincushion – what is left of it – it was broke when you give it me – and now you can 'and over my braces, same's I asked you. May's well be a gentleman for once."

Beaky, with a slightly furtive expression, removed his spectacles – a recent acquisition – and moistened the glass thereof by means at his command. With the assistance of his waistcoat front he dried and polished the spectacles, and replaced them on his nose, and scratched his head, and whistled a note or two from a comic song, and fanned the flame of the coffee urn. Then he spoke.

"If you *must* 'ear the truth," he said, "you may's well 'ave it. I am wearin' the braces *now*."

"I am glad to 'ear you 'are wearin' 'em," she answered. "It'll be pleasant for you in old age to look back on the only decent pair o' braces you ever 'ad, and think that you wore 'em up to the last. 'And the braces over."

"Ain't I tellin' you," rejoined Beaky, with some heat, "that I am wearin' the braces *now*! How *can* I 'and them over?"

"What do ye mean – 'ow can you? They ain't sewed on to you, are they? All the braces what I ever 'ear on was fastened to people by buttons."

"Seems to me," said Beaky, with open malice, "that you know more'n enough for a single young woman."

Miss Hopper takes reflections of this sort very seriously. This is a curious trait in her character, because the air of coffee-stalls is not always encouraging to modesty, and most of the ladies who frequent such places learn early in life to wear their virtue with a difference. The merest commonplaces of converstion at Arthur's are sometimes of such a nature as would pass for outrageous insult elsewhere; but we that are proper to Arthur's would as soon think of judging a man by his language as by his coat or his past.

With Miss Hopper, however, most men were used to exercising some restraint. It was reconised that her modesty was rare and, in some respects, eccentric; but it was also recognised that this eccentricity was of a nature to reflect lustre upon our assemblage. Miss Hopper's weakness, therefore, was, on the whole, encouraged; and certain male admirers of hers had been known to go so far in the matter of curbing their adjectival fluency that each had privately accused the other of having found salvation.

To-night Miss Hopper's mood was more than usually averse from ribaldry. Beaky's observation (shorn of certain picturesque qualifications which accompanied it) might, as a matter-of-fact, have passed muster in one's great-aunt's drawing-room. But Miss Hopper was moved by it to active resentment, and, from being playfully in earnest as affected the braces she became very earnestly in earnest, and stamped her little foot and shook her little fist, and loaded Beaky with epithets.

"It is no good wearing yourself out in that way," said Beaky, when Miss Hopper's eloquence had ended in a choking fit. "You may be too much of a lady to see a joke, and, if so, I am sorry for you. But I am too much of a gentleman to 'and over the braces. Time is not convenient."

"Arthur," cried Miss Hopper, appealing urgently to that gentleman, who did not attempt to discuse his agitation, "Arthur, I call upon you to do your duty. That man there, in your employment, so help your God, is a-wearin' of my braces. I demand my braces back again. He has insulted me, and insulted my boy – Mr. Tuttle, I should say. And he 'as acted like a nog.[197] So I demand my braces back again. And there is the blessed ole sea-shell pincushion what 'e give me o' Christmas an' 'ere is 'is vaccination certificate what I bin keepin' for 'im an' ere is the bob 'e *says* I owes 'im an' so now there is nothing 'e can claim from me an' I done my share o' the exchange full an' square an' so you can make 'im do 'is an' if 'e won't you 'it 'im an' if you won't 'it 'im I will 'cos 'e 'as insulted me. I – I wish I was a man. I – I – wish – I wish – I – w – w wooooh!"

Miss Hoppper's address to Beaky already rendered disconcerting by the utter absence of punctuation, terminated in a flood of tears.

When Arthur saw that Miss Hopper was really crying, he became a very sympathetic and angry man. And whent the COMPANY saw that Miss Hopper was crying, and that Arthur sympathized with her, the company also became serious and angry. So that when Arthur spoke, the company approved. Said Arthur:

"Y' outht to be *ashamed* o' yeself, ole scarecrow you. What do you mean be makin' the lady cry? Take off the braces *at once*, and 'and them over to 'er."

"'Ow *can* I take the braces off, stoopid fools?" protested Beaky, with a pathetic gesture.

"What is to prevent you?" enquired an aggressive member of the company.

"Me trousies!"

"His *trousies*!" repeated Arthur, with a contemptuous emphasis, and a shrug of the shoulders and a sniff.

"'E'll be thinkin' about 'is corsets soon, or buyin' valentines! The silly ole objec' 'as got into 'is second childhood."

The company, taking its cue from Arthur, as usual, also repeated the word "Trousers!" with contemptuous emphasis, and shrugged its shoulders and sniffed. "We will *trouser* you, my nobleman," said the aggressive member before referred to. "'Ere's a bit o' string. Which'd you rather: 'and over the braces an' take this, or 'old on to the braces an' take a slap in the jaw?"

"Neether," affirmed Beaky. "I ain't done none o' you genelmen no 'arm. Very well, then. Leave me alone, an me trousies, too. It isn't much I arst. Leave me in peace an' me trousies, an' I will not quarrel wi' none o' ye."

"Don't make a song about it, ole whiskers," urged Arthur. "Do as you are asked, like a good fellar. Nip round be'ind the stall, an' take the braces off. Look slippy."

"I will *not* take me braces off," roared Beaky, with every appearance of determination. "I will *not* take me braces off; I will *not* run risks wi' me trousies; I will *not* be made a scarecrow of. So there's an end of it. I –"

Before Beaky could finish his sentence, the door of the stall – a little aperture in the back panel of the structure – opened suddenly, and Beaky disappeared from our ken. There were guffaws from the company, and a mild sort of protest from Arthur; then certain sounds, as of combat, and muffled blasphemy issued from behind the stall. And, finally, the aggressive member came boldly forward from some spot in the neighbourhood of the melée, bearing the longed-for braces.

These he politely handed to Miss Hopper whose anger had already given place to a tender regard for the feelings of Beaky. "Where is the silly ole fool?" she demanded, anxiously. "*I* don't want 'is silly braces, really. On'y 'e ought to 'ave kep' 'is mouth shut. Beaky, where are you?"

Arthur withdrew his head from some secret conclave without the door which I have mentioned. "Beaky," he said, "'as gone 'ome to fetch a scarf. 'E is also lookin' for your boy an' a meat chopper. Says this world will be a different place to live in after 'e 'as found your boy."

"Boy? My boy? You are talkin' silly. I 'ave not got no boy. Well you know it!"

"R! I did 'ear somethink about it from Alfred. Tiff, I bleeve!"

"When," said Miss Hopper, "you 'ave apologised to Beaky, an' Beaky 'as apologised to me, an' when I 'ave got time an 'it is a bit earlier in the evenin', I will tell you the ole rights o' the case. At present, I don't wanter talk about the affair at all. Makes me sick, it does. I don't wanter talk about it it all …"

"But what was it, now, that Mr. Alfred was tellin' you about it?"

[8 April 1904]

XXV. Written at the "Meet".

"Go on with you: you are soft," said Miss Hopper to Arthur, as that gentleman made some pointed observations of the subject of broken vows and fickle hearts.

"It is absurd for *anybody* to say that I am tired of 'im, beause when a gal is tired of a bloke she would say, 'Don't talk about the man,' if you mentioned 'im. But you don't find me carryin' on in that fashion. On the contrary, I am quite peaceful and cool-'eaded about 'im, an' far, far from temper. Which on'y shows you that I *can't* be tired of the lad. It do show you that, now don't it? Why, naturally – certainly; you know it shows you that. If I was tired of my boy, like you say I am, I could not bear to breathe 'is name."

Arthur whistled to himself in a most provoking manner. "We won't go into it at present, m' gal, owin' to the nearness of your bereavement. But I wouldn't be surprised if there was more than one way of readin' your symptoms. Meanwhiles, what about this tiff?"

"What about it?" echoed Miss Hopper. "Well, *what* about it?"

"What I mean is," explained Arthur, "why was it? Oo done it? Where? When?"

"And," replied Miss Hopper, "what *I* mean is, mind your own interference. My tiffs ain't *your* business."

"Very true," Arthur answered. "Granted. Correct. We will say no more about the matter. Good evenin', Mr. Walpole. May I arst you your views about these new War Office regulations?[198] Sweepin', eh – very sweepin'?"

But a discussion on the subject of military reforms was not what Miss Hopper had come out for at all. And the tail of Arthur's eye twinkled violently as Miss Hopper exhibited this fact in speech and gesture. "Do give over playin' Parliament, now," she requested, with emphasis. "If you *must* 'ear somethink about this tiff, I may's well tell you. On'y, don't you say a word to Alfred."

Arthur, after wetting his finger and assuming therewith to wet his throat, performed a number of similar evolutions, all designed to suggest the taking of an oath.

"Well, then," Miss Hopper continued, "he – my boy – Mr. Tuttle – 'e called your son Alfred a *bully*."

"Well?" said Arthur, in an entirely inexpressive voice.

"Well!" echoed Miss Hopper, "why, this. Your son Alfred, 'e is *no* pal o' *mine*. Too dark, for one thing, and I *always* 'ated soldiers. But, after all, 'e is a gentleman an' your son, an' always 'as bin polite to me, an' 'e *can* play nap.[199] So I got a lot o' friendship for Alfred, although I do not like 'im – not to say *like* 'im. So when my boy – when Joe Tuttle called 'im a bully, I turned to Joe Tuttle, an' I put 'im through it."

"'Why, bang 'is eyes,' says Joe, ''e *knocked me down!*'

"'Knocked you down?' I tells 'im. 'I should think 'e bloiomin' well *did*. Of *course* 'e knocked you down. That was fur callin' 'im a liar."

"'But,' Joe says, ''e called me a thief!'

"'Called you a thief?' I says. 'Why not? *Ain't* you one?' Joe turned quite red, remembering about my fourpence an' all, an' you would 'a' thought 'e would shut up; but 'e never. 'E looked black an' 'e kicked a stone on the ground, an' rubbed 'is nose.

"'So, it is like this,' says he. 'This bloke ere, this swaddy – 'e can call me a thief, but I may not call 'im no liar; 'e can bloomin' well assault me, but I cannot say bully. Call that justice, I suppose?'

"I didn't get angry, because I love Joe Tuttle, an' when you love a person you can stand a lot from 'im. But Alfred grew angry.

"'Say that again,' says 'e.

"'Say it twenty times,' says Joe.

"'Be careful, now.' I says to 'im. 'Alfred is getting angry.'

"'Alfred can to to Somewhere!' says 'e.

"I lost my temper at that. I don't like Alfred – not to say *like* 'im – and, of course, Mr. Tuttle is My Boy. But you *must* be strict to 'em sometimes.

"'You are a low bounder,' I says, 'an' it would serve you right if Alfred 'it you.'

"That was 'ow the tiff begun."

[15 April 1904]

XXVI. Love in London.

I am sorry to state that the "tiff" between Miss Hopper and her "boy" did not prosper under the healing process of time. Mr. Tuttle, bereft of two teeth and walking in bodily fear of the avenging hand of Trooper Alfred, considered himself to be an aggrieved person.

"I will 'ave the lor on bofe of 'em," he said; and for a while he made a nightly practice of appearing at Arthur's with a young man who kept the books at a leathergrindery, and who wore dirty white cuffs and an air of astuteness. "That is his mahfpiece," we said, one to the other, and conjured up visions of a stuffy police-court and stern warders and a hatchway in a dock, with Miss Hopper and Alfred going down steep steps to penal servitude for life.

But Arthur was not for enduring the patronage of Mr. Tuttle. And the young man from the leathergrindery outraged his sense of human beauty. So he said to Mr. Tuttle: "Pop off from my stall. You are 'ere for no good, and I don't want you." And he said to Mr. Tuttle's friend: "Cow-face – 'op it!" And when both gentlemen displayed an inclination to argue the point, Arthur, in a very audible whisper, requested Beaky to fetch a rozzer. So that for the time being, at any rate, Mr. Tuttle and his mahfpiece found it convenient to depart on a mission of urgency. "But when you *do* see us again," they said, darkly, "you will be sorry for all this."

In the meantime, Trooper Alfred was industriously qualifying for promotion at Aldershot. And Miss Hopper – for whom it was understood by the gossips, he cherished a devouring passion – was attending night school, and keeping good time at the warehouse, and making little shifts for a little baby whose coming had been heralded to Kitty.

And one night, in the dark of the moon, I saw Miss Hopper halt beneath a lamp post contiguous to Arthur's stall, and turn round and giggle. And from out of the blackness there loomed the figure of a tall young man in martial cloak arrayed. His cloak was open to the winds, and I saw that the uniform beneath it was of the square-pushing variety, made glorious by silver-plated shoulder chains. A square-pushing uniform is one of specially ornate production, which warriors of taste and feeling are used to procure for the purpose of enhancing their physical attractions in the eyes of the opposite sex. *This* soldier's uniform was particularly ornate.

The soldier stalked up to Miss Hopper's lamp-post, and in a deliberate, though not unfriendly manner, dug the point of his elbow into the space between Miss Hopper's shoulder-blades. Miss Hopper replied by fetching the soldier a swashing buffet upon his face. Then she giggled again, and walked on.

"Ha!" said I to myself, and stealthily crossed the road. Being on the opposite side of the fairway, I knew myself to be safe from the observation of either Miss Hopper or the soldier, who, in any case, seemed occupied with thoughts more important than those which affected literary persons in spats.

Presently Miss Hopper came to another lamp-post, beneath which she halted as before. And looked round. And giggled.

The soldier strode up and seized her hat – which was decorated with an ostrich feather that would have surprised you – and swung her round and pulled her fringe about her eyes, and lightly thumped her. She spoke, saying: "Give over, you saucy 'ound!" and snatched his cap, and threw it into the road. And while he was gone to retake it, Miss Hopper seized her skirts, and pulled then up above her toes, and ran and ran and ran, like a Greek girl in a picture, until she came to another lamp-post afar off. And here she halted, and looked round, and giggled.

When the soldier came up this time, he put his arm about her waist, and squeezed it rather hard, and rubbed the muddy side of his cap against her cheek.

"Ha!" I said to myself, and began to quote things out of Tennyson.

There is quite a little scuffle – a friendly, but rather noisy scuffle – as the result of the soldier's jest. Then for a little while the two walked onward side by side. But after a little time the spirit of frolic re-asserted itself and they thumped and pushed and scratched each other in a manner most interesting to behold. And I said "Ha!" to myself several times.

Then, of a sudden, the maid picked up her skirts again, and ran forward as before and continued to run so fast and so far that I, on the other side of the fairway, was almost out of breath by the time she had found a satisfactory lamp-post. And as for the solider, weighted down with a martial cloak and marital boots, *he* was actually panting when at last he came up with her. But he was so far from being exhausted that he was able to pull the hat and the feather right off her head, and carried them into the middle of the roadway, and stood there, mocking and flouting her. She could hardly speak for giggling, and she was a little out of breath herself, but she succeeded in conveying a very tolerable infusion of epithets into that which she did say. And then she ran forward, and punched his face, and pulled his hair, and kicked his shins. And he twisted her wrist, and roared with delight. And there they stood, giggling and roaring and kicking and twisting and twisting until, presently, an especially vigorous punch from Miss Hopper sent the soldier sprawling on his back in the messy roadway.

Then I said: "Ha! Ha! Ha! Ha! *Ha!*" to myself. For I was not only amused, but perceived that Primrose Hopper and Trooper Alfred were conducting their courtship.

When Trooper Alfred rose up again he was distinctly a different looking soldier from the one who had initiated this courtship. His overalls were fearful to behold, and the lovelight in his eyes was dim with mire. But his Primrose heeded not: not she. She had, as one might easily discern, the right housewife's spirit, and she dusted him down with vigour, chiding him the while (as a good wife should) because he had spoilt his nice new overalls. And then, being tired and out of breath, and having reached the stage of perfect understanding, they walked on silently side by side. And I re-crossed the road, and followed admiringly in their wake. They stopped outside the portals of an edifice that positively blinded one by the brilliance of arc lights and plate-glass and other appurtenances. And, after a little confabulation with her soldier, Miss Hopper stepped inside, and so, for the first time, so far as I can recall, I saw her entering an ale-house door.

And you may well suppose that I beat my breast, and wept salt tears, and trembled all over, saying, "This is the beginning of the end." If you really *do* suppose anything so foolish, you are a long way from being good supposers. For what I *really* did was to say "Ha!" again, and follow after. Gadzooks! and likewise zoons! If a girl in England may not partake of ale or, as it might be, sherry, on the first day of a spring-time courtship, why, what – which – pah! the thing's absurd. Miss Hopper went into the ale-hourse to sip nectar with her lad; and I that followed after enjoyed the privilege of viewing this operation in process of being carried out. They had one vessel between them – a great, big, unbeautiful quart pot, beastly of design, cheap of material, and badly made. But I'll swear that to my eyes no chalice of alabaster could have looked more comforting than this thing of pewter, as Miss Hopper and Trooper Alfred, holding it between them and sitting close, looked through the thick, foul mist of the tap-room, and saw a fair sunrise and a sweet twilight, and heard the lark and the thrush and the nightingale, and a far-off bleating of little lambs.

* * *

"Well, friend," said Trooper Alfred, as he wiped his mouth with his cap and stood up, right in the tap-room, "well, friend, I tell you square that there's no bloke as me an' the missus 'ere would sooner ha' shared our pot with than yeself. Ain't that so, missus?"

"That is so," responded Miss Hopper. "But ain't you a bit previous with yere 'missus'? Time enough for that if ever I married you. *My* name is Miss 'Opper."

"All right, Primrose," the young man replied. "Time we was gettin' on to Arthur's."

"I'd rather be called 'missus' then 'Primrose,'" expostulated Miss Hopper. "Seems to me you wanter start quarrellin' already."

"Mayn't call you 'missus': mayn't call you 'Primrose.' What the blazes *may* I call you?" Trooper Alfred looked bewildered.

"My name to you, so long as we walk out together," explained the lady, "is Miss 'Opper. I was never one fur bein' familiar. Expect my father was a time-keeper.[200] Even the gels at the war'us calls me properly."

"All right, Miss 'Opper," replied her solider, with an air of gallant surrender. "All right, Miss 'Opper – come along rahnd to father's."

This reference touched Miss Hopper, but she did not show it. "'Ark at the lad!" she said, with scornful intonation and a glance at me. "Father, indeed! Any-body 'd think I was gointer marry you. And 'urry up if you are comin'. What's it that potman is sayin'? Three pots? It's a lie, young man. Don't pay, Alf. 'Ere – you 'ad better gimme your money to o'd. Three pots indeed! And you was 'arf a mind to pay 'im! Anybody 'd think as tuppences rained from 'Eaven! An' do your coat up – rare weather for chills, this is. An' do keep in away from the 'buses, there's a good lad. 'Father,' if ye please! As I say, a person would think, to 'ear '*im*, as I meant to merry the lad!"

When we got to the coffee-stall, this absurd, ridiculous, outrageous sugges-tion was again given expression to – this time by Arthur. "He! he!" said that sinful personage when he looked upon his first-born's face, and "Ho! ho!" quoth he, as he viewed the blushes of Miss Hopper. Then:

"Rare weather for gettin' lost in. Bin gone since six, you two. Workin' at 'ome, I s'pose, Miss 'Opper? Alfred see you safely to your door, like 'e said 'e would when you left the copper-'ouse?"

"Yes, thank you, Arthur," replied Miss Hopper.

"Young 'Erry Vaughan 'as jest looked round," continued Arthur. "Seems you never turned up at the 'armony, after all, young Elf."

"Didn't feel like it," explained Alfred.

"R! I thought you was lookin' a bit pale at tea's afternoon. We must pack you off to Yarmouth for change of hair."

"Pale be sugared!" exclaimed the warrior. "I don't want no rotten Yarmouth. On'y 'ad a 'eadache."

"Rollin' yeself in the mud to cure it, it s'pose?" suggested Arthur.

"Goo-goo-good-night, Arthur!" said Miss Hopper. "Time I was in bed. Good-night all."

But Arthur caught her hand, and held it for a moment and bent over and whispered in her ear. She was blushing like anything as she ran away, and I noticed that her left hand – the one which Arthur had held – was carefully shielded by her other hand from public view. "Belonged to my lad's mother, dearie," was all I caught of Arthur's speech to her.

[22 April 1904]

XXVII. A Valediction.

As I write these words – it would be nicer, perhaps, to have it "As I pen this matter" – I am sighing and groaning in a manner that is most distressing. A Greco-Roman three-armed chalice stands before me on the table, and this vessel bears the following inscription:

> Straight is the line of duty,
> Curved is the line of beauty;
> Follow the straight line
> Thou shalt see
> The curved line ever follow thee.

On the whole, I imagine this to be the most unintelligible effusion that ever vase was decked withal. But there is a pleasing air of virtue about the thing – a sort of suggestion that if you could understand its sentiment that sentiment would appeal to you as being very proper – which somehow has fascinated me. I have been repeating the words over to myself for two days, and they have somehow crystallised themselves into a sort of meaning, and the meaning which I make of them is that it were time I "got a hump on me," and sat down to paper, and quitted me of this, the last instalment of "Little Pictures of the Night."

"Straight is the line of duty," I have said to myself, when not otherwise employed. "Straight is the line of duty." I have whispered it in starry solitudes, and dreamt it in bed, and roared it aloud on waking. Sometimes, of course, I have varied my theme by reflecting that "Curved is the line of beauty"; but, generally speaking, and as a rule, and on the whole, the first precept has done me proudly on all occasions. I have repeated it at least fifty times yesterday, and probably quite as often the day before. And yet – and yet – the Sabbath day has now arrived, and this article, which *ought* to have reached the CLARION office on Friday morning, has hardly been begun. These straight and curved lines that I have spoken of do not seem to have helped me a little bit; and I am an accursed thing. This last instalment will never be finished – not to say *finished* – and that three-armed chalice with its beautiful message will henceforward and for evermore be effigied in lines of fire upon the tablets of my mind.

And, really, when you come to think of it, how *can* I write a last chapter of these records? Little picutres of the night are being painted always in every part of London. I could not put an extinguisher upon them even if I wanted to do so; and you may certainly suppose that I do not want to do anything of the sort, since no man knoweth better than your servant that the *real* pictures of the nght are very curious and wonderful things, which well repay inspection. Furthermore, there is no charge for viewing them, and you do not need a catalogue, and if anybody says "Keep to the left, please!" you hit his eye.

Well, from time to time I have gotten me pieces of paving-stone and lumps of chalk, and I have made things which, in a kind of sense, are copies of these pictures. I have paid no royalties to the owners of the originals, because, generally speaking I did my job at times when the aforesaid owners were asleep or quarrelling. Also, I paid little heed to rules and things, and did it all in a hurry, and to please myself. Apologies are certainly called for, but I am not offering any. I will lose my sleep for no man. And this reminds me that it is a quarter to bed-time, and I am getting off the trail.

What I want to say is this – I have used up nearly all my paving-stones, and nearly all my chalk, and it therefore falls that (for the present, at any rate) I am measuring out the last of these pictures. Now, is it reasonable, I ask you, to suppose that I should conduct the operation on the lines of an early Victorian story-book? Arthur's coffee-stall stands exactly where it did. Arthur's customers are all alive, and all active, and all ready to receive the enquiring stranger – though whether with blessings or with that which is not a blessing depends rather on the nature of the case.

This being so you can hardly expect me to round this record off like a fairy tale. I should perhaps, be doing no violence to the custom of my trade if I were to marry Arthur to a publican's widow. And Tradition and Practice would alike be agreeable to my investing Beaky with a large fortune acquired by reason of the death of a successful brother resident in the Antipodes. But as Beaky is still washing cups for Arthur, and as Arthur happens still to be in love with widowership, that which passes for my conscience prevents me from doing these things.

But, with all honesty and truth, and also with the greatest pride and pleasure in the world, I may say not only that Trooper Alfred and Miss Hopper were duly and irretrievably married, but that I, *ipse*,[201] acted as best man at the wedding.

It *was* a wedding, too, I can tell you. The actual ceremony took place at a registry office; but the really memorable part of the function was conducted subsequently in Arthur's copper-house, most strikingly decorated for the occasion. Trooper Alfred had been granted three whole days' holiday by a sympathetic and grateful country. I say *Trooper* Alfred by reasons of the fact of old associations; but, as a matter of actual fact, the industrious Alfred had worn with modesty the chevrons of a coproral for some weeks before his marriage. And three brother corporals came up from Aldershot for the half-day, and acted respectively as second, third, and fourth best man. Beaky, of course, was present, and delivered five addresses, each a trifle longer and less coherent and more tearful than its predecessor. I almost fear that Beaky had celebrated the occasion by partaking of some liquor other than his benefactor's coffee. The opportunity was certainly present. Our company was a comparatively small one – some twenty-five, all told – but the firkins and flasks and pipkins and casks that were gathered together in the copper-house would almost have satisfired a battalion of German infantry.

The other guests included Mr. Honeybunn, with whom was Mrs. Honeybunn and three juvenile Honeybunns. The three juvenile Honeybunns were appropriately decked with poppies, and their mother was appropriately decked with tear-stains. "She is so very, very young," explained that agreeable lady between her sobs. "It reminds me of my own dear sister Kate, what died in childbirth." When exhorted to brace up and make the best of things, like the rest of us, Mrs. Honeybunn promised to be firm. "But," she added, "it is a contrary world; there is always *somethink*!"

Mr. and Mrs. Robert Walpole were, of course, amongst the guests, and so was Mr. and Mrs. Robert Walpole's new baby. Alfred Hopper Walpole was this new baby's name.

And then – ah! then there was a most striking frock-coat of antique but distinctly tasteful design, with a roll-back velvet collar and ditto cuffs, the whole having black pearl buttons, and being inhabited by Arthur. And Arthur, by common consent, was in his very best form. From the tip of his patent leather boots right up to the shiny bald spot on the top of his head, he shone and glittered and coruscated with animation. He whispered stories of a highly matrimonial character into the ears of all the ladies, and caused them to titter, and say "Go on with you!" Whereafter they repeated these anecdotes in the ears of their husbands, and their husbands roared for joy, and slapped Arthur upon the back, and dug him in the ribs, and whispered other stories in *his* ear: so that he twinkled and coruscated more than ever. And he kissed Miss Hopper at frequent interals throughout the festivities, and assumed to believe that his son was jealous of these attentions. And Alfred said: "Blow me if I ain't beginning to wonder whether this is my weddin' or the ole man's." And the old man looked highly gratifed, and the glint in his eye seemed to suggest that only a sense of parental responsibility restrained him from entertaining the company to some very interesting reminiscences.

And Trooper Alfred made a historic speech, beginning: "WE MARRIED MEN"; and the humour of this utterance so tickled Mr. Honeybunn that that portly gentleman rolled on the mat for joy, whereat Alfred paused in his oration to inform the world at large that if some people wanted a thick ear, they was going the right way to get it.

And then came the departure of the bride and bridegroom for Yarmouth: an event greatly retarded by Mrs. Honeybunn, who thought fit to entertain Miss Hopper to a private recital of some intimate details affecting the death of her sister Kate. "And that," concluded Mrs. Honeybunn, weeping bitterly, and addressing the company at large, "and that is what it comes to – death in childbed and burial at twenty-five. R me, there is *always* somethink!"

Then, of course, Miss Hopper – now Miss Hopper no longer – must give way to tears when bidding good-bye to her father-in-law; so that all the other ladies gave way to tears, too. And Arthur, being connected with a sterner sex, did *not* give way to tears, but turned his back upon the compay, and said "Tut, tut! Silly nonsense!" several times in a husky voice.

Then Corporal Alfred and Mrs. Corporal Alfred clinked into a four-wheeled cab, and were duly assailed with rice; and the most juvenile of the Honeybunns, being possessed of a unrestrainable sense of the congruitites, removed a new tan shoe and threw it after the cab. The shoe alighted upon the roof of that vehicle, and was very nearly lost to the Honeybunn family for ever. The day ended tempestuously for the most juvenile of the Honeybunns.

The company, having exchanged congratulations, proceeded then to divert itself with song and dance. And presently its numbers were swelled by the arrival of an expected reinforcement. This reinforcement took the form of Mr. Joseph Tuttle. That gentleman had caught wind of our proceedings, and came, slighty intoxicated, to demand his "rights." We made him more intoxicated, and put him to sleep upon a couch already occupied by Beaky. What happened next morning has never been fully revealed; but Beaky often smiles the smile of one in possession of secret happiness. And Mr. Tuttle is said to have gone to sea.

And my charge for explaining the geographical situation of Arthur's stall to readers of this paper is one guinea.

Harry Beswick, 'Brother Eli on Tramps' (1904)

"Dost ever peroose t' 'Daily Jellygraff'?" asked Brother Eli of me the other evening.

I had ridden over to Slattox,[1] and had called in the "Hark to Nudger" for a modest beaker. Brother Eli was ensconced in the ingle-nook[2] of the stone kitchen, in company with a long clay pipe, pint pot, and a newspaper.

I explained to the worthy Lancastrian that it was an occasion of some rarity when I gave myself the treat of assimilating the columns of the great Metropolitan organ he named. The frothy lightness of its leaders, the saucy flavour pervading its special scientific articles, the malapertness of its advertisements, and the generally flippant tone of the whole sheet all tended to discourage one who preferred the solid qualities of a "Punch" and the plain, homely commonsense of "Slopperty Slips". "Since," I added, "the 'Jellygraph'[3] departed from its traditional policy of printing descriptions of man-and-dog fights, I have ceased to be a regular subscriber.

"Aw nivver thowt t' 'Jellygraff' wur leet readin'," replied Brother Eli, looking somewhat astonished. "It's allus suggested savvery-ducks to me, and aw cud nivur do ony good after a savvery-duck."

"And what may a savvery-duck be?"

"It's konsidered t' be a greyt delicassy i' Slattox. The'n mak it eawt of fleawer, an drippi', an' other satisfyin' hingrediants."

"What does a savoury-duck taste like?"

"It favvurs a dumplin' when yo fust plant yore teeth inter it; then, as it's gooin into th' bourne fro' which no dumplin' ivver returned, yo get th' idea yo'n swallert a candle."

"But, surely, that's not the flavor of the 'Jellygraff'!"

"Not exackly. Whet aw mean to convey is thet 'Jellygraff' matter sticks again th' ribs, and weyn't digest, just like a savvery-duck does wi' me. Aw'd reyther not be axed t' swoller savvery-ducks, and aw sud purr reet weel if aw wur towd aw mun believe o' as is in t' 'Jellygraff'!"

"As, for instance –?"

"T' editor felly o' t' 'Jellygraff' 's gone stak starin' mad lately becose t' parks i' Lunnon's bein' whet he co's infested wi' tramps. 'Aw conno goo eawt i' t' air o'

Regent's Park,' he ses, 't' geet smell o' t' offis gum eawt o' mi gizzard,[4] an' think o' nasty things t' wreyt abeaut Camel-Bannerman,[5] but whet a narsty, 'orrid pusson, clad i' a tight-fittin' soot o' filth, comes atwixt t' wind an' mi nobillerty."

"Poor gentleman," I commented, pityingly.

"Isno he? Aw symperthise wi' him as mich as onnyone. Then t' readers o' t' 'Jellygraff' – blue-blooded stockbrokers, aristocratic bewk-makers, high financial pimps and company prommoters – raises up their v'ices i' chorus. 'Deawn wi' tramps!' is their motter – an' a good motter it is."

"Hear, hear," I cried.

"One chap wreyts to t' papper leykenin' tramps to t' mowd o' hup-turned graves. He ses he's seen Fattygewed Freddy and Lassichewed Lancerlot trimming their toe-nails under t' greenwood tree.[6] 'They sleep, eat out o' huge pieces o' papper' – 'Jellygraffs', maybe – 'w'ich they leave lyin abeawt." Thet's so leyk t' 'Jellygraff'; is allus lyin' abeaut summat."

"It's a harrowing picture," I put in.

"Ay, and thet's not t' wust. These yer Jaded Josephs en' Ennervated Edwards sups eawt o' t' saame drinkin'-feawnt'in as t' 'Jellygraff' correspondent's kids. They acksherly breathe saame air, too, and use t' saame sun to warm theirsels wi'. 'Ere, hev a goo thisel."

Brother Eli handed me the paper, and I read the following unanswerable impeachment of the tramp:

> There are many groups of finely grown and comfortably dressed children, some of them evidently from wealthy homes, walking, playing horses, or trundling hoops.

But on the seats near by –

> Two or three dirty-looking roughs are stretched upon them, their boot laden with dust, which has stained these rests visibly."

"The brutes!" I commented. "How dare they rest when they're tired."

"Orful depravity!" groaned Brother Eli.

"The writer adds," I went on, "that –

> If our parks are to be the fine-weather refuge of the dregs of the community, then these unwelcome visitors should be confined to spaces where some signal of disease and danger should be raised.

"But wouldna thet be hexpensive?" asked Brother Eli.

"A little," I replied.

"Aw know a mich cheaper wey o' dealin' wi' t' tramp problim," returned Brother Eli.

"Yes?"

"Ay. Whey not sweep aw t' tramps i' t' country into one plaace. Then, when yo've geeten 'em aw i' a mass, fot up a few batteries of masheen guns, and hexterminate 'em. Or gather 'em o' i' a big pit, and dreawn 'em."

"It might be a good thing," I commented.

"Ger off wi' thi coddin'. It ud be neawt o' t' sort. Yo' sall clear t' country o' tramps ter-morrer, and i' six months they'll be as noomerous as dobby-horses[7] at Slattox Weyks."

"Why?" I asked.

"Becose t' soshul system keeps on manufacturin' 'em, and its macheernery for t' job cudno be licked. Put t' 'Jellygraff' editor, i' a city slum, deny him wark, snub and inprison and kick t' manhood and self-respect outern him, and he'll come out o' t' loom as fine a specimen o' a tramp as ivvur starded a neppy-demmick."

"So that your advice to the 'Jellygraff' editor is –"

"Stop makin' tramps, give men a chance i' t' warld, and trey whet a dose of Soap, Sense, an' Sosherlism 'll do."

Robert Blatchford, 'Dismal Dan's Story. "The Only Chance He Ever Gave."' (1905)

"Dirty Dick's been made M.P.",[1] said Corporal Goodchiild, as he thoughtfully shook the beer round in his pot.

"Right billet for him," said Ruggy Brown, "he's a pig."

"It's his nose that's done it," Dismal Dan commented, "a nose like that's just made for poking into other people's business. After you with a pull at the pipe, Ruggy."

Ruggy Brown withdrew his black Cork cutty from his lips, wiped the mouthpiece under his armpit, and passed it across to Dan. "If," he said sagely, "a man isn't a pig when he joins the provost gang they soon make him one."

Dan sucked at the pipe for a moment and then uttered one of his pregnant speeches.

"Most men are; some by nature. If you meet a stranger, dot him down pork; and you'll never be far off the bull's-eye. Look at that driver of the Royal Horse, just coming into the canteen. I don't know him. I never set eyes on him before. But it's ten to one he's a swine. When you've done judging distance with that pot, corporal, p'haps you'll ask a chap if he'd like anything."

"Danny, you're too fond of drink," said the corporal. "It's a nasty fault in a young soldier. Besides – the oof bird[2] isn't singin' in my tree at the present."

"Looks like payin' myself," said Dan, and gave the necessary order.

"The biggest hog in the regiment is the provost sergeant,"[3] the corporal said, resuming the conversation, "but then he mostly is."

"Always," amended Dan. "But our old thief isn't in it with the chap that was chief constable in my old corps."

"The Wessexers?" asked the corporal.

"Yes," said Dan. "He had twenty years service, had been provost sergeant nine years, and never gave a soul a chance – only once."

"That's porky," said Brown, "but what made him spoil his record?"

"It was a case of devil thank him," answered Dan.

"Boots",[4] answered the corporal.

Dan smiled. "There is a yarn in it, certainly," he said "but you can't hear in this noisy hole. When we've finished the beer we'll go for a stroll on the ramparts and I'll tell you the cuffer. My oath, it was funny."

* * *

"I suppose I needn't tell you what sort of a hog old Provost Pegler was: you know the breed. Put extra facings, and extra buttons on the sneakiest beast you ever wanted to kick, and you'll have a flatterin' likeness of Peg. He'd have walked forty miles on an empty stomach to do dirt to his own father. He used to sit up half the night winkin' his rusty eyes, and hatchin' sin. He'd have sold the boots off his feet to buy trouble for another soldier. He couldn't have slept in his bed if he had believed there was a man in the regiment that didn't want to poison him. If he could have got all the sergeants in the corps reduced to the ranks and doing shot drill in short hair, he'd have gone to church and offered up prayers for the crownin' mercy. O, he *was* a swine." Danny paused to strike a lucifer[5] on his trousers.

"Well, there were two brothers, name of Beagle, in the Wessex. One was lance corporal the other private. The corporal was known as the 'Hugly Ducklin',' for his beauty's sake, and the brother, who cocked his cap, and wore a quiff,[6] and fancied himself as a lady-killer, was known as 'England's Pride.' They were silly goats, both of 'em; but not particular wrong un's: not more than the average.

"So the ducklin' got into of Pegler's clutches, and Peggy put him on the peg. It was what you call a 'soft one'; but Pegler had been lookin' for him. Ducky was corporal of the picket. Peggy met him in town and ran him in for 'drunk on duty.' And as old Tommy Strapper, our Colonel, was a mark on 'D. on D.' it meant cells for the Hugly one, as sure as men love women.

"Now, I have to make it plain that old Peggy put three witnesses against the Duck: himself and two of his blighted M.P.'s because that is how it happened that the poor lance Jack, got his chance: the only chance Peg ever gave in all his beautiful life.

"Well, when England's Pride got the griffin he was in a blue funk, you may guess; and he chewed his fingers, and walked sentry-go up and down the barrackroom tryin' to find a hole for his brother to creep through.

"And at last old Jaunty Jobling, who was a four-ringed man,[7] and as full o' wickedness as a pretty woman, he says to the Pride, 'Look here, brat,' he says, 'it's no use snivellin' and swearin'. You can't get old Ducky out up the guard-room chimney, and you can't put natural feelin' nor common dog decency into that old rat Peggy. But there *is* just an off-chance, you've the pluck to try it.'

"'I'm on it,' says poor Pride.

"Well, old Jobling tells him he's a smart young soldier, and has a way with the women and says he, 'there's only one soul o' God's makin' can turn Peggy, and that's his wife. Buck yourself up, sonny, chuck a chest, and try if you can to get the soft side of her.'

"So England's Pride, who was a knocked-kneed, flat-footed little bounder, with a face like a monkey on a stick, washed himself special, greased his quiff, padded his tunic and straddled off to put the comether[8] on to Mother Pegler.

"Now, Mother P. was Peggy's third wife. She was trim and pretty, and full of grit, and was the only living thing that her pig of a husband wouldn't bite.

"But to beg off a prisoner, or get a crime toned down, was more than *she* dare try. So she shook her head, and said she was sorry – and she was a good sort, and very good natured – but it was more than her place was worth to mention it. So England's Pride came back with his tail very much behind him, and went on chawin' his fingers.

"Meantime Peggy was in the doldrums on account of bad biz.[9] Since he ran Ducky in he hadn't landed a solider, and after tattoo, there being nobody absent, he was nosing around seeking mischief, when he spots a civilian shinning over the wall of the married quarters.

"That was tripe and porter to Peggy.

"Back he runs for his bold constabulary, and away to the gate of the married quarters to follow the trail. I was sentry on the magazine[10] post, close by, and I saw the whole performance. Strike me peculiar it if it wasn't great. And I *did* enjoy it.

"Stand inside the gate, Stoneham,' said Peggy to one of his M.P.s, 'stand back out of sight, you flat-headed Bosjesman[11] Baraddle, get round that corner, and squint along the wall this way. Go quietly, you son of a dancin' dervish. You two, come after me, and keep your ugly chops closed, and walk in the shadow, and look three ways at once or you'll blithering soon look the way to the guard room.'

"'Now, sentry,' he says to me, 'there's some sneak-thief blackguard of an officer's servant has gone over that wall after some slut of a soldier's wife. You watch that gate. Let him pass, and by the grace of God I'll have the belts off you before you can count one. Do you *hear*? Stand fast where you are. Don't move an eyelash. I'll have 'em. By this and by that, I'll have the pair of 'em.'

"With that he opened the gate with his key and sneaked through. He was as excited as a cat at a mousehole. I could hear his mouth water, and when he winked his wicked eyes the sparks flew. I'd have given three years' service to stir him up with the bayonet. I thought once of sneezin'; but my good angel didn't let me. Instead, I stood close to the gate and peeped through.

"Sure enough there was a man in mufti,[12] and a woman in a light frock and a dark cloak, standin' a few yards inside the shadow kissin' one another like one o'clock. And in the tinklin' of a bedpost old Peggy was on 'em, and grabbed at the woman's arm. And as quick as turn your eye the man landed him squash on the nose and down he went, and the woman with him. Lovely Paradise, how he did shout. 'Seize that man. Sentry hold the gate.' Up ran the other two provosts, and all four went for the man, and downed him, after the beautifullest scrap you ever saw, and then – and then the hand played. O, my eyes and Betty Martin,[13] such a gettin' upstairs. Soon as Peggy got on his feet he turns on a bull's-eye;[14] and there was as pretty a picture as ever the devil made a frame for.

"Standing among the four M.P.s was sub-lieutenant Vincent Bellamy Walker-Mallock; and full in the flare of old Peg's bull's-eye was Peggy's wife, and no other person, and while all parties was staring with their jaws dropped, except the lady, who was grittin' her teeth and trying to twist her sleeve out of Peggy's fingers, who should walk out of a passage of the married quarters but England's Pride.

"And that's how the Hugly Duckling got a chance. Peggy went up and swore him sober, and he got off with a caution. It was the only time the dirty old scoundrel ever told the truth.

"And I suppose it preyed on his mind. Anyhow, he took his discharge as soon as he could get it, and his wife took her hook; and the young sub-lieutenant went on leave, and stopped there. And, the day Peg left, the bandmaster had the band practicin' the 'Rogues March' by a curious coincidence, just as Peg walked up the lines. And that night the sergeants all sat up in the mess till after one, drinkin' each other's healths, and the rank and file borrowed one another's money, and went out and painted the town a sky-blue scarlet, and Paddy McGinnis, the big drummer dropped on the M.P.'s up a side street and gave them each a black eye, and England's Pride wrote home to his good old mother, and said he and his brother had found salvation, and were going to be good and pure soldiers ever after, and would she send him five bob to buy hymn books. Man alive! The Hugly Duckkin' wasn't sober for a week; and the chaps in cells sang 'Angels Ever Bright and Fair', and asked God to bless good kind Sergeant Peglar, and do unto him as he has done to others. And the end of it was that the Sergeant Major gave the battalion the straight griffin,[15] that if they didn't cool off and begin to soldier, he's ask the Colonel for three marchin' order p'rades a day, and double duties. So we praised the Lord, and took the hint. But we rejoiced in secret for a month o' Sundays. And to this day I can't think of it without wantin' to drink somebody's health. Ruggy: its your turn, darlin', which is the way to the canteen?

"And so Dirty Dick's been made an M.P.! Well: he's a swine."

A. Neil Lyons, 'A Distressed Gentlewoman. A True History' (1906)

This thing is not a fanciful anecdote at all; no "story." It is just a little fact – a true incident; one of those actualities which bump into you out of the gloom in London, and bounce off again, and are more or less forgotten until some similar experience shall recall them.

I do not remember what happening exactly has reminded me of my lady's maid. And it doesn't matter anyhow. The main thing is that I am reminded of her. And it has struck me that she is worth at least a casual column of publicity.

To begin from the beginning, I had been working late. One o'clock had already struck when I came out of Fleet Street and began the usual tedious walk home to my lodgings which were then situated in Camden Town. I walked, as usual, through Fetter Lane, into Holborn, and from there turned into Southampton Row. There is, or used to be, at the corner of Red Lion Square and Southampton Row a coffee stall. I stopped there for some cake – good cake, too, if seedy – and fell to gossiping with some fellow gourmets, and forgot about Time and Duty and all the other important things of this life. When I got started again it must have been nearly three o'clock – cold and clammy at that, and very black.

And half-way up the remaining portion of Southampton Row a woman spoke to me. London was full of women that night – horrible, yellow women, with wicked, miserable, hungry faces. It "doesn't do" to speak kindly to such women. They and "the humanities" have been at odds these many years. And so I answered this woman rather roughly. "Get away!" I said. Whereupon she came closer, and I beheld the face of a Madonna.

She was dressed in black, and there were tear stains upon her cheek. And her eyes were wistful, like a child's; and she spoke in a despairing voice and with an accent of refinement.

"Oh, please, sir!" she said; "please, *please*, don't talk to me like that! I'm not what you take me for – *really* I am not! And I want help. Do you think that I would talk to a strange man in the street at this hour unless my case were desperate? Won't you help me? You have a kind face."

I had heard about my kind face before. Such references to the obvious had long since ceased to move me. But still ... she had a gentle voice and pitiful eyes, and ... the face of a Madonna. So I stopped to hear the rest.

She was a "lady's companion." Her employer had accused her of theft. Her employer drank. She (the employer) had thrust her out into the streets on this pitiless November night. She had walked about these dreadful pavements for hours in thin house-slippers, which I was invited to examine. She was chilled to the bone. She had no money. "What am I to do?" she asked, appealingly; "am I to walk about all night? Oh, I can't do that! I would rather kill myself! – I *will* kill myself! It isn't the cold I mind; it isn't the hunger and the misery, and the loneliness. It is the men – the blackguard *men*. Oh, my God! they are too horrible! The policemen are worse than anybody. I cannot stand these dreadful streets. ... Won't you trust me? Won't you help me? For a few shillings I could get into some decent hotel. And in the morning I can go back to my mistress, who will be sober and reasonable. *Won't* you help me?"

I helped her. Her story touched me deeply.

It touched me deeply for about two minutes. After that I began to think, and the conclusion which forced itself upon me was not flattering to my self-esteem. For, really, her tale was an uncommonly "thin" one. Those pathetic little slippers, the evidence of her sincerity, they certainly did point to a somewhat hasty exit from home. But this haste had not prevented her from donning a hat and cloak and gloves. Also, she had omitted to confide her name to me. And – pah! ... She had the face of a Madonna and the voice of a lady. And if I had been "rooked"[1] what of it? What was all the town but an organized rookery? And wasn't it better to be defrauded twenty times than that one poor girl (with the face of a Madonna) should cry in vain for help? And thus reflecting I went to bed and slept the sleep of virtue.

There, the first chapter of this experience came to an end. Save for what happened afterwards I doubt that the memory of it would have stayed with me at all. But when a whole year had passed, I chanced once more to saunter up Southampton Row in early morning. Only on this occasion I had company. A friend was with me – another journalist – now a Successful Person. Well, there were women about, as usual, and they spoke to us, and sickened us, and we spoke to them roughly. Of a sudden one girl answered back:

"Oh, please don't talk to me like that," she said. "I am not what you take me for; really, I am not. And I want help. I am in trouble. Do you think that I would talk to strange me in the street at this hour unless my troubles drove me to it? You have kind faces. You will help me? *Do* help me. I am a lady's companion."

We had all the rest of the performance – even to the exhibition of those pathetic slippers. And her face was more Madonna-like, more pure than ever. My Successful Person nearly wept with pity. He put his hand into his pocket. He drew forth silver. And then – and then I made a little speech. My Madonna did not stop to hear the end of it. Very quietly, very daintily, with a mincing gait, she walked away. The combination of Christian martyrdom and cultured scorn in her expression was beautiful to witness. There endeth Chapter II.

The last and final scene took place in Chelsea. It was shortly after this episode – three days later, I should think – that I went into Chelsea to spend an evening with some artists. The party broke up a little before midnight, and I set off to catch an omnibus, with one of the artists for escort. Suddenly there emerged from nowhere in particular a pathetic and beautiful maiden, who stopped us there, in the King's Road, and began to speak in broken agitated tones. She had uttered scarcely half-a-dozen words, however, when a sudden dumbness fell upon her. She flushed a little, and stood there blinking at us, wearing on her face a strange expression, part amusement, part anger, part fear. Then she spoke:

"Sort of a dam fairy, ain't you?" she said.

This observation was addressed to me. It's tone, it's form, the girl's manner, and her expression presented such a contrast to the "distressed gentlewoman" of a second before, that both fairy and painter shrieked with laughter. And then the girl laughed too.

"You are a funny little blighter," she observed. "Do you do it on purpose?"

"Of course not!" I answered. 'How could I? Business happens to call us both the same places at the same time. That's all."

She grinned. "Give us a fag, one of you."

We gave her a cigarette, and she walked into the shadow of the wall and lighted it. And then the artist demanded explanations. I gave them to him. "And so," I concluded, perhaps a little boisterously, "after 'having' me and jolly nearly 'having' that other chap, she's all but 'had' you as well." A rather vicious dig in the chest cut short my further utterances "Not so much of your bloomin' 'aves,'" said the lady. ... "'Ow much did I get from you?"

"How do I know? It was a year ago. You're welcome to it, any how."

"Was it a bob?'

"Very likely."

"Was it two bob?"

"I dare say so."

"Was it *five* bob?"

"I should doubt it. But –"

"Never mind about the 'buts.' Suppose we call it two-and-a-kick-me-down?[2] What?"

"Suppose anything you please," I said.

"Then 'ere's the money. *I* don't want your measly 'arf-crowns! Buy a decent 'at."

Before I could realize what was happening, she had thrust a half-crown into my hand. I expostulated wildly.

"My good man," retorted the girl, "don't be silly – don't be tragic." Her manner, her accent had changed as suddenly as before. She was the fine lady again. "I detest argument. It is your own money. Give me another cigarette."

I handed her a cigarette and the money with it. But she dodged the coin. I threatened to throw it into the street. "That would be transpontine",[3] she said (her exact word!) "Much better give it to a beggar man ... I've only paid back what I owe you. ... I hate to be in debt." She looked at me very hard, very shrewdly. It suddenly occurred to me that there was method in her impudence. So I pocketed the money.

She smoked a number of our cigarettes that night talking all the time. Her talk was the most amazing mixture. Sometimes it was frankly ribald, sometimes almost lofty. It was always clever. Her language fluctuated between the exactest Bond Street and the broadest Cockney – with adjectival effect. We learnt nothing of herself, save that she hated children and loved cats. There were "three prize Persians at her place" wherever that might be. She had no lover and sickened at the thought of one.

And she quoted "Omar Khayyam"!![4]

Only Mr. Suthers, with his inimitable "H'm!" could have done justice to the feelings with which we parted from her.

JUSTICE

Joseph Grose, 'The Golden Egg', *Justice*, 13 July 1901, p. 3.

R. B. Cunninghame Graham, 'A Fisherman', *Justice*, 3 May 1902, p. 3.

J. W. B., 'Men and Things', *Justice*, 5 November 1904, p. 6.

Anon., 'The "Smart Set"', *Justice*, 10 June 1905, p. 3.

Henry Mayers Hyndman (1842–1921) and *Justice* (1884–1925) ran the gauntlet of public (anti-Boer) and socialist (pro-Boer) opinion during the Second Boer War (1899–1902) by opposing the war, arguing that the land belonged not to the British or the German colonists but to the indigenous African people. Hyndman withdrew from the SDF in 1900 but continued to write for *Justice*, which continued to be edited by Harry Quelch (1858–1913). Hyndman resumed political activity in 1903. The SDF had withdrawn from the LRC in 1901, and during this period *Justice* maintained its criticism of the LRC's movement towards the Liberal Party. After the 1906 general election, Hyndman wrote in *Justice* that the SDF would be willing to re-affiliate with what was now renamed the Labour Party if they were to embrace even a diluted form of socialism.[1]

Of the authors included in this selection, there have been no biographical or other publishing details found for Joseph Grose while the anonymous author has not been identified, although Jack Mitchell claims there is circumstantial evidence that Quelch contributed to *Justice* anonymously.[2] No biographical details for J. W. B. were found during the research for this project, but the short stories 'Marjoribank's Serenade' (1893) and 'The Man Who Wants to Buy the Labour Party' (1894) were published in the *Workman's Times* under the same initials, while 'An Ancient Manuscript' was published in the *Labour Leader* in 1904 under the pseudonym 'J. Bedubbleu'.

Robert Bontine Cunninghame Graham (1852–1936), the eldest son of William Cunninghame Bontine (1825–83) of Dunbartonshire, was a descendant of the ancient families of Cunninghame and Graham. He was an adventurer and a politician: elected as a radical Liberal for North-West Lanarkshire in 1886, he became the first president of the Scottish Labour Party in 1888. Graham declared himself a socialist in Parliament in 1889, was arrested with John Burns (1858–1943) at the 'Bloody Sunday' demonstration on 13 November 1887, and served six weeks in Pentonville prison for unlawful assembly. He contributed to socialist papers such as James Keir Hardie's *Labour Leader*, Henry Hyde Champion's (1859–1928) *Labour Elector*, Joseph Burgess's (1853–1934) *Workman's Times* and John Trevor's (1855–1930) *Labour Prophet* as well as to *Justice*. After the development of the Labour Party in 1900, he grew increasingly critical of its dilution of socialism.

Notes

1. H. M. Hyndman, quoted in C. Tsuzuki, *H. M. Hyndman and British Socialism* (Oxford: Oxford University Press, 1961), p. 163.
2. See J. Mitchell, 'Tendencies in Narrative Fiction in the London-Based Socialist Press of the 1880s and 1890s', in H. G. Klaus (ed.), *The Rise of Socialist Fiction* (Brighton: Harvester Press, 1987), pp. 49–72, for further details.

Joseph Grose, 'The Golden Egg' (1901)

The Cynic and the Person of Good Intentions walked leisurely along the Embankment. Presently they came to Temple Gardens.[1] On the seat opposite sat one of the co-proprietors of the Municipal wealth.[2] He was, or rather had been, one of the workers, but being either too old in the prime of his years, or more likely still (which was the case) having been competed out of the market by a machine, had developed into a very dilapidated specimen of humanity a veritable piece of flotsam cast about by circumstances hither and thither, and kept in existence only by the charity that is twice cursed, cursing both him who gives and him who receives.

The erstwhile God of Industry and creator of wealth advanced and offered the Person of Good Intentions some bootlaces in exchange for a disc of metal that represented one-fourth of the rent for that night of a couch and shelter. The bargain concluded the Person of Good Intentions observed:

"Poor fellow; evidently unable to obtain a living at his trade."

"Just so," responded the Cynic, "wherefore he should with all convenient despatch and rapidity relieve an unsympathetic world of the trouble and expense of supporting him."

"But he had no doubt produced wealth, been useful in his time, so why should he not strive to live? We all cling to life, you know."

"The tenacity with which such creatures cling to life," remarked the Cynic, "is one of the great paradoxes. When one considers how easily satisfied they are, and how content with small things."

"But," returned the Person of Good Intentions, "the increasing number of this class strikes me as one of the dangers of society."

"It is," said the Cynic, "wherefore you try to buy them off by purchasing bootlaces, and pretty successfully you have been up to now."

The Person of Good Intentions puckered up his eyebrows. "I think," said he, "that legislation should be introduced to prevent machines displacing men."

"Not so," rejoined the Cynic, "let us legislate for men to control them."

"Of course," retorted the Person of Good Intentions, "you must have some roundabout way of settling the matter. Man *versus* machine is a perfectly simple issue which we could all understand, but you would confuse it."

The Cynic smiled. "I do not want Man *versus* the Machine; I want Men *and* the Machine, Man dominating Machinery."

The Person of Good Intentions was posed, but only for a moment; then he brought up all his reserves to smash the argument of the Cynic. "But you want to destroy the relations between employer and employed; you attack property, forgetting that the interests of the employer are also the interests of the employed. The workman is necessary; he produces the wealth."

"Yes," interrupted the Cynic, "he is the goose who lays the golden egg and allows his master to take it from him."

"Then if that is so," said the other, "the master will always have to have some regard for his goose, as you call him; and there will always be a sufficient check in the fact that if he kills the goose who lays the eggs the supply will cease."

Said the Cynic, "The analogy does not hold good in this case, for the means of producing golden eggs are in the hands of the masters; and it scarcely matters how many geese are killed, there are always plenty of others prepared to accept the terms and continue the supply."

Meanwhile the dilapidated one trudged on, content if he could but obtain the barest necessaries of life.

R. B. Cunninghame Graham, 'A Fisherman' (1902)

The steamer scrunched against the pier, the gangway plank was drawn back slowly, and with as great an effort as it had weighed a ton, by the West Highland tweed-clad semi-sailors, semi-longshoremen.[1] The little groups of drovers separated, each following its fugleman[2] to the nearest public house. The ropes were cast off from the belaying pins, and whisked like serpents over the slippery slime-covered boards, a collie dog holding on to one of them by its teeth was dragged to the very edge, amongst a shower of Gaelic oaths.

Then with a snort and plunge the "Islesman" met the south-west swell coming up past Pladda from the Mull.[3] The wandering Willie with his fiddle in a green baize bag, stripped off its cover, and got to work in the wild wind and drizzling rain, at reels, strathspeys,[4] laments, and all the minor music which has from immemorial time been our delight in Scotland, although, no doubt, it is as terrifying to the Southern as when the bagpipes skirl. His dog beside him, a mere mongrel, looking like a dirty mop, and yet with something half pathetic, half ridiculous about him, sat holding round his neck a battered can for pence. The fiddler, bandy-legged and dressed in heather mixture tweed,[5] which gave out fumes of peat reek, snuff and stale whisky, stood by the forebits, and round him clustered all the heterogeneous "heids and thraws"[6] of the population of the West Highlands, Glasgow and Greenock, and the other towns upon the Firth of Clyde. Gently the steamer glided through the Kyles of Bute, left Toward Point on her port bow, and headed for Dunoon.[7] And as she steamed along, passing the varied scenery of mist-capped mountain, and of stormy loch, the peaks of Arran in the distance like a gigantic saddle, hung out-lined in the clouds. The passengers, for the most part, seemed to see nothing but each other's clothes and personal defects, after the fashion of so many travellers, who, with their shells of prejudice borne on their backs as they were snails, go out to criticise that which they could have seen to just as great advantage in their homes. Amongst them was a man dressed in greasy "stan' o' black,"[8] who, at first sight, appeared to be what we in Scotland call a "goin' aboot body",[9] and recognise as having quite a status in the land. His clothes, originally black, had borne the labour, whisky and the rain of many a funeral. He did not seem a townsman, for he had that wizened, weather-beaten look which, once a sailor, never leaves a man this side the grave. At once you saw that he had made his bread in ships, or boats, or in some way upon that element on which those who go down to it in brigs "smell hell," as the old shellback[10] said who heard the passage in the Bible on the wonders of the deep.[11]

Hard bread it is; damned hard, as the old admiral told his sacred majesty, the fourth William, who asked him whether he had been bred up to the sea.

He, at least, cared not an atom for the others on the boat, but seemed to know each inlet, stone and islet on the coast. He carried a geranium cutting in a little pot, hedged round with half a newspaper to shield it from the wind, and as the sun fell on the hills of "Argyle's bowling-green,"[12] broke out into a rhapsody, half born of whisky and half of that perfervidness which is the heritage of every Scot.

"'There shall be no more sea,' no' a wise saying of John, though he was sort o' doited in Patmos;[13] what had the body got against the sea?"

"I followed it myself twal year. First in an auld rickle o' a boat, at Machrihanish, and syne wi' the herrin' fishers about Loch Fyne. Man, a gran' life the sea. Whiles I am sorry that I left it; but auri sacra fames,[14] ye mind. Nae mair sea! Set John up. But the mountains, the mountains, will remain. Thank the Lord for the mountains.

No one responding to his remarks, he turned to me, observing that I looked an "eddicated man."

"Aye, ou aye, I mind I made a matter of five hundred pund at the herrin' fishin', and then, ye ken, I thocht I saw potentialities (gran' word, potentiality) of being rich, rich beyond the dreams of avarice, as that auld arle,[15] Dr. Johnson, said. Johnson, ye ken, he that keepit a skule, and ca'ed it an academy, as auld Boswell said. A sort o' randy body yon Boswell, man, though he gied us a guid book. Many's the time I hae lauched over it. Puir, silly devil, but with an eye intill him like a corbie for detail. Details, ye ken, are just the vertebræ of the world. Ye canna do without detail. What did I do? Losh me, I had most forgot. Will ye tak' an apple? It'll keep doun the drouth. Scotch apples are the best apples in the world, but I maun premise I like apples sour, as the auld leddie said.

"Na – weel, ye're maybe right, apples are sort o' wersh without speerits. Bonny wee islands, yon Cumbreaes,[16] the wee yin just like a dunter's[17] heid, the big yin, a braw place for fishin'.

"Whitin' Bay, ye ken, just beyond where the monument for they puir midshipmen stands.[18] An awfu' coast, I mind three laddies, some five and thirty syne, from up aboot England gaein' oot in a lugail boat from the Largs. Ane o' they easterly haars cam' on. They just come doon like a judgement of God on this coast – ye canna escape them, or irt. Aye weel. I'll no say no, a judgment, a special judgment o' divine providence, just fa's like a haar, fa's on the just and the unjust alike. Na, na, I'm no meanin' any disrespeck to providence, weel do I ken which side my bannock's buttered[19] ... The laddies, the easterly wind just drave them aff the coast, in a wee bit boatie, and had it no' been ane o' them was a sailor laddie, they would ne'er a' won back. Wondrous are His ways, while He saves those that never would be missed, and whiles ... Do I no believe in the efficacy o' prayer. Hoots aye, that is I'm no sure. Whiles a man just works his knees into horn wi prayin' for what might profit him, that is, profit him in this world ye see, and providence doesna steer for a' his prayin'. Whiles a man just puts up a supplication for some speeritual matter, and the Lord just answers him before the man is sure he wants the object of his prayer.

"The Cumbraes, sort o' backlyin' islands, but the folk that live on them hae a guid conceit. Sort o' conceit, the bit prayer, the minister in Millport used to pit up for the adjawcent islands o' Great Britain and Ireland, ye'll mind it, ye that seem to be a sort o' eddicated man.

"Yer lookin' at the bit gerawnium. Sort of tragical that gerawnium, if you regard the matter pheelosophically. I tell't you that I aince made a bit o' money at the herrin' fishin'. Shares in a boat or twa. Man, I was happy then, a rough life the fishin', but vera satisfyin'. Just an element o' gambling aboot it that endears it to a man. Aye, ou aye, the sea, I ken it noo, I see why I lik't the life sae weel. I felt it then though, just like a collie dog feels the hills, although he doesna ken it. I always fancy that collies look kind o' oot o' place in Glesca.[20]

"A collie dog, ye ken, would rather hear a West Heilandman swear at him in Gaelic than an English leddy ca' him a' the pet in the world. It's no his fault, it's no the swearin' that he likes, but just the tone o' voice. A gran' language the Gaelic, profanity in it just sounds like poetry in other tongue.

"Weel, a fisherman is just like a collie dog, he'd rather hear the tackle run through the sheaves o' the blocks than a' the kists o' whistles in the Episcopalian churches up aboot Edinburgh. And then the sea, dam't I canna tell why I still ettle to get back to it. It took ma fayther, maist of ma brithers, and the feck o' a' ma folk. It's maybe that, it's the element o' uncertainty there again, but dam't I dinna right know what it is, except that when ye aince get the salt doon into the soul ye ken, ye canna get it oot again. That is, no' on this side the grave. I wouldna have left it, had it not been ma mither, threep, threepin' on me ... aye, and the auri sacra fames.

"... Bonny the Largs[21] looks eh? Gin it not the view of Cuchullin,[22] the hills of Arran frae the Largs is the bravest view in Scotland. That is for a man that likes the sea. But I see I'm wearyin' ye wi' ma clash. Ye's maybe like to see the *Herald*[23] ... I hae Bogatsky in my bawg; Bogatstky's 'Golden Treasury,'[24] but maybe it's no greatly read in our body. Fine old-fashioned book Bogatsky, nae taint o' latter-day Erastianism[25] aboot it. Na, na, I'se warrant ye the man compiled Bogatsky gied his congregation mony a richt shake abune the pit. Tophet,[26] ye ken, the real old, what I might ca' the constitutional Tophet, before they hung thermometers aboot the walls, in case the temperature should gae ower high.

The steamer, after plunging uneasily beside the pier at Largs for sufficient time to let a knot of drovers, each with his dog led by a piece of twine, and holding in their hands hooked hazel sticks, reel off towards the town, and to allow the passengers (who did not mark it) space to view the beauties of the place, the little river brawling through the town, and the long bit of sea-swept grass on which goats pasture fixed to chains, and get a living on the scanty herbage, eked out with bottles, bones and sardine tins, turned eastward once again towards the Clyde.

She ran past Fairlie,[27] with its cliffs all clothed in oak and hazel copse, the passengers by this time being "michtily refreshed,"[28] as was the chairman of the curling Club at Coupar-Angus, after his fifteenth tumbler, threw sandwich bags and bottles overboard, and took to dancing on the deck. The elders gathered into knots, talked politics, religion, or with much slapping of red hands upon their knees, enjoyed indecent tales, after the fashion of the Puritan, who though his creed enjoins a modest life, yet places no embargo on the speech. So it is said an Irish man in Lent, meeting a friend who remarked that he was drunk, rejoined, "sure, God Almighty never set a fast upon the drink."

My philosophic friend and I watched the athletic sports, and when the lassies skirled as partners pinched them, or in the joy of life, which manifests itself in divers ways, and usually in some unseemly fashion when the two sexes meet, he wagged a moralising head, and free poured out his philosophy.

"Man Rabbie, ... ye'll hae Burns[29] ... Rabbie kenned his countrymen. A fine, free, fornicatin', pious folk we are. Man, Rabbie, kent us better than he kent himsel', I sometimes think. Aye, ou aye, ye anna mak' a saint o' Rabbie. Saints, ye ken, are weel enough in books, but sort o' weary bodies, they must hae been, the feck o' them. I didna tell ye though aboot the bit gerawnium. I hae it in the cabin, for fear they cattle micht sit doon on it; ye mind auld Walter Scott,[30] the time he pouched the glass George IV. drank oot o', and then fair dang it into flinders on the road hame? Kind o' weak o' Scott, pouchin' yon glass; a bonny carle, yon George, to touch folk for the King's evil ... But ou aye, the gerawnium, I mind it.

"Ye see a' my potentialities of growing rich werena just realised. I wrocht two year in Glesca, ane in Edinburgh, syne sax in Brig o' Wier,[31] while takin a bit flutter on the Stock Exchange, ettlin' to mak' their siller without honest toil. Na, na; I ken what ye're goin' to say – if I had won, I wouldna' hae misca'ed them. Pairfectly reasoned, sir; but then ye ken when a man loses, the chap that gets his siller is aye a rogue. Weel, weel, many's the time I wished masel back at Tobermory[32] in the bit boat, wi' the bonny wee-tanned lug, fishin', aye, fishin', like the Apostles. Weel, I ken why the Lord found his first followers amongst fishermen. Simple folk, ye see, and wi' the gamblin' element weel developed; on like yer hinds –

slave, slavin' at the ground – but oot upon the lake, yon sea of Galilee, ye mind; a sort o' loch, just like Loch Fyne, as I ae thocht. When ye sit in the boat, keepin her full and by, fechtin' the sea, your eye just glancin' on the wabes, it kind o' maks ye gleg to risk a wee. Nae fears we'll get another preacher like the Lord; but if we did, there wouldna be a fisherman, from Tobermory doun to the Cruives o' Cree[33] that wouldna follow him. I'se warrant them. Dour folk, the fishers, but venturesome; and a' the time I wrocht aboot thae stinkin' towns, I ettled to get back. I aye went aince a year to see our mither; she just stops aboot twa mile west of Tobermory, and I ay tak back one of they gerawniums in a pot. Why do I no stop there when I win back, ye say? Aye, there's the mystery of it, the sort o' tragedy as I was tellin' ye when we cam through the Kyles.

"Ye se ... Spot yon lassie wi' the sunset hair, and o' the lang backit, short-leggit West Highland kind, built like a kyloe,[34] just gars me think upon yon woman of Samaria[35] ... I'm haverin' ... Weel, the fack is I canna stop at hame. Tak' a West Hielan' stirk and put him in a park, doon aboot Falkirk, or in the Lothians, and maybe, at the first, he doesna thrive, misses the Heilan' grass mayby, and the gran' wind that blaws across the sea. Syne, he gets habeetuated, and if ye take him back to the north, maybe he couldna bide. That's just ma ain case sir.

"Weel do I mind tha auld braw days; a herrin' never tastes saw weel as just fresh caught and brandered in the boat. I mind yon seinin' too, sic splores we had, aye and a feck o' things come back to me when I am in the toon. The peat reek, and a' the comfortable clarty ways we had, the winter nights, when the wind blew fit to tak' aff the flauchter feals[36] o' the old cottage. I mind then o't a'. That is, I dinna care to mind.

And as we talked, the steamer slipped past Wemyss Bay, left the Cloch Lighthouse on the left hand, and passed by Inverkip, slid close by Gourock,[37] and then opened up the valley of the Clyde. Greenock with all its smoky chimneys rose in view, sending a haze of fog into the air. The timber in the bonds upon the shore surged to and fro against the railings as the steamer's swell lifted it slowly, and then settled down again to season in the mud. Dumbarton Rock showed dimly and the river narrowed, the fairway marks showing the channel like a green ribbon winding through mud banks, as the vessel drew towards the pier.

Gathering their packages and parcels, and smoothing out their clothes, the passengers passed down the gangway, laughing and pushing one another in their haste to get away.

The man with the geranium in the pot still lingered, looking back towards the sea. Then gathering up his traps, and tucking his umbrella underneath his arm, prepared to follow them.

"Good-bye," he said, "we hae had a pleasant cract,[38] I'll just be off and daunder up the toon. Doddered poor, and wee thing addicted to strong drink, strong drink, ye ken, speerits, that maketh glad the heart o' man, neither a fisher nor a townsman, a sort o' failure, as ye may say, I am. Good-bye, ye seem a sort o' eddicated man ... Na, na, I will na drop it, never fear. I brocht it a' the way from Tobermory, and ye ken, sir, Greenock is no' a guid place for gerawniums after all."

He stumbled out along the gangplank, his rusty "stan o'black" looking more storm-worn and ridiculous than ever in the evening sun. Holding his flower-pot in his hand wrapped round with newspaper, he passed out of my sight amongst the crowd, and left me wondering if the flower in the pot would live, and he return, and die in Tobermory, by the sea.

J. W. B., 'Men and Things' (1904)

"Lives iv gr-eat min all raymind us 'ow t' make our loife sublime."[1]

The above was quoted by Mr. Terence Malone for the benefit of his particular friend, Mr. Willam Mafeking[2] Gahr (corruption of the ancient name of Gower) in the bar parlour of the Imperial Arms, Edgware Road, W.

"Fill the pot up again," said Mr. Gahr, not much impressed by the sentiment, "an' not so much frorth on it. I'm a little deaf."

"I'd loike t' be a gr-reat man, Bill, and sit in parli-mint," signed Mr. Malone. "I wu'dn't alf squandher me intillic."

"I've niver tho't much abart it," said Mr. Malone, with a wave of his hand, "an' 'asy larn't. Ye take sides. Ye call wan side throo bloo, th' other ye call th' op'sishum. It's loike ring-a-ring-a rosis, only more so."

"I could play fer me nativ' place thin?" said Mr. Gahr.

"No," answered Mr. Malone. "ye-re not iligible, ye-re only a col'eaver. B'sides, ye-re too drunkin an' 'ave no ambi'shun. Ye will not adop' th' rushin' up sistim iv sharin' yer profits, or will ye take ye-re fodder in tablit for-rm in ye-re weskit pocit loike anny other 'orse. Ye ar-re also too foul-mouth'd an' immoral, an' yer conshance is only middlin'. Ye ar-re sivin tinths and a majority, besides bein' a pagan, an' altogether ye-re wan iv th' damdist divils out iv 'ell."

"Who told yer?" asked Mr. Gahr, getting interested.

"Oh, I 'ave it on thrust," said Mr. Malone. "Th' game is only as Shikspere says, f'r th' survival iv th' fit'ist."

"Who might they be?" asked Mr. Gahr, angrily.

"Count tin," said Mr. Malone, "'Ave ye rid th' diff'rinshul cal'kilis?" he continued.

"'Ows this game jined" asked Mr Gahr, irrelevantly

"I admire," said Mr. Malone, "yer Socrishun method iv ans'rin a question."

"It's this way," he continued, "I'm throo bloo. Ye thin lam out yer intrince fee which is rather 'igh, but th' dibs is well invistid. Ye-re thin sint to an' onin'abited islan' w'ere ye wait f'r a man with a bad charicther that wants t' jine. Manew'iles, ye-ve bo't up all th' tea an' wile rabbits ye can lay to, an' 'ave disthributid thim with discrishun among th' desarvin po-ore. Thin ye chalk rude things about ye-re inimy on ther-re frint dures. This counts ye wan. If ye kiss th' ba-abies that ye can't see f'r jam, that count f'r sivril. Ye must wear three shoots per deum an' two watch-chains to the op'sishun's ivery wan, or it gives ye-re convarts the impris'hun that ye'll niver be don at th' game. Th' 'ite iv yer collar too, counts no small beer.

"Thin ye rint th' local primrus' 'abiashun an' 'old phwat they call at 'omes.

"Imparial an 'igh thinkers, ye say, an' frinds iv impire, 'ere stan's before ye Tirrince Malone, th' wan an' only, discinded by 'asy stagis frim th' anthropide apies be Darwin. Not mad' in Jarminy, ye say, like som' wan that shall be namelis, ye say, that's 'oldin' an ad-ock an' ong-mas' 'ooligan ma-a-atin' in an ol' barn.

"Talk to us, says wan iv th' op'sishun, that crawl'd in undher th' curt'in, in lan'widge we can undherstan', 'e says. Hee-haw! ye say.

"Ye 'ave a dhrink w'ile they-re la'din' out th' corpse, an' thin ye conthinue.

"Frinds, ye say, lave us not be onparsh'l, ye say. Look phwat 'e did to that po-ore 'ooman out wist, an' vot strite, ye say. Vote f'r Malone aboo, th' bung'ole facther, 'oos mother is do or be done, an' 'oos crist is a rampin' an' a ro'rin' lion, with a cock-sidid coachman, ye say, in th' int'rists iv lab'er-r, an' lave us be onparsh'l.

"Phwat, ye say, if me two 'undrid aitch-p is a frinch damliar, ye say, 'ow about that sivint'in min'yun 'ooley bis'nis that me rispictid op'onint's mixed up with? I 'ave nothin' agin 'im, ye say, bak iv me 'an' an' the' sol' iv me f'ut to 'im. I rayspict me inimy, ye say, but dham 'is politics. I know nothin' iv 'is antecdints, ye say; 'is for'fath'rs wuz pirit's, ye say, an' this is th' mud that's indoocin' ye t' part ith yer invalu'be suffrage. Don' do it, yer say, with big tears wellin' up in yer eyes. F'r Gawd's sike be ker-e-ful, ye say, an' timp'rit'. 'Old ye-re umbirllas up before it rains ye say, an' take no 'arthquake pills.

"Then ye org'nise a torchli'te pricishun. Th' 'orses ar-re wrenched out iv yer bro'om an' th' toher 'orses rush ye to th' op'sishun barn, we're ye ind th' swaree be sittin' foire to th' roof. They return me," contunied Mr. Maline, "by a majority iv wan iv tea to two iv rabbits an iv'e jined."

"Grand"! exclaimed Mr. Gahr, carried away by the eloquence of his friend; "but 'twud be an ixpinsive game."

"Thrue f'r ye," answered Mr. Malone, "but 'twud be foine to see yer name in th' pa-apers. F'rinstance, in th' *Daily Mail* 'twud be: We larn with 'orror not unmixed with plis'ure, that Mr. T. Malone, em-p wuz sin ag'in all istablish'd pricedince to appear on th' terrace iv th' 'ouse in 'is shirt slaves accoompanid by Lady Ping-pong Bridge from Monkey Bankwit, Chicago, U.S.; this sh'ud mak' im fam'us, th' wither bein' 'ot.

"In th' *Times* 'twud be: Our-re distin'wished war and' spishul cor-r-espondint frim the front, simfores Chifoo t'morrer's date. Ther-re wuz a sacrit interview at Muck-din as this leaves print, vetwane Sir Tirrince Malone, Bart, Rose Beri-Beri, Nancy B, an' Jessie C. Parthy politics wuz avi'did on account iv th' gard'n parthy. Th' 'su'do igypshun wheat spiculat'r held th'dure with 'is pink chif'ong pary'sol up in case it rain'd and 'is pale pills in case iv arthquakes. Oth'r ministers iv th' gospel iv pace wuz prisint, an' an injoyible toime wuz spint, Jessie C. 'avin bro't th' bist dirdd'd doll. Gr-ate things is ixpicted besides three acres an' an ol' cow. Manny iv th' e-lités wuz the-re, clos'ly attended by vallys a-with skippin' ropes, and phwat wuz sid wuz not sid. We 'ear with sadisac'shun that Solimin is t'Sampsin as Tubil Cain it to 60 per cint. iv dhuty, an' thut we must alther th' sistim. Good luck attend th' baronet in is ardo'us unthertakin. The court adjorn'd after rin' drin' the nitional anthim. Were – the – is – that – Scotchman."

"I can't till ye any mor' now," said Mr. Malone, abruptly. "I dursn't till afther the' nixt election."

"Toime, gintilmin."

Anon., 'The "Smart Set"' (1905)

"I see be th' pa-aper," said Mr. Malone, "thet th' smaar-rt set ar-re f'r introjoocin' anither valyable rayform in th' matther iv weddin' prisints. Ye rush in ye-re costly, but invalyable, gifts, which ar-re thin thrun into some char'ty bizaar-re. 'Twill be a foin think f'r ye-re woife, Bill, f'r 'er t' wear a d'mon' necklice over 'er marble for'id 'cordin t' th' noo Parishun fashun, which –"

"Me woife's at 'ome," said Mr. Gahr, "'mendin' me socks. Wot's th' 'smart set'?"

"'Tis little ye know iv politics," answered Mr. Malone. "Any good pa-aper 'll tell ye. Ye 'ave only t' read with intilligence t' larn that they-re th' laders iv th' fash'nable wur-rld. Ther-re phwat they call th' crame della crame iv th' nashun."

"Ain't that a new drink?" asked Mr. Gahr.

"In art," continued Mr. Malone, with a look of withering contempt, "they-re all there; spishally in make-up. In litheraychoor they play an important par-rt, spishally in divorce cases. In th' soiencis they ar-re formust, spishally in th' three car-rd thrick. They-re extremely cliver at law; spishally at making laws an' phwat they call invaydin' thim. Altogether they-re a smar-rt lot, so th' pa-apers say; an' 'ave made the empoire phwat it is."

"Wot is it?" asked Mr. Gahr, like a practical, hard headed man.

"You'll foind it in any good dicshun'ry" said Mr. Malone, "under th' letthers R O T an' T E N. Lind me yer ears," he continued. "This'll give ye an idee iv phwat an impor-r-tint par-rt they 'old in th' 'istry iv th' nashun. Th' frownin walls," he began "iv th' Tower iv London gazed down on a bril'yunt but gorjus spicticle yesterday, whin Miss Flash Oil, th' Amerikin wan-poun'-a-minute 'airess, wuz join' in th' bonds iv wedlock with th' most 'on'rayble Capt'n Stoney Broke, expert ragger in th' classy –th. This 'oly bridal parthy wuz met at th' intrance be nine beefayters, 'oo made a foin ol' wur-rld picthure as they rushed in behind th' two dozin odd broidsmaids, in the'r soft but clingin' drap'ries in white creepy, an' bloo, rid' an white painted shefong. Th' broide wore a simple little thing in velvet, not wuth mor'n two 'underid odd, an' 'er 'eavy lace veil (wuth a princis ransim) wuz ram'd down over natcheral oringe blossoms. Th' bright sun shone be orther on th' moolyun'd windhers, makin' a halo roun' th' broid's bloomin' 'ead, an' lighin' up th' rid coats iv the Coldstrames 'oo contributed pathriotic airs. The cer'mony wuz 'eld at th' chapel iv St. Pather which wuz crowdid insoid an' out with celibrities, many bein' more or liss crushe'd t' dith in ther well-mint, but smart efforts t' offer up prayer f'r th' 'appy couple. Th' service wuz most brief, th' bridegroom wantin t' clear off sivral small dits before rushi' roun' t' empire.

"In th' bril'yunt an' gilded saloons, with a gran' view iv th' slums just 'andy, th' costly an' altogether lov'ly prisints wuz display'd.

"'Rush 'em in,' says th' blushin' broid. 'Nothin' undher goold an' di'mon's, I 'ope, or I'll 'ave it in the pa-apers,' she says. 'Rush 'em in!'

"We regret t' 'ave th' plisure t' announce that we can't give mor'n four columns t' th' names iv dhistin'wish'd guests, 'aving other bril'yunt things t' menshun."

"Ows that f'r smart?" asked Mr. Malone, looking up from the paper.

"Kinder sets yer breath," said Mr. Gahr. "Me an' my ol' woman got spliced on dinner 'our. Ther wuz no Beefeaters at our banquit, we 'ad tripe. We 'ad no prisints, but a man called t' see thet we'd still got th' furnitcher we 'ad on th' 'ire system. Th' rint wint up th' week after."

"Niver ye moind," said Mr. Malone, "ther's a good time comin' f'r ye. Ye must not only think impayrially, but gossip impayrially."

"So I do," said Mr. Gahr, "an' I've bin out of work this last two months. 'Ow do –"

"We wuz talkin' iv the smar-rt set," said Mr. Malone quickly, "ther's lots iv other int'restin' itims 'ere. For instance": –

"We regret to announce that yisterdah 'is most grashus majisty nearly thrip'd over 'is shadow. 'E wuz with th' 'onryble Acres Puglus whin t' ter'ble accident nearly 'appened. Wan physishun, wan surjun, wan p'liceman, wan private yacht, an' wan field batthery were immejutly in athindince. 'Is Majisty 'astens t' assure 'is sorrowin' subjects not t' 'ave fear. 'E will probably take a sea thrip som'where an' shoot rabbits. Mr. Walther W. Cantsmile 'as met with an 'orrid accident while playin' rackits in Buckin'am; snappin' wan iv th' important muscles iv 'is leg, about three an' three quarther inchis above th' ankle. 'Tis 'oped 'is injuries will not privint 'im frim showin' 'is wan leg at th' reassimblin' iv Parli'mit. Th' 'on'rayble Adolphus Paddin Shuffler an' th' little Shufflers have arrived.

"Th' 'op'in' iv Parli'mint in Feb'ry (be th' grace iv Gawd) will be a most bril'yunt funcshun, as all th' rile family will be prisint. 'Tis 'oped that th' peeresses, &c., will not mistake th' House iv Lords f'r a theayt'r 'as they did last time, an' not rush th' door.

"Let's 'ave another pint," interposed Mr.Gahr. "I'm dry. I wish I 'ad nothin' t' do but injoy myself," he continued.

"Ye don't know phwat yer-re askin' for," said Mr. Malone solemnly.

"Well, it's all right t' be rich, ain't it?" asked Mr. Gahr.

"'Tis better t' be comfortable thin to be rich," said Mr. Malone, "an' perhaps 'tis betther t' be rich thin 't be very poor, but 'tis betther t' be poor thin t' want t' be rich an' not be able to. I'll tell ye," continued Mr. Malone. "Th' smar-rt wans ar-re f'r-iver rushi' roun' seekin', as you might say, 'oo they kin devour, like so many little divils. They 'ave no pace f'r all ther money. They turn day into night, and night into 'ell. They spind yisterdsay in thinkin' phwat they'll do t'-day, an' t'-day in thinking phwat they'll do th' day afther. Ther wan intillicital pursoot is thinkin' phwat t' 'ave f'r dinner or p'raps phwat not t' 'ave. Ther fam'ly ties ar-re peculyar, not 'avin' any.

"F'rinstance, Lord Barming Hatch is now at 'ome. Th' 'ous'old is acquainted with th' fact be 'earing' is Lordship wipin' th' flure with 'is valy.

"''Ow dare ye bring me th' same pair iv trousers twice,' e says, 'ye cursed idjot, an' bring thim in with four creasis, ye filthy scum,' e says, 'f'r th' King wears thim like that now. Wad ye 'ave me disgrace soci'ty?' he says. 'Rush about, ye dirthy scoundrel, an' bring me a brandy an' sody f'r me breakfast, or I'll call ye names,' e says.

"In me lady's boodwar, things is ekally plisint an' peaceful. Wan iv th' maids is under th' bed findin' me lady's teeth, an wan's rushin' roun' findin me lady's 'air.

"'Is lordship's at 'ome,' says another wan.

"'Dh—!' says me lady 'that's twice in six months.

"'Bring me me dear Fido,' she says, 'an' orher th' kerrige t' take us in th' park.'

"On the stairs," continued Mr. Malone, "she meets th' governess with th' childer.

"''Oos ar-re these?' she say.

"'Yours, me lady,' says the governess.

"'Indade,' sauys me lady, ''ow intheresin'; let me see thim agin nixt year. Thank Gawd,' she says, 'ther's no doubt about their maternity anyway.'

"'We must burke this free maintenance thing, dear,' she says to a frind in th' park. ''Twud desthroy th' 'ome loife,' she says. 'Isn't Fido 'orribly jolly,' she says.

"'Yis,' says 'er frind, 'e's just too awf'ly swate f'r anything.'

"''Tis an awful bore, bein' 'ere,' says me lady, at the ball in th' av'ning. 'There's that Ferguson woman, niver 'ad a divorce,' she says. 'I wondher they let her in.'

"'We mustn't cut 'er, dear,' says 'er frind, 'she might be 'andy to borrow orf, but she's awfully putrid.'

"'We ar-re 'avin' a monkey bankuit,' says me lady t' th' r-right riv'rant Flapdoodle, 'will you make wan?'

"'Plisure,' says 'is riv'rance, 'awfully, beastly jolly. Be th' way,' e says, 'your Jack iv the Lancers wanted an' appointmint th' other day, but the War Office didn't think 'e 'ad 'ardly expayriance enough.'

"'Oh, didn't they,' says me lady, with a glitther in 'er glass eye, 'I'll see that 'e 'as it, or ther'l be trouble. We shall most prob'ly be Lib'rals nixt year,' she says, 'isn't it just too awfully funny. Be th' way, dear,' she says, ''oo shall we make Prime Minishter?'"

"I'm, goin' 'ome," said Mr. Gahr suddenly, "t' me wife."

"Good man," said Mr. Malone, "an' give 'er that shillin' she axed ye for, an' think yerself lucky ye ar-re phwat ye ar-re."

LABOUR LEADER

Hugo, 'The Blackleg, an Agitator's Yarn', *Labour Leader*, 2 March 1901, p. 66.

Anon., 'The Marchioness', *Labour Leader*, 29 March 1902, p. 102.

Frank Starr, 'The Doll Shop', *Labour Leader*, 15 August 1903, p. 262.

I. O. Ford, 'Aunt Caroline's Christmas Eve', *Labour Leader*, 23 December 1904, p. 449.

Fred Plant, 'Our Story. "The Far Land." (A Fragment of Fact.)', *Labour Leader*, 20 January 1905, p. 506.

J. Bruce Glasier, 'Andrew Carnegie's Ghost. A Red-Letter Day at Skibo Castle. A Christmas Story', *Labour Leader*, 21 December 1906, pp. 481–2.

The *Labour Leader* (1893–1987) continued as the official periodical of the ILP and the LRC, renamed the Labour Party in 1906. James Keir Hardie, along with most socialists, criticized the Second Boer War as being a capitalist-driven conflict, and the periodical supported the Boers over English aggression. Hardie's ownership and editorship was contested during this period, as the group wanted the paper to be held democratically and not controlled by Hardie alone. He ceded control of the *Labour Leader* to the group in January 1904, and John Bruce Glasier took over the editing of the paper in 1905. Under Glasier's editorship sales rose from 13,000 to 43,000, but the content was criticized for supporting the Labour Party's increasingly pragmatic attitude to politics and socialism and its close relationship with the Liberal Party.

There was a gradual decline in the inclusion of serial fiction in the *Labour Leader* during this period, but this is countered by a rise in the number of short stories. Of those authors selected for inclusion during Hardie's editorship, there are only biographical records for Isabella Ford. Neither Hugo nor the anonymous author has been identified; there are also no biographical records for Frank Starr, but he did publish 'An Unpremeditated Crime' in *Teddy Ashton's Northern Weekly* in 1902 (reprinted in this volume, pp. 391–5). Isabella Ormston Ford was born in Leeds to a solicitor and landowner. Her parents encouraged her to take an interest in the conditions of the workers, and she worked as a trade union organizer in Leeds between 1888 and 1890. She was a founder member of the Leeds Independent Labour Party, was an executive committee member of the Women's Trade Union League, and was elected to the national administrative council of the ILP. Her socialism encompassed both class and gender, and she was a member of the executive committee of the National Union of Women's Suffrage Societies between 1907 and 1915, from which she resigned during the First World War to work for peace.[1]

The fiction published under Glasier's editorship included the story by Fred Plant, whose brief biographical details can be found in the headnote for *Teddy Ashton's Journal/Northern Weekly and Teddy Ashton's Journal* in Volume 2, pp. 227–8, and the story by Glasier himself, whose biographical details are given in the headnote for the *Clarion* in Volume 2, p. 228.

Notes
1. For more information, see J. Hannam, *Isabella Ford, 1855–1924* (London: Basil Blackwell, 1989).

Hugo, 'The Blackleg, an Agitator's Yarn' (1901)

Your agitator often makes good company. When he has got past the prosy stage, when he has found out that Society – his favourite abstraction – does not tremble at his bellow, and has achieved his little personal realization of man's place in nature, he becomes a delightful companion. He is not very bookish, but he has been among the stuff that poems are made of; he has read some queer pages in the script of humanity, and he is a living elucidation of the dark saying that the children of men are wiser in their generation than the children of light. I may be indulging the loose practice of describing the type from the individual, but, at all events, my friend Vance, who is secretary of a fighting trade union, answers to the outline. He is always welcome to bed, board, and fellowship when the fluctuating front of labour's battle brings him near my domestic clearing.

In the back-end of the year a dangerous-looking dispute brought him to a northern seaport. Three or four successive paragraphs in the daily papers informed me that mediation had averted war, so on the day after the settlement I was not surprised to see him push open my garden gate.

Late in the evening we sat by a red fire and smoked. He was candidly complacent at having settled the quarrel without a strike.

"Ah," said I, "then you wouldn't get the famous blackleg[1] peroration worked in?"

I should explain that in the prime days of Vance's missionary career as a hot-gospeller[2] of the new unionism[3] he made no scruple about using the "hangman's whip"[4] style of oratory. His presence at a strike was appreciated because, among other things, he could put the fear of hell on blacklegs.

He glanced at me and then at the fire.

"I've had new light on the subject of blacklegs," he said.

"New light? – out with it," I answered.

He sucked at his pipe meditatively for a minute or two, resting his eyes on the back of the fireplace.

"A winter or two, you remember – No, it begins earlier than that. A couple of years ago I spent six months in the C— district organizing. My greatest friend there, both in public and in private life, was James Hall, a steelworker. He was a genuine sort of chap with a parcel of good brains under his very rough pow.[5] He became a very active forward, and as I knew he had staying power, I considered that the cause had a good anchor in Jim. One solid man, I have often noticed, will do more to keep a branch together than a hundred and fifty weathercocks. I left C—, and as time went on Jim slipped more and more from my thoughts.

"Last winter, you recollect, I was at D— in connection with the dock strike. The men had been out nine weeks when I went down, and as the screw began to tighten the leaders got desperately afraid of a breakaway. My remarks on blacklegging, consequently were pointed. I addressed a big mass meeting in the evening in Wharf Street, and though I was fagged to death I managed to get some brimstone worked into the peroration. After that I went along to the Docker's Hall, and talked over the situation. You know what exhilarating places these branch halls are? Huh! After eleven I made weary tracks for my digs. At the end of a shed I met one of the picket parties stamping their feet and cursing the nobs. I exchanged a word or two with them, and learned that some half-dozen men had started to unload the "Golden Horn." It would take them a night or two, I said, and the picket talked of drowning the first scab they laid hands on. I had no more sense than to laugh at theat. It was a miserable night, I remember. A lot of rain had fallen, and the streets glimmered drearily under the gaslamps. I trudged along on the side of Wharf Street, where there is no pavement, too lazy to dodge the puddles, and in that mental state when one's thoughts are a sort of nightmare.

At the far end of the shed there was a break for a cross-river ferry, and a big, three-jet lamp flared out from the opening. As I stepped into the light I was surprised to see a man turn and look sharply at me. Now, there's little in a look, I don't mind being stared at. But I shouldn't like to interrupt a murderer, and get the glare that would flash over his shoulder. That's pretty much what the man's look suggested to me – someone caught red-handed. 'A blackleg,' I thought, and I stepped towards him. I believed I was just opening my mouth to speak when I recognized him, and whatever I was going to say vanished from my mind.

"'Good heavens – James Hall! Are you nobbing?'

"'No,' he said, with a snarl in his voice; 'I'm not nobbing, but I'm going to, and I don't care who knows it.'

"'What's wrong, man,' I said, '*you* haven't gone back on your principles?'

"'Principles be damned!' he replied; 'my principles are all right. My practice is a little off-side, that's all. Nothing uncommon. They do it over there every Sunday.' He jerked his thumb in the direction of St. Peter's steeple.

"You are not to think that this fury was Jim Hall's normal style. He was the soul of courtesy in his heavy way when I knew him before. I didn't see very well what it was, but I knew there must be something very far wrong when Jim tried to bounce it out that way.

"'Why, Jim,' I said, very mildly, 'you and I were friends the last time we met. What's the reason of all this?'

"'Reason? Oh! I've got reasons – good, logical reasons. Would you like to know them? Come along.'

"He took me by the arm, and led me along the quayside to an open shed where a load of Norwegian timber was piled. It was as dark as a wolf's throat. We went round to the back of the pile. Then I saw his 'reasons.' His wife was sitting on a log with her elbows on her knees and her face in her hands. About a yard from her feet was a little black huddle of rags, which, by the sound of breathing, I guessed to be the children. I'm fairly tough, Hugo, but I went rather tight about the chest when I saw her. I have seen hell's despair on a woman's face twice. That was one of the times.

"'Mary,' said Jim, 'here's an old friend of ours – Ned Vance – you remember? – the Socialist.'

"'I'm not likely to forget,' she answered in a general way, and then to me direct she said, 'This is Socialism.'

"'I don't think so,' said I.

"'It's our share of it,' she answered. 'You're at the other end of the stick. You haven't paid so dear for your spouting.'

"'Wants to know why I am going to blackleg,' said Hall, striking in sullenly.

"'If you'd spouted less,' she answered, 'and held your tongue like other men, you wouldn't have got the sack out of Eagles', and we mightn't have been starving tonight.'

"'Were you victimized?' I asked, afraid of provoking anything like recrimination between the two.

"Jim nodded. 'Fired out for being a Labour candidate and leading the agitation against overtime.'

"'Did the Society do nothing?'

"'Society went to the dogs after the lock-out. And old Eagles passed round the word so that I couldn't get a start anywhere. We've come from bad to worse. Oh! we're in luck to-night. Last night we hadn't even a shelter.'

"I hadn't a word to throw at a dog.

"'That's why I'm going to blackleg,' continued Jim. "Oh! I heard your speech to-night, but you can't answer these arguments' – with a wave of his hand towards the ragged miseries on the ground.

"'By heaven, they'll have to be answered some day," I said. 'If I were in your place, I'd be at worse than blacklegging.'

"I got practical after that.

"'You won't blackleg to-night, anyhow,' I said. 'Waken the youngsters, Mrs. Hall, and come along with me and get something to eat. Then we'll see about a night's lodging.'

"Jim was leaning on the timber looking at me.

"'You are very good, Vance,' he said, 'and I'm obliged to you for the sake of Mary and the kids. But I'm going to work. I'll have to work or go mad.'

"'Work! You're not fit. It will kill you.'

"'No fear of it killing me,' he said with a laugh – 'not that it much matters.'

"'Look here, Jim,' I said, 'you'll have none of that blood money to-night. Mine is cleaner. Come.'

"In truth he didn't need much coaxing. The upshot was that they got a meal – it was warm at any rate – and I got them housed in a sort of better-class 'model'[6] for the night.

"I did not sleep very early that night. In the morning I awoke thinking of Jim Hall and his wife, and I got up in a hurry, but before I was dressed the branch secretary called.

"'We've a letter from the masters,' he said. 'They offer to meet us to-day. It's practically a surrender. We'll be working to-morrow.'

"'Thank God!' I said, and I tell you I never in my life put through that form of prayer so heartily.

"You won't wonder now, I dare say, that my opinions on blacklegging have been modified."

"Is that all?" I asked. "You've left them in the 'better-class model,' you know. I want to know what came after."

"Oh, ay! Well, there was no more tragedy. Jim got a job the following day. He joined the union, and I made a few friends for him before I left. He's in the North of England now, in his old line, but he does his agitation quietly."

Anon., 'The Marchioness' (1902)

It was in Normandy, during the shooting season. I had had a long morning's sport, and noon found me, footsore and weary, in the vicinity of an old mill, somewhere between Mortgane and Condé-sur-l'Huisne. It was a comfortable-looking place, and I determined to solicit the owner's hospitality.

The miller received me very courteously, and I was soon stretching my legs under the table and partaking of the most exquisite *déjeûner*[1] that was ever placed before a hungry sportsman. There were trout from the mill-stream, and partridges from the neighbouring moor, cooked to a turn, and accompanied by some really excellent wine, not the *petit vin*[2] of Normandy, but good mellow Bordeaux. This somewhat surprised me, but when at dessert the miller invited me to visit his gallery of family portraits, I was perfectly bewildered.

"What," said I to myself, "a picture gallery in a mill!"

Of course I accepted his invitation, and found that the pictures really existed, and were fine ones, too. There were a dozen of them, representing Louis XIV. courtiers and marquises, and marchionesses of the times of Louis XV. and Louis XVI., the series being closed by a buxom-looking farmer's wife in a white sun-bonnet, next to a delicious little Marchioness.

Stopping before the latter two portraits, the miller said:

"These are mother and daughter."

He appeared to be amused at my surprised expression, and continued:

"Yes, sir, this countrywoman is my mother, and that pretty little Marchioness smiling there is my grandmother. It is a strange story. Everybody round about knows it, and I may as well tell it to you.

"As you have probably surmised from the age of these portraits, the scene is laid during the Terror.[3] The father, mother, and elder sister of yon little Marchioness were arrested, and soon afterwards judged and executed. The little Marchioness, my grandmother, sir, found safety only in flight. The poor orphan took refuge with one of the farmers on the family estate, whom she knew she could trust. This farmer was a young man – he was only about thirty years of age. He had known the Marchioness from her babyhood, and was devoted attached to her. In fact, to be frank with you, sir, in his heart of hearts he loved her.

"He was greatly troubled by the perilous position in which her presence placed him, but he could not turn the poor child away to be massacred by the savage revolutionists. He hid her in the cellar, and the mob vainly scoured the whole country in search of her. But a neighbour, a ferocious Jacobin,[4] had marked the farmer's trouble, and, suspecting the reason for it, denounced him to the Revolutionary Committee.

"In a few minutes the house was surrounded by a horrible mob, howling for the death of the hated aristocrat. They battered in the front door, and poured into the place. Ah! Sir, it was a terrible moment."

Here the miller paused and mopped his brow, while his eyes glistened with excitement.

"The first room was empty," he went on. "They smashed everything in it they could lay hands upon, and were about to break open the door of the next room, when it suddenly opened, and the Marchioness stood before them, beside the farmer, who was half dead with anguish and terror.

"For an instant the mob stopped short. But it was only for an instant. Shrieks of 'Down with the aristocrat! Kill her! Away with her! Burn her! Tear her to pieces!' arose, and the bloodthirsty brutes were about to rush forward, when the little Marchioness was suddenly struck by an inspiration. Ah! sir, it must have come from on high. She made signs to them that she wished to speak.

"'Citizens,' she began.

"Unaccustomed to hearing such an appellation from the mouth of a dainty aristocrat, the mob stopped. She profited by the pause, and continued:

"'Citizens, what do you want with me? Why are you incensed against me? What have I done to you? I am one of you – I am your sister!'

"Murmurs of approval and of protest were heard, but in the main the mob appeared to be astonished and suspicious.

"'She's fooling us, the aristocrat,' shrieked a woman, who, with her disheveled hair, flushed face, and crooked fingers, ready to claw the delicate girl's eyes out, looked like one of the Furies[5] let loose.

"'No, no,' exclaimed the Marchioness earnestly. 'I swear to you that I am no longer an aristocrat, but a woman of the people. In proof of it, here is my future husband,' and she pointed to the farmer, who, too overcome to utter a word, would have bent his knee before the brave young girl, but she prevented him.

"Her remarkable presence of mind was their salvation. The fact that she was willing to marry a simple citizen caused a complete revulsion of feeling, and the wretches who a moment before had been lusting for her blood now applauded her.

"'We must be married under the Tree of Liberty,'[6] she added, 'and, citizens, we invite you all to the wedding.'

"Another burst of applause followed this invitation. Friendly hands seized the little Marchioness and the farmer, and they were straightway shouldered to the Tree of Liberty, escorted by the cheering mob, waving their pikes and scythes.

"The marriage took place, and the crowd, joining hands, danced the Carmagnole[7] frantically around the newly-made husband and wife, and the festivities, with eating and drinking, were kept up till night-fall, when those of the revelers who were not too intoxicated escorted the couple back to the farm.

"As soon as they were alone the assumed familiarity of the farmer immediately vanished. Doffing his hat, he bent respectfully before the Marchioness, and with tears of gratitude in his eyes, exclaimed:

"'Mademoiselle, I thank you from the bottom of my heart. Your sacrifice was our salvation. I beg you to pardon the liberties the critical position in which we were placed compelled me to take. It is, of course, my duty to render you your liberty, and I do so.'

"'Sacrifice! Liberty!' said the Marchioness, 'but I am free, and I have made no sacrifice. Don't you, then, understand that I love you?'

"And thus it was, concluded the miller, that the little Marchioness became a poor farmer's wife, and the grandmother of an honest Norman miller."

Frank Starr, 'The Doll Shop' (1903)

The Boy-child badly wanted a doll, a Man-doll, and the kind Earth Mother, who seldom refuses her children's earnest requests, took his hand and led him to the great World Arcade. Here were toys innumerable, miniature Yeomanry, tiny Venezuelan gunboats, and almost as tiny British and German battleships – everything that a Statesman-child could desire. But the Boy-child wanted a Man-doll, other toys he would not. And so they passed on to the Civilisation Depot of Messrs. Soci, Ology and Co. This, of course was not the only civilisation. All the shopkeepers had Savage and Civilisation Departments, and some few even added Civil branches. At the firm of Diplomacy (Limited), for instance, you purchase your Maxim-gun solution at the Barbaric counter; the Civilisation Store supplied you with the new Christmas Ultimatum Game; while, in the section devoted to civil toys, Penruddocke Enigmas, Penrhyn Anachronisms (or Out-of-date Tyrannies),[1] Trade Union Legislative Anomalies, and a host of other curious puzzles were obtainable.

But Messrs. Soci, Ology ad Co. dealt only in dolls and their belongings, and here it was that the Boy-child stood open-mouthed at the hundreds upon hundreds of different species.

"A nice Man-doll, Ma'am? Certainly. We have all sorts and conditions of Man-dolls. Here is one we call the Proletaire. Rather a cheap article. Spoilt in the making, in my opinion, Ma'am. You see the material's good, but there's not sufficient padding. Indeed, they do tell me a very inferior class of sawdust is used, and, as I said before, not nearly enough of that."

"Talk? Well, you can hardly call it talking, Ma'am. It makes a kind of inarticulate gurgle when pressed very hard. The principal thing I can say in its favour is that it stands a lot of knocking about. Possibly because it has little beauty to lose. But it really is a fact, this common, cheap, half-filled doll with sometimes last out two of the higher priced ones."

"The little boy doesn't like it in those clothes? Oh, but it has many different suits. The one it is now wearing we call the West Ham or Picturesque Rags suit. Then we have the Hodge or Distressed Labourer costume; the Tommy Atkins and Returned Reservist uniforms; the Police or Civil Protector livery, the Jack

Tar, the Lifeboatman, and a hundred other suits.² In fact, the peculiarity of this doll is, Ma'am, that he'll fit almost anything. Why we have one or two specimens arrayed in the M.P. or Representative Legislation dress, and very well they look, but somehow the public doesn't take kindly to them yet."

"Like to look at something more expensive? Here, you see, is a more stylish article altogether. This we call the Middle-class Doll. I can honestly recommend it as a good all-round serviceable doll. Last the little boy a generation or two. It's coming more into fashion every day. Indeed, it is rumoured that entire districts produce nothing else than this kind of goods."

"Oh, certainly, Ma'am, the price is a good bit higher. You see, there's a lot more work put into them. You'll notice the trunks are much more tightly packed, the limbs more shapely, and I have heard that some of the heads take years to make."

"Many suits of clothes? Yes, but not so many as the Proletaire Doll. We never send out what we call 'dangerous suits' with this class, that is, the mining dress, platelayer's uniform, and many others that you saw in the first section. Here, you see, are a number in the M.P. dress – the public takes to it better in this style of doll; others in journalistic and medical attire, while some are even in Navel and Military uniforms."

"Oh, yes, Ma'am, they're all good working dresses, but we put a little better quality into them, a little more gold braid than in the cheaper brands."

"Now, step this way, please. We have a very superior kind in the Gilded Chamber, which I should like to show you."

"All dressed alike? Yes, Ma'am, that's what we call the Hereditary Legislator uniform, and, I'm sorry to say, not very serviceable at that."

"Well, they have other clothes, but we supply very few what you might call hard-wearing suits with this style of doll."

"Very expensive? Yes, indeed, Ma'am, and yet I don't know why, unless it is that the majority are turned out at the old 'Varsity factories. I believe that they employ a lot of obsolete machinery there. Used to produce a first-rate article a few centuries back, and even now they do occasionally send out a tip-topper. But not often. However, it is said, there's a likelihood of some change in the firm shortly, and then we may be able to show you something really first-class."

"The little boy doesn't like any of them? Wants a mixture of Proletaire and Aristocrat doll? Very sorry we can't supply it, Ma'am. We have tried one or two as an experiment. There were the Charles Kingsley, the William Morris, and the John Ruskin³ styles. But they didn't catch on at the time, and were withdrawn. Still, people are beginning to ask for them. Perhaps you'd look round again in a couple of centuries. Thank you. Good morning, Ma'am."

I. O. Ford, 'Aunt Caroline's Christmas Eve' (1904)

The Sunday train was dawdling along the Colne Valley[1] in the reluctant, depressed fashion peculiar to Sunday morning trains, only more so, making me at last wonder if we should ever arrive at all. The number of huge milk cans alternately packed in to the van at one station and dragged out at the next, had increased so much that the guard, and most of us, were becoming profane in our exasperation. To my relief, at the end of the first hour, there got into my carriage two pleasant-faced women dressed in black.

To talk with your fellow-passengers, and especially on a Sunday morning, is never difficult – of course, my knowledge only extends to third-class passengers[2] – and if you have egg sandwiches to share with them you can unlock any heart, however reserved – or, at least, any female heart. Besides, it was close upon Christmas day, when everybody feels a kind of kinship with the rest of the world stirring within them, mostly founded upon the sadness underlying all anniversaries.

"And where be you going to, Missus?" one of my companions asked me as we shared my sandwiches; but, without waiting for an answer, she began telling me the destination of herself and her friend.

"We shall get out at Stalybridge,[3] you see –"

"When we get there," I put in.

"Ay," she went on, "and the train's a bit late now. However, they won't let us in before three, so we don't mind sitting here, these foot-warmers[4] is nice and comfortin'; and these sandwiches is nice, Mary – if eggs wasn't so dear I'd give 'em to Joe sometimes to take for his dinner, he's nobbut weak in his stomach, and meat, he says, seems to sit heavy – he's fondest of a good suet dumpling. But as I was sayin', they won't let us in afore three. It's t' hospital as we're going to, to see Tom, her brother," pointing to Mary, "and my nephew."

Mary drew herself up with a look of pride. "Yes," she said, "Tom's my brother, and good 'un too – and now 'e's gone and lost both his legs."

"Lost both his legs!" I exclaimed.

"Yes, both," said the aunt in a proud and dignified tone.

"'E's a wonderful lad. And 'e's livin' yet; most folks would ha' died when they was took off, but Tom 'e didn't, and 'e's that small to look at as you'd wonder at it more if you saw him. But it's not your big men as has all the go in them!

"It was in this way as it happened. Last Monday night as he wur puttin' on his working clothes getting ready for his journey up north – he's a stoker on an engine – he said to Jennie, that's his wife, 'now Jennie, mind as thou art a good lass while's I'm away, for someways I can't say when I'll be back this time, there's summat strange sitting heavy on my mind, and I can't say what it is, it's summat as I can't make out'; his mother was from Scotland, you see, where they believe in a deal of queer things as you can't see nor explain to other folk, and I'm a bit that way myself, too. But Jennie, she tossed her head and said naught; Mary was there, you see, and telled me all about it. Jennie's one o' them pretty, simpering lasses as men thinks so much of, for she can make the biggest fool think as 'e's wise by the way she just looks at him, and she'll do aught as a man tells her – I've no patience wi' such ways myself, but Tom, 'e's that fond of her as you never did see, 'e thinks all t' world of her. But, then, as I say to Joe, Tom's one o' them as 'ud love aught, and the more folks need helpin' and lovin' to keep them on their feet like, the more Tom cares for 'em. Joe says it's not that at all; it's just because of her way of lookin' and smilin', as Tom sets so much store by her – but, then, as my mother always said, men's that fond o' running each other down to a woman that you can't hardly believe aught they say about each other.

"So off he went," she continued after a minute's pause to eat another sandwich, "and Jennie never so much as looked after him down t' street. Well, I don't rightly understand about engines and such like, my Joe's a carpenter, but while Tom were stoking t' engine that night, he says he heard a voice calling him, and he seemed to know as summat were wrong somewhere wi' t' engine. The driver he heard naught, but 'e's one o' those as niver hears nor sees aught but just what they're doin'. Well, so off Tom must needs go round t' engine to see what was up – nay, it's no use asking me how he did it, only I know as t' driver said as how Tom saved t' train and t' lives o' them in it that night, but as he stepped up on to his place again, something made him stumble, and 'e fell right down and t' wheels went over his legs. 'E was still conscious when they picked him up, but 'e said as 'e hadn't suffered so much, 'e were that comforted by thinkin' o' that voice as had telled him what to do."

"And Jennie?" I asked.

"She's near heart broke, they say, and sits by his bedside gazing at him wi' them big eyes o' hers, and never says a word, poor lass."

"Here's our station, Aunt Caroline, and we're late, so be quick," said Mary, as we drew up at Stalybridge. We had only time to wave our adieus as they hurried to their train.

The following Sunday I was again travelling that same way. Christmas was over, and I was wondering what had happened in the meanwhile to Tom and my travelling companions of last week, when at the same station I saw Aunt Caroline – she hurried to my carriage and got in.

"I'm right glad to see you again, Missus," she said, "for I know as you was interested in Tom, and I want to tell you as he's dead – 'e died on Christmas Eve" – her eyes filled with tears – "and the world seems a lot poorer now 'e's gone – one misses them lovin' ones most. I was there, wi' him and Jennie when 'e died. His mind were clearer that night, and 'e seemed nearly clear o' pain, and we was both feelin' right set up about him, and Jennie, she says to him as she'd never carry on like, never no more, and how she'd be such a good wife to him as never was, and she smiled at him as only Jennie can smile."

"Tom, 'e looks at her, and 'Jennie,' says he, 'it make no manner o' difference to me what yer does, you're Jennie to me, and that means all I want in this world or the next'; and his face was something beautiful to look at, 'and never thou fret, lass, if thou finds th' new leaf thou talks of turning, too hard to do. I often thinks as it's the trying to turn those leaves as is all we can do in this life, and if we try, honest like, God hisself 'ull turn 'em for us at the finish. He's turning mine now, and I'm leaving thee, Jennie lass, but I shall be waiting for thee when thou comes, and whatever thou's done, never fear.'

"He kind o' dozed a bit, and then in a few minutes 'e wur gone."

We sat silently in the carriage, and Aunt Caroline's face was wet with tears.

"It was the beautifulest Christmas Eve as ever I remember," she said, "even though we'd lost him, for there was company sitting round that lad's bed as you couldn't see, and as I've never felt before, and never shall, till my time comes too."

"Jennie, she neither eats nor sleeps, and she sits watching, watching, wi' them big eyes o' hers. I'm going to fetch her home when we've buried him tomorrow."

We said no more, for the train drew up at my station, and I have never seen Aunt Caroline again.

Fred Plant, 'Our Story. "The Far Land." (A Fragment of Fact.)' (1905)

Mr. Samuel Stockson, cotton waste dealer by profession and a staunch believer in the social and economic tenets bequeathed to him by his father (who had "risen" from "little piecer"[1] in a cotton mill to the mayoral chair of the borough), felt on exceedingly good terms with himself and the world – his world – that chill December night, as he sat before his study fire at home, with a partially-consumed cigar between his lips and a glass of straw-coloured something warm at his elbow.

An hour had passed since Mrs. Stockson brought in the three-year-old prattler – their only child – to receive the father's good-night kiss; and now the house was silent.

Stockson mused pleasantly on his banking account, his profitable investments, his child, and he felt good. Strangely enough his wife remained outside the circle of his thought. Two years of courtship and four years of married life found the frail, dark-eyed woman occupying a place in her husband's estimation somewhere between the cook and the cashier at the warehouse.

The waste dealer was chuckling softly to himself, with his glass of grog half way to his lips, when the door opened and his wife appeared.

Stockson wrinkled his brows.

"Well?" he asked.

"I'm going to bed," came the answer; "good-night; that is all."

"Huh! Good-night." Then, looking at her over his shoulder: "What's the matter? Why bed so soon?"

"My back has been very bad to-day."

"H'm, your back to-day, your head yesterday. All right."

As he raised his glass once more the sound of a sob reached him; then the door closed; he was alone.

"Bah! Sniveling again, of course," he muttered; "this thing's getting unbearable. I'll take a turn as far as the club. My night's spoiled."

Flinging himself out of the room, he snatched a tweed cap from the hallstand, put on an overcoat, and was soon striding down the winding roadway into the town.

* * *

It was past eleven o'clock when Stockson left his club to return home, and the public houses had cast forth their friends.

At the corner of the main street a blowsy specimen of womanhood lurched against the waste dealer, and spoke to him.

"Get out, you beast," he said, and walked on. The woman steadied herself, laughed raucously, and shouted after him: –

"It wasn't that once, you –"

Two children, a girl and a boy, shivered along, hand-in-hand, the girl whimpering. On the opposite side of the street a couple of young fellows, arm in arm, wailed piteously:

> "Shall I ever see that dear old home agine?
>   You can see the roses climbing,
>   You can hear the sweet bells chiming.
> How I long to see that dear old home agine!"[2]

Stockson paused.

One word in the refrain lingered with him, the word "cottage." His father had been born in a slum cottage, not far distant from the spot where he was then standing. Its locality had been described to him, but he had never seen it. He would see it to-night! Turning on his heel, he negotiated several corners and came to an alley, at the mouth of which hung a street lamp.

Under the lamp, leaning against it, was a woman. She stood motionless, gazing, so it seemed to Stockson, at the blank wall opposite.

"Is this Bowker's Court?" he asked of her.

"Yes, sir."

"Which is number 4?"

"Second on the right. Why?"

"That's my business. What's yours?"

She laughed, and the sound made him shudder.

"Ah, you are one of them," he said. "I might have known it; but I must say your looks –"

He stopped short and drew his nether lip between his teeth. The woman bore a strong resemblance to his own wife.

"I am not one of them!" she said in a whisper. "I would put them all in a field and set fire to them; but I am at the far end. ... Give me money and I don't care. God forgive me!"

"You are clever," said Stockson, sarcastically, "but your cleverness is wasted. I am not here seeking your sort. I only came to have a look at that house there, Number 4. Here's a copper for you."

She clutched the coins in her hand.

"I beg your pardon, and I thank you, sir; but I only said God's truth. I live at Number 4.

"Indeed! Married?"

"Yes."

"H'm; waiting for your husband, I suppose?"

"No, my husband is at home, in bed; he is ill; dying, so they say. This is why I am here. I tried to go into the street, but I went sick. Then you came."

Stockson wiped his forehead with the back of his hand.

"You are telling me the truth? You left your husband to walk the streets for his sake?"

"But he doesn't know," she replied from behind her hands.

"What is your husband's name?"

"Robinson, James Robinson."

"What trade?"

"No trade; he worked for Stockson's, the waste dealers, until he had to give up. He was late one morning at work; he'd had a bad night, been pumping blood, and was as weak as a kitten. But it didn't matter to his master, Stockson. If it had been the old man, the mayor that used to be – they say he was born in the house where my lad is dying – things would have been different; Ned says they would. I hope young Stockson will die like –"

"Hush," said the man, gripping her by the shoulder. "Lead the way. By God! if your story's true, I –"

He pulled his cap over his eyes and followed her.

She opened the door of the cottage in which his father had drawn his first breath; and he followed her.

In one corner of the room stood an old truckle bed; on it the living skeleton of a man, whose arm encircled a baby girl, aged about three years. The sufferer turned at the creak of the door.

"Where've you been, Nell?" he asked. "I wanted you; I've had a bout. Who's that – the parson?"

Stockson averted his face, plunged his hand into his pocket, brought it forth again laden with gold, silver, and copper, threw the coins on the bed, and departed, without speaking a word.

* * *

Half an hour later the waste dealer entered his home, divested himself of his outer clothing, and ascended to his wife's sleeping apartment.

Her bed was empty.

He passed through the chamber beyond, and saw her knelt by the cot of their little one. She was asleep; her hand was lying against the child's cheek.

"Constance," he whispered.

She did not move.

He turned her face gently to the light, and saw her swollen eyes, the traces of tears on her cheeks.

"Constance!" he said, sinking down by her side.

She awoke with a start. He drew her towards him, and wept on her bosom.

J. Bruce Glasier, 'Andrew Carnegie's Ghost. A Red-Letter Day at Skibo Castle. A Christmas Story' (1906)

> The following account is derived from a source which I cannot divulge, nor can I vouch for the circumstantial accuracy of the story.   J. B. G.

It was Christmas Eve, and Andrew Carnegie[1] was entertaining a house party at his Scottish seat, Skibo Castle, on the Bornoch Firth. His guests were chiefly well-known literary men and Radical politicians. They included Mr. John Morley, Sir Henry Fowler, the American Ambassador, Mr. Samuel Storey, Mr. W. T. Stead, Mr. J. M. Barrie,[2] a Doctor of Divinity, and several Scottish professors.

It was a red-letter night. The ladies had retired, and although not a smoker himself, the host had announced that everyone who wished might smoke with might and main. Andrew himself was in great form, over flowing with brotherly enthusiasm. He insisted that the occasion should be celebrated in real democratic style, and that everyone must either sing a song, tell a story, or give a speech, the forfeit being that the delinquent should stand on his head and name the Kings of Scotland since the Battle of Bannockburn.[3] By way of good example he had done all the first three himself. His favourite song, "Oh, why left I my hame; why did I cross the deep?" he sang with great emotion, striking forth his hands in invocation when he came to the words –

> "And the sun of Freedom shines
> In my ain countrie."[4]

and tears stood in his eyes.

The American Ambassador slily suggested that Andrew had no reason to regret having "left his hame" and having "crossed the deep'; but Andrew protested energetically that but for the hope of doing good with his wealth he would rather a thousand times be a shepherd on the Highland moors than a Pittsburg millionaire, "As I have said in one of my books,"[5] he added, "which, perhaps, you may have read, but for the plays of Shakespeare and the music of Wagner, all my wealth would be as dust and ashes to me."

"Bravo!" cried Samuel Storey, with disturbing emphasis, taking the opportunity of refilling his glass at the same time.

The Doctor of Divinity proved himself a very well-spring of humorous melody. He sang the 'Barrin' o' the door, O!"[6] with topical allusions to women's suffrage, which set the table in a roar – even Mr. Stead laughed, though evidently with reservation.[7] Mr. Barrie told a little story, which he said, he hoped to expand into a book, and afterwards have it dramatised.[8]

John Morley begged to be let off with a speech; but the company yelled the suggestion down opprobriously. So with a shy schoolboy smile and a nervous cough, he said he would try to sing a negro ditty which Mr. Gladstone was extraordinarily fond of; once, indeed, when travelling with him to Edinburgh in the train, Mr. Gladstone sang it over and over again, beating time with his hands and feet, until some ladies in the next compartment complained to the guard of the disturbance. The song, said John, was "Campdown Races".[9] He stipulated they should all join in the chorus.

John started the tune too high, and had twice to begin again; but he was all right when he got to the chorus. The company joined in as one man, and Skibo hall resounded with

> Gwine to run all night!
> Gwine to run all day!
> I'll bet my money on de bob-tail nag,
> Somebody bet on de bay!

"I was always a great admirer of Gladstone," Andrew observed when the chorus had been sung for the tenth time. "He wanted me to stand for Parliament; but I would have had to take the oath of allegiance to the Queen, and you know I am a Republican."

A smile twinkled among the guests, and John Morley and Sam Storey looked a bit uncomfortable.

Mr. Stead's turn came last. He positively declared that he could not sing a song. He had never, he said, sung anything but hymns, and he doubted if a hymn would be suitable for such an occasion. But he would tell a ghost story. It was one, he said, which he had heard from Madame Blavatsky,[10] and he related it to the late Czar of Russia,[11] upon whom it made such a deep impression that but for the fact that he (Mr. Stead) and the Empress had, in the interests of Russian popular freedom, pleaded with the Czar on their knees for nearly three hours, he would have resigned his throne the next day.

The story dealt with the case of a murderer and an Indian priest, who agreed to exchange souls with each other. Thereafter the priest went about committing the most diabolical crimes, while the murderer became noted as one of the most saintly priests of the age. Eventually, the now murderer was caught and put to death, and, strangely enough, the now priest, who was present, fell dead at the same moment.

Told as the story was, with all Mr. Stead's wealth of descriptive power and mystic allusion, it produced a depressed feeling among the company. Professor Patrick Geddes[12] made an attempt to revive the hilarity of the evening by a dissertation on the theory of consciousness; but the company grew sleepy; whereupon Andrew led off with "Auld Lang Syne," and the guests crept upstairs to their bedrooms.

As he sat in deep reflection the sound as of someone moaning in one of the bedrooms above caught his ear. He listened for a moment, and then rising from his chair slipped softly up the great marble staircase, wondering what it might be. Halting in the corridor near the bedroom whence the sound came, he listened near the keyhole.

It was Mr. Stead praying for him!

Andrew returned downstairs greatly disturbed, and dropped into a chair by the side of the fire opposite his own chair, and resumed his troubled reverie. Some thing again roused him, and he looked up. What was that? He started back in the chair with an amazed and terrified expression.

There was a man sitting in his own corner chair by the fireside!

Andrew was transfixed by the apparition. Who was this? Everyone had gone to bed an hour ago. The man was an elderly person, smallish in size, with hard-set face. Andrew stared and stared at the figure until he began to realize that the person was quite familiar to him; but from a sudden lapse of memory he could not recall his name or who he was. A half-amused, sinister smile played on the uninvited guest's features.

"Who – what – how –?" ejaculated Andrew in a thin, hoarse whisper.

The intruder gave a laugh. "Don't be frightened, Andrew. I am an old friend of yours, though at present, as you may perceive, I am only a ghost. I could not do you or anybody any harm, even if I would; I am only capable of being seen and heard."

"I did not believe there were such things as ghosts," said Andrew, more terrified than ever.

"Seeing is believing," the ghost replied bluntly. "But come, let us talk while we may. I am not often allowed the opportunity of playing the ghost with you."

A cold sweat had broken over Andrew, and he felt himself as light as a feather. The voice of the ghost seemed to pass through him.

Then the ghost said: I believe you would give me the slip just now if you could, Andrew; in fact, my grievance is – and this is why I am confronting you face to face to-night – that you have been trying for a long time to cut my acquaintance. And all because you and I take different views about things nowadays.'

Andrew could not speak.

The ghost went on: "Tell me, Andrew, what's the harm in being very rich? Why do you apologise so often for your wealth? Why, after spending your life getting it, should you be so anxious to get rid of it, especially in such foolish ways as you are doing?"

Andrew tried to speak, but his tongue would not move.

The ghost went on: "You are never done saying that you were happiest when you were poor. You declare that you prefer simple living to luxury, and that peasant girls in petticoats charm you more than countesses in gorgeous dresses, and all that kind of thing."

This challenge seemed to recall Andrew's speech, and he stammered in a curious, husky voice: "On my soul I speak the truth when I say so."

"Why, then, don't you become poor and have done with it?"

"Because I cannot," said Andrew, sadly.

The ghost laughed derisively. "No, perhaps you cannot – you would not be Andrew Carnegie if you could. And so you go about talking fine precepts about poverty, with your millions clinging like convict chains about your conscience! The incident of the Homestead strike and the Pinkerton shooting[13] worries you – it casts a shadow over your life. So you told John Burns,[14] and John Burns, of course, tells everybody. You squirm when you are reminded that your 40,000 workmen, in making millions for you, were withered up into old men in ten years. And you gave £400 for Labour candidates once upon a time, and small thanks you got for it, and serves you right, too. The Socialists and Trade Unionists gird at you; they object to your money being accepted for the purpose of erecting heathen altars to you all over the country under the pretence of building free libraries. There is the LABOUR LEADER; it makes you a text for front page comments almost every week."

"I am a victim of circumstances," pleaded Andrew.

"So is everybody, man. You are, in fact, only a circumstance yourself, and I am dealing with you as such. Why don't you become a Socialist at once? Many a better man than you has done so."

"Perhaps it's because they are better men than me," said Andrew, humbly. "I have admitted in my books that Socialism is the noblest ideal of society, but that we would require to be angels to practice it. I'm not an angel. I'm not even a saint, though they call me Saint Andrew sometimes – though more in jest than in earnest, perhaps. John Morley agrees with me that Socialism is impracticable, and he is a good man."

"We won't discuss Socialism," said the ghost. "It is a dangerous thing to do. Arguing against Socialism is like trying to put a fire out by throwing fagots on it."

Bending forward on the edge of his chair, and fixing his eyes keenly on Andrew, the ghost continued: "*I don't believe in Socialism, or philanthropy, or poverty, or fine free library precepts. Epictetus and Marcus Aurelius and Milton*[15] are dead long ago. Besides, they did not make, or want to make, millions, like you or me. I believe in getting rich as fast as possible and by any means possible. I believe in getting the better and the best of everybody. I want to triumph over friends and foes. I wouldn't like to live in a cottage; that's why I am here to-night. I believe in the survival of the fittest, in competition, and inequality. I am all for democracy – excuse me, 'Triumphant Democracy'[16] – as against kings and lords. I am not ashamed of using riots and Pinkerton gangs. I want to keep workmen down and myself up, and, like Mrs. Fisk,[17] I fight them without mercy, as Napoleon did his enemies."

"But," objected Andrew, timidly, remembering he was speaking to a ghost, "we have duties as well as rights, and even workmen are in some degree our fellow men. As I have said in my books, wealth is only a prize. We must help to improve the world."

"Improve the world! As well try to improve the devil."

"But Robert Burns expressed a hope that even the devil might mend,"[18] said Andrew.

"Robert Burns! He was poor devil enough, and didn't mend himself. Improve the world! We did not make the world! Why should we tamper with the work of creation? I believe in evolution, the survival of the fittest. The lion eats the lamb, the spider the fly, and we eat everything and use everything that's good for us. We cannot alter the laws of life and death. We are not gods, but men."

"You are a devil, I do believe," cried Andrew, with an honest throb of indignation.

"Perhaps so, Andrew; you ought to know. At any rate, you and I between us have made as big a hell in Pittsburg as the size of the place would allow, and one no honest devil need be ashamed of."

"Who, then – what are you?" cried Andrew, with a reawakened sense of terror.

"Listen, Andrew," said the ghost, moving towards him; "there is only one person in this room."

"There are you and I," said Andrew, forcing his chair farther away.

"There is only one person in this room," repeated the ghost, advancing nearer to him; "and that one person is you and I. I am your counterpart, Andrew, your other self – and you are mine! Look in the mirror over there."

Andrew looked at the large mirror on the opposite wall of the room, and beheld himself, but could hardly believe it was himself. His face looked strangely mild and beneficent, and his eyes gleamed like stars. The image of the ghost looked black, sinister, and repellant, in contrast with his own. Yet, as he looked from the one to the other he began to doubt which was really the reflection of himself.

"You and I are one, Andrew," repeated the ghost in a husky tone. "We cannot live without each other. See, I come to you, for the cock crows. I cannot longer stay out of you."

A dark shadow came over Andrew's eyes. He uttered a groan and sank in a faint. When he recovered his senses he found the ghost had disappeared. "I must have been asleep," he said to himself.

"What a horrible dream I have had." He rose and looked in the mirror and, with a sigh of relief, he saw his old familiar self – Andrew Carnegie, of Skibo Castle *and Pittsburg*.

SOCIAL DEMOCRAT

Maxime Görki, 'On the Steppes. Told by a Tramp', trans. Emily Jakowleff and Dora B. Montefiore, *Social Democrat*, July 1901, pp. 215–24.

Anatole France, 'Crainquebille', trans. Jacques Bonhomme, *Social Democrat*, October 1902, pp. 312–20.

M. Winchevsky, 'He, She, and It', *Social Democrat*, April 1906, pp. 253–6.

The *Social Democrat* (1897–1913) remained a monthly publication and continued to be edited by Harry Quelch during this period. It also continued to publish short stories, although there was a decline towards the end of this period; only a single short story was published in 1905. There is a distinctly international flavour to the fiction: all fiction included in the *Social Democrat* during these years were by non-British authors, and most were published in translation.

Maxime Görki (1868–1936), also spelled Maxim or Maksim Görky, overcame a childhood spent in poverty to become the founder of Soviet literature, publishing plays, novels and short stories. The publication of *Chelkash* in 1895 began his 'tramp period', of which this short story is a part. He joined the Bolshevik Party in 1905 and became a close friend of Vladimir Lenin (1870–1924), who had shared an office with Quelch in 1902–3 when the SDF helped publish the banned Russian periodical *Iskra* from London. Görki opposed the October Revolution in 1917 and left the USSR in 1921, but returned in 1931. His translator, Dora Frances Barrow Montefiore (née Fuller) (1851–1933), was born in South London and met her husband, George Barrow Montefiore, after moving to Australia in 1874 to keep house for her elder brother. She became interested in women's rights and the suffrage movement after her husband's death, joining a range of suffrage groups as well as the SDF when she returned to Britain in 1892. She was an advocate of internationalism and translated many of Görki's works, working with Emily Jakowleff (n.d.) on most of the translations.

Anatole France was the pseudonym for Jacques Anatole Thibault (1844–1924). He was a prolific writer, publishing in many different forms, although he is best remembered for his novels; he received the Nobel Prize for Literature in 1921. He protested against the Dreyfus case and, at the end of his life, began to develop socialist ideas. This story was adapted to film in 1922, sometimes known as *Coster Bill of Paris*, and starred Maurice de Féraudy as Crainquebille. 'Jacques Bonhomme', the translator of the story, is a pseudonym taken from the nickname for Guallaume Caillet, leader of the Peasant Jacquerie.

Morris Winchevsky was born Leopold Benxion Novokhovitch (1856–1932) in Yanova near Lithuania. After being deported from Germany to Denmark, he moved to London, where he founded and edited the Yiddish socialist newspaper *Dos Poilishe Yidl* (*The Little Polish Jew*) and began writing poetry. He moved to the United States in 1894, where he carried on his work for socialism until his death.

Maxime Görki, 'On the Steppes. Told by a Tramp', trans. Emily Jakowleff and Dora B. Montefiore (1901)

... We left Perekopp in the worst possible humour – hungry as wolves, and angry with the whole world. From early in the morning we had been trying to turn our talents and efforts to account, whether by stealing or earning something, and when at length we were forced to the conclusion that neither one or the other was likely to be crowned with success, we made up our minds to push on ... But where? ... Just on, and on. ... This was the unanimous but silent decision taken by us all; for we were ready to go on, in every sense of the word, along the path of life which we had already for some time been tramping. This decision was no less silent than the previous one, though it flashed forth from the lowering gloom of our hungry eyes.

There were three of us; our acquaintanceship was of recent date. We dropped across one another in a vodka shop in Kherson,[1] on the banks of the Dnieper.

One of us had been a soldier attached to the railway brigade, and later on took service as a platelayer on one of the Viesla lines; a red-haired, muscular man, with cold grey eyes; he could speak German, and had an extensive knowledge of prison life.

Folk like us don't care much to speak of their past life, having always more or less good reasons for not doing so; and all of us believed one another – at least apparently – for inwardly each of us had ceased to trust even himself.

The second one of the party was a shrivelled, dried up little man with thin lips, always sceptically pursed up and when he told us that he was a former student of Moscow University, the soldier and I took it as a matter of course.

As a matter of fact it was all the same to us whether he was a student, a spy, or a rogue. All that concerned us was that during our present acquaintanceship he was our equal; he was hungry, he enjoyed in towns the special attention of the police, and in villages was looked upon by the peasants with suspicion. He hated both town and village with the hatred of an impotent hunted hungry animal, and used to dream of a general vengeance on all and on everything. In a word, as regards his position amongst the chosen ones of nature, and the powerful ones of life, and as regards his disposition, he was one of us.

Misfortune is the strongest cement in the uniting of characters, even divergent ones; and we were all deeply convinced of our right to consider ourselves unfortunate.

The third was myself. From that natural modesty which has distinguished me from my earliest days, I shall not say a word about my own qualities; and not wishing to appear before you as a knave, I shall be silent on the subject of my faults. But as a clue to my character I shall allow myself to mention that I always considered myself superior to the others, and continue to do so till the present day.

Well ... we left Perekopp,[2] and were trudging along with nothing in view but bread, which we might beg of the shepherds, who seldom refused the petition of wayfarers.

I was walking abreast of the soldier, and the "student" was striding behind us. Something that suggested the remains of a coat was hanging on his back. On his close cropped head, adorned with a striking variety of bumps,[3] rested composedly what was little more than a recollection of a broad-brimmed hat. His thin legs were clad in tight grey breeches, with variegated patches; to the soles of his feed he had bound with strips of rag torn form the linings of his clothes the old uppers of a boot he had found on the road; this arrangement he called sandals, and he shuffled along in them, kicking up the dust as he went, and glancing from side to side with furtive eyes. The solider wore a red shirt, which, according to his own account, was actually bought by himself in Kernoneff.[4] Over this shirt he wore a thick wadded waistcoat; on his head, worn with military cock, was a soldier's cap of indefinite colour, and on his legs hung loosely wide moujik[5] trousers; he was barefooted.

I was dressed much in the same style, and was also barefooted. We trudged along ... and on all sides of us stretched the immense boundless steppes, looking like a huge round flat black bowl, under the hot blue dome of a summer sky. The grey, dusty road cut through the distance like a broad stripe, whilst its baked surface burnt our feet. From time to time we came across bristly patches of freshly cut corn, which bore a strange resemblance to the soldier's stubbly cheeks. He stepped along, singing in a rather hoarse voice:

> "The blessed resurrection,
> We greet, and sing its praise."...[6]

Whilst serving in the army he had performed the duties of a deacon in the garrison chapel, and knew an endless number of these sacred songs, to which he always had recourse wherever the conversation flagged.

Ahead of us, on the horizon, rose a delicate sky-line, steeped in tones that shaded from lilac to pale pink.

"These are evidently the Crimean hills,"[7] said the "student" in a dry voice.

"Hills?" exclaimed the soldier. "It's too early in the day to see hills yet, my friend. Those are clouds, nothing but clouds. See how strange they look; they are of the colour of curdled milk and fruit."

I hinted that it would be extremely agreeable if these clouds were in reality curdled milk and fruit. This suddenly aroused our hunger – the bane of our life.

"Damn it all!" cursed the soldier, spitting on one side. "If we could but come across a living soul, but there isn't one ... We shall have to do as the bears in the woods do, and suck our own paws."[8]

"I told you we ought to have kept to inhabited parts of the country," said the "student" didactically.

"You told us so" exclaimed the soldier indignantly. "All your learning is nothing but words. What inhabited places are there here? The devil only knows where they are."

The "student" pursed up his lips silently ... the sun was setting ... the clouds on the horizon were taking on them a variety of colours, indescribable in words ... a mingled smell of earth and of salt arose from the ground ... This dry and savoury smell increased our appetites more and more.

A gnawing feeling took possession of our stomachs – a strange and disagreeable feeling as if from the muscles of our bodies the life juices were exuding, evaporating, and as if the muscles themselves were losing their elasticity. A pricking dryness filled the mouth and throat, the head grew dizzy, and now and again dark spots flashed and danced before the eyes. Sometimes these took the form of hot, steaming meats, sometimes of loaves of bread; fancy attaching to these "silent visions of the past," their own particular smells, and then it seemed as if a knife were being turned in the stomach. Still, on we went, sharing with each other the description of our impressions, and keeping a keen look-out on either side lest a flock of sheep might be seen, or listening for the squeaking creak of the Tartar's cart, carrying fruit to the Armenian market.

But the steppe was void and silent ... On the eve of this unlucky day we three had eaten four pounds of rye bread and five water-melons; after which we walked forty versts[9] ... and, the expenses not equalling the income, we fell asleep in the market-place of Perekopp, and awoke at the call of hunger.

The "student" wisely advised us not to go to sleep, but to take advantage of the night for ... business; ... but in respectable society it is not considered correct to speak of projects bearing on the violation of the rights of property, and, therefore I keep silence ... I only wish to be truthful, but it is not in my own interests to be brutal. I know that people are growing more tender-hearted in these highly-cultivated days; and even when they take their neighbour by the throat, with the evident intention of throttling him, they try to do it with all the amiability in the world, and with the strict regard for etiquette proper to the circumstances. The experience that my own throat has undergone causes me to observe this advance in manners, and, with an agreeable feeling of deep conviction, I assert that everything in this world develops and becomes perfect. More especially is this wonderful process admirably proved by the annual growth of prisons, vodka shops and brothels.

Striving thus to swallow down the saliva of hunger, and making an effort to appease the tortures of the stomach by friendly talk, we tramped along the vast and silent steppes in the ruddy rays of the sunset, ... full of vague hope ... We watched the sun sinking quietly into the soft clouds, richly coloured by its rays, whilst behind us, and on either side, a bluish mist rising up from the steppes towards the sky veiled the gloomy landscape behind us.

"Come, mates, gather some fuel for a fire," said the soldier, picking up a log from the ground. "It seems as if we shall have to spend the night on the steppes ... the dew is heavy ... take twigs, dung, anything you find." ... We scattered on either side of the road, and began collecting dried weeds and anything else that would burn. Each time one of us stooped towards the earth the whole body seemed possessed with an intense desire to throw itself down full length, to lie there motionless and eat ... eat long ... eat to repletion ... and then fall asleep ... Though it might be an eternal sleep ... only to eat, and eat ... to chew ... to feel a warm thick mash slowly sliding down the parched gullet into the starved, contracted stomach, aching with the desire to absorb something into itself.

"If we could but find some roots," said the soldier. "Eatable roots are sometimes to be found."

But in the black, ploughed ground there were no roots to be had. The southern night came on suddenly, and the last ray of the sun had scarcely disappeared, when in the dark blue sky stars began to twinkle, and around us black shadows blended, narrowing the vast extent of the boundless steppes which swallowed us up.

"Brothers!" said the "student" on the left in a low voice; "there is ... a man ... lying down!"

"A man?" laughed the soldier, incredulously; "what can a man be doing lying there?"

"Go and ask! Probably he has bread, if he has made his mind to spend the night on the steppes," exclaimed the "student".

The soldier looked in the direction indicated, and spitting resolutely, said: "Come and see!"

Only the green, sharp eyes of the "student" could discern that the dark heap which lay some hundred yards to the left of the road was a man.

We approached him quickly, striding over the heaps of ploughed ground and feeling that the aroused hope for food had sharpened the pangs of hunger. We had already got near, but the man did not move.

"Perhaps, after all, it's not a man!" the solider gloomily expressed the idea common to us all. But all doubt was at the same moment dispelled, for the heap on the ground suddenly began moving, and we saw that it was a real flesh-and-blood person, who knelt, stretching out his hand towards us.

He spoke in a dull shaky voice:

"Don't come nearer, or I shall shoot you."

Through the misty air we heard the short, dry crack of a pistol. We stopped as if at a word of command, and for several seconds we were silent, taken aback by this uncourteous greeting.

"What a brute!" muttered the soldier.

"That he is," answered the "student" reflectively. "He goes about with a revolver ... one can see the sort of fellow he is."

"I say!" shouted the soldier, having evidently taken a decision.

The man did not change is position and remained silent.

"I say! ... whoever you are. We won't touch you; only give us some bread ... you are sure to have some ... do, for Christ's sake! ... damn ... damn ..." the last words were uttered under his breath.

Still the man remained silent.

"Can't you hear?" continued the soldier, trembling with rage and despair. "Give us some bread! ... do! ... We won't go near you; throw it to us."

"All right," curtly answered the man.

If even he had added "my dear brothers," and if he had poured into these blessed words the most sacred and pure feeling, they would not have touched us and humanised us so much as did this gruff and brief "all right."

"Don't be afraid of us, my good fellow," continued the soldier, with a soft and ingratiating smile, which was lost on the stranger, who was still at least twenty paces distance from us; "we are quiet people, travelling from Russia to the Kouban[10] ... We were out of our reckoning in money matters, and have eaten everything off our backs ... This is the second day since we had a morsel in our mouths."

"Here, catch! ... Here some more ... and some more!"

When the student had finished gathering up this strange alms, we found that it was four pounds of hard wheaten bread; it was soiled with earth and very stale; we paid little heed to the first fact, but the second gave us great pleasure. Stale bread is more satisfying than new bread, for it has less moisture in it.

"Here's for you ... and for you ... and for you ..." The soldier divided busily the pieces ... "Stop! That isn't fair; let me take a bit off yours my friend, for the philosopher, for his share is not big enough."

The "student" put up with the loss of a few ounces of his bread without remonstrance. I fell to my share, and soon found its way into my mouth.

I began chewing it slowly with convulsive movements of the jaws, which seemed ready to crush even a stone. The contraction of the gullet gave me a sensation of keen delight, as did also the slow satisfaction of my hunger. Bit by bit the warm and indescribably delicious food found its way into the hot stomach and seemed there to be transformed into blood and brain. Joy, a strange, calm and vivifying joy, gradually warmed the heart at the same time as the stomach was being satisfied with food, and I fell into a half dreamy state. I forgot the cursed days of constant chronic hunger, and forgot also my companions, engrossed, for the time being, by the sensations I was experiencing.

But when with the palm of my hand I jerked the last crumbs of bread into my mouth, I felt I was still mortally hungry.

"That cursed dog over there, he has got some bacon left, and some sort of meat" ... growled the soldier, sitting on the ground opposite me, and rubbing his stomach with his hands.

"Yes, that's certain for the bread smelt of meat ... And I believe he's got more bread left," said the "student," whilst he added, in a low voice, "If it were not for that revolver."

"Who can he be, I wonder?"

"The chances are he's one of us."

"Dog!" concluded the soldier.

We were sitting in a close group, and glancing askance towards the spot where crouched our benefactor with the revolver.

No sound came from his direction nor any sign of life.

Night was gathering around us its dark powers ... A deadly quiet reigned over the steppes ... We could hear each other's breathing. From time to time was heard the distant melancholy whistle of the shrew mouse ... The stars, the living flowers of the sky, glittered overhead ... We were hungry.

I can say with pride that during this rather strange night I was neither worse nor better than my casual acquaintances. I suggested that we should get up and attack the man; not to hurt him, but to get hold of all the food he had with him. He may shoot ... well, let him ... If he succeeds in hitting anyone, he can only hit one out of the three; and even if he should aim straight a bullet from a revolver would hardly kill.

"Come on!" said the soldier, jumping to his feet.

The "student" rose more slowly.

We went off almost at a run.

The "student" kept behind, and rather away from us.

"Come, mate!" exclaimed the soldier in a reproachful tone.

In front of us we head a muttered threat, the sharp click of a trigger, a flash of fire, the report of a pistol.

"Missed!" exclaimed the soldier joyfully, jumping with a bound on to the man. "Now, you devil! won't I give it you!"

The "student" made a rush at the bag.

The "devil" fell on his back, his arms flung out on the ground, and a choking sound in his throat.

"What the deuce does that mean?" exclaimed the astonished soldier, who had raised his foot prepared to kick the stranger.

"Could he have shot himself? ... Hi! ... you there! ... Hi! Have you shot yourself, or what's the matter?"

"Meat! ... some kinds of biscuits ... and bread ... plenty of everything, mates! ..." sounded the triumphant voice of the "student."

"Well! curse you! ... die if you like! ... let's come and eat, mates!" shouted the soldier.

I took the revolver out of the hand of the man, who lay now motionless, the choking sounds in his throat having ceased. In the barrel only one bullet remained.

Again we fell to and ate in silence.

The stranger lay by our side, also silent, and without moving a limb. We paid no heed to him.

Suddenly we heard uttered in a hoarse, trembling voice: "Dear friends ... can you behave like this just for a piece of bread?"

A shudder ran through us. The "student" choked himself with a piece of food, and bending forward, coughed loudly.

The soldier, having swallowed what was in his mouth, uttered curses.

"Hound! May you burst yourself! Did you think it was your skin we wanted? What use would that be to us, you fathead? You dirty coward ... the idea of carrying arms, and shooting at people. Curses on you!"

He continued to curse and to eat by turns, which in no way interfered with the force of his expletives.

"Just wait till we've done eating! We'll be even with you, then," was the "student's" grim threat.

Then through the darkness of the night we heard loud sobs that frightened us.

"Friends! I didn't know. I fired because I was afraid. I am travelling from New Athon ... to the government of Orel.[11] Oh! dear me! The ague has got me! As soon as the sun sets my torture begins! It was the ague drove me away from Athon. I was a cabinetmaker there ... that's how I earned my living. I've got a wife at home ... two little girls. It's three years ... nearly four, since I saw them. Eat all there is, friends!"

"That's what we mean to do, without being asked," said the "student."

"Gracious heaven! If only I had known that you were quiet, good people, I would never have fired! ... but see friends ... it was the steppes! ... the night! ... could I help it? ... just think!"

He cried whilst he was speaking, or rather uttered a strange, trembling, terrified howl.

"Gammon!" interjected the soldier, disdainfully.

"He must have money about him," suggested the "student."

The soldier screwed up his eyes, scanned him narrowly, and sneered.

"You're a sharp fellow! What I say is, let's have a fire, and go to sleep."

"And what about him?" enquired the "student."

"Oh! devil take him! ... we don't want to fry him, do we?"

"Why not?" nodded the "student," with his long, narrow head.

We went off to fetch the fuel which we had left at the place where we had been arrested by the shout of the cabinetmaker. We collected it again, and were soon sitting round a comfortable fire. It smouldered gently in the quite windless night, and lit up the spot on which we were seated. We were getting sleepy, but we could still have eaten another supper.

"Friends!" called to us the cabinetmaker. He was lying a few steps away from us, and at times is seemed to me he was whispering something.

"Well!" said the soldier.

"May I come near ... to the fire? I'm not far from death's door; All my bones are full of pain! ... Gracious heavens! I shall never reach home again!"

"Crawl in here!" ... said the "student," making room for him. The stranger crawled slowly towards the fire, as if afraid of losing on the way a leg or a hand. He was a tall, exceedingly emaciated man; his clothes hung terribly loosely on him, and his large dimmed eyes spoke of gnawing pain. His drawn face was bony, and even by the firelight showed an earthy, yellow, dead colour. He was shaking from head to foot, and aroused in us a feeling of contemptuous pity. Stretching out to the fire his long thin hands, he rubbed his bony fingers, the joints of which bent stiffly and slowly. The sight of him became at last sickening and revolting.

"Why are you travelling on foot in this sort of state? Is it because you are so stingy?" asked the soldier gloomily.

"I was advised ... they told me not to travel by water ... they said 'go by the Crimea' ... the air they told was so good. And here am I, friends, unable to walk ... dying. I shall die alone on the steppes. The birds will eat my flesh ... and no one will know. My wife ... my daughters ... will await me. I wrote to them ... I told them ... And my bones will be washed by the rains of the steppes."

And he howled with the dismal howl of a wounded wolf.

"Damn it all!" exclaimed the enraged soldier, jumping to his feet. "What's all this about? You don't give us a chance of resting. If you're dying, just die, but be quiet about it. Who wants to bother about you? Just shut up that row!"

"Give him one over the head," said the "student."

"Give us a chance of going to sleep," said I. "And if you want to stay near the fire, stop howling, for otherwise ... indeed."

"Did you hear?" asked the soldier, angrily. "If so, just remember. You think perhaps we are going to bother about you, after you have been slinging bread at our heads, and taking aim at us with your rotten pistol! You whining devil! Anyone in your place would ..." And the soldier spat on one side with a gesture of disgust.

He stopped suddenly and stretched himself full length on the ground. The "student" had already settled himself to sleep. I had done the same. The terrified cabinetmaker shrunk together, and, creeping towards the fire, sat silently watching it. I was lying to the right of him, and I could hear his teeth chattering. The "student" lay on the left, curled up in a heap, and seemed to have fallen asleep suddenly.

The solider, with his hands behind his head, lay on his back, watching the sky. "What a beautiful night ... is it not? ... just look at the stars! ... And so warm!" After some minutes he added, speaking to me: "Look at the sky ... it's really more like a warm blanket than a sky! Oh, how I love this wandering life? Though it means sometimes cold and hunger ... yet the freedom is worth everything. There is no master over one ... one's own life is one's own ... one can even do away with oneself, and no one dares say one nay. It's fine! See how angry and how famished I have been these last few days ... and now, here am I, looking at the sky, with the stars twinkling above me, as if they were saying: 'It's all right, Lakontine; continue to wander about the world, and don't let anyone get the better of you.' Yes, and my heart and soul feel so happy. How are you now ... what's your name ... cabinetmaker? Don't be angry with me now, and don't fear me. It was so natural we should eat your bread, for you had some and we had none ... so, of course, we ate yours! And, fancy you firing at us! Don't you know that a bullet may hurt a fellow? I was very angry with you when you did that, and if you had not tripped up, I should have given you something to be going on with. And as for the bread – why to-morrow you will be at Perekopp, and can buy more ... for you have plenty of money, I know. When did you pick up this ague?

And for some time longer, the soldier's bass tones, and the trembling replies of the cabinetmaker sounded in my ears. The night, dark almost to blackness, fell thicker and darker on the earth, and the fresh scented night air filled all one's lungs.

The fire gave forth a steady light, and an invigorating warmth ... my eyelids grew gradually tired and drooped, and before my eyes something soft and beautiful seemed to hover.

* * *

"Up with you! Look sharp! Let's be off!"

With a feeling of fear I opened my eyes, and sprang to my feet assisted by the soldier, who dragged me up impetuously by the hand.

"Look sharp, I say? let's be off!"

His face showed anxiety and fear.

I glanced around. The sun was rising, and its reddish ray was already lying on the motionless and livid face of the cabinetmaker. His mouth was wide open, and his eyes protruded from the sockets, and seemed to glance upwards with a glassy look expressive of terror. The clothes on his body were torn, and lay in unnatural, tumbled disorder. There were no traces of the "student."

"What's the use of staring? Come along, don't you hear?" said the soldier meaning, and dragging me along by the arm.

"Is he dead?" I asked, shivering with the chill air of the morning.

"Of course he is! If you were strangled, you would be dead?"

"Is he? ... Has he been? ... The 'student'? ..." I exclaimed.

"Why, who else could it be? You don't think it was you or I who did it? ... H'm! ... So much for a man of education! Finished off a man cleverly, he did, and left his mates in the lurch to stand the brunt of it. Had I known it yesterday, I would have killed the 'student.' I'd have done for him with one blow! A knock on the temple, and there would have been one rascal less in the world! Don't you see now what he has done? We've got to make off at once, so that no human eye shall be able to detect that we have been on the steppes! You see what I mean! In the first place they will find the cabinetmaker, and will see plainly that he has been strangled and robbed. Then all folk like us will be watched and questioned ... 'Where do you come from? ...' 'Where did you sleep last night?' And then they will arrest us ... Though you and I have nothing compromising on us. But there's the revolver in my shirt ... that's awkward."

"Throw it away," I advised him.

"Throw it away?" he replied thoughtfully; "it's valuable ... and perhaps after all we shan't be caught! No, I won't throw it away! It's worth three roubles. Ah! With what pleasure I would put this bullet into our friend's ear! I should like to know how much he grabbed ... the dog! ... How much do you think? ... Damn it all!"

"As to the cabinetmaker's daughters – it's all up with their chance of getting it!" said I.

"Daughters? ... what daughters? Ah! Yes! Well, they will grow up; they are sure not to marry fellows like us; it's not to be thought of. Step along quicker! ... where shall we go?

"I don't know, I'm sure. It's all the same."

"No more do I ... but as you say ... it's all the same ... Let's go towards the right, it must lead to the sea."

So we went to the right.

I glanced back ... Far behind us on the bare steppes rose a dark mound, lit up by rays of the morning sun.

"Are you looking to see if he has risen from the dead? No fear, he won't pursue us. That philosopher friend of ours was evidently a clever fellow; he did it neatly. A fine sort of mate he was! He's got us into a rare muddle! ... Ah! ... Ah! ... I see that people are getting worse from year to year," added the soldier despondingly.

The silent and deserted steppes, all inundated with the bright glow of the morning sun, stretched out around us, uniting at the horizon with the sky, suffused with such a clear caressing and soft light that everything black and evil seemed impossible amidst this immense space of free open land shut in with the blue dome of heaven.

"I feel empty still," said my companion, twisting up a cigarette of coarse tobacco. "What shall we get to eat to-day? Where shall we get it ... and how?"

"Ah! ... that's the question!"

* * *

Here the narrator, my neighbour in the next bed in the hospital, finished his story, adding: "And this is all. My friendship with the soldier continued, and together we tramped to Kars.[12] He was a good and very clever fellow, the real type of a vagabond tramp. I respected him. We travelled together as far as Asia Minor, and there we lost sight of each other.

"And do you ever remember the cabinetmaker?" I asked.

"Yes, as you see, or, rather, as you have heard."

"And ... what do you feel about him?"

He laughed.

"Well, what is there for me to feel about him? ... It was no more my fault what happened to him than it was your fault what has happened to me ... For, in fact, no one is to blame for anything, for all of us are alike, beasts!"

Anatole France, 'Crainquebille', trans. Jacques Bonhomme (1902)

Jerome Crainquebille, a hawker, was going along pushing his barrow and calling out "Cabbages, carrots and turnips." When he had any parsnips he called out "asparagus" because parsnips are the asparagus of the poor. Now, on October 20 at noon, when he was coming down the Rue Montmartre,[1] Mme. Bayard, who kept a boot shop (at the sign of the "Guardian Angel") stepped out of her shop and came close to the barrow. Lifting up disdainfully some parsnips, she said:

"I do not think much of your parsnips. What do you want for these?"

"Sevenpence halfpenny,[2] madam. You could not have better ones."

"Sevenpence halfpenny for three bad parsnips?" And she threw them back on the barrow quite contemptuously. Then Policeman No. 64 came on the scene and told Crainquebille to move on.

Crainquebille for the last 50 years had been moving on all day long. He thought this was quite right, and, being anxious to obey, he asked his customer to take what she wanted. She replied hastily, saying that she must choose. And she went on feeling all the parsnips, but at last she took some of the best, which she pressed against her bosom, like the saints in church pictures press on their breast the triumphant palm.[3]

"I am going to give you sevenpence, that is quite enough, and I must go and fetch the money from the shop because I have not got it in my pocket." And holding the parsnips she went back to her shop, where a woman, with a baby, was waiting for her.

At that moment Policeman No. 64 said for the second time to Crainquebille "Move on!"

"I am waiting for my money," replied Crainquebille.

"I did not tell you to wait for your money, but I tell you to 'Move on,'" replied the policeman, firmly.

Meanwhile the lady in the boot shop was trying on blue shoes for a child of eighteen months whose mother was in a hurry. And the parsnips were resting on the counter.

Crainquebille, who had pushed his barrow through the streets during the last 50 years, had learnt the necessity of obeying the police. But just now he was in an embarrassing position, betwixt a duty and a right. He had not a judicial mind. He did not understand that the enjoyment of an individual right did not prevent him from accomplishing a social duty. He thought too much about his right of receiving sevenpence and too little of his duty, which was to push his barrow, to move on, and to keep on doing it. So he stood still. For the third time the policeman quietly and gently ordered him to move on. Unlike Sergeant Montauciel, who always threatens but never acts, No. 64 said little but often summoned. That was his way; though he was rather glum, he was a good officer, as brave as a lion and as gentle as a lamb. He must obey orders.

"Don't you hear me when I tell you to "Move on!'"

Cranquebille had a good reason for standing still, and thought it was sufficient. He said so, simply.

"Hang it all, don't I tell you that I am waiting for my money."

The policeman answered: "Do you want me to summon you? If you do, you only have to say so."

Hearing these words, Crainquebille shrugged his shoulders slowly, and cast a sad look at the policeman; then he raised his eyes towards the sky. That look meant, "Heaven is my witness. Do I break the laws? Do I contemn the rules and regulations affecting my trade? At 5 a.m. I was at the markets. Since 7 a.m. I have been pushing my barrow, calling out 'Cabbages, carrots, and turnips.' I am over 60. I am tired, and you ask me if I raise the black flag of revolt.[4] You are laughing at me, and your jests are cruel."

Perhaps the policeman did not understand this; perhaps he thought that it was not a sufficient reason for his disobedience; so he asked quietly, but firmly, if the man understood him. Now, just at that moment there was quite a block in the Rue Montmartre. The cabs, the brakes, the 'buses, the carts, and the drays seemed to all to be jammed together and mixed up. And there rose cries and oaths. The cabdrivers and the butchers exchanged slowly very remarkable swear words, and the 'busdrivers, thinking that Crainquebille was the cause of the mischief, called him "a dirty parsnip."

Meanwhile, there was a crowd on the pavement looking on at the quarrel. The policeman, seeing that he was being looked at, was determined to uphold his authority.

"All right," said he, taking out of his pocket a greasy note-book and a very short pencil.

Crainquebille was following his thoughts and was obeying his conscience, and now he could neither advance nor go back. The wheel of his barrow had unfortunately caught in the wheel of a milk cart. He called out, tugging at his hair under his cap: –

"But, I keep on telling you that I am waiting for my money! Is it not a shame? What am I to do? It is too bad of you!"

The policeman, by these words, which rather denoted revolt than despair, thought he was insulted. Every insult, according to a policeman, must take a certain form, and certain words must be used; and therefore he felt sure that the man had said, "Mort aux vaches!"* ("Death to the cows!").

"Ah, you have said, 'Mort aux vaches!' All right. Follow me."

Crainquebille, in the excess of his fright and his distress, looked with his large eyes burnt by the sun at the policeman, and with his broken voice, which seemed to come sometimes from his head and sometimes from his heels, he called out, folding his arms over his blue blouse, "I said 'Mort aux vaches!' I?"

This arrest was hailed by the laughter of clerks and little boys. It showed that crowds like repulsive and violent scenes. But a sad-looking old man, dressed in black and wearing a silk hat, came through the crowd and said in a low voice, very gently and very firmly, to the policeman: –

"You have made a mistake. That man did not insult you."

"Mind your own business," said the policeman, without threatening him, for he was speaking to a well-dressed man.

The old man insisted very calmly and very tenaciously, so the policeman told him that he would have to explain matters to the Inspector.

But Crainquebille called out, "So, I have said 'Mort aux vaches!"

He was saying this when Mme. Bayard, from the boot shop, came to him with the 7d. But the policeman had got hold of him and Mme. Bayard, thinking that it was no use paying a man who was being taken to the police-station, put the 7d. in the pocket of her apron.

Seeing that his barrow was going to be put in the pound, that his liberty was lost, that an abyss was under his feet, and that the sun was out, Crainquebeille muttered, "Well, I'm blessed!"

Before the Inspector the old man said that having had to stop owing to the block, he had seen all that took place, that the policeman was quite mistaken and had not been insulted. He gave his name: Doctor David Matthiew, chief physician of the Ambroise Paré Hospital,[6] office of the Legion of Honour.[7] In other days such evidence would have been sufficient to convince the Inspector, but at that time learned men were mistrusted in France.

Crainquebille was kept at the station, and next day he was taken in a Black Maria to the central prison. He did not find it hard to be in prison, he thought it was a law of nature. He was much struck on coming in by the brightness of the walls, and the clean floors. He said: "It is indeed a clean place. Well, I'm blessed:

---

* *Vache*[5] is the classic insult used to irritate a policeman in Paris. – J.B.

I could eat off the ground." Being left alone he wished to pull out his stool, but he saw that it was chained to the wall.

He expressed aloud his surprise.

"What a funny idea. I am quite sure that I would never have invented that."

Sitting down, he twirled his thumbs and was quite still. The stillness and the solitude oppressed him. He was dull, and he thought sadly about his barrow laden with cabbages, carrots, celery and salads in the pound. We wondered anxiously where he should put his barrow.

On the third day, he had a visit from his counsel, M. Lemerle, one of the youngest members of the Paris bar, president of one of the sections of the League of the French Fatherland (Ligue de la Patrie Française).[8]

Crainquebille tried to tell him about his case, but it was not easy, for he did not know how to talk; perhaps he might have got through it, but his counsel shook his head at what he said, saying, while he looked through the papers: "Hum! Hum! I do not see anything about that in the papers." Then, as if he were tired, he said, twisting his fair moustache: "In your own interest it would be better perhaps to plead guilty. As for me, I think your denial of everything is a very bad system." And Crainquebille would have confessed everything if he had known what to confess.

The President,* Bourriche, devoted six full minutes to the examination of Crainquebille. These questions would have brought out the matter more clearly if the defendant had answered the questions put to him. But the prisoner was not used to discussion, and respect and terror quite shut his mouth. He kept silent and the President answered, so the answered were incriminating: "Well, you acknowledge that you said 'Mort aux vaches!'" Then the prisoner answered in a tone as if old iron and glass were rattling: "I said 'Mort aux vaches!' because the policeman said 'Mort aux vaches!' – that is why I said 'Mort aux vaches!'" He wished to say that, astonished by the accusation, he had repeated the words which he was accused of uttering, and which he had certainly not used. He had said "Mort aux vaches!" as he might have said, "I say such a thing, could you believe it?" But the President of Bourriche, would not take that answer. "Do you mean," said he, "that the policeman first said those words." Crainquebille did not try to explain, it was too difficult. "You do not say that you are right," said the President. He had the witnesses called.

Policeman No. 64 – his real name being Bastien Matra – swore to speak the truth and nothing but the truth, and he spoke as follows: "Being on duty on October 20, at noon, I noticed in the Rue Montmartre a person, whom I took to be a hawker, having his barrow stopped at No. 328, and that caused a block in the traffic. I thrice told him to move on, but he would not. Then, when I told

---

* In France there are always three judges – a president and two assessors. – J.B.

him he would be summoned, he replied, crying out 'Mort aux vaches!' which I considered an insult."

This deposition, given in serious and measured tones, impressed the court. The defendant had called as witnesses Mme. Bayard, keeper of a boot shop, and M. David Matthieu, chief physician of Ambroise Paré hospital, and a Knight of the Legion of Honour.

Mme. Bayard had neither seen nor heard anything. Dr. Matthieu was in the crowd which surrounded the policeman telling the hawker to move on.

"I saw the whole thing," he said. "I noticed that the policeman had been mistaken, he had not been insulted. I came near and told him so. But the policemen seized the hawker and told me to come to the police station. I did so, and told the facts to the Inspector."

"You may sit down," said the President. "Usher, call back Matra. Matra, when you arrested the defendant did not Mr. Matthiew tell you that you had made a mistake?"

"Sir, he insulted me." "What did he say?" "He said to me 'Mort aux vaches!'"

There were murmurs and laughter in the crowd.

"You may sit down," said the President, hurriedly. And he warned the public that if these indecent manifestations occurred again, he would have the court cleared. Meanwhile the counsel for the defence was triumphantly puffing out the sleeves of his gown, and it was thought that Crainquebille would be acquitted.

Calm having been restored Me. Lemerle rose. He began his speech by praising the police, these modest servants of society who, for a trifling salary undergo all kinds of fatigue and brave incessant perils, and who daily lead heroic lives. They are all soldiers, and nothing more need be said in their praise. And Me. Lemerle went on in a fine way to praise military virtues. He was one of those, he said "Who would not allow the army to be touched, that national army to which he was proud to belong." The President nodded. For Me. Lemerle was a lieutenant in the reserve, and he was also a Nationalist candidate in the Vieilles Haudriettes quarter.[9] He went on, "Certainly, I do not undervalue the modest and precious services rendered daily by the police to the valiant population of Paris. And I would not, gentlemen, have undertaken the defence of Crainquebille if he had insulted an old soldier. My client is accused of having said 'Mort aux vaches!' The meaning of that word is not doubtful. If you look at a slang dictionary you will find vache – one who is sold to the police, a spy. 'Mort aux vaches!' is said by some people. But the question is, how did Crianquebille say it, and did he really say it? Allow me, gentlemen, to doubt it. I do not say that Matra wilfully said an untruth. But he has a great deal of hard work, and sometimes he is tired, overworked, and driven. In those circumstances he may have had certain hallucinations of hearing. When he comes and tells us, gentlemen, that Dr. David Matthieu, Knight of the Legion of Honour, chief physician to the Ambose Paré Hospital, a shining light, and a man of the world, has also cried out, 'Mort aux vaches!' we are forced to acknowledge that Matra is wrong, or that he does not know at times what he says. Even if Cranquebille had cried out 'Mort aux vaches!' we should have to consider if that word, in his mouth, was an insult. For he is the illegitimate son of a drunken hawker; he was born drunk. Look at him, brutalised by 60 years of misery. Gentlemen, you will say that he is not responsible for his actions."

M. Lemerle sat down, and President Bourriche mumbled out his sentence by which J. Crainquebille got 14 days' imprisonment and 50 francs[10] fine. The Court had believed Matra.

Crainquebille was taken through the corridors to the prison. He spoke to the warder, "If I had been told that this would happen! They speak well, but they speak too quick. I cannot explain to them. Don't you think they speak too quick?" But the warder went on, saying nothing. Then Cranquebille asked him, "Why don't you answer me?" Still the warder was silent, and Crainquebille bitterly said to him, "People speak to a dog. Why don't you speak to me? You never open your mouth; are you afraid of its stinking?"

* * *

Cranquebille, when he was in his cell, sat down full of astonishment and admiration on his chained stool. He did not quite know if the judges had made a mistake. The Court had concealed its weakness by the majesty of the form. He could not think that he was right and that they were wrong; he could not believe that something was rotten in that fine ceremony. As he neither went to church nor to the President's palace, he had never seen anything so fine as the court where he had been tried. He knew that he had not said "Mort aux vaches!" Now he had been sentenced to 14 days for having said it, and that he considered to be a splendid mystery – one of those articles of faith to which believers subscribe without understanding them; an obscure, startling, beautiful, and terrible revelation.

The poor old man felt that he had been guilty of mystically offending policeman No. 64, like the little boy who goes to church feels that he had been guilty of the unpardonable sin. His sentence said that he had called out "Mort aux vaches!" Therefore, he must have cried out "Mort aux vaches," in a mysterious way, unknown to him. He was carried into a supernatural world. His sentence was apocalypse.

If he did not understand his crime, he did not understand his sentence. His sentence was to him as solemn ritual and superior thing, a startling event which is not to be understood or discussed, which is neither to be praised nor blamed. If he had seen President Bourriche with a nimbus on his head,[11] and white wings to his shoulders, come through the half-open ceiling, he would not have been surprised at this new proof of judicial glory. He would have said, "There is my business going on."

The next day his counsel came to see him.

"Well, my good man, how are you getting on? You will soon be out. After all, you did not get on so badly."

"As for that, those gentlemen were very quiet and very polite, they did not swear. I would not have believed it. And the warder had white gloves on. Did you see them?"

"After all, you were right in admitting the offence."

"Perhaps so."

"Crainquebille, I have good news for you. A charitable person has given me 50 francs to pay your fine."

"When will you give me the money?"

"It will be paid to the Registrar of the Court. Do not bother about it."

"Never mind. I am much obliged to that person."

And Crainquebille, thoughtful, said, "This is an extraordinary thing."

"Don't exaggerate, your case is an ordinary one."

"Could you tell me where they have put my barrow?"

Crainquebille, after having been released, was pushing his barrow in the Rue Montmartre, crying out "Cabbages, turnips, carrots!" He was neither proud nor ashamed of his imprisonment. It did not even call up unpleasant thoughts. In his mind it was like the remembrance of a play, of an excursion, of a dream. He was particularly glad of being able to walk in the mud, on the pavement, to see overhead the sky quite watery and as dirty as a gutter, the good sky of his own Paris. He stopped at every corner to have a drink, then, happy and free, he spat in his hands and pushed his barrow along, while in front of him the sparrows, like him, early risers and poor, seeking their food in the road, flew away in bunches when he was calling out "Cabbages, turnips, carrots!" An old woman came near, and, feeling his celery, said to him: –

"Where have you been, Father Crainquebille? I have not seen you for three weeks. Have you been ill? You are a little pale."

"I will tell you, Mme. Mailloche. I have been living on my dividends".[12]

He goes on as usual, except that he goes rather more often to the public house, because he has got an idea that it is a holiday, and he has got to know some charitable people. He comes in the evening back to his garret in a rather lively condition. Stretched on his feather bed, he pulls up the sacks which the chestnut vendor at the corner had lent him and which he uses as a blanket. "Really," he says to himself, "the prison was not bad. I got all that I wanted. But, after all, one is better at home."

His happiness did not last long. He soon saw that his customers did not come to him.

"Nice celery, Mme. Cointreau!"

"I do not want anything."

"You do not want anything? Yet you do not live on air."

Mme Caointreau, without answering him, went back proudly into her fine baker's shop.

The shopkeepers and the concierges, formerly his best customers, would no longer deal with him. Having got near the boot shop ("l'Ange Gardien" – "the Guardian Angel") where his judicial adventures began, he called out:

"Mme. Bayard, you owe me 7½d."

But Mme. Bayard, who was sitting behind her counter, did not even look at him.

All the Rue Montmartre knew that Father Crainquebille had been to prison, and all the Rue Montmartre no longer spoke to him. The news of his sentence had reached even the Faubourg and the noisy corner of the Rue Richer. There, about noon, he saw Mme. Laure, his old and faithful customer, leaning over the barrow of little Martin. She was feeling a big cabbage. Her hair shone in the sun like liquid gold, and little Martin, a good-for-nothing fellow, a dirty chap, was taking an oath that his goods were the finest in the market. This sight broke old Crainquebille's heart. He pushed his barrow against that of little Martin, and said to Mme. Laure, in a sad and broken tone, "It is not nice of you not to buy from me."

Mme. Laure, as she quite agreed, was not a duchess. It was not in the great world of society that she had learnt about "Black Maria" and the central prison. But you should be honest in all trades. Everybody is proud and does not like to talk to a jail-bird. So the only answer she gave to Crainquebille was to pretend to be sick.

The old hawker, feeling the insult, called out, "Go along with you, you strumpet!" Mme. Laure let her green cabbage fall and called out: "Go along, you old jail-bird! He has just come out of prison and takes to insulting decent people." Crainquebille, if he had been calm, would never have told Mme. Laure what her business was. He knew too well that you do not choose your trade in life, and that there are good people in every business. He wisely never asked what his customers did, and he despised nobody; but he was beside himself. Three times he called her that name, and also stinking cat and beastly bird. A crowd gathered round them listening to their solemn winged words, and they would have gone on longer if a policeman had not suddenly appeared, when they both stopped. The each went their own way. But that scene damned Crainquebille in the Faubourg Montmartre and the Rue Richer.

* * *

And the old man went away murmuring, "She certainly is not good. No one could be worse than that woman." But in the bottom of his heart he did not really despise her for being what she was. He rather thought more of her, as she was thrifty and quiet. Formerly, they used to talk together. She would speak about her parents who lived in the country. They both thought it would be nice to have a garden and to bring up chickens. She was a good customer. He did not like seeing her buy cabbages from little Martin, a good-for-nothing fellow, a dirty chap. That had given him quite a shock, and when she had pretended to despise him he had lost his temper and then –

The worst of it was that she was not the only one who treated him like a leper. No one would deal with him. Just like Mme. Laure, Mme. Cointreau and Mme. Bayard would have nothing to do with him. The whole of society was against him. Now, was it right, because he had done 14 days, to say he was not good enough to sell parsnips? Was it fair? Was it even commonsense to make a good man die of hunger because he had had a little trouble with the police? If he could not sell his green-stuff he would die of hunger.

Like bad wine, he was turning sour. After having had a few words with Mme. Laure he was now quarrelling with everybody. He did not spare them. If the women touched his stuff without buying he called them names, and at the public-house he said nasty things to his comrades. The chestnut-seller, his friend, could not make him out, and used to say that old Crainquebille – blast him – was a very hedgehog. It could not be denied he was becoming a troublesome man, with bad habits and given to using too many winged words. You see, he thought society was wrong, and, not being a Fabian bureaucrat,[13] he did not know how to choose his words properly, and his ideas were not properly classified.

Misfortune made him unfair; he revenged himself on those who wished him no harm and sometimes on those who were weaker than he. In that way he boxed young Alphonse's ears, who was the son of the publican and who had asked him how he liked doing time. He said to him, "You dirty kid, your father ought to be dong time instead of selling poison."

That action and that speech did him no honour, for as the chestnut-seller told him, a child should neither be hit nor his father called bad names, for a child does not choose his father.

He began to drink. The less money he made, the more spirits he drank. Formerly he was economical and sober, and he, himself, was astonished at the change.

"I was never lazy," he said. "I suppose I have got less sense as I have got older." Sometimes he used to judge severely his bad conduct and his laziness.

"My old Crainquebille, you are no longer any good but for the drink."

Sometimes he deceived himself and made out that he only drank because he wanted it.

"Sometimes I have to drink a glass to get strength and to quench my thirst. I seem to have something on fire in my inside, and drink is a good thing after all."

Often he got late to the markets and could only get spoiled stuff on credit. One day, feeling his legs tired and no heart for work he left his barrow in the stable and spent the whole day round the stall of Mrs. Rose, the tripe-seller, and in the public-houses near the markets. In the evening he sat down on a basket; he thought, and he felt his degradation. He remembered his old strength and his work, his labours and his profits, all his old happy days full of work and joy; he thought about his walks at night to the markets, and how he waited for the auction to begin; the vegetables which he neatly put on his barrow, the little cup of black coffee drunk burning hot at Mother Theodore's shop, the way he seized the barrow handles, his joyous call as lively as the cock's clarion in the morning air, all his hard and innocent life, and how for half-a-century he had taken to people, worn out with care and watching, the fresh harvest of market gardens. Shaking his head, he sighed.

"No, I am not so good as I was. It is all up with me. The pitcher goes so often to the well that it gets broken. Since my court business I am no longer the same man!"

He was quite demoralised. When a man is like that he is alike a man who has fallen on the ground and who cannot get up, for all the passers by trample on him.

* * *

Then he became poor, dreadfully poor. The old hawker who used to bring back formerly a heap of five-franc pieces to Montmartre had no longer a half-franc. It was winter. He had been turned out of his garret and he slept under the carts in a stable. Rain having fallen for 24 days, the sewers overflowed, and the stable was partly full of water.

Sitting on his barrow, above the stinking waters, with spiders, rats, and starving cats, he was thinking in the dark. He had eaten nothing all day, and he had no chestnut-sacks to cover himself; and he thought of the time when the Government had provided him with board and lodging. He wished he was a prisoner, for they neither knew cold nor hunger, and he had an idea.

"Since I know the trick, why should I not make use of it!"

He got up and went into the street. It was about eleven o'clock, it was dark and miserable; a fine rain was falling, colder and more penetrating than ordinary rain. There were only a few people in the streets.

Cranquebille went along St. Eustache Church and came into the Rue Montmartre. It was deserted. A policeman was on the pavement, near the church, under a lamp-post, and one could see by its flame that little red rain. The policeman got it in his hood. He looked frozen, but whether because he preferred light to shade, or he was tired of walking, he stayed under the lamp, which, perhaps, he looked on as a companion and a friend. That trembling flame was the only person in the solitary night. His quietness did not appear human; the reflection of his boots, on the wet pavement, which looked like a lake, made him seem double, and he was like an amphibious monster, half out of the water. Standing there close-hooded and armed he looked like a monk and a soldier. His features seemed bigger on account of his hood, and were quiet and sad. His moustache was thick, short and grey. He was an old policeman, a man of over 40.

Crainquebille came quietly near to him, and said in a feeble and hesitating voice, "mort aux vaches!"

Then he waited for the result of that sacred word, but nothing took place. The policeman stood motionless and dumb, his arms folded under his short cloak. His eyes, wide open, shining in the shadow, looked on Cranquebille with sadness, with keenness, and with contempt.

Cranquebille was astonished, but still persevered, murmuring, "'Mort aux vaches!' I say to you."

A long silence followed, during which the fine, red rain fell in the cold shadow. Then the policeman spoke: "You ought not to say that at your age; you should know better. Move on!"

"Why don't you arrest me?" asked Cranquebille.

The policeman shook his head under his wet hood. "If I had to collar all the drunkards who say what they ought not to say I should have a lot to do! And what would be the use of it?"

Crainquebille, overwhelmed by that magnanimous contempt, remained for a long time foolish and dumb, with his feet in the gutter. Before going away, he tried to explain: "I did not say that for you – 'Mort aux vaches'! It was neither for you or anybody else. It was an idea of mine."

The policeman replied with an austere gentleness: "Whatever was your idea, you ought not have said it. When a man does his duty and suffers much, you should not insult him with idle words. I again tell you to 'Move on.'"

Crainquebille, with bowed head and lowered arms, passed into the shadow under the pelting rain.

M. Winchevsky, 'He, She, and It' (1906)

He was leaning against It.
He was an old scavenger, a kind of superannuated biped; it was an old apple-tree.
Who was she?
Never mind.
The dense, murky, smoky, suffocating fog that had darkened the sky, and poisoned the air, and saddened every human heart, was gone at last.
Good riddance. Men, women, and children, now breathed a little more freely in modern Babylon. The London autumn resumed its ordinary dismal look. Cabs, carriages and omnibuses. Or rather, since you insist on precision of nomenclature, 'ansoms, fourwheelers, and buses, were again circulating in all directions as freely and unhamperedly as if they had been newspaper lies. The setting sun just peeped through the clouds once or twice, preparatory to bidding the world good-bye, and retiring for the night.
St. John's Wood, a part of London with trees and actors enough to justify the latter and to belie the first portion of its name, was now quiet. The ragged torch-bearers who had been piloting timid pedestrians across the streets, thus earning a 'eap of coppers during the short but, for them, beneficent reign of King Fog, had now disappeared from the surface. Neatly and conventionally dressed, aproned and bonneted young "slavies"[1] were walking, jug in hand, toward the "pubs" for the purpose of obtaining beer in one or the other of its many varieties, eliciting in passing a flattering remark or so from some swell on his way to his club, the theatre, or the music-hall. The neighbourhood being of the shabby-genteel (less genteel than shabby) persuasion, had settled down to feed the inner man, either at supper or at dinner,[2] according to its "station in life". On the whole, then, everybody and everything out of doors was now at rest.
So, too, was the scavenger. For the first time since the lifting of the fog he had just once more swept away the lifeless yellow leaves which the wind had scattered all around him on the side-walk. While the darkness lasts a man literally cannot see his duty; no, not even a p'liceman, let alone a mere legalised beggar in the shape of a street-cleaner, who, unlike the other, gets neither regular pay

nor irregular sixpences from such "unfortunates" as may be fortunate enough to possess that popular coin of the realm.

The old scavenger was now resting, his back against the barren apple-tree, his emaciated, not very cleanly shaven, and self-assertedly-projecting chin on his right fist, while the left, which supported its fellow, was in its turn leaning on the old broomstick, an honest, time-worn implement of the road-sweeping industry, now an integral part of the old man's being.

Thus propped up and "backed" by the tree, he stood there gazing at the stones of the pavement, holding, one would have thought, communion with them.

For the brief space of one moment he dozed off.

* * *

His whole past suddenly arose before his mental eye.

By Jingo, this is queer. Dashed if it ain't!

Here he is, young again, young and vigorous, and as good-looking a chap as any in the whole timber-yard.

Hark! What the deuce is this? What a bloomin' noise? Music, by Gosh!

"Say, gov'nor, where may them red-jackets be going to? To embark for the Crimear, eh![3] Well, I am damned!"

Tis? Why, Soho Square,[4] of course. Any fool knows that. Feels nice to be out of that infernal timber yard. He is now on his way home. Washed and kempt, as bright as a new brass button – a regular dandy. But what makes him carry a broom across his shoulder? Queer, ain't it?

And now he is in Regent's Park,[5] among lofty trees and fragrant flowers, beneath a clear summer's sky. Foggy? Well, it was foggy a while ago, but it seems to be July again.

There is Minnie, emerging from behind a cluster of foliage. The glass roof? Oh, yes, it is that funny old florist's hot-house. Kindest man out; never passes you by without giving a poor man a copper. Thank'ee, Sir, thanks!

Minnie has come to meet him. He know she would come, and that is why he made himself look so spruce. Everybody is fond of Minnie. At the dressmaker's where she works they call her "Queen of Hearts." They say the yard superintendent cheats at cards. What a beast!

"Take me home, Jack?"

Should rather think so. He takes her hand. She blushes. Girls will blush anyhow; they are built that way.

Suddenly it has got very dark, and they are in Bethnal Green.[6] What, already? They didn't ride, though; he is quite sure of that. Here they are, in front of her house, on the doorstep.

"Jack!"

"Yes, dear."

"Good-bye!"

She fumbles in her little bag, gets out her latch-key, opens the street door, looks round to make sure ... and kisses him, sobbing all the while.

"Oh, you silly, little goose!"

He notices some egg-shells. He sweeps them away; that's soon done. Somebody gives him a penny. Confound the man, now Minnie is gone!

Damn the policeman! He catches you by the scruff of the neck and drags you along.

"Say, old fellow, you are choking me!" He digs his iron knuckles into a bloke's neck ...

That gaol is a dreary place, and no mistake about it. Serves him right, though. If she got into trouble through such a mean skunk as that lanky, milk-and-water clerk it was her own look-out. Still anybody would have knocked down a miserable, blooming wretch who fooled a girl like Minnie, and then threw her up like a squeezed orange ...

Hang the little rascals! They will mess up the street with orange-peel and the like! He sweeps it away.

"Sorry, but you can't get your job again," says Plank, Timber, and Co., Limited. Don't want no gaol-birds, not they.

The work on the Underground is downright beastly. Tunnelling don't agree with him. Makes a chap drink, too; he does not booze, not exactly; but he drinks more than what is good for him.

My! How she is rigged out nowadays! And she grins all the time; every customer gets a smile with his gin-and-water. Fancy, Minnie a barmaid!

Is this Le-ster Square?[7] Where, then, would the Underground be? It's all blooming well mixed up, by Gosh! It must be Le'ster Square, for there is the Alhambra,[8] and ... well, Jack may be a trifle tipsy, but, dash it all, he can see all right. There is Minnie coming out of the Alhambra on the arm of a swell. He's got a Scotch plaid over his shoulder. They get into a hansom ... Poor Minnie! Her eyebrows are so very black. He wonders if she paints.[9]

"Look alive, my friend; give us a whisky, will yer?" Here in New York they call their barmen "bar-tenders," and everything is upside down. Seems an age since he crossed the water. Good pay; but, damn it all, they work the guts out of a chap.

"Hextra-a-a! Hextry spesho-o-ol!" That's the Frenchies and the Prooshians coming to blows.[10] Well, it is none of his business ...

Minnie is a ... Confound her! Still, he would never have come back to England but for her ... There, just look, there is a well-dressed, half-drunken woman walking up Piccadilly,[11] who ... He could almost swear it was Minnie. Drunk, eh? Well, he is a bit shaky himself.

Days seem ages in Guy's Hospital.[12] The nurses are fine girls, only they don't sell liquor. What a beast to run his infernal bike into a bloke's ribs! Might have worked to this day ...

"Eh, stop, will yer? Don't ye run away with my broom, don't! ye, blooming idiot! My broom, my broom, help!

* * *

I stop and look at him as he stands there, leaning against the tree. It seems to have a fellow-feeling for the old man. Just now they are both in the same plight.

The autumn had come for both man and tree. Whatever fruit the summer of their lives had ripened has gone into strangers' hands. Now they are both barren of everything; both looking forward to a long, cold, all-devastating winter, with the only difference that while the tree may live to see another spring, the scavenger's winter will have no springtide to follow in its wake.

Presently he shudders at some thought that has just flashed across his mind. Was it the north-easterly that has, perchance, tickled the terrible wound in his heart – the wound which time has been unable to heal?

Nobody knows. The street-lamp has, no doubt, seen a good deal of him. His friend, the apple-tree, may know a thing or two about him. As to the stones beneath him, he was certainly whispering to them all the time. But then, you see, a tree in the fall is too dead to tell any tales. The lamp, again, is like some learned men I knew; it lights everybody's path, and is at the same time a very poor observer. While the stones, low and down-trodden as they are, have, as in the case of the poor, long had their senses deadened.

And so it is all a mystery.

I wonder whether he is dead now – that is, whether he is done dying yet. He probably is by this time.

TEDDY ASHTON'S NORTHERN WEEKLY

Charles Allen Clarke, 'The Cotton Panic', *Teddy Ashton's Northern Weekly*, Introductory, I and II, 6 October 1900, pp. 9–10; III and IV, 13 October 1900, pp. 9–10; V and VI, 20 October 1900, pp. 9–11; VI (continued) and VII, 27 October 1900, pp. 9–10; VIII and IX, 3 November 1900, pp. 9–11; X and XI, 10 November 1900, pp. 9–11; XII, 17 November 1900, pp. 9–10; XIII and XIV, 24 November 1900, pp. 9–11; XV and XVI, 1 December 1900, pp. 9–11; XVII and XVIII, 8 December 1900, pp. 9–10; XIX, 15 December 1900, pp. 9–10; XIX (continued) and XX, 22 December 1900, pp. 9–10; XX (continued), XXI and XXII, 29 December 1900, pp. 9–10; [XXII (continued)] and XXIII, 5 January 1901, pp. 9–10; XXIII (continued) and XXIV, 12 January 1901, pp. 9–10; XXIV (continued) and XXV, 19 January 1901, pp. 9–10; XXVI, 26 January 1901, pp. 9–10; XXVII and XXVIII, 2 February 1901, pp. 9–10; XXVIII (continued) and XXIX, 9 February 1901, pp. 9–10; XXX and XXXI, 16 February 1901, pp. 9–10; XXXI (continued) and XXXII, 23 February 1901, pp. 6–7; XXXII (continued) and XXXIII, 2 March 1901, p. 6.

Teddy Ashton, 'Bill Spriggs an Bet: Their Matrimony an their Marlocks. Bet Turns Bill Eaut', *Teddy Ashton's Northern Weekly*, 16 February 1901, p. 13.

Frank Starr, 'An Unpremeditated Crime', *Teddy Ashton's Northern Weekly*, 18 October 1902, p. 12.

E. Whittaker, 'When Death Crossed the Threshold', *Teddy Ashton's Northern Weekly*, 28 February 1903, p. 10.

Alfred H. Pearce, 'An Angel of Humanity', *Teddy Ashton's Northern Weekly*, 23 July 1904, p. 3.

Teddy Ashton, 'Th' Female Fister', *Teddy Ashton's Northern Weekly*, 4 February 1905, p. 6.

Harford Willson, 'The Scarlet Shoes. (The Story of a Serio-comic Walking Tour and its Tragic End.)', *Teddy Ashton's Northern Weekly*, 3 March 1906, p. 6.

Teddy Ashton's Northern Weekly (1896–1908) continued to be edited by Charles Allen Clarke, and he remained the most prolific writer for the periodical. Nevertheless, he also published articles by others, such as Harford Willson (n.d.), John Tamlyn (n.d.) and James Haslam (1869–1937), as well as two long-running series of articles: Leon Gray's (n.d.) 'Modern Movements and Men' (1902) and C. J. B.'s (n.d.) 'Revelations of a Lodging-House Inspector' (1902). Clarke himself published a series of autobiographical articles in 1905 under the title 'Amongst the Agitators'. In 1903 Clarke started a campaign to put his socialist principles in practice by launching the Daisy Colony appeal, collecting funds to rent a house and land where a communistic colony might be founded. The experiment was launched in 1905, when a house and land in Carleton, near Blackpool, Lancashire, was rented for this purpose. Sales of the periodical began to decline towards the end of the period covered by this volume, and in February 1906 Clarke made the ownership of the *Northern Weekly* a limited company. The threat of closure at the end of 1906 was averted by an appeal to its readership for funds.

Little is known or recorded of the authors included in this selection, except for Clarke, whose full biographical details are given in the headnote for the *Bolton Trotter* in Volume 1, pp. 1–2. However, Harford Willson, Alfred H. Pearce (n.d.) and E. Whittaker (n.d.) were regular contributors to *Teddy Ashton's Northern Weekly*, although Willson published more factual articles than fiction, Pearce published more poetry, and Whittaker contributed both fiction and poetry to the journal as well as the children's column. Frank Starr also published in the *Labour Leader* in this period; see pp. 173–4 above.

Charles Allen Clarke, 'The Cotton Panic' (1900–1)

[6 October 1900]
Introductory

By wonderful yet common laws and processes of the universe acting upon human ways and customs a certain dreadful noise of slaughtering inventions used by men in that animal argument called war, going on in one part of the globe, produced, in another part of the world, a certain dreadful quietness of inventions used by men in making a livelihood and trade; the activity of the machinery of the American War caused a stoppage of the machinery of manufacture in Lancashire. The bullets that silenced fighting hearts in America struck the hearths of Lancashire; the swords that slashed the American armies cut the bread off Lancashire workers; the cannon that blasted the fields of the New World desolated thousands of homes in the Old. Thus are human destinies, near and far, interknit; and the conduct of one country affects the daily life of the nations. Ghastly deadly red strife in America caused in Lancashire the ghastly deathly white inaction known in history as "The Cotton Famine," and in the places where its woes were most felt, the towns and villages of the mills amid the moors of Lancashire, "The Cotton Panic."

This terrible time of starvation is not yet forgotten by those who experienced and endured it; indeed they will never forget it till earthly memories are no more. Amongst the children born in that period of poverty and suffering was the author of this story; who presents this picture of Lancashire's bitterest "hard times" in the hope that its like may never be known again.

I. The Whistler and the Stranger

In the icy January air that was blowing from Pendle Moors and Longridge Fells down the bleak valley of the Ribble[1] an undersized man, middle-aged and clad in all the shabby pathos of poverty, was slowly pacing, in begging fashion, one of the cottage streets of Preston, and whistling shrilly the sad melody of the song

"Hard Times."[2] Those who heard this musician, who had no instrument but nature's, put the words to the tune as it came from his lips.

> "Let us pause in life's pleasures and count its many tears,
> While we all sup sorrow with the poor;
> There's a song that will linger for ever in our ears,
> Oh, hard times come again no more.
>
>   Chorus. –
> "'Tis the song, the sigh of the weary,
> Hard times, hard times, come again no more;
> Many years have you lingered about my cabin door,
> Oh, hard times, come again no more!
>
>   * * *
>
> "'Tis a sigh that is wafted across the troubled wave,
> 'Tis a wail that is heard upon the shore,
> 'Tis a dirge that is murmured around the lowly grave,
> Oh, hard times, come again no more!"

The whistler, about whose face there was a humour, and in whose eyes there was a drollery not subdued by the evident misery of his existence, glanced appealingly at the windows of the houses on each side of him. But none of their inhabitants came to the doors, which were all shut against the bitter cold, though one or two children's faces peeped from lifted corners of thin or ragged curtains.

"It's no use," said the whistler to himself, with a look made half of despair and half of a lean grin, "nobody's nowt to give. They're all as badly off as me, or else worse."

He continued his whistling to the end of the street, then paused, flapped his arms to warm them, and blew his breath on his benumbed fingers.

"My breath would do wi a bit o' coal on," he said. "Th' fire is nearly gone out. I think I'll go an try my music on th' main street."

He made his way into the thoroughfare called Fishergate, from the old days when Preston's fishermen came up this road from the river, and started whistling again.

There were few folks out; the streets were practically empty.

"There's nobody out but them what's obliged," thought the whistler, "or them what's no fire awhum an is tryin to keep theirsels warm by walkin about, poor sowls! I think I'll chuck up, an pike off to my own kennel."

Just as he was whistling the last bars of "Hard Times" a well-dressed stout well-built man, with a considerable dark beard, approached him, and the musician's eyes lit up in the thought that at last he was about to glean a little monetary charity.

But he was disappointed. The gentleman merely inquired, "Can you tell me where Duckworth-street is?"

"Ay," said the whistler. "I'll take yo theer for a penny."

The stranger assented, and the two set off together.

"Dreadful cowd day, isn't it?" said the whistler. "It looks, and feels, like snow. It's no day for whistling – yo heard me whistling as yo came up – whistlin' 'Hard Times,' a tune written by th' chap as wrote 'Th' Owd Folks at Home' – a mon with some music in him – I fetch music out o' my mouth to fetch summat in it, if I can. But times are awful bad, an at the' best o' times, this town's no ear for good music. It doesn't appreciate whistling; but I'd sooner have it mysel than a piano or a brass band. But it's no weather for whistling to-day. Th' winter's whistlin o'er Pendle Hill[3] yon; an a cowd whistle he has too; he's whistling th' snow up. It's a deathly, keen nippin wind to-day; it cuts one like frozen razors."

"We get much greater cold in America," said the gentleman.

"Neaw, I thought yo'd come fro foreign parts by yore twang," said the whistler. "No disrespect," he added quickly. "So yo've come from America? That's where th' war is that's makin all t'bother.[4] How's it goin on? Is th' feightin any nearer an end yet?"

"I don't think it is," said the gentleman.

"I'm sorry for that answer," said his guide. "It's 1863 now; an th' war started in February, 1861. Then t' cotton run short, an th' factories began stoppin in October. We've had fifteen months on it. Do yo think it'll be o'er by next Christmas?"

"I couldn't say."

"So it may last till next Christmas? Eh, dear me, this has been th' unmerriest Merry Christmas and th' unhappiest Happy New Year Lancashire's ever known. Theer's t'new Town Hall, see yo. It's nearly finished now. I only wish they'd finish this cotton panic too. I suppose yo'll have heard o' this cotton panic?"

"Yes, I know the scarcity of cotton, owing to the war, has stopped the cotton trade in Lancashire. Are you a cotton operative?"

"I used to be. But I'm nowt at present. However, I'st be a skelleton soon, if this cotton panic keeps on. I'm a musician; an whistlin's my forte. Everybody calls me Whistlin Will, though my gradely name is Will Redford. I used to addle a fair livin wi my whistling – whistling at fairs, an th' market, an in th' pubs. But my whistlin's down in th' mouth now. However, let's hope that times will soon mend. That's th' parish curch we're passin now. It's hundreds o' years owd – I think it were built by th' ancient Romans when they camped at Walton-le-Dale,[5] across th' river yon – that's lung afore there were any factories or cotton panics. I know a bit of history, yo see. I get sometimes among a company that meets at th' Owd Dog Lad Inn, an there's a hantiquarian chap among 'em – Dicky Langton – an he tells us rare tales o' th' owd times; he knows them days as weel as if he'd lived in 'em. I wonder if anybody had to whistle for a livin in Julius Caesar's day. Though I say it mysel I'm a wonderful whistler, th' best for twenty miles around. But Preston folk has no ear for good music, an I'm not made as much on as I ought to be. Well, I daresay they'll put a monument up to me when I dee. Such things has occurred before wi greit men; neglected when alive, and honoured when dead."

The gentleman smiled.

"This is th' House o' Correction," said Whistling Will, nodding his head at the stone jail with its four martello towers[6] – his hands were deep in his pockets for warmth, "an by gow, I should think them what's prisoned there is better off than workin folks in these hard times."

"Yes, I've seen the building before. Are we far off Duckworth Street?"

"Neow, we'st soon be there now. It is down yon, nearly across th' river and into Walton-le-Dale. Might I ask who you're seechin? Happen I know 'em."

"A family called Milner."

"Oh, I know 'em very weel. I knowed th' father, Mat Milner, as well as I know myself nearly. Poor Mat! He's dead now – this cotton panic's kilt him and brought his family low. They used to live in a nice house, wi a parlour[7] – that were afore th' hard times come. Then they had to flit into a less house, an then a less – like many another family – till now they're in Duckworth Street. They'll be in a back court[8] next. Eh, it's a great pity to see dacent folk come down so, through no fault o' their own. I remember they had a daughter went to America to join th' Mormons[9] – them's em what believes in a man havin several wives. There were quite a talk about it when she went. As for me, I'm sensible enough to have no wife at all, but I should think one's quite as much as any ordinary chap can manage. I know that one's too much for a lot o' henpeckt husbands. But happen these Mormons have a secret for managin women."

"I am a Mormon myself," said the gentleman, "and proud to be a Latter Day Saint."

"Oh!" said Whistling Will, diplomatically; feeing that it would not be expedient to express himself unsympathetically towards the views of the gentleman, with whom he stood temporarily in the relation of employee to employer. He must not risk losing his penny for the sake of an opinion. "Well, there's nowt like bein broadminded."

"Mormonism is the true religion. It is because this country knows not the true religion that it is being providentially afflicted with a cotton famine."

"It may be so," said Whistling Will. "It's said that women's at the bottom of all th' mischief an trouble in th' world. So very likely th' question o' one wife or a batch o' wives may have summat to do wi th' cotton panic."

"There's an unmarried daughter in the Milner's house, is there not?"

"Ay; her name's Ada, an a fine wench she is too; one o' them bonny lasses which only Lancashire can produce. She's courtin, too – for young folks will court even if they're clamming, though love's only a very thin substitute for thick porritch, in my opinion. I know th' young chap very well that she's courtin. His names Sid Clifton, an' he's a hengineer at Wragley's factory – well, he were; but now he's like everybody else, doin nowt but wait for better times. He's a smart, good-looking young felly. I guess that him an his sweetheart would have been married now but for this cursed cotton panic."

The gentleman smiled to himself, but said nothing.

Whistlin Will gabbled on, relating bits of local lore and tales of his own experiences. But he always wound back to the present distress that was desolating the land.

"Dang the cotton panic, say I," he said, "it's makin a rare mess o' t' world. Last year were Preston Guild,[10] too – yo'll have heard o' th' Guild? – what only comes once in twenty year. But it were a strange, sad Guild year; folks had neither heart nor money for rejoicing. An t' Prince o' Wales is getting wed this year too; next month, I'm towd. Well, I suppose Royalty must get wed so's heaw t' poor goes on. I reckon there'll be thousands o' pounds spent in Ryal illuminations an fireworks. I think it would look better on 'em to give t' brass to them what's starving. Eh, I could tell yo such terrible tales o' trouble! Bein a public character like, an whistling about fro one end o' town to t' other, an often to other towns an villages, I sees a lot more than th' average man sees. I could write a book – nay, many a book – on th' sights I've seen since this cotton panic started. – Hello, Billy!" and Will spoke to a figure with pinched, boyish face, yet in girlish attire, which passed by.

"Is that a boy?" asked the gentleman, "I thought it was a girl."

"He's a lad, sure enough," said Will. "He's twelve year owd an gooin in thirteen. I know him an his family well."

"What's he doing in girl's clothes, then, at his age?"

"Th' answer that answers that question," said Will, "is th' answer that answers all the queer an sad questions an things yo see in Lancashire to-day. Th' answer is – th' cotton panic. Billy's parents can't afford to buy him breeches because they haven't even money to buy bread, so Billy's obliged either to go about as naked as a heathen or wear whatever he can catch. So he's got one of his owder sister's black frocks on, an a comic sight he makes, as yo seed; but God knows, there's tragedy under t' comedy. T' other day I saw Billy steiling prato-peelins fro t' back of a farmer's pig-cots, but I turned my head away like a Christian an said nowt nor seed nowt. Later on I called at Billy's house an found that his mother had boiled th' prato peelins wi a bit o' meal an they were havin a rare banquet. Th' Lord Mayor o' London's dinnerin weren't in it for relish. Hungry dogs will eat dirty puddin. Them prato peelins were a regular godsend."

"Matters seem to be getting desperate in Lancashire," said the stranger with sincere sympathy.

"Dal desperate," said Whistlin Will. "Folks are actually eitin Indian meal.[11] It's better than starvation, so' how; an it fills up an it's chep; an them's big considerations in pinchin times. I could tell yo such tales o' trouble. Preston's been a dreary place this last twelve months. Factories idle, standin like skeletons; folks like skeletons too; in fact it's a skeleton world at present. There'll be great rejoicing when t' smook floats out o' t' factory chimleys again. Th' smook nobbut makes black banners, but they're banners o' beauty an glory to them what lives round t' steam-engins. I were in a hovel t' other day an I seed a chap deein on some straw in a corner. Yet that chap were once a spinner getting good wages. In another house I seed a little babby deed in a box. 'Poor thing!' I says, 'theau't weel off. Theau't better out o' this clem-hole.' Happen yo'll have heard o' Sam Laycock,[12] one of our Lancashire singin-brids, an a tip-top throstle at th' job too. He's written a little ballad about a child comin in th' world during these hard times.[13] I'll give yo a verse – I have it aw off by heart, for I do a bit o' reciting as weel as whistling – but as I towd yo afore, these is poor times for th' fine arts. Sam says in his little touchin song, addressin th' new-born babby –

> 'Theau't welcome, little bonny brid,
> But shouldn't ha' come just when tha did,
>   Times are bad;
> We're short o' pobbies for eaur Joe,
> But that of course tha didn't know,
>   Did ta, lad?'

That poem fotches tears in th' een of aw who hear it, because there's hardly a house in th' shire but what's havin th' same experience. I were in a house yesterday, – a young couple what got wed just before the 'panic' started. Th' woman had been confined th' day afore. 'How is she?' I says, for I knowed her, as pratty a weiver as ever thread a shuttle. 'She's very ill!' says her husband, wi tears in his een, 'I fear she's gooin – she wants nourishment – but how am I to get it?' an he clenched his fists in anguish. 'An how's th' babby?' says I. He said no word, but fetched a little owd basket out of a corner. There lay th' little innocence dead. 'That's aw there's left onit,' – an he sobbed from his broken heart. Eh, me! these is weary times. But it's th' same tale everywhere! Just th' same at Bolton, at Blackburn, at Darwen, at Rochdale, at Chorley, at Wigan, – th' same all o'er Lancashire".[14]

"But there is help – there are relief works, public subscriptions, soup kitchens, and so forth," said the gentleman.

"That's so; but yo can't deg a vast droopin garden wi two or three drops o' wayter. However, here's Duckworth-street."

The two had half descended the long slope that runs down from the House of Correction to the river, which it crosses by a low stone bridge.

"That's Milner's, th' third house on th' right hand side," said Whistling Will. "I'll leave yo now."

The gentleman handed his guide his fee. Whistling Will looked at the coin in joyful amazement.

"I said a penny," he said. "This is sixpence."

"It's all right," said the gentleman.

"God bless yo," said Will, clutching the coin as if afraid that it would melt out of his hand. "It's long since I had sixpence to swagger wi. I shall get a fair meal for once. Good day, an thank yo, thank yo!"

Whistling Will turned about, to retrace his steps towards the centre of the town, while the gentleman knocked at the door of the Milners. A girl of twenty, with a sweet face, yet worn and weary-looking for one so young, one who should have been rich and rosy in the glory of youth, opened the door, starting and staggering back when she saw the stranger.

"Mr. Hyde!" she gasped, with a look of fear in her pretty eyes.

"Yes, 'tis I, Ada!" said Mr. Hyde with a seductive smile. "I've had to search long for you, but I've found you at last."

II. Whistling Will Innocently Upsets A Young Man

Whistling Will, gleeful in the windfall of sixpence, started whistling for joy as he walked up London-road. A woman came to a door and offered him a penny. "Dang my button!" said Will, "but I wasn't whistling professionally this time. I was just letting off some jubilee steam, that's aw. But that's t' way o' t' world. It never gives a chap what he expects, though he often gets what he doesn't expect both wi regard to pleasure an pain."

However, he was sagacious enough to take the coin and went on his way whistling merrily. Near the House of Correction he met the sexton of an adjacent church. "Well, Jimmy," he said, "an how's trade?"

"There's nowt doin," said Jimmy, "nowt at aw. Poverty doesn't dee much. Folks is so poor that they corn't afford a funeral. Though i' my opinion there's far more kilt wi o'er-feedin than wi clemmin."

"It's a rum go," said Will. "Folks corn't afford oather to live or dee just at present, so they're doin' noather; they're merely starvin."

"It's weary times," said Jimmy. "I wonder when they'll end?"

"They're bound to end some time," said Will. "Th' greit question is, will they end afore they end us?"

"I've been talkin to Owd Betty Redhead, her as sells Everton toffy[15] made o' treacle, a droll owd soul wi ways of her own, an a temper of her own too; she's th' owdest woman i' Preston, she's ninety or noan far off it, an she says she never knew such a time as this in aw her born days. She remembers strikes an th' plug-drawin riots an t' Chartist riots when t' 72nd Higlanders shot five men deead i' Lune-street,[16] an other dark times an misfortunes, but never nowt like this."

"Ay, this'll be a time to talk about some day, sure enough, for them what manages to live through it. I wonder what yo an me's done to be born t' these days, Jimmy."

Fanciful speculations concerning the period of history in which one happened to be born had no interest for the sexton; and he began to talk about the "relief" works on Preston Moor, a place of wild land the authorities had decided to open out merely to find work for the unemployed cotton operatives, a thousand of whom were engaged in leveling and cutting it up for building purposes.

"Ay, they're tryin to find wark for t' starving folk in other towns too," said Will. "In Manchester an Bolton an Wigan an them places they've set 'em roadmakin an I'm towd that t' spinners is shapin pretty weal at t' job, though pavin an navvyin' is blisterin wark for them that's noan used to it. But owt to earn a bit o' bread. It were i' t' newspaper that t' other week there were thirty theausand folk on t' relief funds at Ashton-u-Lyne,[17] an that five hundert an thirty tons o' coal were given eaut to five theausand poor families i' Blackburn. Clammin's cowd wark i' winter; one can manage beaut fire i' summer an miss a meal or two for t' matter o' that; but it's another hobble awtogether i' winter."

"There's a deal o' money bin collected an given out i' charity tickets," said Jimmy.

"Ay, the London papers, an others is getting their readers to send brass in, though I see that bread is now eightpence a loaf in London; an there's a lot o' money bein sent here fro Australia an India, an other places. Leeds alone has subscribed twenty-six thousand pound. Good Owd Yorkshire! Let nobody call Yorkshire folks skinny after that.[18] Wealth may divide folks, but poverty makes us all brothers. Then there's concerts bein held up an down for th' Famine Fund, which now amounts to over four hundred thousand pounds. But what's even all that money where there's so many wantin it?"

As Whistling Will said, money was pouring in from all quarters of the globe to relieve the famine in Lancashire.[19] All our colonies cheerfully subscribed – New Zealand, South Africa, Canada, and Australia. Everybody was eager to help. Mary Howitt, the poetess, wrote and published a story, "Little Cristal," giving all the proceeds to the famine fund.[20] To their credit, a firm of printers printed and bound the book for nothing. Charles Dickens, too, was at this time giving readings from his works, in Paris and elsewhere, for the benefit of the famine fund.[21]

"Well," said Will, "I'll be getting a bit fur, Jimmy. It's a nippin east wind to stand in. Is it true that th' folks has been riotin for bread at Ashton-under-Lyne?"

"Ay, it's true; an they've been riotin at Stockport and Dukinfield, an other places too. But the worst do were at Ashton. Th' folk were clamming desperate, so they broke into th' relief stores an helped theirsels."

"An I durn't blame 'em," said Will.

"But th' police did," said Jimmy. "They've locked eighty-one folks up, an twenty-seven of 'em women."

"An what'll they do wi 'em?" asked Will.

"Give 'em hard labour," said Jimmy.

"That's noan jannock?" said Will.

"Folk shouldn't breik th' law," said Jimmy.

"There's no law to a starving mon," said Will, "an no law should dare to punish him."

"There's other mischief astair too," said Jimmy. "Th' Fenians[22] is howdin secret meetins. It's said they're goin to blow Lancaster Castle up, or Chester Castle."

"Well, there'll be wark for somebody to build 'em up again," said Will, "so that'll be good for trade."

"Don't let anybody hear thee talk like that or theau'll be getting locked up as a Fenian thyself," said Jimmy.

"It's a free country, an a chap may say what he likes," said Will.

"He may *think* what he likes," said Jimmy, "but he'd best be careful how he says it, free country or no free country."

"I see that th' Bowton Union Clerk has been axin for a rise o' salary because o' th' extra work he has owin to th' poverty o' th' people. I think that's rayther a mean thing," said Will, "to ax for mooar wages off a clamming town."

"There's aw sorts o' folk in a world," said Jimmy, drily. "Well, I'll be pikin off. It's too cowd a wind to stand talkin in. My feet's gootn numb."

Leaving the sexton, Whistling Will went down Church-street and Fishergate; his eyes lighting up with recognition as he saw a young man, over medium height, with a bright intelligent face, coming towards him from the direction of the station.

"Sid Clifton," said Will to himself. "I wonder where he's been. Happen nobbut walking about, like hundreds of others, because he's nowt better to do. Hello, Sid!" and he greeted the young man as the two met.

"Hallo, Will! What are you doing out in this bitter weather?" said Sid Clifton.

"What art thou doin out?" asked Will. "It's as cheerful for me as for thee."

"Oh, I've been to Liverpool on business. Been after a job in fact."

"I hope theau's been lucky enough to get it."

"I have, I'm glad to say."

"That's better. It's time I met somebody wi some good news. What mak of a job is it?"

"Engineering."

"In a factory?"

"No; there's no spinnin factories in Liverpool. It's on a boat."

"So theau'rt goin to be a sailor an see foreign parts. Where's th' boat goin to?"

"I don't know. Nobody knows. There's a deal of secrecy about it. But one can swallow a bit of mystery if the pay's good."

"What's th' boat called?"

"I don't even know that. At present the only name it has is 'Number 290.' It's a new steamer, and Laird Brothers, of Birkenhead,[23] are the builders. I've seen the vessel, and I could see that it's fashioned for speed."

"Ah well. I hope it'll prove a dal fine job for thee, Sid."

"It won't be bad, though I'm only assistant engineer. Would you like to go as a stoker, Will? Perhaps I could get you on."

"No, thank thee. I'm afraid that stoking would spoil my whistle. An such a wonderful whistle as mine – such a whistle as is only heard once in a generation – mustn't be brunt to a cinder in a dirty roastin, stinkin stokehole."

Sid laughed and said, "All right, Will. I'll be getting towards Walton and home."

"I've just been that road myself," said Will. "I were whistling away an hour ago when a strange gentleman axed me where Duckworh-street were. I said I'd show him for a penny. But he were a generous sort, or else he were pleased at findin what he were after, for he gave me a tanner. I entertained him wi buzzes, an sad tales o' th' famine, an odds an ends of owd ancient history, as we went alung, peintin places out to him, an thinkin that he were a total stranger to the town till he flabbergasted me by sayin that he knew th' spots I mentioned. But he didn't let on that he'd been i' Preston afore till I showed him th' House of Correction, an it were on my tongue's tip then to ax him if that were th' house he's lodged in on his former visits here; but I were wise enough not to say owt to lose my job as guide."

"You say you took him to Duckworth-street? That's where the Milners live. What did he want with Duckworth-street?"

"Oh, I know thou'rt vastly interested in Duckworth-street, Sid. Odd to say, this here foreign gentleman were lookin for th' Milners."

"What did he want 'em for?" asked Sid, quickly.

"Nay, now theau'rt askin' me more than I can tell thee, lad. But he said he were a Mormon – a Latter Day Saint."

"Latter Day Devils!" exclaimed Sid, so emphatically that he startled his companion.

"Laws! how yo made me jump!" said Whistling Will. "He seemed a very nice gentleman, an if all the Mormons pays like him, they'll not be bad bosses to work for. Th' Mormons used to have a church i' Preston, so I've heard Owd Dicky

Langton say; it were th' first place in Great Britain to which a Mormon missionary were sent. That were in 1837, when our gracious Queen came to th' throne. They had a place in Vauxhall-road, an after that in th' Cockpit. I've larnt a bit o' Preston history wi listenin to Owd Dicky Langton. But th' Mormons is played out here now. Th' Preston chaps has sense to see that one wife's quite enough to make a man miserable."

Sid had hardly been listening to Will. He was in deep thought, with a troubled look on his face.

"So you took this stranger to Milner's?" he said.

"Ay; he paid me to do it."

"The villain. I guess who he is; one of the same gang of scamps that, with fine lies, enticed Nelly Milner away to Salt Lake City two years ago, since when we have never heard anything of her except through such fellows as this, who only tell what they choose to tell. Did he go into the Milner's house?"

"I left him theer," said Will. "I hope yo're not vexed; I'm sorry to give yo news that upsets yo."

"Good-day, Will," and Sid Clifton hurried excitedly in the direction of his sweetheart's home, while Whistling Will said to himself, "Well if ever! He's off like a thunderbout. I didn't think my bit o' news would flust him off like this. What a gunpowder thing it is to be in love; I hope him an th' Mormon doesn't' get feightin."

[13 October 1900]

III. The Lovers

Sid Clifton was certainly considerably agitated in heart as he made his way, at a very vigorous pace, towards Duckworth-street. And there was some cause for his excitement. Mr. Willard Hyde, the Mormon missionary, had, on two previous occasions, sought out the Milners, his undisguised object being to persuade Ada to go to Salt Lake City, where Mr. Willard Hyde was an elder of the church, and there become one of his wives – he already had three. Just before the beginning of the cotton panic he had paid his first visit to the Milners, ostensibly calling to deliver a message from Ada's sister, Nellie, who six months previous, had gone to America with a Mormon friend of Mr. Hyde's. On this occasion Mr. Hyde had seen Ada and taken a fancy to the girl. As Ada at that time was at an age when the glamour of sex is strong upon a maid, she had, childishly, purely, without any thought, been friendly and familiar with Mr. Hyde, just as she was with her brother or her father (who was then alive.) She liked Mr. Hyde, because he was a man; and the magic of the masculine on the feminine, though she knew it not, was beginning, with subtle strength, to assert itself in her being. Of course

Ada, at this time, had not begun "courting," she was only just turned seventeen; indeed she had not yet met the young engineer, Sid Clifton.

When the American war commenced Mr. Hyde had called again upon the Milner's, who were then living in another part of the town, in a pleasant cottage the father being alive and earning good wages as a spinner and the family consequently enjoying a happy, though humble, prosperity. Mr. Hyde was evidently in love in his expansive Mormon way with Ada; but the girl, who had now begun "keeping company" with Sid Clifton, who went to the same Sunday school, was shy of him and in a slight degree afraid. He tried to make love to her one occasion but she had courteously repelled him. Then he held before her the example of the Old Testament patriarchs who had several wives, and tried to show Ada that polygamy was commended by God. Ada listened to him silently, having no talent for theological argument, and wished that he would let her alone; she was quite content with her lover, Sid Clifton, whom she loved truly and passionately, though with the cool propriety that characterises an English wooing, which has not in it the volcanic elements of the amorous hearts of hot southern climes. Mr. Hyde loved like a Turk;[24] but Ada preferred the undivided devotion of one English lover; and told the American so.

"That is because you do not understand," he had said. "Your sister is quite happy as one of the wives of my friend Mr. Brigham Bouncely".[25]

"Why doesn't she write and tell us so herself then?" asked Ada.

"What need to write when she can send word of her bliss by messengers?"

Mr. Hyde talked eloquently and used all his powers of persuasion on Ada, but he made no impression on the girl, except to scare her. Then he had gone away and she had heard nothing of him for over a year. But now he had turned up again.

Of these things Sid was thinking as he walked towards Duckworth-street. His sweetheart had candidly told him all that had passed between her and Mr. Hyde. Sid had never seen the man; but he disliked him in a natural jealousy, for trying to woo Ada; and he hated him because of his Mormon principles. Yet he had no fear that his sweetheart would give the least encouragement to the Salt Lake City wholesale husband. Sid knew that Ada loved himself and would be true to him. But all the same he felt very angry towards this Mormon who had already, being a wealthy man and a leading light in the Mormon church, at least three or four wives.

"I'd like to kick the beggar," said Sid to himself as he knocked at Milner's door and entered the house, denuded and desolate, for most of the furniture had been sold to buy bread.

His first glance was directed to his sweetheart, who was sitting on the hearthstone, though there was no fire in the grate. Opposite Ada sat her mother, shivering and drawing her clothes tightly about her for warmth. Against the bare table sat the Mormon visitor, Mr. Hyde; his good clothes and well-fed appearance contrasting pathetically with the poverty-stricken aspect of the room.

Ada, rather flurriedly, and with a blush, introduced Sid to Mr. Hyde. Sid half scowled, and did not hold out his hand, while Mr. Hyde merely interjected a suspicious "Ah!"

Then Mr. Hyde rose to go, saying to Mrs. Milner, "Well, you will think over what I have said. I shall remain in England some months, and will call again."

Sid wished to speak, but was checked by the thought that he had no right to interfere; he was not yet one of the family. He had no business to poke into Mrs. Milner's affairs. But it was hard work to hold his tongue back. He felt that he would like to give this man a "good talking to," as we say in Lancashire.

"Very well," said Mrs. Milner to Hyde. She spoke in a weak and vacillating manner: she was worn-out and despairing by the terrible struggle for bread. "I should like," she went on, "to have some news of Nellie from herself – in her own writing. I wish she would write to us, and let us know how she is going on."

"I have informed you that she is all right," said Hyde. "I left her happy and in the best of health."

Sid could hold himself no longer. "Why doesn't she write to us herself?" he asked.

"I beg your pardon, sir," said Hyde, "but I am not aware that you have anything to do with this matter. I was addressing my conversation to Mrs. Milner."

"I have some right to speak," said Sid. "If I am not mistaken – and I know I am not – you have come here to entice this young lady –" he laid his hand on Ada's shoulder – "to your vile Mormon den of deceit and immorality. And as this young lady's sweetheart, I have a right to interfere; to warn her against listening to your lies. I speak straight to your face; and I fear you not."

Hyde smiled, but there was the look of an impending thunderstorm about his smile. "Perhaps you are afraid that Miss Ada Milner may be attracted to Mormonism," he said. "I grant that it is a tempting and beautiful creed, despite your ungentlemanly denunciation of it. And, further, as Miss Ada is by no means your wife, she has a right to please herself in disposing of her charms."

"I shall never marry anybody but Sid," said Ada, and her lover looked at her proudly and joyfully, "so you need not bother me any further, Mr. Hyde. If you are a gentleman you will take this refusal, and never come here again."

Mr. Hyde smiled. "We shall see," he said. "Good afternoon, Mrs. Milner, and good afternoon Ada."

Glaring at Sid, he opened the door and passed out.

"If ever he comes again," said Sid, "I'll kick him out if you'll only give me permission, Mrs. Milner."

Mrs. Milner made no answer; she only rocked herself to and fro and sighed. All the strength was gone from her, prostrated by poverty and semi-starvation she was indifferent to everything.

"Cheer up," cried Sid, producing some food from his pocket. "We'll have a feast. I bought these sausages in Liverpool. Get 'em cooked, Ada; where's the bread?"

"We have none," said Ada. "And we've no fire for cooking."

"Then fetch some bread," said Sid, giving her sixpence, "and I'll find some coal."

"Hast thou come into a fortune, Sid?" asked Mrs. Milner in surprise.

"No, but I've got work, and been paid some of my wage in advance."

"But your folks are hard up too, Sid," said Ada.

"I'm not forgetting them," said Sid. "While you're going for the bread I'll just slip down to my mother's. I'll be back by the time you have the sausages cooked, and we'll have a jolly tea together."

Ada went out to purchase the bread, and Sid, after getting a small wheelbarrow full of coal from the next street, hurried home. He was back, however, at the Milner's just as the sausages were frizzing nicely brown before the fire.

"Now this is something like a Christian smell," said Sid, sniffing the odour.

"It's long since I smelt so good a smell," said Mrs. Milner. "Keep that door shut, Ada. If the clamming neighbours smell this, there'll be a riot."

"I wish we'd sufficient to divide with all the poor folks in the town," said Ada, as she set the cups on the table, and cut the bread.

"Shall I put butter on the bread, mother?" she asked.

"No, no," said Mrs. Milner. "We've very little butter left. Sausage is good enough without butter. We'll be fain o' dry bread again before long."

While they were enjoying the meal, the door opened and in came a girl of fifteen, a younger sister of Ada's.

"Why it's our Lily," said Mrs. Milner. "What's brought thee here to-day?"

"Missus said I could have a bit of a walk, so I thought I would slip down to see how you're getting on. I've brought something for you," and she opened a little parcel, revealing some cold potatoes and meat.

"It's very good of thy missus to remember us," said Mrs. Milner.

Lily did not explain that the food was her own dinner, of which she had deprived herself in order to feed her mother and sister. She was employed as servant in the house of Mrs. Treebarn, wife of a dissenting minister. Though on this occasion the food brought by Lily was the girl's own dinner, Mrs. Treebarn had sent many things to the Milners, for she was a kindly, sympathetic woman. Had she known that Lily was going without dinner in order to give it away she would have gently chided the girl for her excessive self-denial and given her food to take out of her own larder. But she did not know.

"Well, Lily," said Sid, "we'll share the cold beef and potatoes on condition that you share the sausages with us," so Lily got something to eat after all, and was soon laughing heartily at the lively talk of Sid, who could be noisily droll, in a simple humorous way when he chose.

There was a knock at the door.

"I'll open it," said Sid, springing to his feet to save his sweetheart the trouble. "Why, it's old Chartist Grimshaw," he said.

"Right lad," said a tall, thin old man with deep bright eyes and grey head, "I've come to see if Mrs. Milner has a match she can spare. I've been out and piked a bit o' wood an coal, so I want to make a fire. This weather's bitter for old chaps whose blood is freezing thin with old age."

"Here's a match," said Sid.

"Come in, Chartist Grimshaw," cried Ada, "and have a cup of tea."

"Nay, lass, I should be robbin you," said Grimshaw, longingly.

"While we've a bit we'll spare a bit," said Ada, and Sid looked admiringly at his sweetheart.

"Ay, come in, Chartist," said Sid, "Come and sit down a minute."

Grimshaw's real Christian name was Henry, but everybody called him "Chartist Grimshaw," because of his connection with that body of reformers which had fought for "The People's Charter".[26]

Chartist Grimshaw sat near the table, and Ada gave him some tea and some sausage on some bread.

"Thank you, thank you," said the old man, "this is certainly a better meal than the one I was going to have. This is royal fare."

"What were you going to have, Chartist?" inquired Sid.

"I hardly like to tell you," answered Chartist. "However, there's no shame about starvation. I'd stolen some stuff out of a pig-trough, and some potato peelings out of a swilling-tub, and I was going to boil the lot."

Chartist was living with his son-in-law next door. But the son-in-law was afflicted, like everybody else, with the cotton famine, and his wife and family were suffering; so Chartist had to shift for himself and catch what he could.

"Oh, how I wish we could feed everybody," said Ada.

"It's very hard times," said Chartist, "some of the hardest I've known, and I've known a few. But we mustn't grumble. The war is a just war the Northern States of America are fightin to give freedom to shackled slaves, an we must bear up in the thought that we are helpin by our sufferin. I've fought for freedom all my life, an I'll not turn coward or traitor in my old age."

"Goo lad, Chartist," said Sid.

"The world improves but slowly though," said Chartist. "I remember the beginning of the Chartist movement – from which I get the nickname that I'm proud on – I remember orators, an writers, Ernest Jones, Feargus O'Connor,[27] an others, an what glorious dreams we had, an how we faced peril an feared not prisons – I've been in gaol myself – for the sake of our cause; an where is our cause now? Fizzlin out like wind out of a pricked bladder. Where are all our songs an our music an our banners? Where are our ringin speeches an our fiery souls? There seems nothing left.[28] Yet I hope; I'll not despair. If not in our time, the good time shall come someday."

Chartist babbled on, of great meetings long forgotten by all but him, of rousing speeches, of secret assemblies, of conflicts with police and soldiers, of all that he had seen and known of the Chartist movement. Then, having finished his talk and his meal, he went away to his own desolate cot.

Sid whispered to Ada that he would like her to go out with him for a brief walk; so presently the two went out together into the street.

IV. On the River-side

The winter afternoon had darkened into dusk, rapidly thickening into night, as Ada and Sid made their way down the road towards Walton-le-Dale. The air was very cold, the wind blowing keenly from the north.

"We'll not stay out long," said Sid, "or you'll be frozen. But I wanted us to be by ourselves for a few moments. Let me see if I can't keep you warm," and he smilingly put his arm round her waist.

"I am not cold, Sid," said Ada, trying to keep from shivering, for her clothes were thin and old.

"Let us walk sharply for a few moments," said Sid. "I'll see that you don't fall."

They walked briskly along the river-bank, over the ground where they had often loitered lovingly in the sweet summer nights, when the river ran brightly by, and all the valleys and the mountain-sides[29] were fair. But now the dale and hill were bare and bleak; the trees were wintry and the flowers all fled. The river rolled by, with little sobbing splashes against the slimy banks. They could see the water dimly gleaming in the darkness.

"When I am on the sea," said Sid, "I shall think of our river and try to recognise its waters in the vast deeps."

"On the sea, Sid? What do you mean?"

"That's what I brought you out to tell. I've got a berth on a Liverpool steamship."

"Then you are going away, Sid?"

"There is no help for it."

"Where are you going?"

"I don't know yet. Australia or America. The ship's rigged out for a long voyage. But I don't know the port yet. However, that doesn't much matter."

"How long will you be away?" asked Ada with quivering lips.

"I can't even tell that. But not very long, I hope."

"Oh Sid, and do you want to go?"

"No need to ask that, sweetheart! – But I must be doing something. Our folks are feeling the pinch of the hard times now. They cannot keep themselves, much less me. I shall be able to keep them now, – and you too. In fact, if that hadn't been my notion, I shouldn't have taken the place. Be brave, Ada; I shall soon be back. And then this war, and cotton famine will be over, maybe, and there'll be no need for me to go to sea again."

"Where is the ship?"

"Liverpool."

"Oh yes. You said you'd been to Liverpool."

"Yes, the ship's been made in Liverpool, – well, Birkenhead, to be correct. She's manned chiefly by Fylde lads – I know several of 'em – Dick Bickerstaffe, from Lytham, Billy Parr, from Blackpool, Harry Thornton from Kirkham, and others".[30]

"And when do you sail, Sid?"

Sid's face saddened. "To-morrow!" he said.

"Oh, Sid, how soon! To-morrow!"

"It is soon, dreadfully soon, but it can't be helped, sweetheart."

Ada was crying.

"Don't cry, Ada! Don't! or you'll make me want to give the berth up. I wouldn't have taken it, only I thought I might make some money, and so be enabled to get married. Don't cry, I shan't be away long. Be a brave lassie now."

Ada dried her tears, clinging closely to her sweetheart.

The night was black; not a star to be seen.

"Now there's another thing," said Sid. "That fellow, Hyde? What did he want?"

"You know, Sid," said Ada fearfully.

"Ay, I know. Curse him. What's he been saying this time? The same old tale, I guess."

"Yes. He wanted me to go back to America with him. He said I should be as happy as our Nellie –"

"Lies, lies!" interrupted Sid. "I'll warrant your Nellie's miserable, if we only knew the truth. But we've only this fellow's reports."

"He's trying to influence mother, Sid. He said that if I went with him, mother would never want; in fact, she could go with us, if she liked. And trouble and starvation have made mother wavering. It's hard for her to be firm when she knows that by yielding she can gain at least a secure living. If this famine lasts much longer I am afraid mother will do anything to keep from dying of poverty."

"But she can't force you to marry him," said Sid. "Ada, I don't know what to do. If there were time, and I had money, we would be married by special licence to-morrow, and then you would be safely mine. But there is not time, and I have not money. I have to go to Liverpool to-morrow afternoon."

"And God knows when you'll see me again," said Ada, breaking into tears.

Sid kissed her and consoled her.

"Has Hyde gone away?" he asked.

"Gone out of Preston, do you mean? I don't know," said Ada. "I wish he had, and I wish he would never come back again."

"Ugh!" said Sid, "It makes me shudder to think of my sweetheart being one of that fellow's half-dozen wives. It's too horrible to think of."

"They must be queer women, Sid, who can share a husband so," said Ada.

"They'd probably argue that that proved their unselfishness," said Sid, grimly smiling.

"It's wickedness," said Ada.

"It's hoggishness; piggishness," said Sid. "I think I shall kick Mr. Hyde if ever I come across him again. If he should call while I am away don't let him in, Ada. Keep the door bolted against him. Or if he does chance to get in you must go out."

"I shall do all I can to avoid and discourage him," said Ada, "but he's a dreadfully obstinate man."

"Anybody can see mule in his face," said Sid, with the reckless exaggeration or misrepresentation prejudice makes of facts. "But I know you'll be true to me, Ada."

Kissing and caressing, and repeating vows of love the pair turned about and retraced their steps towards the bridge that crosses the river at Walton-le-Dale.

The night was at its depth of darkness and silence now. The weird gloom and loneliness frightened Ada, who had heard many tales of robbery latterly. With the severity of the cotton famine crime had increased, and drunkenness and prostitution; while significant on the bill-posting hoardings loan-office advertisements were plentiful.

"Let us hurry, Sid," said Ada, "I don't like being here."

"Surely you're not afraid while I'm with you," said Sid, laughing.

"No; but this is an awfully desolate place."

They now felt damp specks on their faces.

"Snow," said Sid. "I thought we should have it sometime to-night. It's been coming up all day."

The white flakes gave the night a ghostly semblance.

"The snow will make starvation worse," said Ada.

"It may find a few men work to clear it away," said Sid. "It looks as if it was going to be a heavy fall."

They were now nearing the bridge. Across the river, unseen in the night, Walton church stood on the hill, above the trees on the slope. Far behind them the river wound through the wide and fertile valley, so beautiful in spring and grand even in winter. Most of the walks up the river and the highways that led to the neighbouring towns were well known to Sid and Ada, who had rambled them often in their lovers' ramblings. Both were thinking of these sunlit walks now; recalling sweetest memories.

"Do you remember that day we walked to Houghton Tower?' said Sid, "and the splendid view we had from the hill?"

Ada recollected. The day was a clear, autumn Sunday; and from the hill ascending towards Houghton Tower they had had on turning round, a magnificent view of the estuary of the Ribble, the shining sea in the western distance and all the green and wooded land between them and the shore, with the farms amidst the trees and the villages in the valley, and across the river to the north the fairness of the quaint and quiet Fylde land. As Sid said, in joy of the sight, such a view made a man feel that he wanted to kneel down and thank God for the beauty of the earth. And Sid's words were no empty fine phrase; he was not a man who never said what he did not mean; he expressed the emotion he truly felt.

Silent for a moment in these happy memories, and each wondering sadly when they would stroll together these ways again, they reached the bridge, and began to ascend the path leading up to the road. They heard voices, and saw two figures, a female and a male, emerge from behind the buttress of an arch, but could not distinguish them because of the dark and the thick whirling snow. These two preceded them up the path to the street. Then in the pale scanty light of a lamp Ada recognized the female.

"It's Lucy Clayton," she said, "and the man with her is young Wragley, the factory master's son. What does it mean, Sid?"

"It means suffering and shame," said Sid, "and all through this cursed cotton panic."

Lucy Clayton was one of Ada's weaving-shed companions. She was the daughter of very poor parents, who had a big family, Lucy being the eldest.

"Don't let her see us," said Ada, "it would hurt her to think I had seen her."

But Lucy and her companion stopped near a lamp, and Sid and Ada passed the pair. Despite the fact that the snow, now covering the ground, muffled their footsteps, Lucy saw Ada and Sid as they approached, and turned away her face.

"Poor Lucy!" said Ada, "and she was going to marry Ted Banister."

Sid said nothing, but his fists were clenched; and the two walked on in silence till they reached the corner turning into Duckworth-street.

Then Sid said, "Now Ada, sweetheart, after tomorrow I shall see you no more for a time. Oh, how I wish I had not to go – I will slip in tomorrow morning. I shall have to be off soon after dinner. – I want you to promise me that whatever happens you will not listen to that reptile Hyde."

"There's no need to promise, Sid, but I promise. Nothing shall break me from you."

He clasped her in his arms and kissed her.

"I shall soon be back – and I will send money to help you," he said. "And the cotton panic must end soon – it cannot last much longer."

One more embrace, and then, covered with snow, they entered Ada's home.

[20 October 1900]

V. The Virgin's Inn

While Sid Clifton and Ada Milner were spending their good-bye evening together, – the last time they would see each other for they knew not how long – Whistling Will, trudging through the still-falling snow in the dark and desolate night, made his way to an old tavern called The Virgin's Inn, noticeable as the only thatched tavern in the borough, – the only ancient roof in the midst of a town of modern roofs; like an old-fashioned knee-breeched rustic standing amongst a crowd of factory artisans – situated in a short narrow turning called Anchor Weind, off Friargate.[31]

Whistling Will entered the tavern and went straight to the half open door of a room where a great pleasant fire was burning.

"Whistling Will!" cried several voices as Will stepped forward.

"Here's a seat for thee, lad!"

The room was full of men, mostly of the working class, who had come here, not to spend money in drink, for they were penniless, but to enjoy the warmth of the fire, the landlord, a good-natured fellow, making no objection; for these men had all been regular customers of his in the days before the "hard times" came upon Lancashire.

In one corner sat Chartist Grimshaw, and next to him, a soldierly-looking middle-aged man with a war medal on his breast.

Whistling Will had hardly greeted this man with "How do, Billy Richardson!" when the landlord came into the chamber, and cried, "Now gentlemen, as yo all know, perhaps, an if yo didn't know before yo know now, we're here to-night to give a right royal farewell to Billy Richardson, what's goin across th' Atlantic to fight in this Meriky[32] war! Three cheers for Billy Richardson!"

After the cheers had been given – Whistling Will remarking that their friend Billy must excuse the cheers "for being a sort o' clemmed cheer, as men couldn't raise full-fed cheers in starvation days" – the landlord went on to say, in homely compliment, that he had no doubt the "hard times" would soon be over now, for as soon as Billy Richardson got fighting the war would be settled in no time, and very likely less.

"Which side's Billy fightin on?" asked Chartist Grimshaw.

"The North," said Billy.

Chartist rose and gripped Billy's hand. "Then good luck to thee," he said, "for thou'rt on the right side o' righteousness an justice."

"Question?" cried somebody. Several of the company hissed the interrogator.

When the American civil war started in 1861, though the majority of people in Lancashire were in favour of the North, many thought the South was in the right; but as the war went on, and the workers of England understood that the North was fighting to free the Southern Slaves, whose miserable doom had been depicted in the vivid pages of "Uncle Tom's Cabin,"[33] all the sympathy of factory Lancashire was with the North; though many of the middle classes, and almost all the upper classes, supported the Southern cause with encouragement and money. But working-class Lancashire, to its credit, stood by the slaves and suffered starvation in the cause of freedom – stood by the slaves though it perished of poverty and hunger.[34]

At the cry of "Question?" Chartist Grimshaw rose erect, in a rude yet eloquent dignity, his eyes flashing as in the old days when he had stood on Chartist platforms denouncing tyranny and oppression. "Who says 'Question?'" he asked. "Who dares to say "Question?" when the shackles are being struck from the slave? There can be no question about it. The Northern States are in the right, and the right will win. Here's long life and health to President Lincoln, and success to the Federal Army!"

Chartist Grimshaw's little speech was received with cheers.

"Let's have a few words fro' Billy Richardson," said the landlord, "an then, as it's a cowd snowy night, I'll give yo all a pint o' warm ale apiece, just to celebrate Billy's farewell."

There was applause for the landlord's generosity, and then Billy Richardson stood up. "I'm no talker," said Billy, "except with a gun or a sabre, but I'll do my best."

"Tell us about th' charge o' th' Light Brigade",[35] cried somebody.

Billy, who was one of the famous Six Hundred which had charged the Russian guns in the Crimea, in that deed of reckless daring at which "all the world wondered," as Tennyson's popular poem puts it, narrated, for the thousandth time, his experience of that memorable day but he was very brief; he was a soldier, nor a story-teller. "We got the order to charge," he said, "and we went at the Russian guns, helter-skelter. We ran into hell, made a slash at the devil, and then backed out again – all in a jiffy. That's all. Any other British soldiers would have done the same if they'd been ordered. 'Trot, gallop, charge!' shouts Lord Cardigan, 'give 'em the points, lads; it's no use slashing at em!' So we crashed into the smoke of the guns; I couldn't see where I was going. My horse was shot, and I fell under him. I got to my feet and used my musket, loading as fast as blazes. Two Cossacks pricked me with their lances. I fought my way out, and struggled back to the British lines on foot. In my regiment a hundred and sixty of us rode out together – only twenty-three of us got back. That's all."

"And now your country allows you to go to the dogs," said Chartist Grimshaw. "Such is the glory of war, and the gratitude of a warlike nation."

"War isn't all picture-book," said Billy Richardson. "There were lots of disgraceful things about the Crimean war – bad food and rotten clothes for the soldiers, owing to the swindling of army contractors, – they ought to be hanged, the wastrels."

"Did you get any stripes?" asked a short, thick-set, middle-aged stranger, with a full head,[36] and great intelligent forehead, with deep humourous eyes thereunder, who had just entered the room, shaking the snow off his broad shoulders as he spoke.

"Only on my back, sir," replied Billy Richardson. "I am supposed to be discharged for misconduct. I'll tell you what the misconduct was. It was when I was in Hulme Barracks, a few years ago. I was absent for six days, and the adjutant,[37] when I returned, called me a vile scamp. That got my blood up, and I hotly answered, 'Whatever I am, I'm not like you – a coward. I saw you run away from a mounted Cossack in the Crimea – and I saw you slink out of the charge of the Light Brigade.' Well, after saying that, which was only the truth, I was always up to the neck in trouble, thanks to the adjutant. He made it hotter for me than ever the charge of the Light Brigade was."

"The mean varmint!" said the stranger emphatically.

"Eventually," said Billy, "the adjutant goaded me into disobedience, and obtained his end. He got me flogged."

"Shame!" said the stranger.

"I got fifty lashes with the cat, and flogging is a fearful thing."

"Barbarous!" said the stranger. "It ought to be abolished."

"You'd say so if you'd felt it," said Billy Richardson. "I got fifty lashes as I said. My back was all a hideous jelly of flesh and blood. The cat-o'-nine tails had cut to the bone. I've known it, in some cased to go through the bone, and the spinal marrow has been mixed with blood. It's the most cruel punishment in the world. And it does no good. It only makes a man worse. In my own case my back took bad ways, and festered, and I was in hospital for a month."

"And they flogged like a dog a soldier who rode in the charge of the Light Brigade!" said the stranger.

"I was the last man flogged at Hulme Barracks," continued Billy. "Then I was put in prison, but my father wrote to the Duke of Cambridge, who ordered me to be released at once."

"Disgraceful treatment of a brave soldier!" said the stranger. "Are you a native of Preston?"

"No, sir; I was born at Carlisle."

At this juncture the landlord brought in the warm ale, and served the company round.

"And now," said the landlord, "as it would be a sin to be stingy on an occasion like this, I'll give a pipe o' 'bacco to every man that sings a song, or tells a tale, or otherwise does anything to amuse the company, an keep things convivial. It's hard times, we know, but let's do our best to be convivial. If we can't be convivial, what's the good o' livin?"

With a significant glance at the sturdy stranger, somebody said, "tuttling."

"No, no," said the landlord, "none o' that sport to-night."

"And might I ask what is this 'tuttling'?" said the stranger.

The landlord smiled. "It's a marlock these gam divvles plays sometimes on strangers," he said. "In the bar there is a stool – the tuttling stool. Tuttle is birdlime."

"Yes, I know that," said the stranger. "I am pretty well acquainted with every form and phrase of the Lancashire dialect. What's the trick with the birdlime?"

"It's a favourite lark in Preston. We get the tuttling stool ready, then I or some other fellow sits near, smoking a pipe and invites any unsuspecting stranger to have a drink with us. Of course he sits down on the tuttling stool and that's where the fun comes in."

"Um!" said the stranger with a laugh. "I suppose the green bird leaves most of his tail feathers attached to the stool."

The company grinned and the stranger said, "Well, I'll thank you for sparing me the comicality of becoming a victim to the tuttling. I can't afford new breeches at present. It's a pity you couldn't send some tuttling stools to Parliament. There's a good twothree M.P.s that ought to be thoroughly tuttled – that is to say, lose their seats!"

There was laughter at the jest and everybody voted the stranger a merry fellow and good company.

"Well now," said the landlord, "who's bein first to win a pipe o' bacco?"

"I'll sing "Th' Shurat Weiver,""[38] said a man. "I'm deein for a smook."

"Brast of then," said th' landlord, "an to the divvle wi 'Shurat.'"

The candidate for the pipe of tobacco began to sing "Th' Shurat Weiver," one of the many dialect songs sold in broadsheets during "the cotton panic:"

"Confound it! I ne'er were so woven afore,
My back's welly broken, my fingers are sore;
I've been starin an rootin among this Shurat
Till I've very near getten as blind as a bat.

* * *

"I wish I were far enoof off, eaut o' th' road,
For o' weivin this rubbitch I'm getting reet stawed.
I've nowt i' this world to lie deawn on but straw,
For I've only eight shillin this fortneet to draw.

"Neaw I haven't my family under my hat,
I've a wife an six childer to keep eaut o' that;
So I'm rayther among it at present, yo see,
If ever a fellow were puzzled, it's me.

"If I turn eaut to steil folk ull caw me a thief,
An I conna put th' cheek on to ax for relief;
As I said in eaur heause t' other neet to my wife,
I never did nowt o' this soart i' my life.

"One doesn't like everyone t' know heaw they are,
But we've suffered so long through this 'Meriky War,
An there's lots o' poor factory folk getting t' far end,
An they'll soon be knocked o'er if th' times dunnot mend.

"Oh dear, if yon Yankees could only just see,
Heaw they're clemmin an starving poor weavers like me,
I think they'd soon settle their bother, and strive
To send us some cotton to keep us alive.

"We've been patient an quiet as long as we con,
Th' bite o' things we had by us are welly aw gone;
I've been trampin so long my owd shoon are worn eaut,
An my holiday clooas are aw on 'em 'up th' speaut.'

"It were nobbut last Monday I sowd a good bed, –
Nay, very near gan it – to get us some bread;
Afore these bad times come, I used to be fat,
But neaw, bless yore life, I'm as thin as a lat!

"Mony a time in my life I've seen things lookin feaw,
But never as awkward as what they are neaw;
If there isn't some help for us factory folk soon,
I'm sure we shall aw be knocked reet eaut o' tune.

Though the company was inclined for gaiety, and though no hearts can be so cheerful – and pathetically humorous – under depressing conditions as Lancashire hearts, the song that expressed the trouble of the suffering weaver and his family touched the listeners deeply, for it reminded them more acutely of that which they were all more or less enduring at present, and could not forget even in the tavern's convivial glow.

"That's a good song o' Sam Laycock's," said the stranger. "It set me thinkin o' that other poem o' Sam's about th' owd barber bein eaut o' wark because o' the' cotton panic, – men couldn't afford to get their hair cut or to get shaved."

"That's true," said Whistling Will, "th' length of a chap's beard neawadays shows th' shortness of his pocket. There'll be less whiskers soon when there's moar bread i' th' cupboard. Lung hair's noan a sign o' poetry neaw, but a mark o' poverty. I know Sam Laycock. I once heard him recite a teetotal poem at a tay-party."

"Ah, Preston's the cradle o' teetotalism,"[39] said the stranger, who had now lapsed into the dialect. "Here's th' place where a stutterer, – vowing that he'd be totally without intoxicating drink, could only say that he'd be 't-t-t-totally without,'[40] an so added a word to th' language. An it's Joe Livesey's town too – th' father of th teetotal movement. Well, though I like a glass in reason myself, I've nowt again temperance; an I know that Joe Livesey's a dacent chap wi a gradely heart."

"Did you ever see his paper, – *The Struggle*[41] it was called?" asked Chartist Grimshaw.

"I used to take it in till it deed," said the stranger.

"I took every number," said Chartist. "There were some good writing in it, an a champion cartoon every week. An every picture told a tale, an a good tale too. Eh, if th' people would only take notice o' their teachers what happy times there might be."

"Hold on," said the landlord, "let's keep out of the dismal key. Let's be convivial. Who's being the next to win a pipe o' bacca?" He turned to the stranger, "Might I ask you what part of the country you come from?"

"I'm a Rachda'[42] lad," said the stranger. "I was born in th' air that Tim Bobbin[43] breathed. I've rambled over Blackstone Edge some an oft – an thowt poetry myself, ay, an written it, though I say it."

"You said you knew Sam Laycock?"

"Sam an me's owd pals; an Ben Brierley,[44] too."

"Surely you're never Ned Waugh!"[45]

"That's my name, an I can't help it if it's noan good enough."

"Hurrah, chaps!" cried the landlord, "here's our Lancashire King o' poets, Ned Waugh. We're honoured to-night."

After the surprise and excitement caused by the revelation of the stranger's identity had subsided, the landlord said to Waugh, "And might I ask you what's brought you to Preston?"

"I'm on a bit of a scribblin errand," said Waugh. "I've been sent down here to describe th' scenes of th' cotton famine for a Manchester newspaper; an a heartbreakin job it is too. If my pen only felt th' half o' what I feel it would cry as it writes! I wish times would be sharp an mend. However, I'm glad to see that help's comin in fast. There's somebody that signs hissel 'A Lancashire Lad,' writin some clinkin appeals in a London paper."

"Dare we ask yo to give us one of your own songs?" asked the landlord; and the company thundered endorsement of the question.

Waugh good-naturedly complied, "As you're all singin or recitin," he said, "I'll not be out o' th' fashion," and he sang his sweetest, tenderest, homeliest song

"Come whoam to thy childer an me."

Then a man recited one of the poems of Billington, the Blackburn poet[46] – "Nobody knows but mysel," which concludes thus –

> I started o' keepin a shop;
>   Eaur Tummy geet tacklin; an then
> Eaur Peter just happened to pop
>   On a snug shop o' managin, when
> This 'Merica bother begun, –
>   This world o' misfortune befel,
> An what loss an what lumber it's done,
>   Let Lancashire speik for itself."[47]

"Good," said Waugh, "Billy Billingotn's one of eaur true throstles. Like Sam Laycock, he too has a song about this cursed Shurat cotton. But he's rayther moor savage than Sam in his language, – he goes at it ding-sweep, in a terrible temper, for he says –

> "I onst imagined death's a very
>   Dark an dismal face,
> But neaw I fancy t' cemetery
>   Is quite a pleasant place!
> For sin we took eaur Bill to bury
>   I've often wished Owd Scrat
> Ud fotch aw t' bag o' tricks, an lorry
>   To hell wi aw t' Shurat!"[48]

"Billington's quite reet, an noan hauve strong enoof in his language," said Whistling Will.

A little man next recited one of Ramsbottom's poems about "The Lancashire Emigrants"[49] for during the cotton panic many families had been assisted to go out to Australia, in one case a hundred young women alone going out to Melbourne.[50]

"It's a gradely concert of all th' Lancashire throstles to-neet," said Waugh. "We're havin 'em aw. We only want a lay fro Critchley Prince[51] an one or two mooar, an then we'st have had aw th' hatch."

"Now, Whistling Will, I think it's thy turn," said the landlord.

"Well, I'm longin for a pipe o' bacco," said Will, advancing into the middle of the room. "Now chaps, I'm goin to give yo summat yo've never hear afore. Yo aw know I'm a rare whistler – an Preston ull find it eaut when it's too late – but I'll astonish yo to-neet. Durin this cotton panic, an especially last summer, I've been trampin o'er hill an dale, listenin to my little brothers, the singin birds in tree an copse, an larnin their music; an they're generous teichers, for they never charge owt for their lessons. Well, I've lain in th' fields, an on th' moorsides, an in th' cloughs by the' singin brooks, an in th' grass, among th' wild flowers, under th' hedges, at dawn an gloaming, in light an dark, in sun an rain, an I've larnt a lot o' things, includin some music which I'll give to yo. An I never were happier in my life – though my pockets were empty an my back nearly bare – than when takkin music lessons off th' little brids, bless their sweet sowls! Now listen – here's some of th' songs I larnt – there is no words to 'em – they're above words – but if yo understand yo con put th' words to yoresel as yo listen – yo'll hear songs o' joy, songs o' courtin, songs o' spring an summer, songs o' sun, moon, an stars, songs o' flowers an butterflies,' songs o' lullaby, songs o th' mother singin o'er th' little brids – an sometimes songs o' sadness, songs o' mournin an lamentation, for th' brids has their times o' trouble an sorrow just like human beings. Now listen!"

Whistling Will started the silver flute of the thrush; then he changed into the blackbird's golden note; and presently, suddenly, there came the glad call of the cuckoo. Next came the shrill soaring song of the skylark, followed by the song of the hedge-sparrow, and the robin's merry spring carol, varied by the same bird's plaintive autumn requiem.

Whistling Will imitated to perfection the songs of over a dozen warblers, with a little humorous interruption of chanticleer's crow and farmyard cackle of hens, and concluded amidst loud clapping of hands.

"Bravo!" cried Edwin Waugh, "well done, my friend. You're a regular woodland choir, and quite as good as nature. As you whistled I was in the glen with the thrush, and in the willow-trees with the robin, and on the bonny moorlands with the lark. And I know all the words to all the songs you whistled. Well, done, my friend!"

Whistling Will was pleased at the praise poured upon him.

"He's well earned his pipe o' bacco," said the landlord. "Nay, dang it aw, he shall have two pipes. If I were thee, Will, I should see some concert-room manager. Theau ought to be able to make a fortune out o' that whistle o' thine. That performance would take anywhere."

"It certainly would," said Waugh; "it's original and beautiful." Though Waugh spoke thus he had little hope for Whistling Will's future. His keen eyes saw at once the whistler's weakness that would ever fetter him to failure. Whistling Will was poor in will-power and application; he lacked persistence; he was easy-going; and so long as he got comfortably through one day was content to let the morrow shift for itself. He had great dreams but not the strength to realize them; high ambitions, but not the determination to climb towards them.

"Oh, if I'd only some money to give me a start," said Whistling Will. "That's what I want. But I'm one o' th' unlucky ones. I'm not one o' them as can get howd o' th' brass – like Luke Wragley for instance. He's makin a fortin out o' this cotton panic; an he was nobbt a bit of a waste dealer afore this 'Meriky war started. But he got a lot o' chep waste in – at about a farthin a pound – an sold it at sixpence a pound, I'm towd. Then he bought a weivin-shed, an he'll be a greit factory-master afore he dees, no doubt."

"The cotton panic is making fortunes for more than one," said Waugh, now speaking in English, "Though it seems strange that men should be making money out of a people's misery. But some men would cut out their mother's heart and sell it for butcher's meat if they could grow rich thereby. Ever since the American war started there has been great excitement on Liverpool Exchange; and vast money-making; cotton brokers riding now in carriages and their sons on horseback. For, you see, they're selling all sorts of cotton at high prices. In other words, there' a lot of swindling going on – thieving's the plain English for it. But there's two sorts of thieving in the country – rich thieving and poor thieving. Rich thieving is called business and is out of the reach of the law; while poor thieving is criminal stealing and means prison if you're caught at it. But in my opinion the cotton broker who palms off an inferior cotton as another sort is quite as deserving of jail as the poor factory operative who got a month's hard labour for taking a loaf of bread. The latter has my sympathy and is innocent before God, if guilty before man; but the cotton brokers though innocent before man are guilty before God."

"Hear, hear!" cried the company heartily.

In accordance with the unvarying discursiveness of general conversations the talk drifted to first one topic and then another in spontaneous miscellaneousness, and presently Whistling Will got an opportunity of mentioning the Mormon gentleman, which brought up the strange elopement of Nelly Milner a couple of years ago, which event had been a nine days' wonder in the town.

"Let me see," said the landlord, "she was courtin young Sandy Aspinall o' Penwortham, wasn't she? I hear that Sandy's not been the same lad since. He doted on the wench, and I reckon she was a pretty lass."

"She was that an all," said Whistling Will. "I could never understand her doin a trick o' that sort. What made matters worse, th' banns were up for her an Sandy, an they should have been wed on the Saturday as she disappeared on the Wednesday. Sandy took it very hard. Happen our friend Billy Richardson will be meeting Nelly Milner in America."

"If I do," said Billy, "I'll bring her back with me if she's had enough; and I'm told that there's many a poor woman longing to escape from Salt Lake City. But the Mormons watch the women too well for any of em to get away; they've spies and agents everywhere; and if a woman does chance to get out of the city she's soon trapped and taken back, or else done away with, so that she can't blab anything. Them Mormons must be fascinatin chaps to lure women away from England as they do."

"Sid Clifton," said Whistling Will, "that's courting Nelly Milner's sister Ada, is gooin on a boat to work as an engineer. He towd me so hissel; I met him to-day. Maybe he'll be getting to America too. He's gooin on a steamer fro' Birkenhead, but he doesn't know th' name o' th' boat; there seems to be a bit o' mystery about it."

Waugh smiled. "You'll hear a deal about that vessel ere long," he said. "I've heard more than one whisper already. That steamer is to be a privateer – to cripple the Federal Fleet and help boats to run the blockade with cotton. I'm told that there's more than one pious and respectable Lancashire factory master got shares in that steamer."

"Shame on em!" said Chartist Grimshaw.

"They don't mind the shame so long as they're makin brass," said Waugh. "How's the neet, landlord?" and Waugh slipped into the dialect again

"Still snowin fast," said the landlord. "It's better indoors than out to-neet."

"Then let's make eaursels awhom a goo on wi eaur tale-telling," said Edwin Waugh, and he began to relate droll anecdotes – "buzzes" he called them – in his own inimitable way – stories of humorous incidents and folk, varied with a weird tale of old Pendle Forest, or Witchland, and the hags that superstition once believed rode on broom-sticks over the midnight moor.

"Well," said Waugh, jovially, as the night wore on, "I con say that I've fairly enjoyed myself i' this town o' Preston, where Arkwright, th' founder o' th' cotton trade, an th' builder o' th' first factory' used to do knobstick shavin, – pity that he didn't stick to his shavin, for he's speilt Lancashire with cotton factories, – but I suppose we can't do with out 'em, though we're in a sad plight wi 'em today, – th' town o' th' Stanleys an Houghtons,[52] – didn't King Jimmy visit Houghton Castle an knight a loin o' beef theer, since which day that loin has been dubbed Sir Loin? – Well, well, times is bad, but we've this consolation, 'We'st never be lower i' this world I'm sure,' as it say i' Jone o' Greenfelt's song,[53] referring to Bill o' Dan's an their Margit clutterin on th' floor when the bailies took th' only stoo they had in th' heause from under 'em. Sup up' chaps; let's be merry while we may; let's kill care wi tale an a song."

"That's the ticket," said the landlord, "let's be convivial. What's th' use o' livin if we can't be convivial?"

VI. Sid Clifton's Departure

The snow ceased to fall in the night, and in the morning the January sun rose on a white world.

Sid Clifton, after a hasty farewell visit to his sweetheart's, – he had left her in tears, and his own eyes were not dry – was making his way towards the station; the time being shortly after noon.

There were few people out, and Sid met nobody he knew.

But as he was turning the corner of London-road into Fishergate he was disagreeably surprised to see Mr. Willard Hyde advancing towards him. "He'll be going to Milner's," said Sid to himself angrily.

As Hyde passed he half-smiled, half-sneered at Sid. In an instant Sid stepped up to him, and touched him on the shoulder.

"What do you mean?" cried Sid.

"Take your hand off me," said Hyde, insolently. "What do you mean?"

"Where are you going?" said Sid.

"That's my business."

"You're going to the Milners."

"What if I am?"

"Then keep away, or it will be the worse for you," said Sid, who was now in a hot rage.

Mr. Willard Hyde laughed derisively. Sid crashed his fist into the Mormon's face, right between the eyes, and the fellow went sprawling on his back in the snow.

[27 October 1900]

VI. (Continued)

Sid hurried on, not stopping to see how Hyde picked himself up.

But the Mormon had assistance. Whistling Will, who chanced to be emerging from the street corner opposite, had seen Sid knock Hyde down, and, in a Good Samaritanism not altogether unmixed with the idea of a reward – perhaps another sixpence – hastily crunched through the snow and helped the stout Mormon missionary to his feet.

"Thank you," said Hyde.

"Yore nose is bleedin'," said Whistling Will, "an yore eyes is bungin up badly. Yo'll have two bonny black een in a twothree minutes. I'd advise yo to get a piece o' raw beef an clap it on 'em straight away. Raw beef's a champion plaster for black een. It taks th'swellin down wonderful. Yo'll find a butcher's shop down Fishergate. What did Sid Clifton hit yo for?"

"You know the villain then?" asked Hyde, wiping his bleeding nose tenderly.

"Well, well," said Whistling Will, deeming it policy not to appear too much a friend of the enemy's, "I know him in a way, so to speik, same as I know almost everybody in Preston. He were allus a hot-tempered youth, allus ready to strike off wi his fists. He's got in more than one bother through that same trick."

"He shall rue that he ever struck me," said Hyde, vindictively. "He has struck me on the face; but when I strike, I shall strike him in the heart."

"Howd on neaw," said Whistling Will. "Surely you're not meeanin murder. A fair feight is aw reet, but I'm again manslaughter."

Hyde laughed grimly. "Oh I don't mean to murder him," he said, "but what I do shall be worse than murder to him."

"I durn't underston yo," said Whistling Will.

"You needn't do," said the Mormon, curtly. "I must get off and get my face bathed. Curse the fellow! I shan't be able to appear in public for a week. Here's a copper for you, for helping me up."

Will took the coin, saying to himself, "It were silver afore; now we've got down to copper." But aloud he said, "Thank yo; I'm fain I were near to help yo."

"I've seen you before, haven't I?" asked Hyde.

"Yah, I took yo to Milner's in Duckworth-street yesterday."

"Ah, I remember you now. Do you mind going to Duckworth-street and telling Mrs. Milner that I have met with a slight accident which will prevent me calling for a few days? Tell her it's nothing serious; and that I shall soon be all right. Here's another copper for you."

Hyde hurried away, holding down his disfigured face, while Whistling Will trudged off to Duckworth-street, and delivered his message to Mrs. Milner, who was seated in the house with Ada, on whose face there were still traces of the tearful parting from her sweetheart.

"Mr. Hyde met with an accident!" said Mrs. Milner. "Whatever has he been doing?"

"That's not for me to say," said Whistling Will. "I've towd yo what he towed me, an that's my errand. But I may say that it's nowt to bother about. He'll be aw reet again in a twothree days. He's nobbut run his nose against a man's fist."

"Run his nose against a man's fist," said Mrs. Milner. "What do you mean?"

Ada appeared quite unconcerned about the account of the Mormon's misadventure.

"I see that I'd better tell yo aw I know about it," said Whistling Will, seating himself in a chair. "For yo're a woman, Mrs. Milner – no offence – an yo'll not be satisfied till yo have aw th' tale an the tale's mestur. Th' fact is, that this Mestur Hyde an Sid Clifton has been feightin."

Ada started, and was suddenly interested in Whistling Will's narrative.

"Sid Clifton and Mr. Hyde fighting. Whatever about?" cried Mrs. Milner.

"That's more than I can tell yo," said Whistling Will. "All that I seed was Mestur Hyde and Sid talkin, an then Sid shot out his fist, an down went Mr. Hyde on his back in th' snow. Sid walked off quick, an I run to help Mestur Hyde to his feet. He had a brasted nose, and two pratty black een."

"Disgraceful!" said Mrs. Milner, the exclamation being one of sympathy for Mr. Hyde. Ada, however, smiled, and seemed not displeased.

"Oh, Mestur Hyde's not much hurt," said Whistling Will. "He'll be none the worse in a day or two. He only looks as if he'd been having a bit of matrimonial discuss with his wives, – I don't know how many he has."

Ada laughed outright, and her mother reproved her. "You oughtn't to laugh, Ada; it's a shocking thing that Sid Clifton should thus treat a respectable gentleman. Whatever may be Mr. Hyde's religious views, and no matter how many wives he has, I must speak of people as I find them, and I can say that Mr. Hyde has always conducted himself as a gentleman when he has been here."

"Very likely, no doubt," said Whistling Will, "no offence, Mrs. Milner. I'm nobbut telling yo what happened to Mestur Hyde, an how he looked after it. Happen I've been rayther too merry i' my language; maybe I have; for I were at a convivial do at th' Virgin's Inn last neet, – good company and good doins. For though we're in the' midst of' th' cotton panic we murn't give way to mopin awtogether; we must do summut to keep eaur hearts up. I've nowt again Mestur Hyde – indeed I'm sorry for him because of his matrimony. An I've nowt again Sid Clifton noather; in fact, I rayther like th' lad, though I admit that he's hasty tempered betimes. But that's not a bad fault sometimes. I'm towd that Sid once kicked a tackler out o' th' weivin-shed for hittin a little tenter-lass.[54] Well, that weren't a bad thing to do. I'm sorry that Sid an Mestur Hyde geet agate scrappin, an I'm very sorry for Mestur Hyde's squashed nose an damaged een. What more can I say? Or heaw can I speik fairer."

"Did Sid say anything to you?" asked Ada.

"No, he was off in quicksticks. An I think I'll be gooin too. How are you getting through this cotton panic, Mrs. Milner?"

"Badly; we're nearly at the far end. If our Lily's missus – Mrs Treebarn – was not good to us I don't know what we should do."

"It's th' same wi everybody" said Whistling Will, "though that's noather help nor consolation. I've felt th' pinch myself, an I'm feelin it still. I never thowt I should see times like these. Th' world seems all out of flunter. As if th' cotton panic weren't enoof, there's talk o' Fenian secret meetins, plottin mischief an rebellion. There's been extry souldiers on guard at Fulwood Barracks for many a week, to see that no Fenians get near an blows th' place up wi gunpowder, like Guy Fawkes tried to do wi th' House o' Commons once upon a time, when th' Fifth o' November were invented for the benefit o' th' firework trade. An then there's trade union riots an outrages – especially in Sheffield;[55] th' world seems getting to a bonny pitch; I raly don't know what we're comin to. An then, wost of aw – to us anyhow, what' in it – there's this cotton panic.

"Well, it can't last for ever," said Mrs. Milner.

"That's what everybody says," said Whistling Will, "though I must say that it looks very like lastin for ever, an happen a twothree days longer. We'st be gloppent if, when we get up on th' Resurrection Morn, th' first thing we hear is that th' cotton panic's still gooin on. It's makin some terrible distress everywhere, as yo can guess. An them what can get away is leavin th' country. There's been public subscriptions to pay th' passage money of a thousand factory operatives to

Queensland – an th' Australey Government is finding brass too. So there's lots leavin their native land. Lancashire will be empty soon, if there isn't a halteration. An it must be a sad an wrenchin thing to leave yore owd home – th' place where yo went a-courtin – th' steet where yore childer's played – an go to a far-off an strange land to start life anew."

"We might have to do it ourselves yet," said Mrs. Milner.

Ada looked quickly at her mother in surprise, but said nothing.

"When I look back o'er this last eighteen months," said Whistling Will, "I wonder how folks has scrat and scraped through it. Just before the cotton panic began, aw th' South Lancashire weivers were on strike – I darsay they'd ha kept to their work an saved their brass if they'd only known what were comin. Then there were collections for th' India famine fund; and we little thowt, as we gave our mite to that, that we should soon be sufferin a famine of our own. Then th' Meriky war began, an England nearly got entangled in it o'er them two Confederate chaps, Mason an Slidell[56] – there were bustle an rubbin th' Liverpool battery up, seein if th' guns were aw reet, an then it all fizzled out to nowt an a dal good job too. For other folks's wars is bad enough without havin one of our own. Th' papers warned us that three million folk in Lancashire would be without daily bread if th' war lasted any length o' time. An it's lasted, reet enough. First th' factories went on short time, four, three, an two days a week, then stopped altogether; we'd six months o' poverty, an starvation ever since. We can't say we hadn't plenty practice in clamming before th' worst came' but clammin's one o' them contrary things that th' more practice you have an the' worse you get at it. Not withstandin this, th' Bolton folks started a subscription for a statue to Sam Crompton – what's responsible for th' factory trade; but I think Sam would sooner th' brass were given to starving childer. I'm sure he'd say so if he were alive. But he's lucky; he's dead. I have aw th' history off, yo see. Blackburn were th' first place to begin to feel t' pinch, then Wigan, then Darwen, an Preston, where it's the wurst of aw, Glossop an Ashton bein next; an we're enduring it yet, though God knows how. As if things weren't bad enough, th' Darwen colliers came out on strike too, an wanted th' public to help keep them. I think they might ha put their strikin off till th' cotton panic were o'er. But some workin-chaps is foo enough for owt; I get out of aw patience wi 'em. It's reet enough for 'em to go in for better wages – an I wish 'em aw good luck at th' job – but there's sensible times to strike, an silly times to strike. Well, well, there'll be an end to it aw some day, I darsay. I see that fifteen thousand pound has been collected in Liverpool for th' factory folks; that's good."

"How you do rattle on, Will," said Ada, smiling.

"Oh, I have all th' history off," said Whistling Will. "I picks all th' news up wi knockin about so much. There's many a book hasn't half as much in it as me. I gathers all sorts – good news, bad news, quare news, rare news, false news, true news, wise news, an foolish news. Talkin o' quare news, what do you think o' men breikin into th' cemetery an steilin corpses for th' doctors to cut up? Body-snatchin it's called, an there's been a lot of it goin on lately – especially at Sheffield.[57] That Sheffield seems a rum auction – trade union outrages an body-snatchin both goin on theer."

"But what do the doctors want the dead bodies for?" asked Mrs. Milner, with a slight shudder.

"Oh, I dunno," answered Whistling Will. "I'm towd they experiment to find things out. Happen they're trying to see if it couldn't be contrived for folk to live without meat, seein that this cotton panic is takkin th' bread off so many. If they could only discover the secret it would be a dal fine thing for Lancashire."

"But how would the bakers and grocers go on if nobody wanted anything to eat?" inquired Mrs. Milner seriously.

"Well, in that case, done yo see, as they wouldn't want nowt to eat noather there'd be no need for 'em to keep shops to make a livin? However, I'm sorry to say there's no chance of such a patent bein found; so we'st e'en have to peg along as we are, an clam as comfortably as we can. Good-souled folk all o'er t' country are doin their best to raise money for Lancashire, an I thank 'em heartily; there's concerts, there's soup-kitchens an I see that in plenty o' chapels they're collectin cast-off clothes to give to them what has noan an corn't afford to beigh any. There's lots o' honest folk bein driven to steilin food by this cotton panic an it's a shame to see t' magistrates sendin 'em to jail. Only t' other day too, a poor factory chap got sent to prison for seven days for beggin. That's not jannock, is it hek as like. It's noan fair when a hungry mon daren' ask for bread. – Well, there'll be an end to it some time. I see that foreign countries on t' continent is feelin t' scarcity o' cotton too an doin a bit o' riotin – them foreigners weren't stand things as quietly as us – though their state is not to be compared to ours for hardship. Well, I'll be gooin. I think I've said so afore. Th' gift o' t' gab's on me to-day. Anyheaw, I've given yo a bit o' th' history o' things; an I don't think it'll do yo any harm. I'm a wonderful chap but folk doesn't seem to appreciate me. There's talents about me; not just one talent, but several. But i' th' Virgin's Inn last need th' grait Lancashire poet, Ned Waugh, praised me sky-high. He's a good judge is Waugh. Well, I'll be getting off. I'm really gooin this time. Good-day."

VII. Off With The "Alabama"

Sid Clifton paced the Preston station platform, awaiting the arrival of the Liverpool train. He walked to and fro briskly, partly to keep himself warm, for there was ice in the air, and partly because he was still excited from his encounter with Mr. Hyde. "I wish I'd let the fellow alone," he said to himself. "He'll seek to injure me now from a motive of revenge and persecute Ada with greater vigour in order to hurt me. It would have been better if I had restrained myself." He took a few more steps, then said, "Well, I couldn't help it; the slight of him irritated me. I wish I'd never met him. And yet – I'm not sorry. He'll not be able to visit the Milners for a few days; I've spoilt his face for a week, anyhow."

Though it was not a morally elevating feeling, Sid felt a very human satisfaction in the thought that he had knocked Mr. Willard Hyde out of the field for a short time. "But he'll fetch up for lost time and do his best to pay me out," reflected Sid; and was much disquieted, as he pictured the Mormon like a stealthy serpent, craftily putting his coils round Ada.

His uncomfortable reverie was broken by a voice behind him. "Hello; Sid Clifton, what are you doing here?"

Sid turned round and faced a young man of his own height and about his own age, with a ruddy face and bright eyes saddened by some great trouble.

"Sandy Aspinall!" cried Sid. "I thought you had gone out of England; I heard so, anyhow. What are you doing here?"

"I'm going to Liverpool," answered Sandy.

"So am I," said Sid.

"And from Liverpool across the river to Birkenhead," said Sandy.

"I too," said Sid, beginning to make mental comments about this coincidence.

"I'm going as second mate on board a boat whose only name at present is the '290!'" said Sandy.

"And so am I," said Sid. "This is strange."

The conversation was interrupted by the coming of the train. When the two young men were seated therein, having a compartment to themselves, Sid said, "Well, I never dreamt that one of my shipmates would be Sandy Aspinall, who once courted my sweetheart's sister."

A look of painful memory came upon the face of Sandy Aspinall.

"Forgive me for mentioning that matter if it hurts you," said Sid. "I meant no harm, Sandy. But I'm always making some blunder with my impulsiveness. I knocked a man down as I came to the station – and now I wish I hadn't. But it served him right. I know you'll agree with me when I tell you that he was one of the dirty gang that took Nelly Milner away."

"A Mormon!" exclaimed Sandy.

"Elder Willard Hyde, of Salt Lake city; a sleek and slimy creature. It seems that once the Mormons get a foothold in a family they pester it till they've absorbed every female member of it. The villains are after Ada now. This dog I thrashed wants her to go away with him. As I was coming to the station I met him – going to Milners. The look in his eyes made my blood boil. I spoke to him; we had a few words and I finished the debate by knocking him on his back in the snow."

"You did quite right, Sid. I wish I'd been there to see."

"What worries me is the fact that Ada is left at his mercy."

"God grant that she doesn't follow her sister," said Sandy, fervently.

"She is firm enough to be true to me," said Sid.

"These Mormons have devilish powers of persuasion. Who would have thought that Nelly Milner would have been enticed? – I can't understand it. Day and night I have tried to think how she could be led away, and I can't fathom the riddle. I am convinced some dark trick was done. It is said, I know, that she went willingly, of her own accord, but I don't believe it. I can't believe it, I won't believe it. For, only the night before, she had been loving and happy with me, looking forward to our wedding – it was only three days off, Sid! Ah, how it is off now – far beyond the impossible for ever! – looking forward to our wedding with joy. And then, and then – when I went to see her next night she was gone, and I haven't set eyes upon her since. – In one instant all my heaven was turned to hell."

Sandy's agitated voice ceased, and he gazed mournfully though the carriage window at the snow-covered fields, and the hills in the distance. Sid, feeling that words were useless to soothe, kept a sympathetic silence.

Then Sandy said, "If ever I meet the man who took Nelly Milner away, there'll be more than knocking-down, Sid, if I hang for it. I am hoping to get to America somehow, sometime, and when I do I shall make my way to the Mormon colony."

He paused, and Sid said, "What then?"

"First, punishment of the villain; and then – nay I know not what then – for if Nelly be still alive – if – this thought is agony, Sid – she cannot be the same lassie who was stolen from me two years ago. – But, what'er she is, and wherever she be, I love her still; and love works miracles. But can it make one forget all that is foul and only remember what is fair? – Excuse my rambling talk, Sid; but when I think of this affair, I feel that I am going mad!"

Once more there was silence. The train was puffing through dreary, desolate marshlands, where wild-fowl plashed in the rushy pools, ringed with thin wind-blown snow.

"Let us talk of other things," said Sandy, with an effort. "You're surprised to find me going to sea."

"Well, a little," said Sid. "How comes it about?"

"You know I am a fisherman; one of a fishing family. I was at Southport before I came to Penwortham; and I know all the Lancashire coast. Nine months ago a gentleman friend of mine – a man I have often taken out for a night's fishing experience in the Irish sea – told me that men were wanted for a new steamer building at Birkenhead, and said he could get me a good berth on the boat if I were agreeable. I jumped at the chance – for since I lost Nelly I have not cared what became of me. So I went to Birkenhead and was engaged on 'the 290.'"

"There seems to be a mystery about the vessel," said Sid. "What is it? And I thought she was quite a new boat. Yet I understood you sailed on her nine months ago."

Sandy smiled.

"I think I may enlighten you a little," he said. "As you're going straight to the ship there's no chance of you doing any indiscreet blabbing. You've heard of the *Alabama*?"

"The *Alabama*!" cried Sid. "Who hasn't heard of her? She's the vessel that's cruising about doing all the damage she can to Federal shipping. Federal men-of-war are after her, and if they once get hold of her, she's booked for "Davy Jones".[58]

"They'll have to catch her first," said Sandy, "and she's a greyhound in a race."

"Here I was thinking that this 'No. 290' I was going on was an entirely a new boat," said Sid, "and it appears she's been at sea for months."

"For nearly nine months. She's practically new though. She's put into Liverpool for repairs. She got knocked about a bit last month. One of the Federal war-ships, the *San Jacinto*, nearly caught her napping. We were steaming through a fog, and almost ran into the *San Jacinto*. We were seen, and the call came 'What vessel there?' Our captain's only answer was 'Full steam ahead' to the engineer. The *San Jacinto* blazed after us with her guns, and I thought it was all over with the *Alabama*. We got a cannon-ball in the stern; it only just missed our rudder. Then part of the captain's bridge was blown away, and other damage done. But, fortunately for us, we ran just then into another dense bank of fog, and succeeded in giving the *San Jacinto* the slip. But it was a close shave. Our captain made for Birkenhead to get the vessel repaired. Of course we dare not enter Liverpool port as the *Alabama*; that would lead to bother with the Federals, and perhaps land England into a war. We got in as a trader from the West African coast – badly storm-tossed in the Bay of Biscay. The tricks and disguises we have to adopt will astonish you. Our painters are always busy. Of course, there are gentlemen in Liverpool who know that the *Alabama* is lying at Birkenhead, but they may be trusted to keep secrecy, for they are interested shareholders. We leave the Mersey to-night; and when we shall see England again, God knows. Perhaps never. For, as you will have gathered from what I have said, we're on a risky business, and if the Federal men-of-war can only manage to trap us we're done for. They'd sink us in a minute."

"I see that I'm in for adventure, anyhow," said Sid. "Well, I'm getting more than I expected, but I'm ready for it. I'm sorry, though, that the *Alabama* is against the Federals, for all my sympathy is with the north in this war."

"So is mine for the matter of that," said Sandy, "but in this job we're on business – we're merely workmen, and have nothing to do with either one side or the other. Our only duty is our duty to our ship."

When Sandy and Sid reached Liverpool with its nautical smell of tar and ships, and its thousand spires of masts from all parts of the earth, they made their way straight to Prince's landing stage, and were soon on the Birkenhead ferry boat, crossing the river that is perhaps the most important, and certainly the busiest, estuary in the modern world; the port whence so much is ever coming in, so much ever going out, in myriad vessels of all sorts and sizes, manned by men of all colours and language, a mighty babel of ships and sea-farers.

But Liverpool was sad, and Lancashire suffering, because at present the most necessary cargo of all, the cotton cargo, was not coming in, owing to the American War. This fact suggested a question to Sandy, who put it to Sid. "How are the Milners going on in this awful cotton famine?"

"It's hard times for them," said Sid. "As you know, there is no father now."

"I know," said Sandy. "He died soon after Nelly went away – she was his favourite child. Perhaps the cotton famine helped to finish him, but I think it was a broken heart."

"It's said there's about fifteen thousand cotton operatives unemployed in Preston now," said Sid, "so you can guess how things are. And no signs of the end of the war yet."

"None!" said Sandy. "The Federals seem to have got the worst of it so far, though I hear they're pulling up now."

"The North is bound to win in the end," said Sid.

"It hasn't looked like it. The Southerners have had it all their own way, defeating the Federals every time they have met."

"According to the news this last two or three months the fortune of war has turned in favour of the North, and the Confederates are being beaten everywhere. Only a week or two ago they were driven back from Fredericksburg with great loss."

"I've missed recent news with being away," said Sandy.

"Once the North gets the upper hand the war is over," said Sid. "Then Lancashire will thank God and rejoice."

Reaching Birkenhead, the two young men made their way to the river-side where 'No. 290,' or the *Alabama*, lay ready for putting to sea, and settled themselves on board.

In the dark winter night, the engines of the *Alabama* began to thud, thud, thud, and, with the rising tide, she crept out of the river, past the New Brighton battery, and into the open sea.

Sid and Sandy stood leaning over the taffrail;[59] the water swishing along the vessel's side in the great lonely silence.

"There's Southport lights," said Sandy, "and round the bend of the coast, Preston – proud Preston."

And Sandy sighed and fell a-thinking of the lassie he had once wooed on the banks of the Ribble; the lassie who had gone from him so darkly and cruelly. And Sid was thinking of a fair lassie too.

[3 November 1900]

VIII. The Sewing Class[60]

In the grey wild dawn on the lonely water, the *Alabama* passed a large vessel making for Liverpool. By the help of his glass, the captain of the *Alabama* made out this ship to be the *George Griswold* from New York. Though he had no fear of this boat, for it was clearly nothing but a merchantman, the captain of the privateer gave it as wide a berth as possible. Had he met it on the Atlantic he would no doubt have attacked it, and sunk it; in which case he would have robbed his own countrymen in starving Lancashire of generous gift of bread. But he was too near Liverpool, and the British coast, to risk an engagement which might result in serious international complications, and probably turn out very awkward for himself. Yet as he looked at the wake of the *George Griswold* he regretted that prudence prevented him sending a shot at her.

Sid Clifton and Sandy Aspinall, who were on deck both guessed what was passing in the captain's mind. Sandy was indifferent whatever course the captain took; but Sid was indignantly excited, though he kept his emotion in check.

"If he fires at that peaceful merchantman," said Sid, "I shall be tempted to spring at his throat."

"Harassing and destroying peaceful merchantmen is our game," said Sandy nonchalantly.

"I didn't think I was shipping on a thundering pirate," said Sid.

"Don't let the captain overhear you, or you'll be clapped in irons," said Sandy.

"It's a vile business," said Sid.

"It's all in a war," said Sandy. "I'll admit I'm rather sorry for it; in fact, I don't relish it; but what can we do? We've shipped to serve in this boat; and it's our duty to do our work. We've nothing to do with the boat's object."

"I wish I'd never engaged," said Sid. "I fear I've made one of the biggest mistakes of my life; and shall have to suffer for it."

He was thinking, as he spoke, not so much of the conduct of the *Alabama* as of the fact that by taking a position on this oat he had left his sweetheart open to the amorous attacks of Willard Hyde, the Mormon elder.

While the *Alabama* was cleaving her way into the watery vastness of the Atlantic Ocean, the *George Griswold* entered the Mersey; and two days later her arrival was the theme of talk at Mrs. Treebarn's Sewing Class in the Preston Sunday School which Ada Milner attended. During the "cotton panic" in all Lancashire towns sewing classes had been started by the ladies of the middle and upper classes, the object of these sewing classes being to find the unemployed young factory women and girls something to do as well as to raise money for the famine fund by the sale of the articles made. At the sewing classes many factory lasses learned how to sew and make garments, and were, in addition, by contact and communion with the educated and refined ladies who took charge of the work, improved much in general manners and conversation. Probably both rich and poor benefitted by the companionship: they certainly learned to understand each other better, and a desirable sympathy was generated between those who had hitherto been distantly socially separated, though dwelling together in the same town, and deriving their living or income from the same industry. Besides the sewing classes for the women, there were schools formed for the men; and for the first time many old people learned to read and write. It was amusing, yet pathetic, to see grey heads struggling with A B C and pothooks. There were many willing teachers, chiefly clergy and ministers; and, because of the cotton panic, many a workingman got an education that would not otherwise have fallen to his lot. In many pupils a talent that touched genius was developed, as the painting and decoration, done by tenders of spindle and shuttle, of the halls and rooms in which the men assembled for their lessons, testified.

Mrs. Treebarn, wife of the Rev. Arthur Treebarn, was one of the first to commence a sewing class in Preston, and three days after Sid Clifton's departure, she was telling the young women, as they plied their needles, of the arrival of the *George Griswold* in Liverpool.

"The vessel got its name," she said, "from a New York merchant named George Griswold, who resolved to send the boat to England with a huge cargo of flour and provision paying all the expenses. When the ship reached Liverpool, the Custom House officials did not board the vessel, no dock dues were asked, and everybody employed in unloading her, down to the dock porters, refused to take any payment for their services."

The girls and women stopped their sewing to clap their hands.

"It was the same in New York," continued Mrs. Treebarn. "Captain Lunt, who commands the vessel, says that the New York dockmen all heartily worked to load the boat for nothing. Pilots and tug-boats would not make any charge, but vied with each other in offering their services. Lancashire's suffering has made the whole world kin. England and America have shaken hands as brothers. Wealth may divide man, but misery brings us all close together; and if the world is now full of sympathy, of brotherly feeling, if all men realize that we are all children of one Great Father, even out of the sorrow of the cotton famine will have come blessing and Lancashire's tribulation will not have been evil, though it has been painful. The kindly charities pouring into Lancashire from all quarters, the universal sympathy from all peoples and nations make me think of the motto of

Mr. Joseph Livesey, the teetotal reformer of whom Preston may be proud, for it now seems that the sentiment of this motto is ruling men's hearts everywhere: –

> Stretch forth your hand like a brother,
>   Remember that life's but a span;
> It's our duty to help one another,
>   And do a good turn when we can.[61]

When this cotton famine is over, when all Lancashire's spindles and shuttles are busy again, and cupboards full of bread, may we not forget these lines, but always act upon them, remembering how, in Lancashire's hard times, all the world held out a helping hand. Now, lasses, we'll have a song. Start the singing, Louis," and Mrs. Treebarn turned to a dark young woman who sat next to Ada. In a rich contralto voice Louis began the following song of Laycock's,[62] the rest of the sewing class quickly joining in: –

> Come lasses, let's cheer up an sing, it's no use lookin sad,
> We'll make eaur sewin schoo to ring, and stitch away like mad;
> We'll try an make th' best job we can of owt we have to do,
> We'll read an write, an spell an rest, while here at the' sewin schoo.
>   *Chorus.* – Then lasses, let's cheer up an sing,
>   It's no use lookin sad.
>
> Eaur Queen, th' Lord Mayor o' London too, they send us lots o' brass,
> An neaw, at welly every schoo, we've got a sewin class;
> We'n superintendents, cutters-eaut, an visitors an o',
> We'n parsons, cotton mesturs too, come in to watch us sew.
>
> Sin th' war begun, an th' factories stopped, we're badly off, it's true,
> But still we needn't grumble, for we've noan so much to do;
> We're only here fro nine to four, and have an heaur for noon,[63]
> We noather stop so very late, nor start so very soon.
>
> We're welly killed wi kindness neaw, we raly are, indeed,
> For everybody's tryin hard to get us aw we need;
> They'n sent us pudding, bacon too, an lots o' dacent clothes,
> An what they'll send afore they'n done there's nobody here that knows.
>
> God bless them kind good-natured folk what sends us aw this stuff,
> We conna tell 'em heaw we feel, nor thank 'em hauve enuff;
> They help to find us meat an clothes, an eddication too,
> An what crowns aw, they give us wage for goin to th' sewin schoo.
>
> We'n such a chance o' larnin neaw we'n never had afore,
> An oh, we shall be rare an wise when th' Yankee wars are o'er;
> There's nobody then can puzzle us wi owt we'n larned to do,
> We'n getting polished up so weel with goin to th' sewin schoo.

* * *

Come lasses, then, cheer up an sing, it's no use lookin sad,
We'll make eaur sewin school to sing, an stitch away like mad;
We live in hope afore so long to see a breeter day,
For th' cloud that's hangin o'er us neaw is sure to blow away.

During the afternoon other songs and hymns were sung, and in the intervals Mrs. Treebarn went about the room, chatting with individuals here and there, and giving every one a friendly word or smile.

Seating herself besides Ada, she said, "I'm sorry to say that your sister, Lily, is not well to-day. She as grown very thin and pale lately."

"I have noticed it myself," said Ada.

"I can't understand her illness," said Mrs. Treebarn. "I told her to lie in bed to-day."

"I am sure she has every kindness at your hands," said Ada.

"I treat her as I would treat one of my own children. But she is a very sensitive child; she thinks deeply. The sight of the starving people in the town seems to affect her very much. I can see that she is always thinking about them, though she doesn't say much."

"I'll go up and see her when the sewing-class is over," said Ada.

"She wants to go home," said Mrs. Treebarn. "Perhaps for some things she would be better at home for a few weeks. The little change might do her good. How is your mother?"

"As well as can be expected," said Ada.

"Tell her not to despair. These hard times will perhaps be over soon."

Mrs. Treebarn went to talk with others, while Ada thought of Lily as she sewed, and then of her lover, her mental picture of Sid being naturally associated with a ship on the deep sea. She wondered where he was now; and what he was doing. Was he thinking of her as she was of him? She smiled to herself at the query. Of course he would be thinking of her.

At the dismissal of the sewing-class Ada set off for Mrs. Treebarn's house. Mrs. Treebarn would have gone with her, but she had a few charitable errands to do ere going home; she had to call on several poor families who were to be supplied with clothes.

As Ada went through the streets, from which the snow had been partially cleared, though it still lingered meltingly on the housetops, toppling over the water-troughs in places, she met Lucy Clayton.

"Have you given up the sewing-class, Lucy?" asked Ada.

"I can't forshame to come," said Lucy.

"Why?"

"You can guess why. You saw me with young Wragley the other night. – I wish I were dead."

Tear trickled down Lucy's face; and Ada understood. She felt a great sisterly compassion for the girl.

"You can be helped, Lucy."

"Not now; it's too late. I am fallen."

Ada knew not what to say.

"Don't think harshly of me, Ada. I was forced to it. My little brothers and sisters were crying for food, and young Wragley had long pestered me. – It's a terrible thing to have a pretty face and be poor! – Young Wragley watched well for his opportunity."

"He's a scamp," said Ada.

"He is not the only one of his sort, nor alas, am I the only one of my sort. There's many more going there – God knows how many there'll be before this cotton panic's over. – And I wish I were dead. I feel that I am going mad when I think – I dare not think. Ten Banister was courting me, and I had dreamed, like every other girl, of a little cot, and Ted and I husband and wife there, with little ones, may be, – but never now. – I could throw myself into the river and end it all thus!"

What hope could Ada hold out to this despair? She stood in sad silence.

"But I must keep my little brothers and sisters till the hard times are over," said Lucy, – "and then – ah God what then? – There is only one thing or it – Curse the cotton panic, for it has ruined me for ever! – But I have saved the little ones. Perhaps when they are safe in heaven God will let them think sometimes of the sister who for their sakes went to hell!"

Lucy's strange words and excitement awed Ada.

"Lucy," she said, "Come to our house to-night and –"

"I have to see *him* to-night. He promised to give me some money to-night. He's promised that ever since – but he has lied to me. That's the bitterness of it. I know now that he never meant to help me. – Yet I'll try him once more. That's the agony of it, to think that I fell for nought. – Not from him, but from other men has the money come. – Curse him! – I could kill him, for he's more than killed me."

And Lucy Clayton hurried away distractedly, while Ada sorrowfully resumed her way to Mrs. Treebarn's house.

IX. One Who Had Been On Tramp

Ada found Lily in bed. The girl certainly looked very ill. Ada kissed her and said smiling, "Now Lily, what are you doing here?"

"Mrs. Treebarn made me stay in bed," said Lily, "but I'm not ill."

"Well, you'll be better in a day or two," said Ada.

"Is the cotton panic over," asked Lily.

"No; I wish it were." Said Ada.

"Isn't the suffering awful?" said Lily. "Ah, I've seen so many poor little babies crying for bread – I can hear 'em all the day and night as I lie here. Don't you think England's a sad and wicked place, Ada?"

"When people suffer they are paying for past wickedness. I think. Just after the cotton panic began, when I was at mother's one day, old Chartist Grimshaw came in, and he said that England was beginning to pay for the crime of the Russian war. Don't you remember?"

"Yes, I remember," said Ada.

"But why should innocent little babies and children have to pay?" asked Lily. "If I were God, I wouldn't punish *them*. Mr. Treebarn – and Mrs. Treebarn – say often that God's too good to be cruel to anybody. But what about the cotton panic, Ada?"

"Hush, Lily, you mustn't talk like that."

"I only want to know what God means," said Lily.

She lay back exhausted; and her manner was feverish.

"Don't excite yourself," said Ada, "or you'll never get well."

"I don't know that I want to get well – if I'm ill –" said Lily, wearily. "I only want to see the little children happy. – If ever you have a baby, Ada –"

"How strangely you talk," said Ada, smiling.

"Go and live where there are no cotton panics. Tell Sid I say so; for you'll marry Sid some day; won't you? Let me see, he's gone away, hasn't he?"

"Yes, he's gone away."

"But he'll come back again. I like Sid. Sid's brave and sticks up for the helpless ones and the little ones. When I was a tenter in the weaving-shed, before I came to be Mrs. Treebarn's servant, Sid wouldn't let any of the overseers say a hard word to me. And he thrashed one overseer for hitting little Polly Farrington. Sid's a man, Ada. When you and he are married I should like to be at the wedding."

"Of course you'll be at the wedding, Lily. You shall be bridesmaid."

Lily shook her head. "I don't think I shall be there, Ada."

"Certainly you will."

"Not as you think, Ada. But I shall watch over you and Sid – and your little babies. Perhaps you'll call one Lily, after me."

"You mustn't talk like this, Lily," said Ada. "You're low spirited. But you'll be all right when you're well again, and then you'll laugh at this talk."

"Ah, you don't know what I know, Ada. The angels don't come and talk to you as they do to me. They come while I'm lying here. I've seen them many a time. My father is with them. He smiles, and says I shall soon be with him. And he tells me what work to do – but that's the secret. Oh, how I wish I was able to do more. But I've done all I can; and I've done my best."

Ada thought that Lily was deliriously rambling in her speech, and grew seriously alarmed on her account. She stayed with the sick girl, who fell into a restless doze, till Mrs. Treebarn came home. Ada told Mrs. Treebarn what had occurred.

"We will have the doctor in at once; I'll fetch him myself this evening," said Mrs. Treebarn. "I didn't think Lily's case was so bad."

"I'll come again in the morning to see how she is," said Ada.

"Come as often as you like," said Mrs. Treebarn. "And bring your mother. It may cheer Lily up to have you near her."

Ada went upstairs to see Lily again ere departing for home. Lily was awake.

"I'm going now. Lily," said Ada, "but I shall see you again in the morning."

"Will you do a little errand for me, Ada?" asked Lily.

"Yes, what is it?"

"Take this little parcel," and Lily pulled a brown paper package from under the bed-clothes, "to Mrs. Martin, 43 Mill-street. She knows what to do with it. She has a big family, and nothing at all coming in. Tell her I'm very sorry I couldn't come myself, as I promised."

"I'll take the parcel," said Ada, wondering what business Lily had with Mrs. Martin. "Now go to sleep," and she kissed her tenderly, "get a good rest; and I'll call in the morning to see how you're going on."

On her way to Mill-street, Ada met Ted Banister, the sweetheart of Lucy Clayton. The young man was lean and ragged; a very picture of poverty. He hung his head as if he would have passed, glad to be unrecognized but Ada said cheerily, "Nay, nay Ted: you wouldn't run past me, would you?"

"I feel ashamed to meet anyone," said Ted, glancing significantly at his clothes.

"Why should you feel ashamed? What ill have you done?"

"None that I know of," said Ted, "and folks say that poverty is no crime, yet, somehow – and it's a strange fact – them what's poor nearly always feels that they are guilty of something or other. How is it? It's a puzzle to me. However, I'm not the only ragamuffin in Lancashire. I could have had some clothes, but they weren't the sort for me. The other day I was in Manchester – some clothes were being given out –cast-off clothing o' rich folks – but I should have looked a bigger guy in them things than I look in my tatters. There were hunting breeches, red hunting jackets, swallow-tail coats, white waistcoats,[64] and I don't know what. One chap got a red waistcoat, and a groom's coat, all buttons, and a pair o' breaches a yard too long for him; but he put 'em on; beggars musn't be choosers – an rare an comic he looked. He knew it hissel, an admitted it. 'I look a bonny mongrel, I know,' he said, 'but odd clothes is as warm as a gradely suit, so what's the odds?"

"You've been in Manchester, then, Ted?"

"I've been all over the land this last month. I set off four weeks ago to look for work. I've been in Wigan, Chorley, Bolton, Farnworth, where the Co-op had just gone smash through the cotton panic; then Manchester, and on to Ashton, Hyde, and Glossop; but no work could I get. And it's dreary trampin in this weather;

snow, puddles, wind, and freezin. Ay, I've been all over, an met bony starvation starin at me everywhere. I was in Ashton-under-Lyne when the riots were on."

"What riots?" asked Ada.

"Bread riots. There were thousands o' clamming women an men clamourin round th' Relief Stores. They'd had food given 'em; but it weren't enough; they were still hungry. Th' policemen tried to keep th' crowd back, but it were too big a job for 'em. Like mad folks th' men an women stormed th' relief stores an broke into th' market, an helped theirsels. 'We want bread!' they yelled, 'an we'll have it!' There was terrible excitement. The police used their bludgeons, an more than one starving chap got his skull cracked; an th' police got badly mauled too. Th' folks were like wild beasts. Then th' Riot Act[65] were read, an more police fetched – an there were talk o' bringin th' soldiers to shoot th' mob – to give 'em bullets an bayonets for fightin for bread. There were nearly a hundred rioters locked up, twenty-seven on 'em bein women. Two days after, the prisoners were taken in 'buses, – lookin to their friends to free 'em – for what crime had they done except bein hungry? – I thought that if one o' them men were my brother or father, or one o' them women my mother or sister, I shouldn't stand quietly by an see 'em carted to jail for nowt, so I upped wi a brick an knocked a bobby off his hoss. I was lucky that I didn't get catched, or I might have been now in Chester Castle too. Th' Riot Act was read again, an more arrests made. There's also been bread riots at Dukinfield and Stockport."

"And what will be done to the rioters taken to Chester Castle?"

"They'll get sent to jail for one, two, or three months; happen more. That's a grand state of things for England, isn't it? Maybe some of 'em will get transported – but no, they can't transport folks now; I heard a chap say that transportation was done away with in 1857".[66]

"You've seen something in your tramping, Ted."

"I've seen enough to make me cry for years," said Ted. "I've met bands o' factory folks in every place, singin hymns an beggin. Yo know the tunes, Ada; they're what we have at th' Sunday school – 'Burton,' 'French,' 'Luther's Hymn,' 'O'd Hundred,' and 'Kilmarnock,'[67] – them's the commonest. For years after th' Cotton Panic's o'er – if it ever is o'er – there'll be few folk in Lancashire that will sing them tunes without tear in their eyes, an bitter memories in their hearts. But th' favourite tune of all seems to be 'Warrington,'[68] – written by a Manchester Unitarian minister. I heard one lot sing that at Bolton; an it touched all who heard it; then they sang one o' Leach's tunes – a Rochdale chap were Leach – beginnin' –

And am I born to die,
And lay this body down?

But th' best singer I heard was in Manchester; a young fellow, all by hissel; didn't look like a workingchap at all. He was singin, 'The Cry of the Unemployed' by a poet-chap called Gerald Massey.[69] I remember a line or two –

> Gold! Art thou not a blessed thing? a charm above all other,
> To shut up hearts to Nature's cry, when brother pleads to brother?
> Has thou a music sweeter than the voice of living kindness?
> No, curse thee, thou'rt a mist twixt God an men in outer blindness.
> "Father, come back!" my children cry. Their voices, once so sweet,
> Now quiver, lance-like in my bleeding heart; I cannot meet
> The looks that make the brain go mad, from dear ones asking for bread –
> God of the wretched, hear my prayer! I would that I were dead!

I wish I could just sing it as th' singer did. It made fine ladies stop in th' street, cryin, to open their purses; an business gentlemen, what's generally as hard in th' heart as in th' head, sniffle and look human for once as they gave money to th' singer. That last line – 'God of the wretched, hear my prayer, I would that I were dead!' seemed to cut through hard hearts wi a sword o' sweetness, while it made th' soft hearts blubber like babbies. Folks said that this singer were some greit man – some famous singer – that were doin this singin in th' streets to raise money for th' poor. There were certainly some mystery about him. Well, how is Sid going on, Ada?"

Ted Banister was surprised to hear that Sid had gone away. "I hope he'll do well," she said, "an come back wi a fortune. Has anybody else gone away?"

"Nobody that you know, I think, except the Walkers. They've flitted into Yorkshire.

"There's a good twothree flittin out o' Lancashire into other parts o' th' world just now, said Ted. "It'll not be th' same country when th' cotton panic's done with it; it'll never be th' same again. There'll be faces missin; some flitted into Yorkshire, some to Australey, an some to th' cemetery."

Ted paused ere saying what now rose to his lips; a question that he had been wishing to ask some time.

"There's no change wi' th' Claytons?" he asked anxiously.

"I've not heard of any," said Ada.

"That's better. My heart's up again now. I've only been away four weeks, but there's a good deal can happen in a month, as I know."

Ada's face saddened, as she thought of how much had happened since Ted had been away; what would the poor lover do when he learned the dark truth?

"Lucy's all right, I suppose?" he said. "Have you seen her lately, Ada?"

"I saw her this afternoon," said Ada.

"Ah, that's good news," said Ted. "I'll get off home, and see if I can't get some other clothes to rig myself up in before I go to see her. I'm a bonny sight to go a-courtin, eh?" and he laughed. "I've come back as poor as I went away – nay, poorer – but Lucy will be glad to see me, anyhow. Poor lass; how I do wish I could help her! There's a big family o' little uns at their house. An my own brothers and sisters are on the starve too. – But I'm fain to hear that Lucy's all right. It does a chap good to know he's a sweetheart waitin' for him, even if they've nowt but love to live on."

Ada was silent; her heart sorrowful and troubled; she was full of a great pity for Ted so happy, even in his poverty, because of thoughts of his sweetheart. What agony would be his when he knew what had happened since he went away?

"Well, good-day, Ada," said Ted, gaily, "I'll go an dress myself up for my courtin. For I shall be off to see Lucy as soon as I've washed this road-slutch an travel-dirt off me."

[10 November 1900]

X. Before the Guardians

Mill-street was typical of the workingclass streets to be found in every manufacturing town. It consisted of two rows of cottages, facing each other, twin oblong piles of brick monotony utterly devoid of picturesqueness or any architectural beauty. The street was like a tunnel without top; one end being blocked by a transverse row of houses, and the other, after crossing an intersecting street, being a continuation of Mill-street itself, seemingly, to infinity. Standing in Mill-street one could hardly imagine that if one only walked far enough, through street after street, he would ultimately find, beyond this depressing arrangement of dreariness, the invigorating beauty and free symmetry of nature – fields, and trees, and brooks and perhaps woods and hills, immune from the miserable measurements and building economies of profit-pilfering man.

All the doors and door-knobs, and even the key-holes, in Mill-street were alike; the separate houses in the blocks were as like as the stamps on a sheet of penny stamps; the interior of the houses and the furniture – a table, a chair or two, cheap fireirons, and in some cases a chest of drawers or dresser, and perhaps a washing machine in the back-kitchen – were all alike; the children playing in the gutters seemed all alike; and the men and women, in all rising to go to work at the same time, coming to meals at the same time, and having the same leisure time at night, were practically all alike. Mill-street's distinguishing feature was severe sameness; and it had few other features.

Indeed, Mill-street, and the companion streets comprising the whole district, made a sort of workhouse; the inmates having a little illusory liberty of a sort, but really no more liberty than that of the privilege of changing, under certain restrictions, at certain times, one set of taskmasters, – variously called employers of labour, town councillors, guardians, and members of parliament[70] – for another set of taskmasters, in no whit different from the others. Yet, practically Mill-street district was one huge workhouse, the workers being bound, in more or less degree, to certain labours and employments, having, it must be admitted, the one great liberty of starving if they did not choose to submit to the conditions of their existence, and blindly supposing themselves free while in reality they were fettered in a thousand ways to landlord, worklord, law-maker and creed-jobber. For the great ones in cunning know that the surest way to enslave a nation is to give it the semblance of liberty; thus the wily few secure the substance while laughing secretly at the earnest attempts of the deceived many to tinker the shadow; which is commonly called politics.

Ada, however, had no thought of these things, – though she had often heard Chartist Grimshaw speak in such a strain, – as she entered Mill-street. She was not even thinking of Chartist Grimshaw – who had many strange ideas, saying that where there was only liberty by law there was very little true liberty, and that the object of all government should be to do away with government, – but of her sister Lily, and her lover Sid.

As she passed down the street Ada noticed that many houses were empty, and soon guessed the reason why. Many families, unable to pay a full house rent in these hard times, had given up their cottages and joined together at one dwelling. Consequently there were, in many cases, three or four families living together – "pigging together" Chartist Grimshaw called it, – in a house barely large enough for one ordinary family. When better times came, and rents could be paid again, these little communities would, of course, break up into their own family groups, and have their own houses once more.

Ada found Mrs. Martin's tenement[71] and knocked at the door. Mrs. Martin herself, a middle aged woman, with a harassed face, came to the door, two young children at her heels; and the voices of other children could be heard inside the dwelling.

Ada quickly explained that she had brought a parcel from Lily Milner, who was servant at Treebarn's.

"Come inside a minute!" said Mrs. Martin, "it's cowd in th' street."

Saying "I mustn't stop long," Ada entered the house.

"We're all jammed an crammed, as yo con see," said Mrs. Martin. "Sit yo deawn. There's only one good chair in th' heause; t'others has aw been turned into bread, – an we're hungry yet. There's two families of us livin here, to save rent – I've heard of landlords that's letting their tenants off for rent while the panic's on, but I'm sorry to say our landlord isn't one o' that sort; he's for all he can get, an a bit mooar, if he can only manage it, – as I were sayin, there's two families livin here; an another family comin in to-morn, so yo may guess we shall be throng. Well, I suppose we shall have to put up wi it. We con stand a bit o' hutchin an thrutchin, if we've only summat to eit. There's nobody knows what we've gone through this last twelve-months; – it were'nt bear thinkin of; indeed

I can't tell how we have got through it; I can only say that we have pulled through so far, an here we are. It's like that song o' Natterin Nan's[72] as my husband sings –

> 'No livin sowl atop o' th' earth's
> Been tried as I've been tried,
> There's nobody but the Lord an me
> That knows what I've to bide.'

My husband's doin a bit to-day on Preston Moor – navvy[73] work, an eh's noan used to it, same as a lot mooar. He says his honds ull be utterly speilt for ever doin spinnin again. He were tellin me this morning that some o' th' men were grumbling at Jackson, t' labour-master, that walks about in his white jacket seein that th' men do their jobs reet, an one on 'em said, 'Let's talk to th' divvle,' an Jackson, just passin them, overheard him. 'All right, my lads,' says Jackson, 'let's talk; that's just what I want.' So they talked, an Jackson listened, an said that he wanted to do fair an just wi everybody, an he'd put things reet. He fair won the grumblers o'er by this straightforwardness. He can't be a bad sort, through he's a boss; an there's some men has to be kept in their place, or they'd upset aw law an order. But how I'm rambling; let's oppen th' parcel yo've brought. Is Lily yore sister? Yo've a greit favvour of her."

"She's my sister," said Ada, as Mrs. Martin opened the parcel.

"I thought I weren't mistan," said Mrs. Martin. "And I know what she's sent – some bread an beef, an pratoes, see yo. She's a good un is that sister o' yores. She's given lots o' things to Mrs. Wheelton, what used to live next door, but is now livin wi us; her husband's name is Bill, an he's very down in th' mouth, just now. He's a greit affecton for poultry, an he kept hens, tendin 'em just like childer. But soon after th' cotton panic begun, he had to start killin his hens, an it nearly broke his heart. He said he felt like a murderer. It were very hard for him certainly; but I must say that the; hens come in handy, an were very good, for I had a taste. His owdest lad, Rafe, has got a job drivin th' 'quality' in a waggonette to Lytham an Blackpool – but that's off now till th' summer comes again. It's lucky to be quality folk, isn't it – nowt to do or think about but gallivantin after pleasure. Rafe were tellin me that he drove owd Wragley an his family to Blackpool last year. Theer's a upstart for yo – I mean Wragley. Used to be as poor as dirt, an were born up a back entry.[74] He were a child when I were. But laws! How he's but got on wi his scrapin and schamin, an his thowt for nowt but hissel. I suppose he's a gentleman now though I remember th' days, when he were a lad, that my mother gan him eaur Daff's owd breeches. An now he walks by me in th' street, an weren't look at me, struts by as peart as a pynot,[75] an never cheeps. But he's no 'casion. I knowed him when his hair suck out at th' to of his hat, an his shirt would have hanged out behin like a Wigan lantern[76] – if he'd had a shirt."

Ada smiled and said, "You say my sister has sent you food before; and also sent to others?"

"She's been doin it for months," sad Mrs. Martin. "Th' first time she came was with Mrs. Treebarn."

"Then she's been depriving herself of food to feed others," said Ada, now understanding Lily's illness.

"I'm sorry to hear that," said Mrs. Martin. "To tell yo th' truth, though, I suspected it, an axed her if it were so; but she denied it so strongly that I could hardly help believing her. Yet I've had my doubts all along. She's a good lass, a grand lass, but she shouldn't have made herself ill. This parcel o' stuff she's sent isn't for me. It's for a Mrs. Gregory, what was confined last week. Your sister heard us talkin about this Mrs. Gregory and their hard circumstances, an she said she'd come round to our house an bring some food, an I could go with her to Mrs. Gregory's. An she's stuck to her word as far as she could; though she can't come herself she's sent th' stuff. But perhaps you'd better take it back."

"No, no," said Ada, "let Mrs. Gregory have it. Lily would never forgive me if I took it back; she would be worse ill than ever."

"I've no doubt she would," said Mrs. Martin, "she's one o' that tender-hearted sort that would kill herself to keep others alive. Not only has she given food, but clothes, an very likely – I begin to think now – th' clothes off her own back. She gave a jacket to Mrs. Wheelton's wench, an a scarf to Bill Wheelton, th' fayther. He'll tell yo so hissel. He's gone afore th' Guardians to-day – he didn't like doin it. But there's no choice. I'm expectin him back any minute. Eh, dear me – this cotton panic; it's a weary time. An Mrs. Dobson – she lives on t' other side – says it'll last a while yet. She's took up wi that new table-rappin religion fro Amerikky,[77] as believd i' spirits comin back an tellin folk things. I'd believe in t' spirits myself if they'd only bring summat substantial – would be th' best road for th' spirits to help us, wouldn't it? Well, as I were tellin yo, they had th' table turnin – it seems a silly marlock to me – at Mrs. Dobson's, an Mrs. Dobson went in a trance, as they call it, an she said that th' Amerikky war wouldn't end gradely for two or three year; an then – this were her prophecy – the divided shall be united by sympathy for th' tragic end o' th' divider. What that means I can't tell yo, but that's what she said. I was there. But I don't care for prophecies an them quare things; they're all right in th' Bible, which is their proper place, but they're out o' place nowadays. I think this here spirit business is nowt but tomfoolery an wickedness; that's my opinion. We've quite enough trouble wi th' livin without botherin about th' dead. Hello, here's Bill Wheelton come back. I wonder how he's gone on wi th' Guardians."

As Mrs. Martin was speaking the door had been opened from without, letting in the chill air of the darkening winter afternoon and there entered a man whose aspect was defeated and despairing.

"How's ta gone on, Bill?" asked Mrs. Martin and Mrs. Wheelton, who had been upstairs, now came down with a baby in her arms and two more children at her heels. The baby was ill and fretful and wailed incessantly.

"How've I gone on?" said Wheelton fiercely. "Why, I'd rayther go to jail than face yon lot o' cowd-blooded beasts again."

"Raly now!" cried Mrs. Martin in dismay.

Wheelton went on, the baby's painful crying forming a shrill accompaniment to his speech. "Them guardians is th' awfullest set o' men i' t' world. They look on yo as a thief an question yo like a criminal – heaw owd are yo; where were yo born? – it's funny they durn't ax what we were born for an whether we did it on purpose or not – where had I been workin an heaw lung – who did I marry an heaw mony childer had I – did I tak ale – were I careful – were my wife thrifty – an a theausand other things. For two pins I'd ha cussed 'em an towd 'em to tak their charity to h— an warm it theer. As an owd Irishwoman said, that went before 'em when I did, "A man had better be transported than go before them guardians; they'll try you, an try you as if you had done a murder, when you're only askin for bread!' An th' owd Irishwoman were reet too. I'll die in a ditch afore I'll ax for relief again. There were another chap up afore 'em when I were; an he fair shrunk i' shame. When we coom eaut he says to me, 'I dunnot like them guardians. One doesn't like to lay one's bareness naked afore such men ... I'm fain there's four of our childer dead ... They're better off! An we should aw be better off if we were dead!"

"But surely aw t' guardians isn't hard-hearted," said Mrs. Martin.

"There mayn't be one of 'em hard-hearted when he's by hissel," said Wheelton, "but take a dozen men and make 'em into a Board to examine unlucky starving other men, an ostid o' bein a dozen ordinary men they become one soulless, heartless, methodical machine that grinds eaut charity like cowd stones. But we con hardly expect any different fro 'em when even t' poor theirsels is full o' spite an nowtiness agen one another. Th' guardians were readin some letters – anonymous letters they cawed 'em – tellin 'em to stop So-an-so's relief as they drank, or were too lazy to wark, an so on."

"Who'd ha thowt there were sich meanness i' t' world?" said Mrs. Wheelton. "Happen somebody's been sayin summat abeaut thee, Bill."

"Did th' guardians allow thee anything?" asked his wife.

"No; they said they'd consider my case an I must see 'em again next week."

"An while they're considerin my child is deein," sobbed Mrs. Wheelton.

"It'll be better off," said the father, but his voice choked as he spoke. "But we'll aw dee afore I'll go before yon guardians again. I'm sorry I ever went. We've struggled on for above a year, in th' pride that hides its misery, while others were runnin for relief th' very first pinch; an this is our reward. Them that's cheeky an sheauts eaut gets what they want; them what suffers quietly an says nowt is denied. Well, it's t' way o' t' world. – What must we do? What must we do?"

"We'st ha' to bide as best we con," said Mrs. Martin. "We're not th' only ones."

"Neow, we're no th' only ones," said Wheelton, "but that doesn't mend things. While I was before th' guardians I heard a few other cases. There was a clean old woman with a white cap on her head. 'Well, what do yo want?' says t' cheermon. 'I could like yo to give me a bit o' summat, for I need it,' she says. 'But yo've some lodgers haven't yo?' 'They pay me nowt; they're aw eaut o' wark.' 'Well, but yo live with yore son, durn't yo?' 'Nay; he live wi me an he's eaut o' wark too. We're hard put to it.' Then another old woman, with a thin shawl reaund her head, came up. 'Well,' said t' cheermon, 'there's only yo an yore husband, isn't there?' 'That's aw,' says th' owd woman, 'me an eaur John.' 'What age are you?' 'I'm seventy.' 'An what age is your husband?' 'John's goin in seventy-four.' 'An where is he?' 'I left him deawn t' street yon, getting a load o' coal in.'"[78]

"An owd chap like that getting coal in. It's shameful!" said Mrs. Martin.

"Let me tell yo of another case," said Wheelton, forgetting for the moment his own trouble in narrating the pathetic hardships of others, "an this proves to them what says us workinfolks is lazy, how we'd rayther do owt than beg or tak charity. There were a decent but totterin owd chap coom up afore these guardians an t' cheermon knew him, for he says, 'What's brought you here, Joseph?' 'Why I've nowt to do, nor nowt to live on,' says Joseph. 'An what's your daughter Ellen doing?' 'She's eaut o' wark – I'm helpin her if I con.' 'An what's your wife doing?' 'She's been bedfast above five year.' Well, they gave Joseph a ticket for relief, an th' owd chap looked at th' papper an turned it o'er, an then looked at th' guardians an said, 'Couldn't yo let me be a sweeper i' th' streets ostid?'"

These simple records of the suffering and noble spirit of the poor brought tears to Ada's eyes. She could recall many similar instances.

After a few words with Mrs. Martin and Mrs. Wheelton – and wishing inwardly that she could help them – she bade them good-day and left Mill-street.

XI. The Sacrifice

Next morning, when Ada went to Treebarn's to see how Lily was goin on, she told Mrs. Treebarn what she had learned the previous afternoon in her visit to Mill-street.

"That explains everything," said Mrs. Treebarn. "The noble self-sacrifing child has been giving her own food and clothes away, and clamming and starving herself in order to help others. God bless her! – though she should not have gone to such an extreme as to punish herself. And yet –"

Mr. Treebarn, a pale man of studious looks, with bright sympathetic eyes, finished the sentence for his wife – "the child is an example to us all," he said.

"She is doing what Christ would have done. If only all others would give a little she would not have had to give so much. She is worthy a place in sacred history alongside the widow who only gave her mite, yet gave more than those who gave much gold.[79] God bless the child! – Nay, God has already blest her in giving her such a heart."

"If we had only guessed what Lily was doing," said Mrs. Treebarn. "I would have seen that she had other food and clothes – though we are but comparatively poor ourselves. It is hard times for us, as well as for the factory operatives. But I never dreamt that the girl had given her clothes away. I noticed that she was very thin, and could not account for it; it must have been because she had given her underclothing away. And a few Sundays ago, when she should have dressed to got to chapel with us, she lay in bed, saying she was ill, as indeed she must have been; yet I now suspect that the chief reason was that she had no change of clothes for Sunday. We will ask her."

Mrs. Treebarn and her husband, and Ada went upstairs to the little room in which Lily lay in bed. The girl started as they entered; and stared at them, wondering what they wanted.

"It's all right, Lily," said Ada, sitting by her sister's side, and holding her hand. "But you shouldn't have done what you have done."

"You've done right, Lily," said Mr. Treebarn, "I cannot say that you have done any wrong. Even I, with all my learning, am in a quandary to say how far self-sacrifice must go. Learning cannot answer the question; only the heart, and Christ is the heart, can answer it."

"Jesus says we must give all we have," said Lily.

"And hard though it seems to us, that is the only answer," says Mr. Treebarn.

"We've found out what you've been doing, Lily," said Mrs. Treebarn, gently, "and though we think you were quite right in spirit, we think you went a little too far in practice."

"That is not for us to decide," said Mr. Treebarn. Lily looked at him gratefully. He was a good man, and an earnest preacher, and whatever the rest of his congregation had done in rejecting or accepting his precepts, Lily had seriously endeavoured to make her life harmonise as fully as possible with that of the Christ he preached. There were no "but's" or "if's" in her religion. She gave, not a little thithe, – hers was not the charity that simply gives what it can do without, the comfortable charity that never inconveniences itself, – she gave all she had, she gave herself, as she would give even her life, if need were, for the sake of Christ and humanity. And, in her pure simplicity and faith, this great thing she did, thinking she was doing nothing at all.

"In men's eyes least and last in all my congregation," said Mr. Treebarn to himself, "and yet in God's sight – and in mine – she is first. Not the well-dressed and moneyed, not the young ladies who dispense charity with a great flutter, and make their workshop a fashionable spectacle, are the glory of my little harvest for God, – but this poor and obscure child. She is the star, and all the rest are rushlights."

"Lily," said Mrs. Treebarn, "when you lay in bed and missed chapel the other Sunday, was it because you had no clothes to go in, having given them away?"

Lily hid her face in the bed-clothes for a moment; then she looked up and said, "Don't be vexed at me, Mrs. Treebarn; the girl I gave 'em to needed 'em."

"God forbid that I should be vexed at you!" cried Mrs. Treebarn, bending over Lily and kissing her. "But you should not make yourself ill."

"Well, you were giving help, and Mr. Treebarn, and your children were giving money they could have spent in toys, and so I felt that I must give too, or Jesus would not be pleased with me," said Lily.

"This child is nearer God than any of us," said Mr. Treebarn softly.

"You took me with you to the soup-kitchens, and to visit the poor in their homes, and when I saw the hungry little children, I could not help but give all I had," said Lily.

Then she lay back, exhausted, being very weak.

Mr. and Mrs. Treebarn retired, leaving Ada and Lily alone.

"How's mother going on?" asked Lily.

"Don't talk, dear," said Ada, "lie down and rest; try to go to sleep. Mother's all right. Try to got to sleep now; I'll sit by your side."

Lily shut her eyes, and was silent. Ada looked at her, noticed her short sharp breathing, and was troubled in mind.

Then the doctor came, and after examining the patient, said he would send some medicine up.

"The child is very weak," he said to Mrs. Treebarn. "She is utterly run down, and all her vitality gone. She must have been starving herself for weeks. In that condition she was peculiarly liable to contract disease. I fear that pneumonia is beginning."

"But surely she will get better," said Mrs. Treebarn, in alarm.

"I can't say," said the doctor. "If she were stronger she would have had a chance. But she has no reserve strength to fall back upon. Her system is completely enervated. I'll look in again to-morrow."

Lily rapidly grew worse daily. In three days the doctor said there was no hope for her. Her mother, tearful, and Ada, came to see her.

"I know I'm dying," she said. "Father keeps coming to see me, and there are beautiful angels with him, and little happy children playing with flowers. Many of them are children that have died during this cotton panic, and they want me to go and play with them, Some of them I know; there's little Jane Ardwick, and Polly Clinton, and Jackie Moorhouse, and many, many more, and they're all joyful, not hungry and cold any more."

Ada tenderly laid her hand on Lily's hot brow.

"Don't excite yourself, Lily," she said. "Try to rest."

"I shall be at rest in the Lord soon," said Lily. "I can hear singing; it's the hymn I liked most of all at the Sunday School –

> 'For ever with the Lord,
>   Amen, so let it be;
> Life for the dead is in that word,
>   'Tis immortality.
>
> Here in the body pent,
>   Absent from Him I roam,
> Yet nightly pitch my moving tent,
>   A day's march nearer home.
> Nearer home! Nearer home!
> A day's march nearer home!'[80]

"Don't you hear the music, Ada? Don't cry, don't cry – I'm sorry to leave you, and I would like to stop to help the little starving children – but perhaps I shall be able to help them all the more when I'm a spirit. Listen! Don't you hear the singing?"

Ada strove to keep her tears back; her mother was sobbing.

"Ada, when I'm gone," said Lily, "but I shall be with you though you can't see me, – when I am gone, you must go to the poor little children and starving people, and help them. There's Mrs. Martin – and Mrs. Wheelton – and Mrs. Gregory – that's her that had a new baby – why do people have babies in such times as these? – well I suppose God sends 'em, and He knows best, – you must help Mrs. Gregory – the new baby will need no help – for it's dead now – I know, though nobody's told me – it died yesterday – I've seen its spirit – it comes and kisses me, – you must help these folks, Ada and as many more as you can, – for I don't think I can be happy in heaven knowing there are suffering children on earth – so you must help them, and I'll be with you, and help you – I wish I could help everybody –'

She suddenly stopped, and painfully gasped for breath.

"Don't talk, dear," said Ada.

"I haven't much more to say," said Lily. "Oh how I wish this dreadful cotton panic was over; and all the misery ended. Well, earth's only for a short time; and there's no cotton panics in heaven."

The next day Lily was mostly unconscious. Ada and her mother were there, but she only recognized them once or twice. Mr. and Mrs. Treebarn were in the room constantly, and Mrs. Treebarn, seeing that the girl was dying, suggested to Mr. Treebarn that he should pray for the child.

"There is no need to pray for her," he said. "In her case it is superfluous – it would be almost an insult. No, we have no need to pray for her. Let us pray for ourselves."

Mrs. Milner and Ada stayed all night at Treebarn's, sitting by Lily's bed. They felt that she would not last till morning.

Soon after midnight, she opened her eyes and looked at Ada and her mother. "Kiss me Ada, kiss me mother," she said. "Father has come for me."

Weeping, they kissed her.

She closed her eyes and sank into unconsciousness.

Once her lips moved, and she whispered 'Father!" Her days upon the earth were done.

[17 November 1900]
XII. The Minister "Brought to his Knees"

The Rev. Mr. Treebarn buried Lily, and though the tears trickled into his eyes in mortal grief as he went through the solemn service in the cemetery overlooking the winter-wild valley of the river, his faith was strong in the immortal joy that the girl was now in a better place than earth, near to God, and far from the cruel touch of the miseries made by man. Ada and her mother were the only mourners in the bleak afternoon which a straggling sunshine, feeble and with no warmth in it, seemed but to make more desolate and dreary.

Soon after the little funeral party returned home Elder Willard Hyde knocked at the door, and Ada admitted him. One of his eyes, to a keen observer still showed a little bruised discolouration.

"I came to tell you how I condole with you in your sorrow," said Mr. Hyde to Mrs. Milner, and his tone was sincerely sympathetic. He glanced at Ada, but she was apparently paying no heed to him.

"It is good of you to remember us," said Mrs. Milner. "When friends are few, one good friend is much. I feel that I have nothing to live for. Husband gone, Lily gone, home gone – what is there left, only a broken heart and sad memories?" Hyde had the tact to make his visit brief. "I merely called to show you that I felt for you in your grief, though I can do nothing to lessen it – would that I could! And this I wish to say, too – if you need help, let me know. I am at your service."

He put on his hat and went to the door. Ada thought it would be ill-natured not to reply to his "Good-day"; she was too sad to be resentful, much less hostile.

On the Sunday morning Mr. Treebarn preached an eloquent funeral sermon on the life and death of his little servant-girl, whom he held up as an example for his congregation to imitate.

"Poor she was in earthly goods," he said, "yet rich in the measures of heaven, which are not measured by men's measures, nor counted as men count coins.

Humble she was in estate, a servant, what the world calls a drudge, yet high in a glory and honour beyond all the titles and orders and distinctions kings confer. One of the least amongst us in our eyes was she, yet in God's sight one of the greatest. Hers was not the comfortable charity which gives what it does not need itself; but the true charity which will itself suffer to lessen the sufferings of others. She did not content herself with giving a tenth of her income; she gave all that she had. She did not merely give her cast-off clothes; she took the clothes off her own back and gave them. She was a truer Christian than any of us; she did not argue – how much can I afford to give? – she obeyed and gave all she had. She gave herself, her whole life. Contrasting ourselves with her, we stand small and set in shame; we stand accused of neglect of our duty to our neighbour and our God; by her side we seem Pharisees and hypocrites; full of words and barren of deeds. Our religion is only on our lips; hers was in her life. And though her life was her death, her death is her life. We all of us hope to become angels when we are dead; she was filled with a nobler idea; she made herself a ministering angel while she lived. Let us do the same. We shall make none the worse angels in heaven for practising being angels on earth. Let us go about doing good, doing our duty to our neighbour, not stintingly, nor grudgingly, nor condescendingly, but brotherly and sisterly, generously. Let us not in sinful pride sit in judgment on our fellow-men – hunting their defects and mistakes, and making them excuse for not doing our duty – let us do our obvious duty and leave all judgment to God, who alone knows all things, and who can alone decide whether any man is worthy or unworthy. There are many amongst my hearers who think themselves Christians, yet do nothing to make other people think them so. It is true they come to Sabbath worship, and pay their pew-rent, and are diligent in all forms and ceremonies, but these things, though greatest to them, are least in the eyes of God; and will not save them. My words may offend some; but I mean no offence; I must speak what I believe, else I, too, shall have failed in my duty to my people. In this sad cotton famine, though many men and women are nobly doing their duty to help the poverty-stricken and afflicted, there are others to whom God has entrusted money and goods, who are doing nothing at all, or next to nothing. I tell you that these will have to answer for their selfish conduct; I tell you that in sitting in a church or chapel and pretending to be servants of God, these men defile the temple of their Master; and God will remember them. If there be any such here this morning – and your hearts and consciences will tell you whether there are or not – may they from this moment see themselves in God's truth and become changed. God makes true Christians of us all; may He honour us by making us all such servants as the little servant who has inspired my sermon. Amen."

During the delivery of this discourse, one of Mr. Treebarn's congregation, Mr. Jabez Wragley, a little pudgy man, with a fat, almost bloated, face, and quick cunning eyes, had manifested by slight sneers, and angry looks, considerable dissatisfaction with the homily; and, when the minister was perorating, he muttered to himself, "the man's daft," and half rose in his seat, as if to leave the tabernacle in a sharp feeling of personal insult. Then he controlled himself, smiled grimly, and looked contemptuously, and revengefully at the preacher.

Mr. Treebarn had evidently some misgivings as to the effects of his sermon, for, as he went home with his wife he said to her, "I fear that my outspokenness will have offended more than one member of my congregation. Mr. Wragley didn't look pleased. He hurried off home without waiting to exchange greetings with me. Well, I felt that it was my duty to speak out; and so I spoke."

"Your sermon was certainly very bold – I dare say to some it would seem personal. It is better to be prudent."

"There are times when prudence is a crime, or at least cowardice. No; I feel that I have done well, though the earthly effects may be ill for me."

"And we can hardly afford to offend the supporters of our church," said Mrs. Treebarn. "As you know, I am almost at my wit's end how to keep our household going."

Mr. Treebarn knitted his brows in a moment's thought. Then he said smiling, "We must be brave, wife. Nay, you have always been brave; and stood by me;" and he looked at her in playful affectionateness, touched with a shadow of regret that she, by reason of being his wife, had to make sacrifices which most women do not like to make, – "You have never even murmured when you have had to go without a new dress, but had to trim the old apparel up instead."

She looked at him, half-sadly, and smiled.

"I thank God for giving me such a helpmate," he said.

Mr. Treebarn was one of those ministers who manfully do their best, in a hindering and indifferent world, to live up to the ideals they preach. His profession was not to him an approved fashionable mode of getting an easy livelihood, but a real duty of service to God and humanity. He had become a minister, not from any motive to live upon labour of others, but in order to have full opportunity to labour for others. He not only preached his religion, he believed it and strove to live it. Christ was not to him a pulpit picture for conventional praise one day a week, but a practical, every-day standard of righteousness. Mr. Treebarn never quibbled with his own conscience, nor equivocated with God or God's Word. He upheld that every man who called himself a Christian must practice Christianity to the fullest of his ability and power; else was he worse than those who knew no God. He maintained that to one styling himself a Christian neither business expedients, nor the ways of commerce, nor the neglects and, omissions of other men, nor the customs of the world of trade nor the fact that certain things claimed to be sanctioned by long establishment, nor the plea that one must do as others do and conform to the laws and usages of society and the community, nor other excuses were any extenuation or of any avail; the Christian must daily, hourly strive to make his Christianity his existence, else he is a traitor to God and a hypocrite to men.

Holding such views and endeavouring to be such a Christian, Mr. Treebarn naturally found his path beset with difficulties. He was, of course, popular with the poor, with those who could give him least assistance in his work; but the rich regarded him with no affection and in some cases with positive dislike because he walked not in the orthodox grooves, but was a raiser of unsettling questions, a disturber of creeded tranquilities, a ruffler of pew-cushioned peace.

His wife, to her credit, loyally stuck steadfast to him in his struggles and harassments and frictions; though at times, being human and feminine, she could not help a little sigh as she saw the wives of other parsons going affluently and gorgeously along the rosy path while her own way lay amidst the thorns. And, as she once said to her husband in a mirth that was plaintive – like so many smiling jests whose soul is a sob – "No man can conceive how hard a thing it is for a woman to give up a new bonnet for a crown of thorns."

But she gave up much, for she was brave and proud of her husband, though she knew that as ordinary men reckoned success and failure, he was a failure. But in his wife's eyes – and in God's – no failure he, but a success beyond all mortal computation.

At night when Mr. Treebarn came home from evening service he said to his wife, who had not been to the chapel, "Mr. Wragley was absent to-night."

"You think he is vexed at your sermon of this morning?" asked Mrs. Treebarn.

"I think so."

"It is a pity; but you have done no wrong."

"I don't like to hurt any man's feelings. Yet I must speak the truth."

"It is not your sermon that's scourging him, but his own conscience," said Mrs. Treebarn. "If his soul were all right, your words would not have hurt him; but, in the contrary, rejoiced him. Not your sermon, but the evil in himself, hurts him."

"You are right, wifie," said Mr. Treebarn. "The word of God, by a divine mystery, is both a terror and a joy at one and the same time; the very same words that are whips to the wicked are rewards to the righteous."

"If we do our best, we may hope for the best," said Mrs. Treebarn.

"I am glad you are not cast down," said her husband. "I don't mind my own suffering, but I don't like to bring others into it. – It's a fearful thing to have a flock."

He smiled wearily as he mused of the daily and weekly events of his ministry – the mean little jealousies amongst the members of his church, the spiteful critics who watched him keenly only to seek flaws in him, the auditors who listened eagerly to his sermon only to discover offence or error, not to get blessing and benefit, the one or two employers, and shopkeepers, who were personally insulted if he attacked the evils of the social system or spoke against unjust profits and usury, or pleaded for the downtrodden and oppressed who were, at least in the fact of contiguity, their own neighbours.

"How amusing, and yet how pitiful," he said, "to think how mightily careful a minister must be if he wishes to 'get on well,' in the common acceptation of the term, with his flock. He must be ever thinking, not about God and God's work, but of the hundred little mischief-making whims and oddities of the people who assemble to worship under him; he must humour this man, flatter that woman, not say anything to offend the susceptibilities of this one, be careful not to say anything in his sermon that will touch on the raw this other man who is harsh with his employees, or the other one who neglects his wife, or some else who is a sweater, and a dozen more sorts of human being, who all think that it is their parson's duty to please them whether he pleases God or not. I can understand how any young ministers, starting upright, with the noblest intentions to do their duty, have been gradually bent and distorted, and tempted till, after much fraying of spirit and weariness of flesh, they have given up the nagging gnawing struggle; and allowed themselves to be dragged down to the level of their flock. I cannot blame them; I am sorry for them. Their strength was not equal to the task. God give me strength always to keep upright."

He needed that strength. Next morning, just after he had had breakfast and gone into his study to attend to some correspondence, Mrs. Treebarn went to him, and with a significant smile, said, "Mr. Wragley has called, and wishes to see you."

"Send him in," said Mr. Treebarn.

Mr. Jabez Wragley entered, in all the chinking insolence of a vulgar cash importance, recently acquired, and unrefined or unsoftened by a generation of two's possession. He seemed the human embodiment of a cheque for twenty thousand pounds, and with no more qualities or intrinsic value than such a cheque, apart from the monetary stamp on it, possessed. If we could imagine a cheque, puffed and swollen into the size of a man, and put into human shape, then dressed up in hat, clothes, and boots, and walking about saying, 'I am a cheque for twenty thousand pounds,' we should have some idea of Mr. Jabez Wragley; who, breaking on the minister's speculation, glanced aggressively at Mr. Treebarn's pale, earnest face, and said, "Ah, it seems a nice easy thing to be a parson, sittin in a study, readin an writin, while other people are busy keepin the universe goin."

"Take a seat, Mr. Wragley," said the minister.

"I haven't much time to waste," said Mr. Wragley, "I am a busy man. And I can talk as well standin as sittin. To get straight at the point, I have called about your sermon of yesterday mornin."

Perhaps it was because Mr. Wragley was such a busy man that he hadn't time to pronounce his final "g's," but omitted them entirely from his conversation; and otherwise neglected his grammar.

"Yes," said Mr. Treebarn, "about my sermon."

"That ought to be apologised for," said Mr. Wragley. "That's what I've come about. An I've not come in any temper, or haste. I don't do things rashly. I thought the matter over last night – I slept on it, as the saying is, an that's a wise thing to do; an if other people would only do the same – even in regard to sermons – there'd be less unpleasantness in the world. That sermon was a direct personal insult to me; an it ought to be apologised for, an apologised for in the place where it was made – the pulpit."

"The sermon wasn't meant as such," said Mr. Treebarn.

"It was took as such," said Mr. Wragley. "Not only by myself, but by others. I heard of folks sayin yesterday afternoon, how the parson had been rappin at old Wragley, an tellin him that he was on the way to perdition."

"I never said such a thing, Mr. Wragley."

"No, but your sermon implied it, an that's food enough. If you make a sermon that people can pour all sorts of dirty slops into, that's your fault. The talk about me has been disgraceful."

"I'm truly sorry for that," said Mr. Treebarn.

"An this is the way you treat your friends," said Mr. Wragley. "I've been a friend to you an the chapel – I've given plenty money – I built an extra classroom all out of my own pocket; an then you tell me, in front of a public congregation, that I must give more. Tell me who's given half as much at our place? An further, you insult me by sayin I'm not to be compared to the servant who washed your pots and mopped your floors. I'd like to know what you think of yerself."

Mr. Treebarn smiled innocently.

"An now you're laughin at me. Instead of goin down on your knees an beggin my pardon, you laugh at me. Well, my fine fellow, you may laugh when you want some more help. You'll laugh on the other side of your face then. I'll keep my money to myself, or give it where it'll be more appreciated. That reminds me that you've more than once hinted in your sermons about makin money out of sweated workpeople, an I'm told that you meant me. You've also spoke of people actually usin the cotton panic for their own ends. It's a nice thing to call a man because he takes opportunities God has given him, isn't it? Allow me to tell you I've made my money honestly, an I'll not be insulted about it. In my opinion it's nothing but mean jealousy and envy. I've kept my eyes open and made the most o' my chances, an I shall stick to what I've got. I shan't give it to help to keep idlers an wasters, like most poor folks are. If they'd only saved their money when times were good instead o' spendin it in drink,[81] there wouldn't have been a quarter the distress there is, even with a cotton panic."

"Mr. Wragley," said the minister, "I assure you I am very sorry if I have hurt your feelings. But I must preach God's word; and, so far as I know, I have never preached any other. Will you kneel down with me an pray to God to guide us in this dispute or difference?"

"Certainly not," said Mr. Wragley, in a flush of indignant amazement at such a proposal. "I want no humbug. It's Monday to-day, not Sunday."

"God is the same everyday," said Mr. Treebarn.

"Let's have no pulpit cant now," said Mr. Wragley. "I'm here as a business man. And you know that the world can't get on without business; that not even a church or chapel can pay unless it's run on sound business lines."

"What we call 'paying' and what God calls 'paying' are two very different things," said the minister.

"It's no use discussin anythin," said Mr. Wragley. "I've come to tell you that I cannot support your chapel any longer. I shall in future patronize some other place of worship."

"You really mean this?" asked Mr. Treebarn.

"I mean it. A man that's got on as I have, that is a Board of Guardians, an a J.P.[82] can't go to a chapel to be insulted. I've done with you."

"I am very sorry, Mr. Wragley, not for my own sake, nor even for the sake of our chapel, but for your sake. You may find a different minister at some other place of worship, but if you look rightly, you will find the same God everywhere. You may change your minister, but you cannot change God."

"I haven't come to listen to a sermon," said Mr. Wragley, in an anger born of a consciousness of guilt and meanness. "I have had sufficient sermons from you. Many a Sunday you've preached at me, as if I was the greatest rascal in the world instead of a respectable gentleman, a man of wealth and position, honoured by his fellow-citizens."

Mr. Treebarn looked Wragley right in the eyes. "Let us talk to each other straight," he said. "yet not in haste, but in love. I bear you no personal malice, Mr. Wragley, though I hate many things you have done. – Nay, don't go; it is the last time I shall preach to you. – May God inspire me to speak so that you will understand, even though you don't like my words, that I am speaking in love, not in any ill feeling. You say that you are a man of wealth and position – I grant that. You say you are honoured by your fellow-citizens. That I deny. What your fellow-citizens honour is not yourself, but your money. Your workpeople fear you; many, I regret to say, hate you –"

"You've been listening to lousy dirty back-biters!" cried Mr. Wragley. 'You call yourself a gentleman, and yet you let people who I find bread for come an slander me behind my back. You ought to be ashamed of yourself for listenin to their tales an lies."

"I can sift the true from the false," said Mr. Treebarn, "and I may say that it is no pleasure to me to hear evil of any man. After making a generous allowance for exaggeration and distortion in the reports brought to me I have concluded there was a sufficient foundation of fact at the bottom of them."

"I'll sack every man, woman, an child in my place an get a fresh lot," said Wragley, vindictively.

Mr. Treebarn felt that it was hopeless to talk with this man. He deemed himself an appointed authority in the world, a man set over his fellows: he was one accursed with arrogance and poisoned with power. The laws of God, the laws of humanity were naught to him; he was a law unto himself. The product of an age of machinery, he was merely a great and terrible human-machine; having strength but no sympathy, power but no pity.

"I believe," said the minister, "that God gave us any talents we have to use in the service of mankind, not for our own selfish ends. The aim of men should not be to make money for himself, but happiness for others."

Wragley sneered. "We're not living in the New Testament," he said, " but in England, anno domino[83] eighteen-hundred an sixty-three."

"Do you know what those words 'anno domini' mean?" said Mr. Treebarn, slightly emphasising the last syllable of the Latin, but the mill-owner did not notice the correction. "They mean 'The year of our Lord'; even though we are not now living in the New Testament. But there will never by any real 'year of our Lord' till men like you, Mr. Wragley, learn and do their duty to their neighbour."

Wragley fumed. "Insultin me again," he said. "I won't stand it. I've not come here to argue, or have sermons pitched at me. An I don't want to talk. I'm no spouter. I'm no parson who's nothing else to do but talk. I prefer action to talk."

Mr. Wragley rather under-estimated himself in the matter of talk. He liked hearing himself talk. He had been Sunday school superintendent for two years, and had used his opportunities to the full for indulging in long discourses to the scholars. But he only loved to talk because it fed his pride to have an audience listening to him. His object in orating was not to teach anything, but to gain glory.

He had now strode to the door of the minister's study, and stood with his hand on the knob.

"I hope we part in goodwill," said Mr. Treebarn. "I wish you well. I pray God will soon enlighten you."

The last remark was unfortunate; it irritated Mr. Wragley still more. "You must be an oily hypocrite," he exclaimed. "How can you wish me well when you keep insultin me with every word you say? You talk as if you were always looking down on me; as if you were a superior angel while I was only a miserable worm. But you'll have the conceit taken out of you; you'll be brought to your knees. I shan't forget your insults and your success. I'll bring you to your knees!" And Mr. Wragley bounced abruptly and vigorously out of the room.

Mr. Treebarn laid his head in his hands and thought; and was very sad. He critically examined his own conduct; he reviewed his words. Perhaps he had not spoken as he ought to have spoken; he was only a faulty, fallible mortal. There might be truth in Mr. Wragley's contention that he, the minister, had unconsciously posed as a superior being loftily correcting an inferior. If so, God forgive him; he had never meant such an attitude.

Mrs. Treebarn, who had heard the vicious departure of Mr. Wragley, wondered what had happened. She guessed there had been an unpleasant scene. She knew Wragley and she knew Mrs. Wragley; the latter being a coarse, narrow-minded, illiterate woman, who, since her husband's acquisition of wealth, had put on great airs and often made herself ridiculous by her aping of what she considered aristocratic manners. Like all such upstart women she was suspicious that she was a laughing-stock, and jealous of those whom she imitated. She did not like Mrs. Treebarn because the minister's wife had that educated polish she lacked, and further, because Mrs. Treebarn did not bow down and worship her. Mrs. Treebarn shrewdly reasoned that Mrs. Wragley, by peevish scandal and innuendoes had largely influenced the mill-owner in his resentment against the minister.

Fearing that some crisis had come Mrs. Treebarn went to her husband's study and quietly opened the door.

Her husband was on his knees, his eyes closed in prayer.

She waited a moment; then bent over him and kissed him on the forehead.

"Thank God!" he said; and rose to his feet with a smile of courage.

[24 November 1900]

XIII. Genteel Trouble

Because of their own financial embarrassments, none the less tragic, but perhaps more so because they had, on account of their social position, to hide their poverty under an appearance of prosperity, as is the case with many middle-class people, Mr. and Mrs. Treebarn could not now give the Milners the help they had given them while Lily was alive. The defection of Mr. Jabez Wragley from the chapel had serious effects on the pecuniary standing of Mr. Treebarn. The chapel, quite in accordance with the popular fashion, was heavily in debt:[84] and a great part of the minister's current salary was owing. There was a chance of this being paid while Mr. Wragley's purse was at the disposal of the deacons; but Mr. Treebarn despaired of getting the money now. And the grocer, and other shop-keepers, compelled to look sharp after their debts to pay their creditors, who were in turn pressed by other creditors, in that ceaseless circle of business which seems to be composed of a string of rats each holding on grimly by his teeth to the tail of the one on which he is dependent, were becoming ominously clamorous at the minister's door.

One day, being in the neighbourhood, Mr. Treebarn called at Mrs. Milner's, with the object of explaining, to some extent, how it was that Mrs. Treebran had ceased to send gifts of food. When the minister entered he found Mr. Willard Hyde talking with Mrs. Milner. Ada was out, at the sewing-class.

"I thought you'd forgotten us quite, Mr. Treebarn," said Mrs. Milner. "It seems quite an age since you were here."

"It is hardly a fortnight," said Mr. Treebarn, glancing at Hyde.

Mrs Milner saw the look, and said, "This is Mr. Hyde, a sort o' parson too, Mr. Treebarn. He's been a good friend to us."

Mr. Treebarn said, "I have heard of the gentleman, but never been introduced to him before."

"I am pleased to make Mr. Treebarn's acquaintance," said Hyde, defiantly.

Mrs. Milner noted the tacit antagonism betwixt the two men, and said, with a smile, "How you two scowl at each other, like two rival dogs or tomcats. How is it that two parsons, of different sects, yet both preaching the same peace and love, always look at each other as if they could tear one another's throats?"

One of Mrs. Milner's chief traits was a candour which often made awkward situations in any company in which she happened to be.

Mr. Treebarn smiled, and said, "I'm sure I bear Mr. Hyde no animosity. I differ from – and strongly oppose – the religious views he holds; but I have nothing against him as a man."

"That is precisely my feeling," said Mr. Hyde.

"Mr. Hyde has explained his religion to me," said Mrs. Milner, "and I don't see that it's any worse than any other. Indeed, in lots of things it's better. The Mormons don't let each other starve; they share all they have with each other. In that they do what Christ commanded."

Mr. Treebarn immediately guessed that Hyde had been trying to convert Mrs. Milner; and, to judge by her remarks, was succeeding in his object. Evidently Mr. Hyde had had more than one talk with the woman. Now what could his motive be in endeavouring to win Mrs. Milner over to Mormonism? Mr. Treebarn concluded that it was to secure Ada. He knew that Ada's sister Nelly had been persuaded to go to Salt Lake City; and reasoned that the Mormons were also desirous of capturing Ada; probably Hyde had marked her out for his own harem.

Having thus thought, rapidly, Mr. Treebarn quite as quickly decided on his duty.

"Mr. Hyde will excuse me being quite frank," he said. "I will say what I have to say to his face, honestly. I should be sorry to see you inclining to Mormonism,

Mrs. Milner. Your daughter Ada is in my charge: I am her pastor. If she were drawn into Mormonism – into polygamy – I should believe she had gone to mortal and immortal ruin. Therefore, I advise you, – even in Mr. Hyde's presence, – to listen not to his wily words."

Mr. Hyde smiled combatively. "You are certainly very frank, Mr. Treebarn," he said. "I will be the same. Mrs. Milner and her daughter know your views; they know my views; let them judge for themselves what is best for them. You assert that Mormonism means ruin to a soul. What proof have you? None. On the other hand, we Mormons can easily prove that we are much closer to the spirit and letter of the Bible than any other existing Christian sect. Even our belief in polygamy – which is only one of the minor articles of our creed – is in thorough accordance with the Bible. The old patriarchs had many wives. We believe in God, we believe in Christ, we believe in the gifts of tongues and prophecy; we believe all that the Bible teaches. And we practice what we believe. We live as brother and sisters; we help each other; we let no man or woman in our colony starve. What other Christian community can say as much? Or half as much?

"I do not deny the good points in Mormonism," said Mr. Treebarn, "but in my opinion, whatever good there is in your religion is utterly nullified by the evil of polygamy. Christ did not teach polygamy."

"He said nothing against it," said Mr. Hyde, "so we may fairly assume that he sanctioned it, or else thought it such a trifle that it might be left to the discretion of His followers. That is our opinion. With Christ a good life was the main thing; and it did not matter whether a man had one wife or a dozen wives so long as he treated them well and did his duty to God and his neighbour. As I have already told you, polygamy is only a minor tenet with us. Our enemies magnify it and make it our whole creed."

"Polygamy is the little part which corrupts the whole," said Mr. Treebarn, "and makes all the rest of your beliefs only a cover for lust."

"You take a prejudiced and grossly distorted view, sir," said Mr. Hyde.

"Polygamy means perdition," said Mr. Treebarn.

Mr. Hyde smiled contemptuously. Then he laughed. "If polygamy is wrong," he said, "let me say that it is its own punishment, as say the humorists and comic scribes, who certainly do not more misunderstand and misinterpret Mormonism than those who argue against it seriously. I contend that a man has a natural right as well as a sacred right, to more than one wife. Of course some men are content with one wife; that's all right. Others want more than one wife; that's all right too. Each to his taste and his desire. But let me put the Mormon position truly. A man finds the labour of his household increasing. His wife needs domestic help. Instead of engaging a servant, who is to be a despised drudge, he marries another woman, who becomes, not a kitchen-slave, but the companion and equal, as well as the help-mate, of his wife. If, as his household grows in size and importance, he finds that more female labour and superintendence is necessary, he marries another woman, and another – as many as are required; but not more than he can afford to keep comfortably. No Mormon is allowed to take a second wife till he can prove that he can maintain her. Now what is wrong about that method? In addition, it gives every woman opportunity to enjoy the beauty of marriage, which your system, condemning many maidens to be 'old maids' and cruelly disenfranchising them of the rights of sex, does not give."

"It is lust, and nothing but lust," said Mr. Treebarn excitedly, emphatically.

"What's in a name?" said Mr. Hyde. "What is lust? What is love? The two are so intermixed in most men and women that there is no difference; they are merely what I may call thermometric gradations of one same passion. Further, I may ask, which is better – open polygamy, or concealed polygamy?"

"What do you mean?" asked Mr. Treebarn.

"I mean this. In England here, in your righteous, respectable England, how many rich men have their servants for mistresses? The practice is the same here as in Salt Lake City, with this difference, which is in our favour, that we marry our servants and call them equal wives, while in England you have only one wife, and servants who are fully entitled to be called such. We are honest, while you are hypocrites."

"'Tis a foul slander," said Mr. Treebarn.

"I congratulate you on your innocence, and your ignorance," said Mr. Hyde. "I can prove what I say."

"There may be cases, I admit; but they are uncommon," said Mr. Treebarn. "They are the exception, not the rule."

"That's all you know," said Mr. Hyde. "I know different."

"And I say that you are grossly libeling a nation which, whatever its faults in other ways, does uphold the purity of the ideal marriage – monogamy," said Mr. Treebarn, warmly.

Mrs. Milner here interfered with one of those clumsy unfortunate utterances, which, while it may mean only an innocent little to the speaker may be construed into a mischievous much by the hearer.

"I wish you wouldn't come here to quarrel, Mr. Treebarn," she said.

The minister started, flushed, and rose to his feet.

"I will not thrust myself anywhere I am not wanted," he said.

"I never said you wasn't wanted," said Mrs. Milner. "I only said I wish you wouldn't quarrel."

"I will leave you in peace," said Mr. Treebarn, and he hastily quitted the house.

He felt that all the world was against him. When a man is worried by a pinched purse, and gnawed by the small, but keen, miseries of domestic impecuniosity, his views of greater things are pessimistically affected and distorted out of all true proportion; as an insignificant batch of dancing biting midges may annoy and mar a person's view of a vast tranquil summer scene. The saying is trite enough, but its truth is justification for its repetition, that a little thing in the eye makes a vast difference to a man's outlook on life for the time being. The importunity of the greengrocer anxiously after his account may even cause a devout minister of religion to take a darkly doubting view of an eternally Benevolent Providence. The divinity of human nature is often made mocking ruin of by the diablerie of human affairs. If Mr. Treebarn's exchequer had been in flourishing condition, and there has been no rupture between himself and Mr. Jabez Wragley, he would have paid very little heed to Mrs. Milner's treatment of him or to her careless words.

As he walked homewards, however, and thought things over calmly, he began to think that he had been too precipitate at Milners.

"We are all weak and prone to err," he said to himself. "I ought not to have taken offence. But my nerves are all upset; and a man with disordered nerves is easily irritated." He smiled to think what havoc nerves play with souls.

When he told his wife what had occurred, she said, "I am surprised at Mrs. Milner. We had better leave her alone till she comes to her senses. Surely her sense of gratitude ought to have restrained her. She knows how much we have done for her."

"She implied that we had forsaken her because we have not visited her for two weeks," said Mr. Treebarn.

"Oh these selfish poor people, who are always expecting to receive, yet never think of giving, – never even think of making the least kindly allowance for their benefactors if the well of their charity fails for only a day or two. Surely they might consider that we too have our difficulties and debts. But the poor don't think, – they only devour, and devour, and expect to have everything done for them."

From which outburst it will be seen that recent monetary troubles and domestic affairs had also had some effect on Mrs. Treebarn as well as on her husband.

"Wife," said Mr. Treebarn, "we must say nothing rashly. We are in a disagreeable, depressing mood because of the gloom on our own house. We are weak and frail. We must pray for the Divine Strength to help us; else we shall begin to take miserably mean views of the world and of the people in it. We must get the heavenly sunshine of Christ on our earthy despair lest we despair and in our despair become despicable. We must not forsake the Milners."

"I think it would do Mrs. Milner good to leave her alone for awhile," said Mrs. Treebarn. "She has lately said things I don't like. The last time I was with her she said she knew of a religion where the rich shared all they had with the poor."

"That's the Mormon's doing," said Mr. Treebarn. "The man is deluding Mrs. Milner with exaggerated if not altogether lying pictures of Mormonism. But you see, my wife, if we abandon Mrs. Milner now we leave her open to the wiles of this Mormon missionary. That is just what he wants. – No; I thought of keeping away from Mrs. Milner myself; for I hate to force myself on people; but I see now that I should not be doing my duty if I stayed away. And we must do our duty and submit to a few insults and snubs, not alone for Mrs. Milner's sake, but for Ada's. It would be a horrible thing if Ada should embrace Mormonism."

"Ada can take care of herself," said Mrs. Treebarn. "Besides, she is constantly under my care at the sewing-class. As for Mrs. Milner, I think it would be best to leave her alone for a time. I am not speaking in any malice, but I believe, in wisdom."

"When our wisdom accord too well with our personal inclinations we had best be wary how we accept it," said Mr. Treebarn. "But we must not quarrel, wife; you and I, at least, must not let ourselves be dominated by the demons of the empty purse; we must fight them, saying, 'Get thee behind me, Satan.'[85] Perhaps these are some of the temptations to try us. Let us remember ourselves and show true mettle. Don't fret, wife; I know the days are hard for you just now; but if only we have faith and fear not, trusting in God, all will be well with us, whatever betide."

XIV. The Horror of the Workhouse

Chartist Grimshaw, dismal as the rainy winter day that made the town look miserable, sat in the house of the Milners, sadly telling a sorrowful tale. Ada had seen him walking about the street just before noon in a disconsolate way, and asked him to come in and sit down; and now she and her mother were listening to his outburst of lamentation. "Th' horror has come at last," he said. "Joe's goin to th' warkheause to-day; an his wife an childer with him. Th home is to be brokken up. But I'll no go wi 'em; I'll die in a ditch afore I'll go to th' Bastile!"[86]

Joe – Joe Hagan – was the son-in-law with whom Chartist lived. As his name showed, he was of Irish descent; his parents having come to Lancashire, like many more sons and daughters of Erin, when the rise of spinning and weaving inventions and multiplication of machinery caused the wonderful development of the cotton trade in the first half of the nineteenth century. People flocked to Lancashire from all parts of England, Scotland and Ireland, with a vision of good wages and plenteous days before them; and Lancashire villages became towns, and towns became thickly populated manufacturing centres. John Bright,[87] the Rochdale orator, immigrated a deal of Irish children to labour in his mills; and the sweet brogue of Ireland mingled with the whirring dialect of Lancashire; both tongues and peoples being curious akin in one thing, their happy and droll humour under all circumstances, even in times of trouble and despair. There is at least a close cousinly relationship betwixt Irish wit and Lancashire humour; and a general family likeness can be traced in their features. The Irish peasant and the Lancashire worker are equally pat with droll repartee.

Yet Lancashire regarded the Irish as foreigners; and looked with some disdain on that quarter of each of its towns where the Irish clanned together, this locality being nicknamed – and even to-day there is one such district in almost every Lancashire town – "Little Ireland." For years and years too, the Lancashire folks labeled all foreigners, or outsiders, even natives of their own country from other counties, as "Irish," a term of opprobrium, which, despite the broadening influence of railways and the increase of education and knowledge, has not yet quite passed away with the end of the nineteenth century.

There were in course of time intermarriages between the Lancashire cotton workers and the Irish factory hands; Lancashire is full of the descendants of such alliances, which often resulted in bitter, religious family feuds, caused by the antagonism between Roman Catholicism and Protestantism.[88] Thus it often happened that what love brought together, religion – or rather theology – sundered.

The daughter of Chartist Grimshaw had married Joe Hagan. Unfortunately, when the American war started, Joe was in a transition stage as regards employment; he had left the hand-mule spinning, to which he had been brought up, to learn the new self-acting mule method,[89] with which he was only getting familiar when the cotton famine began. Consequently, he had no money, no savings to fall back upon having only had apprentice wage while he was learning how to manage the self-acting mule. In addition, his wife was but weakly in health, and he had three little children. Further, with the generosity of his race, he had insisted on supporting and finding a bed and home for Chartist Grimshaw, who had got too old to earn his own living, though he was willing enough to work at anything he could do.

And now, after fifteen months of pinching and starving of the Hagan household, existing they hardly knew how, Joe Hagan had himself fallen seriously ill, pulled down by privation and lack of food. He lay bedfast, unable to stir; his wife was near confinement: – there was nothing for it but the workhouse.

"An it'll kill Joe," said Radical Grimshaw bitterly, "th' very thought o' th' workhouse will finish Joe off, for he has a great independent spirit an would sooner go to hell than to the union. But what can he do? An I can't help him. I only wish I could. But they shan't take me to th' Workhouse. It shall never be said that Chartist Grimshaw ate workhouse bread. An I'd give my life this minute if I could only keep Joe out."

"When have they to go?" asked Ada sympathetically.

"I'm expectin th' prison-like van every minute," said Chartist. "They want me to go too. But I'll not go. I'll tramp till my feet are worn to th' bone, – but in no workhouse I'll never live nor dee."

"Many others have had to go," said Mrs. Milner.

"Curs wi no spirit in 'em," said Chartist, emphatically, "or else they'd never submit to such a doom. If only this country were rightly governed there would be no need for anybody to go to the workhouse, – nay, there'd be no need for any workhouses. But th' people is cowards an curs; they've neither sense nor pluck. Joe Hagan's willin to work, ill as he is, if they'd only find him work. He went to get work at th' Corporation job on th' Moor, but he didn't succeed. There's a prejudice against him, because of his Irish blood; he's been called a Fenian. That tells against him everywhere. But Joe's no more a Fenian, believing in bloodshed an outrage, than I am, though he naturally has great sympathy with his country, an wants to see justice done to Ireland. And I dare say he's talked rashly bitter against English oppression at times, but that's excusable. Th' English would talk more than the Irish, and do more too, if they were in their place. But Joe's no Fenian; he's too gentle a sowl. Yet, he's even been followed an watched by th' police; an our house has been watched."

"He has no relations here?" said Ada.

"He has parents at Chorley, but they're hard put to it theirsels, like everybody else just now. His brothers an sisters are all factory hands; an so out o' work too. His younger brother, Bob – Bob Hagan – a wild young cowt he is too, a little youth, with surprisin long arms an big hands – he's th' hand of a man twice his size – has gone for a sailor on th' *Alabama*. Let me see, Sid Clifton's gone on th' *Alabama* too, hasn't he?"[90]

Ada nodded affirmatively, and blushed.

"Then Bob Hagan an Sid will have met," said Chartist. "The sea will suit Bob better than th' factory. I remember Joe tellin me that Bob thought nothing o' strippin naked an racin o'er th' Nab moors near Chorley. A rough lad, yet not bad-hearted. He'll just be suited wi a sailor's life. If Bob had been at home, an workin, Joe an his family could have gone to Chorley for a bit; but Chorley's every whit as poor as Preston is to-day, – an so is all Lancashire. Yet it needn't be – it needn't be. If folks were only wise there would never be any hard times; if trade were only gradely governed an regulated there'd be ample stores made in th' good times to last out any bad time that may come.[91] Oh, if th' people would only go in for th' Chartist programme. But th' workin-classes cannot see beyond th' end of their nose, nay, they cannot even see th' end of their nose, though they're everlastingly led by it, an pay through it. But Chartism's droopin.[92] And th' same may be said of th' Socialism of Robert Owen, and th' Owenites;[93] they had a Hall of Science in Preston twenty years since, – but that's fizzled out now. An there's folk that says Robert Owen's work has been all in vain. They're blind that says so. For though Owen's ideal hasn't been realized, yet there's much good an reform been done by his work, – let us never forget that he started infant schools, an th' system of education that's now in general use,[94] besides bein indirectly th' inspiration of th' Co-operative movement that began in Rochdale twenty years since, an which has done a bit for them that has good wages an is thrifty, but doesn't go right to th' root o' th' social evil, like Owen wanted. Real Co-operation would, but this sort doesn't; it only gives shoon to them that can stand up and walk; it doesn't help them what's tumbled down in barefeet an rags. Progress is very slow. It seems to me that th' world crawls forrud an inch, like a snail gooin up a pole, an then falls down to th' bottom wi a fullock[95] every time it gets a little height. But I believe it'll get to th' top some time."

There was a rattle of wheels in the street, and Chartist Grimshaw stood up and looked through the window.

"Th' workhouse van," he said. "it's come. It's just like a funeral. I'll go an see what's agate."

He went out to his own home, – soon to be no longer his home, nor anybody else's.

Ada said suddenly, "I'm very sorry for old Chartist, mother."

"He's an old talkbox," said Mrs. Milner. "He can't get out of his spoutin tricks. He used to stand gabblin at street corners, and on spare land, an sometimes on waggons an carts, with gapin crowds listenin to him; an much good it's done him, hasn't it? So he's got in the habit of talkin an can't get out of it. I wonder what he'll do when Joe Hagan's gone to the Bastile."

"Mother," said Ada, "I should like to help old Chartist. He's a good old man. Couldn't he live with us?"

"Mercy! how? What can we do?" exclaimed Mrs. Milner. "Haven't we enough to do to keep alive ourselves just now?"

"We could at least give him shelter," said Ada "and as to food, he can have half of mine."

Mrs. Milner looked at her daughter as if she thought the girl had suddenly lost her senses.

"If Lily were here," said Ada, "she would say 'Help old Chartist.'"

Mention of her dead daughter set Mrs. Milner crying, and in this softened mood she said, "Well, well; we'll have him a day or two. Perhaps in a few days he'll find somebody who can better afford to take him in."

"Lily is rejoicing this minute," said Ada. "She is looking down on us with approval."

"Ay, ay," moaned Mrs. Milner, "my poor lass in the cemetery – I wish I were there too. She killed herself for others."

Ada rose, tears of remembrance and mourning in her eyes, and looked through the little window. A small crowd of women, children, and men, despite the rain, had gathered about the door of Hagan's house to see the luckless inmates taken away to the workhouse. Ada saw the dreary vehicle, looking still more dreary in the rain, and the house that appeared to have many miserable memories of similar occurrence on his mind. Then a couple of bailiffs, who were taking Hagan's few goods for rent and debt, as soon as the family were removed, came up with a couple of handcarts, drawn by two hungry-looking men belonging to the unemployed class.

"It's just like a funeral," said Ada to herself, "only I think it's worse, really. This looks as if somebody were being buried before they were dead. God help poor Joe Hagan and his wife and children!"

She stood watching the depressingly pathetic scene for a moment, then turned to her mother quickly, and said, "There's something to do.[96] The people look dreadfully awed. And here's old Chartist rushing across the street to our house, and he looks strangely wild."

The door opened, and Chartist Grimshaw walked in; and said in a breaking voice, "Joe Hagan won't die in the workhouse. He's dead. The very thought of going to the Bastile has killed him. When they went upstairs to fetch him he lay on his poor bed, dead! Died of a broken heart! – a broken heart!"

[1 December 1900]

XV. Some of Chartist Grimshaw's Opinions

The winter was nearly over; the sun had arisen to light the morning fire of spring; the month that is the vernal dawn on the winter night, partaking of the nature of both, was upon the land; flowing February that loosens the soil for flowering March; the month the Romans devoted to ceremonies of purification, typifying the cleansing of the winter-lumbered earth for the fair festivities of spring.

On an evening in the mild end of February Chartist Grimshaw walked to the Virgin's Inn. He was an abstemious man, with no liking for drinkers or their company, but he loved to hear the news of the world and talk of the day; and went occasionally to the Inn for this purpose. He had been living with the Milners since his son-in-law's funeral – a parish funeral[97] – and the removal of his daughter and her children to the workhouse; for Ada had insisted on helping him, though this kindness tended to fix her in a tangle she had not dreamt of; for even the little addition to the household expenses caused by the lodging of the old Chartist had made it impossible for her and her mother to "keep the house door open" as the saying is, without monetary assistance from somewhere or other. This made Mr. Hyde's great opportunity. He offered all the help he could; his purse was at the disposal of Ada and her mother, he said. Ada did not like the idea of being indebted to Mr. Hyde; she uneasily suspected that another motive than pure charity prompted his philanthropy. She said to her mother, "I'd rather we didn't have Mr. Hyde's help."

"We can't do without it," said her mother.

"We might try to manage. Perhaps things will mend in a short time," said Ada.

"Things look like mending, don't they?" said her mother fretfully.

"I don't like being beholden to Mr. Hyde," said Ada.

"Well," said her mother, "we've either to get rid of Old Chartist or be beholden to Mr. Hyde."

Ada saw how she had unwittingly played into the hands of her mother and Mr. Hyde. She was in a dilemma. But she stuck staunch to her nobler instincts. She would not desert Old Chartist though she suffered for her standing by him. "We'll let things be, then," she said. But she had an ever-increasing fear. Intuitively she guessed the aim of Mr. Hyde's tactics, yet she trusted to the future to extricate her from her uncomfortable position.

Mrs. Treebarn, counselled by her husband after his argument with the Mormon, had spoken to Ada of her mother's encouragement of Mr. Hyde; and warned the girl not to be led away by his fine tales and blandishments, as her poor sister Nelly had been by another of the sect.

"I shall never become a Mormon," said Ada.

"The man who visits your house will do his best to make you one," said Mrs. Treebarn. "Already, my husband says, he has gained a deplorable influence over your mother."

"I daresay that's true," said Ada. "But mother is not me. I detest Mr. Hyde and his doctrines."

"That's right," said Mrs. Treebarn; and when she reported her interview (which had taken place in the sewing class) with Ada to her husband, he was pleased.

Chartist Grimshaw was utterly ignorant of the situation in which he had innocently placed Ada; else he would have immediately undone it.

When the veteran reformer got to the Virgin's Inn he found Whistling Will, and many others he knew in the company. Then, presently, Edwin Waugh, who was making weekly visits to Preston, came in; and there was a great noise of merry talk.

"That's it," said the landlord, "let's be convivial. There's nowt like bein convivial."

"Well, what's the news? Owt fresh?" asked Chartist Grimshaw.

"There's plenty news to-day," said the landlord. "Th' Prince o' Wales was married[98] the day before yesterday."

"I know that," said Chartist, "an a bonny lot o' money that would have been better spent in feedin starving folks was squandered in fireworks. How many pounds did our council spend on such tomfoolery?"

"Not much," said the landlord. "They were economical. It wouldn't do to let such an occasion pass without a bit o' show, yo know; we must be loyal. Lancashire spent nowt to what were spent in London."

"It would have looked better o' London to have sent its fireworks brass to Lancashire," said Chartist.

"Nay, let's not grumble at London; it's done well for Lancashire. An we can't let th' weddin of our prince go by without a bit o' buntin an bonfire. It wouldn't be natural, would it hek as like. There's nowt like bein convivial any time, an especially when a queen's son is bein wed."

"More royal childer for th' country to keep," said Chartist. "What starin fools folks are! But th' world seems getting all topsy-turvey. Even them what had sense is losin it. Last night I went to hear Joe Barker,[99] the Secularist lecturer; and he spoke dead against the North in this war, an upheld the South and slavery. There was nearly a riot among the audience. I was staggered wi surprise myself. For I've heard Joe Barker lecturing many a time, an thought he was a man of broadminded views, – but it seems he's as bad as any Christian."

"Here, howd on," cried the landlord, "I won't have Christianity run down. I'm a Christian myself."

"Oh, there's good Christians as well as bad ones," said Chartist. "If there hadn't been one good Christian in Preston, I shouldn't have got to hear Joe Barker's lecture."

"Now here's a tale," said the landlord, "let's have it, Chartist."

"I was walkin about the entrance to the hall where the meetin was held," said Chartist, "longin to go in, but havin no brass to pay for admission, when up comes a minister – well-known in Preston for his sunshiny heart an bounteous good works – Charles Garrett[100] – I'll not disgrace him by calling him reverend; I prefer to think of him as a man – which he is – and not a parson. He saw me, an knew me, for in the old Chartist days Charles Garrett an me had stood together on many a Chartist platform, for he's a man that always had the cause of the people at heart – an a big brave heart his is too. He says to me, 'Well Chartist, are you going to the lecture?' 'I'd like to,' says I, 'but –' 'I understand,' says Garrett, 'hard times; no money. Well, I'll pay for you Chartist; though I don't know whether I'm doing right or not in encouraging you to listen to an atheist,' and he smiled. However, he paid for me to hear Barker an left me."

"He's a champion is Garrett," said Edwin Waugh, quietly. "He's worked like an angel durin this cotton panic. He's a walkin gospel; a grand preacher, an a thousand times grander practiser."

"Well," continued Chartist, "he paid for me to hear Barker, an I wish I'd never gone to hear the fellow. I was disgusted. A man who has derided the Bible because it upholds slavery; yet now speaks in favour of slavery himself. He's nothing but an old turncoat. A man that's preached liberty, justice, and equal government for all – an yet he's in favour of slavery. He ought to be a slave himself."

"Oh, let's noan talk about such a wastrel," said the landlord, "let's be convivial."

Waugh, evidently with a wish to tease the landlord, said, "I was reading in the paper this week a suggestion that all the folks who are working full-time should pay a penny a day to the Famine Fund and do without intoxicating liquors."

"An what would th' poor lanlords do then?" demanded the landlord. "There'd be us to keep then," and the company roared at his sudden excitement, as he went on, "That notion has come fro Joe Livesey,[101] or one of his tribe, I'll warrant; them as wants everybody to be teetotal. But I say that men weren't made to be teetotal; else Providence wouldn't ha created hops and vines. Let a man drink in reason, say I an be convivial when he's a chance."

"There's nowt like speikin for oneself," said Waugh good-humouredly. "However, we'll let our landlord off this time, as he's a good sort. How's this new pier goin on at Blackpool?[102] It's to be opened in May, I hear. Well, I daresay a pier will improve Blackpool shore; just as a good nose sets a man's face off. But for my own part I like to see Nature unspeiled – even by piers. Th' sea's grand enough itsel, without gridirons stuck on it. They'll ruin Blackpool by improving it too much, if they're noan careful. For my part, I prefer quiet little Norbreck, just beyond Blackpool, where there's nowt but sea an nature, an th' next best thing to nature, farms. I were down there three years since to see the high tides – an th' show didn't come off. It's allus th' road when Blackpool advertises its special high tides. There were mooar disappeinted besides me. There were no wind, so th' tide were little higher than ordinary; and the visitors, what had come in their theausands to Blackpool to see th' waves dashin o'er t' promenade, went whum grumbling an growlin thinkin th' whole gam were nobbut a hoax. I met an owd gentleman in th' train – he'd be close on seventy – a gradely owd Lanky gentleman, what talked th' dialect an weren't ashamed on it, – an he declared that he wouldn't come to Blackpool again for th' next fifty years, sink or swim. He had aw th' company in th' carriage roarin at his drowl talk. He said he were gradely sea-sick neaw if he never were afore. Their greit tide were nowt in th' world but an arant sell, getten up by lodgin-heause keepers, railway chaps, newspapper folks, an sich-like wastrel divvles, a purpose to bring country folk to th' sea-side an pike[103] aw th' brass eaut o' their pockets. It wer a land tide what Blackpool folk were after, – an they wanted to get it up i' winter as weel as summer. He could see through it weel enough, he said. But they'd done their do wi him. He'd too much white in his een to be humbugged twice i' th' same gate, or else he's worn his head a greit while to vast little end. But he'd come no mooar a-seein the their tides, nor nowt else, – neow, not if th' whole hole were borne away, folk an aw, bigod! He didn't blame th' sae much, not he. Th' sae would behave itsel reet enoof if a ruck o' thievin divvles would let it alone, an not go an belie it shamefully, just for ther love o' ill-getting, an nowt else. He coom fro Bowton, he did, an he were beaun back to Bowton, an if anybody ever seed him in Blackpool again they met tell him on it at th' time, an he'd ston a bottle o' wine for 'em, so's who they were. They had a sope[104] o' wayter aside o' whum, i' Bowton – it were nobbut a bit of a brook, but he'd be content wi it for th' future, tide or no tide. They met tak their sae an sup it for him, – trashy divvles! Bowton folk had brass enoof to buy salt an wayter an make a sae o' their own, beaut being behowden to a ruck o' grabbing cockle-catchers."

Waugh's jolly narrative of the chargrined Bolton tripper made his audience laugh heartily.

Then Whistling Will said, "I think when this pier's oppened at Blackpool I'll ge deawn an see if I can't get engaged as a whistler. I'm towd there's to be a concert hall on th' pier; an I think I could entertain a company as weel as here and theer one."

"I daresay they'll be engaging that mite Tom Thumb, if Barnum, th' Yankee[105] showman, brings him o'er to England," said the landlord. "He's th' littlest dwarf ever known, I'm towd."

"Blackpool will be up-to-date, never fear," said Waugh. "It's allus up-to-date, an generally a day or two before."

The talk then turned on the awfully brutal murder of an old fireman, near Wigan: he was found, almost burnt away, in the boiler furnace of a colliery. His slayer had been found, and the news caused quite a sensation. The murderer, who was serving a term of imprisonment for theft when his identity was discovered by means of his victim's watch, which he had given to his brother, had confessed the crime to the policeman who fetched him from Portland prison.

"He'll get hanged safe enoof," said the landlord, "an sarve him reet. He's a callous beggar. He stood on th'canal, watchin th' men while they dragged it to find th' deed owd mon's watch, which it were thowt had been thrown into th' wayter. An he'd th' watch in his pocket all th' time."

"Crime has increased fearfully durin th' cotton panic," said Waugh, "especially thievin an drinkin. I see too that the Bowton chief constable says that he never knowed a time when there were mooar women on th' streets."

"Folk gets into mischief when they've nowt to do," said Whistling Will. "If th' people were only workin, there'd be less crime."

"I don't know about that," said Chartist Grimshaw. "It seems to me that th' increase o' crime proves what the Chartists have long contended, an that is – that poverty's t' chief cause o' crime. Do away wi poverty, as that drives folk into drink."

"Teetotal Joe Livesey says quite different," said Whistling Will.

"I don't care what Joe Livesey says," said Old Chartist Grimshaw, "he's a good man, an doin good, but that doesn't say he can't be mistaken as to the cause of drunkenness. I say that it's the grindin dreary lives o' th' poor – all work an bed, an no chances to improve their minds – that drives folk to drink; it's their dismal surroundins an lives that drives 'em to th' alehouse. Give folk fair work, fair wage, wi fair play, build clean healthy towns, an make honest amusements, an folk will become sober. You cannot get figs off thistles, and you cannot get decent citzens out of such hideous towns o' slavin work as we have to-day. That's my opinion."

"An yo're not far out," said Waugh.

XVI. The News in the Market Place

Mr. Treebarn was reading the morning newspaper in his study. There was nothing but war news. The minister's face was sad.

"And this is the eighteen hundredth and sixty-third year of the Prince of Peace," he said. "When will Christ really begin to reign?

He turned to the Parliamentary news. There had been some discussion about the *Alabama* in the House of Commons. Mr. Laird, M.P., ship-builder, and the maker of the *Alabama*, declared that he would rather be the builder of a dozen *Alabama*s than set class against class, like Mr. John Bright, who had spoken scathingly on the fact of an English firm equipping a privateer to harass the Federal shipping.

Mr. Treebarn went out to make certain calls, and met Ted Banister, who tried to avoid him, near the Market-place. Ted looked very destitute, and haggard in the fitful sunshine of the cold March morning; when to stand in the sun was to feel a touch of summer, while out of the sun one was chilled with winter.

"Ted," said Mr. Treebarn, kindly, "you shouldn't seek to evade me. You hurt me. It makes it look as if we were not friends. How is it you've not been to Sunday school lately?"

"I've no clothes to come in," said Ted, surlily.

"What do clothes matter? It's you I want, not clothes. But perhaps I can find you some clothes. I have at least an overcoat I will give you. The days are becoming warmer and I can dispense with it."

"I'm not going to rob a delicate chap like you of his overcoat," said Ted. "And don't think that I've anything against you, Mr. Treebarn. I've not. You're a good sort, and I like you."

"Then come to school, where we can chat together."

Ted shook his head.

"You're in trouble," said the minister. "What is it?"

"Everybody that's poor is in trouble nowadays," said Ted.

"But yours is special trouble, Ted. I can see it in your eyes."

Tears were trickling into Ted's eyes.

"Don't talk to me so – or you'll make me break down!" he cried. "Talk to me harsh, so that I can keep my heart hard an curse all the world!"

"Ted," said Mr. Treebarn, "there is something serious. Come, talk with me as a chum. Perhaps I can help you."

"You can't help me," said Ted. "Even God would have a job to help me now. God can't undo what's been done."

Mr. Treebarn led Ted gently down a quiet side-street. "Now, let us talk together," he said. "Tell me your trouble. It will ease your trouble. It will ease you to confide in me."

"Nothing can ease me," said Ted, "but I'll tell you. Just after Christmas I went up and down Lancashire tramping in search of work. I couldn't get any work anywhere. When I went away I was courtin."

Ted paused with emotion. "Yes," said Mr. Treebarn, "I know your sweetheart, Lucy Clayton. Mrs. Treebarn tells me that Lucy hasn't been to the Sewing Class lately. Perhaps you know why."

"Yes, I know why," said Ted, bitterly, "an you shall know too. The villain ought to be exposed. As you know the Claytons are poor, with a big family, an this cotton panic made starvation times for 'em. While I was away, they were clamming. Well, Lucy couldn't bear to see th' childer cryin for bread, an so – well, you know Mr. Wilfred Wragley, him that goes to our Sunday school – nor for any good, but only to be a big man an make mischief and wickedness – he said he'd help Lucy – on condition – on condition – oh my God! I can't tell it, for it won't bear thinkin of! He's a d— scamp!"

Mr. Treebarn was silent while Ted's excitement cooled. But he began to understand the story; and was shocked and sorrowful. He knew young Mr. Wragley and his character. Wilfred Wragley was an only child, and the spoilt son of his mother; indeed both parents had let him have too much of his own way. In their ignorant idea that vulgar display and pride meant social superiority they had let the lad lead a moneyed idle life, with, of course, its inevitable lapse into dissipation and gambling. He had flashed and flaunted his parents' wealth; he had squandered money in foppery and freakishness; and his mother foolishly and fondly imagined that he was an ideal gentleman, unsoiled by any plebian labour or poverty. Mr. Wragley, senior, though, in his secret heart had been angry and disgusted at the spendthrift ways of his son; but if he ever suggested checking the young man, the mother almost went into hysterics and wondered why he should wish to be so hard-hearted with his offspring. "If we're to make a gentleman of him," she said, "we must let him have plenty of money to spend. He can't go into gentlemen's company, and go gentlemen's ways, without spending money." Mrs. Wragley's notion of a gentleman was the common one, that a gentleman is a man who ostentatiously parades and spends wealth that he has never worked for;[106] and she sneeringly despised all who had to labour for their living as "low and ungentlemanly."

"Now Ted," said Mr. Treebarn, "will you go on with your story."

"When I came back from my trampin about," said Ted, "I was, though miserable in poverty, happy in thoughts of Lucy. Ah God! I didn't know what had happened while I had been away. I went down to the Clayton's, full o' longin to see my sweetheart, full o' joy to know that she would give me welcome, no matter how poor I was. But when I got there an opened the door – she was sittin with her head in her hands –, she looked up, saw who I was, an began sobbin somethin terrible. Her mother was too fagged with her own worries an clamming to take much notice; an then Lucy got up quickly an put her shawl on her head, an said: 'Let's go outside; I want to speak to you,' but she never said my name, an she never looked me in the face, but walked about with her head hangin down. When we got outside I said, 'Lucy, whatever's to do?' but she only cried harder than ever, an her tears filled me with agony. 'Lucy,' I said, 'why don't you look at me?' Then she spoke. 'I can never look at you again! Oh, Ted, Ted, why ever did you come back?' I tried to hold her in my arms, to comfort her, but she pushed me away an says, 'Don't touch me – I'm foul! I'm not fit to touch!' An then she told me how the villain had 'ticed her saying he'd help her mother an the childer – but he only lied to gain his end, for he's doin nothin for 'em –, and so she sacrificed herself for nothin, which makes it worse than ever, if worse could be –, an she was broken-hearted, an so am I."

"God help you both!" said Mr. Treebarn. "Ted, my lad, my heart bleeds for you. Would to God this horror could be undone."

"It's as I said," said Ted, in a calmness of despair that was terrible in its quiet hopelessness, "there's nothin can be done. Even God can do nothin now!"

"Don't talk like that, Ted, don't talk like that." Yet as he spoke, Mr. Treebarn himself felt the utter helplessness of religion in such a situation. "We must pray now."

"This thing's past prayin," said Ted. "I feel that I shall go mad if I keep thinkin about it; an yet I can't help thinkin about it. God help Wilfred Wragley if I meet him!"

"You must do nothing rash, Ted. Further evil will not mend the evil that is done. Leave Wilfred Wragley to God and his own conscience."

"Conscience he has none," said Ted, grimly, "an as to leavin things to God – they've been left to God as it is, an you see the result."

"Ted, you must not talk such blasphemy," said Mr. Treebarn. "I admit there seems no good in this tragedy; but we do not know all; we must hope and trust."

"Sunday school talk's no use in this case," said Ted. "I feel that there's no God, no nothin in all the world, or in all the skies and starry deeps beyond."

"Come home with me, Ted, and we'll pray together."

"I don't want to pray," said Ted. "I don't want to do anythin – except – I feel at times that I could kill somebody."

"I will get Mrs. Treebarn to see Lucy too. The poor girl must have somebody to comfort her. You haven't seen her since the night you came back."

"I haven't," said Ted. "I've tried to go to her – but I couldn't. Not that I love her less – for I love her as much as ever, that's the awful sorrow of it – an pity her an want to help her; but she said I'd best not see her any more, but forget all about her – as if I could forget; as if forgettin an rememberin were as easy as pullin one's clothes off – an though I've tried to go an see her again – I couldn't – I want to see her an I don't want – but I've heard that she's gone away – anyhow, that she's not been at home for several days an her mother's anxious about her. She said she was goin away to look for work at Darwen or Blackburn – but I've had my fears too; an if they're true, then God help – no, devil help Wilfred Wragley!"

"You must come home with me, Ted," said Mr. Wragley, "I can't let you go in this mood."

The two walked back to the Market-place. It was market-day, though there was not much business doing. But there were many people about, including some Fylde farmers, who had been disposing of cattle. Three or four of them stood together talking about cows – the Fylde farmers have hardly any other topic of conversation. One of them was gravely informing his companions and a few town listeners, ignorant of the mysteries of cattle and agriculture, that "there were nowt like peppermint an new butter to cure cows that had the bellyache. Get that into 'em an they would be aw reet in a twothree minutes."

This doctoring remark caused considerable laughter, and then the voice of Whistling Will was heard saying that any cow of his, – but unfortunately he was too poor to possess such beasts – would have "to dee o' th' bellywarch two or three times afore he'd waste new butter on it. He found it hard wark to get even chep owd butter for hissel in these hard times, let alone chuck it away on walkin milk-cans."

The market jocularity caused no smile on the face of Ted Sandiford; indeed it pained him by its contrast with his own woe.

He still heard the voice of Whistling Will as he and Mr. Treebarn passed by. "Oh, have you heard the news?" said Will, to the group about him, "there's been a young woman's body found in th' river."

Mr. Treebarn would have pulled Ted on; but he stopped listening, with his mouth set hard and his hands clenched.

"Ay, who is it?" asked somebody.

"A poor weaver lass," said Whistling Will. "Her name's Lucy Clayton; in fact I knowed her. It's said she's drowned herself because o' this 'cursed cotton panic. They found the body early this morning – washed up by the tide."

Mr. Treebarn hurried Ted Sandiford away; he went quietly enough now, but there was a strange wild look on his face.

[8 December 1900]
XVII. The Easter Egg-Rolling Carnival

In spite of wars, famines, pestilences and other social and nautical disturbers of peace and pleasantness, the human heart, in reponse to the vital instinct for happiness that ever strives against all marrings and miseries, forgets not its holiday periods of festival and carnival but keeps up their celebration, though of course with some inevitable lack of the usual exuberance, under darkest skies and in the gloomiest outlook.

So, when Easter came, even the starved and suffering factory operatives of Lancashire remembered the occasion, and kept it according to old custom, as far as their contracted and scant means would allow; taking, instead of the usual trip to the seaside, a country walk round home; while the children had to be content with merely looking and longing for the toys in the shop-windows instead of buying them.

Conciding with the advent of spring, Eastertide in Lancashire is no doubt connected, in a traditional and fading survival of Nature-worship, quite as much with the vernal resurrection of earth's flowers and herbs as with the tragedy of the Messiah's burial and rising from the dead.[107] The fact probably accounts for Easter being, with the majority of the inhaitants of the north, not so much of a religious holy-day as a merry holiday, – an old carnival with much of its ancient and original meaning and rites lost in the lapse of ages. Thus, the Lancashire people, in going forth to the woods and seaside at Easter, though in modern railway carriages and waggonettes, are only, in a fashion changed and corrupted by the spent centuries, keeping up with the joyful festival with which their Druid ancestors, in an adoration easy to understand by all who yearly feel the first sweet thrill of spring, greeted by the return of the sun from his winter tomb and the arrival of fair Flora and her rainbow train, to the glad music of the wooing birds.

In Preston, on Easter Monday, is observed the singular custom of "egg-rolling," a sight not to be seen in any other town in England. On this day, soon after noon, the children of the town make their way, in twos and threes, and larger groups, to the great natural ampitheatre which makes Avenham Park, on the bank of the river Ribble. The children carry baskets containing more or less eggs, dyed various colours. These eggs they trundle down the grass slopes amidst vast juvenile excitement, and fun for the onlooking elders. When the eggs smash, which happens in a very short time because of their rough treatment, they are eaten, and oranges substituted in the rolling game.

On Easter Monday morning, which fortunately was fine, Chartist Grimshaw asked Ada and Mrs. Milner if they were going to watch the egg-rolling by the river-side. "I only wish I could take Jane an her childer," he said. "They were there last year, – an so was Joe – poor Joe."

Jane was his daughter, the wife of Joe Hagan who had died just as the workhouse van came for him. Jane and her three children, with a new baby now added, had gone to the workhouse; where they were at present.

"I never thought any kin o' mine would drop into the workhouse," said Chartist, sadly. "I wish I could get 'em out. Old as I am, I'd tackle any job that was offered me if I could but find one."

"Don't fret, Chartist," said Ada. "Times will mend ere long. Then Jane and her children will be able to get a little home, and you'll all live happily together once more."

"I can't bear the thought of 'em bein in the workhouse," said old Chartist. "I'd as leif they'd gone to jail; an I too, as livin on charity. It galls me."

"You can't help it," said Ada. "And we are glad to help you."

"Ah, but I don't like it, I don't like it, though I thank you from the bottom of my heart, for your kindness to a poor old man, – but I don't like it," said old Chartist, sorrowfully. "I'd rather earn my own livin. It's always been my pride to be independent – I never thought I should have my spirit broken like this. And yet – and yet," and there was a manly ring in his voice now, "I've always worked when I could, and am honestly entitled to a living now. If I only had all I'd earned I could keep myself as long as I shall live. But no workingman gets what he earns; he lets the master take a shilling for every penny he gets as wage. These big factories are only swindling dens. In the old days, especially the days of handloom weaving, things were different. Every weaver was his own master, and himself got what he made. I used to be a handloom weaver myself; and it was a grand trade; a man could please himself when he started work, and when he gave over, and all that he did was under his own hand and eye, and he had a joy and a pride in his work. It wasn't the same as it is now – a lot o' weavers set together in a big room, each fixed to two or more machines, and all going together like clockwork, all starting at once, all giving over at once; and all tied to a steam-engine and a factory bell. The modern factory system destroys all individuality, it makes the worker only adjuncts to machines. The old handloom system developed character and independence; and gave a man time to think and turn the prolems of life over for himself. But nowadays even the thinking is done for folks by papers; and it's a bad job, too. We shall never have another race like the old handloom weavers – the fathers and sons of Chartism. Chartism grew out of the handlooms; it was woven on the handlooms. There's as much difference between a present-day factory hand – 'hand' is a good true description; that's all they are, 'hands' – not heads – as I was saying, there's as much difference between a present-day factory hand and an old handloom weaver as between a stunted town shrub and a vigorous village oak. The old handloom weavers had time to think for themselves; they'd time to read and study; time to walk out into the fields and make friends with Nature; and so their views were broad, and there was a touch of poetry in their souls. Their idea of reform wasn't like modern co-operation – simply to make divi.[108] – but to make opportunities for man to develop himself to the highest and take an intelligent interest in the universe in which he was a part. – But I'm like all old men – I'm rambling in the past, forgetting myself, and thinking I'm talking from a platform to a crowd, as in the good old days, when men were not machines but minds."

This tendency to harangue was Chartist Grimshaw's chief weakness, if such it were.

"We were talking of the egg-rolling," said Ada, to bring the old man back to the subject.

"So we were," said the Chartist, "and I expanded the egg into a whole poultry-yard. Shall you go to see the sight? I'll go with you."

"Yes, I think I'll go," said Ada; thinking of Lily, who had accompanied her to the egg-rolling last year, but this Easter was invisible to earthly eyes.

After having their small midday meal old Chartist, Ada, and her mother set off for the riverside. The day was sweet and the sun shone. Ada was happy to see the merriment of the children hastening along with their eggs to the field of sport. Her mind was less troubled, too, than it had been lately, for Mr. Hyde had not been to their house for a week; he had gone away to Liverpool. And during the past few weeks, though he had not made any uncommon demonstrations of his passion, Ada knew that he had been trying to make himself amorously agreeable unto her. She was, therefore, well pleased to be rid of him for a week. She knew that he had got "a great hold," as the saying is, of her mother, and suspected that he had lent or given money, to keep the household going. But she had shrunk from questioning her mother on this point, though she thought of it every time she partook of food. And she wondered who had paid the rent, with which they had got in arrears; for certainly it had been paid; the absence of the scowl on the collector's face was proof.

However, Ada forgot these things, and the Mormon, in the charm of the holiday excitement; though she remembered Sid, and wished he was with her.

There were many people making their way towards the river.

"But they don't look as gay as they used to do," said Old Chartist. "There's a look o' th' cotton panic even about their pleasurin; they can't forget that they're hard up an nothin comin in, nor likely to have for a long time, by all accounts."

They passed Whistling Will, who was busy with his mouth-music, hoping to draw a few pence from the crowd.

"Well, Will, an how's business?" asked Chartist.

"Not so brisk," said Will, pulling a long face, "there's plenty of folk, as yo may see, but they've nowt to give. For my part, I'd sooner have less folk an mooar brass. However, I mustn't call 'em; I darsay they'd give if they had it to give. I'm very sorry for th' poor beggars. Though I must say they didn't use to patronise me anything extraordinary when th' factories were all at work an regular wages were comin in – they couldn't appreciate my music somehow. But they'll miss me when I'm dead an gone. Th' rarest whistler that ever were known in Preston. They'll make a lot on me when I'm deead, see if they don't. It's th' way o' th' world."

Leaving Will and his whistling the trio soon found themselves on the top of the green slope leading down to the river; a beautiful view before their eyes; the broad ribbon of water winding up the fair alley, and, in the other direction, westward to the sea; the whole scene permeated with the joyous spirit of spring.

"Grand, grand," exclaimed Old Chartist. "It's a bonny world, when all's said and done. How sublime is spring on the hillls, how glorious in the valleys! A day like this puts new life into a man. If he could only get new limbs and other body tackle as well, he would be all right. But I'm getting old, and my day is done. My spirit says 'Let's dance,' but my body says 'Hold on, I've no legs.' I can remember coming here nearly sixty years since, when I was a lad, and rolling my eggs down this hillside. – Ah, I've had to roll big stones down this hill since then. – Bless the childer, may they never have aught heavier to roll than eggs.

"Sixty years since I romped here, and my memory can leap back to those days in a second – a marvellous thing is memory. At that time the councillors and gentry hadn't begun to make a park of this place; it was called Avenham Walk,[109] and was a promenade with seats here and there along the river bank. It's been a favourite walk of Preston folks for hundreds o' years. Generations in all styles o' dress have walked here – and they're all passed away now, just as we shall pass away. I used to come a-courtin down here too – an now she whom I courted is sleepin in the cemetery, waitin for me to go an lie by her side. Ah! If this spot could only make us hear all the children's shoutings it has heard and all the lovers' sighs and vows what a strange clamour there would be. But all those voices now are silence; as ours will be anon."

Old Chartist's mention of his sweetheart days brought to Ada recollections of herself and Sid, wandering along the river side in the tranquil summer evenings, or taking a boat and sailing up the stream. She had dearest memories of Avenham Walks and Park; of sitting clasping her lover's hand while watching a splendid sunset or listening to the song of the thrush in the gloaming.

Old Chartist, Ada and her mother went amongst the people and the children – the world seemed full of the youngsters and the antics of their eggs.

"I'm glad to see it all and yet I'm sad," said Old Chartist, "for last year Joe an his wife an childer were here enjoyin themsels – an now – Joe's in his grave an his wife an childer's i' t' workhouse. What strange an terrible things can come to pass in one brief year!"

Ada has a similar mourning thought of her sister Lily. Perhaps there was not a family in all the multitude but had some such grief, or shadow of a bygone sorrow or lamentation on the holiday hour. For Weaver Death, whose flying shuttle, strangely enough, has been wrongly called a fatal arrow by primitive poets and others who could only make similies from weapons of war and slaughter, is ever busy taking individual spools of thread – for what else are human beings? – to weave into the immortality of the Deitiy. And he speaks not at his work; being deaf and dumb; yet not unkind; deftly and lovingly tending life's eternal loom. For such in truth is Death. No destroyer – not even a reaper with a scythe – but the Silent Weaver at the Loom of Life.

"Look at the childer, all so happy," said Old Chartist. "Wouldn't it be a great thing to make the childer as happy every day in the year as they are to-day? And it can be done, I'm sure of it. Some day it will be done. I've fought for reform and tried to teach thickheads sense, and I've been reviled; and I've suffered becaue I've preached to do away with suffering, but I don't regret it; I'd bear all I have borne all over again, and more too, to help make the world a happy place for children – to see every child well fed, well drest and well provided with playthings. At times I feel depressed and despairing, like all men, like greater men than I, but the sight of the children revives my courage and my hope; and for them I'd work and die."

Across the river there were many people with more children; the crowds on both sides of the banks would total at least fifty thousand. They were not all inhabitants of Preston; many folks had come from the adjacent townships and out-lying villages on the moors amidst the hills; and there were, from more distant places, many strangers who had come far to behold this famous Easter Monday spectacle on the banks of the Ribble. The sight of the river, which was packed with pleasure boats full of folks, old and young, singing and joking, set Ada thinking of poor Lucy Clayton and her fate – this calm, beautiful water had floated her into the arms of Death.

The tragedy of Lucy Clayton's end had been the sensation of weeks. The coroner's inquest resulted in a verdict of "Committed suicide while temporarily insane." Ted Banister, who was summoned to attend the inquiry as a witness had caused a scene in court by declaring that Lucy had been murdered and was proceeding to expose the wickedness of Wilfred Wragley when the coroner interrupted him and said that matter had nothing to do with the case. "All right," said Ted, "cloak it up if you can – hide the villain because he's rich – but the truth will come out some day."

Mr. Wragley, senior, certainly exerted himself to keep his son's name out of the affair; and by means of his monetary influence succeeded so far as the coroner's investigation and the public press were concerned. But the whole town knew the truth of the tale and talked of it, though Mr. Wragley threatened to take legal proceedings against anyone who, as he put it, "dared to slander his son."

Ada's tear-touched recollections of Lucy Clayton were made all the keener this Easter Monday because on the Easter Monday a year ago Ada and Sid had met Lucy and Ted, happy in their sweethearting, on the river side, and walked and talked with them, keeping together the whole afternoon, and going home together. And now Lucy was darkly dead, and Ted – no one knew where he had gone, – he had left the town after Lucy's funeral, – while Sid was far away at sea, in foreign places and perils: – and where once four blissful lovers had strolled, now only Ada walked alone.

Ada was roused from her melancholy reverie by a sudden outburst of singing.

Some woman, unable to forget even on this day that the horrors of the cotton famine were all around them, grimly shadowing their little holiday, had started singing "Hard Times,"[110] and the vast concourse, with sobs in many throats, and tears in many eyes, had taken up the chorus and continued the pathetic air.

> "'Tis the song, the song of the weary;
>   Hard times, hard times, come again no more;
> Many years have you lingered about my cabin door –
>   Oh hard times come again no more!
>
> 'Tis a sigh that is wafted across the troubled waves,
>   'Tis a wail that is heard upon the shore;
> 'Tis a dirge that is murmured around the lowly grave,
>   Oh, hard times, come again no more!"

Ere the song was done, there wasn't a dry eye in the whole multitude, and the last chorus died out more like a choking wail than vocal music.

Then all at once the grown folks stared at each other, and smiled, as if they thought themselves exceedingly foolish for giving way to such weakness; while the children looked on, in awe and surprise, unable to undersrand this curious topsy-turvy sort of holiday, and wondering whatever everybody was crying about.

And next, somebody with a faith and hope that rose above the dolours of the day – it was Mr. Treebarn and some members of his choir – commenced Dr. Watts magnificent hymn of trust and assurance,[111] to the noble simplicity of the tune "St. Stephen"[112] which was heartily taken up by the crowd –

> "O God our help in ages past!
>   Our hope for years to come!
> Our shelter from the stormy blast,
>   And our eternal home.
>
> Before the hills in order stood
>   Or earth received her frame,
> From everlasting Thou art God,
>   To endless years the same.
>
> Time, like an ever-rolling stream,
>   Bears all its sons away;
> They fly forgotten, as a dream
>   Dies at the opening day."

The mention of "hills" and "rolling stream," and the fact that the people who were singing were standing amidst hills and a rolling stream while they sung, caused the throng to realise the grandeur of the hymn more vividly than ever they had done before; a mighty emotion possessed them, – the thrill of thousands of voices singing together in devotional service; and for once, at least, they felt what they sung; forgotten were hard times, empty cupboards, children crying for bread; – and their souls were uplifted gloriously above the toils and turmoils of this dusty strife to a vision of the ever-lasting peace of heaven.

> "O God our help in ages past,
>   Our hope for years to come;
> Be Thou our guard while life shall last,
>   And our eternal home.

With traces of tears still upon its face, yet mightily comforted in heart now, the multitude resumed its holiday making.

XVIII. By the Midnight River

While Ada Milner had been thinking mournfully of Lucy Clayton, another personage, a man, on the other side of the river, had been thinking in anguish of the same dead girl. This man was Ted Banister, Lucy's lover. After aimless wandering about the shire he had tramped back towards Preston, reaching the river-side on the Easter Monday afternoon. The sight of the egg-rolling festival, the crowd of holiday makers, the lovers arm-in-arm, filled him with agonising recollections.

He did not mingle with the throng. Travel-stained, unkempt, with a wild look in his eyes, he kept aloof, hovering about the top of the slope. Children who chanced to get near him, ran frightened back to their parents or friends, and said there was a "bad man" up the hill.

Seeing that people began to notice him, and stare at him, and knowing too that he looked a forlorn and weird object, Ted Banister, after one absorbing glance at the holiday-making by the river, and a thought of her who had been there – he could see the very place where he had sat with her – only a year ago, – turned away with a terrible sigh, and made his way towards Walton-le-Dale.

He went up the hill, and past the church standing above the river, and then along the road high above the water, yet following its course towards its source, in the direction of Cuerdale and Samlesbury, with its old hall said to be haunted by a white lady.[113] The day was alive with the dawn of spring, the birds were merry of song in bush and brier, and the earliest wayside flowers were fair in the sun, but Ted had no eye nor heart for these things.

Wherever he walked, he walked in gloom; taking with him his own desolate world, wherein there were no flowers, no birds, no sun, no spring, no hope.

He rambled far, going foodless, – indeed, he had no thought of food, – till the sun set, and night crept over the lonely hills and down the quiet valley. In the stillness, under the stars, Ted walked on; then abruptly turned about, and began to retrace his steps towards Preston.

The time was midnight when he reached the top of the hill which descends into Walton-le-Dale. The few houses about, mostly villas of business men, were in darkness; the inmates having gone to bed.

Down at the bottom of the steep declivity on his right, through the great whispering trees, was the river, – the deep mysterious river.

He thought of his sweetheart and groaned.

He fancied that the trees were whispering dirgefully of her; the river, lapping its bank in solemn plashes, was sobbing for her – and for him, the heartbroken lover.

Suddenly he heard a voice, – a voice that was noisy with drink, – trying to sing a roistering ditty.

> "Champagne Charley is my name,
> Knocking down the bobbies is my game."[114]

and beheld a man's form staggering towards him.

Ted Banister started as he recognised the man. It was Wilfred Wragley. Ted remembered that the Wragley's lived at Walton. Wilfred Wragley was returning home from an Easter carousal.

The two met.

Ted grabbed Wragley by the collar of his coat, and said, "Now we've met."

"Who are you?" said Wragley drunkenly.

"I'm the man whose sweetheart you ruined – she drowned herself in that water," and Ted nodded his head towards the river.

"Ah!" exclaimed Wilfred Wragley, partly sobered by a fear of this man. "What do you want?"

"I want to tell you what a rat you are!" cried Ted, shaking the young man fiercely. "You got your damnable way with the poor girl by promising to help her, – and then, you cur!" – Ted spat in Wragley's face, – "having gained your vile end, you even slunk out of paying the price! – you toad, you mean miserable piece of dirt!" and Ted spat in his face again.

Wragley gasped. "Let go!" he said, "You're choking me!"

"What do you deserve but choking! You ought to be hanged, for you are nothing less than a murderer, and as foul and slimy a murderer as ever committed crime. Ah, you infernal coward! Bah!" and Ted spat in his face once more.

"What do you mean?" cried Wilfred Wragley, struggling to free himself, and he struck Ted in the face. Ted hit him back, with a heavy crash of his bony fist; the two gripped esach other; and fell to the ground together; gradually rolling towards the trees on the river-bank. In a frenzy of rage Ted pounded away at

Wragley; then, under a savage impulse, began to drag him through the trees and down the slope towards the water.

In terror guessing Ted's design, Wilfred Wragley made frantic efforts to free himself, but in vain. Ted dragged him on; down; down; down. The night was gruesomely gloomy and lone; thick clouds had come and hidden the stars.

With manic strength Ted pulled the panting, exhausted young man to the very brink of the river; down, down, down.

Then, with one great push, he toppled the body over the edge.

There was one awful shriek, then a splash – a brief struggling and bubbling – and then the old silence.

[15 December 1900]
XIX. The Adventures of the "Alabama"

The day following Easter Monday Chartist Grimshaw, who had been having a walk in the town, returned to his home at the Milners' dwelling with news which greatly interested Ada – news of the sea fight betixt the *Alabama* and the Federal cruiser, the *Hatteras*.

Sid liked his life on board the *Alabama*, and came to regard the mission of the boat in a broader and more tolerant spirit; recognising the obvious, yet not forgotten fact, that there are at least two sides to every question.

During the passage of the boat down the Irish Sea and Bristol Channel into the Atlantic,[115] Sid became acquainted with two or three of his ship-mates, and learned much from them. He found that he knew several of the crew, including the brawny lads from the Fylde, and nimble Bob Hagan, with his remarkably big strong hands, all the more noticeable on a man who was small of stature, from Chorley.

Sid's superior, the chief engineer, was Miles Freeman, a dark man with much hair on his head, and a striking resemblance to Charles Dickens, his moustache and beard completing the likeness to the novelist.

Freeman, in the course of many chats, gave the history of the *Alabama*, and her commander, Captain Semmes, to Sid.

"Raphael Semmes," he said, "or to give him his due title, Admiral Semmes – for that was his rank in the United States navy, – believes fully, as you may guess, in the cause of the South. When the war broke out in '61, after the secession of the Southern States – not alone on the slavery question – there were many other reasons and causes,[116] – he was appointed by the Confederates to take charge of a vessel to damage the northern shipping. We knew that we could strike the enemy sore blows by playing havoc with its commerce. Accordingly the steamship *Sumter* was prepared and commissioned for the work. The South had practically no navy; and there the North had the advantage of us. They blockaded all the southern ports, preventing vessels going out or in. This, as you know, is the cause of the cotton famine, which is so terrible in Lancashire, the spinning market of the world."

"The privations of the Lancashire factory operatives are awful," said Sid. "I've been in the cotton famine."

"The blame rests on the North," said Engineer Freeman. "The *Sumter* was got ready for sea as quickly as possible. She was only a small propeller steamer of five hundred tons of burden, with a low-pressure engine, but sound, and capable of carrying four or five guns. Her speed was about nine knots an hour, though sometimes I got ten knots out of her. The *Sumter* lay at New Orleans, in the Mississippi; and we soon got our crew; there being far many more offering themselves than we could take. At last all being ready for sea, we had to watch for a favourable opportunity to get out of the river. The northern warship the *Brooklyn* was outside the river mouth on the look-out to intercept us. After several attempts we managed the feat; and in broad daylight. The *Brooklyn* had gone off in chase of a sailing vessel trying to enter the river. We seized our opportunity, and were soon steaming past the lighthouse and over the bar. Up went the Confederate flag with a cheer from the men. Our pilot bade us good-bye, saying to our commander, "Now, captain, you are all clear; give her hell, and let her go." But, now we saw the *Brooklyn* in sight. She had been spying on us all the time, and, soon as she saw our tell-tale smoke, had given up the pursuit fo the sailing-vessel, and turned about to meet us. When we crossed the bar she was three or four miles away – we were just out of the range of her guns. We were now going at nine and a half knots an hour; I was doing my very best; though we had a little draw back in the 'foaming' of our boilers, caused by the suddenness with which we had got steam up; as this 'foaming' subsided, I gradually increased our rate by half-a-knot. The *Brooklyn* loosed her sails, bracing them sharp up on the starboard tack. We set our sails too; knowing that we could lay nearer the wind, being able to have our yards sharper. Then a rain-squall came on, enveloping both ships. When this cleared away the *Brooklyn* seemed quite near, and a beautiful and majestic sight she was, – broad flaring bows, clean symmetrical run, masts and yards all taut and square as those on an old-time sailing frigate. We could see the officers on deck, with telescopes. Captain Semmes feared that it was all over with us, and told the paymaster to get ready for throwing our papers overboard, – but at this critical juncture the 'foaming' of my boilers ceased and I sent up to the captain the welcome word that the engine wss working splendidly, giving the propeller several more turns a minute. The breeze helped us too; and slowly the *Brooklyn* fell beind us. She was beaten; we were safe; and the Brooklyn gave up the chase. Our crew shouted and cheered the Confederate flag, – "the little bit of striped bunting," – that had flown from our peak during all the exciting time, and then sang lustily the new national anthem of the Confederate States.

"In Dixie's land I'll take my stand,
I'll live and die in Dixie."[117]

So we got into the open sea, the sailor's glory, the home and empire of the British race, to whom we, as well as the English belong; the mighty mysterious sea, whose magic draws our hearts as it does those of all English-speaking people, the strange old sea, which with all its renowned tales of adventures and exploits and heroism and battles theron, is the common hertitage of all who hold England as the birthplace of their forefathers. I'm of a good old English stock myself – my very name, Freeman – shows it. I'm a freeman born of an ancestry of freemen."

The chief engineer had traces of poetry in his composition; in this respect being like his captain, Commander Semmes, who was fond of quoting Byron, Moore,[118] and other famous singers of the century.

Engineer Freeman, in snatches at various times, gave Sid the whole history of the *Sumter*. "Our first capture," he said, "was a vessel called the *Golden Rocket*. We were running with the English flag hoisted, between the Cuban coast and the Isle of Pines, of notorious piratical memory, one afternoon, when the cry of 'Sail Ho!' was heard from the mast-head. There were two vessels in sight. The nearest proved to be a Spanish boat bound for Vera Cruz. After boarding her to make sure what she was, we let her proceed on her course; and went for the other sail, which was plainly an American boat; though she had not yet shown her colours. We fired a gun at her, and she unfolded the 'Stars and Stripes.' We hauled down our English flag, and ran up the new Southern banner. The *Golden Rocket* made no resistance, knowing it was useless. Our officers boarded her and returned with the master and his papers. He was tremendously astonished; he had never dreamt of finding the Confederate flag in these seas. Then Captain Semmes did his duty – and a painful one it was – to burn the vessel we had captured; as all our ports being so rigidly blockaded, we had nowhere to take her. All the crew of the *Golden Rocket* were fetched off in boats, and the torch applied to her. It was night when this was done; and the burning of the ship was a sadly magnificent spectacle. She was fired simultaneously in several places. The flames soon lept up into the rigging and all the yards began to blaze; pieces of burning cordage and sail falling into the sea. The captain of the *Golden Rocket*, apparently calm, watched his noble vessel burn; but his soul must have been full of emotion at the sight of her terrible dying agonies – it almost breaks any true sailor's heart to see his ship perish, whether by tempest, accident, or fire. We treated our prisoners well; and made up a purse for the shipless captain, when we landed him. That was the beginning of our work of devastation and vengeance; the *Sumter*'s task came to an end six month later at Gibralter, where we had run for coal. Three of the enemy's vessels blockaded us. Captain Semmes left the *Sumter* and proceeded overland to England, to look after the *Alabama*, then in building, and near completion. During the six months of the *Sumter*'s cruise we captured seventeen ships, and did dreadful damage to the enemy's commerce. That was a grand record; but the *Alabama* has beaten it. The *Alabama* will be famous in the annals of the sea forever."

From Sandy Aspinall and Bob Hagan Sid got the story of the *Alabama* previous to his joining her.

The *Alabama*, as already mentioned, was built by Laird Bros., of Birkenhead, at a cost of about £60,000. She was a screw steamer, of 900 tone burthen, 230 feet in length, 32 feet in breadth, and 20 feet in depth, with a speed of 10 knots an hour, though she once did 13 knots (not very much larger than the *Queen of the North*, a pleasure steamer now at Blackpool (1900), which was also built by Laird Bros, – the dimensions of the *Queen of the North* being, length 220 feet, breadth 26 feet, depth 12 feet. The *Queen of the North* also differs from the *Alabama* in being a paddle-steamer; her speed being about 18 or 19 knots, or 20 miles an hour).

Sid found that he was one of a total crew of 149 men; there being 24 officers – captain, four lieutenants, surgeon, paymaster, marine officer, four engineers, four master's mates, a captain's clerk, boatswain, gunner, sailmaker, and carpenter.

The armament of the *Alabama* consisted of eight guns, – six 32 pounders, in broadsides, and two point-guns amidship – one of these latter two being a 100 pounder rifled Blakely,[119] situated on the forecastle, and the other, abaft the mainmast, a smooth-bore eight inch. But the gunner said that the Blakely gun, on account of being deficient in metal, compared with the weight of the shot it threw, was of no use after the first few discharges, as, when it became heated, the charge of powder had to be greatly reduced because of the recoil.

"The *Alabama* is a beautiful boat," said Engineer Freeman, "she's a perfect Venus of the sea for shape – light and graceful as a swan – not a line nor a curve out of proportion – 'She walks the waters like a thing of life,'[120] as Captain Semmes says, quoting Byron's poetry. Her engine is grand too; there's 300 horse power behind the propeller. She's built to act either as steamer or sailing vessel, barquentine rigged,[121] with three long lower masts, enabling her to carry large fore-and-aft sails, as jibs and try sails, which are of the utmost importance to a steamer in an emergency. Her sticks are of the best yellow pine – they bend in a gale like a willow wand, without fear of breaking, – and her rigging is of the best Swedish iron wire. She's a perfect steamer and a perfect sailing vessel at one and the same time; neither of her two modes of locomotion being dependent on the other. The *Alabama* is so constructed that in a quarter of an hour the propeller can be detached from the shaft and put in a well made for the purpose; high enough out of the water to make no impediment to her speed. This done, and the sails spread, she is to all intents and purposes a sailing ship; and a model at that. But if the wind be adverse all we've to do is lower the yards to the wind, start the fires, lower the propeller, and there she is going along merrily as a steamer. She's a beautiful and wonderful boat, and whatever may be her ultimate fate, will live for ever as one of the most picturesque vessels in the romance of the sea."

Sid found his duties pleasant on the whole; and life on the *Alabama* was enjoyable and exciting. Commander Semmes, though strict, was not unkind; but he would be obeyed and he would have no shirking. He was a tall man, with strong features, the upward curl of his moustache indicating a strain of self-control, or at least egotism. He was aristocratic in thought and aim; he despised democracy. Coming of a Southern family he was naturally bitter against the North, which he was fighting. He said that the New England people – the Northerners – being of Puritan descent, derived from their religious doctrines a gloomy asceticism of character and a remarkable tolerance of other people's opinions. The Puritan leaven[122] had at last "leavened the whole loaf" and the descendants of those who had come over to America in the Mayflower, to escape persecution in England, were now, having got power, using it to persecute others who differed from them. "Rebels when in a minority they had become tyrants when in a majority." By unjust taxation the North caused the slave-owning planters of the south to so mortgage their property that to make ends meet they had to become almost as terrible slave-drivers as the manufacturers and merchants of the North.[123] Majorities always had a tendancy to become injurious; liberty was always destroyed by the multitude in the name of liberty.

Such were the views of Captain Semmes, who earnestly believed in the justness of the Southern cause and gallantly fought for it. For the South was his native land, and, as he often quoted,

> "Breathes there a man with soul so dead,
> Who never to himself hath said,
> This is my own, my native land!"[124]

Yet Captain Semmes, though honourable and a gentleman, became brutalized to some extent, as all military men are and always will be, by the fever of war; and his fine feelings of broad humanity were blunted by his narrow patriotism, as is always the case. He lowered his moral gods down to the excuse that "all's fair in war." Writing to the Federal Congress of the South, he said, explaining his views of an irregular naval force, "I mean private armed ships, called privateers ... It is at ships and shipping that we must strike, and the most effectual way to do this is by the irregular force of which I speak. Private cupidity will always furnish the means for this description of warfare... and you can prevent it descending into sheer privacy."

He did not hesitate to use the base passion of "private cupidity" to secure his ends and the cause of the south. He also firmly believed that white men had a right to own black men, as slaves; though in his contention that the manufacturers of the north were really and truly as much slave-drivers as the cotton-planters of the South there is perhaps more truth than most people would suppose. There is more than one form of slavery and the most open form is not always the worst.

Yet Captain Semmes strove always to be a gentleman and generally proved such even under the most trying circumstances. He had a taste for science as well as poetry and took great delight in gardening when at home on shore; and no man who is touched by the gentle grace of gardening can become base.

All was not work and fighting on board the *Alabama*. There were days of rest and holiday. On such occasions the discipline of the ship was relaxed while the men entertained themselves with fiddle and concertina, or that most favourite pastime of sailors and soldiers – yarn-spinning. More than one of the crew could extemporise tales that would have made the fortune of a business-like novelist. Occasionally the men had a dance, some of them taking the part of ladies, and putting on ribbons, and a mimicry of maidenly shyness to act the part thoroughly; to the huge amusement of their shipmates and officers. On these days of enjoyment Captain Semmes sould sit smoking a cigar on the bridge, with his officers about him, in social chat and literary and scientific gossip. One time he quoted the following lines with all a sailor's enthusiasm for the sea, to his companions: –

> "Ours the wild life in tumult still to range,
> From toil to rest, and joy in every change.
> Oh, who can tell? Not thou, luxurious slave,
> Whose soul would sticken o'er the heaving wave;
> Not thou, vain lord of wantonness and ease,
> Whom slumber soothes not – pleasure cannot please;
> Oh, who can tell, save he whose heart that tried,
> And danced in triumph o'er the waters wide,
> The exciting sense, the pulse's maddening play,
> That thrills the wanderer of that trackless way?
> .... Death!
> Come when it will we snatch the life of life;
> When lost – what recks it – by disease or strife?
> Let him who crawls, enamoured of decay,
> Cling to his couch and sicken years away;
> Heave his thick breath and shake his palsied head;
> Ours the fresh turf, and not the feverish bed;
> While gasp by gasp he falters forth his soul,
> Ours with one pang – one bound – escapes control.
> His corpse may boast the wan and narrow cave,
> And they who loathed his life may gild his grave;
> Ours are the tears, though few, sincerely shed,
> When ocean shrouds and sepulchres our dead."[125]

"But," and Captain Semmes laughed, "We're far from dead yet, my lads; we're very much alive, as our enemy, – the Puritan plague hatched from the cockatrice's egg brought over in the *Mayflower* – is finding out to its cost.

> Howl, ye ships of Tarshish,
> For your strength is laid waste.[126]

That's out of the book they descecrate; the book which they only value for the profit they can make out of it; as witness that New York vessel we captured carrying contraband Bibles and tracts to Portugal, with a note amongst the captain's papers that all orders for Bibles could be sent to a certain New York firm. But we burned the cargo of cant; and pleased God by our deed, I am sure. For God is no lover of hypocrites. I believe in the Bible myself – an eye for an eye; a tooth for a tooth; and these we'll have from our foe. One ship we found full of marketable religion; another one burned was loaded with patent medicines. The burning of the latter ship was an act of humanity; we thereby saved many lives. – Bring me another cigar, Bartelli."

Bartelli, who was an Italian, was the Captain's steward; he was a model servant; he knew always exacty what was wanted of him, and did it thoroughly and beautifully. There were many foreigners in the crew of the *Alabama* – Germans, Danes, Dutch Malays, and others, but the bulk were English and American. Once there had been a little drunken mutiny, some of the crew having too much liquor while ashore at Port de France, in the Island of Martinique; but Semmes soon quelled the insurrection by tying all the offenders up and dousing them with buckets of cold water till they were sober.

[22 December 1900]

XIX. (continued)

Sandy Aspinall told Sid the story of the career of the *Alabama* up to the time of Sid's joining her at Liverpool.

"When she first left Liverpool she crossed the Atlantic," he said, "till she got into Confederate waters. Then, to a band of music, she was christened, the English flag being hauled down and the confederate flag hoisted. Next day we started off to strike at the whale fishery off the Azores. We caught several Yankee whalers and burned them. The destruction of one of them, the *Dunbar*, was a fine sight. There was a gale blowing when the torches were put to her and the wind made wild banners of the flames, scattering sparks far over the sea; then she sank, all aglow, a victim, as I heard Captain Semmes say, 'to the passions of war and the fury of the elements.' But our chases didn't always end in havoc; there was fun about some of them. Once we were after one ship all night – and she could rip away too – and when we caught her we were vexed to find she was a Danish boat.

Of course we had to let her go; we dare not war on any but Federal vessels. From another ship we took the black lad who attends on our doctor – Doctor Galt. The black lad is really a slave; but, as you know, he couldn't have kinder treatment; and he won't leave the doctor. Dr. Galt offered to put him ashore at one place but the lad preferred to remain the doctor's happy slave than become a miserable freeman under some employer of labour. Dr. Galt says the people of the Northern States are unable to understand the sympathy between Southern masters and their slaves; if they had understood it there would have been no war."

"Has the *Alabama* been in any storms?" asked Sid.

"In several," said Sandy. "But the worst was a cyclone in the Gulf Stream last October. I thought it was all over with us. All the hatches were battened down; and if life-lines had not been put along the deck for us to cling to we should all have been swept overboard. We got right into the vortex of the cyclone – a terrible thing; the winds running round and round us in a circle, but, where we were, almost a dead calm – like the point of rest in the centre of a whirlpool – calm as regards wind only, the sea being all agitation caused by the winds outside the vortex; the clouds were writhing and twisting low over us like awful serpents; it was an appalling sight; while the waves were bobbing up and down as if there were giant engine-pistons under them. The *Alabama* was thrown over – just as we got out of the vortex – then her fore stay-sail was split into ribbons and the main yard went overboard, the winds screeching like ten thousand demons; and blinding spray everywhere. We were in the cyclone about four hours and never thought to get out of it. But we were lucky; and the *Alabama* behaved magnificently; she's a champion."

Sid had begun further to understand the two sides to the American war and comprehended that from their point of view the Southern States was really a small man fighting a big man for his rights and liberties; and he certainly developed a sympathy for the South, though he hoped the North would compel the South to abolish slavery.

Though Sid at first thought he was joining the *Alabama* under a deception he was pleased to find he was mistaken. Before he signed his papers he was given the chance, if he wished it, of going back to England in a steamer, which, by appointment, met the *Alabama* to supply her with coal. Captain Semmes said he didn't want to engage any men under false pretences. Sid decided, for several considerations, chief being that his friend, Sandy Aspinall, was one of the crew, to stay on the *Alabama*.

While Sid had been on board the *Alabama* she had taken over a dozen prizes, the last being a New York vessel called the *Ariel*, which had ladies on board. But Captain Semmes treated the females very courteously, and though they were frightened at first, when the *Alabama* boarded the *Ariel*, the ladies, with the romance and curiosity of their sex, soon began to find a pleasure in the adventure of being captured by the "pirate" *Alabama*, of which so many tales were now being told all over the world, and actually persuaded the sub-officers to give them brass buttons, cut off their coats, as souvenirs of their thrilling episode. One of the *Alabama* lieutenants hadn't a button left on his coat!

After leaving the Arcas Islands, Yucatan, where deep in the clear waters was to be seen a forest of sponges, a marvellous and lovely sight – Bartelli, the steward, fished some sponges up, one for the captain's use – the *Alabama* got along the coast of Texas, and neared the port of Galveston, which had been captured by the Federals.

Captain Semmes steered towards the lighthouse. The look-out cried, "Land ho! sail ho!"

He saw five steamers, suspiciously like ships of war. There was excitement on the *Alabama*. Presently one of the steamers threw a shell which burst over the city of Galvaston. Captain Semmes at once concluded that Galvaston had been re-taken by the Confederates, as the enemy would not fire into his own people. Then the look-out called from aloft that one of the steamers was coming out to the *Alabama*.

Captain Semmes turned his vessel about, and got up steam, – she had been under sail though the water was still warm in her boilers. The pursuing steamer came on, though cautiously; but the *Alabama* kept up her game of decoy, to draw the steamer away from her consorts. She was a large paddle-steamer, rather bigger than the *Alabama*. The chase continued till pursued and pursuer were twenty miles away from the fleet; then the *Alabama* prepeared for action; sails were furled, the drums beat to quarters;[127] and Captain Semmes wheeled his boat round to meet the foe, the United States ship, the *Hatteras*, which now hailed the *Alabama* – "What ship is that?" "Her Brittanic Majesty's steamer *Petrel*" was the false reply. "We will send a boat on board to verify," came the answer from the *Hatteras*.

Captain Semmes turned to his first lieutenant, "All ready for action?" he asked. "Yes, sir; the men are eager to begin." "Then tell the enemy who we are," said Captain Semmes, "for we must not strike her in disguise." The trumpet of the *Alabama* rang out. "This is the Confederate steamer *Alabama*!" and Gunner Kell, turning to the crew, all standing at the guns, the gunners with their sights on the *Hatteras* and lock-strings[128] in hand, gave the order to fire; and instantly a broadside was poured out.

Night was on the sea now, but the night was clear, there being no moon, but sufficient starlight to make the ships distinctly visible to each other at the distance of half a mile.

The *Hatteras* returned the broadside; and the battle began. Both ships being under steam, and heading in the same direction, the conflict became a running fight – the *Alabama* fighting her starboard-broadside and the *Hatteras* her port-side. For neary a quarter of an hour there was the notes of guns, the flashing and the smoke of power; dreadfully disturbing the beautiful night; then the *Hatteras* hoised a light, and fired an off-gun as a signal that she yielded. What a cheer went up from the *Alabama*, as she drew near the defeated *Hatteras*, and Captain Semmes asked Captain Blake if he had surrendered. "Yes," said Captain Blake, "and we want help; my ship is sinking fast."

Captain Blake was brought on board the *Alabama*, where he gave up his sword to Captain Semmes, who immediately set about saving the crew of the *Hatteras*, which was fast going down.

The *Alabama* succeeded in saving every soul; and two minutes after the last boat-load came away the *Hattras* went down, bow first. The *Alabama* was hardly injured at all in the fight; there was not a shot-hole required plugging; and only one man was injured.

The last news was joyful news to Ada, to whom Chartist Grimshaw had been telling the foregoing story of the *Alabama* and the fight with the *Hatteras*; his information being got from newspapers and public talk; for Ada was now assured that her lover Sid was still alive and well.

"The *Alabama*'s making quite a name as the terror of the seas," said Chartist Grimshaw. "Every merchant vessel that crosses the Atlantic is in dread o' meetin her; for she's done wreckin wark on many a dozen. Th' insurance companies has raised their prices, too, for Northern vessels; an th' *Alabama* is in one way an another makin a mess o' th' United States commerce. At first, when tales of this strange steamer, that scoured the ocean, pouncin on harmless traders, were heard, folks said they were wild sea yarns, like th' story o' th' Flyin Dutchman;[129] but there's no getting behind the fact now. The *Alabama* is a reality; an she's fought, an beaten, an sunk a United States man-of-war.[130] Of course I'm against the *Alabama* and her privateer doins; an yet if there were no war there'd have been no *Alabama*. It's a pity that th' North an South couldn't settle their differences without fightin. If they had, there'd have been no *Alabama* as I've said. Neither would there have been any cotton panic. War's a foo's game for th' nation that allows it; a thief's game an a murderer's game for them that's fightin in it; an hell's game all o'er for everybody else concerned.

"What will become of the *Alabama*?" asked Ada.

"That's an anxious question for thee, lass," said Old Chartist, kindly. "But I can't answer it. I don't know. Shes in war, an will have to risk the fortunes of war. If any great Federal battleships trap her she'll be sunk – not without desperate fightin no doubt. But for thy sake, Ada, an for Sid's, thy sweetheart, I hope that the *Alabama* has the best of luck, an comes out of all the strife safe. An the sooner the better, the sooner the better, for America an Lancashire, an all of us."

XX. A Timely Intervention.

The news that Mr. Jabez Wragley had severed his connection with the Hosanna Chapel, as Mr. Treebarn's tabernacle[131] was called, soon became public amongst those who atteneded that place of worship. Mr. Jabez Wragley himself had indignantly denounced Mr. Treebarn to several of his friends, and emphatically asserted that he would never set foot again in Hosanna Chapel; his wife also, in still more vulgar fashion, had spread the tale, with slanderous additions, telling how her husband had been insulted by the minister when he went to talk matters over with him in a calm and reasonable manner. The majority of the members comprising the Hosanna congregation were of the opinion that they were well rid of the mean up-start manufacturer; some, however, kin to him in character and conduct, sympathised with him and expressed their intention of following his lead in the matter of secession.

The girls and women at the Sewing School talked of the event; and looked at Mrs. Treebarn to see how she was affected by it. But the minister's wife showed no signs of fear or uneasiness; she chatted as cheerfully as ever; hiding her own despair to bring out the courage of others.

She came and sat by Ada, and began to talk about the *Alabama*; and its recent fight with the *Hatteras*. "It was a dreadful thing," she said, "according to the newspapers one of the shells from the *Alabama* fell in the sick bay of the *Hatteras*, where several seamen were lying ill; but fortunately, no one was injured. I am glad the *Alabama* won, for the sake of you and Sid, Ada; and I am gladder still that no lives were lost, the *Alabama* being able to rescue all the crew of the *Hatteras* before the latter vessel sank. Everybody is talking about the *Alabama*; she is quite famous; schoolboys are longing to go to sea to emulate Captain Semmes; the romance of the story of the *Alabama* enthralls them. I suppose you haven't heard from Sid?"

"No; I've had no letter yet," said Ada.

"It will be difficult for the *Alabama* to post letters; she is roaming all over the ocean, and has to be careful what ports she enters. But I daresay you'll be having a letter before long. I hope so."

Ada told her mother and Old Chartist, who was still living with them, about the difference between Mr. Treebarn and Mr. Wragley. Old Chartist Grimshaw listened intently to the recital, and then said, "So th' minister stuck up to th' bullyin capitalist, did he?"

"He must have done," said Ada. "He must have talked very straight to drive Wragley away. But Wragley's long had a notion that he should rule the chapel and everybody in it because he has money."

"I'm fain th' parson stuck up to him," said Old Chartist. "There's no mony ministers like that. Most of 'em think far more abeaut keepin in wi t' rich than tellin 'em th' truth an doin their duty. A minister like Mr. Treebarn deserves supportin. I'm no chapel goer, nor church-goer,[132] myself, believing that men's first business is this world, but I'd walk a mile or two to hear a mon like Treebarn, an give him th' help o' my presence. If there were more men like him there'd be less misery in th' world. I'll go to hear Mestur Treebarn on Sunday."

"I shall be very pleased to take you," said Ada.

"I've criticized cantin creeds, an called trick theology as much as anyone in my time," said Old Chartist, "for I've always stood up again th' domination of either priests or lords or any other arrogant authority. I've pitched reet an left into silly superstitions, an been as bold as any mon in arraignin[133] God, if there were one, for bein guilty o' makin this muddle[134] of a world, an openly given my ideas as to where I could have improved on creation if I'd only had th' job in hand, – but I might have had different ideas an approached th' subject of religion in a different attitude if there'd only been more ministers o' Mr. Treebarn's stamp knockin abeaut. In my opinion parsons make more atheists than anybody else. Heawever, Mr. Treebarn's evidently one o' th' reet soart; he's a mon, an that's a better thing than a parson anyday. I think of him as a mon, not as a parson; an I couldn't give him higher praise than that."

During the week, on a fine clear sunny day, Old Chartist inwardly fretting because he was a burden on the Milner's, set off on the nine-mile walk from Preston to Chorley, to visit his son-in-law's relations there, and see if he could find anything to do. He started early in the morning, crossing the river by the old stone bridge into ancient Walton-le-Dale, with its old inn where the Jacobites used to meet,[135] and so on through the narrow winding thoroughfare, past the blacksmith's shop in the corner, up to Bamber Bridge; where he overtook a carrier who gave him a ride in his wagon, through Clayton-le-Wood, Whittle Woods, and into sleepy little Chorley. As the carrier was returning the same day, and offered to give Chartist a seat in his wagon back to Preston, the old man was home again by sunset.

"But I've had no luck," he said sadly. "I couldn't get any work. They're makin a cemetery at Chorley to find work for the unemployed – makin a place for th' dead in order to find th' livin a bit o' bread, – indeed, they're making cemeteries at other places, too, an parks – one at Stockport, – th' cotton panic will have its memory kept alive by cemeteries and parks, an roads, all o'er Lancashire. But they wouldn't take me on at Chorley; said I was too old. It's a pitiful thing to be old, – an poor; an yet I'd rather be what I am, poor as I be, than them that's made their money out of th' cheatin an enslaving of th' poor."

Recollecting the joy of nature connected with his little outing, he continued in another strain, "But it's a bonny world, after all; an would be a glorious world for everybody if men weren't such fools. When I got up the hill goin to Bamber Bridge, an under the trees in merry bud, an among th' wayside grass, green wi new life, a th' spring flowers openin here and there, an th' sun bright an th' sky blue, an away to th' left Pendle Hill an th' wild moorlands, an everythin full of th' glory o' spring, th' larks an throstles, pipin away like little good uns, – I thought how beautiful th' world was, an how grand a thing human life might be if only men had a bit of sense how to arrange th' government an trade of a country. It's a pretty road from here to Chorley, – o'erhangin trees, grass and flowers on either hand, woods plantations, an farms, an mansions among 'em; cottages nestling in wayside nooks, or under trees, wi sweet patches o' garden in front of em; in one garden there was a cat dozin in th' sun on th' top of a rain-tub, – then, on the left, across th' valley, th' hills an moors runnin down to Chorley an Rivington Pike;[136] a grand sight o' grand country. England were made to be a happy land – but folks spoils it; we ought to have more sense an pluck than let 'em. Risin up th' hill at Whittle Woods, fro th' Sea View Inn, where we had a bit o' refreshment, we caught a glimpse of th' sea, across th' fields, shinin in th' sun, miles away. These were glad sights to see on th' road; but there were sad ones too; – out-o-work men trampin, an sometimes women an children wi 'em; an groups wi a two-three musical instruments, beggin. Eh, what tales that Preston road could tell if it could only talk! – tales o' tramps, an travellers, an carriers jolly at wayside inns, and children frolicking in road-side gardens and orchards, an coaches drivin th' genry to Blackpool an Southport, an courters clingin under th' trees, an happen tales o' crime, too, an boggarts an ghosts, for there's one or two old halls on th' road."

Ada listened, interested, but Mrs. Milner yawned at Old Chartist's long-windedness, as she called it; she said that it always took him an hour to tell a minute's tale. However, he drew on to an incident that excited Mrs. Milner's curiosity.

"Just when we got into Walton, in th' gloaming," he said, "we heard that a dead body had been found in the river."

"Who was it?" asked Mrs. Milner.

"Nobody knew for certain; the features were disfigured, or decomposed; th' body had been in th' water several days. But some said it were young Wragley, who's been missin about a week."

"What a terrible thing if it is," said Mrs. Milner.

Ada thought of Lucy Clayton, who, because of Wilfred Wragley's villainy, had sought death in the same river, and, assuming that the corpse found was that of the mill-owner's son, saw a divine retribution in the end of young Wragley; though she was sorry that he should come to such a fate.

As the evening, which was Saturday, passed on, Mrs. Milner went out on a little errand, while Old Chartist betook himself for a stroll to the Virgin's Inn, to hear the latest news of the cotton famine, and the *Alabama*.

Ada was thus left alone, but not for long; for presently there was a knock at the door, and Mr. Willard Hyde entered, with a very wooing look about him. He was evidently pleased to find Ada in the house by herself. With a civil familiarity, he drew up a chair, and sat near Ada, in front of the little fire.

Ada was silent, uneasily quiet.

"Won't you speak to me, Ada? Have you nothing to say to me?" said the Mormon. "There was a time when you were not so shy with me; a time when you talked freely and laughed with me, and even romped in a pretty innocent girlish way; why have you changed?"

"I am older now," said Ada. "I was young and thoughtless then."

"How should a year make so much difference?" asked Mr. Hyde. "In those days – the days of that free and joyous time, ere you put on restraint and coldness – you caused my heart to thrill with a great hope. The hope is there still."

Ada drooped her head from his burning eye.

"You are very beautiful, Ada," he said. "Shall I tell you what my hope was?"

"I would rather you didn't," said Ada.

"You guess it then; you know it. All the same, I will tell you. This is a favourable opportunity. My hope was that you would love me enough to become my wife."

"You already have three or four wives," said Ada, wishing that her mother or Old Chartist would return.

"That is my religion," said Hyde softly, "the religion of the old patriarchs of the Bible, the religion approved by God and the prophets. But if you will become my wife, you shall be chief and queen of my spouses."

Ada shuddered.

"You think it is wrong for a man to have more than one wife," said Hyde. "That is because you do not understand; and because you have not seen the happy workings of the system. If you had been reared amongst polygamy you would think nothing of it."

"I should loathe it," said Ada.

Hyde was silent for a moment. Then he said, "I love you so much, Ada, that for your sake I will do anything. Be my wife, and you shall be my only wife. I will dispose of the others. No one else shall share my heart with you."

While he was speaking, he had left his seat and stood beside Ada, putting his hand on her shoulder and bending his face down towards hers.

[29 December 1900]
XX. (Continued).

"Please don't," said Ada, pushing his hand away. "Please leave me alone. It's not right of you, Mr. Hyde. You know that I have – a sweetheart."

"But you knew me before you knew him," said Hyde, scowling to himself as he recollected the black eyes Sid Clifton had given to him, "and before he came on the scene you were kind to me. Your passion for him is only a girlish fancy. Besides, he has left you."

"He will come back," said Ada.

"Perhaps," said Mr. Hyde. "Young men are fickle. Your lover will find other lasses and woo them. It is the way of masculine nature. Every man is a Mormon at heart."

"I don't believe it," said Ada.

"Simply because you don't want to believe it," said Mr. Hyde. "But it is a fact. I repeat that every man is a Mormon at heart, though most men hypocritcally conceal the truth, and, while ostensibly living in a monogamous union, are practically polygamous. Women don't like this truth; they refuse to look at it; but it's a truth all the same. However, as I said, I am eager to give up my polygamy for your sake."

"I wish you'd let me alone," said Ada. "I don't want you."

"But I want you, and so I cannot leave you alone," said Hyde. "Ah, how fair you are, Ada; how tempting your eyes, your lips. I –"

He tried to kiss her. Ada rose to her feet and struggled. Her chair was knocked over. Hyde clasped his arms about her and held her fast, trying to place his lips to hers. Ada felt weak against his amorous strength.

To her relief there came a knock at the door.

"Come in!" called Ada, as the baffled Mormon released her, and she, panting, seated herself hurriedly, while Hyde glared at the intruder, in came Mr. Treebarn.

XXI. Strange, Awful News

Chartist Grimshaw, true to his word, went on the Sunday morning to Hosanna Chapel to hear Mr. Treebarn preach. He had also had a talk with the minister on the Saturday evening, for he had returned home about an hour after Mr. Treebarn's accidental, but timely, arrival had saved Ada from the forcible caress of the Mormon missionary, and found the pastor of Hosanna Chapel chatting with Ada.

Mr. Hyde had just departed. He had glowered at Mr. Treebarn's sudden coming upon the scene, but, suppressing his excitement, had said to the minister, coolly, "Good evening. May I ask you what's brought you here again?"

Mr. Treebarn, glancing at Ada, and noting her confusion and guessing what had been astir, determined to stand his ground for her sake, and not quit the house till the Mormon left it. He said, "I called to see Miss Milner."

"How do you know but that you're intruding on a lover's meeting?" asked Mr. Hyde, with bold jocularity.

"If Miss Milner wishes me to go away, I will go," said Mr. Treebarn.

"I've no objection to your presence Mr. Treebarn," said Ada. "I'm very glad you've called."

Hyde scowled aside; then turned to Mr. Treebarn with a laugh and said, "I see you are a favourite with the young ladies. I hope your wife isn't jealous."

Mr. Treebarn perceived that Ada was upset; and divined that she would have told him more if Mr. Hyde were not there. Though the situation was uncomfortable, he sat down, resolved to sit the Mormon out.

Hyde made the best of the positon. He kept up an awkward rasping conversation with Mr. Treebarn, mainly contrasting Mormonism wth the religion of England, satirising and making fun of the hypocrisies and shortcomings of parsons he had heard of or read about; and making a very black picture of all churches except the Mormon church.

At last he rose, and went away; and Ada, held by maiden shyness, made no confession of his rude conduct to Mr. Treebarn, who discreetly thought it best to ask no questions, though he told her to beware lest the Mormon persuaded her to join his sect.

"You needn't warn me," said Ada. "I don't like Mr. Hyde and I hate his doctrines."

"I'm pleased to hear that," said Mr. Treebarn. "I was afraid he was getting some influence over you."

"None," said Ada, "though I admit that I feel frightened of him at times. And I must say that he seems to have great influence over my mother."

"Do you never hear from your sister, Nelly?"

"We have never had a letter from her since she went away," said Ada.

"Then there is something wrong, I fear," said Mr. Treebarn. "Probably she is dissatisfied with the polygamic life, and so the Mormons won't let her write. No doubt she regrets that she ever let herself be led away. It is a great pity."

"But can't she leave if she wishes?" asked Ada.

Mr. Treebarm sadly shook his head. "You don't know the ways of the Mormons," he asid. "When one once enters Salt Lake City there is no hope of escape. They watch you like a cat watches a mouse, especially if they suspect that you want to get away. And if one does succeed in eluding their vigilance he or she is followed by a band of Mormons called The Destroying Angels,[137] and killed."

"It's horrible," said Ada. "But doesn't the law punish the Mormons if they murder anybody?"

"The law has first to catch them at it – they work very mysteriously. They have secret agents and spies all over America. It is said that nobody ever escapes them and nobody has managed to fasten even one of their crimes upon them."

"This is a terrible thing," said Ada. "Poor Nelly! she's practically imprisoned for life."

"If she is not already dead," said Mr. Treebarn, mournfully. At this point Old Chartist came in and was introduced to the minister by Ada.

"I've just been talkin to Whistlin Will," said Chartist. "He was down in the dumps an began to talk about his funeral as if he could see it comin. He said he'd like to have a tombstone when he's dead; it seemed to worrit him that he couldn't afford one. He has a notion of his own for a sort of picture to be carved on his gravestone an it's a notion that's not without a touch o' poetry. It'll tell yo what it is. 'These hard times is killin me,' says Will, 'an I've a thowt o' my tomb. When I'm deead an gone I should like a gravestone – I can't afford one mysel but happen somebody will be kind enough to gie me one – an on this stone I should like this picture to be carved – a lark risin up to th' sky eaut of a little cage, th' door o'which was just been opened by an angel hand – th' Angel o' Deeath settin a lark free fro th' cage o' this world!"

"A beautiful and touching image," said Mr. Treebarn, "and what is more, a perfectly true one."

"It's beautiful an touchin certainly," said Old Chartist, "an I never thowt that poor owd Whistlin Will had such fairy fancies in his head; but I'm not so sure abeaut it bein true. I've always been of an investigatin and inquirin turn an I've studied long an thowt deep on this question – th' immortality o' th' soul. And I must say that I can't see it yet."

Then Mr. Treebarn opened out; and he and Old Chartist ran round and round the circles of argument, touching every point of the circumference but never getting any nearer to the centre, as is generally the case. Ada listened, keenly interested; for Old Chartist, in his glory when debating, waxed wonderfully warm and astonished the minister by his knowledge and reasoning.

"I believe," said Old Chartist, in his pride of learning and intellect, and pleased with himself at the way in which he had puzzled a parson, "that I could put posers to the Almighty."

"Speak not so, my friend," said Mr. Treebarn, reverently, "for God overhears you."

"You've not proved God's existence to me yet," said Old Chartist, triumphantly.

"Perhaps I cannot," asaid Mr. Treebarn. "God is not to be demonstrated by mortal reason and logic. How can you measure the Eternal by the transitory, or explain the Incomprehensible in mortal sppech? Perhaps no man can prove God's existence to another man. God reveals himself to every man separately, in His own way, in His own time. Perhaps your time is not yet. But it will come. Someday you will know there is a God, not by reason, but by feeling, by the awakening of the soul."

"Then it's no use arguing?" said Old Chartist.

"I'm afraid not," said Mr. Treebarn. "God cannot be put into argument."

"You're certainly very candid an honest, Mr. Treebarn," said Old Chartist, heartily, "an I like you for it. I wish there were more parsons like you. But I've heard that you're brave an outspoken in other things, an for that reason I'm comin to hear you preach to-morrow."

"I'm very glad to hear it," asid Mr. Treebarn. "But don't expect too much from me. I'm only a weak vessel."

"It's years since I went to a place for worship before," said Old Chartist. "But I like an honest man, whether he's parson or anything else, that stands up for the poor an oppressed an denounces the tyrants an money-grabbers."

"I only do what is my duty," said Mr Treebarn, "and I fear that I often fail in that."

"You do your best, an that's a lot more than most does," said Old Chartist. "I'm very fain to know you, Mr. Treebarn."

After the two had talked for some time, Old Chartist telling his story of the Chartist days and his own part in the movement for uplifting the people and securing justice for all, Mr. Treebarn took his departure.

On the Sunday morning Old Chartist attended Hosanna Chapel with Ada; and enjoyed the sermon. Mr. Treebarn preached well, perhaps for one reason because his mind was less embarrassed about his pecuniary difficulties, for, on reaching home after leaving the Milners he had found a visitor waiting for him. This was Mr. Livesey, the teetotal pioneer; a man noted quite as much for his unostentatious philanthropy as for his total abstinence views.

Mr. Livesey soon explained his errand. "I heard how you were fixed, Mr. Treebarn," he said, "because you did your duty as a servant of our Master, and so I have come to offer you any assistance I can give you. If your chapel needs any help, call on me. We cannot afford to let you be crushed. You have done good work for the teetotal cause in Preston; not to mention your preaching for other reforms; and as an old Chartist, who has in his day battled as hard as anybody for the cause of the people, I am always pleased to encourage any other man engaged in the same struggle."

So Mr. Livesey had insisted on rendering substantial help to Hosanna Chapel and its pastor; and there was no load on Mr. Treebarn's mind when he preached to the congregation in which Old Chartist was a unit.

"If all parsons," said Old Chartist, as he and Ada walked home, "would only tackle th' problems of our own day in their preaching, an not bother so much about Abraham an Isaac[138] an other dead and gone old Jews, who are of no interest to us an our time, their churches an chapels wouldn't be half as empty as they are. But they daren't; they're too cowardly; too afraid of offending th' squire an th' landlord an th' moneylord. The old prophets of Israel weren't so; they stood up an stuck up for th' people, no matter what happened, not even if they vexed th' kings an lords till they clapped 'em in jail an in fiery furnaces. But th' parsons of to-day cares for nothing only a nice easy livin, – all except this Mr. Treebarn an a few others. I'm not surprised that Jabez Wragley couldn't stand that chap's talk. There were one or two others i' th' congregation that'll have had enough, too, ere long, or else I'm vastly mistaken. There were Winkster, th' pawnbroker, for one. He's a rascal is that."

"Many families have found the pawnshop a help during the 'panic,'" said Ada.

"Ay, I daresay," said Old Chartist. "There's lots o' things gone to pawn that'll never be got out again, – an th' pawnbrokers have got 'em cheap. I've seen more than one woman nearly heartbroken as she's been taken some cherished article – some family heirloom, or something belonging to somebody loved an dead. Hello, here's Whistlin Will."

There was on Whistling Will's face the look of one who has great news to tell. "Have yo heard?" he said.

"Heard what?" asked Ada.

"Th' body that were found in th' river last night were young Wragley's. His father's identified th' body this morinin. Th' young fellow's been missin for nearly a fortnight."

"It's a very sad thing," said Old Chartist. "But th' world can very spare such families as th' Wragleys."

"I'm towd that th' owd chap was awful cut up about it," said Whistling Will. "An they say his wife – th' lad's mother – is nearly out of her mind."

Mr. Jabez Wragley was certainly smitten sore by his son's tragic end. The young man was his only son, his only child; and the father had meant to make much of him. Probably it was for his son's sake, as much as for his own, that he had set himself to acquire riches, regardless of how he got them. Counting money, and the might of money, the chief thing in the world, Mr. Jabez Wragley had determined to make his son a man of money, that he might have social influence and eminence. He would have laughed at the notion that it is better to make a child honest and noble, and intelligent, than wealthy. He belived that money was everything and could do everything. He gave his son money in order that the lad might lord it over his associates; though it was often irritating to him to see the money he had slain his soul to accumulate being squandered by is son's reckless profligacy. Mrs. Wragley, too, had spoilt her son. She had let him have all his own way, and it was a willful way, and often a bad way. Yet, in her own fashion, she loved the lad, and was in frantic grief at his sad and sudden death.

"How did this young Wragley get in the water?" asked Old Chartist.

"There's all soarts o' tales abeaut," answered Whistling Will. "At first it were thought he was goin whum drunk, an tumbled in th' river hissel; but th' police has found some bits o' clothes, and signs of a desperate struggle, on th' steep riverside near Walton, just before yo get to Wragley's house. They say it's murder."

"And have they any idea who's done it?" asked Ada, with a strange fear upon her.

"Th' police is after Ted Banister!" said Whistling Will.

"I was afraid so," said Ada.

"Ted Bannister's not been seen since Easter Monday, – an it was on th' night o' that day, or th' day after that young Wragley was chucked into th' river. An th' police know that Ted had a grudge again young Wragley because o' Lucy Clayton drownin herself. So they're after Ted."

"I hope they'll never catch him!" said Old Chartist.

XXII. The Whitsun[139] Procession

The Lancashire Whitsuntide of 1863 was darkly clouded by the cotton famine. There was yet practically no cotton coming into the country; the spinning mills and weaving sheds were still closed, or in a very few instances working one or two days a week; and severe poverty was prevalent. Streams of charity, big and little, were still pouring into Lancashire. Even the London Shoeblacks' Brigade sent its mite.

Because of the warmth of the sun and the cheefulness of the light penury is not quite as bitter in summer as in winter. When snow and rain and freezing cold are taken away from poverty, they make it less hard to bear; starvation in summer is not quite so bad as starvation in winter.

But in Whitweek, 1863, the Lancashire working-classes could take no advantage of the holiday time and weather because their pockets were empty; the majority of them were living on charity. They could not even take a proud part in the Whitsuntide Sunday school procession, usual in most of the Lancashire towns; for neither parents nor children had any clothes fit for such a festival. Yet the processions were held, and pathetic enough they were, in many cases; the old clothes having to serve in place of new finery. The children who were used to having new garments – the girls new frocks and hats, and the boys new suits of clothes, – for the Whitsuntide parade were very much disappointed.

"It's cruel on th' little childer," said Whistling Will, who was one of the crowd watching the Whit-Monday morning procession at Preston. "Even childer doesn't like to processionate poverty. I'm downreet sorry for th' poor little things. An yet there's rich folks goin to Blackpool an Lytham; I've seen th' trains whistling through Preston station. An what hideous whistles they have. Why couldn't railway engines be made to have a musical whistle, like me? Then it would be a joy to hear 'em, as they shot across th' land, an we could call 'em th' iron nightingales."

Whistling Will's fantastic notion struck him as a very good and practical one, though it only amused his hearers, among whom were Old Chartist and Ada, who had come out to see the Sunday school-children "walk."

"By gow," said Will, "there's summat in that idea. I'd patent it if I'd brass. It's a champion idea. 'Iron nightingales.' There might be a fortin in it."

"Them as runs railway trains," said Old Chartist, "runs 'em to make a profit, an not to be things o' beauty an pleasure. They don't care what screechin din they make so long as they're makin money. So I'm afraid they'll not take thy idea up, Will. Where have you been lately? I've not seen you in Preston for some time."

[5 January 1901]

"I've been knockin about th' country a bit trying to pick up a whistling livin," said Will. "I was at Rochdale all last week; an I had a look at Tim Bobbin's[140] grave. An I got nearly as much off deead Tim as I did off th' livin. Very few gave me anything. But Tom Livesey were good to me."

"If it's Tom Livesey the Chartist, he's a good sort," said Chartist Grimshaw.

"That's the mon," said Whistling Will, "an he is a good sort, too, though he is an Alderman, an there's talk o' makin him Mayor; but, fro what I hear, there's a lot o' th' big men against that, becaue Tom's allus been one that's stood up for th' workin-classes."

"Tom can do without their paltry honours," said old Chartist. "Rochdale might honour itself by making Tom Livesey mayor, but it cannot add any honour to Tom. He has the honour of a good life, lived for the good of his fellow-men; an neither corporations nor kings can give a man a greater honour than that. I was in Rochdale in 1842, th' time when th' plug-drawing riots[141] were on, all o'er Lancashire, – when mad excited crowds were scramblin o'er factory gates, opening engine-boilers, and letting the water and steam out – the steam hissing an screaming as if full of the fury of the plug-drawers themselves. Tom Livesey did his best to stop the Rochdlae folk doin such mischief, for he knew that destruction would do no good; an he succeeded more than once. The Riot Act was read in Rochdale, an the soldiers stood ready to charge the mob, one day, when Tom Livesey sprang in front of the magistrates an said, 'Howd on, Mr. Chadwick; surely you don't mean to have these poor hungry folk murdered all of a ruck. Leave 'em to me, an I'll persuade 'em to go away. You know what th' Bible says about angry words stirrin up strife?' 'That's all very well, Tom,' says t' magistrate, 'but we can't allow such work as this?' "'No, I dunnot think yo' con,' says Tom, 'un there'd be no need o' such work if these poor folk could ony get their ballyful o' meat. However, draw your soldiers off; an I'll get these people to go home in peace.' The magistrates had sense enough to let Tom Livesey try his method; and Tom succeeded in coaxin the people into quietness."

"That's true that there wouldn't be much bother if folks only geet their ballies filled," said Whistling Will.

"Tom Livesey was a gradely champion of the working-classes," said Old Chartist. "He did great work against the Corn Laws. I recollect a good bit in one of his speeches. After he'd shown up the evil of the Corn Laws, he said, 'But O, how much more could be said against the present trade system? We all know that the cart-horse has to work to keep the hunter; so you, if you like, may be content to work from morn till night, to keep your master in state. But will you do it?' The crowd shouted 'No, we'll see 'em hanged first.' Yet the crowd soon forgets; and keeps on being the carthorse to support the idle hunter. As long as this is so there will be discontent, rebellions, and riots. The history of the working-classes would make strange and terrible reading. As long as I can remember there's always been struggle – a few struggling to induce the multitude to do its duty to itself and its neighbour. There was the fighting for the Reform Bill, then for the Factory Acts for children, then for Trades-unionism, then for Chartism, then for the repeal of the Corn Laws, besides lots of little things that don't get put into history. And the men at the top, the generals and arisotcrats, and all other butchers and thieves and scamps in authority and power, have always, almost to a man, opposed every attempt of the workers to better themselves. The Duke of Wellington, in 1830, declared in the House of Commons, that 'while he remained in power there should be no reform.' Yet that blockhead of a butcher – for what else is any soldier? – is held up as an English hero. He was a man who would have shot the English peasantry when they opposed his notions, if he had dared, just as readily as he fought the French soliders. And I can't see that even his victories in war gained England much, if anything. What better off were the people after Waterloo? None. But they got massacred for quietly meeting to demand their rights at Peterloo.[142] No, there's no sense in war. This cotton panic's another proof of that; nations oughtn't to be allowed to fight, no more than individuals are permitted to break the peace with impunity."

"Ay, ay," said Whistling Will, 'There's certainly summat in what yo say'n, Chartist. To Owd Nick wi aw wars, say I. Though Dicky Langton tells me there used to be wars i' this country, on this very spot. He says that Oliver Cromwell's army once did some fine fightin down in Walton-le-Dale."[143]

"That's two hundred years since," said Chartist. "Surely we ought to have improved a bit in two centuries. War is mainly due to folks' ignorance; people are led away by lies. Parsons and politicians keep the nations in darkness. The average parson will say anything to keep the people under him. Look at Canon Parr for instance, in our own town. Only the other day he said, at his Sunday school, that Jesus Christ was a Tory, and that the devil was the first Dissenter. That man's had hundreds of pounds spent on his education, and talks like that, and misleads folks what cannot read and ferret truth out for themselves. Fancy daring to call Jesus Christ a Tory. Christ was nearer a Chartist than anything else. But he couldn't be either, for there were neither Tories nor Chartists in Christ's time. There were scribes and Pharisees, we do know that, – and they haven't died out by a lot. There's some of 'em stands in pulpits every Sunday."

"Th' procession's a long while comin this road," said Whistling Will. "But it can't be far off now. I can hear music; though the band sounds as if th' players had been on short rations lately, like everybody else. But times are mendin a bit here an theer. There were some cotton come into Farrington t' other day; an th' women o' th' village went out to meet th' wagon, an began cryin for joy, an actually kissed th' bales o' cotton. So may be th' war's getting to an end. I wonder how Billy Richardson's goin on among it. We've heard nowt from him since he went away. Hello, here's th' music an banners."

The long procession of Sunday school children, headed by a brass band, came up the street. The faces of the majority of the children were pinched and pale; and they made a pathetic sight.

"My heart bleeds for the children!" said Old Chartist.

"Damn th' cotton panic!" said Whistling Will, with tears in his eyes. "Look at that little lass, wi her thin shoon an thin frock – poor thing; an that little lad, wi his sad thin face. Yet how little it would tak to make 'em happy!"

"And rich England can't afford that little – or rather won't," said Chartist Grimshaw. "The high and mighty folks can do nothing for the poor and low – they're cheap; there's always plenty of 'em; fast as they die off there's no lack of 'em; for they breed faster than they die. Ah if they'd only sense enough to know their strength. The man with a whip can keep a hundred of 'em i' cowering dread."

"Especially if he lives in Mainsprit Weind,"[144] said Whistling Will. "That's where all our moneyed men live. More Mayors o' Preston have come out o' Mainsprit Weind than all our other streets put together."

Ada was watching the procession, paying no heed to the chatter of Chartist Grimshaw and Whistling Will. She was thinking of the happy childhood's time when she had walked in the procession; and of the later years when her dead sister Lily had been one of the throng; also of her sweetheart Sid, who used to march along with the boys. Then there was Lucy Clayton too – she was dead and gone now; while Ted Banister, her lover, was in hiding, nobody knew where, the police searching for him with a warrant to arrest him on the charge of murdering Wilfred Wragley.

As Ada looked at the new faces passing before her, she thought of the old faced vanished. Other spectators in the crowd had similar thoughts. While some parents were gleefully calling out, "There's our Jackie," or "our Sissie," others saw only deathly gaps in the procession, and remembered those who walked therein no more. Little children who had smilingly and gleefully taken part in last year's parade were in the graveyard now; and the hearts of those who loved them knew woe and mourning. "God bless them all, seen and unseen, here and beyond," said Ada to herself.

"If the sight of a procession of children like this won't stir men to battle for the bettering of the world, then men are cowards that nothing will stir to fight," said Old Chartist Grimshaw. "How selfish folks must be when they won't even strive to get benefits for their children; when they are content to let things go on as they are, making no attempts to make life better and sweeter for the next generation, than it has been for them, but saying, 'What's been good enough for me will have to be good enough for my children. I've had to slave an sweat as they must do th' same.' Such folks are fit for neither earth, heaven, nor Wigan."

Sometimes Chartist Grimshaw talked ordinary English, sometimes the undiluted Lancashire dialect, and sometimes a mixture of both. Like most educated workingmen in Lancashire he could speak either English or dialect fluently, using either according to the company he chanced to be in.

"Th' band didn't sound as weel to me as usual," said Whistling Will. "It seemed short o' force. Aw the result o' th' cotton panic. Men corn't blow brass instruments off empty ballies. Some o' th' band chaps looked as if they hadn't had a good feed for a twothree hunded year. I think I should ha made a champion musician myself if I'd nobbut been browt up to th' job. I've a natural talent for music. But I've had no opportunity. Yet as it is I'll whistle any mon in Lancashire, an that's summat."

So the long Suday school procession passed by, with the black shadow of the cotton famine dark upon its banners that used to be so gay, and sad upon the faces of the children.

XXIII. The Love Letters from the Sea.

When Ada got home she found that a letter had just come for her. The envelope bore a strange stamp, and was marked with the postmarks of foreign places. She immediately guessed that the letter was from Sid, and she was right.

After a greedy glance through the letter, which was a very long one, she decided, as the day was so warm and fine, to go, after she had had a little noonday meal, down to the park, and then, by the river-side, on the seat where she and Sid had often sat together, enjoy the delight of her sweetheart's letter all alone, fancying that he was with her again.

"Is it a letter fro Sid Clifton?" asked Mrs. Milner.

"Yes," said Ada.

"What's he got to say?"

"I've only just glanced through it; I'm going to read it slowly after dinner. But Sid says he's all right."

"He says nothing about coming back, I suppose?"

"No," said Ada.

"Perhaps he never will come back," said Mrs. Milner. "When once a man starts rovin there's no getting him back home. I shouldn't be surprised if he didn't pick up wi' some woman in one of them far-off places, and settle down there."

"Mother, you shouldn't talk like that," said Ada. "How can you say such things of Sid?"

"He's nobbut a man, and all men's alike when they're out o' sight. Look at the case of Jennie Moscrop. Her young man only went to work at Blackburn, a twothree mile away. Yet in less than three months he picked up with a lass there, and threw Jennie over. Of course, it doesn't make much difference in the long-run. Jennie will find another fellow, and all will be well. I only want you to be prepared for any disagreeable surprises that might come, Ada; that's why I'm telling you these things. Young men are very changeable. They never know when their mind's made up. And this affair of Sid and you is practically only a children's affair; one of those green courtships that generally means nothing and ends in nothing."

Ada made no reply to her mother; though she wondred why she was talking in this strain and suspected that Mr. Hyde was at the bottom of it.

Early in the afternoon Ada went to the park. The day was bright and beautiful; the land was full of the glory of spring in merry maturity. The trees in the park were pretty in foliage; the banks and gardens were sweet with flowers. In several small orchards she passed the apple trees were in bonny pink bloom; and the blossom of the pear trees was like the winter's snow – but without its coldness – hung upon branches. And the almond trees were a rosy splendour. The winding valley of the river, fair in the sunshine, seemed inviting one to stroll happily and far amongst its wonders and pictures – to wander far and away, in a vision of flower and grass, thrilling with the music of birds, towards the distant hills and moorlands, grand with all the enchantment of distance.

As Ada entered the park she was somewhat surprised to see the Rev. Mr. Treebarn and Mr. Jabez Wragley seated talking together on a form. She was curious to know what had brought the two together, knowing of the difference there had been between them. She noticed that Mr. Treebarn was talking earnestly and that Mr. Wragley was listening intently, with a softened look on his face quite different from his usual aspect.

The meeting of the minister and the manufacturer had been altogether accidental. Mr. Treebarn, passing homeward through the park had met Mr. Wragley walking about disconsolately. The minister looked at him and pitied him exceedingly; for the look on the manufacturer's face was the look of one mourning for the loss of all he valued in the world. The awful death of his son had striken him sorely in the very heart.

Moved by a great compassion Mr. Treebarn stopped and said, "Mr. Wragley – I am very sorry for you. I beg your pardon for any words of mine that offended you when last we conversed together."

Since the interview thus alluded to by Mr. Treebarn Mr. Wragley had always passed the minister without recognition. He now looked at Mr. Treebarn, uncertain whether to speak or not. Then he opened his mouth, but all the utterance he had was a low sob.

"Let us sit down and talk together," said Mr. Treebarn.

"I want my lad back!" said Mr. Wragley, wildly.

Mr. Treebarn led the grieving father to a seat and talked with him as consolingly as he could.

"I did a wrong to you, Treebarn," said Wragley quietly. "I know now that money, position are nothing. I would give all my fortune and all my honours to have my son back again. For I did wrong to him too. I trained him up with the idea that money was everything – and his end was what it was. Ah! my God! I shall go mad if I think of it. Oh! would that I could have him back again to train up aright. I have ruined his soul and sent him to damnation!"

"God is merciful," said Mr. Treebarn, "and will not judge as men judge. God knows everything, and will make all allowances. You may safely trust your son to God!"

"But he lived a vile life, and I let him, thinking I was making a gentleman of him. And now I am accursed."

"God is merciful," said Mr. Treebarn.

"I feel that I have sent my lad to hell," said Mr. Wragley. "Oh! how I wish I had listened to you, Treebarn. Your sermons were right and honest; but I was lured by pride and vanity, and the pomp of this world. I beg your pardon for insulting you that morning I visited you and said I had done with you. I will atone to you a thousand-fold. I will come back to your chapel, – you shall have all the help –"

"Let us not talk of that," said Mr. Treebarn. "What I want to do now is to comfort your soul." And so, gently, lovingly the minister talked to the afflicted manufacturer; and was thus talking when Ada passed them.

Ada went to the favourite seat of her lover and herself, and took out Sid's letter; reading it slowly and absorbingly.

"Dear Ada," the letter said, "you will be wondering, I know, why you have not heard from me sooner; but this is the first chance I have had of sending a letter to you. I am on board the confederate cruiser *Alabama*, and you will be glad to know that amongst the crew are many friends of mine, and some you know, including – who do you think? – Sandy Aspinall, and several Fylde lads from Kirkham, and Lytham, and Bob Hagan – Joe Hagan's brother – from Chorley; and I can assure you that we are all a happy family together. I like my berth very well; and life on the sea is a grand thing, even when reckoning in all the hard work we have, and we have plenty. Then there's the excitement and the variety. As you know the business of the *Alabama* is to capture and destroy Northern trading ships, and thus cripple the enemy. We have caught and burned many vessels, and it is a great sport – though it is also a pain. It is a sad thing to see a beautiful ship perishing in flames; it looks like some great live creature with something human and loveable about it, writhing in an agony of fire. The Northerners would do the same to the Southerners if they could. Our captain – Captain Semmes – is a thorough gentleman and a brave man; and I can see that he, too, is sorry to have to burn vessels. For, like all sailors, he loves a fine ship as if it were a brother. My boss[145] – that's a Yankee phrase – Mr. Freeman, is a good sort of chap, too, though he has his moods like all of us. Then the captian's steward, an Italian named Bartelli, is a very nice, gentle fellow. When we are not chasing northern vessels we sometimes have a holiday on board and great fun. We have a rare fiddler – Michael Mahoney, an Irishman; who can also sing and spin some of the funniest yarns that ever came out of mortal mouth. Another member of the crew has a concertina; so we're not short of music, you see. Sometimes the band – that's our fiddle and concertina – plays for dancing, and we have jolly jinks, I can tell you; some of the men comically taking the part of ladies, and simpering, and giggling and pretending to be shy – it would make you laugh your head off to see 'em. Captain Semmes and his officers sit on the bridge watching us dance; and they enjoy the sight. Captain Semmes is a very clever fellow and has read a lot. I have heard him quoting poetry and other books when chatting with the officers on these festive occasions. I recollect two lines he said once – two lines which give you in a few words a picture of our free sea life:

> 'Far as the breeze can bear, the billows foam,
> Survey our empire, and behold our home.'[146]

But though Captain Semmes is genial enough at play times, and always just and often generous, he is strict on discipline, and won't allow any drinking, except the usual allowance to the men.[147] One day we captured a vessel laden with wine; but he made us throw the thousands of bottles into the sea. After burning the vessels we take, we convey the prisoners generally to Flores, in the Azores, and leave them there; we have nearly filled the island. I am writing this letter in Cape Town harbour, where we have just come after capturing a northern vessel, within a few miles of the land, – the hills on shore being lined with thousands of spectators watching the *Alabama* circle round her prey. And I should say it was a splendid sight to watch, for the *Alabama* is as beautiful and shapely a ship as ever sailed, and her master handles her as if she were a well-trained mare under him. The folks at Cape Town are making a great ado of us, and inviting Captain Semmes and his officers to banquets, ladies presenting 'em with bouquets, and so on. A few days before we reached here we caught and burned one vessel in a storm. It was a magnificent spectacle; the ship on fire in the dark, the sea roaring and rolling, thunder booming, and lightning flashes whipping the heavens. From Cape Town we are making towards the East Indies and China Seas, and I do not know from what port I shall send my next letter. I have, in my sailings, seen many new and strange things; and I have always wished you had been there to enjoy the sight with me. There was the port of San Domingo, in the West Indies, an old city, with the ruins of a very old cathedral. On one crumbling tombstone were carved a mitre and crosier, showing that a bishop was buried beneath; but the name was worn away – had faded off the stone. I heard Captain Semmes, as he looked at the gravestone, say to the officers with him, 'What a sermon there is in this stone. The record of a bishop, carved upon the enduring marble, and placed upon the floor of his own cathedral, has been lost! 'What is man, O lord, that thou should'st be mindful of him?'[148] You'll remember that passage; Ada it was Mr. Treebarn's text the last time we were at chapel together. – I wonder when we shall sit there together again. May it be soon! – Another little island we saw, off the coast of Brazil, is the famous peak of Fernando de Noronha, – it looks just like a cathedral, with a steeple, as you sail towards it. And, oddly enough, this island that looks like a church, is the penal colony for Brazil. We landed, and saw many convicts, some sentenced for life. Yet they didn't seem much different from other folks. You wouldn't have known they were criminals if you hadn't been told; yet there were forgers and thieves, and one or two murderers amongst them. They work on the island and dress and go about like ordinary people; and have their parties, and so on. But they can't get away. There was one pretty young woman there with her father, who was a forger; yet he seemed a nice respectable old gentleman. But if I try to tell you of all the things I have seen I should have to write a book; so I'll keep the rest to tell you about when I come home. I have got several little foreign curiosities for you – they will do to ornament our cottage when we are married, sweetheart. I fancy I can see you blushing so prettily as you read that – I wish I were there to see your face and kiss the blush off. But I don't know when I shall get home. We have no idea when the war will be over. But I think the North will win in the end, and I hope so, too, though since I came on the *Alabama* I have learned that there are two sides to every tale; and that the Southerners are honestly fighting for their rights and independence, for which I cannot help but admire them, as it's like a little lad fighting a big man. And I find my sympathy going with with lad, who is brave and true. It isn't only the 'slavery' question that's at the bottom of the war; there are a lot of other things, though the slavery question is put to the front to get the sympathy of the world. But I am really beginning to think, as Captain Semmes says, that money is at the bottom of the war. The lean north, he says, envies the rich south and wants to tax its money off it; for the Southern States have flourished much more than the

Northern. However we'll not talk about the war in a love-letter. And I must now draw to a close. Give my respect to your mother and to all friends; and beware of that rascal Hyde. He has a grudge against me, for I met him on the day I want away, and struck him, because of his sneering. I'm sorry I hit him – but I couldn't help it; and he deserved it. I hope that he isn't pestering you. If he is, keep him off till I come back, and I'll soon shift him. God bless you, sweetheart, God bless you.

Your affectionate lover,
SID

As Ada finished the letter, and sat, in a sweet reverie, musing of her lover, she heard an advancing step, looked up, and beheld Mr. Hyde.

She put the letter into her pocket as Mr. Hyde said, "I am glad to meet you here. May I sit beside you?"

Ada rose. "I must be going," she said.

"Why should you go?" asked Hyde. "There is no need."

"I would rather go," said Ada.

[12 January 1901]
XXIII. (Continued)

"Why are you afraid of me?" said Hyde. "I would not do you the least harm; I mean well to you and your mother; I am extremely anxious for your welfare. Why may I not sit beside you this summer day?"

Ada made no reply.

"It is out of deepest affection for you," continued Hyde, "that I would take you out of this place of famine to a land of plenty – to a land blest by God because the true believers abide there."

"I would rather stay where I am," said Ada.

Hyde suppressed his anger and talked amiably and persuasively. But he made no impression on Ada, whose only thought was a wish that he would go away. She heard footstpes, looked up, saw Old Chartist Grimshaw approaching, and was glad. "Sit down, Chartist," she said and the old man seated himself beside her. Hyde, chagrined, after a few more words, went away.

"I don't like that man, Ada," said Old Chartist.

"Neither do I," said Ada, smiling.

"Yet he likes you," said Chartist, speaking in English, not the dialect, "but don't have anything to do with him. He's a Mormon, and the Mormons have done terrible things."

"I can believe it," said Ada, "though Mr. Hyde says the Mormons are all saints. You might tell me what you know about the Mormons, Chartist. I know you can, for I think you've read about everything."

"I've read a lot, certainly," said Old Chartist, "but I've not read everything by many a million books. Ay, there's several I would like to read yet if I could only afford. There's some books – novels I think they're called – written by a parson called Charles Kingsley,[149] which I should like to read. I've read extracts from his tales and he seems a very decent fellow for a parson. His stories are full of good teaching and exposure of tyrants and wrong-doers. He's full of sympathy for the poor and wants all men to be brotherly. He's too good to be thrown away in the pulpit. However, you were asking me about the Mormons."

"Yes, I'd like to know some of their history," said Ada.

"They're a religious sect that came to the fore about fifteen years ago – in 1847, I think – under a man called Brigham Young. Of course they'd been started long before that, by a man named Joseph Smith, who pretended to have received divine revelations straight from heaven, and similar nonsense.[150] But in 1847 Brigham Young led a party of Mormons, in America, in search of the Promised Land. Fancy looking for the Promised Land in America. Well, the Mormon emigrants went across the big praries – often attacked by Red Indians – and founded a colony called Salt Lake City."

"That's where our Nelly went to," said Ada.

"God help her!" said Old Chartist. "From all accounts the Mormons prospered where they planted themselves, and many of them were good folks, kind, and peaceable, and industrious; and ever ready to give each other a helping hand. I must give 'em their due. But about five years ago the Mormons committed one of the vilest butcheries in history – The Mountain Meadow Massacre. I should tell you, before giving you the details of this crime, that many of the Mormons were robbers, and considered it a righteous game to despoil and slay all unbelievers – that is, all who did not believe as they did. All religious sects have always considered difference of opinion a capital offence. But I'll give you the circumstances of the massacre – the world rang with the horror at the time. A party of rich emigrants was going from the United States into California. They had to pass through Salt Lake City. The Mormons let them go through unmolested, noting the wealth of the splendid wagons, and outfit of the caravans. But, though the Mormons let the emigrants pass through their city, they determined to kill and rob them before they got out of Mormon territory. Word was sent to John D. Lee, a Mormon bishop of a district further along the track the caravan had to pass, that he was to slaughter every man, woman and child in the emigrants' party. In order to do the crime, and yet appear not to have done it, the Mormons disguised themselves as Indians, and attacked the caravan near a small stream. The emigrants drove the sham Indians off; but the latter took up a position behind some rocks, guarding the stream, and cutting off all communication with it. Then they waited, day after day, till the emigrants ventured out for water; and as each one came forth, he or she was shot. You can imagine the awful positon of the people comprising the carvan surrounded by a hidden murderous gang of supposed Indians, and dying for water. Yet if they went for water they died by a bullet. The emigrants sent their girls and children with pails to the stream thinking that the assassins would not shoot innocent little ones; but they were mistaken. Every girl and child who stepped forth from the caravan was shot. So this hideous work went on for days, till not a soul of the caravan was left alive."[151]

"What a strange sad tale," said Ada.

"Then the Mormon scoundrels made off with the plunder, and thought nobody would ever know of their crime. The massacre would be attributed to Indians. But the truth got out. The United States government sent soldiers to the scene, to bury the dead, and chastise the Mormons. One of the scouts, named Nelson, tells of the horrible spectacle that met the gaze of the soldiers when they reached the fatal spot – skeletons all about the ground, the bones picked as clean as ivory by vultures and wolves. Beside some of the skeletons were buckets for carrying water, showing how the victims had fallen. Here and there on the bushes were tresses of women's hair. The soldiers shed tears at the sight."

"And did they catch the Mormons who had done the foul deed?" asked Ada.

"Not for a while; nobody would give any information. The Mormons, of course, shielded the criminals of their own creed. But the soliders searched the houses, and found in one a little fair-haired girl of three years of age. This child pointed to one of the Mormon women, and said, 'She got my mamma's frock on. Naughty Indians come and kill mama, papa, and auntie.' That little girl was the only survivor of the hundred and odd people who had comprised the caravan. But the perpetrators of the outrage could not be caught; they were well concealed. However, John D. Lee, the Mormon bishop, was captured last year, and executed.[152] And that's the tale of the Mountain Meadow Massacre – a ghastly blot for ever on Mormonism. If Mormon Hyde ever comes bothering you again, just ask him if he had any share in the Mountain Meadow Massacre. Perhaps he was one of the gang that committed the massacre. Ask him if he ever played Red Indian in a wholesale murder."

"And my sister Nelly is among such folks!" said Ada. "Poor Nelly! I wish she could get away!"

"There's no escaping from the Mormons after once you've joined 'em," said Old Chartist. "They have most diabolical and ingenious arrangements for disposing of all runaways. There's a secret band called The Destroying Angels, and, if anybody succeeds in getting away from Salt Lake City, these Destroying Angels are instantly on the track, and they do not give up the trail till they have found and silenced for ever the marked person. They have been known to follow some persons all over the world till they have caught and killed them. And nobody has ever been able to catch the Destroying Angels at the job. The victims have disappeared mysteriously, and never been heard of again, or been found dead – stabbed, strangled, or poisoned – sometimes in bed, sometimes in the street, but never a clue to the perpetrator of the crime."

"Oh, how dreadful!" said Ada, shuddering in a chilly, uncanny sensation, as she thought of murderers with masked faces, suddenly pouncing out on their victims in lonely places, "then there is no hope for Nelly. She is doomed for life!"

"I won't say that," said Old Chartist. "There is always hope. And the Mormons cannot pursue their nefarious games as they used to do – there are more police in the world. I don't think the Desroying Angels have the chances they used to have nine or ten years ago."

"What an odd, wild land America must be," said Ada.

"It's a new country, and that explains a lot," said Old Chartist. "But even in England, a very old place compred with America, we still have our secret societies. The trade-union outrages that's been in the papers lately are the work of secret societies. There's always secret societies when men are not allowed fair liberty. If the law would only allow workingmen to combine openly to secure justice in a peaceable constitutional way, there would be no secret societies and outrages. Trade-unions have had a hard struggle, and are struggling yet for their rights. And this in a free country. Of course, the aristocracy and employers don't like trade-unions; they wouldn't allow the people a voice or thought in anything if they had their way; but that day of damnable domineering has gone by. If masters had only done what's fair to their workmen, there would never have been any trade unions, nor any need of 'em. But in an unhealthy state, as in an unhealthy body, sores are bound to break out somewhere. Make men healthy and government clean and there'll be no bother. But I think things are mending, though, only at a small gallop. I've seen some changes in my time, and some of 'em are changes for the better, and improvements. Our gas-lamps are better than the old dingy oil-lamps that only seemed to make the streets darker. Preston was the first town out of London to be lighted with gas, – I was a lad at the time, and remember it well, and what a wonderful thing everybody thought it was. That was nearly fifty years ago – about 1816, a few years before the Peterloo Massacre[153] in Manchester – the Mormons are not the only folks who have done massacres. The cotton trade was only in its infancy then, machinery was only beginning to come in to drive men out. Little children were working in the factory at five years old; and the factories were regular hell-holes. I could tell a long and lamentable tale – the story of the cotton trade; of the invention of machines for making money out of men, the tragic tale of the horrible sufferings of little children, the moaning of women, the crying of a few for reform, the burning songs of poets on the inhumanity of man to man, the sickening sympathy of the rich for the slaves abroad, whose freedom they purchased out of profits on a worse slavery at home; the war with Napoleon and the French, the people paying for the war as they pay for everything, bread dear, food scarce, poverty everywhere, – but in my opinion there never was much glory yet but was dyed in the blood of the poor and ground out of their bones. – Ay I could tell a long and lamentable tale, of the struggle of the workingclass leaders and friends, generally unheeded and reviled by those they strove to help, – of the getting of the Reform Bill, – that was about the time the self-acting mule was invented, and when the first railroad in England was opened, between Manchester and Liverpool – laying iron on the land, and putting iron in factories, – the beginning of the age of 'misery and iron,'[154] as the Psalmist says, – and then the first Factory Act, due to the agitating by Lord Ashley and Oastler and others; and soon after this the first screw steamer was made – iron on the sea now; then then Queen Victoria came to the throne, and Chartism started, and we got Penny Postage, though newspapers were still dear, having to pay a tax. Then came machine-breaking riots – the poor folks hated the machinery that was driving 'em out of work, – and the Co-operative Movement, and the Abolition of the Corn Laws, and more Factory Acts, – opposed by John Bright – like most other politicians ever ready to legislate about other people's interests, but resenting all interference when Pariament came to his own trade. And all this time Chartism was struggling, and doing a little; and sowing seed. Then came the great Peace Exhibition at the Crystal Palace, followed of course by the booming of guns and war – the Russian war; more glory for historians to write about, but bitterness and woe for the poor, and even for the soldiers despised and thrown on one side when they had done their butcher's work. Ay, the history of the cotton trade is a strange one, and mingled with strange events, and when I consider its rise and growth, how its course has always been marked by tears and cruelties and death I cannot see that any good will ever come of it. And now its in the biggest crisis of its history – this cotton panic, from which it may never really look up again. What good can come of a trade built up on slavery and the agony of little children, and whose track is marked by the oppression and punishment of the poor? But I'm rambling again in my usual fashion. Ay, I could tell a long and lamentable tale if there were only time to tell it all. But what does it matter? It will be all forgotten some day – all the lads at the spindles, and the lasses at the looms, and all they knew and suffered, and us and all, with our little stories that are only a part of the big story, – will all be vanished away and remembered no more.[155]

XXIV. Old Chartist Gets Work

In the summer of 1863 the effects of the cotton famine began to be less severe in a few towns, though there was no decrease of struggling poverty in other places. Some of the towns, like certain ships, were better able to weather the storm than others; but even these which, by more fortunate circumstances, or good luck, did not suffer as much as the rest, were like tempest-stricken vessels that could only just crawl into port.

According to statistics, the number of persons employed in the Lancashire textile trades in 1861, just before the beginning of the American war, was 426,000, of whom 230,000 were females. On New Year's Day, 1861, there was a few month's supply of cotton in the Liverpool warehouses.

In Feruary, 1861, the Southern States seceded, and the American civil war began. There was no anxiety in England concerning the cotton trade; the opinion being that the war would soon be over, that at longest it would only last a few months. But wars, like many other things, have a trick of playing havoc with prophesy; and short beginnings have often very long-drawn endings. In most wars before and after the American war this has proved the case. For it is always a much easier thing to begin a war than to end it.

As the war went on, far beyond the "ninety days" as predicted for its duration by those who had only wisdom enough to prophesy, people said that a bad time was coming upon the Lancashire cotton trade, owing to the ports of the Southern cotton-growing states being blockaded by the vessels of the North. There was no cotton coming into Liverpool; and the inland factories were getting "spun up." In the October of 1861 the mills were forced to run "short time;" and the trouble began. Applicants for poor relief increased in number. By December the whole county was in a state of pauperism. At Ashton-under-Lyne the excess of pauperism was 213 percent. over the usual amount; at Stockport 263 per cent.; at Blackburn 270 per cent.; at Glossop 300 per cent.; and at Preston – the highest figure of all – 320 per cent. In Ashton there were over 3,000 persons utterly without food, in Stockport nearly 9,000, and in Preston nine thousand and a half. And these people, being decent hard-working people, with the independent spirit that dreads the workhouse, refused to go to the Guardians for relief. They would rather earn their bread than have charity; all they wanted was work, the means to keep themselves.

But – strange thing – in a well-governed land – there was no work for these people; no means by which they could keep themselves, except by selling their labour in the factories; and the factories were shut and silent the engines still, and the fires gone out. In the desolate spinning rooms the spindles twirled not; in the weaving sheds the shuttles clacked no more; the patter of clogs in the early morning was heard not in the streets, and even the occupation of the poor knocker-up[156] was gone. There was nobody to knock up; and thus fate knocked even the knocker-up down.

What could be done for these people? They could not be allowed to perish of hunger and starvation. Benevolent persons started soup-kitchens, agencies for the free distribution of clothes, sewing classes, and other means of amelioration; while Town Councils and other authorities began to make parks, cemeteries, roads, and undertake other public works, in order to find a little employment for those who would rather work hard for a dry crust than have a buttered loaf given to them. For such a brave and honest race, and for the children of such, there should be hope. Surely the descendants of the sturdy endurers of the cotton famine will not prove the despair of social reformers. Surely another generation of machinery manufacturing, and the factory system cannot have crushed out of the Lancashire people all that sweet independence and labouring honesty their fathers possessed and bequeathed to them.

Inevitably, the poverty of the workers made hard times for the shopkeepers; many small tradesmen, after sore striving to ward off the woe, became bankrupt. And with increase of destitution came increase of crime; theft, drunkenness, prostitution; proving, if it need be proved again, that poverty is the chief father of ill. If succeeding generations would only study the lessons written by events in the lives of their fathers and forefathes they would have the wisdom that would bless the world. But each generation plods on in its own pain, learning in long-suffering from its own experience what it might learn in a short time from the experience of its predecesors.

In the spring of 1862 local relief committees were formed in many Lancashire towns; by August, 1862, these committees numbered a score; and the seekers for relief were increasing by thousands a day. In Manchester a Relief Committee became necessary, not so much to help the cotton operatives as to help those indirectly dependent on the cotton trade, – clerks, porters, small tradesmen, warehousemen, and even owners of cottage property, who could, of course, get no rents from their penniless tenants.

With the approach of winter, 1862, there was much anxiety as to how the starving people would fare; and philanthropy public and private, was busy doing great things to mitigate the great distress. Subscriptions poured in from all parts of England and the world. India, so often fiercely stripped by famine itself, contributed much; let this fact be remembered when India is appealing to Lancashire for help. Yet, in spite of all the charity and help of kind hearts and open hands, the Lancahire Christmas of 1862 was a dreary and dismal one; as was the New Year, which, in Lancashire, is generally a period of holiday-making and merriement and Sunday-school tea parties. But the Lancashire New Year's day of 1863 was ushered in with no cheerful celebration and human rejoicing; it came in with rags and fireless grates, and starved beings, and little children crying for bread.

But, as is shamefully usual in all periods of general distress and ruin, there were cunning and unscrupulous men, who, all head and no heart, turned the trouble of the land to their own pecuniary profit and made money out of the cotton panic; cotton dealers who held their store back till they could get top prices for it, caring naught that in the meantime the workers were perishing of hunger, because the mills were idle; manufacturers who sold "shoddy" at "cotton" prices; and chuckled over their opportunity; and sundry others, of whom the least said the better in any self-respecting history. Many a Lancashire "gentleman's" fortune was founded in "the cotton panic," and founded on the agony of the people. Of such men, what shall be written? Only this, of each and all of them, "He made money," – the most execrable epitaph, and the meanest memory for any man. Far better is it to write of a man, as may be written of the majority of men who had means to help during the cotton famine, "He pitied the poor, and made misery less."

[19 January 1901]
XXIV. (Continued)

So dragged the cotton famine on to the early summer of the year 1863, the time with which this story is dealing at this point. The war, which had now lasted nearly two and a half years, was still going on redly, with alternating success and defeat to both sides; and even yet no man could foretell the end of the fighting, though the North seemed to be gaining ground.

The distress was still deep in Preston, though a few mills had begun to work several hours a day. But there were thousands and thousands of workers still unemployed; and dreading the coming of another winter. At Chorley the relief fund was exhausted; and the little town was in desperate strait.

With the Milners there was, so far, no change. They managed to struggle along; secretly helped, as Ada was certain, by Mr. Hyde, who now visited the house very frequently; and did not offend Ada by pressing his attentions on her. But the girl guessed that he was playing his game all the same; and loathed the man.

One day Hyde met Ada near the Mill-street district, where Lily Milner had given her life for charity's sake. Ada, though she could give little help, had, keeping the promise made to her dying sister, gone often to see the people Lily has sacrificed herself in assisting. Hyde, thinking to step into Ada's favour thus, had asked her about her philanthropic errands, and offered her money to dispense to the poor objects of her compassion. Ada gently declined his money, but told him she would be glad if he would call upon the people himself and give it them.

One day Old Chartist came in joyful with a pound of black puddings wrapped up in paper, and a flour cake. "I'm very fain that I've been able to do a bit at last towards keeing the house-door open;" he said. "I've been working a bit."

The old man's pride in the fact that he had been able to earn a little money, and his greater pride in bringing what he had therewith purchased to help the home of those who had befriended and sheltered him, touched Ada.

"Why, what have you been doing?" asked Ada smiling.

"I've been acting as a guide to Ned Waugh; he's going to write a book about Preston and Lancashire, and tell all the tales of old and historic places.[157] He gave me a shilling to show him round Walton-le-Dale; and tell him all I knew. And I knew a bit – I told him how Walton had been a Roman station, nearly two thousand years ago; and how there had been a Roman temple at Ribchester, seven or eight miles away; and the richest find of old Roman coins ever found in England, at Cuerden; and all about Cromwell's battle at Walton, when he captured Preston; and then about the Jacobites, a hundred and fifty years since; how some of em were executed, the head of one, a man called Shuttleworth, being stuck on a pole in front of the old Town Hall in Preston; then how the Jacobites, when all hope of putting the Stuarts on the throne was lost, gathered a club together at Walton's old Inn under the disguise of a Corporation, and had a mayor, huntsman, poet laureate, slut-kisser, jester, custard-eater, physican, and all those other old-time officers, and consoled themselves for their defeat by drinking the health of 'the king over the water,' – Walton being one of the last places where the friends of the Royal Stuart line met in this country. But Walton's old Jacobites are all dead and gone now; and only a tale for folk to tell. And I told Ned Waugh how Preston had always been a town for sticking to the Royal Family and that there's more Roman Catholics in Preston[158] than any other town in England and they're thick all about the neighbourhood and all over the Fylde. And Ned Waugh's going to put it all in a book; and he said I was a well-read man, a very well-read man for a workingchap. That's true, too; I've read a bit and thought a lot; and I know something about the history of things and the common sense of things as well. However, all this is only dry talk for a young lass, Ada, and I'm rambling again. But I've something better to tell you – better than anything."

"And what is that?" said Ada.

"I've got work!" shouted Old Chartist, standing up in glee. "I've got work!" and it was pathetic to see how glad at the thought of working for his livelihood was this grey old man, whose age ought to have ensured him an easy end to his days without any labour or fear of want in any civilised land.

"I met Mr. Treebarn," continued Old Chartist, "coming back from Walton, where he'd been to visit the Wragleys – I'm told that Mrs. Wragley is in an awful way over the death of her son – and he asked me if I would like a job at caretaking for a chapel. I said I would jump at it; where was it? It was their own chapel, he said; the old man that had been doing the work had died and I could have his place if I would. I said I didn't reckon to be a religious chap but I'd take the job and do my duty; and then Mr. Treebarn said it wouldn't be a bad world if everybody were as really religious as me. So we clinched the bargain and I've got work. I could dance for joy if I were young enough for such marlocks! For I shall be able to get our Jane out of the workhouse now and make a little home for her and the children!" and happy tears came into the old man's eyes as he spoke.

"I'm very, very glad," said Ada.

"Perhaps I'll be able to pay you back for all you've done for me," Chartist began, but Ada interrupted him. "If you ever speak about paying back I'll never look at you again," she said and Old Chartist smiled.

"Mr. Treebarn told me that there was a rumour out that Ted Banister had been caught," said Old Chartist, "but he inquired at the police-station and found it wasn't true. I hope they'll never catch the lad to hang him. He's suffered enough."

Ada said nought but sat in a sad silence full of sorrowful thoughts and memories.

Hyde called in the evening. He was chatty and genial, concealing the disappointment he felt at not making any favourable influence on Ada. He was getting tired, not of Ada, but of the task of trying to win her to himself. Yet he determined not to give up; by some means or other he meant to have her for his own.

XXV. The Capture of the "Golden Star"

Meanwhile, the *Alabama*, in a world of her own, largely unconscious of the doings of the world beyond its horizon, yet eagerly grabbing newspapers to learn tidings, from the vessels she captured, went on her way of adventure and destruction; making her name a terror on the sea and a tale on the land. Merchant vessels feared to venture forth lest they should meet the *Alabama*; while on land, in England especially, schoolboys read the story of the *Alabama* and glorified it with romance; longing to emulate its captain, whom their hearts held as the hero of the time. Many lads ran away to sea, expecting to find *Alabama*s to join; while many more wrote letters of worship and admiration to Captain Semmes, some of which he received and treasured as curiosities.

Sid Clifton saw much and learned much on the *Alabama*, and though there is really a deal of hard prose in the life of a sea-sailing man, he found much of the poetry of change, of travel, of seeing strange lands and peoples, in his life; and ever the great mystery of the ocean – the loneliness of its solitudes, the sublimity of its solemnity and joy; the grandure of its winds and tempests, the fairness of its freedom, the beauty of its days and nights, the sun, and moon, and stars, and the charming contrast of the wild, untrammelled sea-life to the tame, coffined existence in towns on shore.

And yes – thinking of a sweet lassie who was struggling against poverty and all the plagues of "hard times" in a certain town on a river by the sea – he often longed to be back on shore, to clasp his sweetheart in his arms once more, and feel the witchery of her love again.

The *Alabama* crossed and recrossed the Atlantic many times; darting between the West Indies and the African coast, on the tracks most frequented by merchant ships. Captain Semmes knew the highways of the sea well; to a good sailor they are as well defined and as easy to find as the roads on land. But Semmes also knew the byways and short cuts; and in this knowledge lay his strength and his safety, and his power to do the work he had in hand. After capturing and destroying ships on one busy trade-way of the sea, he would scurry across to another route, and so well had he calculated his points that he would hit exactly the spot he wanted, and pounce upon his amazed prey, who had supposed him, from other reports passed by one vessel to another, in another part of the sea altogether.

During the cruises of the *Alabama* Sid visited Jamacia and Kingston; then right across the Atlantic to Table Bay and Cape Town;[159] where the crew and officers of the *Alabama* had a royal time of it, being feted and feasted by the inhabitants; ladies sending bouquets daily to Captain Semmes. Off Cape Colony, the *Alabama* chased and captured a vessel, in sight of thousands of spectators on the land; crowds assembling at every good point of vantage to watch the spectacle which a South African editor described in a very eulogistic article on the skill of Captain Semmes and the beautiful sailing qualities of the *Alabama*. Leaving Table Bay the *Alabama* met a British cruiser, whose captain had a chat with Semmes through his speaking trumpet; then the *Alabama* crossed the Indian Ocean, where she met a vessel full of pilgrims going to Mecca; but even these strange folks had heard of the *Alabama*; and their notions were amazingly odd. They supposed that she was propelled by a giant in the hold. Then the *Alabama* went through the Straits of Singapore into the Chinese seas; capturing and destroying several Northern trading vessels on the way. But as soon as the merchantmen heard that the *Alabama* was about, they discreetly stuck in port.

The *Alabama* called at several Chinese ports, and Sid had opportunity of noting the curious Chinese, whom Captain Semmes described as "the most gentle and pacific people in the world," not given to war, but loving peace; a simple and frugal people, the cheapest producers on the earth. Speaking to his officers one day Semmes said that the Chinese had had very few wars, compared with western nations. For centuries and centuries the Chinese had been at peace except for the Tae-ping rebellion, which was a just rising against a military tyranny and lazy soliders who sought to live at the expense of the hardworking producer.[160]

Crossing the Pacific Ocean, the *Alabama* encountered a terrific gale in rounding Cape Horn, and Sid believed that the doom of the vessel was upon her. The night was pitch dark, and icebergs were drifting about; while the fury of the storm tossed the vessel about like a cork. Captain Semmes gave order to "tie all fast and let her rip;" and with good fortune the vessel succeeded in "ripping through" the tempest. But she was badly damaged; and her captain decided to cross the Atlantic and make for the port of Cherbourg in France, where she could be repaired and put in fine trim again, if need were. The "if need were," was a sad and troubling thought. Captain Semmes had gathered, from the latest reports he had heard of the war, that the North might win a great and decisive victory any day; and if so, there would be no further use for the *Alabama*; her duty would be ended and her day done.

"Well, well, if that be so," he said to his officers, "we will content ourselves with the work we have done, and face the future cheerfully. We have done our best, and done it well. Ah, if the South had only had a fleet! The result of the war would have been different. A fleet's the thing for a nation that's kissed by the sea. Britain's Empire depends solely upon her ships – upon her ships and colonies. Cut them off, and Britain will fall. Well, if there is nothing more for the gallant little *Alabama* to do, I think she had done her share splendidly."

But the *Alabama* was fated to make another capture ere her career was ended. Just before the Irish Coast came into sight, the look-out saw, early one morning, a sailing vessel ahead, evidently making for one of the Irish ports. Captain Semmes immediately gave chase, and soon overtook the ship. A shot from the *Alabama* caused her to take in sail and heave to. Sid was one of the boarding party.

This vessel proved to be the *Golden Star* from New York, laden with grain for the Irish and English ports.

Captain Semmes gave orders that she was to be burned, so the captain and crew were brought off in the *Alabama*'s boats. With the crew were two male passengers, and Sid started as he recognised one of them as Billy Richardson, the old Crimean veteran who had left Preston to enlist in the Northern Army. Sid also fancied that somehow he had seen the features of the other passenger before – he was a young man, seeming almost a boy with a clean hairless face.

"Where have I seen that face before?" he said to himself; and strove to recollect, yet could not.

Sid noticed that Billy Richardson limped, as if he had been wounded in the leg and resolved that he must quietly put the old man on his guard against letting Semmes know that he had fought for the North. Luckily, Billy Richardson and his young companion were put next to Sid in the boat. Sid was puzzled to see the young man blush – yes, very decidedly blush – as he sat down.

"Well, Billy Richardson," said Sid, softly, "who'd have thought of meeting you here, and in such a way."

"Why, it's Sid Clifton," said Billy Richardson, with a sharp side glance at his young companion, who again grew extraordinarily red in the face.

"Billy," whispered Sid, "just a word of caution. Before I left Preston to join this vessel I heard that you were going to fight for the North. If that's what you have been doing, say nothing about it for this is the Confederate steamer, *Alabama*."

"I guessed as much," said Billy Richardson, once more glancing strangely, interrogatively, at his young companion. Then he said to Sid, "Do you know who this is with me?"

"I've a strong idea I've seen the face before," said Sid, "but I can't remember where."

The young man, blushing again, looked into Sid's face, and said, softly, sorrowfully, "I am Nelly Milner!"

Sid gasped. "And Sandy Aspinall's on the *Alabama*," he said, "where you'll be in a few minutes."

[26 January 1901]

XXVI. The Story of Nelly Milner's Escape from the Mormons

When the boat containing the crew and two passengers of the captured *Golden Star* reached the *Alabama*, the former vessel was already in flames, having been fired in several places by the men from the latter.

Sid, full of strange delight and wonder at the events of this day, stood on the deck of the *Alabama*, Billy Richardson and Nelly Milner, still in male attire and keeping up the disguise, besides him, watching the conflagration on the *Golden Star*.

Then Sid started as Sandy Aspinall approached. What would happen now?

Sandy greeted Billy Richardson and stared hard at Nelly Milner, with a vastly bewildered expression in his face.

Nelly Milner hung her head; not wishing to look her old lover in the face.

Then Sid whispered the secret to Sandy. Sandy uttered a low exclamation, looked at the young man, with downcast head, standing beside Billy Richardson; then sighed deeply and hastily walked away. Sid, glancing at Nelly Milner, saw, as she looked up, that her eyes were full of tears.

He followed Sandy, who was hiding his emotion in a deserted corner of the deck.

"Sandy," said Sid, "you never said a word to her. Why did you rush away in such a fashion?"

"I felt that I wanted to speak to her – and yet that I didn't want," said Sandy, "and so I couldn't speak at all. I don't know what to do. It's all so strange, so horrible. She is Nelly Milner – but not the Nelly I loved and lost."

"But you ought to say a kind word to her. She has suffered – she must have suffered."

"My feelings, my thoughts, are all of a confusion. I feel dazed. I don't know what to do, – I never dreamt that I should see her again. – And she is not the same, not the same. When I knew her she was a pure maiden; she has been a wife, one of many wives, since then – and now she is neither wife nor widow. – I am glad she has got away from the Mormons; but there's a sort of sickening horror mixed with the gladness – a repugnance – I hardly know what. Yon ship that's burning to destruction now – lost, hopeless – is like the love that once was mine and hers."

Sid thought it best to leave Sandy alone for a time. He quitted him and rejoined Billy Richardson and Nelly Milner.

"What will be done with us?" asked Billy.

"You'll be landed at Cherbourg, no doubt: – that's where the *Alabama*'s making for, – and then be left to shift for yourselves. But you'll make your way easily from Cherbourg to England, – to Southampton I should think. Captain Semmes always puts his prisoners ashore, to get rid of them, as soon as possible. But now, tell me how you and Nelly came to be on the *Golden Star*; and you, Nelly, how you escaped from the Mormons. I have been told that nobody ever gets away from Salt Lake City."

"I was very fortunate," said Nelly Milner, "I found a good friend, or else I should have been in Salt Lake City still." She paused, and looked at Sid; evidently wishing to speak of what was troubling her most keenly. Then she said, "Why did Sandy turn away from me?"

"He was so astounded that he did not know what to say. But – he'll be all right by-and-bye."

"I did him a great wrong, and I deserve his coldness and scorn," said Nelly, in quiet sadness, "but, but, – it's very hard."

"Oh, Sandy will be all right in time," said Sid.

"How are Ada, mother, and Lily getting on?" asked Nelly. "I'm longing for a sight of their faces."

"They were all right when I left Preston," said Sid. "Lily was working for Mr. Treebarn, the minister." (Sid, of course, did not know of Lily's death.)

"I'm glad Lily's got such a nice place," said Nelly. "Now, what about Ada?"

Sid told Nelly about Mr. Hyde, the Mormon missionary.

"Oh, I'm all anxiety to hurry home now, to warn Ada to beware of him!" cried Nelly. "To go to Salt Lake City is terrible – the life of a decent woman there is hell!"

"Oh, Ada's all right," said Sid. "There's no fear of her being won over by Mormon yarns. You can rest easy on Ada's account. Your case was enough example for her. Now tell me how you got away from the Mormons."

'I soon had my eyes opened," said Nelly. "Perhaps the man who had married me wasn't bad, but he would have his own way always. He was very nice to me till he got me fast. And I must say that I loved him, or at least was fascinated by him. He was a wonderful wheedler – I don't think any ordinary woman could have resisted him if he had set himself to win her. Indeed, when I got to Salt Lake City I discovered that two of his wives were women he had enticed away from their husbands; and I was disgusted with these women. It may be a cruel thing to forsake a sweetheart; but it's a bad thing to elope from a husband."

"But you eloped from yours," said Sid, smiling.

"He had enough wives before he got me," said Nelly. "I was going to tell you that I began to feel very sorry for Sandy Aspinall, and reproached myself for having treated him wrongly, soon after we left Liverpool. But it was too late to turn back then. And, to be honest, I can't say that I really wanted to turn back then. I pitied Sandy; but I was infatuated with the Mormon. I needn't tell you about the voyage. We got safely across the water, and then from New York set out for Salt Lake City and the Promised Land. A deal of the journey was done by caravans across the prairies, and we saw Indians occasionally, and once were attacked, but drove the assailants off. When we got to Salt Lake City I was soon made one of the wives of Runshaw – that was my husband's name – and he was a big man among the Mormons. The other wives were jealous of me, and made me uncomfortable. I must admit, too, that I detested them. I couldn't bear the idea of sharing a husband and a home; and was soon sick of the whole business. Then I did not like the Mormons and their ways. Some of them were good decent folks, but the majority were ready for any game or crime. They attacked and robbed many caravans; and considered that they were pleasing God by slaying any persons who did not accept the Mormon religion."

"Did you see Brigham Young? What sort of a man is he?" asked Sid.

"I saw him several times. He didn't look anything out of the common, but he was very sharp and shrewd, and quick at reading the thoughts of people. And he could manage a crowd well. He wouldn't have any questioning of his authority; his word must be obeyed. I think he wanted to make himself a king as well as a prophet. He told the truth when it paid him to do so, and did justice when it was policy. There was a deal of style about him; he put on unapproachable airs, as if he were a royal and sacred person."

"Well, he must be a curious chap considering the notions he's got," said Sid. "But go on with your tale."

"Loathing the Mormon life, I made up my mind to try to escape," said Nelly. "I knew it would be a very difficult task; for the Mormons have spies everywhere; and the gang of executioners called The Destroying Angels are soon on the track of any runaway. I believe my husband was one of the Destroying Angels. There was a young woman, quite a girl, who had been abducted from a caravan by the Mormons, and married to an old wretch named Slimter, who had already six wives. This girl, whose age was not more than seventeen, and whose name was Alice, often got in conversation with me; and, – after I was sure that she was not a spy – we got very friendly, and confided our troubles to each other. Alice hated the Mormon life as much as I did, and told me she should run away, no matter what the risks. Well, one night she disappeared and the next day the Destroying Angels were after her. I guessed that my husband was one because he left home that day, and returned the day after the news came out that the Destroying Angels had done their duty. That was in three days. Alice was never seen or heard of again. She must have been captured and put to death. Later on her skeleton was found in a lonely valley – the bones picked clean by wolves. My husband said grimly to me, 'That's the fate of all who try to forsake the true religion.' And I then knew from his tone, and the threat in it, that he had had something to do with the murder of poor Alice. He thought that her doom would perhaps scare me out of any hopes I had of escape; but he was mistaken. After the death of Alice I had no friend to talk to and I was not allowed to write home to England. If I wanted to communicate with my mother my husband said he would write for me. Then Elder Willard Hyde left for England and said he would call at my mother's. What sort of a tale he told I don't know, but I can guess."

"He said you were quite happy – so happy that you advised your sister Ada to follow your example."

"What a lying villain!" said Nelly. "I hope he only calls at my mother's when I get back home. I'll astonish him."

Sid laughed. "Oh! you women! how you love revenge."

"If we go on like this I shall never finish my story," said Nelly. "There came to Salt Lake City a young man named Hawkins; he professed to adopt Mormonism, was baptised into the faith, and put in charge of Hyde's household while the Elder was away in England. And I'm rather afraid that Elder Hyde will be very suspicious when he returns to his nest; for Hawkins made love to the youngest and prettiest of the wives. As the Hyde house was near mine I sometimes had a chat with Hawkins and one day found out that he was no more a Mormon at heart than I was. He had simply joined the sect for fun and in order to 'get on' in Salt Lake City. He confessed that he was as sick of the Mormons as I was and he talked of planning my escape. But we had to be very careful; we were well watched. My husband, however, supposed that the ghastly end of poor Alice would frighten me out of all thought of escape; he told me more than once that such a death would certainly befall any woman who tried to run away from Salt Lake City. Perhaps thinking that I should be too terrified after this even to dream of escape, his vigilance was somewhat relaxed. But even under the most favourable circumstances, it was a tremendous task to elude the Destroying Angels. I think I am the only one who has managed to baffle them. And I couldn't have done it but for Hawkins, who was as cute as could be. He had lived with the Indians, and been made a member of one of the tribes; and had married an Indian squaw in Indian fashion, though rather against his will, he said. He had all the tricks of the Indians off; and it was lucky for me that I found him for a friend. It was he who suggested that I should don male clothes, – and I'll keep up the part till I get to England. It was in broad daylight that Hawkins and I made our escape – thanks to the scout's ingenuity. He had got the clothes for me the day before; and said there was no time to waste; the elderly wives of Hyde were going to complain to Brigham Young of Hawkins' carryings-on with the youngest wife; and there would be a rare scandal and hullabullo. The clothes Hawkins had got for me belonged to Hyde's son, a youth of seventeen, just about my height, and complexion. In order to give us a chance to get away from Salt Lake City before our absence was discovered and the pursuit raised Hawkins had carried out a deep dodge. He had taken Hyde's son out shooting, on the outskirts of Salt Lake City, for several days in succession, generally returning after sundown. Then, early in the morning of the day we had fixed for our escape, he had taken the lad out again, stripped him of his clothes, and tied him up and gagged him in a lonely cave. Returning at noon without the lad, he gave me the bundle of clothes, unobserved fortunately, and told the Hyde household he had left the lad shooting, having merely come back himself for some more ammunition, as they had gone short. Soon after noon, dressed in the lad's clothes, I joined Hawkins in the street, and was by many people mistaken for Hyde's son. Thus we got away. We went to the cave where the lad lay bound; Hawkins loosed him and let him eat some food; then tied him up again securely; and, with the lad's rifle slung over my shoulder, I trudged quickly along with Hawkins. Before our flight was discovered we were far away, and practically undiscoverable in the prarie, of which Hawkins seemed to know every foot. Even if I had got away from Salt Lake City myself I should most assuredly have been lost in the prarie, and either recaptured, or devoured by wolves. By trails only known to himself and the Indians Hawkins took me to the tribe to which he belonged; we reached its camping ground after a week's travelling over the prarie. Hawkins kept us both in food by means of his rifle. He could have got along faster but for me; I was not used to such tramping."

"And what then?" asked Sid.

"I stayed with the Indians a few days to rest. I must say that I found them a brave and noble people. They don't hanker after money like white men. They've no wish to pile up a fortune. Amongst them the man who gives away most, not hoards most, is reckoned the best and bravest. It's a pity such a race is being killed out by white men; white men who are making money out of the ruin of these children of the prairie. After I had been in the Indian camp a week Hawkins saw me safe to a caravan that was bound for the nearest railway and gave me money to continue my journey to New York, where I was delighted to drop across Billy Richardson, who had been wounded in the war. I told my story to Billy, and, dreading that the Destroying Angels might even be in New York searching for me, kept to my male disguise. Then Billy and I booked passages in the *Golden Star*; and the rest you know."

"It's a very interesting story," said Sid. He looked at Nelly, started to speak, hesitated, and at last blurted out, "During the week you and Hawkins slept out on the prarie together what relationship did you hold to each other?"

Nelly blushed. "He was my deliverer," she said. "And he was a man, and I was a woman; and we were alone together. – It was not my wish, but what could I do?"

Sid was silent; thinking that when he told Nelly's story to Sandy he would have to tell this item too. But he decided not to mention it, unless Sandy questioned him directly on the point.

As he anticipated, Sandy, after listening intently to Sid's narrative of Nelly Milner's disillusionment, horrors, and her escape from the Mormons, did put the question. And when Sid answered it Sandy's face looked sadder and gloomier than ever.

"She is a wanton," said Sandy, bitterly.

"No, no," said Sid, "you must consider the circumstances of the case and make allowance."

"No allowance can undo what's done," said Sandy. "She is not what she was, and never can be again. She is not the lass I loved, though she wears her shape and bears her name."

"She's just the same lassie, only purified and ennobled by suffering," said Sid.

"Did she say anything about me – of the old time when – when we were sweethearts?"

"No."

"And do you think she wants me to love her?" asked Sandy.

"I don't know," said Sid. "But I don't think she is throwing herself at you. But she has suffered, and wants sympathy."

Sandy sat with his head in his hands, and Sid left him to his thoughts.

The man who had once wooed Nelly Milner sat mournfully wondering whether he loved her still, asking himself, in anguish, if he could love her still."

She deserved to suffer, he said to himself. She had by her own folly wrought all her own misery; and woe for others as well.

While the *Alabama* was making for Cherbourg Sandy passed Nelly Milner on deck several times; but did not stop to hold any intercourse with her. He merely gave an ordinary greeting and passed on. And the heart of the woman was sad. She longed to beg Sandy's forgiveness; she yearned to hear him say that he forgave her, even if he could not forget the pain she had been to him. She felt that in some degree he loathed her while he pitied her; she read his feelings from his looks, his attitude towards her.

Once, when the fair coast of France came into sight, she ventured to speak to Sandy.

"Sandy," she said, "can't you forgive me? I am very sorry for the wrong I have done you; no one regrets it more than I do. I acknowledge my fault, and ask you to forgive me."

He silently turned his face from her.

She bit her lip and continued, "Don't imagine that in talking thus, I am trying to patch up what has been torn, to mend what is broken, to ask you to have me back again, and be as we were before, – no such thing. I only wanted to say that I am very sorry for the way I treated you, and I beg you to forgive me."

Sandy clenched his fists and walked away.

Nelly Milner went to a lonely corner of the deck, and leaned over the taffrail. And the salt sea was salter by a woman's tears.

[2 February 1901]

XXVII. The "Alabama" Entrapped

The *Alabama* steamed past the Channel Islands, round Alderney Isle and Cape de la Hague into Cherbourg harbour. As the vessel passed Cape de la Hague Captain Semmes saw amid the fishing-boats and other channel craft, a large steamer far astern. "What do you make of the stranger?" he said to Evans, the master's mate.

"Yankee man-o'-war – and on our track," said Evans, who in addition to a long sea-faring existence, had a marvellous observation, so keen and accurate that one would have said it was more an extraordinary intuition than mere observation. Evans could tell at a glance the nationality of any ship at a fair distance; he knew the distinctive shape, rigging, features and general appearance of the ships of all climes.

"Then we're in for a fight," said Captain Semmes, as the *Alabama* dropped anchor in the port of Cherbourg.

Semmes soon learnt that the vessel he had seen was the United States battleship, the *Kearsage*, under Captain Winslow.[161] The *Kersage* took her station outside the harbour, waiting for the *Alabama* to come forth. But Captain Semmes would not hurry; he was resolved to put his vessel in as good trim as possible before engaging in what might prove the *Alabama*'s last fight. She would have to sink the *Kearsage* or be sunk herself. It would be a battle to the death.

Captain Semmes sent an officer ashore to the Port Admiral of Cherbourg, with a request to land the prisoners the *Alabama* had on board. Permission was readily given and the two passengers from the *Golden Star*, Billy Richardson and Nelly Milner, who was still in masculine disguise, were told they could depart with the rest.

Nelly Milner, with some timidity, approached the commander of the *Alabama*. Billy Richardson stood beside her. "Captain Semmes," she said, "I should like to stay on the *Alabama* in this fight."

"Why?" asked Semmes, smiling.

"I have a friend on board – Sid Clifton; I should like to stay with him."

"The fight may end in the destruction of the *Alabama* and perhaps in many deaths," said Semmes.

"I understand that," said Nelly.

"You are but a youth," said Semmes, kindly but admiringly, for he honoured pluck, "wouldn't you be better on shore?"

"I beg of you to let me share the danger of the *Alabama*," said Nelly earnestly.

"And I too," said Billy Richardson.

"You would not be so eager to volunteer for this work if you knew its fatal possibilities," said Semmes.

"I'm an old soldier," said Billy Richardson. "I fought in the Crimea; here is my medal," and he unbuttoned his coat and showed the disc of distinction fastened on his vest. "So you see, captain," he went on, "I'm not altogether a novice at this business."

"If we are captured by the *Kearsage* you'll be treated as prisoners of war."

"We'll risk that," said Billy. "At least I will. As for this young man," and Billy touched Nelly on the shoulder, "I almost wish myself that he'd change his mind. But if he wishes to fight, let him fight. He'll be of use to help the wounded, anyhow."

"Very well, then," said Semmes. "You can stay with the *Alabama* till the great issue is decided. I will have you entered on the ship's books as members of the crew. Give me your names."

"Billy Richardson and Mat Milner," said the Crimean veteran, acting as spokesman for both himself and Nelly.

And so that matter was settled. Sid was not very joyful when he heard the result of Billy and Nelly's interview with Captain Semmes. "A battleship in action is no place for a woman, Nelly," he said.

"You forget that for the time being I'm a man," said Nelly, smiling.

"If Semmes should discover that you are a woman there'll be a rumpus," said Sid. "I think you ought to have told your tale and revealed your sex when we took you off the *Golden Star*."

"And I think you are quite mistaken, Sid," said Nelly. "You are not a woman, and you don't understand. My male disguise was my shield and protection from many things. Not that I care to pose as a man. I'm longing to cast off these clothes, and be a woman once more. But not till I get on English soil again. Till the *Alabama*'s fight is over I am a man."

"I think Sandy would have thought less harshly of you if you had appeared to him as a woman," said Sid.

"Sandy, like you, has only the understanding of a man; not the sense of a woman," said Nelly.

Mention of Sandy, however, set her thinking of her one-time lover, sorrowfully. He still maintained towards Nelly a cold and contemptuous attitude; though in his heart he loved her still. But the strangeness of her in male attire helped him to be chilling and unyielding. If she could have stood before him in maiden apparel, his love for her would have risen and he would have worshipped her as of old; forgiving and forgetting; and only loving. But this creature, though wearing the face of Nelly Milner, was not she; it was a grotesque mockery of her! it was his sweetheart dead and come to life again in the form of a man. Sandy was puzzled, grieved, forlorn, like one perplexed and vexed by tricks and illusions. When Sid informed him that Nelly and Billy Richardson were remaining on the *Alabama* he scowled, but said nothing.

By this time the arrival of the *Alabama* at Cherbourg had been telegraphed to Paris, and thence transmitted all over Europe and America. The newspapers were full of sensational headlines, and articles; and the public thrilled in the expectancy of the sea-fight that was now inevitable between the *Alabama* and the *Kearsage*.

Chartist Grimshaw, hearing the exciting news in the street, hurried home to tell Ada. "The *Alabama*'s at Cherbourg, a French port," he said.

"Then I shall be having another letter from Sid," said Ada.

Chartist Grimshaw, not wishing to alarm Ada said nothing of the fight that was to be; but began talking about his new work as chapel-keeper; he had commenced duty that day.

"I'm managing all right," he said, "an I like the job. It's not hard work, it's good money, an I shall stick to the shop.[162] I'll have Jane an her childer out of the workhouse again in a few weeks, an we'll be happy again, – nay, not all, for Joe will not be with us, – poor, poor Joe – how we shall miss him. It'll be a heartbreakin thing to get th' home together again, an him not in it any more. Well, I suppose we shall get used to it. There's more homes than ours that'll be strange an sad when they're started again after this cotton panic's o'er. There'll be familiar furniture missin, – sold or gone to pawn, – ay, an little childer's faces missin too, an other faces. But let's bide our bitterness an face our fate, an not talk things worse than they are. Perhaps all will be well sometime, somewhere. An as it is we shall get used to it. Folks get used to everythin – to clammin, to sufferin, to poverty, to bereavement, – ay, folks gets used to everythin except livin on for ever, an happen it's a good job they can't get used to that."

Next morning Ada got a letter marked "Cherbourg," form Sid. She opened it eagerly, caressingly, and read: –

"Dear Ada, – after many adventures on the great seas, the *Alabama* is now lying at Cherbourg, but this, I suppose, you will know already, as I guess the news is now all over England. Captain Semmes has been to see the port admiral to get consent to dock our ship for repairing, but I understand there is some difficulty in the way, as Cherbourg is a naval station. The port admiral says it would have been better for the *Alabama* to have gone to Havre or some other commercial port, where she would have found private docks. The port admiral is afraid that docking her in Cherbourg might lead to what he calls 'international complications' whatever those may be; so he is of opinion that it would be best not to harbour 'a belligerent vessel,' – more big words, Ada. These big men always use big words to cover up little things. However, the port admiral is writing to the Emperor of France, to see what he says; but Captain Semmes tells Freeman that the Emperor is away and won't be back home – or to his palace I should say – for several days. Captain Semmes intended, if he could get into dock, to give us leave for a couple of months, in which case I should have come to Preston to see you; but I'm afraid that pleasure will have to be postponed now. The absence of the Emperor has put us into a little hobble, which may lead to a sea-fight. The United States cruiser, the *Kearsage*, is lying outside Cherbourg, off the breakwater, with her eye on us. If we have to quit Cherbourg – as I fear we shall – there is nothing for it but a battle with the *Kearsage*. The captain of the *Kearsage* has already communicated with the port authorities, protesting against them permitting us to enter Cherbourg; and asking for the prisoners sent ashore from the *Alabama* to be delivered up to the *Kearsage*. This Captain Semmes will not allow. – Just as I am writing this, Freeman tells me that Captain Semmes has sent word to Captain Winslow of the *Kearsage* that if he will wait till the *Alabama* has got some coal on boad we will sail out and give him battle. The challenge has been accepted, and the *Alabama* is coaling immediately. The *Kearsage* is rather a bigger boat than the *Alabama*, and is better armed, having seven guns, two 11-inch Dahlgrens,[163] four 32 pounders, and a rifled 28 pounder. We carry one gun more than the *Kearsage*, but the battery of the latter enables her to throw more metal at a broadside, and this is greatly to her advantage. The *Kearsage* has also more men than the *Alabama*. But we are sanguine that we shall come off victorious in the fight. Don't be afraid. I had also some very good news for you – joyful news you never dreamt of – but it is to be kept secret for a short time. You'll hear of it by-and-bye. Just amuse yourself by trying to guess what it is, till I come and tell it you. I shall have such a long tale to tell you when I see you. I shall make it an excuse for seeing you every day for weeks – and then there'll be another thing. You can tell Mr. Treebarn to be getting the marriage service off,[164] so that he'll make no slip over the job, but tie us up properly. I have made much money on board the *Alabama*; and I don't see why there should be any delay about our wedding. Let it be as soon as I come home. Oh, we'll be so merry. I enclose you some paper money,[165] which you can change at the post office, so that, in case the cotton panic has left you penniless, you'll not be lacking cash to buy the pretty dressing tackle that's so necessary for a bride. I hope, though, that the severtity of the 'hard times' had decresed, and that trade is mending. God knows it's been a terrible time for Lancashire. But I think the war will soon be over now; and Lancashire will quickly pull up again. Give my kind regards to your mother and a brotherly kiss to Lily – you're not jealous are you? I don't like to make any mention of that Mormon snake, but I trust he has left you in peace while I have been away. If he's hovering around when I come back, I'm afraid I shall let him feel my foot; and sea-travelling has made it very strong. I've learnt a lot about the Mormons lately from some passengers we took from a ship we burned; and I find they're as vile a lot of folk as ever practised villainy in the name of religion. Their doings are awful. However, let's not spoil this letter with talk of such people. – And now, a concluding word. To-morrow or the day after, the *Alabama* goes forth to fight. Though I think all will be well with us, yet one never knows what will happen in a battle. If it should be that I do not come out of the fight, be a brave lassie, Ada, and keep your heart up. I kiss this paper I am writing on – I kiss it for you to put your lips to it that I may feel the kiss returned. Kiss it, and I shall know. And so, if the worst should befall – but no, it cannot! – I feel that I see you again and hold you in my arms, my sweetheart. – Good bye and God bless you. Till we meet again. SID."

Sid had made no mention of Nellie Milner at her own request; she said she would rather no word should be sent home; she would take the news of her deliverance herself and give her mother and sisters a glad surprise.

Ada sat silently, Sid's letter in her hand, thinking with troubled and anxious soul of her lover, who was going into a dreadful battle, and whom she might see again no more on earth.

XXVIII. As Strange a Lover's Re-union as Ever Was.

The day in which the *Alabama* went forth to fight the *Kearsage* was Sunday. The morning was bright and beautiful with summer. Sweet calm was on the sea and genial peace on the land. Nowhere was there any hint of the hateful tumult that was about to burst on this tranquility with shot and shell and battle-smoke. Small boats and white-sailed fishing-smacks[166] made a picture on the blue sea. The coast of France smiled fair; the cliffs of the Isle of Alderney[167] seemed asleep in the sun.

All being ready, the *Alabama* steamed out of Cherbourg, being accompanied part of the way by the French ironclad frigate, *Couronne*,[168] to see that the neutrality of the French waters was not violated.

The *Alabama* had sent all her pay-rolls and other papers to shore that they might be safe in the event of the ship being lost. The crew were all astir and alert; they had had a good night's rest. Sid, after a few words with Sandy, went to talk with Nelly, who in her male attire, was looking at the receding coast-line. Sandy stood a short distance off eyeing Nelly sulkily yet longingly.

"Nelly," said Sid, "we are running the great hazard now; we may never set foot on shore again."

"That's as it will be," said Nelly. "Life is not much to lose after all. What is there on shore for me anywhere?"

"Friends and home," said Sid.

"Friends and home are naught to a ruined life," said Nelly dejectedly. "I am not particular whether I live or die. I don't know whether I've anything to die for but I'm cerain I've nothing to live for."

"Let's not talk funeral talk," said Sid. "Let's be cheerful."

But he, too, was thoughtful, if not melancholy. He was thinking of Ada. He might never see her again. This might be his last look on shining sun and bright earth. Ere the close of this day he might by lying dead at the bottom of the sea.

Billy Richardson came up. "Look at the crowds of spectators on shore," he said.

Sid and Nelly glanced at the heights of Cherbourg, which were thronged with people. Wherever a view of the sea was to be had was a multitude of eye-straining watchers, come to see the sea-fight, as to a holiday show. Excursions had run to Cherbourg from Paris and other inland towns. On the rocks of Alderney Isle were many folks, too watching the *Alabama* steam towards the *Kearsage*.

"This is a bit like a circus," said Billy Richardson contemptuously. "'Come and see the great naval battle. Admission one shilling. Front seats extra.' Faugh! We might be only a dog-fight, not two ships going to fight to the death in grim earnest."

Whether the event was tragedy or comedy, the crowds had come to see it as they would go to a play. The stage was the real sea, and the scenery real nature; and the combatants real men at real warfare, not mimic; that was the only difference.

A little way out at sea were many yachts, and sailing vessels, and a few steamers, all packed with spectators. One of the steam yachts, a beautiful boat, was the *Deerhound*, belonging to John Lancaster, Esquire, of Hindley Hall, Wigan. Mr. Lancaster had his wife and several young children on board, having been making a holiday cruise along the English Channel.[169]

The *Kearsage* lay six or seven miles out; and the *Couronne*, after leaving the *Alabama*, anchored just outside the harbour.

The *Alabama* went gallantly on, the Confederate flag flying, full of challenge, from her peak. The time was ten o'clock of the Sunday morning.

As the *Alabama* approached the *Kearsage*, Captain Semmes had all his crew called aft, and, standing on the gun-carriage, thus addressed his men: "Officers and seamen of the Alabama, – You have at last another opportunity of meeting your enemy, the first that has been presented to you since you sank the *Hatteras*. In the meantime you have been all over the world, and it is not too much to say that you have destroyed and driven for protection under neutral flags, one-half of the enemy's commerce, which, at the beginning of the war, covered every sea. This is an achievement of which you may well be proud, and a grateful country will not be unmindful of it. The name of your ship has become a household word wherever civilization extends. Shall that name be tarnished by defeat? (Enthusiastic cries of 'never, never,' from the crew). The thing is impossible. Remember that you are in the English Channel, the theatre of so much of the naval glory of our race and that the eyes of all Europe are at this moment upon you. The flag that floats over you is that of a young Republic, who bids defiance to her enemies, whenever and wherever found. Show the world that you know how to uphold it."

The seamen cheered loudly, and then disperesed to their quarters; ready to do their duty.

[9 February 1901]
XXVIII. (Continued)

In half-an-hour the *Alabama*, with her guns pivoted to starboard was within a mile of the *Kearsage*, which suddenly headed inshore presenting her starboard side, contrary to the calculations of Captain Semmes, who was rather nettled at this manœvre. However, the *Alabama* opened fire with a broadside of solid shot; the *Kearsage*, after a few minutes' interval, replied with the same kind; and there was the greatest activity on both sides.

As the *Kearsage* pressed forward, under a full head of steam, it was necessary for the two vessels, in order to keep their respective broadsides bearing on each other, to fight in a circle; the two ships steaming round a common centre, and keeping about a distance of half-a-mile from each other. There was great work in the engine-room, but Freeman and Sid, and their assistants, performed their task excellently; Sid wondering all the while how the fight was going on, and how Nelly Milner was faring. Sid could see nothing of the combat, of course; he could only hear the boom of the broadsides and the shouts of the men. Then came a short silence which seemed ages in length; and the next instant there was the scream of a shell fired from the *Alabama*. It hit its mark, striking the *Kearsage* in the forepart of the hull; but it did not burst, and Captain Semmes was astonished and annoyed. Next there was cry on the *Alabama*. The spanker gaff[170] was carried away by a shot from the *Kearsage* and the Confederate ensign fluttered down with a rush; which caused a cheer of delight on the *Kearsage*. Presently, after the battle had been raging half-an-hour cries of pains and groans were heard; many men being wounded, and several killed. Nelly Milner was doing her best to tend and bandage the injured. Sandy Aspinall, busy assisting at one of the guns looked swiftly at her as she came to help to carry away one of his comrades shot dead. Perhaps he thought that Nelly would faint, after the fashion of her sex, at the sight of blood and horror; but she did not flinch though her face was very pale. She looked at Sandy and said, "I am glad you are all right yet." Sandy made no answer.

Shot and shell were now pouring from the *Kearsage* into the hull of the *Alabama*, whose fire seemed to have no affect on the enemy. "I can't understand it," said Semmes, suspecting some dodge, "we've struck her more than once where we ought to sink her; yet our shot flies off harmless." He got his glass and examined the *Kearsage* closely. "The dogs!" he exclaimed, "they have made the vessel ironclad by hanging chains over the side. To hide their meanness they have boarded the chains over. But one of our shots has knocked some of the boarding away, and I can see the chains. Look for yourself," and he handed the glass to one of his officers. [171]

"It's true," said the officer.

"So really we are a wooden vessel fighting an ironclad," said Semmes. "It's a dishonourable thing the *Kearsage* has done. But I suppose Captain Winslow would only call it a 'cute Yankee trick.' We are at a terrible disadvantage, but we'll fight to the finish."

After an hour's ceaseless combat the *Alabama* was riddled with shot; many wounded and dead were strewn on her decks; and the carpenter came up to say that she was sinking, and nothing could be done to save her, as she was leaking in more than one place, and filling very rapidly.

Semmes shouted down to Freeman to make full steam ahead for the French coast, hoping to reach it before the *Alabama* sank. Freeman replied that the water rising in the hold was putting the boiler fires out.

"Then set all fore and aft available sail!" roared Semmes.

Freeman, Sid, and the engineers now came on deck, and saw for the first time the havoc that had been wrought. The beautiful *Alabama* looked like a dying cripple. Sid rejoiced to find Nelly Milner, Sandy Aspinall, and Billy Richardson were safe and unhurt.

Captain Semmes, seeing that it was impossible for the *Alabama* to make the coast in time, and not wishing to sacrifice more life needlessly, hauled down his colours, as a sign that he yielded, and despatched a boat to the *Kearsage* to inform Captain Winslow of the sinking condition of the *Alabama*.

But though the two ships were now less than a quarter of a mile from each other, and after the *Alabama* had struck her colours, the *Kearsage* sent five more shots into the settling wreck.

"Despicable!" said Captain Semmes. "Surely Captain Winslow cannot be doing this deliberately."

Exertions were now made to get the wounded men of the *Alabama* into the boats; then all the boys and men who could not swim.

"The rest must jump and swim for it when the order is given," said Semmes. "The *Kearsage* is evidently in no hurry to send help. I was not so with the *Hatteras* when we sank her. Yet," added Captain Semmes, bitterly, "Captain Winslow calls himself a Christian gentleman. And he'll stand by and see us drown! I thank heaven I am not a northern Yankee!"

Sid, Nelly Milner, and Billy Richardson stood together; the *Alabama* swiftly sinking under them, by the stern, which was now almost level with the water.

"Nelly," said Sid, "why didn't you go in one of the boats?"

"I'll take my chance here," said Nelly. "I'm not afraid. If I live I live, and if I die I die."

Sandy Aspinall, standing near by, heard the words, and was moved. But he kept silence.

"Sandy, what of you?" said Sid.

"I'm all right," said Sandy, quietly.

He seemed to be keeping a protecting guard on Nelly. A strange conflict was going on in his mind.

The *Alabama* quivered – shook – like one in a fatal spasm.

"Poor old *Alabama*!" said Captain Semmes. "She's done. Now, my lads, jump, and save yourselves."

As Semmes spoke, the bow of the Alabama rose high in air, and down she went into the depths of the sea, stern-first; making a whirlpool and a bubbling where she sank.

The water was full of bobbing heads and swimming bodies.

Steaming rapidly towards the men in the water came the yacht, *Deerhound*; bent on rescuing as many as possible. Captain Semmes, an excellent swimmer, struck out for the *Deerhound*. As he did so, he heard a gurgling cry behind him. It was Bartelli, the steward, sinking for the second time. Semmes turned about, but he was too late. Bartelli sank again before he could be reached. "Poor Bartelli!" thought Semmes. "I thought he could swim. The faithful fellow has sacrificed himself in order to stand by me to the last!"

Captain Semmes and many of his crew were picked up by the *Deerhound*;[172] others by the little yachts and fishing boats but a dozen were drowned. Sid Clifton made for a fishing boat, and was helped in. He glanced round him, and beheld Nelly Milner, a few yards away, and Sandy Aspinall close besides her. Nelly was quite exhausted. "Surely Sandy will not let her drown," said Sid, and was about to plunge in to save her himself, when Sandy swam up to her, and held her up. Only her head was out of water; her male attire could not be seen; and now she appeared to Sandy the real Nelly Milner he had known, though with a face changed by sorrow.

"Let me be, Sandy," she gasped. "If you can't forgive me, let me drown!"

Sandy looked into her eyes; then he grasped her firmly; and made for the boat in which Sid sat watching this strange re-union of two lovers.

XXIX. No News.

The news of the destruction of the *Alabama* spread swiftly all over England, and reached Preston. Ada was all anxiety as to the fate of Sid; and Chartist Grimshaw went out to make inquiries. He found Edwin Waugh at the Virgin's Inn, reading a description of the fight and sinking of the *Alabama* from a Manchester paper.

"Who's lost and who's saved?" asked Old Chartist.

"Captain Semmes and about forty men of the *Alabama's* crew were picked up by the *Deerhound* and taken to Southampton, thus escaping capture by the *Kearsage*, which seems to have been very slow at making any effort to rescue the men in the water. The captain of the *Kearsage* is wroth at the escape of Semmes; and says he ought to be delivered up as a prisoner of war. He futher accused the *Deerhound* of being in arrangement with the *Alabama* to help Semmes away. But I think that's all nonsense. Captain Semmes indignantly denies the charge. And he may rest assured that Britain won't give Semmes up to his enemies. Indeed, the public at Southampton are making quite a fuss of him. He's the hero of the hour. Gentleman, clergymen are vieing with each other in offering him hospitality. Ladies are writing sweet congratulatory notes to him."

"But who's saved and who's lost?" repeated Old Chartist.

"As I have said," continued Waugh, "forty or fifty of the *Alabama's* crew were picked up by the *Deerhound*. The paper says that the bulk of the remainder ware saved by a couple of French pilot boats which happpened to be about, while sundry other surviors were rescued by some fishing-smacks. Nine men on board the *Alabama* were killed during the engagement, and twenty-one wounded. When the boat sank, eleven or twelve men were drowned."

"Is the name of Sid Clifton amongst the killed?" asked Old Chartist.

"No," said Waugh, "nor among the drowned. Sidney Clifton and Sandy Aspinall, both of Preston, are reported amongst the missing. But as no tidings have been heard of them, it is assumed that they have been drowned."

Old Chartist sighed.

"They were both swimmers," he said.

"But they may have been wounded, and so disabled from swimming," said Waugh, "or drawn into the vortex made by the sinking ship and sucked down. A great many more would have been drowned, no doubt, but for the timely humanity of the *Deerhound*."

There was no mention of Billy Richardson and Mat Miner (that is Nelly Milner). In the rush of preparation for the fight the paymaster had omitted to enter their names onto the *Alabama*'s roll. Billy Richardson, however, was lying in a hospital at Southampton; he had been picked up, exhausted, by the *Deerhound*.

"It seems to me," said Waugh, "that the *Alabama* would have won but for the Yankee captain's trick of protecting his vessel's sides with chains. Within thirty minutes from the beginning of the combat Semmes says he had sent shots which would have sunk the *Kearsage* but for the chain dodge; and according to all evidence he is quite right. It took the *Kearsage* an hour and ten minutes to get home the shot which sunk the *Alabama*. Captain Semmes was heavily handicapped; and unfairly, he says. Well, so ends the career of the *Alabama*. After all her renowned adventures she has found a fitting and worthy tomb in the English Channel, the grave of so many of the gallant ships once commanded by Britain's sea-kings; the scene of so many brave fights and British victories in the old days; the water where Drake and his worthy comrades chased, harassed and defeated the Invincible Spanish Armada. The *Alabama* is honoured in her end; she lies in the English Channel, the Westminster Abbey of the seas, in great and glorious company."

Chartist Grimshaw rose and sadly left the Virgin's Inn. He had a doleful tale to take home and he shrank from the task of telling it. More than once as he neared Duckworth-street, where the Milners lived, he turned back, unable to proceed with his fatal message, and wandered aimlessly about the town.

He met Mr. Treebarn returning from Higher Walton.

"I have been to visit Mrs. Wragley," said Mr. Treebarn, "and I am much concerned for her; Mr. Wragley has begged me to see her often and give her what consolation I can. But I make no impression on her. She sits mourning, gloomy, silent, oblivious of all things but two – that her son is dead and that she longs to see his slayer executed. She is heedless to all talk of forgiveness, of mercy; all gentler thoughts are dead within her. She sits like a living stone, petrified by a cold mania for revenge. It is only the hope and desire for the capture and hanging of her son's murderer that keeps her alive. But for that she would die."

"Her son was as much a murderer as Ted Banister is – and more," said Chartist.

"It is a world of strangely tangled deeds," said Mr. Treebarn. "So awful is the mystery that it is best for us not to presume to judge anyone. I am sorely grieved for the woman."

"So am I for the matter o' that," said Old Chartist. "I am sorry for all who suffer. And I've got to take home a tale that will make more suffering. There's no news of Sid Clifton."

"No news is good news," said Mr. Treebarn.

"That can hardly be in this case. I'm afraid to face poor Ada. I'm no coward, but I dare not break such news as this."

"Shall I go with you?" asked Mr. Treebarn.

"I'd be glad if you would," answered Old Chartist.

The minister and the old man went to the Milner's cottage together.

Ada started and looked piteously into Old Chartist's face as he entered. "Tell me," she whispered.

"There's no news, my lass," said Old Chartist.

Ada burst into tears.

"Hope, hope!" said Mr. Treebarn, and he talked all the hope he could.

But Ada only wept.

[16 February 1901]

XXX. Hurrying Home

Sid Clifton was lying ill in the house of the French fisherman whose boat had saved him and Nelly Milner and Sandy. Coming from the hot engine-room to be immersed in the sea had struck a chill into Sid and when he was got ashore he began to feel very ill. Then pneumonia attacked him and he became feverish and delirious.

The French fisherman was a good and generous soul, and fortunately could speak considerable English. He fetched a doctor; and he and his wife did all they could for the invalid.

But Nelly saw that Sid would be laid up for several weeks and resolved to stay with him till he was well. She had no fear of a fatal issue; the doctor, too, said he believed Sid would pull thorough his illness all right; he was young and strong and had a healthy constitution.

"Well, if you stay, I'll stay," said Sandy to Nelly. "Indeed I should stay with Sid in any case. He has been a good chum to me."

"If I'm any impediment to your staying – if you'd rather I went away," Nelly said to Sandy, "I will go."

Sandy smiled. "I'll stay with you, Nelly," he said. "That's if you'll let me – and – and – if you'll not run away from me again."

"No fear of that," said Nelly solemnly. "Oh! Sandy, I was a fool – but I have learned my lesson. I can never forgive myself for the wrong I did you."

"I have forgiven you," said Sandy.

"You are not myself," said Nelly. "But I am glad I have your forgiveness, Sandy; I must have been out of my senses when I went away. I must have been bewitched. Indeed, I was; but the spell was soon broken. Before I got to Salt Lake City I realised what an error I had made – and knew that I only wanted one man in all the world and that man was you."

They were alone. Sandy kissed her.

With her lover's arm still about her Nelly went on, "And when I knew that I still loved you and that in a wild, passing fancy I had given myself to another man I wished I were dead."

"Let us not talk of this any more," said Sandy, a shadow on his brow. "Let us try to forget it. I am trying hard to remember it no more; it is not pleasant. I have forgiven you everything; let it rest at that." He was gloomy for a few moments; thoughts of his sweetheart's past, whether voluntary or by force of circumstance, were exceedingly painful to him. But he looked in Nelly's eyes, now true and faithful, and brightened up.

"Our life begins afresh from this time," he said. "We will have no past; we will have only the present and the future."

Sandy felt that though this joy could not be the same as it might have been if his sweetheart had not forsaken him for a period, there was still enough joy left to make a happy future for him and her; and he was content. He felt too, and was glad, that Nelly loved him more sincerely and deeply, and clung to him more than ever she had done before. He could safely trust his heart to her now. All flightiness, all fickleness, were taken out of her by trial and sorrow and though, in one sense, she was less pure, materially, than when he had first wooed her, she was in the highest sense, spiritually, purified by her affliction, and was a nobler and better woman than ever he had known her.

"I am longing to see you in woman's attire," said Sandy. "The oddity of seeing you dressed as a man was a shock to me – and it is so still. Perhaps it's only a whim; but I'm sure I should feel better to see you as you ought to be."

"I am eager to make the change myself," said Nelly; "and would effect it at once if I could. But it wouldn't do to make it now as you will admit. Our good French friends would be surprised, and not know what to make of us. But, soon as we get to England, I'll be a woman again in quicksticks –"

"And then I'll marry you," said Sandy smiling, "for, you know, I cannot marry you while you are a man."

She nestled her head on his shoulder worshipingly; and Sandy thrilled as he realised that he was her sole idol now.

"Sandy, you are too good for me," she said. "I am not worthy of you."

"You are quite good enough for me," said Sandy.

"I will always strive to be," she said, tears in her eye, "nay, I will be."

Sandy caressed her.

"Are you sure you can trust me again?" she whispered.

Sandy's answer was an emphatic kiss. Nelly was silent. But though she spoke not, Sandy knew her thought, he felt it. She was saying to herself that such a noble trust should never be betrayed. Thus trust makes fidelity.

"Now, what about Sid?" said Sandy. "His friends in Preston – your sister Ada, – will believe that he perished with the *Alabama*. Hadn't we better send some word? Sid is unconscious and can't do anything himself. But I know, that if he could speak a message, it would be this – 'Write to Ada.'"

"We will send some word," said Nelly. "And we will send it at once. But I don't wish Ada to know who the sender is. I don't want our folks to know anything about me till I appear before them in person."

"What shall be done then?" asked Sandy.

"We will send a note just saying that Sid and yourself are all right. We will not sign any name; and we'll address it to Ada."

This was done, and an envelope containing only the following lines, "Sid Clifton and Sandy Aspinall are saved and all right. Tell their parents," addressed to Ada Milner at Preston.

"Now let us get to our patient," said Nelly.

The doctor called shortly afterwards, and said that Sid was progressing favourably. The worst was over now. It would be safe for him to set off for home in a week or ten days.

This was nearly a month after the sinking of the *Alabama*.

Sandy, hearing one day that the English steam-yacht which had done such good service when the *Alabama* went down, was again in Cherbourg, went down to the docks, and found the *Deerhound*. He asked to see the owner, Mr. Lancaster, and was ushered into his cabin. Mr. Lancaster, a genial type of the Lancashire squire, was pleased to find there were more survivors of the *Alabama*, and said that he should be delighted to convey Sandy and his companions to Liverpool in the *Deerhound*. Sandy told the narrative of Sid's illness, and said he would be ready for removing in a week.

"Well, the *Deerhound* will be here for that time," said Mr. Lancaster, "and can wait longer, if necessary. I shall be happy to do you and your chums this little service."

Then Sandy, shyly, and in some confusion, related the story of Nelly Milner.

"This is quite a romance," said Mr. Lancaster. "The young woman was very fortunate to get away from the Mormons. And how strange she should be a passenger on the very last vessel captured by the *Alabama*. You must bring her down here to-morrow. My wife will be pleased to see her."

"But she's in men's clothes," said Sandy.

Mr. Lancaster laughed. "My wife will find her some female rig-out," she said. "She has plenty to spare."

Sandy thanked Mr. Lancaster, and went to tell Nelly and Sid the good news that the *Deerhound* would take them to Liverpool, whence they could quickly proceed by railway to Preston.

"That's all right, then," said Sid, who was convalescent. "Won't we make a surprise in Preston?"

XXXI. On the Landing Stage

But Ada Milner had not received the message sent by Nelly and Sandy. Mr. Hyde had it in his pocket.

The Mormon had rejoiced at the news of the destruction of the *Alabama*. He had rejoiced still more, secretly, when he learned that Sid Cifton was amongst the missing. And his rejoicing was at the height when, after the lapse of three weeks there came no tidings of Sid Clifton, and everyboy concluded that he must be drowned.

Even Ada herself had given up hope, though she sometimes thought that her lover must somehow have escaped death, and would yet turn up.

But her mother said, "I wish I could think so Ada, but I can't. If he was alive, something surely would have been heard of him, or from him. I'm afraid he must be dead. Don't fret lass, don't fret."

Mr. Hyde had been constantly at the Milner's cottage since the loss of the *Alabama*. But he was tactful; and made no mention of the matter of Ada's mourning. He kept an attitude of quiet respectful sympathy. He firmly believed that Sid was dead; and that now there would not be very much difficulty in persuading Ada to go to the Mormon City. She would not care what became of her now.

And the Mormon had now a very strong ally in Mrs. Milner; who truly had a yearning to go to America to see her daughter Nelly, who had been her favourite child. She had no idea that Nelly had succeeded in getting away from Salt Lake City. Hyde knew this fact, but, for his own purposes, he kept it back from Mrs. Milner. He had had a private letter from Salt Lake City, informing him of Nelly's escape, and instructing him to keep a look-out for her, and, when he found her, if he could not compel her to return, to get rid of her so that she could tell no tales. Hyde, in fact, was now commissioned to act as a Destroying Angel and knew that he would be put to death himself, by other Destroying Angels, if he failed to do his duty. He was not quite a novice at this secret murder game, though, for he had more than once assisted the Destroying Angels in America, and had taken a part in the Mountain Meadow Massacre. He had spies out in Liverpool and Preston, on the watch for Nelly Milner. If she eluded the vigilance of his hirelings and got home, he knew that all hope of securing Ada for himself would be gone. He took every precaution to prevent this event happening.

Mrs. Milner said to Ada, a fortnight after the loss of the *Alabama*, "Ada, let us go to America, and see Nelly. There's nothing to stay here for now. You've nothing to stay for neither. Sid is dead. Let us go away."

Ada, tearfully, in her despair said she was not particular where she went. But if she went to America she would not have anything to do with Mr. Hyde.

"Nobody's asking you to have anything to do with him," said her mother. "I think he's a very nice man, but you can please yourself what you think about him. But, you've no objection to his going back on the same boat that we take, have you?"

"I don't care about anything," said Ada.

"Well, I've made up my mind to go to see Nelly," said Mrs. Milner. "You'll go with me, won't you?"

Ada did not wish to desert her mother; she knew her parent's weakness, and her gullibility, and how easily she could be imposed upon by plausible persons. If her mother got to Salt Lake City she might even become another of the numerous wives of some Mormon. Ada shuddered at the thought; it would be enough to make her father turn in his grave. Therefore, though she had no desire to go to Salt Lake City, she said she would accompany her mother, who was not to be persuaded from making the journey.

And Hyde rejoiced. For he knew that if he once got Ada in Salt Lake City there would be no escape for her; she would be his.

"What shall we do with our furniture?" Ada asked her mother.

"We'll sell up," replied Mrs. Milner.

"I have another idea," said Ada. "Old Chartist is fetching Mrs. Hagan and her children out of the workhouse next week. He has not got a house for them. Let him have this house, and pay the rent for it."

"But what about our furniture?" said Mr. Milner.

"It will thus be all right for us when we come back."

"But supposing we don't come back?"

"There's no supposing about that," said Ada; and her mother thought it best to keep silence. For Hyde, in order to gain his ends, had actually told Mrs. Milner that it was she he really wanted to marry, and not Ada; that he was merely being as agreeable as possible to the daughter in order that she would not object to her mother's intended second husband; and the silly woman believed him.

Chartist Grimshaw was delighted with Ada's proposal that he should take the cottage; but he said he would rather there was a different cause for his opportunity, and begged Ada not to go near Salt Lake City.

Mr. Treebarn, hearing the news of Mrs. Milner's determination to go to America, also had a serious talk with Ada; his wife adding her pleadings to his.

"If you once get among the Mormons you are doomed, Ada," he said.

Ada seemed indifferent to the minister's arguments and entreaties. "I think I can take care of myself," she said. "Further, I intend to bring Nelly back with me. And I must go for the sake of mother. She has set her heart on going, and I cannot let her go alone. I must do my duty towards her. I know you wouldn't have me break the commandment which tells us to honour our parents. But have no fear for me. I shall certainly come back, though I have nothing much to come back for. But I promise you I shall come back."

"The despair of your bereavement has made you reckless, Ada," said Mr. Treebarn kindly. "But bear up, and hope. Sid may be found yet."

"You know there is no hope now," said Ada.

"Hope or no hope," said Mr. Treebarn, "do not trust this Mormon."

"I don't trust him, and never shall," said Ada. "I shall only go to Salt Lake City with some caravan of non-Mormons that is passing through. I will not be trapped, I assure you."

"Planning is one thing, but carrying out is another," said Mr. Treebarn.

However, Aa was not to be moved from the decision to go with her mother.

The day after Mr. Treebarn's talk with Ada the postman had a letter for the Milners. It was the letter from Cherbourg; and was addressed to Ada, who was out at the sewing. As it happened Mr. Hyde was with Ada's mother when the postman deliverd the letter.

"Ths letter's for Ada," said Mrs. Milner. "I wonder where it's from."

"Let me see," said Hyde. Mrs. Milner handed him the letter.

"Cherbourg!" he said with a start. "I think you had better open this letter, Mrs. Milner.

"You open it for me," said Mrs. Milner.

Hyde needed no second telling. He tore the envelope open, extracted the sheet of paper and read aloud: "Sid Clifton and Sandy Aspinall are saved and all right. Tell their parents."

"If Ada gets that letter she won't go to America," said Mrs. Milner, significantly.

"Then I'll take charge of it," said Hyde, putting the letter into his pocket.

He was prepared to descend to any villainy now to make sure of the prize which was so near at last. He swore to himself that he would not have all his scheming brought to naught at the last minute – just when the treasure, long coveted, long striven for, was within his grasp.

The news that Sid Clifton was alive after all filled Hyde with a vicious feeling. "He had better have died," he said to himself savagely, "it will be worse than death for him to come back from the grave and find his beloved gone – and gone with me. I would like to see his face when he returns and learns. I am having a grander revenge than ever I dreamed. He struck me once on the face when he was going away; I shall have struck him through the heart, not with a merciful material weapon to end his tortures, but with an invisible agony that will make his soul writhe in torment as long as he lives."

Hyde turned to Mrs. Milner. "We must hasten our departure," he said.

"I am ready now," said Mrs. Milner.

"Fortunately our vessel sails in four days. However, we will get to Liverpool as soon as we can; we can lodge there till the ship sails. We can tell Ada that it is necessary to go to Liverpool for a few days to make arrangements. We must not delay now. The persons who have sent the note I have now in my pocket may return any day; we must make all sure."

Ada, unsuspecting that there had been any message from or about her lover whom she mourned as dead, had no objection to going to Liverpool; so a couple of days afterwards Ada and her mother stood on Preston station platform awaiting the train that was to take them to the great busy seaport at the mouth of the Mersey. Hyde had gone to Liverpool the day before. With considerable cunning he had told Mrs. Milner that it would be best for him not to be seen going away with her and Ada; it would be folly to excite suspicion. Nobody need know that he was returing to America by the same boat. But, that he might not lose any delicious morsel of his revenge he meant to write from New York to Mr. Treebarn, telling him to inform Sid Clifton that Ada and her mother were on their way to Salt Lake City with Elder Willard Hyde, Mormon missionary. This intended letter would serve a double purpose; it would also be a whip on the back of Mr. Treebarn, who had dared to scandalise the Mormon religion and personally insult one of its respected missionaries – to wit, Elder Willard Hyde.

The morning of "Good-by to England" came. The day was dull, but without rain; a strong south-west wind was driving the water back up the river, and lashing the waves into a foam.

Ada and her mother and Mr. Hyde stood on the landing stage waiting for the passenger-tug that was to take them out to the big American liner lying in the river. Mr. Hyde was all smiles and chat. But Ada paid no heed to his words. She was thinking of how Sid had set sail from this very river – his eyes had surveyed this scene – the long line of docks – the ferry-boats crossing between the two shores of the river, to Birkenhead and New Brighton, – the little boats darting up and down – all the busy life and motion of the great waterway – the city spires and domes behind, the forest of masts in the docks, all these Sid had seen when he set sail from this port – when he sailed away and came not back. Perhaps he had even stood on this very spot, thinking of her, as now she thought of him. And now he was dead, and could think of her no more.

Tears trickled into Ada's eyes as she stood in this sad reverie.

"Here's our tender coming," said Hyde. "Ah!" he chuckled to himself, Ada would soon be safely his now.

A steam-yacht was seen coming up the river, and making for the landing stage just before the passenger tender for the Armeican boat. The tender edged along to get a little further down the landing stage.

"This way," said Hyde to Ada and her mother, "here's our tender."

Mrs. Milner and Ada turned to follow him.

Then Ada heard a voice that thrilled her through.

"Ada!" It was the voice of Sid Clifton.

Trembling with emotion, doubt, joy, Ada turned and beheld Sid leaping along the gangway of the steam-yacht, and running towards her, and behind him was – could she believe her eyes? – her sister Nelly and Sandy Aspinall!

[23 February 1901]

XXXI. (Continued)

Mrs. Milner had turned round too; and when she beheld the daughter she thought was thousands of miles away she uttered an exclamation of surprise and joy, and fainted on the landing-stage. Nelly Milner ran to her mother and knelt by her side; raising the fallen woman's head.

"Thank God! she's only fainted," said Nelly, fearing at first that the shock might have had more serious consequences.

Hyde stood a couple of yards off, alone, his face full of awful emotions, and his hands clenched and restless, despite the strong self-control he had over himself.

Though there were many people on the landing-stage, hurrying this way and that, in their own directions, they were so engrossed in their own affairs that only a few idlers, in curiosity, paused to watch the little drama in which Ada Milner, Nelly Milner, their mother, Sid Clifton, Sandy Aspinall, and the Mormon were taking part in such a startling and unexpected impromptu way. The usual landing-stage frequenters and officials were too used to strange scenes to take any particular notice of the incident.

"Nelly!" said Ada, "is it really you?"

"As you see me!" said Nelly, embracing Ada and kissing her.

"And have you escaped from –"

"I have escaped," interrupted Nelly.

"This is wonderful and joyful," said Ada. "And Sid – oh Sid – we thought you were dead!"

Sid folded his sweetheart in his arms and kissed her. "How's that for dead?" he said, laughing.

There were smiles, tears, excited exclamations, broken speech, amongst the friends and lovers thus so curiously brought together again. Mr. Lancaster, leaning over the side of his yacht with his wife by his side, was enjoying the occasion excellently.

Then Mrs. Milner opened her eyes; and looked like one awakening from a bewildering dream. "It's true," she said, "it's true," as she looked up into Nelly's face.

Sid and Sandy helped Mrs. Milner to her feet.

Hyde, still watching the group with feelings of one in the very hell of disappointment, saw, with a side-glace at the water, that the passenger tender was filled, and ready for starting for the Atalantic steamer. – And all his schemes had come to naught and he was defeated and down.

He looked maliciously at the group of re-united ones; who had all forgotten him, and noticed him not.

Ada, Sid, and Nelly were standing on the edge of the platform, against the chains that ran along the edge of the stage.

Hyde thought that if he ran at them with a strong push he could knock the three into the river.

And as a Destroying Agel he was commissioned to slay Nelly Milner. If he let her escape, he would have to suffer death himself.

On the impulse he made up his mind, and in a paroxysm of hate ran at the three he had marked out for victims. They were turned sideways towards him and saw him not.

But Sandy Aspinall, who had just chanced to look at the Mormon, saw him, and guessed his intention. Sandy with a shout leapt forward and just managed to deal Hyde a blow on the shoulder as he was crashing into the trio he had doomed. Sandy's blow caused Hyde to swerve and reel aside but did not check his terrible impetuous rush; and with a startled cry, the Mormon fell over the edge of the landing-stage into the water, right under the bow of the *Deerhound*.

Instant efforts were made to save him; a life-belt was thrown; but in vain; he sank.

Nelly Milner turned to Sandy Aspinall.

"Twice you have saved my life now," she said.

"Give it into my care, and I will save it a third time – for life," said Sandy smiling as only a lover smiles.

Ada, touched by the horror of Hyde's end, and the excitement at the accident, clung to Sid in a half-fainting condition.

Mr. Lancaster called to Sid, "Come on the yacht," he cried. Sid led Ada on the boat, and Mrs. Lancaster made a cup of tea for her and for Mrs. Milner and Nelly.

"Better stay on the yacht to-day and go home to-morrow," said Mr. Lancaster.

"I'd rather get to Preston, thank you, Mr. Lancaster," said Sid. "My parents are longing to see me, you know."

"Only natural," said Mr. Lancaster. "Well, we won't detain you."

"We must thank you for all the services you have done us," said Sid.

"Nothing to make a speech about," said Mr. Lancaster, "You and your sweetheart have had a strange time of it, – and just missed being parted for ever by this Mormon. I hope the future will be bright and happy for you."

Presently, when Hyde's body had been recovered and taken to the mortuary, and the curious crowd had cleared off the landing-stage, Sid and Ada, and Sandy and Nelly, and Mrs. Milner, left the *Deerhound* and made their way for the station, where they booked for Preston.

In the train, gleeful in the reunion, misdst many questions and explanations, and exclamations of wonder and congratulation and delight, the lovers told the tale of what had befallen them since they last saw each other; and how the *Alabama* had taken Nelly from the *Golden Star*; and how Sid had been ill at Cherbourg; and how Mr. Lancaster has offered the use of the *Deerhound*, and many other things, including the sad death of Lily.

And Nelly said, "But we sent a message from Cherbourg saying that Sid and Sandy were alive and well. Didn't you get it?"

"I never got any letter," said Ada.

Mrs. Milner, in some confusion and shame, faltered out, "Mr. Hyde got the letter – it came when he was in and you were out, Ada – and he kept it. I was weak enough to let him. I've been an old fool. That man bewitched me, I think."

"Well, all's ended well, and we forgive you, mother," said Sid, cheerfully.

"But you shouldn't have done a thing like that, mother," said Nelly. "How terrible it would have been if the *Deerhound* had not reached Livepool when she did, and Ada had gone to the horrors of Salt Lake City."

"I should not have stayed there," said Ada.

"That's all you know about it," said Nelly, and proceeded to tell her story.

Indeed, there was so much to tell and talk about that not half the histories were told by the time the train reached Preston.

Coming out of the station, the party heard a well-known sound, and saw "Whistling Will" plying his shrill vocation in the street. Will rejoiced to see Sid and Sandy, and was very much surprised to behold Nelly Milner. "Though I heard yo'd escaped fro th' Mormons," he said.

"Who told you?" asked Nelly.

"Billy Richardson, in th' Virgin's Inn, last neet. He arrived home fro Southampton yesterday; an said that he'd met yo, though he were feart that yo'd been lost wi th' *Alabama*, alung wi Sid an Sandy. He'll be rare and fain to know that yo're all alive."

"Well, an how's the whistling business goin on, Will?" asked Sid.

"It's mendin a bit," said Whistling Will. "As yo know, th' cotton panic's getting o'er neaw, one factory after another is startin wark, an they'll soon aw be busy again. An about time they were, too. There's been some clammin i' Lancashire this last twothree year. I've done a bit myself, an it's noan a thing I like. But, like plenty mooar, I've getten so used to short rations that a good square meal would be hard wark for me neaw. My jaws is eaut o' fettle wi havin so little to do."

"You shall come home with us, Will," said Ada, "and we'll have a merry feast of welcome home."

"Well, I think I'll risk it," said Will. "Better dee o' summat than nowt. But I'm doin better than I were doin three months sin. Trade's briskenin, an there's mooar brass stirrin. Last week but one I drawed a ha'penny mooar than I had done for two year. I thowt that were a good sign. An last week I took a penny mooar; so this week I'm expectin I shall make twopence extra than th' cotton panic wages."

Whistling Will's hearers laughed good-humouredly, and took him along with them.

When they reached Mrs. Milner's cottage, and entered, Old Chartist Grimshaw could not speak for rapturous astonishment. When, after a minute's amazed silence, he managed to produce his voice, he shouted "Hurrah!"

XXXII. The Answer

The weather was crisp cold, December time. The valley of the Ribble was bare, and the river crept through wintry fields and by flowerless hillsides. But the stars were bright at night, and cheerful Christmas was approaching.

Sid and Ada were man and wife now; as were Sandy and Nelly. There had been a double wedding, Mr. Treebarn officiating. The minister held that Nelly Milner's Mormon marriage was not binding, as the man had already several wives before she went away with him. He thanked God that Nelly had escaped, and got safely home.

Sandy and Nelly had a small house of their own; but Sid and Ada had lived with Mrs. Milner, not wishing to be left all alone, for some months till she died. She had never been quite well since her return from Liverpool. The scene on the landing-stage and the shock of Hyde's awful death, had affected her. She died when Ada and Sid had been married three months.

Old Chartist Grimshaw and his daughter, Mrs. Hagan, and her children, were living in a small cottage not far from the house of Sid and Ada.

The war was over; the Southern States having been vanquished; and the cotton mills and weaving-sheds were hard at work again; and the people knew the joy of "pay-day" once more. Sid was engaged as engineer at Mr. Wragley's spinning factory; and was paid excellent wages. Mr. Wragley was a changed man since his son's death; a better and more considerate employer, and kindlier with all with whom he came in contact.

But Mrs. Wragley was strange and morose. Day after day, night after night, she sat brooding in her desolate home, thinking only bitterness and revenge. Every morning her question was, "Is the murderer yet caught?" And then she was silent for the day. She took no interest in anything; would not converse with anyone. Her husband was alarmed for her sanity. He had doctors to see her, but she repulsed them.

Thus she sat, week after week, month after month, absorbed only in one thought, "Is the murderer yet caught?"

There came Christmas – the merriest Christmas Lancashire had known for three years, for all the cotton mills were at work now and people were recovering, though only slowly, from the effects of the cotton panic – and Christmas passed and the New Year came, with ringing of joyful bells; but this woman had no thought of Christmas, with its sweetening memories; nor of New Year, with its good fellowship and forgiveness of the past; she only sat in her lonely room as in a living tomb – mourning, mourning mourning and longing for the law's revenge on the wronged man who had slain her son. "Is the murder not yet caught?"

She never thought, having no imagination, that she herself might not be altogether blameless to the matter of her son's death. She never asked herself had she trained him rightly; had she set his feet in the path of righteousness? She never saw that by spoiling him with money, by teaching him to think that he was superior to the common people, by letting him believe that all the world was only a plaything for him she had put him in the path which led to his ruin and tragic doom. She blamed everything but herself and him. She had no idea that whatever a man reaps he must have sown[173] somewhere, sometime. She thought that God and the universe had dealt cruelly and unjustly with her and her son. She would have risen in rage if anyone had hinted that she and her son, she by her over-indulgence to him, he by his vicious life, had brought their fate upon themselves.

But of such considerations, moral and social, she never thought. She had only one all-absorbing thought and desire; and that a base one: to have an eye for an eye, a life for a life.

"Is the murderer not yet caught?"

Sometimes she railed at the police. What was the law doing that it was so slow in laying its hands on the guilty wretch? Were the police asleep?

There came a warm, wet spring night, dark, with a drizzing rain; that gentle pattering, caressing rain which is only the moist kiss of the sun to the earth; the rain that rouses flower and bud to vernal greenery.

Mrs. Wragley sat in her room alone. Her husband was away in Manchester on business and would not be home till ten o'clock; the time now being eight o'clock. She was all alone in a sitting-room whose windows opened on to the garden. One of the side windows was unfastened and slightly open because of the warmth of the night. The servants were all in the rear of the house.

The forlorn woman, with her hard, coarse face, heavy jaw, low forehead, thick nose and lips, and hair grown grey, sat all alone thinking only one thing. "Is the murderer caught yet?"

She was dressed in black; a heavy gold watch chain on her bosom; and glittering rings on her hands. She has always had a love of jewelled display; and now, even when she had no more thought of these vulgarities, wore them because she had got in the habit of wearing them.

The doctor told her husband that the thought of revenge was the only thing which was keeping Mrs. Wragley alive. That desire satisfied, or gone, and she would collapse and die.

Mr. Treebarn, at Wragley's earnest request, visited her frequently, but he could not move her in any way. Sweet preaching, pure prayers, compassionate fellowship, had no effect on her. "Let God do justice on my son's murderer," she said, "and then I will think of dealing with Him."

This utterance, and many similar ones, shocked the good Mr. Wragley. He strove to coax the hard bitter feelings of revenge out of this woman; but in vain. She said she did not care about her soul; all she wanted was law on the murderer. But as a rule, she refused to speak with Mr. Wragley; and when he talked with her, her ears heard him not.

On this damp dark evening she sat alone, thinking, as she thought every hour of the day and many hours of the night, how she had sat up alone, on the night of the murder, waiting for the midnight coming of the son who never came. She remembered how she concluded that he was only staying out all night in a gentlemanly fashion, with gentlemen, as he had often done before; and went to bed with very little uneasiness. She remembered how she grew anxious when next day brought him not home, nor the days following; and how a horrible anxiety had grown upon her that something awful had happened to him. She remembered the dreadful discovery of the body, and the cruel agony that had struck her with the news of his death. He had suffered; she had suffered – all her proud hopes of seeing her son high and great in the land because of his riches were darkly dashed to pieces; and so his slayer should suffer, "a life for a life."

When would those stupid police catch the murderer?

There was a slight scraping sound near the half-open window. She started. She was about to call for help when the side-window opened wide, and a white face and wild eyes, and thin bony hands, sprang into the luxurious room.

"You needn't be afraid," he said. "I shan't hurt you. You're Mrs. Wragley, aren't you?"

"Who are you?" asked Mrs. Wragley. "How do you know me? What do you want?"

"I want many things, but most of all, – peace. My name is Ted Banister, and I am the man who killed your son."

[2 March 1901]

XXXII. (Continued)

Mrs. Wragley tried to shriek, but the sound was crushed into a startled squeak. "Oh, where are the police?" she said to herself.

"I have come to ask you to forgive me for my deed," said Ted Banister, piteously. "I am miserable and want to die. I am very sorry that I killed him. I wish I could undo that night's work. I didn't mean to kill him. But we met, and we fought, and I was in a passion, and I have broken his mother's heart, – but I beg you to forgive me."

Mrs. Wragley's voice was strained and harsh. "You deserve to die," she said.

"I know it," said Ted Banister, wearily, "and I pray for death."

"And you shall die!" she exclaimed.

"Then you won't forgive me? For your own sake, for his sake, as well as mine, I ask you to forgive me."

"I will never forgive you till I see you going to the gallows," said Mrs. Wragley.

"Say that you forgive me. You will never have another opportunity of saying it. I have done wrong, I know; but it is wrong, too, to be unmerciful. You will only do evil to me and evil to yourself by being hard. Crime and evil can only be undone by love and forgiveness; this I have learned while hiding in the woods in the night, – the trees have told it me, the stars have told it me; God had told it me."

"This man is mad," said Mrs. Wragley to herself and began to be afraid of him.

Ted Banister strode towards her sharply, and seized her wrist. "If you shout," he said, and his manner was strange and fierce now, "I will choke you. I have asked you to forgive me, and you will not. Well, you shall be accursed as I have been accursed; and when your soul is longing to forgive me, for its own salvation, it shall long in vain."

He released her hand, and she fell back in her chair, overcome with fright. She tried to call out for help, but no sound came from her lips. What had happened seemed to have paralysed her speech. After a time she managed to rise from her chair, and ring the bell. A servant-maid entered the room. Mrs. Wragley opened her mouth to speak but could make no sound. Horrified she went to a little desk, and took out a sheet of note-paper, on which she wrote, in bad spelling and grammar, "The murderer of my son as been here. I am all upset. Send word to the polise at once. He came in at the window, an we was together a while. He went out throo the window. It as struck me dum."

Mrs. Wragley never recovered her speech; she was dumb to the day of her death, which was only a few months after this incident.

While the police were being communicated with, Ted Banister had made his way to the river-bank. In a sort of frenzy he plunged into the water, and, as if by a miracle, could not drown, but eventually found himself on the other bank.

Sid Clifton and Ada were just having a slight supper ere retiring to bed when there was a slight knock at the door.

"Sounds like a beggar," said Ada, "give him this piece of cake."

Sid opened the door and started as he saw in the light cast from the gas of the house on the gloom of the street, a weird, dripping, mud-daubed object, like a man, with a pale, piteous face.

"It's Ted Banister," said the desolate being. "The police are after me – let me in, Sid."

"My God!" said Sid; and Ada, who had come and stood behind him, shivered under a sudden thought of a scaffold and hangman.

"Come in, Ted," said Sid, "we'll not give you up, anyhow. We'll hide you and get you away if we can," and he dragged the outcast inside the house and shut the door.

"Give him a drink of something warm, Ada," Sid went on. "Sit down against the fire, Ted old chap. I know your tale and I pity you more than I blame you. Where've you been?"

"Everywhere, but chiefly in hell," said Ted. "I wish I hadn't killed him. I didn't know what I'd done till it was done. But I had some justification; he dealt worse than death to me. I was merciful and only gave him death."

Ada handed Ted a cup of hot tea. His teeth chattered against the edge of the cup as he sipped the liquid. "I've rambled up and down everywhere," he said, "ever since that night. I met him accidentally and I couldn't help telling him what I thought of him. It would have been best to have passed him by; I wish I had. He was half-drunk and we quarrelled and fought on the river-bank. Fury filled me – I was a demon for the time – and I had thrown him into the water before I knew what I was doing. I heard a splash – I heard his cry; and I knew his blood was on my soul. But you don't think badly of me, do you, Sid? You don't really think that I'm a deliberate murderer, do you?"

"Most certainly not," said Sid kindly.

"I rushed away from the spot like a madman," said Ted. "I ran and ran the night out; all day long I hid in a wood; afraid to stir for fear of seeing a policeman. I hid many days and I starved. Then hunger made me bold and I wandered into the Black Country[174] – which is full of fires and furnaces, just like hell. It was real hell to me, anyhow. I got a bit of work in the Black Country – all the blacksmiths were busy making contraband of war; making bullets for the Confederates.[175] The place was busy and prosperous; quite a contrast to Lancashire, where I had left the people clamming in a famine. I worked for a while myself, but I was always uneasy; always dreading to feel a policeman's hand on my shoulder; always feeling my guilt and thinking that everybody could see the brand of

Cain on my brow.[176] – I worked day and night; I was never tired; the folks were amazed at me. Ah, they did not know that I was working so that I could not hear my conscience. I felt a great desire to come and confess my crime to his mother, and beg her forgiveness. So I made my way back here. I have seen her. She would not forgive me; but she will have put the police on my track, I know. I've come through the river – the river that drowned him – at the very spot – but I could not drown! I –"

The cup dropped from his fingers, and broke on the floor with a crash, while the tramp fell back in a fainiting condition.

"Oh, Sid! he looks as if he were dying!" cried Ada. "See how his eyes roll!"

"We must get him to bed," said Sid. "We can put him into the bed that was your mother's."

Mention of her mother reminded Ada of her mourning; her mother had only been buried a month.

Sid roused Ted up and helped him upstairs; and into bed. Ted was in a dazed semi-conscious state; and talked oddly.

"Try to rest Ted, old chap," said Sid. "You're all right here. Get a good night's sleep, and we'll consider what to do tomorrow."

"I can't sleep," said Ted, feebly. "I've never slept properly since that night. There's only one sleep that will sleep me now. Kiss me, Lucy! kiss me to sleep, to the same sleep as yours."

He fell into a doze, and Ted crept softly downstairs.

"Is he asleep?" asked Ada. "Poor Ted Banister! How he must have suffered!"

"He was murmuring about Lucy when I left him," said Sid, "his talk brought tears to my eyes."

There were tears in Ada's eyes too, as she thought of poor betrayed and drowned Lucy, and her lover now in this plight, with the police after him, seeking to take him to execution. And once these two had been happy lovers, – never dreaming that their wooing should come to such a tragedy as this.

Sid and Ada sat up talking about Ted till near midnight. Then they heard the sound of feet on the footpath, and the next instant there was a sharp knock of authority on the door.

Even with the knock, there flashed on Sid what was coming.

"It's the police," he whispered. "I'll run upstairs to warn Ted – to get him away if possible. Don't open the door till they knock again," and Sid, in his stocking-feet,[177] silently passed into the back kitchen towards the foot of the stairs.

There was a louder and still more imperative knock, and Ada opened the door.

Two policemen entered. "We have a warrant for the arrest of Edward Banister," said one, "and we believe he is in this house. We must search the place. Where is your husband?"

"Upstairs," said Ada.

"Then we'll go upstairs," said the policeman, and Ada knew not what to do. The voice of Sid was heard in the back kitchen.

"It's all right, Ada," said Sid, solemnly, stepping forth, and, addressing the policeman, "you can come upstairs. I'll take you."

Ada was bewildered. She sat down in a chair, overcome with emotion, while Sid, followed by the policeman, went upstairs.

Then Ada heard Sid's voice once more, and though she wept, rejoiced. "There's the man you are after," said Sid. "You cannot take him now. For God has taken him. Let God judge him!"

XXXIII. The Song that is a Prayer

A bright summer afternoon. The sunshine is sweet upon the land; and even in the streets of the great manufacturing towns, now brisk with business once more, for the cotton panic is over, and the people are well in work. From the open door of a neat cottage on the green edge of the town of tall smoking chimneys comes the sound of a rocking-chair, and the voice of a mother singing to her beloved babe. On the little table in the little cottage the "tea things" are laid ready for the evening meal; the kettle is singing on the hob; the tea-pot is simmering on the top-bar of the grate. The time is just after half-past five, when the big factories cease work for the day, and the engine rests from its throbbing till the dawn.

The voice of the mother is heard talking to her babe. And surely we know that voice; it is the voice of Ada Clifton, once Ada Milner.

"Dada will be here in a minute now," she says. "Clap hands, dada come!"

Then she laughs as the child smiles, and rocking the chair again, begins to sing the chorus of the song that was sung for many years afterwards by many mothers in Lancashire – for many years after the 'cotton panic' was over – the song that is also a prayer –

> "'Tis the song, the sigh of the weary,
>   Hard times, hard times come again no more;
> Many years have you lingered about my cabin door,
>   O! hard times come again no more."

Teddy Ashton, 'Bill Spriggs an Bet: Their Matrimony an their Marlocks. Bet Turns Bill Eaut' (1901)

On Wensday neet there were a reglar hullibulloo i' Tum Fowt.[1] Bet Spriggs, what had just yeard abeaut Mrs. Jackson, o' Clitheroe,[2] an heaw as women con do what they want neaw, an con please theirsels whether they obey their husbands or not, chucked Bill eaut, an towd him hoo wouldn't keep him any mooar. He'd been eaut o' wark three days, havin geet stopt for speilin a tombstone by writin th' truth on it. Th' tombstone were abeaut a factory-mestur what were a reglar skinflint an bad un. Bill's boss, Owd Stonechopper, forgettin th' mess Bill had made of a previous job, or else thinking Bill had mooar sense neaw, left him to finish th' epitaph, which where "Gone, but not forgotten." Owd Stonechopper had cut the' letterin thus far –

"Gone, but –"

An Bill Spriggs finished it as follows –

"Good Shuttance!"[3]

Th' result were that Owd Stonechopper in a rage sent Bill whum. "Why I've nobbut towd th' truth," says Bill. "Th' truth has no business in this world," says Owd Stonechopper. "Anybody as thinks th' truth will do i' this world is a foo an were better deead. Off wi thee whum, an never let me see they face again."

But Bill had hopes that Owd Stonechopper would tak him on again after he'd cooled deawn a bit.

Meanwhile, Bill had been doin nowt for three days, as yo'n just been towd, an while Bet were eaut on this particular Wensday afternoon he'd made his own tay, and geet a new-laid egg to it. This egg Bet had put on one side for herself, and when hoo come whum an fun it gone, hoo geet in a bonny temper. Bill darsent say that he'd etten th' egg. "I darsay theau's mislaid it," he said to Bet. "Nowt o' t' soart," said Bet, "I'm positive I put it i'th' sugar-basin o' this shelf. Theau's had th' sugar-basin, so theau should ha' seen th' egg." "Happen th' egg's hatched into a chicken an flown away while theau's been eaut," said Bill. "Shut up, theau gobbin!" said Bet, "theau talks like a idiot!" Just then Bet seed a bit o' yallow on Bill's waistcoat. "What's this?" hoo said, coppin howd o' Bill by th' collar of his jacket; "why, it's yolk! Theau villain, theau's etten that egg!" "If I have," said Bill, pathetically, "I know nowt abeaut it, I must ha' done it in my sleep, or been mesmerised." "That tale weren't go deawn wi me," said Bet, beginning to peil Bill, "theau's stown that egg, an had it aw to thy own guts, theau desaver an wastrel! An eaut o' wark too an noan brining a penny in, an wantin new-laid eggs. Clear eaut o' this heause! Th' law says that a woman con chuck her husband eaut neaw, so eaut theau goes! Go to that hussy theau were wi at Blackpool, an see if hoo'll keep thee," an Bet bundled Bill eaut into th' street; Bill noan bein sorry to get eaut of her clutches.

This were abeaut seven o'clock o' th' neet an happened when Sam Snidey, t' bobby,[4] were just slouchin past Spriggs' door. Sammy were suddenly hit wi summat an sent flyin on his back. When he geet up to see what object had struck him, it were Bill Spriggs what had just been slung eaut by his fifty-hoss power wife, who were stood fierce an threatenin in t' door-hole, wi t' rowlin-pin in her hond.

"I'll ha thee locked up for this," said Sam to Bet Spriggs as he brushed t' dust off his uniform; while Bill picked hissel up an seet off runnin for his life, and a twothree inquisitive neighbours gathered reaund.

"Well, lock me up if theau con," said Bet. "Theau darn't try."

"Durn't aggravate me, woman, or yo'll see whether I will or not," said Sam, but he didn't oss for t' goo any ner.

"Shunt, afor I blow thee away," said Bet wi contempt.

"What has yo broken t' peace for?" axed Sam.

"I'll break thee if theau doesn't clear off," said Bet.

"An what han yo thrown yore lord an mestur eaut into t' public 'ighway for?" continued Sam, tryin to talk i' dignified English.

"If t' women o' Tum Fowt had any sense they'd aw do t' same as me. Th' judge has said as women's not to be slaves no mooar. I'm gooin to manage beaut him; let him goo an keep hissel. I'm noan gooin to have a idle chap on my honds. Let him goo to Ameriky wi that brazen thing he ware so thick wi at Blackpool."

Sam made a step forrud an Bet struck him wi t' rowlin-pin. Poor Sam howled an scuttered away.

Meanwhile th' Members o' th' Menociation[5] were at th' Dug an Kennel, lookin at th' President's empty cheer. We'd yerd heaw he'd been turned eaut an tan his hook.[6]

"I think th' world's comin to a end," said Ben Roke. "What wi Mrs. Jacksons, an th' influenza, an bad ale, an one thing an another, it strikes me as t' universe is comin to a collapse."

Just then Bill crept in. He lookt freekunt to death. "By gum," he said, wi chatterin teeth, "this aw comes o' new-laid eggs an a chep trip. Never no mooar. Let's lock this dur."

We bowted t' door an Bill took his seat. "Neaw," said Bill, "what mun I do wi my wife?"

"Theau mun turn on her," said Ben Roke.

"Oh, tis aw very weel sayin 'turn on her.' Hoo doesn't gie thee time for t' turn. Theau't lucky if theau con turn an run."

"Theau's no pluck, Bill," said Joe Lung, "I wish I had her for t' deeal wi."

"So do I," said Bill earnestly. "But, well, there'll be a chance for some on yo to try yore hond at tamin her. I think as it's one o' t' rules o' this Menociation as when a member's wife wants to wear his clooas,[7] as a deppytashun be sent to argue wi her. Isn't that so, Teddy? Let's have a look at th' quarter-of-an-heaur book; it were entered i' theer."

"Theau means t' minute book," I said.

"Ay, that's it," returned Bill.

"An theau't quite reet," I continued, "accordin to t' rules o' this 'ere Menociation theau con insist as a deppytashun o' three members visits thy refractory wife."

"Then I insist," said Bill.

Greit looks of alarm gathered on t' faces o' t' members when they yerd this.

"Who volunteers for't goo?" I axed. Nobody spoke. "We'll ha to draw lots then, that's aw," I said.

So we drawed; an it fawd on Ben Roke, Joe Lung, an Sammy Snokes, an didn't they look sayrious.

They armed theirsels wi a thick stick a-piece.

"Neaw Ben," I said, "theau reckons as theau't proficient i' lodgick. No bullyin an blusterin; just sit deawn an talk till hoo hasn't a leg for to stond on."

"That's noan so bad," observed Bill, "but it would be better if he'd talk to her till hoo'd noan a fist for to strike wi."

"I'll have a gill[8] for to keep my courage up," exclaimed Ben.

"So will we," said t' others.

They'd abeaut four gills apiece afore their courage were satisfied.

Th' lonlord lent 'em his bulldug, an they seet off, Bill Spriggs bein i' t' rear. They marched very timidly deawn th' lane, till they geet opposite Spriggs' dur.

"Thee knock," whispered Joe Lung to Ben.

"Neow, thee," said Ben, shoving him forrud, while Sammy and Bill slunk at t' back.

Ben an Joe kept pooshin one another tort t' dur, but nayther on 'em darst knock. They could see Bet's big shadow on t' blind as hoo walkt abeaut t' flure. It seemed as if hoo were moppin wi t' lung mop.

Well, Joe an Ben kept pooshin one another forrud till suddenly Joe cluttered o'er t' step an his yed went straight throo t' dur.

"Murther! murther!" he screamed, while for t' make matters wuss th' bulldug gripped him by his wudden leg.

"Durn't desert me, chaps," pleaded Joe. "Stond by me neaw I'm in difficulties."

"I con stond by thee when theau'rt i' difficulted, but noan when theau'rt in a dur," muttered Sammy, perparin to tak his hook.

"Hello! what's up?" yelled Bet, when hoo seed t' yed come flying throo t' dur.

An hoo coom an oppent t' dur, nearly wrenchin poor Joe's yed off. Theer he were stuck fast; aw th' jagged pieces o' wood cuttin his neck, an th' bulldug fast howd of his wudden leg.

"Oh, Bet! dear good kind Bet!" said Joe, "It weren't me what did it. It were t' others."

"What do yo want?" axed Bet, savagely. "Come, be clearing off, or I'll help yo."

"Well, Betsy," begun Ben Roke, pompously, "we're a depputayshun o' three intelligent sober men, as drunk as new-born babbies, bless their pratty faces; an we're sent to thee for t' prove by lodgick, fair an square, an reaund, an oblong too –"

"What are ta meitherin abeaut?" interrupted Bet.

"Wait a bit; theau'll see. Neaw when th' Almighty made mon, well he made him aw reet; he didn't make him eaut o' some other animal, did he?"

"Neow, neow!" said Sammy Snoakes. "I think not, but not bein theer at t' time I corn't swear to it."

"Here, poo me eaut," whined Joe.

"Well," resoomed Ben, waving his honds abeaut like a orator, "but when th' Almighty made a woman he made her eaut o' Adam's rib. That were for t' show as hoo were part o' t' chap an belongs to him, an should love, honour an obey him in that station –"

"Howd on, what station?" cried Sammy. "Is it Mosesgate or Lostock Junction?"⁹

"Shut up, theau leatheryed. – As hoo must love, cherish, an obey him i' that station o' life which her godfaythers an godmothers gan us in eaur baptism in t'litany where it says fro cowds, an plague, an fro them females and pestilences what walks o' two legs, good Lord deliver us."

"Theau't drunk," said Bet. "Go whum wi thee!"

"I've a duty to do fust," said Ben, "a duty to a fallow-creacher what's bin turnt eaut in t' street," an he begun wobbling abeaut unsteadily.

"I've to convince thee, Madam," he went on, "by sublime lodgick as theau'rt a brute to thy husband."

"Oh is that thy game?" said Bet, an beaut sayin a word hoo went inside. But in hauve a minnit hoo were at t' dur again.

"Madam," Ben were beginning; but he geet no further. He geet th' lung mop dabbed in his meauth; an then afore he could stir Bet clapped t' bucket full o' dirty wayter reet o'er his yed, and theer it stuck like a hat. Nearly choked, he tumbled to t' greaund, rowlin abeaut wi awful explosions o' bad language.

Sammy Snokes took to his heels, but he were soon stopt, for t' bulldog left Joe Lung an darted after him. It grabbed him by his treausers seat an howded him fast, while he were skrikin like a stuck pig.

Bill were off o'er t' fields, an hud issel again a haystack aw neet. He says he geet th' fust good neet's rest he'd had for years.

Joe Lung in his terror geet his yed eaut o' t' dur and crept away. His neck were scrat an bleedin badly.

Then Bet went in, triumphant, an locked t' dur.

"An if there's any more depptashuns comin," hoo sheauted, "tell 'em t' be sharp while I'm i' t' humour for tacklin 'em."

"Why Ben," I said, as I helped him whum, "thy lodgick murn't ha' bin strung enoof for her. It mun ha' bin wake."

"I durn't know," replied Ben, "but what th' lodgick were strung enoof an weel put together, but it weren't as strung as her arm."

Frank Starr, 'An Unpremeditated Crime' (1902)

On returning from a prolonged holiday tour last year I received a communication from a firm of solicitors acquainting me with the death of my old friend Nevison. The letter stated that he had died from injuries incurred during a fire, and that a package accompanying the letter was forwarded according to instructions left by my friend.

The packet I found contained papers revealing a period in Nevison's history which had hitherto been to me a sealed book. As the story proved to be so remarkable, and I have been careful to alter names, I offer no apology for making it public: –

"My dear Trevor," the manuscript commenced, "I never dreamed during the happy days at Oxford that I should live to pen these words. Indeed, I would not do so now but that I feel I owe you an explanation – one that I could not make in life.

"You will remember, long ago as it is, my engagement to Mildred Devenish. Indeed, from your frequent attempt to turn the conversation into that channel, I know that its mysterious breaking off has always been an enigma to you. Knowing my love for her you must have believed that I should never have voluntarily broken our engagement, and I, poor coward, have allowed you to thinking that Mildred was responsible for the separation. But I, and I alone was the cause. As you know, we loved each other sincerely, and until my last term at Oxford, nothing had occurred to mar our happiness.

"You may recollect, too, that at that time I had a great antipathy to field sports, and, although brought up in a hunting county, resolutely set my face against fox-preserving.[1] Indeed, I had boasted that I would certainly shoot a fox if ever I suffered from its depredations. Such an opportunity occurred during the long vacation, when one of these animals killed a number of my tame pheasants. But my constitutional cowardice stayed me from shooting it, for I knew my father did not share my views on this subject. I was, however, none the less resolved to kill it, although by a different method. Therefore, saying nothing of my intentions, I dosed the body of a dead pheasant with strychnine,[2] and hid it at night in some undergrowth near the lair of the animal. I did not return to the spot until the following evening, when I was delighted to find the pheasant had disappeared. But there were no traces of the fox, although I had used poison enough to kill and elephant, and I only hoped the animal had not been found, but had crawled into a hole to die.

"Two days after, while we were at breakfast, my father, without looking up from the *Times*,[3] remarked, 'That's a queer story the servants have got hold of. They tell me the wife of that poaching rascal Laurence was found dead in her chair at dinner-time yesterday. I hear, too, that the remains of a pheasant were found upon the table. Possibly Laurence is the fox that is responsible for the disappearance of your birds.'

"My God! The truth flashed across me in an instant. Laurence or his wife had found the poisoned pheasant, and this was the result. I don't understand why, but I knew instinctively that this was the truth. How I preserved my presence of mind I cannot surmise, but at last I mustered up sufficient courage to ask, 'What does Laurence say about it?'

"'Oh, he's away, it appears. Left the previous day on one of his peddling trips. After stealing a few pheasants, I suppose.'

"I sat for some time making a pretence of eating, and revolving different schemes in my head, but ere I rose from the table I resolved that at any cost I would leave England. My natural cowardice made me afraid to face the result of my own action, – I dared not look upon the face of that dead woman. I was in no mood to reason calmly upon the matter; horror of the dead was strong upon me, and my one desire was to get away. But how could I leave Mildred? And yet, with such a crime upon my conscience, thought of wedding her seemed hopeless.

"Words cannot describe the day and night that ensued. A thousand times I was on the verge of confessing to my father, a thousand times my heart failed.

"Next morning I told him I contemplated spending the remainder of the vacation in Jamaica, and hoped to return with some choice botanical specimens.

"'Rather a sudden resolve, isn't it?' he commented dryly.

"I did not reply, but maintained a silence which he mistook for obstinacy.

"'H'm. Well, I suppose if you want to go you will go, though why on earth you couldn't find enough botanising in England, I cannot understand. By the way, Dr. Ewan tells me he believes that woman Laurence has been poisoned.'

"I muttered something about packing, and got away, only to induce further hours of self-reproach and remorse.

"Before evening my trunks were in order, and I was in the Southampton mail.[4] My father evinced some surprise at my hurried departure, but I explained it on the score of a boat leaving next day.

"A night at an hotel followed, spent in concocting a letter to Mildred, telling her I hardly know what in explanation of my journey, hinting at possibilities of my having ceased to love her, and making such puerile excuses that I knew her love must see through.

"Morning saw me aboard the steamer, and at noon I stood at the taffrail[5] watching the Needles[6] disappear, and gripping a newspaper containing this paragraph: – 'Mysterious Death of a Woman. – At an inquest held yesterday at Blitchford upon a woman found dead at dinner, the doctor in attendance said he believed the deceased died from strychnine poisoning. The inquest was adjourned for further evidence.'

"I need not detail my sufferings during that short voyage, nor can I offer any excuse for my conduct. Even now I do not know whether it was horror at the deed or fear of the result that was the determining factor of my fright. I only know that the nervous timidity, inherited, I think, from my dead mother, has been a characteristic which years have failed to entirely eradicate.

"Arrived at Jamaica, I wrote to my father, telling him that I was going up country. Then, after a night at an hotel in Kingston, where I left most of my luggage against an indefinite return, I engaged a negro and a couple of mules and started inland.

"The tropical scenery interested me but little. Luxurious banana and sugarcane plantations soon became monotonous and I realised that change alone would not banish the memory of the dead woman. My restlessness drove me forward, and after spending a night at a wayside hotel morning saw me again in the saddle.

"Hitherto I had taken little stock of my guide, but as the country became wilder and my usual nervousness asserted itself I could not help noticing his forbidding aspect and decided to dismiss him next day. My fears were further aroused by his persistently keeping close to my mule through the jungle of tree-ferns and palms into which we were now penetrating. It was a wild, uninhabited piece of country, but the guide assured me that we should reach an hotel before nightfall. As it was then late in the afternoon and I knew twilight was almost unknown in the tropics, I urged the mule into a faster pace. At the time we were travelling over a rocky, broken bridle-path and as I touched the animal with the spurs it started suddenly and stumbled. Instinctively I threw myself back only to receive from the treacherous guide a blow which knocked me senseless from the saddle.

"When I recovered consciousness I found myself stretched upon a rude mattress in some kind of hut, and a black but not unkindly face bending over me.

"'How mas'r doin' now?' asked the negro.

"I strove to speak, but failed to utter any articulate sound, and my efforts only produced a relapse into unconsciousness.

"The second stupor must have lasted some time, but eventually I returned to life to learn that my host had found me lying in a mountain path, with a gaping wound in my head, and nothing beyond the clothes I wore to indicate my identity. He gave me to understand that I had had fever, and when I asked how long I had been there, he replied,

"'Two-tree, week.'

"I begged him to hurry to Kingston and procure a doctor, but his he resolutely refused to do, as by reason of some misdemeanour, he was 'wanted' by the police.

"I recovered slowly, and had relapse after relapse, but at length mended sufficiently to make my way back to Kingston. The negro accompanied me as far as he dared, and at parting implored me to say nothing of his whereabouts. My weak condition made the remainder of the journey very painful; but I succeeded in reaching the hotel, where I was received with mingled consternation and rejoicing by the landlord. My indefinite arrangements had prevented him from feeling alarmed, nor had he taken any steps to discover my whereabouts. Consideration for my black saviour led me to conceal as much of my adventure as possible, and also deterred me from asking too pointedly after the scoundrelly guide.

"Two letters from my father awaited me. The first contained a welcome remittance, and told me of the evidence at the inquest, while the later one was filled with upbraidings for not writing and fears for my safety. These I answered, explaining the reason of my long silence, and asking for further particulars of the adjourned inquest on Laurence's wife. Of Mildred I dared not write, for I knew my father resented our engagement, and would wonder why I wrote to him for information.

"After despatching this letter, I spent several weeks exploring the surrounding country, being careful, however, in my choice of guides. By the time my father's answer arrived I had quite recovered my strength, and time and my own adventure had helped to ease the weight from my heart. But I received no line from Mildred. I knew my brutal letter must have hurt her terribly, but still hoped, unreasonably perhaps, that she would write. The longing to see her, to hear her voice again, grew so strong that I had almost decided to return to England, confide in my father, and ask his guidance as to my future conduct. For I knew that without her life held nothing for me, and although she could never be my wife, yet a vague hope arose that I might see her, the rest I left to Providence.

"No prescience, however, warned me of the coming horror, besides which my former trouble sank into insignificance. The memory of it will never leave me until death summons me to meet my victims. Better I had perished in the forest than lived to learn the ghastly intelligence my father's letter brought.

"It was the only package, besides a newspaper or two from the same source, that I received. I read it eagerly, hoping for news of Mildred. Paternal wishes for my recovery there were in plenty and hopes for a speedy return, but no word of my darling. But before the end of the letter, father and Mildred alike were forgotten, for in the last few sentences appeared words that stopped the beating of my heart, and froze on my lips the cry I strove to utter. These are the lines, seared deep into my memory, that will live with me so long as life remains: –

"'I am glad to tell you that scoundrel Laurence was hanged yesterday for the murder of his wife, a fate he richly deserved. Am sending paper with report of trial.'

"Merciful heaven! Could it be true? Was another life added to my account? Would the result of my cowardice pursue me with an ever-increasing tale of victims?

"Frantically I tore open one of the papers, and rushed through the account of the trial. Read, with straining eyes, how, after the analysis, the coroner's jury returned a verdict of "murder." Read how the police arrested the husband when returning home; and how he had been heard, when drunk, to threaten his wife. Read that strychnine was found in his house, which he protested, was for destroying vermin. Read how the prisoner swore that he had not even shot the pheasant, but had found it under a hedge; and read how the prosecution derided his tale. Read finally the verdict of the grand jury, and the judge's awful sentence, and then fell fainting to the ground.

"The rest of my story needs little telling. On my return I sought Mildred and told her everything, but that scene I dare not attempt to depict. Then I enlisted as a private in the — Regiment, and served through the Afghan and Soudan campaigns.[7] My fatal cowardice left me. Twice during my service I rescued men at the risk of my own life; but since leaving the army no other opportunity has presented itself. I hope, however, ere death overtakes me to save two lives for each one I have taken, and thus, perhaps, make amends for the cowardly crime of my youth."

E. Whittaker, 'When Death Crossed the Threshold' (1903)

Life and Death came together to the door of a four-roomed dwelling in a congested, poverty-stricken neighbourhood. Life, young, full of hope and promise, gathered her garments together and stood aside to let the sable-apparelled, venerable Death pass in before her. Death raised his grisly forearm to his cowled face and glanced out gravely, and bowing to the fair visitor, held the door that she might pass in before him. Down the street, in great haste, came a gentleman in a suit of black cloth, and a silk hat, accompanied by a ragged lad, much out of breath with the pace he had to make to keep up with his companion. They come to a stop at the house where Life and Death had entered, and the lad knocked.

A white-faced man, with shirt collar undone, exposing his throat and chest, opened the door and admitted them. He hurried the boy through a connecting door into the scullery and closed it tight. The gentleman removed his silk hat and glanced round.

A four-roomed cottage is decided in its limitations, and it is a perplexing riddle to those who do not know how the mysteries of birth, and the solemnities of death, have the necessary considerations and decencies they demand. The gentleman with a brief glance passed over to an impoverished bed, where a woman well on in years lay, with agony strained features and set teeth, looking towards him.

"It's time, doctor," she murmured.

The gentleman smiled pleasantly and nodded his head, and turning about, directed the white-faced man to retire and send some woman to be of assistance if necessary. The white-faced man passed into the scullery where a number of children, like a cluster of frightened sheep, huddled together half-dressed. Dispatching one of them to bring a neighbour-mother's assistance, he drove the rest upstairs, and paced the scullery's narrow limits in an agitated state of mind. The neighbour-mother came and passed into the house-place, and then all became quiet, save for a restrained moan of pain, and the short, crisp utterance of the gentleman in black.

Life had accomplished the purpose of her visit, and beckoned to Death to accompany her away. Death stood silent and watchful, at the bed-head, his head resting upon his bent arm.

"Come with me," said Life, pleadingly. Death motioned his refusal silently, and Life observed, in the disturbed folds of his robe, his scythe.

"It's been sadly too much for her," said the gentleman in black, referring to the sick woman who lay white and unconscious upon the rude pallet.

"She was too old," said the neighbour-mother, who was now nursing a red speckled atom of mortality in a yellow piece of flannel.

"Perhaps so; perhaps so," assented the gentleman. "How many more are there, did you say?"

"Nine! God help them!" answered the woman. The gentleman uttered a subdued exclamation and paced the floor, his hands behind him.

Life laid one hand gently upon Death's shoulder, and clasped his bony wrist, which held the scythe, with the other, and pleaded for the sick woman's life. "For the children's sake," she said. Death's scythe hand trembled.

The gentleman paced up and down the hearth-rug waiting for some change to take place in his patient. At length she opened her eyes and looked enquiringly round. The gentleman approached her, and gently moved back the sweat-dewed hair that lay upon the woman's forehead. "Do you feel better?" he asked.

The sick woman feebly smiled, and looked enquiringly at the neighbour-mother, who drew near and laid the new born baby alongside the sick woman. "It's a boy," she said in answer to the other's low-voiced enquiry.

"Are you going to look after them," asked the gentleman.

"I'll do what I can," said the neighbour-mother, "but I've five little ones of my own to look after."

"The child must not have the breast. See to that, my good woman," said the gentleman.

The white-faced man was admitted to the house-place, and with a few general instructions the gentleman took his departure.

The white-faced man, the sick woman's husband, made himself ready for work, and two hungry looking lads appeared and made similar preparations. The two girls of twelve and sixteen respectively came into the room. The elder girl also dressed her self to go out, while the sick mother directed the younger one in the household management, and breakfast preparations for several younger children upstairs.

Death kept up his silent watch unmoved by the entreaties of his companion.

"For one year," begged Life.

Death remained silent.

"A week then – one little week," pleaded Life. Death raised his skeleton hand to his cowl and opened it to gaze at the bold questioner, and slowly shook his head.

"Well, a day or two."

"Two days," said Death, and gathering his robes together about him, he crossed the room to the street door, as the twelve year old girl wound up the blind to let in the pure daylight.

Slowly the July day went on its wearisome course followed by the short hot night and the dawn of another day. The white-faced man who had slept fitfully in a chair beside his wife's bed, rose up, and called his two lads and two eldest daughters and went off to work hollow-eyed and weary.

As the day advanced towards noon, the sun shone with a fierceness of heat that baked the pavement of the street. Indoor, the air was sultry and oppressive, and the weak, faint woman lay gasping for breath; outdoor the dogs and cats lay gasping on the heated pavement, suffering the passer-by to walk over them. In the afternoon, the doctor came carrying his hat and mopping his brow with his handkerchief.

"Phew, it's hot! How do you find it my good woman?" he asked, feeling the sick woman's pulse.

The woman murmured something which the gentleman took no notice of. He knitted his forehead, and looked solemnly thoughtful. "You're very weak," he said. "Have you any pain?"

"None," answered the woman.

The gentleman paced about much perturbed. The voices of several children quarrelling amongst themselves, followed by sounds of hard smacks, and crying, caused the woman to turn uneasily in her bed. The gentleman went and silenced the rebellion amongst the unruly urchins, and returned to the bedside.

"My good woman," he said, in a low tone, "I have done all I can; and it is as well you should know. You are nearing the end."

The sick woman betrayed no emotion, save the brought her worn hands outside the coverlet and tugged at its ragged fringe.

"You understand me?" questioned the doctor.

"I understand! Doctor?" said the woman.

"Well?"

"Say nothing to the children or my husband."

The gentleman gave the sick woman a glance of admiration. "Can I send a minister to you?" he asked.

The woman shook her head. "I haven't thought much about God, perhaps, but I haven't been a bad woman and I rest on that. I've prayed in my heart for what is good and best; not in a set form of words, but sincerely for all that. Don't send no minister, I wish to pass on quietly."

"You are a brave woman and I do not doubt a good one," said the doctor. "May the end be equally peaceful."

"How long may I expect to live, doctor?"

The doctor glanced at his watch. "It is three o'clock now; about twelve hours or so," he said. He then prepared to take his leave, and at the woman's request called the children out of the scullery into the kitchen so that she could keep her eye on them. The doctor observed a large tear from and slowly roll down her cheeks without her relaxing a muscle of her features.

When her husband and the rest of the children returned from work in the evening they talked over the kitchen fire in hopeful whispers as the sick woman in a gaiety of spirit smiled and talked cheerfully of better days to come when her family was grown up.

As the last red flush of declining day painted the sky, evidences of a storm's approach were made apparent. The lightning flashed and the thunder followed at intervals; large drops of rain beat against the window or fell hissing and steaming up from the sun-baked pavement. Nearer and nearer came the thunder, and soon the lightning flash and the thunder were simultaneous. The sick woman would not have the blind drawn, but lay gazing up thorough the kitchen window at the play of the lightning in the rent clouds. Brave with courage born of years of fortitude she betrayed no sign or word of her passing on. The husband and father, irritable and meddling, forced food and medicine into her mouth and occasionally loudly be rated the children in the scullery for raising their voices above a whisper. The battle of the elements ceased at length and a procession of soft, fleecy clouds drifted across the heavens like a glad triumphant throng of angels.

Midnight approached, and the moon became shrouded in a thick black cloud. An invisible Presence entered the room and approached the bed.

"So soon?" said Life.

"Even now," said Death.

The man started up from an unrestful slumber in a chair and hurriedly lit a candle that was upon the table. The lamp had burnt out and left the room in darkness save for the dull sombre glow of the dying embers of the fire.

"My baby! My baby," moaned the woman.

"The baby, fetch the baby," shouted the man. His eldest daughter entered the room with hair dishevelled, and half asleep. "Fetch the baby," roared the man seizing her by the shoulder, and pushing her into the street. The girl went to the house of the neighbour-mother, who had taken charge of the baby, and knocked her up. The neighbour-woman brought the baby which shrieked loudly and lustily at being so rudely awakened, and at finding itself among so much commotion.

"You're starving the child," cried the man, evidently under the impression that babies never cried for anything else but to be fed.

"I've done more for it than you've done for her," said the woman a little angrily.

The man uttered some contemptuous remark.

"Thank God, I'm not your wife," answered the woman. "That's something to be thankful for whether you thank me for my services or not."

What promised to be a wordy quarrel was cut short by the return of the two lads. The doctor had said he could not come, but had sent a powder for the sick woman to take. The man emptied the powder into a cup, and added a little water to mix it and then forced it between the sick woman's lips. The sick woman moaned a small complaint, and the liquid oozed out of the corners of her mouth.

A change like the cast of a shadow passed over the sick woman's features, "She's going," said the neighbour-mother, who in her experience, had seen the death-shadow on several occasions. Life grasped the wrist of Death and stayed his hand.

"Another doctor, another doctor," cried the man gazing round with flaring eyes. The two lads and a girl ran into the street, and hurried together to find a doctor to come at their call.

Several refused, but at length, a young practitioner, new to the profession, and earnestly energetic to do his very best, was found coated and booted, just from a similar case and willing to go. He hurried alongside the children asking questions as they went along, and arrived at length into the street where they lived. The raving sobbing of a frenzied man, notified the house to the young doctor, before the children had brought him to the door.

"Calm yourself," said the doctor, entering: "Quietness is an essential in all sickness." He passed over to the sick woman's bed. "Too late, too late," he said, in an audible whisper, as he bent with his ear over the woman's face.

"Can you do nothing?" cried the nigh frantic husband.

"Nothing," answered the doctor.

The younger children were brought to the bedside and held over the sick woman to kiss her and then followed frightened anguished silence. The young doctor, visibly perturbed, watched the last flickering of a parting life. He was not yet hardened to indifference, and keenly felt his utter powerlessness.

The sick woman moved, and half rose, supporting her body on her hand; she drew a deep breath and part opened her lips, and then the breath of life, like the long sweep of a scythe passed from her, and she fell back on her pillow, silent and still.

"She has gone," said the doctor, quietly.

"Dead, dead," shrieked the husband, falling on his knees beside the bed.

The spell of silence was broken, the children and neighbour-mother terrified, raised their voices in discordant wailing anguish. The doctor, no less weak, buried his face in his handkerchief, and sought the door, and he and Death passed out together, whilst Life remained sorrowing with the bereaved.

Alfred H. Pearce, 'An Angel of Humanity' (1904)

I.

"I tell you, sir, I will go!"

"And I say, Marian, you must not."

She had been fascinated by a touring actor at the little seaside theatre, and he was the bone of contention.

"Must not! Sir, what mean you? Is this the manner in which to treat your not-yet-twelve-months wife? Am I not to make any friends? Am I to be a nun?"

"He is no fit man for you to meet."

"I hope I am neither an infant nor a dunce. I say he is a splendid man, full of high sentiment and good breeding. What debased man could so finely utter the noble sentiments of the characters he undertakes?"

"That is no guide. He is an actor, and speaks by the book."

"He lives, moves and has his being in an atmosphere of refinement. Think you the Mervyles would know him, or would offer to introduce me to him if he was the dreadful character you seem to apprehend? It is preposterous, sir. Whether you choose to accompany me or not, I shall go to the theatre to-night and avail myself of the introduction offered by the Mervyles."

"Who are these Mervyles? People without a history – people who come from no one knows where –"

"Sir! Are you determined to flout all my friends? I tell you I will go, so there, there, *there*!"

A stamp of the foot and an outburst of tears clinched the matter irrevocably.

* * *

Ronald Thurston had had previous experience of his wife's hasty temper and impetuous manner. She was romantic and had the passionate nature that romanticism gives. He, fond to weakness of her, sincere, good-hearted, seldom ventured to cross her will. He took matters in an easy-going spirit, bowing his head only too often in order to escape the tempest that a bold front would inevitably arouse. However, on this occasion, when his wife announced her intention of making the personal acquaintance of the popular and somewhat notorious actor, Bertram Clifforde, he had deemed it his duty to assert his authority. With what little success we have already seen.

II.

Marian Thurston was not bad at heart. Her mind only was somewhat warped. She had been a deeply-indulged child. The old aunt with whom she had passed her girlhood spent untold money in the gratification of her protégée's whims and fancies. And when she died she left more in order to continue the indulgence. Therefore, Marian had naturally grown up to be impatient of restraint. Opposition roused her. Had Ronald behaved as he usually did she would not have cared half so much for the promised introduction. His breath of opposition fanned her romantic spark into flame. It was a glorious opportunity to indulge one of her most ardent fancies. To make the personal acquaintance of one of the idols of the stage – a man whose mellow voice and fine acting and splendid figure had fascinated her – was a delightful thing. To talk with him in the wings whilst he was in all the glory of his "war paint," or to talk with him off the boards just as with an ordinary human being, was an experience ever to be regretted if missed. Ever since that first appearance of his on the local stage nearly a fortnight ago, she had night after night listened rapturously to his splendid voice, and watched his lithe figure move gracefully about. Now that her recently-made friends, the Mervyles (who knew everybody), had offered to bring her into actual contact with this ethereal being, was she to be robbed of the triumph because of the insane ideas and prejudices of her husband? Hoity-toity! he must not think, because she happened to be married to him, that she was to be chained to his side, and to ask permission for every little thing she desired to do. Tush! the days of matrimonial slavery were over, and a good job too!

III.

She was duly introduced to him that night, and she returned home in a dream of rapture. His stage voice and manner were his real voice and manner. He was gentle and courteous; cultured too, with a fund of original anecdotes about the many famous people he had met. At least she was sure they were original, for she had never heard or read of them before.

She met him again and again despite her husband's threats and entreaties. She urged him to make the actor's acquaintance. She said Clifforde himself had desired it. Ronald, full of vague stories he had heard about the man, point-blank refused. She condescended to entreat. He was a magnificent man, whose friendship it would be an honour to cultivate. He was only to be at the theatre a month – until the late season closed in this little out-of-the-way watering place – and such an opportunity to meet him was likely never to occur again. Note how the papers praised his performance of Iago¹ in the recent production. As for herself, she doubted if Irving² could have transcended it. – "Surely such a man as Mr. Clifforde –"

"Could play Iago well? – naturally" interrupted Ronald, with a bitter inflection in his voice.

"Not so well, however, as you play the jealous Moor," retorted Marian. "He smothered Desdemona – true, but you, sir, shall not be allowed to smother me!"

Ostentatiously she repaired to the theatre that very night, and he, next morning, returned to London in a tearful rage.

She remained, gave out that business called him back, and attended the future performances six times out of six.

She met the actor furthermore at many of the little functions that the limited society of the little town could boast. She introduced him here and there, extending his circle of acquaintance and patronage. She sold benefit tickets for him. Full to the brim of his praises and excellences she made him the lion of the little theatrical world. People who had looked shyly at his acting suddenly discovered untold beauties in it. So powerful is a pretty woman possessed of a mint of money in her own right.

IV.

Bertram Clifforde was perhaps three times as black as the devil, these days, is painted, though very few people knew it. This because, within limitations, he was a born actor. That is to say, traitorous parts were his forte. Hotspur³ he would have miserably mulled; Iago was his masterpiece.

His subtleness and dissimulation turned inside out the soul of his feminine admirer. He flattered, petted, cajoled her, the while he dissected her piecemeal. Her friends, relatives, fortune, passed through the metal crucible, and came out golden. They were worth the effort.

The effort? – That of making her Mistress Iago.

He played his part with consummate skill. Soft words, honeyed phrases, sighs, wishes, inferred and half-expressed, rained their artillery upon her. She sighed, fluttered, hesitated, before him. In her room she stamped, raved, protested hysterically. In his presence again she fluttered, hesitated, stammered, fell. It was easy to elope out of the country, and – well, easier still to arrange a fresh marriage. As for money, she had plenty at command. He took care to be sure of that. They arranged to fly at the end of the week – the close of his engagement.

V.

She lived in paradise that week; fearful perhaps of the serpent, but not much. Her eyes had neither time nor capacity for looking at such a lowly thing; they were too occupied by the glorious halo round the head of her idol. As for someone she used to know as – what was his name? – oh, Ronald – he was far – far off. He had not written to her from his town house, nor had she communicated with him. The silence suited him, presumably, and – well, yes, it suited her. Quite a case of mutual accommodation.

Friday night – they were going on Saturday – was a busy one. So many preparations had to be made. It was past nine when she started for the theatre. He knew she would be late, so that was all right. It was a glorious evening and she decided to walk.

On she went, musingly. How quiet all seemed. Scarcely anyone about. The little town was emptying fast. Audiences were getting smaller; but engagements entered into had to be kept, so he remained. But after this week – Elysium.

Her meditations were interrupted by a small voice behind her. She turned to behold a little girl, seemingly nine or ten years of age, approaching her with an inquiring face.

"If you please, ma'am, can you tell me the way to the theatre?"

"The theatre, child. I'm going there myself. But what do you want at the theatre?"

"I've got a letter from my mammy."

"Oh. For whom?"

"Please ma'am, for my daddy."

"Oh, and does your daddy work at the theatre?"

"Oh, no, ma'am; he doesn't work – he plays there."

"Plays, oh? Innocent child. One of the minor actors your daddy is, I suppose. Come along, I'll show you the way. What did you say his name was?"

"Please, ma'am, it's on the letter. See – Mr. Clifforde."

Whatever made the lady shriek and stagger and turn so white? The little girl was puzzled and alarmed.

The lady dropped on a promenade seat and gasped for breath, clutching the letter in her hand. The child began to cry.

"Hush, my child, do not cry. Did you say this – this letter is addressed to – your daddy?"

"Yes, if you please, ma'am."

"And your mammy wrote it?"

"Yes, ma'am."

"I – I know your daddy, and he doesn't want this yet. Where do you live?"

"Please ma'am, in Stanton-street. It's a long way from here, and I got lost."

"I know where it is. Come, I must see your mammy at once. Your daddy can easily wait."

They entered the house half-an-hour later.

VI.

"Mrs. Clifforde?"

"At your service, madam."

"I – I found this little girl of yours near the theatre, towards which I was going. She was lost, and enquired the way of me. She had this letter addressed to – to Mr. Clifforde, the great actor, I presume. Is – is he – your –"

The word stuck in her throat.

"My husband, madam? Yes, he is, unfortunately for me. What of it? Lily, why did you not deliver the letter, as I told you?"

The poor child faltered.

"It is my fault," interposed Marian. "May – may I speak to you in private, please?"

The woman bowed and dismissed the child. Protestations, questions, answers, tears and temper permeated the room for fifteen minutes by the clock. An hour later an outraged and deserted woman frantically hugged her child, and cast occasional glances at a bundle of small-amount banknotes resting on the mantel.

At a corresponding time a woeful-faced lady laid her throbbing head wearily on the cushions of a luxurious railway-carriage. She was alone, save for the tumultuous thoughts surging in her brain. After a while they poured in words from her mouth.

"And this is the man for whom I spurned my deeply-doting husband! The man who already had a wife, treated so cruelly as to be forced to obtain a judicial separation, and even now to be compelled by want to demand the grudged alimony by means of his neglected little daughter! Oh God, I thank Thee for thus opening my eyes to the course I was pursuing; for sending to me in the very crucial moment that little angel of humanity, whom I will well look after. As Thou didst guide her footsteps to me, so do Thou in Thy further goodness guide my erring footsteps to my husband, instilling into his mind the knowledge that his erring wife is truly repentant, resolved to be ever submissive and true."

VII.

Telegram No. 1: –

"Beloved – The scales have fallen from my eyes, and I, humbled and repentant, am thine, if thou wilt, for ever. – Marian."

Telegram No. 2: –

"Beloved – come! – Ronald."

Teddy Ashton, 'Th' Female Fister' (1905)

At one Tum Fowt Wakes[1] - which generally faws oather on th' thirty-second o' March or pancake Wensday, or else th' fifth Monday after the sixth Sunday i' May[2] – there were a bit of a Fair, including a fat girl show – th' Rose of England hoo were styled in th' bills – shootin galleries, caocoanut shyin, a three-yeaded cauve,[3] a reaundabeaut swing-boats, some little hobby-horses, turned by a hondle for childer, an reaund th' umbrella top o' which were this inscription – "Pongo's Farmyard, including Banthams an gondolas" – just as if gondolas were a breed o' poultry, which reminds me o' that yarn that's towd abeaut a certain Owdham teawn ceauncillor. I'll tell it yo, though I darsay you known it; but if yo done, greet it wi a smile, same as yo done aw owd friends; an if yo'n never yeard it afore – why ax yoresel where yo'n been livin this last twenty year that your eddication's been so neglected. It were at a Teawn Ceauncil meetin in Owdham, an somebody had proposed that th' Corporation should purchase a gondola for one o' th' lakes i' th' park; wheereupon this certain teawn cauncillor, full of economy an foreseet, and desirous o' keepin th' rates deawn as much as possibile, geet up an said: "Mestur Mayor, – Why not get two gondolas, for suppose they're composed o' cocks and hens, same as any other wayter-fowl, an then they'd breed, an we should soon have a good stock beaut any further spendin o' brass."

Well, to get back to th' Tum Fowt Wakes. In addition to t' things I've aweady mentioned, an a twothree as I haven't, for there's no need, there were a penny show, which had eautside it a big placard summat to this effect: –

MADAME MASHEM!

THE LADY PUGILIST!

The Pride of Britain, and Lady Champion Boxer of the World

Is open to have a Sparring bout with any gentleman who comes forward!

Come and see her! She's a regular knock-out!

All Classes One Penny!

There were no extra charge for front seats, or rather front stondin. Yo paid yore penny, an geet where yo could.

Th' tales o' this woman boxer's skill, an heaw hoo bashed every mon as stood afore her, were soon aw o'er th' Fowt, an were th' theme o' talk at th' Dug an Kennel, where th' Menocation met.

"Well," said Tommy Dod, "it's a greit reflection on eaur monhood that a bloomin woman should be knocking men abeaut as if they were dolls and dummies. Hoo owt to be put a stop to. If hoo isn't, th' women ull tak a tip fro her, an henpeck ull become mooar terrible than ever"

"Moaas women's no need to tak lessons off nobody at that game," said Bill Spriggs.

"It's eaur duty to check this 'ere female," said Ben Roke. "It's th' object of eaur Menociation. This woman's makin mon an inferior beast to his wife. Reet on eaur own doorstep, too, as one met say. We'st ha to do summat – or else never howd eaur yeads up to no mooar."

"But what con we do?" axed Tum Bibbs.

"Let's aw goo to th' show," said Jack Tyke, "an see this woman for eaursels."

"Hear, hear!" said everybody.

So they went to th' boxin-show, an th' woman stood up in a little space, roped reaund, an th' gaffer o' th' show inquired if there were any gentlemon as were inclined to have a dust wi her. He'd guarantee that hoo wouldn't hurt 'em much, an he'd supply th' injured wi a bit o' stickin-plester, if necessary.

This skittin an tauntin rather galled th' Menociation crew; an when th' lady boxer, a shapely, strappin young woman, looked reaund wi a sniff o' scorn, Ben Roke said, "This is too aggravatin. This woman's makin us aw look like little kids."

There were a bit of applause as a farmer's son, a very raw youth, stepped up an put th' gloves on in answer to th' lady's challenge.

Th' lady smiled, an soon sent him flyin. After three raunds he didn't know where he were. He axed where he lived, an said he'd be fain if somebody would lead him whum, as booath his een were bunged up."

"This'll never do," said th' Menociation lot. "We murn't let this female romp o'er th' king o' beasts like this."

They whispered among theirsels, an Joe Lung said it were Bill's place, as president o' th' Menociation, to have a smack at this woman, to redeem th' honour of his sex, an so on.

Bill had had a pint or two, an felt that he could feight owt as walked, especially if it wore frocks.

But someheaw he didn't relish th' idea o' facin this female.

However, egged on by his mates, he put th' gloves on, an stepped into th' ring.

"Though I think I'd better not," he said. "I dun't want to hurt th' woman."

Th' showmon said Bill needn't worry on that acceaunt; th' boxin lady would tak care of hersel.

An so hoo did. After playin wi Bill for a minute or two, hoo gan him a whack on th' yerhole that loosened aw th' screws in his yead, an he felt that his face were comin undone. He'd ha' crept eaut o' the show, an run whum, but his mates wouldn't let him, but forced him up to th' scratch[4] again. Meeanwhile, some little lads eautside th' show, yeard what were gooin on within, an one on 'em were Bill's own son, Baccarat.[5] Baccarat rushed off whum – it were only a twothree yards away – an brasted into th' heause cryin, "Oh, mother, th' lady boxer's killin my feyther!"

"Laws! What's th' silly foo doin neaw?" said Bet. "He's allus i' some lumber or other. But I weren't have him banged abeaut by no woman – except me – that's my privilege. I weren't have my matrimonial reets usurped by nobody, an I'st allow nobody to peil my husband but myself."

So Bet put on a shawl an hurried to th' boxin-show. Just as hoo crashed in, poor Bill had geet a blow on th' chin that made him feel sure that he's swallowed his own jaws an that aw his teeth were driven through his yead, an flyin eaut, like a beiler explosion, through th' back of his neck. He flopped to th' flure as if he'd done wi England an Tum Fowt for ever.

"Here, stop this gam," said Bet, breastin up to th' lady boxer and givin her a welt on th' yead.

"Put yore dukes up, missis," said th' lady boxer, landin Bet a crack on th' neck that made her stagger.

This made Bet mad, an hoo went for th' boxer wi aw her might. But hoo'd no chance. Bet, wi aw her size and strength, lacked skill, an this were a battle o' science agen mere force.

Bet fowt wildly, but hoo'd no chance; th' lady boxer made rings reaund her – to th' vast amusement o' th' audience – an in a twothree minutes th' amazed Bet had a black eye an a bleedin nose; an then hoo geet a whack that made her think hoo'd been run o'er by an electric tramcar. Hoo were licked.

Hoo sit up, dazed – wonderin what had happened.

"Come on whum," said Bill, "this do ull happen do her good. It'll happen mak her a bit mooar considerate of her husband."

Bill were a bit fause o'er this event. He made a bit o' sly capital eaut of it. When folk met him an said, "We'n yeard that yore Bet has to keep indoors because hoo's a black eye – is it true?" Bill replied, wi a wink, "Oh, ay! It aw very weel to be good-natured wi eaur wives – but we murn't let 'em goo too far. A chap mun assert his authority sometimes."

But aw th' same, he hoped that this explanation would never get to their Bet's yers.

Harford Willson, 'The Scarlet Shoes. (The Story of a Serio-comic Walking Tour and its Tragic End.)' (1906)

"What do they know of England, who only England know?" sings a modern poet.[1] But how many of those who pride themselves upon being English really know England itself?

John Skeat put the latter question to himself as he sat in his room one morning in the early part of May. The table before him was crowded with maps of all sizes, guide-books, newspaper cuttings and pictorial postcards. Mr. Skeat was to start upon a four months' walking tour on the morrow, and he was busy planning out the details. He was finding the task a more difficult one than he had anticipated. If the four months were to be spent to the best advantage a careful itinerary was necessary.

"Seems to me," thought Skeat, as he looked at the littered table, 'that what I want first of all is a guide-book to these maps and papers. The rest would then be comparatively easy. Two heads are better than one, so I'll wait until Hargold arrives. He'll help me to straighten things, and besides, he ought to have a say in the matter."

Mr. Skeat leaned back in his chair, placed his feet on the table and lit a cigarette. The next moment there was a knock at the door.

"Talk of the old lad,"[2] said Skeat, "I'll be that's Hargold. Come in! I was just thinking of you. Why –"

Mr. Skeat's cigarette fell from his fingers to the floor and he stared in astonishment at his visitor. Had the "old lad," to whom he had just referred, been standing there in the doorway instead of his old school-chum, Henry Hargold, his surprise could not have been greater.

What's the matter?" asked Skeat's visitor, laughing. "A moment ago you said you had been expecting me and yet you seem as flabbergasted at my appearance as if I had dropped from the skies."

"I *am* flabbergasted at your appearance," said Skeat. "Really, Hargold, whatever made you come in so hideous a disguise?"

"No disguise at all, old chap. This is my real self, this is my usual attire. Rather striking, is it not?"

It certainly was. Skeat had never seen anything like it before. He knew that artists took liberties in the matter of dress, and he knew also that Hargold (whom he had not seen for several years), was not over particular as to his personal appearance. But he had never thought it possible for anyone to go so far as his old friend had done. To look at Hargold, as he stood there, still smiling, one seemed to forget that one was in England, and that it was the twentieth century. His fantastic apparel irresistibly reminded one of the stories of Hans Christian Andersen and the Brothers Grimm.[3] When Skeat had invited Hargold to join him on his walking tour he had never expected to have such a scarecrow for companion.

Hargold was a thickset man of rather over medium height. His hair, a tangled tawny mass, hung down and covered his shoulders. His untrimmed beard resembled nothing so much as a rough-edged piece of cocoanut matting.[4] These partly-natural advantages would alone have attracted attention. Apparently, however, they were not sufficient for Hargold for he adopted a style of dress that served to make him still more conspicuous.

His cap was of a strange shape, with a stranger metal ornament stuck in the front of it. His coat was of rust black velvet, his vest a bright blue, his knee-breeches of a large check pattern, outrageously loud, and patched and darned in several places. His stockings were brown, with a green and yellow design running through them. And, to complete the picture, Hargold's shoes were of brilliant scarlet leather.

"Well," said Hargold when Skeat had finished his survey. "How do you like my get-up?"

"I can't say that I care for it," replied Skeat. "Are you going on tour in that eccentric costume?"

"Certainly. It's the only one I've got and – you'll pardon my saying so – but I think it's rather unique in its way."

"I was just selecting routes and halting-places," said Skeat, changing the subject. "If you'll draw up to the table we'll soon settle the job, and then we can have a good talk about things. We can start to-morrow morning – if you're agreeable."

"Before we do anything," said Hargold, laughing and pointing towards the window, "you had better go outside and send that crowd of kids away. They followed me all the way from the station."

* * *

For three weeks Skeat and Hargold journeyed together, tramping highways and byeways, skirting large towns and passing through small villages. Those three weeks would have been the happiest time of Skeat's life but for the presence of Hargold. Personally the latter was all that could be desired – clever, witty, good-humoured, an ideal travelling-companion. But his appearance – why, that had been the talk of every place they visited.

Skeat disliked Hargold's costume the first time he had seen it, and the dislike had grown into repugnance and hate as the days went by. He had remonstrated with Hargold, but that gentleman smilingly brushed aside all pleas for a more rational dress and even hinted that Skeat would be well advised in discarding his ordinary tourist suit and copying his own picturesque clothing.

But though he had put up with the annoyance so far, Skeat was beginning to get tired of Hargold's needless exhibition. The tourists had been followed in their journey through the towns and villages by troops of jeering children. The people they had met had stopped and stared at them as if Hargold were some new kind of wild animal and Skeat its keeper. Hargold had taken the taunts and the sneers of the crowd in good part; indeed he seemed to delight in the fact that he was being taken so much notice of. But Skeat was becoming thoroughly ashamed of his companion. Once or twice during the last few days he had approached a populous district, pretending to have no connection with the strange figure in front. He could scarcely have done anything that was better calculated to disturb his peace of mind still further. Walking by Hargold's side he saw only the crowd. Walking behind he saw Hargold in addition. And the back view of his companion was even worse than the front. The sight of Hargold's red heels kicking up the dust was peculiarly irritating.

As the two neared Chester, where they had decided to spend a few days, Skeat renewed his entreaties that Hargold should sink his aggressive individuality and descend to the commonplace of ordinary dress. Hargold, however, only shook his head and smiled. Skeat determined to make another appeal to his friend before they left the ancient city, and if he failed to persuade Hargold, well – he should throw up the trip.

The next morning the two men went sight-seeing, and, as usual, Hargold attracted great attention. It was the same in Eastgate-street and in the Park, in the Rows and on the city walls, in the Cathedral as well as in the Grosvenor Museum.[5] In the last-named building the visitors seemed to take far more interest in the appearance of Hargold than in the fine Roman relics stored there.

In the afternoon Skeat proposed a few hours' boating on the river, believing that they might better escape observation there. Hargold readily assented, for it was years since he had handled an oar. Soon they were pulling up the broad stream, and Hargold enjoying the change of exercise. Skeat found that they had not gained anything in the way of quietness by leaving the city, for it was holiday time, and the Dee was crowded with trippers and pleasure parties. The occupants of the steamers going to and fro between Chester and Eaton Hall[6] were particularly sarcastic in their remarks, and the sight of the scarlet shoes in the bottom of the boat added greatly to their mirth.

"What is it?" asked one red-faced fellow, staring at Hargold.

"It's th' Duke o' Westminster," was the reply of a stander-by. "He allus dresses like that on a Monday."

Hargold smiled, but Skeat felt angry. They had to run the gauntlet, however, and at one or two stopping-places along the river banks their appearance was the signal for a great ovation from the waiting crowds.

They rowed on, on past Eccleston Ferry, and left the crowd behind. They had the fine, broad stream to themselves. It was a perfect day, a warm sun and a cloudless sky. The placid river, the rich green meadows behind the tree-lined banks, the floating swans, the cattle cooling themselves in the stream, all made up a picture that delighted the artistic soul of Hargold. But Skeat was thinking of other things – he was thinking of the taunts he was having to bear through his companion's vagaries, thinking of the scoffing crowds, of the return to the city and the renewal of these offensive references.

"Look here, Hargold!" he said, suddenly. "I'm not going to stand this nonsense any longer. I'm about tired of this unnecessary pantomime. You've either got to get a respectable suit of clothes when we get back to Chester, or I'm going to finish this tour alone."

"Oh!" replied Hargold, "you needn't reopen the subject, old chappie. We've got to wear something, and I shall wear what I like. I don't interfere with your style of dress, though, from an artistic point of view, it has many shortcomings. Why should you interfere with mine? I should be sorry to see this delightful tour brought to a premature conclusion, for I'm enjoying myself greatly. Look –"

"But I'm not," broke in Skeat, angrily.

"Well, that's your own fault," said Hargold, smiling. "If I can stand the remarks of the vulgar herd, surely you ought not to mind them."

"If you'd only list to reason –"

"Reason? Who is reason? What is she? Looking at my shoes? What is the matter with them?"

"Everything. Look at their hateful colour. No man ever wore red shoes on a walking-tour before."

"Perhaps not. Great are the pioneers. Thousands of people wear brown shoes, however, and it is not quite so great a step from brown to red as from black to brown, is it?" And Hargold smiled again at his friend.

Skeat felt he was being laughed at, he lost his temper and raised his oar to strike his companion. Hargold, still smiling at his friend's outburst, tried to avoid the blow. The next moment the boat was overturned and the two men found themselves struggling in the water.

Skeat, who was a good swimmer, soon reached the river bank, but Hargold, less able, was carried helplessly down the stream.

The tour was ended.

* * *

Early next morning John Skeat gave himself up to the police for the manslaughter of his friend, Henry Hargold. His tale was coherent enough up to a certain point, if somewhat strange, but when he began to ask why had everybody taken to wearing scarlet shoes, the sergeant looked astonished.

"I saw him drown before my eyes," said Skeat, resuming his story, 'and I made no effort to save him. I saw him sink, and then, as I gazed at the river, I saw a pair of big red shoes come walking over the water towards me. I turned and ran, but they have followed me all night. See! They are there again! See –"

* * *

A month later John Skeat went to prison for ten years.

EDITORIAL NOTES

Thompson, 'The Labyrinth. A Caution to Husbands: a Warning to Wives'

1. *Lieber. Himmel*: respectively 'Dear' and 'Heaven'. Andy is exclaiming at his wife's intentional clumsiness.
2. *chimney-pot*: a tall hat with a flat brim worn by men throughout the latter half of the nineteenth century.
3. *wollüstige*: voluptuous or lustful.
4. *verflüchte gardens of the Teufel*: the cursed gardens of the devil.
5. *Gott in Himmel*: God in Heaven.
6. *a momentary respite from despair*: Arthur Murphy (1727–1805), *Alzuma: A Tragedy* (1773), Act I: 'Kind sleep affords / The only boon the wretched mind can feel; / A momentary respite from despair.'
7. *Sancho Panza*: fictional character from *Don Quixote de la Mancha* (1605, 1615) by Miguel de Cervantes (1547–1616). The pragmatic character Panza is often the voice of reason in Don Quixote's madness.
8. *Mein Gott*: my God.

Suthers, 'The Adventures of a Drop of Water'

1. *My finger's wet, my finger's dry*: ... I'll cut my throat before I lie. A childish vow of honesty.
2. *Lebaudy*: Jacques Lebaudy (1868–1919), the son of a Parisian sugar magnate who declared himself Emperor of Sahara in 1903. The drop of water is unable to differentiate between the political aspirations of Napoleon and those of a delusional rich man.
3. *battledore and shuttlecock ... ping-pong*: Battledore and shuttlecock are early versions of badminton; pitch and toss is a game of skill with the aim to get the penny nearest to the mark; shinny is a form of ice hockey; ping pong, also known as table tennis, is played by hitting a ball back and forth across a table with small, solid bats. The point is that the experience was both fun and skilful.
4. *Niagras*: Niagara Falls, the collective name for three large waterfalls (Bridal Falls, American Falls and Horseshoe Falls) on the Niagara River at the Canadian/US border. Approximately 550,000 litres of water per second move over the falls. The drop is emphasizing the power of water en masse.
5. *Where was Moses when the light went out*: a schoolchild riddle, the answer to which is 'in the dark'. Noah would not know where Moses was because Noah existed earlier than

Moses: the story of Noah is told in Genesis, chapters 5–9, while Moses is found in the later books Exodus, Leviticus, Numbers and Deuteronomy.

6. *Arabian Nights chap*: *One Thousand and One Nights*, often called the *Arabian Nights* in English, is a series of stories collected over centuries by many authors and translators. The 'chap' referred to by the drop of water is probably Andrew Lang (1844–1912), who published a collection of the stories under the title *The Arabian Nights* in 1898.
7. *lachrymal duct*: the tear duct that carries water to the eyes.
8. *on report*: placed on a disciplinary charge for misconduct. In this instance, to report to a teacher or headmaster.
9. *Tommies*: short for 'Tommy Atkins', a generalized term for a British soldier of lower rank.
10. *Afridi*: inhabitant of the mountainous region between Pakistan and Afghanistan. The narrative could be set in either the First (1838–42) or Second (1878–80) Anglo–Afghan War, as Russian expansion in Central Asia worried British colonial interests in India, and Afghanistan, if annexed to India, would be a bolster against a Russian threat.
11. *official 'Gazette'*: a publication that disseminates information authorized by the government and the Crown. In Britain the *London Gazette*, founded in 1665 and originally entitled the *Oxford Gazette*, would publish official information for England and Wales; the *Edinburgh Gazette* (1699) would serve Scotland; and, until separation in 1922, the *Dublin Gazette of Ireland* (1705) would serve Ireland. Reports of British military engagements, narratives such as the soldier's 'heroism' read by his mother back at home, would be part of the role of the *Gazette*.
12. *Rainbow Minstrel Troupe*: A minstrel troupe was a group of performers, whether white or black, in blackface (the application of burnt cork to the face), who would perform songs, comedies and sketches. Although there was little format to the minstrel groups' performances, at the heart would be the interlocutor, who would act the straight man and speak with 'proper' diction, and two endmen, who would caricature African-American speech for comic effect. The drop of water plays one of these comedic characters.

[Lyons], 'Little Pictures of the Night'

1. *Montressor Albert*: The parents have named their baby 'Monstressor', presumably unaware that this is the name of the murderous character in Edgar Allen Poe's (1809–49) story 'The Cask of Amontillado' (1846). Whatever the name and whatever the achievements of the baby, he will always be referred to by the colour of his hair.
2. *bewrays*: an archaic term meaning to expose or reveal. One look at the baby is enough to forecast how he will be referred to for the rest of his life.
3. *Waterloo Bridge*: Designed by John Rennie (1794–1874) and opened in 1817, the bridge suffered from settlement, as the scour of the Thames undermined the foundations. It was closed in 1924 and demolition was begun in 1934, inaugurated by Labour London County Council leader Herbert Morrison (1888–1965). The new bridge, designed by Sir Giles Gilbert Scott (1880–1960), was completed in 1945.
4. *Benjamin Disraeli*: Disraeli (1804–81) was the British Conservative Prime Minister in 1868 and 1874–80 and also a successful novelist. He was made Earl of Beaconsfield in 1876. Lyons's reference to 'Beaky's' similarity to Disraeli is alluding to Disraeli's Jewish heritage and the association of a large, Roman nose with Judaic ancestry, despite his repeated assertions of innocence on how 'Beaky' got his name.
5. *ormenack*: almanac, an annual publication of calendars, astronomical tables, tides timetables, anniversaries and holidays. Beaky's complaint is that despite the publication of

almanacs setting out the four annual equinoxes, the summer still does not know when to start.
6. *old clay*: a pipe made of clay. Clay pipes were often the cheapest form of pipe and of inferior quality.
7. *Any news ... about the 'Ouse, guv'nor*: Beaky is lamenting the lack of discarded newspapers in Surrey as that is his only access to current affairs, being unable to afford to purchase newspapers. The narrator is sceptical that a tramp should be interested in the affairs of the country, a scepticism that is proved correct later in the conversation.
8. *interested in stocks*: The narrator distinguishes between 'House', which could refer to the two Houses of Parliament, Commons and Lords, and 'Bourse', meaning a place for the meeting of merchants and specifically the London Stock Exchange.
9. *Played there ... pullin' of it down*: The Lyceum Theatre in Wellington Street, off the Strand in the City of Westminster, London, was closely associated with actor and manager Henry Irving (1838–1905) between 1871 and 1902. After Irvine left, the theatre was rebuilt in 1904, retaining only the façade. Beaky's comment is published just before – or just as – work starts on the rebuilding.
10. *squash 'at ... blighted sooper*: A squash hat is a soft, less rigid hat; a super is a casual or extra for a theatre production. Beaky is offended that the narrator, in his unconventional attire, has mistaken him for a member of the background cast.
11. *'Er Late Lamented*: the recently deceased Queen Victoria (1819–1901).
12. *Astley's*: Astley's amphitheatre in Lambeth, London. Philip Astley (1768–1821) founded the amphitheatre in 1773, and it survived a number of fires in the nineteenth century. Far from being the high-class theatre Beaky claims to have been employed at, Astley's was an equestrian show and circus – an employment Beaky takes pains to separate himself from. Charles Dickens (1812–70) used Astley's as a basis for Sleary's circus in *Hard Times* (1854).
13. *chaw*: chew. Beaky finds chewing rather than smoking the tobacco more effective at staving off hunger pains.
14. *Gaudelpus*: gawdelpus, a helpless or exasperating person; *OED*.
15. *white spats*: a covering for the top of shoes. There is a comic juxtaposition between the image the narrator gives of himself (as a worldly man with a large vocabulary) and that described by Beaky's mate Miss Hopper and other characters in the serial (as a young man trying his best to look mature). This disparity counteracts the possibility of offence when the narrator's descriptions of the unemployed and working classes appear to move into pomposity.
16. *It isn't long whiskers ... rich city merchant, 'oo –*: clearly not Shakespeare; probably an unidentified popular music hall song. Beaky's understandings of the high and low arts are comically overlapped.
17. *Liberty green*: the same shade of green as that of the patina covering the copper that forms the Statue of Liberty in New York. The exposure of the girl's arm to the rain and cold has affected the circulation of the blood to the surface of the skin.
18. *tract merchant*: a seller of religious tracts. Miss Hopper reads the narrator's clothing as not those of a worldly man but those of a religious zealot.
19. *playin' the ox*: a variation of the better-known phrase 'acting the giddy goat', meaning to act irresponsibly or foolishly.
20. *the cokernuts*: Miss Hopper was born and brought up in a travelling fair. She worked on the coconut shy until she and Beaky ran away after Beaky had tried to defend her from the attentions of the males she names and they planned to kill him.

21. *round 'ats an' leggin's*: the costume of agricultural labourers in Norfolk or farmers in the Yorkshire Wolds. The costume would be perceived as 'old fashioned' by this time.
22. *fur a look at the papers*: The 'Shipping Intelligence' or 'Shipping News' was carried by many newspapers taking information from *Lloyds List*, which began in 1734 as a collection of information about merchant vessels. Miss Hopper is placed in a long history of fictional heroines who scour the shipping news for information on their loved ones, from Anne Elliot following Captain Wentworth through the navy lists in Jane Austen's *Persuasion* (1817) to Mina Murray consoling herself about her fiancé Jonathan Harker's absence from the lists of shipwrecks in Bram Stoker's *Dracula* (1897); see M. Rubery, *The Novelty of Newspapers: Victorian Fiction after the Invention of the News* (Oxford: Oxford University Press, 2009), ch. 1 'The Shipping Intelligence: Shipwrecks and Secret Tears from Dickens to Stoker', pp. 23–46.
23. *Arthur's coffee-stall*: Coffee stalls were mobile vehicles that would be pulled by pony or manpower to its official location (Arthur's pony appears in Chapter IX), where they would serve coffee and sweet cakes to Londoners. Mayhew noted the profusion of coffee stalls in *London Labour and the London Poor* earlier in the century, and there were many concerns raised about coffee stalls providing a breeding ground for criminality among the customers. Richard Machrey described the problem of disreputable coffee stalls who attract 'bad men and bad women of the lowest type' (*Night Side of London* (Philadelphia, PA: Lippincott, 1902), p. 39), but Peter Jones recognizes that through his fiction 'Lyons clearly wanted to encourage his readership to recognize the misperceptions and assumptions upon which these reformist accounts were grounded' ('A. Neil Lyons, "Arthur's"', *London Fictions*, at http://www.londonfictions.com/a-neil-lyons-arthurs.html [accessed 29 October 2012]). Although Lyons is vague about the location of Arthur's coffee stall, Arthur laments his separation from 'the Walworth Road on a Saturday night' in Chapter XXII.
24. *O spare me ... go on*: not identified.
25. *"Returns" ... to me*: The narrator, being in the newspaper trade, is distressed by the conversation of newspapers being returned unsold to the wholesaler.
26. *a "come-down" ... high white collar*: a destitute clerk who is trying to maintain a semblance of class difference through clothing but who is alienating himself through the perpetuation of class division. His situation is more dire than those surrounding the coffee stall, but his instilled class instincts cause him to fear the workers at the stall, who, as the narrator knows, would probably treat him with kindness and humanity if they were aware of his presence.
27. *God save the mark*: originally used as an expression of contempt and/or to soften something that might be offensive. The narrator is referring to the prostitutes who are part of the coffee stall crowd, not because he finds their presence offensive, but because he is rather ironically sparing the delicate sensibilities of the reader.
28. *"Superba" cigar*: a slim cigar, not expensive but a significant gift from Arthur to Beaky.
29. *curate-in-charge*: used in the colloquial sense of an unofficial arrangement, giving Beaky substantial responsibilities in the running of the coffee stall.
30. *clobber*: clothing, personal belongings or equipment; *OED*. In this sense it is used to refer to a new set of clothes.
31. *As worn by the King*: Edward VII (1901–10).
32. *Trilby*: a soft felt hat with a narrow brim and indented crown; *OED*. The hat is named after the eponymous character of George Du Maurier's (1834–96) phenomenally popular novel published in 1894.

33. *a ripe fourpenny*: a cigar.
34. *Mosenstein's*: possibly a Jewish dealer in second-hand clothes or a pawnbroker selling uncollected items.
35. *Progressive*: The Progressive Party was the title taken by the Radicals of the Liberal Party in the 1890s who advocated municipal reforms. Arthur is making a point on the reactionary nature of Progressive politics according to socialism.
36. *Labour Member*: a Labour Party Member of Parliament in the British House of Commons. It is presumed that the reference is to the consternation caused by James Keir Hardie (1856–1915), the Independent Labour Party MP who attended parliamentary sessions dressed in the clothes typical of a respectable working man rather than in the frock coats and top hats traditionally worn in the Commons.
37. *Kitty the Rake*: Kitty's story is told in the earlier tales published in 1901.
38. *a vote for the School Board*: In Britain women were not entitled to vote in political elections until the reform Act of 1928 gave all women over the age of twenty-one a vote. Before this act, the 1870 Education Act had given unenfranchised British women the right to vote and sit on the school boards.
39. *circs.*: circumstances.
40. *put him in the Pound*: a term usually referring to an enclosed area used to hold stray cattle or, more recently, dogs until their owner claims them. Miss Hopper has placed Beaky somewhere safe while he recovers from his tobacco-related delusions so she can collect him when she has found food for them both.
41. *Claverin' Gaol*: Clavering is a picturesque village in northwest Essex, twenty miles from Cambridge.
42. *Then they ... five bob*: Miss Hopper is brought before the magistrates' court and fined for the assault. The magistrate is a local citizen who volunteers time to pass judgment on summary cases that can be resolved in the magistrates court – Miss Hopper's case would be classed as a minor assault – or to pass more serious (indictable) cases on to the crown courts. Because the magistrates are not trained in law, they are advised on legal issues by a justice's clerk – the 'interferin' bloke'.
43. *chalked*: marked; the magistrate's leniency towards Miss Hopper and his bias against those made wealthy by industry will be noted to his discredit.
44. *pipe your dial*: to punch in the face; a slang term, despite Miss Hopper's earlier statement.
45. *'avin' you always 'andy*: to have someone's support.
46. *The Party*: the Labour Party. At this time the parliamentary branch of the socialist movement, financially supported by the Trades Union Congress, was named the Labour Representation Committee and consisted of James Keir Hardie and Richard Bell (1859–1930). Hardie and Bell had been voted into Parliament in the 1900 general election, but Bell would join the Liberal Party in 1904.
47. *Stone 'Ands*: a colloquial term in the printing trade for the compositor who constructs the type for the imposing-stone.
48. *sweet Kate O'Connor*: unidentified.
49. *Number Forties*: shoe size. Miss Hopper is pointing out to Kitty that even if she were of a mind to curtsy, it would be almost impossible while she is wearing oversized, heavy men's boots.
50. *'The Last days of Something or Other,' by Lord Somebody*: *The Last Days of Pompeii* (1834) by Edward Bulwer Lytton (1803–73). The novel, Lytton's most successful work, used the imagery of Roman decadence to form a critique of his contemporary world. Kitty has clearly never read the book despite her later declarations.

51. *Fetter Lane*: At this time Fetter Lane was the address of the Samson Low printing and publishing company, and in 1904 the Socialist Party of Great Britain was formed in Bartlett's Passage off Fetter Lane. This is an appropriate place for a tryst for the printer of socialist newspapers.
52. *start you at fourteen*: The pay starts at fourteen shillings a week, which was a low wage at less than a pound. Kitty and Miss Hopper are glad for the regular wage, but this is still significantly lower than the pound a week that Maud Pember Reeves's (1865–1953) 1913 survey *Round About a Pound a Week* considered insufficient for a family.
53. *lagged me*: to make a convict of somebody; an old lag is someone who was transported or sentenced to prison. Although Miss Hopper has not been imprisoned, she has been found guilty of a crime.
54. *"An' the serpent tempted 'er!"*: Genesis 3:13. The word 'tempted' is not used in Eve's excuse to God; 'deceive' or 'beguile' is more usual. Mr Honeybunn, aware of the wiles and cunning of these women, wonders at the possibility of a snake being even more manipulative.
55. *airey*: area, the small courtyard space in front of a house at the basement level, which would be accessed by steps to the side of the main entrance. This would be the entrance and exit for servants and tradesmen, which is why the milkman had delivered the milk there.
56. *rozzer*: policeman. According to the *OED*, the origins of this term are unknown but it may be a corruption of Sir Robert Peel's (1788–1850) name; as Home Secretary, he created the official full-time professional police force by passing the 1828 Metropolitan Police Act. Bobbies and peelers are other colloquial names for policemen also derived from Peel's name.
57. *dooks*: dukes, meaning fists or hands; to put your dukes up is an invitation to fight.
58. *resterong*: restaurant.
59. *Cully*: meaning one who is duped or fooled. This insult is revenged as the waiter charges the toff an exorbitant fee for cooking the cabbage.
60. *two thick 'uns*: possibly two half-crown coins. These were the same diameter as the penny but thicker in depth. The half-crown was worth two shillings and sixpence or thirty pence in decimal currency. The toff is being overcharged for having his cabbage cooked in the restaurant.
61. *swaddy*: a slang term for a soldier, now more usually 'squaddie'.
62. *Vine Street*: a London street best known for the police station opened there in 1829 at the creation of the police force, and which remained in use until 1940. It was at Vine Street police station that Oscar Wilde charged the Marquis of Queensbury with criminal libel.
63. *Scraps*: possibly a reference to George Cruikshank's (1792–1878) *Scraps and Sketches* (1828–32), a series of comic and satirical images, or Charles Dickens's (1812–70) *Sketches by Boz* (1836), which Cruikshank illustrated. Neither would have been deemed suitable reading by the average parson.
64. *colics*: not identified, but possibly a humorous reference to the catechism.
65. *Ambleworth*: a fictional place name.
66. *Daniel ... little 'orn*: Daniel 6: King Darius puts Daniel in the lion's den for praying to God and not to him, but Daniel is saved by God shutting the lions' mouths. The image of the lamb refers to Jesus Christ, the Lamb of God; the lamb's seven horns is from Revelations 5:6: 'Then I saw a Lamb, looking as if it had been slain, standing at the centre of the throne, encircled by the four living creatures and the elders. The Lamb had seven horns and seven eyes, which are the seven spirits of God sent out into all the earth'. The tract is encouraging meekness and obedience.

67. *Pennorth ... blanket fund*: The parson is replacing religious guidance with material help for the homeless by buying the tracts off those to whom they had been given and therefore providing financial aid (after first checking that it was not to be spent on drink) and making a profit by reselling them back to the rector at an inflated price. The profit is then spent on blankets for those forced to sleep rough. The parson is acting in the true Christian manner and ensures the rector pays for the aid.
68. *Broomfield Squire*: a popular ballad dating from the early eighteenth century (*c.* 1711–32) entitled 'The Merry Broomfield, or The West Country Wager'. The squire wagers with his love that if she visits the broom field the next day she will not return a maid, but he sleeps through her visit and loses his bet. Miss Hopper's encounter is not so chaste.
69. *Obelix*: the obelisk on the Victoria Embankment of the Thames, a famous landmark brought from Egypt and erected in 1878 and colloquially known as 'Cleopatra's Needle'.
70. *linch-pin*: a metal pin to connect a wheel to its axle; a much larger, heavier and more dangerous pin than the boy's scarf pin.
71. *toke*: usually refers to a piece of bread, but is used by characters in this story to refer to food in general.
72. *Tho' ... oft-a*: not identified.
73. *Good-den*: good evening, sometimes used as good afternoon. This is not the case here, as the Broomfield Squire encounters Miss Hopper in the morning.
74. *darkling*: in the dark; wondering about the end of the story.
75. *Jew girls on a Saturday night*: There are a number of fasting days in the Jewish calendar, including Yom Kippur, but there is no expectation for fasting on the weekly Sabbath on Saturdays.
76. *May bush*: hawthorn. The May blossom is generally associated with freshness and exuberance as the flowers herald the beginning of summer. Shakespeare's Sonnet 18 contains the phrase 'the darling buds of May'.
77. *Some 'ad got ... stood eels*: pink stuff is probably smoked salmon; red stuff is possibly some form of fish paste; stood eels are stewed or jellied eels, a delicacy of the southeast of Britain. The eels would be boiled, and the water would be flavoured with vinegar and parsley and left to cool and form a 'liquor' or jelly.
78. *gimlet*: a tool used for boring. The Toff Boy cannot eat such hardened food and selflessly gives his own good-quality sandwiches to Miss Hopper.
79. *Tommy Brooks ... rhyme*: 'As Tommy Snooks and Bessy Brooks / Were walking out one Sunday, / Says Tommy Snooks to Bessy Brooks, / "Wilt marry me on Monday?"'
80. *moniker*: a slang word for name. The class differences are apparent in the language used by both characters as well as the difference in wealth.
81. *lady-smocks ... an' that*: wild flowers that bloom in the late spring and early summer and grow in woodland areas. Lady smocks are also known as Cuckoo Flower, Meadowcress, Pigeon's Eye, Lucy Locket, Mayflower and Bittercress; dog violets are scentless wild violets; enemies presumably refer to wood anemones, which grow on woodland floors.
82. *Song o' the Jolly Beggars*: Robert Burns's (1759–96) 'Love and Liberty: A Cantata', also known as 'The Song of the Jolly Beggars', are six songs by beggars at a revel. The six songs – by the old soldier, his woman, a tinker, a fiddler, a pickpocket and a fool – celebrate the abandonment and lively existence of those at the very bottom of society. However, the lyrics given by Miss Hopper are not those of Burns but a misremembered version of the first and final stanzas of a traditional song attributed to Richard Broome and entitled 'A Beggin' I Will Go, the Jolly Beggars'.

83. *Sir Tristram, an' a lady named Isalt*: Tristan and Iseult, the legend of the Cornish knight and the Irish lady whose love continues despite her marriage to King Mark, and one which is thought to be the inspiration for the story of Arthur, Lancelot and Guinevere. The legend was the basis for Richard Wagner's (1813–83) opera *Tristan und Isolde*, which premiered in 1865. The Toff Boy might be reminded of the legend, thinking of love that crosses insurmountable barriers, while enamoured with Miss Hopper.
84. *tin weskit*: tin waistcoat, meaning a suit of armour. The Toff Boy is sounding out Miss Hopper about her feelings for him.
85. *Suited me! ... I cried*: The Toff Boy imagines that the power of the landlord is left in the past but uses his sense of entitlement to seduce Miss Hopper.
86. *Sir Godfrey's Bride*: by Ruth B. Yates, published in 1903.
87. '*Noble Sir Arthur an' Pretty Mollee*: a traditional song originating in Northumbria, alternatively titled 'Sir Arthur and Charming Mollee'. The 'Sir Arthur' of the song is believed to be Sir Arthur Haselrigg, governor of Tynemouth Castle during Cromwell's Commonwealth. Miss Hopper correctly recalls the verses she recites.
88. *broom-stick business*: meaning a sexual relationship outside of marriage. The phrase refers to the saying 'living over the brush' or 'jumping the broom', a practice that signifies a couple beginning a life together without the official or religious sanction of marriage. Mollee refuses to be Sir Arthur's mistress.
89. *Lord Lytton*: see above, p. 423 n. 50. The opening line of Lytton's *Paul Clifford* (1830), beginning 'It was a dark and stormy night', has been held as an example of poor writing and purple prose. The Toff Boy shows his ignorance about literature, creating an irony between his fantasy of educating Miss Hopper and her wider knowledge of the origins of the poor-quality novels he reads.
90. *tow-pickin' job*: meaning she would be sentenced to penal servitude for the crime. Tow picking or oakum picking, an occupation prisoners and workhouse inmates were set, prepared fibre for spinning or for use on ships.
91. *Barbara Allen*: a folk song originating around the late seventeenth century, also known as 'Barbara Ellen' or 'Barb'ry Allen', about a young man dying of unrequited love. The Toff Boy is teasing the woman by suggesting his unrequited love for her.
92. *he*: Editor Robert Blatchford had set the intended reader as male when he addressed his *Merrie England* series (1893) to the fictional reader 'John Smith'.
93. *"Forty shillin' ... starve*: The man is fined or threatened with prison for not sending his child to school. Since the passing of Mundella's Elementary Education Act of 1880, school attendance was compulsory between the ages of five and ten. The man's declaration of starvation might refer to the forty-shilling fine or the loss of his son's earnings.
94. *pristine gander ... frenzied satiety*: reference to the goose clubs, where working people would save regularly over the year to ensure they could afford a bird for Christmas dinner. There were also burial clubs, which saved towards an elaborate funeral. Middle-class philanthropists, who would urge thrift in the workers, were dismayed that efforts to save would be spent on what were considered fripperies.
95. *Party politics ... Bernard Shaw*: an ironic list for the socialist reader, as party politics divided the worker between parties working for the enrichment of the employer and landowner; the British Constitution is unwritten; the Gaming Act of 1845 had criminalized gaming houses and organized card or dice games; the mainstream press was biased against the socialist movement; Bethlem Hospital in St George's Fields, London, was renowned for its brutal regime for psychiatric patients during the first half of the nineteenth century; George Bernard Shaw (1856–1950) occasionally contributed to

the *Clarion* despite promoting Fabianism, a more theoretical form of socialism than the *Clarion* group's jollier style. The narrator humorously wonders how some of the working or underclasses could have such an uncivilized attitude to Christmas with all these august institutions in the country.

96. *pantomime fairy's "trip"*: not as elegant as the pantomime fairy. The good fairy is a traditional character in the long tradition of pantomime and enters and exits stage right to signify her goodness. The pantomime's association with Christmas is an example of the relationship between religious festivals and carnival; see M. Taylor, *British Pantomime Performance* (Bristol: Intellect, 2007).

97. *Salvation Army*: a Christian Methodist movement founded in 1865 by William (1829–1912) and Catherine (1829–90) Booth in Whitechapel, London. Members of the group were organized in a hierarchical fashion similar to that of the army, and it sent men and women into urban slums to convert the inhabitants to Christianity. There was also some relief work carried out to alleviate some of the sufferings of poverty, but generally the socialist movement was critical of the Salvation Army for elevating the soul above the body's material sufferings and therefore distracting the poor from working towards social, political and economic change; see, for instance, the March 1888 exchange between Henry Hyndman and John Law (Margaret Harkness) in *Justice* after the publication of her novel *Captain Lobe: A Story of the Salvation Army* (1888; republished 1890 under the title *In Darkest London*). Arthur's brother-in-law would be an important man in the group, which was the reason why he had little time for his paid work.

98. *weatherproof eye*: The soldier either has a false eye or is wearing an eye patch.

99. *'ome from the front*: a reference to the returning soldiers after the Second Boer War, which had ended with the signing of the Treaty of Vereeniging in May 1902. Mr Ducker proceeds to claim instrumental actions in the significant battles of the war.

100. *swagger cane*: a stick carried by senior officers in the police or military and not by privates, who are the lowest ranking soldiers in the British army.

101. *Voetsvlei*: In Afrikaans, voetsek means 'get lost' while vlei means 'valley'; perhaps an Afrikaans joke played on the soldier over the name of an area.

102. *First Man ... Commander-in-Chief*: Mr Ducker claims to have been instrumental in all the important parts of the war: the captures of Pretoria in 1900 and Belmont in 1899, and the battle of Graapan in 1901.

103. *Magersfontein*: The battle at Magersfontein was fought in December 1899, and so Soap-Suds 'Erry could not have been a witness to Mr Ducker's successes in later battles.

104. *Paardeberg*: fought February 1900, so not much later than Magersfontein, and still long before many of the battles he claims Soap-Suds 'Erry to have been involved in.

105. *Ladysmith*: The battle of Ladysmith was a victory for the Boers and led to the siege of Ladysmith between October 1899 and February 1900.

106. *Sanna's Post*: a Boer victory over British troops in early 1900. Mr Ducker's comment on 'those who come back' refers to the capture of over 400 men by the Boers as well as the 115 killed.

107. *Catford ... Ilford*: suggesting that people came from far and wide to greet Alfred. The location of Arthur's coffee stall is not made clear, but we know it is south London because in Chapter II the narrator, Beaky and Miss Hopper walk south from Waterloo Bridge. If we guess the stall is around the Newington area, it is unlikely that people are going to walk the nine or ten miles from Walthamstow or Ilford to drink coffee with Alfred. The narrator is indulging in exaggeration in the same manner as Mr Ducker.

108. *black cutty*: a type of clay pipe.

109. *Ollendorf*: Heinrich Gottfried Ollendorff (1803–65), grammarian and author of the new method of learning languages that brought together exercises for reading, writing and speaking. The narrator does not claim to have studied language formation but focuses instead on the production of his work.
110. *Thackeray's view of George VI*: William Makepeace Thackeray (1811–63) was highly critical of what he considered the superficiality of George VI (1763–1830), and this reference is to his lecture series *The Four Georges*, delivered in the USA in 1855, Scotland in 1856 and England in 1857. In the George IV lecture, he described George through his identification with clothing: 'But this George, what was he? I look through all his life, and recognize but a bow and a grin. I try and take him to pieces, and find silk stockings, padding, stays, a coat with frogs and a fur collar, a star and blue ribbon, a pocket-handkerchief prodigiously scented, one of Truefitt's best nutty brown wigs reeking with oil, a set of teeth and a huge black stock, under-waistcoats, more under-waistcoats, and then nothing.'.
111. *Alaska jewellery*: possibly jewellery made of moose horn and etched with pictures of Alaskan wildlife.
112. *fashinate*: an affected pronunciation of fascinate. Alfred wants the narrator to distract the woman while he gives his attention to Miss Hopper.
113. *Khedival Government*: Khedive is the title of a viceroy or governor of Egypt, an Arab equivalent of king.
114. *Commander-in-Chief ... Prussia*: The multiplication of confidence by an increased number of young ladies, taken to its conclusion, would raise Trooper Alfred to the commanding officer in an eastern country (Sirdar) and in Ireland (Cork), present him with the freedom of the City of London, raise him to a major in the Prussian army and a knight of the realm (Knight Commander), decorate him with the highest military honour (VC) and make him a member of the Royal Victorian Order (MVO). The final set of letters appended to Alfred's name refer to the General Post Office (GPO), as the narrator gets carried away with the abbreviations.
115. *Breacherprom*: breach of promise. Until the early twentieth century the agreement of a woman to marry a man was viewed in law as a binding contract. Alfred has proposed to Miss Cobworthy and is now trying to extricate himself from the engagement.
116. *And here comes ... my head*: the final line of the children's nursery rhyme and game 'Oranges and Lemons'. In the game, two children form an arch with their arms, and others walk through singing the song. On the final line the arch is dropped and the child caught is 'out'. Here the narrator is referring to the length of his chapter in relation to his allotted space and the 'chopping' of the end of the page at the middle of his story.
117. *corpuscular swain*: Corpuscular is literally a minute particle but probably used here as a reference to blood corpuscles; swain is a lover or, probably in this instance, a man of low standing. Miss Cobworthy is accusing the narrator of acting the 'bloody fool'.
118. *'Ere we go round the mulberry bush*: an English nursery rhyme dating from the 1840s, which would be sung, holding hands, moving around in a circle. To Beaky, the participants in this dance are circling around each other.
119. *seidlitz powder*: a compound of tartaric acid, sodium bicarbonate and potassium sodium tartrate that acts as a mild laxative.
120. *This is the grave ... 'er like again*: not identified; possibly a real, parody or pastiche of a popular music hall song or ditty.
121. *Festina lente*: commonly translated as more haste, less speed. Mr Fothergill is demonstrating his repetitiousness and pedantry, which will annoy the narrator later in the chapter.

122. *St. Boniface of the Benighted*: St Boniface (Winfrid/Winfryth, d. 755) brought Christianity to Germany. Fothergill imagines the coffee stalls 'civilizing' and educating their customers.
123. *honest ... bark*: but no coffee.
124. *vine leaves ... hair*: The sailor is drunk; the vine leaves suggest Dionysus, god of the grape harvest, and intoxicated revelry.
125. *poll*: her hair; poll can refer to the whole skull or the part of the head where the hair grows. The narrator is referring either to the faded beauty of her naturally blonde hair or to the fact that she dyes it blonde.
126. *cop the pleeceman*: a suggestion that Mr Fothergill, returning home unexpectedly early, might find his wife with a policeman. The suggestion is greeted with hilarity by the coffee stall regulars, but the meaning is opaque to Mr Fothergill.
127. *Nunquam*: Robert Blatchford; see the *Clarion* headnote in Volume 2, pp. 1–3.
128. *So theer 'e sot ... the pur-ah-pul Joe*: In *Oddities: A Book of Unexplained Facts* (London: Philip Allen, 1928), the author, Rupert T. Gould, claims that this part of the song refers to the murder of Marat by Charlotte Corday.
129. *Bloemfontein*: a city in central South Africa, 300 miles from the sea. Trooper Alfred is teasing the drunken sailor, and the game is joined by the other coffee stall regulars, who proceed to name places a long way from coastlines.
130. *sither*: zither, a string instrument introduced to Britain in the 1850s.
131. *cake-walk*: Originally a competition for graceful walking among African Americans with a cake as the prize, it became a dance based on the movements of cake-walking. Albert is walking with unusual movements along the tram lines.
132. *quartern*: a quarter of a pint; Albert is supplying the woman with large mugs of coffee.
133. *a man and a brother*: 'Am I Not a Man And a Brother', the slogan of the movement advocating the abolition of slavery. The regulars at Arthur's coffee stall are practitioners of human equality.
134. *fever-van*: a forerunner of the ambulance and used to transport people with infectious diseases, usually scarlet fever or diphtheria, to the isolation or infectious diseases hospital. The 'drawbacks' would be the very real possibility of catching a potentially fatal infection.
135. *carbolix*: carbolic; carbolic acid was used as a disinfectant in the vans to try to minimize the chances of passing the infections on to others.
136. *Fred Archer*: jockey (1857–86). Archer caught typhoid after weakening himself dieting to race the horses and committed suicide by gunshot on the second anniversary of his wife's death.
137. *zareeba*: zariba or zareba from the Sudanese, a defensive enclosure – usually of wild bushes – to withstand an attack by enemies or wild animals. The red-faced man is accusing Arthur of hiding behind his stall.
138. *welsh*: meaning to cheat or dupe. Considering the red-faced man's association with horse-racing and betting, it was probably meant specifically to refer to the refusal to pay a lost wager.
139. *Christmas box*: a gift of money at Christmas from those to whom the receiver has performed a service; a seasonal and often substantial tip. The red-faced man is indicating that those for whom he worked were suitably appreciative of his efforts.
140. *take a month*: The overseer is giving the red-faced man a month's notice of the termination of his employment.

141. *a Jew for its secretary*: The figure of the Jew was a problematic one for British socialists because of the very visible examples of extreme wealth and extreme poverty. Henry Mayers Hyndman of the SDF was the most outspoken against the Jews, many of whom had migrated to Britain after the Russian pogroms following the assassination of Tsar Alexander II in March 1881. Hyndman blamed Jewish financiers for the Second Boer War and attempted to justify his criticism of the Jews by emphasizing the economic, rather than religious, aspects: 'Attacking Jewish monopolies would not lead to a hate of the Jewish proletarian, and so far as these were concerned Socialists were anxious to work in harmony with them for any objects held in common ... unfortunately we could never attack the wealthy Jews without the poorer ones came to their defence'; Hyndman, *Justice*, 10 March 1900. The *Clarion* was not so overt in its criticism of the Jewish race; nevertheless, Robert Blatchford's serial 'No. 66' (7 January–1 April 1893) featured a Jewish employer who is given a beating by the protagonist for overworking his employees.
142. *Sheenies*: an abusive word for a Jew.
143. *stiver*: a penny. A cab driver would hire the cab and horses from his master and would pay between fifteen and sixteen shillings a day for the equipment before he could start earning his own money.
144. *Taxameter*: a machine to calculate the fare according to distance travelled, which could be seen by the passenger. The machine standardized fares and prevented overcharging. The red-faced man recognizes that the opportunities to make a greater return from passengers and to raise his earnings after the hire fee had been paid was being made impossible.
145. *Jap business*: the Russo–Japanese War, 1904–5.
146. *Bowers*: Boers. The red-faced man is referring to the massive loss of horses during the Second Boer War and the commissioning of domestic horses to be sent to the battles in South Africa. The loss of horses during the war was the highest ever recorded, totalling around 300,000 between 1899 and 1901.
147. *square-rigged mariner*: A square-rigged sail is rectangular and held to the mast by a horizontal spar; the mariner is described as being both tall and wide.
148. *The Word*: the word of God. The sober mariner is preaching to the public, a hobby at odds with sailors' reputation for drunken revelry.
149. *When the wicked man ... soul alive*: Ezekiel 18:27. God, in this chapter, places the responsibility for sin on the individual and promises salvation for those who repent their sins. The mariner's partner is assuming the cabmen have sinned and is exhorting them to repent.
150. *coal tickets*: The cabmen are only interested in the material help offered by the church. Concerns about the low levels of church attendance in the working classes were exacerbated by the motivations for attendance being based on the receipt of charity in the form of money, food, blankets and tickets for coal. When a church ceased giving material aid, the congregation would often move on to another church that was giving charity. Gareth Stedman Jones commented that 'It is a pleasant irony that the poor should adopt a thoroughly utilitarian attitude in the one realm in which the middle class considered it to be inappropriate'; *Languages of Class* (Cambridge: Cambridge University Press, 1983), p. 196.
151. *Limus Reach*: Limehouse Reach, an important part of the London docks. The sailor, when drunk, has the respect of all other sailors.
152. *firemen*: the stokers of the ship's boiler, renowned for being the toughest of the mariners.
153. *Joe Golightly an the captain's spine*: The sailor's partner is the singing sailor in Chapter XV.

154. *Shadwell*: a part of Limehouse Reach and so a convenient place to board for sailors on shore leave.
155. *St. Vitus Waltz*: usually St Vitus's Dance, a historic name for Sydenham chorea, a disease of the neurologic system that results in spasmodic movement of the limbs.
156. *soverink*: sovereign.
157. *I 'ave ... to me*: a children's poem entitled 'My Little Sister' included in the collection *One Thousand Poems for Children* (1903) edited by Roger Ingpen, but without a note of the author.
158. *Artz Mountain*: The Hartz Mountain strain of canary was bred in the Hartz Mountain region of Germany and was one of the most popular pet bird breeds. The shop owner is making the most of the visitors as potential customers.
159. *'Vast heaving*: a nautical term meaning to stop immediately. The shopman uses the language of the sailor, including an earlier reference to the narrator and Trooper Alfred as 'lubbers' and the later exclamation of 'shiver me timbers', because of his location within the maritime area of Shadwell but in the manner of a caricature of the language, as the narrator goes on to note.
160. *throstle*: thrush; presumably the man is selling a song thrush alongside other song birds.
161. *Captain Marryat*: Frederick Marryat (1792–1848), a sailor and naval officer from 1806 to 1830, who retired to become a novelist and writer. He is remembered for his many novels of naval life based on his own experiences.
162. *dicky-birds*: small birds such as canaries, robins and, presumably, thrush.
163. *breeks ... marlinspikes*: breeks: breeches; peak-halyards: tackle for lowering a sail; marlinspikes: a tool used to splice rope. True sailors do not spice their language with references to the tools of their trade.
164. *Ratcliffe Highway*: or Ratcliff, an ancient road in the East End of London dating back to the Roman period. In the nineteenth century it was notorious for crime and violence and was the place of the Ratcliffe Highway murders of 1811, when two families were murdered in the area within days of each other. Joe Tuttle's association with the area suggests an unsavoury nature.
165. *four-ale*: ale sold at fourpence a quart; the Friendly Grip is a public house selling cheap beer.
166. *cake-walker*: see above, p. 429 n. 131.
167. *coon dance*: the cake walk.
168. *beer engines*: pumps for dispensing ale from the cask into the glass.
169. *Hebrew patriarch ... spotted cows*: Genesis 25:43. Jacob is denied his wages of the spotted and speckled sheep and goats by Laban, who removes them from the flock tended by Jacob. Jacob breeds a stronger flock of spotted and speckled animals, leaving Laban the weaker part of the flock. Mr Tuttle looks as though Jacob has bred him especially for his spotted skin.
170. *bull-throated ... strabismus*: bull-throated: having a thick and heavy neck; *retroussé*: usually used to describe a nose turned up at the tip, a feature considered attractive on a woman; strabismus: misalignment of the eyes, commonly known as a squint. Mr Tuttle is not considered an attractive man by either the narrator or Trooper Alfred.
171. *picture hat*: a large, elaborately trimmed hat that became very fashionable in the late Victorian and Edwardian periods.
172. *Ow Dinah ... 'Cos*: This song is unidentified but presumed to be a pastiche of the blackface minstrelsy that had been popular with working-class audiences since the 1830s.

Nasal obligato: the obligato is an essential part of the musical work but is subordinate to the main melody. Mr Tuttle's nose is making a whistling noise as he is singing.
173. *Rangitang*: orang-utan; the man is deemed a lower species for disliking Joe's entertainment.
174. *next fur stripes*: Alfred is in line for promotion to lance corporal, the next rank after trooper.
175. *This life ... we're not*: not identified.
176. *peg tops*: spinning tops, a child's toy. Trooper Alfred, for all his age and experience, is still seen as a wilful boy by his father.
177. *pink rat*: also sometimes pink elephant, a hallucination caused by delirium tremens after a sudden withdrawal from alcohol by someone who drinks heavily.
178. *Melincourt*: Thomas Love Peacock's novel of 1817 about an orang-utan mimicking humanity and standing for Parliament.
179. *bankrupts at Brighton*: Brighton, fifty-four miles from London, would be a pleasant place to escape the demands of debtors.
180. *Mrs. Sherwood*: Mary Martha Sherwood (1775–1851), novelist and author of children's stories renowned for their evangelical Christian themes.
181. *bump of caution*: a reference to phrenology or craniology, the science of telling a person's psychology by looking at and feeling the shape of the skull. It was believed that the configuration of a person's skull would relate to certain faculties associated with certain areas of the brain. It was commonly known as 'having your bumps felt'. Lyons is playing with this idea, naming the result of a former injury in the language of phrenology.
182. *Baden-Powell waistcoat*: a reference to Robert Baden-Powell (1857–1941), lieutenant-general in the British Army, garrison commander during the Siege of Mafeking (1899–1900) during the Second Boer War, from which developed the boy scout movement. Arthur's waistcoat is made of the khaki wool of the British Army uniform.
183. *Albert chain*: a watch chain with a T-bar that would be tucked into a buttonhole from which would hang another length of chain to which charms would be attached. The narrator suggests that Arthur is a member of a Masonic Lodge, alluded to in the conversation between Arthur and Mr Honeybunn in Chapter X, and a high-ranking member with the status of Worshipful Master.
184. *Fleet Street soup*: a reference to the association between the journalism profession and high alcohol consumption.
185. *tee-totaller*: one who abstains from alcohol. Early temperance advocates focused on encouraging the refusal to drink spirits while allowing beer, but later advocates promoted total abstinence (teetotalism). On 1 September 1832 the 'Seven Men of Preston' who formed the Preston Temperance Society, including the working-class journalist and reformer Joseph Livesey (1794–1884), pledged to abstain entirely from drinking alcohol, except for medicinal purposes. There were other, earlier temperance societies, but Preston was the first to abstain entirely. There is an unsubstantiated story that the term 'teetotal' was coined by Richard Turner (1790–1846) of Preston, whose stutter, when taking the temperance pledge, became the word used for abstinence from alcohol. Turner's *Oxford Dictionary of National Biography* entry points out that while Irish labourers had used the term to mean complete or absolute, Turner's use gave it a specific meaning that has lasted for almost two centuries.
186. *London-be-the-Sea*: a popular nickname for Brighton as the favoured holidaying destination of the inhabitants of the capital.
187. Pimlico: a generally affluent area of London in the City of Westminster and close to the Houses of Parliament. Arthur is missing the working-class areas of London, where he feels more comfortable.

188. *stones ... water*: Brighton seafront, with its shingle beach, entertainment and the sea.
189. *Bath chairs*: an early version of the wheelchair that was used by the elderly or the infirm. Arthur's comment reinforces his statement of Brighton as a town with a quiet and sedate atmosphere.
190. *Brighton methylated*: methylated spirits, pure alcohol with additives to make it unsuitable for consumption but which is sometimes consumed by those in the last stages of alcoholism. Even Brighton's whisky is unpalatable to Arthur.
191. *Walworth Road*: a main road in South London that runs through Walworth from Elephant and Castle to Camberwell.
192. *Dame – Grand – Falconer of the Primrose League*: The Primrose League (1883–2004) was an organization that promoted the principles of the British Conservative Party. The head of the League was termed the Grand Master, and the position was held by important male members of the Conservative Party. The narrator's aunt was not the head of the League, but the point is that her politics and social position would be incompatible with Arthur and Arthur's mode of dress.
193. *Waiting for his share of Daniel*: see above, p. 424 n. 66.
194. *circs.*: see above, p. 423 n. 39.
195. *'ot-cross-bun maker*: a trade only occasionally useful, like the later-mentioned leap year almanacs and glass for viewing an eclipse. In Mr Walpole's opinion, Joseph Tuttle is a shirker.
196. *owdy clone sachy*: eau de cologne sachet.
197. *nog*: a wooden peg or a wedge used for structural support in mines. Miss Hopper is accusing Beaky of being as incapable of persuasion as a piece of wood.
198. *War Office regulations*: Concerns about the efficiency and training of volunteer regiments and soldiers were raised during and after the Second Boer War. A Royal Commission on Militia and Volunteer Forces was set up in early 1903, and Hugh Oakley Arnold-Forster (1855–1909) was appointed to the War Office to address the problem. He planned to introduce a two-tier system of enlistment: a two-year short service which would train soldiers to defend the nation on home ground, and a nine-year long service for defending the empire. His lack of political diplomacy and Prime Minister Arthur Balfour's (1848–1930) resignation in 1905 prevented his plans being implemented.
199. *'e can play nap*: a game of cards where players forecast the number of tricks their five cards will win; *OED*.
200. *timekeeper*: one who records arrivals, departures and progress of work by employees before the advent of automated clocking systems. A timekeeper would need to maintain a professional distance from other employees to ensure strict impartiality.
201. *ipse*: himself; truly himself, in his right mind; *OED*.

Beswick, 'Brother Eli on Tramps'

1. *Slattox*: Slattocks is a small town situated between Rochdale and Oldham, Lancashire.
2. *ingle-nook*: 'ingle', meaning fire, and 'nook', a corner. Eli is sat inside a large fireplace that has seating on either side of the fire.
3. *'Slopperty Slips' ... 'Jellygraph'*: *Jellygraph*, a mispronunciation of the *Daily Telegraph* (1855–present). The description of its apparent levity is ironic as the *Telegraph* has a reputation for seriousness in its journalism, whereas *Punch, or the London Charivari* (1841–1992, 1996–2002) was a satirical magazine. There is no record of *Slopperty Slips*, but the word 'slopperty' is listed in John Collier's (1708–86) *The Miscellaneous Works of*

Tim Bobbin (Salford: Cowdray and Slack, 1812). Collier was the first Lancashire dialect author, writing under the pseudonym of 'Tim Bobbin', and the title of this 'paper' may be a reference to him.

4. *gizzard*: a bird's second stomach; used generally to signify something distasteful.
5. *Camel-Bannerman*: Sir Henry Campbell-Bannerman (1836–1908), Liberal politician and Prime Minister after Balfour's resignation in 1905. Campbell-Bannerman would be political fodder for the editor of the *Telegraph*; his Liberal politics would offend the Conservative paper, and his early Conservative allegiance before his move to the Liberal Party would exacerbate animosity.
6. *Fattygewed Freddy and Lassichewed Lancerlot ... greenwood tree*: The *Telegraph*'s correspondent draws a picture of tramps as lazy (Fatigued Freddy and Lassitude Lancelot) and living a life of pastoral indolence, referencing William Shakespeare's (1564–1616) poem 'Under the Greenwood Tree' in *As You Like It*, Act II, scene v: 'Who doth ambition shun, / And loves to live i' the sun, / Seeking the food he eats, / And pleas'd with what he gets'.
7. *dobby-horses*: 'Dobby' means 'stupid', but in this context it refers to the wooden pole with a horse-shaped head that children ride at play; an older term for a hobby horse. These would be 'ridden' by children either at play or in the parades for Whitsun Walks, or 'Weyks'. Whitsuntide is the week following Pentecost, the seventh Sunday after Easter, and a religious holiday for Christians. The holiday was celebrated throughout Lancashire, with towns organizing walks or parades of Sunday-school children through the town, brass band displays and competitions.

Blatchford, 'Dismal Dan's Story. "The Only Chance He Ever Gave."'

1. *M.P.*: a member of the Royal Military Police, the corps responsible for policing servicemen (and now women). Formed as an official corps in 1877, the military police have a reputation for being tough.
2. *oof bird*: a wealthy person or a source of money; *OED*. The corporal is referring to either his own lack of money or his inability to find someone to pay for his drinks. The hint is taken by Dan, who replenishes his corporal's drink.
3. *provost sergeant*: a sergeant in the military police.
4. *Boots*: Blatchford, when recalling his time in the army, described the storytelling (known as 'cuffers') indulged in by soldiers after lights out. In order to check if his listeners were awake, the narrator would periodically call out 'Boots', which would be returned by his listeners in a chorus of 'Spurs'. The corporal's 'Boots' suggests that Dan has a story to tell.
5. *lucifer*: a friction match. The original 'Lucifers' contained sulphate, but later matches used phosphate. The 'safety' match, which could not be lit on material other than that on the box, was invented in 1844 and produced by British company Bryant and May from 1862, but it is not used by Danny, who lights his match with his army trousers.
6. *quiff*: a curl of hair plastered to the forehead; *OED*.
7. *four-ringed man*: a reference to the embroidered rings around the cuff of the uniform to indicate rank. Four rings would indicate Jobling's rank as a colonel, and the antipathy for Peggy was shared across the ranks. The cuff rings were introduced in 1902, so Blatchford is indicating rank through the current army uniform and not as it was during his own period in service.
8. *comether*: to wheedle, coax or persuade; *OED*.
9. *biz.*: business. Peggy has no one to arrest.

10. *magazine*: a storehouse or hold for goods. In this context the store will probably be ammunition.
11. *Bosjesman*: a South African term for an African bushman. It is used here as an insult to the soldier.
12. *mufti*: civilian clothes.
13. *my eyes and Betty Martin*: usually 'all my eye and Betty Martin', meaning something is nonsense. Here it is used as an exclamation of surprise and joy.
14. *turns on a bull's-eye*: turns on a lantern. The lantern was known as a 'bull's-eye' because of the convex glass that spreads the light in a cone shape.
15. *straight griffin*: a griffin usually means a hint or signal; *OED*. In this context, the Sergeant Major is issuing a direct warning for the soldiers to cease their celebrations.

Lyons, 'A Distressed Gentlewoman. A True History'

1. *rooked*: to cheat or swindle; *OED*. The author is making a play on words when he describes the swindle as a 'rook' and the city as a 'rookery', the latter meaning both a place of cheats and a densely populated area, usually a city slum.
2. *two-and-a-kick-me-down*: presumably rhyming slang for a half-crown (which the woman hands back to the narrator), worth two and a half shillings or thirty pennies.
3. *transpontine*: in this context, meaning melodramatic or sensational; *OED*. The woman's vocabulary is more sophisticated than is usual for a street swindler.
4. *Omar Khayyam*: *The Rubaiyat of Omar Khayyam* is a series of poems attributed to Omar Khayyam which were translated and published by Edward FitzGerald (1809–83) in 1859.

Grose, 'The Golden Egg'

1. *Embankment ... Temple Gardens*: Opened in 1870, the Thames Embankment, the collective name for the Victoria, Albert and Chelsea Embankments, reclaimed around thirty-seven acres of marsh land at the side of the Thames between Westminster and Chelsea Hospital. The Embankment, like Trafalgar Square, had become a place where the homeless gravitated at night to sleep, and it was an image of the problem of poverty in London at the end of the nineteenth century. Sociological surveys of poverty in the capital included descriptions of the Embankment homeless in works by Charles Booth, George Sims, Andrew Mearns and others. The image was also drawn into fiction by other socialist authors, including A. Neil Lyons and Robert Blatchford. Middle Temple and Inner Temple Gardens sit beside the Victoria Embankment between the Blackfriars and Waterloo Bridges.
2. *co-proprietors of the Municipal wealth*: a worker; somebody who creates municipal wealth and has a right to its disposal.

Graham, 'A Fisherman'

1. *semi-sailors, semi-longshoremen*: The men are employed to both sail the steamer and unload its cargo. In this case it is the cattle and their drovers.
2. *fugleman*: somebody who is well drilled and acts as an example; *OED*. Usually a military term, but here used to describe the main drover of the group.
3. *Pladda from the Mull*: an island to the south of Arran in the Firth of Clyde with a lighthouse designed by Thomas Smith dating from 1790 near the Mull of Kintyre, rather

than the island in Loch Linnhe between Lismore and Ardmucknish Bay between the mainland and the Isle of Mull.
4. *strathspey*: a reel for two dancers; *OED*.
5. *heather mixture tweed*: a form of Harris tweed made by twisting different coloured strands of wool.
6. *forebits ... thraws*: forebit, to the front of the foremast where the ropes are secured; 'heids and thraws' means 'from heads to tails', as the fiddler plays to the high and low of local Scottish society on the steamer.
7. *Dunoon*: a resort town on the Cowal Peninsula, Argyll, on the Firth of Clyde.
8. *stan' o' black*: the dress of a minister or church elder. Graham had criticized the calcification of Scottish literary character, which 'is composed of ministers, elders, and maudlin whiskified physicians'; *Saturday Review*, 1896, quoted in A. Nash, *Kailyard and Scottish Literature* (Amsterdam and New York: Rodopi, 2007), p. 45.
9. *goin' aboot body*: meaning of no fixed abode. In England, the man would be referred to as a tramp.
10. *shellback*: a sailor.
11. *wonders of the deep*: Psalm 107:24: 'These see the works of the Lord and his wonders in the deep'. The sailors question the wondrousness of the element that may be the death of them.
12. *Argyle's bowling-green*: a range of peaks between Loch Long and Loch Goil. The misnomer 'bowling green' is not an indication of the area's flatness but a corruption of Baile na Greine, which is Gailic for 'sunny hamlet'. See *Gazetteer for Scotland*, at http://www.scottish-places.info [accessed 7 February 2013].
13. *There shall be no more sea ... Patmos*: Revelations 21:1: 'And I saw a new heaven and a new earth: for the first heaven and the first earth were passed away; and there was no more sea'. 'John' is John the Revelator, who is referred to by modern scholars as John of Patmos; doited means to be muddled. The old sailor is questioning the wisdom of John's prophesy.
14. *auri sacra fames*: the lust for gold. The phrase relates to St Paul's declaration that money is the root of all evil (1 Timothy 6:10). The fisherman is referring to his quest for riches, which took him away from the sea.
15. *arle*: usually used as the verb of earnest money; used in this context to signify the earnestness of Samuel Johnson (1709–84), lexicographer.
16. *Cumbreaes*: Great Cumbrae and Isle of Cumbrae, two islands in the Firth of Clyde.
17. *dunter's*: usually meaning to hit or blow in Scots dialect, but here used as a term for a porpoise or dolphin.
18. *Whiting Bay ... midshipmen*: Whiting Bay is a coastal town on the Isle of Arran, an area renowned for shipwrecks.
19. *bannock's buttered*: unleavened bread, usually made with barley or pease in Scotland. The fisherman is showing he knows the power of providence and will.
20. *Glesca*: Glasgow, the largest city in Scotland.
21. *Largs*: a town on the Firth of Clyde
22. *Chuchullin*: Cú Chulainn, the Irish hero and Hound of Ulster, is trained to fight by female warrior Scáthach in Alba, the Gaelic name for Scotland.
23. Herald: The *Herald* is a Scottish newspaper founded in 1783.
24. *Bogatstky's 'Golden Treasury'*: Carl Heinrich von Bogatzky (1690–1774), author of devotional literature for children, including *A Golden Treasury for the Children of God* (1718).

25. *Erastianism*: Erastianists hold that the state is superior to the church, a misinterpretation of the argument of Thomas Erastus, who argued that sinners should be punished by the state rather than the by church through withholding sacrament.
26. *Tophet*: Jeremiah 7:31–2. Topheth is the high place where sacrifices were made and burnt offerings presented to God. The sailor laments the toning down of the 'fire and brimstone' teaching of the Bible.
27. *Fairlie*: on the eastern shore of the Firth of Clyde looking towards the Isle of Arran.
28. *michtily refreshed*: a polite term for drunk.
29. *Rabbie ... Burns*: Robert Burns, celebrated Scots poet, also referred to in the dialect as Rabbie. He was the son of a ploughman, and his poetry used the Scots language and dialect. His poem 'A Man's a Man for a' That' was a favourite with British socialists for its egalitarian sentiment. His birthday, 25 January, is now celebrated as Burns Night.
30. *Walter Scott*: Sir Walter Scott (1771–1832), Scottish author who organized the visit of King George IV to Scotland in 1822, the first English reigning monarch to do so since 1650. The visit was theatrically organized, and Scott intended it to be a celebration of Scottish tradition and a gathering of the clans; even the king wore tartan. Scott dined with the king and requested the king's whisky glass as a souvenir. One of Scott's biographers, John Buchan, tells the tale of the broken glass as being the result of Scott's enthusiastic greeting of George Crabbe (1754–1832), while the sailor's version makes Scott a nationalist.
31. *Brig o' Wier*: Bridge of Weir, a village in the lowlands of Scotland.
32. *Tobermory*: fishing port on the Isle of Mull.
33. *Tobermory ... Cree*: Tobermory is situated on the north coast of Mull, and the River Cree enters the sea at Wigtown on the southernmost coast of western Scotland. The sailor makes the point that the fishermen of the west coast are committed in their religion. Cruives are fish traps set in the river.
34. *kyloe*: breed of West Highland cattle.
35. *woman of Samaria*: John 4: Jesus speaks with the Samaritan woman at Jacob's well and tells her that she has five husbands. The sailor is making the same accusation of the woman on the boat.
36. *flauchter feals*: flauchter is possibly faluchter, meaning a spade for cutting turf; feals is fail, meaning a turf or sod used as roofing material. The wind is enough to take the roof off a house.
37. *Weymess Bay ... Gourock*: coastal towns, as the boat rounds to its final destination at the mouth of the Clyde.
38. *cract*: crack, to talk or chat.

J. W. B., 'Men and Things'

1. *Lives iv gr-eat ... loife sublime*: Henry Wadsworth Longfellow (1807–82), 'A Psalm of Life' (1838): 'Lives of great men all remind us / We can make our lives sublime'.
2. *Mafeking*: now Mahikeng. The siege of Mafeking during the Second Boer War was the most celebrated British victory during the conflict. The strategically important town of Mafeking was held against the Boers for 217 days by British troops under the command of Robert Baden Powell. The relief of Mafeking caused wild celebrations in Britain. The word 'mafeking' became a term for riotous celebration.

Hugo, 'The Blackleg, an Agitator's Yarn'

1. *blackleg*: a slang term for a strike breaker, a worker who will do the work of others on strike.
2. *hot-gospeller*: to evangelically preach, to acclaim fanatically; *OED*. The term is used here to suggest the enthusiastic promotion of New Unionism by Vance, not religion.
3. *new unionism*: the unionization of previously non-unionized, unskilled trades. Trade unions were traditionally formed around skilled trades such as weaving, spinning and mining, but the 1888 matchgirls' strike at the Bryant and May factory in London showed that unskilled workers could also benefit from collective action. There was a flurry of unionization at the end of the 1880s as dock workers, gas workers, boilermen, shop assistants and many others were encouraged by a series of successful strikes led by socialists like Tom Mann, Ben Tillett and John Burns. See also 'Citizen' [James Sexton], 'The Blackleg' in Volume 2, pp. 265–347. A downturn in the economy in the early 1890s saw the decline of the new unions through the development of employers' federations such as the Shipping Federation and Engineering Employers' Federation, alongside the National Free Labour Association formed of non-union workers. The realization that union success depended on a strong economy and the power of legislation wielded by the employers, culminating in the Taff Vale decision in 1901 which made unions liable for damages and made picketing illegal, turned socialist and trade union attention to parliamentary representation.
4. *hangman's whip*: Robert Burns, 'Epistle to a Young Friend' (1786): 'The fear o' hell's a hangman's whip / To haud the wretch in order'. Vance keeps the workers in order through fear of retribution.
5. *pow*: a mispronunciation of 'poll', meaning head or hair. See above, p. 429 n. 125.
6. *better-class 'model'*: possibly a reference to philanthropic (model) housing built and run by private companies such as the East End Dwellings Company.

Anon., 'The Marchioness'

1. déjeûner: morning meal, breakfast; *OED*.
2. petit vin: an inferior wine; the term literally means 'small wine' and is used in the same derogatory way that 'small beer' would be used in England.
3. *the Terror*: the Reign of Terror from 3 June 1793 to 28 July 1794, which began with the fall of the Girondin and ended with the arrest, trial and execution of Robespierre. During the Terror hundreds of thousands of people were put to death by guillotine, at first for resisting the revolution and later for their class position; the proportion of aristocrat and upper-middle-class executions rose throughout the period.
4. *Jacobin*: a member or sympathizer of a French political group, founded in 1789, to establish society on the principles of equality and democracy; *OED*. The term suggested extreme political opinions; thus the farmer's neighbour is willing to see the farmer put to death for harbouring an aristocrat child.
5. *Furies*: According to legend, the Furies were dreadful goddesses who were sent to avenge wrongs and punish crimes; *OED*. The revolutionary woman's insistence on killing the Marchioness is likened to the inexorable punishment of the Furies, a likeness reinforced by her dishevelled hair, reminiscent of the snakes the Furies had for hair or within their hair.

6. *Tree of Liberty*: Liberty trees were planted after the revolution and were inspired by the Liberty Tree in Boston, Massachusetts, an elm tree signifying resistance to the Stamp Act imposed by George III.
7. *Carmagnole*: a lively song popular with French revolutionists; *OED*.

Starr, 'The Doll Shop'

1. *Penrhyn Anachronisms ... Tyrannies*: a reference to George Sholto Gordon Douglas-Pennant (1836–1907), second Baron Penrhyn, who founded the North Wales Property Association in 1886 to resist land nationalization plans promoted in the press. He rescinded the 1874 Pennant Lloyd agreement at his slate quarry, which allowed workers to control wages and management and to set wages by collective bargaining. The Penrhyn dispute between owner and workers, lasting between 1900 and 1903, saw riots and the use of troops against the workers and ended only when the workers' funds ran out.
2. *West Ham ... hundred other suits*: clothing associated with the poor working class: the worker in the slums of London, the agricultural labourer, the low-ranking soldier, the police, the sailor and the lifeboatman. All are essential to create and protect the wealth and body of the rich but are regarded as inferior to those they protect. The worker will 'look very well' as an MP, but the public is not yet ready for the worker in a position of power.
3. *Charles Kingsley ... William Morris ... John Ruskin*: Charles Kingsley (1819–75), the son of a Hampshire country gentleman, was ordained in 1842 and worked to alleviate poverty; he practised Christian socialism by setting up co-operative workshops as well as preaching the ideas of the movement. He declared himself a Chartist but rejected the revolutionary aspect, and he drew his moral Chartism and Christian socialism into novels such as *Yeast* (1849) and *Alton Locke* (1850). William Morris (1834–96) was the eldest surviving son of a wealthy City financier; he first found fame as a poet and began the move towards socialism after reading Ruskin's chapter 'On the Nature of Gothic Architecture' in *The Stones of Venice* (1853). Morris went on to join the SDF in 1883, Unhappy with the parliamentary direction Henry Hyndman, chairman of the SDF, was leading the group, he left the SDF to form the revolutionary Socialist League at the end of 1884. John Ruskin (1819–1900), son of a prosperous sherry merchant, was a critic of both art and society. Although not a socialist, declaring himself an old-school Tory, Ruskin's work combined both the aesthetic and the social, and he criticized the conditions of manufacture that dehumanized the producer. All three men were from a class of society that benefited from the status quo but who relentlessly criticized the social structure and its effects on the worker.

Ford, 'Aunt Caroline's Christmas Eve'

1. *Colne Valley*: an area of the east Pennines in West Yorkshire between Oldham and Huddersfield along the route of the River Colne.
2. *third-class passengers*: During the early years of British rail travel, there were separate carriages – and at stations separate waiting and dining rooms – for first-, second- and third-class passengers. By the end of the nineteenth century and the early years of the twentieth, rail companies, with dwindling first-class passengers, ended the expensive first-class carriage and renamed second class 'first' while third class became 'second'. The Scottish and north-eastern railway companies were the first to change the class system,

so the reference to third-class passengers may be a referential hangover from the three-class era or used to emphasize the narrator's position in relation to the other passengers.
3. *Stalybridge*: Now a part of Greater Manchester, Stalybridge is to the east of Manchester and an early centre for the industrial production of cotton. The train the passengers are on is travelling southwest.
4. *foot-warmers*: Early trains provided foot-warmers for first-class passengers, which were formed of a metal or wooden box containing hot water, hot bricks or chemicals. It is unlikely that this would be provided for third-class passengers, so the woman is probably referring to the heated pipes that ran through the carriages and were served by the boiler driving the engine.

Plant, 'Our Story. "The Far Land." (A Fragment of Fact.)'

1. *little piecer*: children employed in the cotton factories who would repair broken threads. The work was arduous and poorly paid; a little piecer in Bolton in 1906 would earn 10s. 7d., while the spinner in charge of the machine would earn 45s. 9d.
2. *Shall I ever see ... home agine*: unidentified.

Glasier, 'Andrew Carnegie's Ghost. A Red-Letter Day at Skibo Castle. A Christmas Story'

1. *Andrew Carnegie*: Carnegie (1835–1919) was born in Fife and made his fortune as a steelmaker. The family emigrated to the United States in 1848 and settled in Pittsburgh. Carnegie worked his way up from bobbin-boy in a cotton factory, through interests in oil, rail, bridges and horses to iron and steel. In 1900 he bought the Skibo estate in Sutherland, Scotland, for his retirement, where he promoted himself as a radical, Chartist and philanthropist despite his ruthless use of his workers and destruction of their unions. Carnegie, like Lord Overtoun, is criticized for the partial redistribution of wealth to the poor after having made vast sums of wealth through his pitiless use of his workers.
2. *John Morley ... J.M. Barrie*: John Morley (1838–1923), journalist, editor and Liberal politician; Henry Hartley Fowler, first Viscount Wolverhampton (1830–1911), Liberal politician; Whitelaw Reid (1837–1912), American ambassador to Britain in 1905–12, Liberal Republican and grandson to the editor of the *New York Tribune*; Samuel Story (1841–1925), founder of the *Sunderland Echo* and Liberal politician; W. T. Stead (1849–1912), newspaper editor and Liberal supporter; J. M. Barrie (1860–1937), playwright and novelist, given a peerage by the Liberal government in 1910. The guests reflect Carnegie's involvement in Liberal politics in Britain and his ownership or control of seven British newspapers.
3. *Battle of Bannockburn*: 23–4 June 1314, a Scottish victory in the First War for Scottish independence.
4. *Oh why left I my hame ... ain countrie*: 'The Exile's Song' (1831) by Robert Gilfillan (1798–1850).
5. *one of my books*: After making his fortune, Carnegie published *Triumphant Democracy* (1886), *Wealth* (1889) and *The Gospel of Wealth* (1900) on the benevolent distribution of wealth by the rich to the poor.
6. *Barrin' o' the door, O!*: an old ballad about the stalemate between a husband and wife as to who should bar the door.

7. *Mr. Stead laughed ... with reservation*: Stead was a strict Congregationalist and was renowned for his views on the ungodliness of the theatre. He would, therefore, be discomforted by the performances of the men.
8. *Mr. Barrie ... dramatised*: Barrie was a playwright and novelist whose most famous character is Peter Pan, who first appeared in *Peter Pan in Kensington Gardens* in 1906. The date of this story could suggest that Barrie is testing his work on the audience before publication or production.
9. *Campdown Races*: minstrel song 'Camptown Races' by Stephen Foster (1826–64), first published in 1850. William Ewart Gladstone's (1809–88) enthusiasm for the song reminds the reader that his father's fortune was founded on slave labour working his plantation in Demerera and that Gladstone had not initially supported the abolition of slavery in the 1830s. Blackface minstrelsy had been popular in Britain since the 1830s, especially with working-class audiences.
10. *Madame Blavatsky*: Helena Petrovna Blavatsky (1831–91), founder of theosophy. Stead was fascinated by spiritualism and had introduced Robert Blatchford to the belief. Blatchford was sceptical but turned to spiritualism after the death of his wife in 1921.
11. *Czar of Russia*: Stead developed a deep interest in Russia and met both Tsar Alexander III and Tsar Nicholas II.
12. *Professor Patrick Geddes*: Sir Patrick Geddes (1854–1932) brought his ideas of social evolution and sociology to bear on town planning, publishing *City Development: A Study of Parks, Gardens, and Culture Institutes. A Report to the Carnegie Dunfermline Trust* in 1904. The title 'professor' may be ironic, as Geddes did not complete his degree.
13. *the Homestead strike and the Pinkerton shooting*: Carnegie and Frick's response to a strike by workers at his Homestead Steel Mill in 1892 was to hire Pinkerton guards to allow non-union strike breakers through the strikers' picket line. The Pinkerton guards were an offshoot of Allan Pinkerton's detective agency and were hired out to guard banks and commercial businesses. Frick ordered 300 guards, who attempted to enter the mill by the river. Both agents and strikers were armed, and the clash left ten men dead and scores of people wounded.
14. *John Burns*: Burns (1858–1943) was a leading member of the socialist and new union movement, a member of the SDF and one of the organizers of the London dock strike of 1889. He had originally entered Parliament as an independent labour MP in 1892 and again in 1901, but he gravitated towards Liberalism, being the first working man to achieve cabinet status as president of the Local Government Board in Campbell-Bannerman's administration in 1905. At the end of his political career, in 1918, Burns was supported by a Carnegie pension.
15. *Epictetus and Marcus Aurelius and Milton*: Epictetus (AD 55–135) declared that everything was controlled by fate and humans should attempt only to control what is in their power; Marcus Aurelius (AD 121–80), emperor and Stoic philosopher whose *Meditations* urge self-reliance and the importance of duty and service; John Milton (1608–74) was a Republican and poet whose epic poem *Paradise Lost* (1667) lamented the loss of the republic and aimed to 'justify the ways of God to men'. These men had tried to enhance human existence in their different ways, while Carnegie made money and subsequently aimed to enhance his reputation.
16. *Triumphant Democracy*: Carnegie's book; see above, p. 440 n. 5.
17. *Mrs. Fisk*: possibly a reference to Minnie Maddern Fiske (1865–1932), the famous American stage actress.

18. *Robert Burns ... devil might mend*: for Burns, above, p. 437 n. 29. Burns shows in his poetry the human propensity to carry out evil actions, and the reference might be to Burns's poem 'Address to the De'il' (1785). Although there is no sense of the Devil 'mending', the narrator blasphemously taunts the Devil with God's promise of universal salvation, thus deflating Satan's power.

Görki, 'On the Steppes. Told by a Tramp'

1. *Kherson*: a city in southern Ukraine.
2. *Perekopp*: Perekop, a village on the isthmus connecting Ukraine to the Crimean peninsula.
3. *striking variety of bumps*: a reference to phrenology or craniology; see above, p. 432 n. 181. The 'student' is a particularly unusual man.
4. *Kernoneff*: possibly a reference to Kharkiv, a city in the northeast of Ukraine, or Kaniv in central Ukraine.
5. *moujik*: a variation of muzhik, meaning peasant. These were trousers cut wide on the upper leg and tapered to fit into knee-high boots.
6. *The blessed resurrection ... its praise*: possibly a fragment of a znamenny chant of the Russian Orthodox Church. There were three types of znamenny chant: the Stolpovoi, used for Sundays and festal hymns; the Maly, used for weekday services; and the Bolshoi, used for great events in the church and important festivals.
7. *Crimean hills*: A peninsula in southern Ukraine, the Crimean hills – or mountains – run parallel to the coast on the southeast side of the peninsula. The hills had been an important factor in the Battle of Balaclava (25 October 1854) during the Crimean War (1854–6), as the British Light Cavalry Brigade were ordered to charge the Russian position at the end of South Valley and had to pass the Russian redoubts on the Causeway Heights and Canrobert's Hill.
8. *suck our own paws*: The myth that a bear can assuage hunger by sucking its paws is also applied to the badger in England.
9. *versts*: an old Russian measurement of length equating to two-thirds of a mile; *OED*. The tramps had walked roughly twenty-seven miles.
10. *Kouban*: Kuban, a Cossack area in southern Russia bordering the Black Sea. The tramps must intend to travel by ferry from Crimea to Kuban, which is separated by the Kerchns'ka gulf.
11. *New Athon ... Orel*: New Athos (Novyy Afon) is a city in Abkhazia on the Black Sea; Oryol is a city to the south west of Moscow. The distance between the two cities is roughly 1,400 miles.
12. *Kars*: a city in northeast Turkey.

France, 'Crainquebille'

1. *Rue Montmartre*: a main road in Paris that runs from the junction of Rue Saint-Lazare, Rue Des Martyrs and Rue de Maubeuge to the Église Saint-Eustache.
2. *Sevenpence halfpenny*: The currency has been translated along with the language. 7*d.*, roughly worth £1.70 today, was an important amount at a time when bread would cost just over a penny a pound, and Joseph Rowntree's calculation for subsistence wages was the ability to purchase 4.22 pounds of bread per day.
3. *triumphant palm*: a Christian symbol of victory and an emblem of Christ's triumphant entry into Jerusalem, which is celebrated on Palm Sunday.

4. *black flag of revolt*: The black flag is usually associated with anarchism. Crainquebille is arguing that he wants only the money he is rightly owed and not anarchy.
5. Vache: cows; the English equivalent to insult the police would be 'pig'.
6. *Ambroise Paré Hospital*: Clinique Ambroise Paré is a university hospital in west Paris that is named after Paré (1510–90), the influential French surgeon.
7. *Legion of Honour*: The *Ordre national de la Légion d'honneur* was established by Napoleon Bonaparte in 1802 and is the highest decoration in France. The doctor's word should carry authority.
8. *Ligue de la Patrie Française*: Formed in response to the League of Human Rights, Ligue de la Patrie Française drew together right-wing anti-Dreyfusards who took the side of Esterhazy in the scandal. A solicitor with such political leanings would not take care to give Crainquebille the best representation.
9. *Vieilles Haudriettes quarter*: The Rue des Vielles-Haudriettes is in the Third Arrondissement of Paris. The right-wing nationalists surround Cranquebille within the court.
10. *50 francs*: The currency for this figure has not been translated into British imperial coinage.
11. *nimbus on his head*: A nimbus is a luminous cloud surrounding a deity; *OED*. Crainquebille imagines the courts to be as powerful and unquestionable as gods.
12. *living on my dividends*: Shareholders, who advance money to a business, draw regular dividends from the profit of the company. Crainquebille will not own shares, but the comment may refer to the taxes he has paid, which have been used to build and maintain the prison in which he was incarcerated.
13. *Fabian bureaucrat*: The Fabian Society in Britain, founded in 1884, was renowned for being the socialist group of the intellectual elite, and counted George Bernard Shaw, Beatrice and Sidney Webb and H. G. Wells as members. The Society is given the term 'bureaucrat' here as a reference to their policy of permeation, which aimed to draw socialist policies into the existing political structure of Britain.

Winchevsky, 'He, She, and It'

1. *slavies*: servants, usually female, who carried out general housework instead of being assigned specific duties. 'Slavies' would generally be the only servants employed in a household and were employed to indicate the status of a lower-middle-class family of the 'shabby-genteel' type, as the area is later described.
2. *supper ... dinner*: The vocabulary used for the main meals of the day is an indicator of social class.
3. *red-jackets ... Crimear*: The Crimean War between the Russian Empire and an alliance of the British, French and Ottoman empires was fought between October 1853 and February 1856. The British army uniform was the red coat, except for the artillery, rifles and light cavalry, and 'red coats' was the general term used to indicate a British soldier.
4. *Soho Square*: a square and park located near Charing Cross Road and Tottenham Court Road, London.
5. *Regent's Park*: a park to the north of Soho Square. It was designed by John Nash (1752–1835) on the orders of the Prince Regent (later George IV), and work began in 1818. The park is Crown property.
6. *Bethnal Green*: a slum area of East London renowned for the Old Nichol rookery used by Arthur Morrison (1863–1945) as the setting for *A Child of the Jago* (1896).
7. *Le-ster Square*: Leicester Square, London.

8. *Alhambra*: Alhambra Theatre and Music Hall, Leicester Square. Built in 1854 as the Royal Panopticon of Science and Arts, it became the Alhambra in 1854 and was demolished in 1936.
9. *Her eyebrows ... she paints*: The wearing of makeup was one of the signs of prostitution, which is reinforced here by setting the scene outside a theatre. There has been a historical association between the theatre and prostitution, as Jeffrey Kahan points out in his biography of John Kean (1811–68): 'Prostitution in London was nothing new, nor was its association with the theatre'; *The Cult of Kean* (Aldershot: Ashgate, 2006), p. 84. See also K. Pullen, *Actresses and Whores: On Stage and in Society* (Cambridge: Cambridge University Press, 2005) for her consideration of prostitution and performance.
10. *Frenchies and Prooshians coming to blows*: The Franco–Prussian War was fought between July 1870 and May 1871.
11. *Piccadilly*: Piccadilly, along with Leicester Square, the Haymarket, Oxford Street and Pall Mall, had some of the highest levels of prostitution in the capital, as 'the West End of London was the epicenter of commercial sex in the metropolis in the decades after 1885'; see J. Laite, *Common Prostitutes and Ordinary Citizens: Commercial Sex in London, 1885–1960* (Basingstoke: Palgrave Macmillan, 2012) for further information.
12. *Guy's Hospital*: Founded by Thomas Guy and opened in Southwark, London in 1725, the hospital originally cared for the incurably ill, but by the nineteenth century Guy's practised medicine rather than simply palliative care.

Clarke, 'The Cotton Panic'

1. *Ribble*: The river Ribble begins in the northwest of Yorkshire and runs through Lancashire to the estuary at Lytham. The width of the river at Preston enabled the development of the Port of Preston in the city, and around 1,100 acres of land were reclaimed from the river by the First and Second Ribble Navigation Companies between 1806 and 1853.
2. *"Hard Times"*: The song 'Hard Times Come Again No More', written by Stephen Foster and published in New York in 1854, was popular across the United States and Europe. The song being whistled in Preston, a Lancashire port and mill town, encourages the association of this scene with Charles Dickens's industrial novel *Hard Times*, which is understood to give a fictional account of the Preston weavers' strike of 1853–4.
3. *Pendle Hill*: a hill to the east of Clitheroe, Lancashire, roughly twenty miles from Preston. Pendle Hill is famous for being the site of Henry Power and Richard Towneley's barometer experimentation with air pressure and air density in 1661; of George Fox's vision of the Lord in 1652, with Pendle Hill still associated with the Religious Society of Friends or Quakers; and of the witch trials of 1612, when twelve people from the Pendle area were accused of murder by witchcraft. For further information, see R. Poole, *The Lancashire Witches: Histories and Stories* (Manchester: Manchester University Press, 2002).
4. *th' war is that's makin all t'bother*: the American Civil War, 1861–5. The election of Abraham Lincoln to the American presidency in November 1860 caused division between the southern pro-slavery states and the northern abolitionist states. Southern states such as Alabama, Georgia, South Carolina and Mississippi seceded from the Federation of United States and formed the Confederate States, demanding autonomous government and rejecting federal rule. Most of the cotton-growing states were part of the Confederacy, and it was the revenue generated by the sale of cotton that gave the Confederate States the financial power to be taken seriously by the northern states and Europe. The northern states blockaded the southern ports to prevent the exportation of cotton, and

Britain's dependency on American cotton meant that the blockade had a serious effect on the cotton mills, many of which were in Lancashire.

5. *ancient Romans when they camped at Walton-le-Dale* :Walton-le-Dale is located to the southwest of Preston. A Roman fort was discovered in the nineteenth century at the fork between the river Ribble and the river Darwen.
6. *martello towers*: round defensive towers usually found on the south and east coasts and built to defend the shores from a possible invasion during the Napoleonic Wars, 1803–15. The towers of Preston jail are a defence only against escape rather than attack.
7. *parlour*: a reception room other than the kitchen-living area. The possession of a parlour was a mark of status and relative wealth. The room would be used only on special occasions and kept as 'best' while daily life was conducted around the kitchen-living area.
8. *back court*: tenement buildings built around a central court that would often hold a communal lavatory and water tap for the residents. Courts were usually overcrowded slums, and the Milners' trajectory is to the bottom of society.
9. *Mormons*: also known as the Church of Jesus Christ of Latter-Day Saints (LDS). Founded by Joseph Smith in the United States in 1830, the LDS sent missionaries to Britain in 1837, and in Preston they were given access to the pulpits of a number of Nonconformist churches. The drive was successful, and many were converted; by 1840 there were more Mormons in Britain than there were in the United States.
10. *Preston Guild*: The Preston Guild dates back to 1179, when Henry II granted Preston a royal charter and gave permission to have a Guild of merchants and traders. Periodically the Guild needed to gather and add the names of those who had moved to Preston to begin trading. It was decided that this needed to be carried out at twenty-year intervals. Freedom of trade in Preston was established in 1790, but the tradition of civic procession of trades, feasting and celebration was maintained. Today the Preston Guild is the only Guild celebration still held in Britain.
11. *Indian meal*: a ground grain or pulse usually used as cattle feed for fattening the animals.
12. *Sam Laycock*: Samuel Laycock (1826–93), Lancashire dialect poet, renowned for his dialect poetry and relevant here because his *Lancashire Lyrics!* were published during the cotton famine.
13. *Ballad ... these hard times*: 'Welcome, Bonny Brid' is a dialect poem of a father's welcome to his new baby and his concerns for the child's future, as the baby was born during the difficult times of the cotton famine.
14. *Bolton ... Lancashire*: All are major textile towns in Lancashire. Bolton is twenty-four miles southeast of Preston, Blackburn is nine miles east, Darwen is fourteen miles southeast, Chorley is twelve miles south, Rochdale is forty miles south east, and Wigan is twenty miles south.
15. *Everton toffy*: a sweet confectionary originally made and sold by Molly Bushell in the Everton area of Liverpool. The original recipe was made from loaf sugar and flavoured with lemon. The inclusion of treacle is a later addition to the recipe. The Everton football team is known as the Toffees.
16. *plug-drawin riots ... Lune-street*: the Chartist disturbances. Chartism was a movement that aimed to give the British working-class man the vote, standardize voting constituencies, give salaries to MPs, introduce the secret ballot for elections, abolish the property qualification for the franchise, and introduce annual parliamentary elections. The movement was at its most influential between the years 1838 and 1848, especially in times of deep economic depression, and there were periods of unrest after the huge petitions sent to Parliament were rejected. The Plug Riots or Plug Plots were part of the call for

a general strike in response to the rejection of the Chartist petition of 1842, and they aimed to halt factory production by removing the plugs from steam engines. The riots in Lune Street, Preston, occurred over 12 and 13 August 1842. Magistrates read the riot act to the mob, who were attacking factories. When the crowd began to throw stones at the military instead of dispersing, they were fired upon, and seven men were shot.

17. *Ashton-u-Lyne*: Ashton-under-Lyne. The incredibly high levels of unemployment in the areas affected by the cotton shortage meant that the money that would have been used to support the unemployed through indoor (workhouse) and outdoor relief provided by the Guardians through the Poor Law was woefully inadequate. The riots that Will goes on to discuss occurred at the height of the famine between 1862 and 1863 – when this story is set – and were in response to the threat to reduce relief in the Lancashire towns of Ashton, Dukinfield and Staleybridge. The government passed the Public Works Act of 1863, which gave authorities more money to create work for the unemployed in order to quell the rising unrest. But by the time the Act was implemented, the worst of the crisis was over.

18. *Good Owd Yorkshire ... skinny after that*: Yorkshire's textile industry was predominantly wool- and worsted-based and therefore not as affected by the blockade of cotton as Lancashire. Many unemployed cotton operatives relocated to Yorkshire to work in the woollen trade. Will's reference to calling Yorkshire people 'skinny' refers to the stereotype of Yorkshire folk as being mean with money. The willingness of the Lancastrian to promote the negative image of Yorkshire people originates in the counties' rivalry during the War of the Roses (1455–87) between the House of Lancaster and the House of York.

19. *money was pouring in ... famine in Lancashire*: According to the *Sydney Herald* in 1874, the total sum collected for the starving workers throughout the world was almost £150,000. By the time the money had been collected and sent, the crisis was receding and only £58,000 had been distributed. It was decided that it would be impossible to return the remaining money and that the £90,000 should instead be used to build or maintain convalescent hospitals in the cotton districts.

20. *Mary Howitt ... famine fund*: The writer Mary Howitt (1799–1888) was most famous for the poem 'The Spider and the Fly'. She was the wife of William Howitt, the proprietor of *Howitt's Journal* (1847–8), which employed William Lovitt at its publisher in 1847. The Howitts were connected to some of the prominent Chartist agitators, including Thomas Cooper and W. J. Linton as well as Lovitt. Mary also published her poem 'The Eye of God' in Isa Craig's collection of poetry, *Poems, An Offering to Lancashire, 1863*, which was similarly sold for the benefit of the cotton operatives.

21. *Charles Dickens ... famine fund*: Dickens's biographer John Forster notes that Dickens gave four readings 'at Paris in January 1863, given at the Embassy in aid of the British Charitable Fund'; J. Forster, *The Life of Charles Dickens*, 2 vols (London: Chapman and Hall, 1876), vol. 2, p. 295.

22. *Th' Fenians*: an armed organization fighting for the independence of Ireland from British imperial control. The origins of the Fenian movement were founded with the Young Ireland group after the Great Famine in 1848. Two members of this group, James Stephens and John O'Mahoney, went on to form, respectively, the Irish Republican Brotherhood in Dublin and the Fenian Brotherhood in America in 1858. The 1860s witnessed a number of attempted Fenian uprisings: in 1866 the British authorities in Ireland intercepted a planned uprising before it could happen, and in 1867 Thomas Kelly and other Fenians tried to attack Chester Castle but were caught and arrested. Kelly was taken to Manchester for trial and rescued by a group of Fenian members. A policeman was killed during the

rescue, and three of the rescue group were caught and hanged for murder. Later in 1867 the Fenians exploded a bomb at Clerkenwell Prison, killing several people. This spate of violence began the Home Rule movement to give Ireland independence from Britain.

23. *Laird Brothers, of Birkenhead*: shipbuilders based at Birkenhead on the Wirral. William Laird founded the business in 1824 and was joined by his son, John, in 1828. The company became famous for building iron ships and for making progress in propulsion mechanisms. The company merged with Johnson Cammell & Co. in 1903 to become Cammell Laird, one of the country's most successful shipbuilding firms. In 1862 Laird & Sons & Company built the CSS *Alabama* for the Confederate States Navy. The ship was commissioned by the Confederate foreign agent in Britain, James Dunwoody Bulloch, and was built in secret at the Laird docks in Birkenhead under the hull number '290'. The ship acted as a 'commerce raider' and destroyed or captured sixty-five Union merchant ships as well as the warship USS *Hatteras* before being destroyed by the USS *Kearsarge* off the coast of France in 1864. The history of the *Alabama* is accurately recounted in 'The Cotton Panic', except for the dating; the history of the *Alabama* is condensed to fit the chronology of the story.

24. *loved like a Turk*: an extreme example of the 'amorous hearts' mentioned, but also a suggestion of his cruelty in love, as the word 'Turk' would be used to describe something savage and barbarous.

25. *Mr. Brigham Bouncely*: an allusion to Brigham Young, the Mormon leader who replaced Mormon founder Joseph Smith, Jr after Smith was murdered in jail at Carthage while under arrest for riot. The Mormon practice of polygamy is roundly denounced in 'The Cotton Panic', and Young's role in the 1857 Mountain Massacre, recounted by Chartist Grimshaw in Chapter XXIII, is still debated by historians today.

26. *"The People's Charter"*: see above, pp. 445–6 n. 16.

27. *Ernest Jones, Feargus O'Connor*: Ernest Jones (1819–69) was born into the landed gentry but became involved in Chartism after a property deal collapsed and left him in financial difficulties. Jones worked closely with Chartist leaders Feargus O'Connor and George Julian Harney, the latter introducing him to Karl Marx and Friedrich Engels in 1848. Jones was imprisoned for two years after speaking at the last great Chartist demonstration on 10 April 1848. After his release in 1850, Jones attempted to reinvigorate the Chartist movement through his periodicals *Notes to the People* (1851–2) and the *People's Paper* (1852–8); he was working towards election as an MP for the Liberal Party when he died of pleurisy at the age of fifty. Feargus O'Connor (*c*. 1796–1855) was born in Cork to a Protestant landowning family and became involved in radical politics after the passing of the 1832 Reform Act working for the repeal of the Act of Union between England and Ireland. One of the founding members of the Chartist movement, O'Connor began the Chartist periodical the *Northern Star* at Leeds in 1837. He was imprisoned for seditious libel after speaking at the Chartist convention in 1839 and imprisoned again for eighteen months in 1840. He was the driving force behind the Chartist Co-operative Land Society, established in 1845 with the intention of making workers independent through the creation of smallholdings – an idea Clarke was later to attempt through the Daisy Colony scheme, which he founded in 1903 but which had failed by 1907. O'Connor was the speaker before Jones at the April 1848 demonstration. He suffered a mental breakdown in 1851, which some have attributed to syphilis, and remained in an asylum in Chiswick until immediately before his death.

28. *Where are all our songs ... There seems nothing left*: Chartism's period of influence had come to an end after the failure of the large demonstration of 10 April 1848. Chartism's

popularity had been closely aligned with the series of economic depressions suffered by Britain during the 1840s, and with the upturn in the economy during the 1850s the perceived necessity for Chartism dwindled. The last Chartist convention had been held in 1858, three years after O'Connor's death. Chartist Grimshaw's lament suggests the short-term perspective of the workers, who abandoned the movement when the economy improved without any thought that the economy might once again fail.

29. *mountain-sides*: The hills of the Lake District are clearly visible from Preston and make a significant juxtaposition with the dirty, unnatural industrial landscape of Preston and other northwest English towns.
30. *Fylde lads ... Kirkham, and others*: The Fylde plain sits on the western side of Lancashire, north of Preston. It runs north from Preston to Lancaster and east from Blackpool to Garstang. The characters named cover the traditional Fylde occupations of fishing (from Lytham and Blackpool) and agriculture (Kirkham).
31. *The Virgin's Inn ... Friargate*: This public house, known as Lea's Virgin's Inn, stood where Clarke describes until its demolition in 1894. A brief history and a reproduction of Edwin Beattie's painting of the building can be found at the *Pubs in Preston* blog at http://pubsinpreston.blogspot.co.uk/2012/03/virgins-inn-anchor-wend.html [accessed 29 January 2013].
32. *Meriky*: American; the American Civil War.
33. *"Uncle Tom's Cabin"*: an anti-slavery novel written by Harriet Beecher Stowe (1811–96) and published in 1851. It was phenomenally popular in both the United States and Britain and helped to change attitudes to slavery. In an apocryphal story, Abraham Lincoln is said to have greeted Stowe in 1862 as 'the little woman who wrote the book that started this great war'.
34. *When the American civil war started ... poverty and hunger*: There was a class divide in Britain between those who supported the southern Confederate states (predominantly the aristocracy, with whom southern leaders were at pains to identify, and the factory owners who were reliant on the cotton trade for their business) and those who supported the northern Union (predominantly industrial workers who identified with the plight of the slaves). This division is most clearly illustrated by two statues erected after the war: the first of Stonewall Jackson in Richmond, Virginia, which was paid for by British subscription, and at its unveiling Governor James Kemper emphasized the ties between Virginia, as the first Confederate state, and the British aristocracy; the second of Abraham Lincoln, located in Platts Fields in 1919 and relocated to Lincoln Square to commemorate the support for the north by the workers of Lancashire. For further discussion, see R. J. M. Blackett, *Divided Hearts: Britain and the American Civil War* (Baton Rouge, LA: Louisiana State University, 2001).
35. *th' charge o' th' Light Brigade*: On 25 October 1854, during the Battle of Balaclava in the Crimean War, a series of poor decisions and misunderstandings by the commanding officers led to the charge of the 11th Hussars, 13th Light Dragoons, 17th Lancers, 4th Light Dragoons and 8th Hussars along a valley to the east of Balaclava rather than along the ridge of Causeway Heights. In the valley Russian cavalry, troops and guns surrounded the British Light Brigade on three sides. Figures of the death toll are contested, but it is thought that only around 110 of the 670 who charged returned, and almost as many horses were killed or wounded. The Russians held control of the area. The event was immortalized in poetry by Alfred, Lord Tennyson (1809–92) in 'The Charge of the Light Brigade' (1855). Billy Richardson would have been among the few survivors of the action, a survivor of disastrous leadership by the aristocratic officers.
36. *full head*: meaning a full head of hair, not balding or thinning.

37. *adjutant*: an aide to a senior officer.
38. *Th' Shurat Weiver*: by Samuel Laycock, one of the poems forming *Lancashire Lyrics*. Shurat is a type of cotton from India that was used to replace American cotton, which was initially withheld from Britain by the Confederate states to force Britain into supporting their cause and was later prevented from being transported to Britain by the northern states. The narrator is lamenting the loss of the good-quality cotton from America and the state of the poor-quality cotton he has to work on during the cotton famine. This poem was written and circulated during the cotton famine but was not published in book form until the 1883 collection *Lancashire Songs*.
39. *Preston's the cradle o' teetotalism*: on the Preston Temperance Society, see above, p. 432 n. 185.
40. *t-t-t-totally without*: on Richard Turner's stutter, see above, p. 432 n. 185.
41. The Struggle: Livsey published a number of political and temperance periodicals, including the *Struggle*, a weekly halfpenny anti-Corn Law paper he published from December 1841 to 1846, when the Corn Laws were repealed.
42. *Rachda'*: Rochdale is situated to the northeast of Manchester and in east Lancashire. Inspired by Robert Owen and his ideas of a Co-operative Commonwealth, the weavers of Rochdale formed the Rochdale Friendly Co-operative Society in Toad Lane, Rochdale, in 1832. This society only lasted two years, but in 1844 the weavers again formed a society, and these 'Rochdale Pioneers' were the originators of the co-operative movement.
43. *Tim Bobbin*: the pseudonym of John Collier (1708–86), cartoonist and satirist. Collier was apprenticed to a weaver in Newton's Moor, Lancashire, but became a schoolmaster in Milnrow near Rochdale, where he supplemented his earnings by producing cartoons. He published *A View of the Lancashire Dialect, or Tummas and Mary*, the first dialect publication, in 1746 under the name of Tim Bobbin. Collier was revered by many dialect writers who followed him, including Clarke.
44. *Ben Brierley*: Brierley (1825–96) was another famous and revered Lancashire dialect author who published poetry, drama and short stories. Brierley was most famous for his dialect character Ab-o'th-Yate.
45. *Ned Waugh*: Edwin Waugh (1817–90), dialect author and contemporary of Brierley. Waugh's most famous poem is 'Come Whoam to thi Childer an Me' (1856). Clarke published a series of articles in the *Liverpool Weekly Post* in 1926, which began with Tim Bobbin and included articles on Brierley and Waugh. For more on Clarke and the Lancashire dialect tradition, see Salveson, *Lancashire's Romantic Rebel*, ch. 3.
46. *Billington, the Blackburn poet*: William Billington (1825–84), a dialect poet from Blackburn, Lancashire.
47. *Let Lancashire speik for itself*: 'Nobudy Knows Bud Mysel', published in 1862. Like the authors mentioned earlier in the chapter, Billington was one of many who produced dialect poetry in response to the cotton panic. 'Nobudy Knows Bud Mysel' is a narrative of the effects of both the factory system and the American Civil War on the lives of a Lancashire family, representative of all those affected by the cotton shortage.
48. *To hell wi' aw t' Shurat*: 'Th' Surat Weyver's Song' (1862), a poem about the difficulties of weaving Surat cotton and the necessity of it during the cotton famine. It is, as 'Waugh' says, a much more angry poem than Laycock's lament. Clarke changed Billington's spelling 'Surat' to 'Shurat'.
49. *Ramsbottom's poems about "The Lancashire Emigrants"*: Joseph Ramsbottom (1831–1901), from *Phases of Distress: Lancashire Rhymes* (1864). Little is known of Ramsbottom's life except that he worked in a dye factory and became a contributor to newspapers and periodicals.

50. *Australia ... Melbourne*: There had been emigration from Lancashire to Australia to relieve unemployment since the growth of machinery in the cotton trade had affected handloom weavers from the 1840s onward. The cotton famine caused a substantial increase in emigration, with towns such as Stockport offering to pay for passage and to clothe emigrants for their journey. There were also substantial funds allocated by Australian towns, such as Sydney and Melbourne, to assist the emigrants on their arrival. The Operative Cotton Spinners Union was supportive of the emigration project, but many employers and government ministers objected, concerned by the loss of skilled workers for when the crisis ended. Despite Sid's employment on the ship, emigration is not considered by any of the characters; rather, there is the desire to improve the conditions for all Lancashire workers rather than remove the individuals.
51. *Critchley Prince*: John Critchley Prince (1808–66), Lancashire poet, essayist and author, was born in Wigan and died in Hyde, Manchester.
52. *th' Stanleys an Houghtons*: Stanley is the family name of the Earls of Derby, who lived in Lancashire from the fourteenth century. The thirteenth Earl was MP for Preston and Lancashire in 1796–1832, and the fourteenth Earl served as Tory Prime Minister three times (February–December 1852, 1858–9 and 1866–8). The Houghtons lived at Houghton Tower since the Norman conquest, in the area named after the family to the southeast of Preston. James I famously knighted a loin of beef Sir Loin during a banquet held in his honour, as Waugh goes on to note.
53. *Jone o' Greenfelt's song*: the famous dialect ballad character Jone o'Grinfilt, or John of Greenfield. In *A Book of Scattered Leaves* (Cranbury, NJ, London and Mississauga: Associated University Presses, 2000), J. G. Hepburn dates the original Jone ballad to around 1805 and names the author as Joseph Lees of Glodwick, south of Oldham. The character of Jone – sometimes spelled Joan, John or Johnny of Grinfilt, Grinfield or Greenfield – became a popular character in Victorian broadside balladry, successfully combining the specific regionalism of Oldham with commentary on national and international events. Later Jone ballads feature his comments on such current events as Queen Caroline's trial, the 1832 Reform Bill, the New Poor Law, the Crimean War and the effects of the American Civil War on the British weaver. The last mentioned version of the 'Jone' ballads is the one referred to by 'Waugh' and is a scathing attack on employing manufacturers and religious teachings on patience and acceptance.
54. *tenter-lass*: A tenter was a young girl who would work with the weaver and learn all the skills involved in the trade. Children would work half-time in the mills from around the age of eight and would spend half the day in school and half the day in the mill. School would finish at the age of thirteen, and they would then begin work full-time. Young boys would start at the same age as 'piecers' assisting the spinners. It was hard work, and Clarke argued vociferously for the end to the half-time system, understanding (from his own personal experience of the system) how exhausting it was for the children. Sid Clifton's attack on the tackler (an adult who tended the power looms) indicates his violence is only unleashed onto those who attack the vulnerable.
55. *Fenian secret meetins ... especially in Sheffield*: for Fenian unrest, see above, pp. 446–7 n. 22. 'Sheffield' refers to the Sheffield Outrages in 1865 and 1866, when there were a number of attacks against strike-breakers, or blacklegs, involving gunpowder.
56. *Mason an Slidell*: James Murray Mason (1798–1871) and John Slidell (1793–1871) were Confederate diplomats travelling to England on the mail packet the RMS *Trent*, which was intercepted by the Unionist USS *Jacinto* and the diplomats removed. The

Union threatened war with Britain, and the Confederate states hoped a war with the Unionist states would see Britain side with the Confederate cause. Britain was offended by the Unionist impingement of its neutrality and demanded the release of the prisoners. As Britain mustered its forces at the Canadian border, the Unionists eventually avoided war by releasing the prisoners. Mason and Slidell completed their journey to London but failed to convince the British government to recognize the Confederate states.

57. *Body-snatchin ... at Sheffield*: In 1862 there was a riot at the Wardsend Cemetery in Sheffield when it was suspected the sexton was disinterring bodies for sale to medical staff and students. The mob damaged the house, the incumbent Rev. John Livesey was found guilty of falsifying burial records, and the sexton Isaac Howard was imprisoned for three months for disinterring bodies.
58. *Davy Jones*: a euphemism for the sea floor. Resting in Davy Jones's locker means being drowned and buried at sea. The federal navy aim to sink the *Alabama* so she rests in Davy Jones's locker.
59. *taffrail*: the rail at the rear of a ship on the poop deck, the highest point of the ship; *OED*.
60. *The Sewing Class*: As described later, sewing classes were organized by upper- and middle-class women to occupy unemployed factory women, who would make items for sale, the money from which would be used to relieve some of the suffering in the cotton towns. It is also a reference to Samuel Laycock's (1826–93) poem 'The Sewing Class', which Gerald Massey (1828–1907) described as having 'the true twinkle of Lancashire humour'. This was one of the poems Laycock composed to thank those who contributed to the relief of the poor Lancastrians during the cotton famine, and it is sung by the class later in the chapter.
61. *Stretch forth ... when we can*: 'Do a Good Turn When You Can' by Bella Fennimore. The earliest version I have found is the poem's inclusion in *The American Manual, or, The Thinker* in 1854.
62. *song of Laycock's*: see n. 60 above.
63. *We're only here ... an heaur for noon*: The length of the working day in factories and mills had been a cause for concern for reformers for much of the nineteenth century. Successive Factory Acts had limited the working day for women and children to ten hours, and from the mid-1880s the SDF member Tom Mann was campaigning for an eight-hour day for all. Many factory owners extended the working day by omitting to count meal breaks as part of the working day, so women and children might still be in the factory for twelve hours. Clarke's concern over long working days was expressed in his book *The Effects of the Factory System* (1895–6).
64. *hunting breeches ... white waistcoats*: forms of clothing signifying the aristocracy. There is an ironic humour here, as those forced into idleness by the removal of their productive independence through the factory system are being clothed by those who flaunt their idleness as a symbol of their class position.
65. *Riot Act*: The Riot Act was passed in 1714 and was used to disperse unlawful groups. Magistrates were given powers to forcefully disperse crowds by military force once the Riot Act had been read and the crowd given an hour to disperse voluntarily. The law was not repealed until 1967.
66. *transportation was done away with in 1857*: Transportation had been a form of punishment in Britain since 1717. At first convicts were taken to America, but after the United States had declared independence from Britain, convicts were transported to Australia. Transportation was seen as a lesser punishment than hanging, but conditions on board the early forms of transportation, rotting vessels known as 'hulks', were so bad that

many convicts died on the journey. Transportation ended as a punishment in the mid-nineteenth century when emigration to Australia grew, and it was seen as unfair to send convicts there to build a new life when people were voluntarily paying to emigrate.

67. *'Burton,' ... 'Kilmarnock,'*: tunes to which hymns would be set. 'Burton' is possibly John Burton, Jr (n.d.), composer of children's hymns, who published *One Hundred Original Hymns for the Young* (1850) and *Hymns for Little Children* (1851); 'French' is a tune taken from the early Scottish and English psalters after the Reformation; 'Luther's Hymn' was composed by Martin Luther (1483–1546) *c.* 1529–31 and was also known as 'A Mighty Fortress is Our God'; 'O'd Hundred' (1561), attributed to Loys Bourgeois (*c.* 1510–*c.* 1560), is based on Psalm 100 and begins 'All people that on earth do dwell'; 'Kilmarnock' (1831) was composed by Neil Dougall (1776–1862).

68. *'Warrington'*: composed in 1784 by Ralph Harrison (1748–1810). Harrison was a member of the Unitarian Warrington Academy, after which this tune was named. This and the hymns mentioned above are all Protestant or Nonconformist hymns. Nonconformism was noted for its 'hands-on' approach to ending material and earthly suffering, especially among the poor, as well as spiritual guidance.

69. *Gerald Massey*: Gerald Massey (1828–1907) was a poet and radical who had been attracted by the Chartist movement and radical politics after his move to London from his birthplace of Tring in Hertfordshire. He founded a Young Men's Improvement Society with printer John Bedford Leno in 1845, and the society published the manuscript newspaper *Attempt* between 1845 and 1849. He was sacked from his employment for his involvement in Chartism, and he turned to writing, founding the periodical the *Uxbridge Pioneer* in 1849 as an educational paper for the working classes and then the *Uxbridge Spirit of Freedom* which published his poetry and articles on the labour question. See D. Shaw and I. Petticrew, *Gerald Massey: Chartist, Poet, Radical and Free-thinker* (1995/2009), *Minor Victorian Poets and Authors*, at http://gerald-massey.org.uk/massey/biog_contents.htm [accessed 25 February 2013].

70. *town councillors, guardians, and members of parliament*: Although ratepayers had been given a vote for their parish vestry in the Sturges Bourne Act of 1818 – which had been widened in the 1834 Poor Law Act to allow ratepayers to vote for the Board of Guardians who would decide upon and distribute the relief – this was restricted to owners of property up to £50 and additional votes for additional properties up to £25. This gave the vote to property owners rather than those who rent property, as would be the case in working-class Mill-street. Clarke's story is set in 1862–3, before the 1867 Second Reform Act that gave some working-class men paying £10 rent for their lodging the parliamentary vote, and changes in the franchise in 1867 and 1869 gave the vote to ratepayers in the borough election if their rates were paid through the landlord rather than direct to the borough. Clarke's comment on the illusion of the democratic vote would not be appropriate for his characters for at least another four years.

71. *tenement*: The term 'tenement' could refer simply to a dwelling, but in this case it refers to a building that is separated into multiple occupancy. As Mrs Martin goes on to explain, the poverty caused by the cotton crisis means that families are no longer able to reside in individual dwellings and move in together to share costs. There is often a suggestion of squalor in the use of the word.

72. *Natterin Nan's*: 'Natterin Nan, be a Yorkshur Likenass Taker' (1856), a long dialect poem by Benjamin Preston (1819–1902) of Bradford.

73. *navvy*: an abbreviation of navigator, a construction worker employed in the building of roads or canals; *OED*.

74. *back entry*: meaning either the back door to a house or the passageway behind a row of terraced houses. Both meanings suggest the lowly birth of Wragley.
75. *peart as a pynot*: Peart means cheerful and self-confident but is used in this sense to mean arrogant and superior; pynot means magpie. The impression is of Wragley strutting about with an attitude of superiority but with an association of criminality, as the magpie is known for its attraction to, and hoarding of, shiny objects.
76. *Wigan lantern*: this phrase is unidentified.
77. *that new table-rappin religion fro Amerikky*: spiritualism. This form of entertainment-cum-religion began with the Fox sisters in Hydesville, New York, in 1848, when they claimed to be able to communicate with the spirit world. Although the sisters later stated that it was a hoax and that the rapping noise supposedly made by spirits was actually made by them, the phenomenon of spiritualism had spread across America and Europe. Spiritualism in Britain had many prominent believers, including author Arthur Conan Doyle, journalist W. T. Stead and, in the British socialist movement, Robert Blatchford and Charles Allen Clarke – both of whom had become involved with spiritualism after experiencing bereavement.
78. *getting a load o' coal in*: Her husband is temporarily employed unloading coal, possibly as a delivery to a house into the coal cellar or shed. The elderly are being forced to engage in heavy labour in order to survive.
79. *the widow ... gave much gold*: Mark 12:42: Christ in the temple compares the gifts of money given by the rich to that given by the poor widow. Although her gift is small compared to those of the rich, in relation to her poverty her gift is all she had, not what she could afford to give. Lily's sacrifices are akin to the widow's money – both give more than they could afford.
80. *For ever with the Lord ... nearer home*: 'At Home in Heaven ("For Ever With")' (1835), words by James Montgomery (1771–1854). Montgomery's words have been set to a number of tunes, including the traditional English tune 'Terra Beta' by Franklin L. Shepherd (1852–1930) in 1915. Lily's version will be the score composed by I. B. Woodbury (1819–58) in 1852 and which was later harmonized by Arthur Sullivan (1842–1900) in 1874.
81. *instead o' spendin it in drink*: The socialist movement in Britain, despite many and serious doctrinal differences, defended the working classes from the accusation of drink being the cause of their poverty. Teetotal James Keir Hardie wrote articles on the percentage of working-class money being spent on drink in relation to that of other class groups, and in *Merrie England* Robert Blatchford lamented the lack of alternative entertainment for workers outside of the public house.
82. *J.P.*: justice of the peace, a citizen of some local standing who sits in the magistrates' court and presides over summary cases carrying up to two years' imprisonment. JPs have no legal training and are advised on legal matters by a justices' clerk. See also above, p. 423 n. 42.
83. *anno domino*: anno domini; a deliberate mistake to reinforce Wragley's unfounded sense of self-importance.
84. *heavily in debt*: Mr Treebarn's chapel is a non-specific place of worship that is presumably one of the many Nonconformist sects of Protestant Christianity popular in Britain (Methodist, Baptist, Congregationalist, etc.). Because it is outside of the Church of England, it does not have the resources that supported the established church (large congregations giving money regularly during worship, revenue from land income, etc.) and will be entirely reliant on donations from wealthy donors such as Mr Wragley.

85. *Get thee behind me, Satan*: Matthew 16:23: Christ's rebuke to Peter for putting his own earthly interests before God's. Similarly, Mr Treebarn understands that they must put earthly difficulties to one side and focus on their spiritual duties.
86. *Bastile*: The workhouse, or 'indoor relief', was intended as a last resort of the poor and was run in such a way as to deter any person seeking to avoid work. While those opposing the foundation of the workhouse system spread rumours about starvation and flogging that were unfounded or untrue, it is the case that the workhouses were uncomfortable and seen as degrading to the independent working class. The application of the name of the French fortress destroyed during the French Revolution to the workhouse is evidence of the feeling workers had of the system being oppressive, unfair and organized for the benefit of the ruling class.
87. *John Bright*: John Bright (1811–89), born in Rochdale, the son of a factory owner whose cotton mill he inherited, moved into politics through his involvement with the Anti-Corn Law League, working alongside Richard Cobden (1804–65). He became the MP for Durham in 1843, and in 1847 he became MP for Manchester when he argued in parliament for franchise reform – although not full manhood suffrage, as the Chartists demanded. He lost his seat in Manchester in 1856 but was returned for Birmingham in the same year. Bright spent his political life arguing for reform – of the franchise, Ireland, India, church rates – and he supported the northern states over the Confederacy during the American Civil War. However, he spoke against Lord Ashley's proposed Factory Act and believed that businessmen should be free from state control to manage their own business. It is conceivable that Bright employed Irish children in his cotton mill, either through a sense of benevolence, believing that employment would enable them to support unemployed members of their family, or by taking advantage of the cheap labour on offer.
88. *Roman Catholicism and Protestantism*: The historical antagonism between Catholic and Protestant in Britain after the Reformation was exacerbated by the spike in Irish immigration during the Potato Famine between 1845 and 1852. Lancashire had a larger population of Catholics than most English counties and a history of low attendance at Church of England services.
89. *hand-mule spinning … self-acting mule method*: Joe is making the transition from independent manual spinning to employed minder of the spinning machinery in a factory. His independence has been undermined by the factory system, and at the point of transition his hopes of employment are removed.
90. *Sid Clifton's gone on th' Alabama too, hasn't he?*: a narrative inconsistency. Sid did not find out that 'boat 290' was the *Alabama* until Sandy Aspinall enlightened him on their journey to Liverpool, and Ada gets her first letter from Sid in Chapter XXIII.
91. *If folks were only wise … bad time that may come*: Chartist Grimshaw's lament reveals the difference between Chartism and socialism. The earlier Chartist movement believed that the working-class vote would change Parliament, which would result in a change in circumstances for the working-class experience. The extension of the franchise to some working-class men in 1867 and 1884 had not changed the existing political party system, and working-class men were offered a choice of two parties, both of whom were perceived as working primarily for landowners and employers. Chartists' dreams of trade reform as an answer to poverty would seem woefully inadequate to the *fin-de-siècle* socialist.
92. *Chartism's droopin*: see above, pp. 447–8 n. 28.
93. *Robert Owen, and th' Owenites*: Robert Owen (1771–1858) acted on his theory that environment informed character, and in 1799 he and several partners bought the New

Lanark mills and set out to improve the moral and physical welfare of his employees. He improved working and living conditions for his employees, introduced communal cooking and so improved nutrition, founded welfare and pension funds, and used encouragement rather than punishment to motivate his workers. He widened his scope to include national poverty and worked with Robert Peel to restrict the employment of children in factories by age and time. By the time the Queenswood project bankrupted the Rational Society in 1844, the power of Owen's influence had begun to wane as his reluctance to large-scale organizations contrasted with the popularity of the Chartist movement.

94. *th' system of education that's now in general use*: Clarke had strong opinions on the form of education children were subjected to at the end of the nineteenth century, based on his own experiences as a pupil and as a teacher. He was critical of the rote-learning method and believed that children should not begin school until the age of seven; the early years of a child's life should be given to play. For further discussion of Clarke's ideas on education, see Salveson, *Lancashire's Romantic Radical*.
95. *fullock*: possibly an alternative spelling/pronunciation of 'fuzzock', meaning an idle fat woman.
96. *There's something to do*: a Lancashire phrase meaning something is wrong or something is happening.
97. *parish funeral*: To be buried by the 'parish' was to have a pauper's funeral paid for by the Guardians of the Poor Law and was akin to going to the workhouse in terms of perceived degradation. Many working-class families would pay into a burial club to save for their funerals; see above, p. 426 n. 94.
98. *Th' Prince o' Wales was married*: The Prince of Wales, later Edward VII, married Alexandra of Denmark on 10 March 1863, at the height of the cotton famine.
99. *Joe Barker*: Joseph Barker (1806–75) was renowned for changing his views. Born near Leeds, he began as a Wesleyan, became a Methodist – from which he was expelled – moved through Quakerism, Unitarianism, republicanism and Chartism, and was elected MP for Bolton. He moved to the United States in 1851, where he joined the anti-slavery movement, before moving back to Britain in 1860, becoming an advocate of secularism, before returning to the Methodists in 1868. Barker's speech in Preston would shock those who knew of his support of the abolition of slavery a decade before.
100. *Charles Garrett*: Rev. Charles Garrett (1825–1900) was a Wesleyan preacher who lived in Preston during the cotton famine and raised funds for the relief of the cotton operatives. He was a temperance advocate and became the Wesleyan Conference president in 1882.
101. *Joe Livesey*: Joseph Livesey; see above, p. 432 n. 185.
102. *new pier ... at Blackpool*: North Pier, the first of Blackpool's three piers, was opened in May 1863.
103. *pike*: see Glossary in Volume 1. The old gentleman applies the term to the movement of money by the 'divvles'. The man is accusing those who have promoted the high tide of taking his money under false pretences.
104. *sope*: a variation of soof, sough or suff, meaning a drain or sewer.
105. *Barnum, th' Yankee*: Phineas Taylor Barnum (1810–91), American showman, hoaxer and founder of the Barnum and Bailey Circus. 'General Tom Thumb' was the exhibition name of Charles Stratton (1838–83), the dwarf who was billed as eleven but was in fact four years of age when he began touring with Barnum. Barnum brought his circus, with Stratton, to Britain in 1844, and he appeared before the queen twice.

106. *Mrs. Wragley's notion of a gentleman ... never worked for*: The idea of what makes a 'gentleman' has never been a fixed set of criteria, and the class basis for being a 'gentleman' expanded during the nineteenth century to include the now-wealthy mercantile classes alongside the hereditary aristocracy, gentry and landowners. There was a sense of aspiration in many of the newly enriched to be perceived as 'gentry', and so their image of the 'gentleman' was that of the idle rich, conspicuous consumption and wealth. Mrs Wragley's ambitions for her son are based in ignorance and vulgarity, seeing only the riches of the gentleman and none of the gentleness and social responsibility recognized by John Ruskin and John Henry Cardinal Newman in their descriptions of 'the gentleman'.

107. *Coinciding with the advent of spring ... rising from the dead*: Clarke had a broad approach to religion and spirituality. He was a member of John Trevor's Labour Church, which sought to combine socialism and Christianity; as a young man he defined himself as an atheist but withdrew from such claims; in 1887 he became interested in spiritualism; in 1905 he claimed a leaning towards Pantheism; and in 1927 he published a book on comparative religion that discussed the beliefs of Celts, Druids, Buddhism and Islam. See Paul Salveson's biography of Clarke for further details.

108. *simply to make divi.*: The foundation of the modern co-operative movement was to collectively manage wholesale food sales for the benefit of members. Dividends shared the profits made by the business with the shareholders so that food was kept at an affordable price and profits were distributed fairly. Chartist Grimshaw criticizes the narrowness of such co-operation: people working for the benefit of a small group rather than the nation as a whole.

109. *Avenham Walk*: Avenham Walk, later Avenham Park, is a public space in Preston on the north side of the river Ribble. Preston Council first acquired land in 1697 and created the walk with gravel walkways, seats and gates. The park was formerly Jackson's Gardens, private gardens open to the public. The corporation bought the gardens in 1843, and they were expanded in 1844 and landscaped between 1864 and 1867. Avenham Park opened in 1867, five years after the outing of Chartist and the Milners.

110. *"Hard Times"*: see above, p. 444 n. 2.

111. *Dr. Watts magnificent hymn of trust and assurance*: Isaac Watts's (1674–1748) hymn 'Oh God our Help in Ages Past' was published in 1719 and is based on Psalm 90:1. It is best known and sung to the tune 'St Anne', composed by William Croft in 1708, rather than 'St Stephen' as noted here.

112. *St. Stephen*: composed by William Jones and published in 1789; a more upbeat tempo than the Croft tune usually accompanying Watts's words.

113. *Samlesbury ... haunted by a white lady*: Samlesbury Hall, situated just outside of Preston, beyond Ribbleton, claims to be the most haunted stately home in Britain. The white lady is said to be the ghost of Lady Dorothy Southworth, member of the Catholic Southworth family who owned the hall. Lady Dorothy fell in love with a son of the local Protestant de Houghton family, and her brothers were said to have killed her lover on the night of their elopement; she died of a broken heart. Lady Dorothy's story is an echo of Lucy Clayton's life and death.

114. *Champagne Charley ... my game*: a popular music hall song written by George Laybourne and Alfred Lee in 1866, so an anachronism in the serial. Wilfred Wragley has adapted the original lyrics to reflect his own antisocial pleasures, as the original chorus followed the first line with 'Good for any game at night, my boys'. The reference to 'bobbies' is a slang term for the police; see also above, p. 424 n. 56.

115. *Irish Sea ... into the Atlantic*: This suggests that the *Alabama* sailed south from Liverpool, but Sandy's description of the coastline in Chapter VII, as he and Sid sail out of port for the first time, points out the lights of Southport and Preston and so indicates the ship sailing north.
116. *not alone on the slavery question ... causes*: The American Civil War, although historically associated with opposing attitudes to slavery between the northern and southern states, was also fought over states' rights, taxes and tariffs. However, the South Carolina Declaration of 1860 justified its secession on the grounds of fourteen states refusing to fulfil their 'constitutional obligations' – meaning the fugitive slave clause – and growing hostility towards slavery. See J. W. Loewen and E. H. Sebesta (eds), *The Confederate and Neo-Confederate Reader* (Jackson, MS: University Press of Mississippi, 2010).
117. *In Dixie's land ... in Dixie*: Known as 'Dixie', 'I Wish I was in Dixie' or 'Dixie's Land', this song was the unofficial anthem of the Confederate states. Although the authorship of the song is not known, the words have been credited to Albert Pike (1809–91) and the music to Daniel Decatur Emmett (1815–1904). It was a popular song in the blackface minstrel shows of the 1850s.
118. *Byron, Moore*: George Gordon Lord Byron (1788–1824) and Thomas Moore (1779–1852). Moore's 1806 volume *Epistles, Odes and Other Poems* was denounced by Francis Jeffrey in the *Edinburgh Review*. A subsequent failed duel with Jeffrey was ridiculed in the press, and the story was repeated by Byron in *English Bards and Scotch Reviewers* (1809). Although Moore also challenged Byron, Byron was out of the country at the time and the two became close friends.
119. *100 pounder rifled Blakely*: a cannon designed by British army captain Theophilus Alexander Blakely but sold mainly outside of Britain and popular with the Confederate army. There were two manufacturers of the Blakely rifle in Liverpool, where the *Alabama* was built: Fawcett, Preston, & Company and George Forrester and Company.
120. *She walks the waters like a thing of life*: Byron, *The Corsair, a Turkish Tale* (1814), Canto 1, stanza 3.
121. *barquentine rigged*: a ship with three or more masts and square-rigged only at the foremast, making it possible to sail the ship with a smaller crew than a fully square-rigged vessel.
122. *The Puritan leaven*: Leaven is a fermenting agent. Here Semme describes the Puritans in America as imposing their will and religion on other immigrants, exercising the same level of power in the New World that they left the Old World to escape.
123. *as terrible slave-drivers ... of the North*: The wealth of the US southern states was founded primarily on agriculture, and the south was not as industrialized as the north. Part of the reason for the south's resistance to the union of all states under a federation was the desire to defend the south from industrialization. Those suffering from the effects of industrialization in Lancashire would feel some sympathy with this effort, but this would be overlaid with their sympathy for, and identification with, the slave population forced to work in agriculture. The slave-owning south was fighting for its own independence from the industrial north while simultaneously denying slaves the same benefit.
124. *Breathes there a man ... my native land*: the opening lines of the sixth Canto of *The Lay of the Last Minstrel* (1805) by Sir Walter Scott (1771–1832); the first stanza celebrates patriotism.
125. *Ours the wild life ... sepulchres our dead*: Byron, *The Corsair*, Canto 1, stanza 1.
126. *Howl ... laid waste*: Isaiah 23:14. Isaiah 23 is a warning against the sin of pride.
127. *the drums beat to quarters*: a signal to the crew to clear the decks and ready themselves for battle. Quarters are also beaten when life is endangered by storms.

128. *lock-strings*: the mechanism for firing the cannons.
129. *th' Flyin Dutchman*: the legend of a ghostly ship doomed never to land. The stories of the *Alabama* were first thought a myth similar to that of the Flying Dutchman.
130. *man-of-war*: an armed warship developed in Britain in the early sixteenth century.
131. *tabernacle*: Originally a term for a temporary dwelling or place of worship, in this sense it is used to distinguish a place of Nonconformist worship from the Church of England, as Chartist Grimshaw separates church and chapel in the next note.
132. *no chapel goer, nor church goer*: Chartist is neither a member of the official Church of England, nor of any of the dissenting sects.
133. *arraignin*: arraign, a legal term for the reading of charges before the defendant in a court of law. Chartist Grimshaw has accused God – if there is one – of making life hard when He had power to make life better.
134. *guilty o' makin this muddle*: another echo of Dickens's *Hard Times* through Stephen Blackpool's lament that 'aw's a muddle'. Chartist Grimshaw is more proactive in terms of looking for a solution, in contrast to Stephen's passive acceptance of a system, which eventually kills him.
135. *Walton-le-Dale ... Jacobites used to meet*: possibly the old building that was locally called 'Jacobite House' and demolished in 1900. Jacobite forces had mustered in Walton-le-Dale in 1715 and had recruited a number of local men for an attack on Preston, but the town was successfully defended by a blockade at Walton-le-Dale Bridge. The leader of the defence was James Wood, the Presbyterian minister of the chapels at Atherton and Chowbent in what is now Greater Manchester, and Chartist Grimshaw notes the area as one where a minister fought against the potential oppression of Nonconformism by the restoration of James VII of Scotland and II of England. James was a practising Roman Catholic and had previously been antagonistic to the Scottish Covenanters. James Wood's physical rejection of monarchical oppression is akin to Mr Treebarn's moral rejection of Mr Wragley's capitalist power.
136. *Rivington Pike*: a summit on Winter Hill near Chorley, Lancashire. The Pike summit has one of a series of beacons across England to send warnings over the country. The beacon system was devised in 1139 and last lit in 2012 to celebrate the Diamond Jubilee of Queen Elizabeth II.
137. *The Destroying Angels*: a group within the Mormon religion also known at the Danites, originally formed by Mormon founder Joseph Smith, Jr as the Armies of Israel to protect the Mormon community during its early days in Missouri. Smith later denounced the Danites as an evil secret sect and excommunicated the leaders. Mr Treebarn's point is that Mormonism is undemocratic and oppressive.
138. *Abraham an Isaac*: Genesis 22:1–19: Abraham obeyed God's command to offer his only son, Isaac, as a sacrifice to God. Before Isaac was sacrificed, God sent an angel to stop Abraham from killing his son and reward him for his obedience to God's commands. Chartist Grimshaw raises this Old Testament story as an example of the blind obedience to the teachings of the Bible expected by the church.
139. *Whitsun*: The seventh Sunday after Easter, Whitsun is celebrated across the northwest of England with parades and Whitsun Walks to herald the beginning of summer. The Whitsun holiday is a relic of feudal society, when the lord would allow his serfs time away from work. The cotton factory workers are portrayed as the modern-day serfs. See also above, p. 434 n. 7.
140. *Tim Bobbin's*: pseudonym of John Collier. See above, pp. 433–4 n. 3 and p. 449 n. 43.
141. *plug-drawing riots*: see above, pp. 445–6 n. 16.

142. *As long as I can remember ... Peterloo*: A meeting on 16 August 1819 in Peter Street in Manchester city centre, addressed by Henry Hunt and protesting against the poverty caused by the corn laws and the restricted franchise, was attacked by local Yeomanry, Hussars and infantrymen. The Riot Act had been read but was unheard by most of the protesters. Eighteen people died and 700 men, women and children were seriously injured. Percy Shelley's (1792–1822) 'The Mask of Anarchy' (1819) was written in response.

143. *Oliver Cromwell's army ... Walton-le-Dale*: Oliver Cromwell's (1599–1658) New Model Army lost the Battle of Preston in 1648 to the royalists and Scots.

144. *Mainsprit Weind*: Main Sprit Weind is a narrow lane in the centre of Preston that runs between Church Street and Sykes Street near Avenham Park. Whistling Will's point about the number of mayors originating in Main Sprit Weind is, presumably, referring to the lane being one of the Burgage plots in Preston. The Burgage plot was land given to a Burgess, one who had permission to trade within Preston boundaries and was a member of the Preston Guild. Will's point is that most mayors have been associated with trade and will facilitate business over the good of the people.

145. *boss*: the American form of 'master' originating from the Dutch 'baas', now widely used in British English to signify an employer; *OED*.

146. *Far as the breeze ... behold our home*: Byron, *The Corsair*, Canto 1, stanza 1.

147. *the usual allowance to the men*: The spirit ration of 2–4 oz. of whisky, brandy or rum for United States troops had been discontinued in 1832 and replaced with coffee and sugar. The spirit ration was reinstated in 1846 and again discontinued in 1865. During the Civil War, the Confederacy's move towards prohibition was hampered by the military demand for alcohol. Semmes, like some others, saw the limited drinking of alcohol as beneficial for men in action.

148. *What is man ... mindful of him?*: Psalm 8:4. The Psalm considers the wonder of God taking notice of man and sending his son to save mankind. Captain Semmes is reminded of the Psalm in the irony of the bishop – presumably a rich and powerful man in his life – now wiped from history along with his forgotten flock.

149. *a parson called Charles Kingsley*: see above, p. 439 n. 3.

150. *Joseph Smith... nonsense*: Smith (1805–44) claimed to have been visited by the angel Moroni, who showed him the place where buried gold plates told of the former inhabitants of the American continent and the everlasting Gospel. The content of the plates was translated into the Book of Mormon.

151. *The Mountain Meadow Massacre ... was left alive*: Clarke/Chartist Grimshaw has most of the facts correct here, although the Mormons had continued to claim that the attack was made by the Southern Paiute tribe until the beginning of the twenty-first century. The Mormon attackers of the wagon train in September 1857, aided by the Paiutes, had disguised themselves as Native Americans. The wagoneers were surrounded by the Mormons and attacked until food and water ran low, when they were approached by John D. Lee offering to negotiate with the Paiutes to free the train. This was a trap, and Lee led the slaughter of around 140 men, women and children. Only seventeen children were spared, as the Mormons believed that children under the age of eight were holy. There was a conspiracy of silence to hide Mormon involvement and to blame the Paiute. It was only when a federal authority was established in Utah that any criminal proceedings were brought – in 1875 – and then only Lee was tried, found guilty and shot near the sight of the massacre. Many believe that he was used as a scapegoat for Mormon leader Brigham Young. See S. Denton, *American Massacre* (New York: Vintage, 2004);

J. Krakauer, *Under the Banner of Heaven* (New York: Anchor, 2004); and the LDS-approved version, R. W. Walker, R. E. Turley, and G. M. Leonard, *Massacre at Mountain Meadows* (Oxford: Oxford University Press, 2008).

152. *captured last year, and executed*: This is a chronological inaccuracy, possibly deliberate so that Chartist can give the full story. Clarke's tale is set in 1863 and Lee was not tried until 1875. His first trial (23–6 July 1875) ended inconclusively, with the jury evenly divided on its decision. His second trial (14–20 September 1876) found him guilty of murder in the first degree, and he was executed by firing squad on 2 March 1877.

153. *Peterloo Massacre*: see above, p. 459 n. 142.

154. *'misery and iron'*: Psalm 107:10: 'Those who sat in darkness and in the shadow of death, Bound in affliction and irons'. The Psalm refers to the misery of those who have rebelled against God, but Chartist sees the 'misery and iron' inflicted on the innocent, who are undeserving of such punishment.

155. *It's a new country ... remembered no more*: Chartist Grimshaw's lengthy speech is not the 'ramble' he declares it to be but a potted history of the British working class across the first part of the nineteenth century. Chartist covers the Napoleonic Wars, which affected the price of food; the 1819 Peterloo massacre (see above, p. 459 n. 142); the introduction of machinery and factories in production, which shifted the balance of power from independent workers to factory employers; the 1832 Reform Bill, which gave the franchise to the upper-middle-class male and caused a divide between the middle and working classes, who had campaigned together for manhood suffrage; the Factory Acts of 1833 (which was not the first, but the third), which placed a minimum age of nine on children employed in factories, 1844, which restricted the working day of the child to six hours, and 1847, which introduced a ten-hour working day – the latter two were resisted by Bright (see also above, p. 454 n. 87); the Chartist movement; the Anti-Corn Law movement; the co-operative movement; and the Crimean War. Chartist Grimshaw's point is that although the factory system brought poverty and hardship for the workers, there is a gradual movement towards improvement and working-class independence. Readers in 1900–1 would have seen even greater improvements in working-class life and even more hope for independence with the development of the British socialist movement, socialist MPs such as James Keir Hardie, and the foundation of the LRC in February 1900, which would be re-named the Labour Party in 1906.

156. *knocker-up*: a person employed to wake factory workers before the advent of cheap alarm clocks. Clarke is showing the domino effect of the cotton famine beyond the mills themselves and includes the Lancashire shopkeepers in a following paragraph.

157. *Ned Waugh ... tales of old and historic places*: Edwin Waugh published a number of books containing sketches of Lancashire life, although none appear to deal with Walton-le-Dale as Chartist Grimshaw claims.

158. *Roman Catholics in Preston*: Although Henry VIII closed the Friary at Preston during the Reformation, the town and surrounding areas remained loyal to the Roman Catholic church.

159. *Jamacia and Kingston ... Table Bay and Cape Town*: Sid is visiting British colonies in the southern states' privateer ship. That the *Alabama* is not only being allowed to dock and disembark, but the crew is also celebrated on arrival, illustrates the close relationship between Britain and the seceded states during the period of the American Civil War when the former was supposed to be maintaining its neutrality.

160. *Tae-ping rebellion ... hardworking producer*: The Taiping Rebellion (1850–64) in the northeast of Guangxi was led by Hong Xuiquan (1814–64), a member of the lowly

Hakkas social group. Influenced by Protestant Christianity through missionaries, Hong believed himself the younger brother of Jesus. He believed God wanted him to found a new kingdom on earth, and his followers repelled imperial troops sent to arrest him. The movement grew and became political, capturing villages and forcing them to accept Taiping ways. It was not until the British and French launched the Arrow War (1856–60) and joined the Qing Empire's army against the Taiping that the rebellion was ended. Semmes's sympathy for the Taiping on grounds of class omits their oppression imposed on others, in the same way that the Confederate states projected their fight as one against the oppression of the north while simultaneously maintaining slavery.

161. Kearsage, *under Captain Winslow*: USS *Kearsarge*. This was the first United States warship to be named after Mount Kearsarge in New Hampshire, and subsequent ships named *Kearsarge* were named in honour of the first and its destruction of the *Alabama*. The *Kearsarge* was built in 1861 during the emergency shipbuilding programme for the Civil War, and it was captained by John A. Winslow. The ship was wrecked in the Caribbean Sea in 1894.

162. *shop*: meaning work generally and the place where an occupation is carried out; *OED*.

163. *Dahlgrens*: a popular gun during the American Civil War, designed by John A. Dahlgren for greater accuracy and better safety for those firing.

164. *getting the marriage service off*: memorizing the wedding service, learning it off by heart.

165. *paper money*: Paper money or bank notes are a form of promissory note where, in exchange for the note, the bank will supply the bearer with the equivalent value in gold or coins. Bank notes were backed by the country's gold reserves until the Great Depression in the 1930s, when the gold standard was removed and the worth of a bank note is now derived through fiat, i.e. government regulation and law.

166. *fishing-smacks*: vessels used for fishing in Britain and America up to the nineteenth century. These traditional vessels are the peaceful backdrop to the modern firepower of the two battleships.

167. *Isle of Alderney*: the northernmost of the Channel Isles, Alderney is about forty-three kilometres or twenty-six miles from Cherbourg.

168. Couronne: meaning 'crown', a popular name for French battleships, starting with the first French man-of-war built in 1636. This vessel was made entirely of iron rather than being 'iron clad' and was launched in 1861.

169. Deerhound ... *along the English Channel*: The connection between the *Alabama* and the northwest of England are continued.

170. *spanker gaff*: a triangular or square-shaped sail flown from the mizzenmast of a tall ship.

171. *The dogs! ... officers*: The hull of the *Kearsarge* was reinforced by concealed iron chains, so shells that should have hulled the ship did not and so confused and frustrated the tactics of Semmes. This tactic is perceived as underhand and unfair. The battle was the subject of a painting by Édouard Manet, '*The Battle of the U.S.S. "Kearsarge" and the C.S.S. "Alabama"*' (1864).

172. Deerhound: The *Deerhound* was owned by John Lancaster (1815–84) (as mentioned in the fiction), a Lancashire businessman who became MP for Wigan in 1868. He and his family had been sailing around the Channel Isles on holiday before they sailed out to watch the fight, after having docked next to the *Alabama* in Cherbourg harbour. Those rescued by the *Deerhound*, including Semmes, were taken to Southampton. As a neutral ship, the *Deerhound* had no obligation to hand the *Alabama* crew to the *Kearsage*. The accusations of the *Deerhound* colluding with the Confederate states which followed the rescue were, as Waugh says below, nonsense.

173. *reaps ... sown*: Galatians 6:7: 'Be not deceived; God is not mocked: for whatsoever a man soweth, that shall he also reap'. The 'man' in this sentence refers to both Wilfred Wragley, for his dissipated ways, and to his mother, for encouraging them.
174. *Black Country*: This is an undefined area to the west of Birmingham located generally between the towns of Walsall, Dudley and Wolverhampton. The Black Country earned its name because of the high concentration of coal mines and iron foundries – the latter being the 'fires and furnaces' seen by Ted Banister.
175. *making bullets for the Confederates*: There was support for the Confederate states in Birmingham and the Black Country, from businessmen and leaders such as William Schofield, a manufacturer and MP for Birmingham, and from workers, who formed pro-Confederate clubs.
176. *the brand of Cain on my brow*: Genesis 4:15. Cain killed his brother Abel, jealous of Abel's offerings to God. In his remorse, Cain wandered the land hoping for someone to murder him, but God branded Cain so that no one who met him would kill him, and so he would have to live with his crime to the end of his life. Ted feels similarly branded that his crime would be visible to others.
177. *stocking-feet*: without shoes, with only his socks on his feet. Sid can pass the door without the police hearing movement because he can move silently without his shoes.

Ashton, 'Bill Spriggs an Bet: Their Matrimony an their Marlocks. Bet Turns Bill Eaut'

1. *Tum Fowt*: Tonge Fold. Now part of Bolton's urban sprawl, at the time of Clarke's writing this was a small village to the east of Bolton, Lancashire.
2. *Mrs. Jackson, o' Clitheroe*: The case of Mrs Emily Jackson of Clitheroe was a legal battle over the control of a woman's body. Mrs Jackson's husband, Edmund, had left his wife the day after their wedding in 1887 to travel to New Zealand, with the expectation she would follow later. In their correspondence she asked him to return to England, but the couple quarrelled during their communications. When Mr Jackson returned his wife would not live with him, and he brought an action for conjugal rights. When she refused to live with him despite the court finding for her husband, Mr Jackson snatched her on her way home from church in 1891 and locked her in his house. Mrs Jackson's family brought a writ of habeas corpus, but the Queen's Bench decided that he had a right to the custody of his wife's body unless he intended misconduct. The Court of Appeal overturned this decision and directed the release of Mrs Jackson by her husband. The decision was seen by feminists as a victory in the emancipation of women from the control of men, giving women the right to decide whether they live with their husbands or not. Both Bill Spriggs and narrator Teddy Ashton see this as a dangerous freedom for women.
3. *Good Shuttance*: good riddance.
4. *bobby*: slang for policeman; see also above, p. 424 n. 56.
5. *Menociation*: The Kock-Krow Menociation formed by Bill Spriggs and his friends, so called because they did not want to be known as an association, with the connotation of 'ass', but rather as men, hence men-ociation. Bet later forms a women-ociation.
6. *tan his hook*: To take or sling your hook means to leave, to go away. It is believed to have a nautical origin, where 'hook' refers to a ship's anchor.
7. *wear his clooas*: The phrase 'to wear the trousers' in a relationship means to hold authority, and a wife who 'wears the trousers' is one who dominates her husband.
8. *gill*: a measure of liquid, a quarter of a pint.
9. *Mosesgate or Lostock Junction*: railway stations on the outskirts of Bolton.

Starr, 'An Unpremeditated Crime'

1. *fox-preserving*: Nevison is making the distinction between hunting (tracking wild animals on horseback and killing by dog-pack) and shooting. Although he is no enthusiast for hunting the fox, neither does he support the growing criticism of blood sports, evidenced in Henry Salt's formation of the Humanitarian League in 1891, which encompassed animals in its ethic of 'universal kinship'. The shooting of a fox in a hunting area would be frowned upon as inappropriate.
2. *strychnine*: a very strong poison, with a reputation of being the preferred poison of murderers. It is a product of the nux vomica tree (*Strychnos nux-vomica*), and its incredibly poisonous properties were discovered in the early nineteenth century.
3. Times: The *Times* is a British daily newspaper that was founded in 1785 and is still in publication today. It has held Conservative leanings since its beginning, and Nevison's father is situated as a Conservative by his association with the paper.
4. *Southampton mail*: a fast train carrying mail to Southampton. Nevison takes the quickest form of travel to escape the country.
5. *taffrail*: see above, p. 451 n. 59.
6. *Needles*: a series of hard chalk rocks off the western coast of the Isle of Wight.
7. *Afghan and Soudan campaigns*: for the Second Anglo–Afghan War, see above, p. 420 n. 10. The Anglo–Egyptian Wars of the 1880s and 1890s saw British power in Egypt rise and fall as Mahdi forces overwhelmed the British army and executed Governor Charles Gordon in 1885. Britain withdrew its control until 1898, and the scramble for Africa saw Britain reassert its power through the machine gun under the direction of General Kitchener.

Pearce, 'An Angel of Humanity'

1. *Iago*: the antagonist in Shakespeare's *Othello* who convinces Othello of Desdemona's infidelity. Ronald's comment on Clifforde's ability to play Iago well is a suggestion of the actor's perfidy as well as the character's.
2. *Irving*: Sir Henry Irving (1838–1905) was the most famous and acclaimed actor of the late nineteenth century, and Marian's comment places Clifforde's talent above even Irving's.
3. *Hotspur*: Henry Percy (1364–1403), who was referred to as Henry Hotspur, was the eldest son of Henry Percy, first Earl of Northumberland, and was renowned for his courage and chivalry. As a character in Shakespeare's *1 Henry IV*, Hotspur is brave and impetuous but too unpredictable to be a successful monarch if his rebellion of 1403 had succeeded. While Clifforde could play the traitor with aplomb, his own treacherous personality would prevent him from playing the honourable characters successfully. The word 'mull' in this context means to turn to dust or ashes; *OED*.

Ashton, 'Th' Female Fister'

1. *Wakes*: Whitsun Walks or Wakes; see above, p. 434 n. 7.
2. *thirty-second o' March ... sixth Sunday i' May*: a humorous aside on the complicated calculation that sets Easter. Easter Sunday is the first Sunday after the ecclesiastical full moon following the northern spring equinox. Whitsuntide (Whit) or Pentecost is the seventh Sunday after Easter.
3. *three-yeaded cauve*: three-headed calf. Travelling fairs would often have side-show or freak-show exhibits of biological oddities, which would include humans as well as ani-

mals. John Merrick became an exhibition in Tom Norman's freak show and was billed as the 'Elephant Man'.
4. *up to th' scratch*: the line drawn in the ground from which boxers would start the match, each with a foot on the line. A number of idioms come from this, including: starting from scratch, meaning to begin again; being up to scratch, meaning being adequate for the role; and toeing the line, meaning to conform to rules.
5. *Baccarat*: Bill's son is named after a card game that was illegal in Britain at this time, although it was brought to public prominence in 1891 with the Royal Baccarat Scandal, alternatively known as the Tranby Croft Scandal, when William Tranby Croft was accused of cheating during a weekend house party with a group of aristocrats, including the Prince of Wales.

Willson, 'The Scarlet Shoes. (The Story of a Serio-comic Walking Tour and its Tragic End.)'

1. *What do they know of England ... modern poet*: 'The English Flag' (1891) by Rudyard Kipling (1865–1936): 'Winds of the World, give answer! They are whipering to and fro – / And what should they know of England who only England know? – / The poor little street-bred people that vapour and fume and brag, / They are lifting their heads in the stillness to yelp at the English Flag?' Kipling's poem celebrates the global power of England, asserting that those who only know England cannot understand its worldwide strength; Skeat uses Kipling's question as a motivation to discover the beauties of England.
2. *old lad*: not Hargold, Skeat's old friend, but a slang term for the Devil.
3. *Hans Christian Andersen and the Brothers Grimm*: authors of fairy tales. Andersen (1805–75) was the Danish author of tales such as 'The Ugly Duckling' and 'The Emperor's New Clothes'; the Brothers Grimm (Jacob, 1785–1863; Wilhem, 1786–1859) were the authors of stories such as 'Cinderella' and 'Snow White'.
4. *cocoanut matting*: a rough and hard-wearing material made from coir. The term is used to indicate the unkempt appearance of a person's hair.
5. *Eastgate-street ... Grosvenor Museum*: The historic Roman city of Chester has many sites of interest to Skeat and Hargold. Eastgate Street, running either side of the east gate of the city walls, is the site of the Victoria Clock, which was erected in 1899 to celebrate Victoria's diamond jubilee. Grosvenor Park, on the banks of the Dee, was designed by the renowned landscape gardener Edward Kemp (1817–91) and was opened in 1867. The Rows are covered walkways at first-floor level running along the four main streets of the city above the ground-level shops. The origin of the medieval walkways is unknown, but they are unique to Chester. The city wall dates back to the Roman occupation and is the most complete set of city walls in Britain. The building of the Gothic structure of Chester Cathedral was begun in 1260, although there had been religious buildings on the site dating back to the Druids. The Grosvenor Museum was opened in 1886.
6. *Eaton Hall*: Eaton Hall, about six miles south of Chester and a mile south of the village of Eccleston, is the country house of the Duke of Westminster – hence the reply to the 'red-faced fellow's' question. The house is situated near the River Dee, which runs through the city of Chester.

SILENT CORRECTIONS

[Lyons], 'Little Pictures of the Night'

p. 33, l. 11	g.m.] a.m.
p. 46, l. 4	go] got
p. 62, l. 13	as] as one
p. 81, l. 10	Wherefor] Wherefore
p. 89, l. 11	contained] contained the
p. 91, l. 14	had] had not
p. 106, l. 33	condition.] condition."
p. 118, l. 38	of] of the

Görki, 'On the Steppes. Told by a Tramp'

p. 200, l. 31	it all] it's all
p. 201, l. 22	me to to] me to

Clarke, 'The Cotton Panic'

p. 226, l. 25	there] there's
p. 233, l. 22	I] I am
p. 264, l. 22	overseers] overseers say
p. 306, l. 6	Will an] Will and
p. 357, l. 11	salt] salter